Also by the Author

Business Thesaurus
Business Writer's Book of Lists
Complete Secretary's Handbook
Complete Word Book
Elements of Correspondence
Encyclopedic Dictionary of Business Terms
Encyclopedic Dictionary of Style and Usage
Guide to Better Business Writing
How to Run a Meeting
Internationally Yours: Writing and Communicating Successfully
in Today's Global Marketplace
Legal Secretary's Complete Handbook
New American Dictionary of Abbreviations
New American Handbook of Letter Writing
New American Three-Step Vocabulary Builder
New Robert's Rules of Order
Office Sourcebook
Practical Writer's Guide
Prentice Hall Style Manual
Professional Secretary's Book of Lists & Tips

Contents

Assistants • Certified Professional Secretary® (CPS®) • Ethics • Etiquette • Firing • Gifts • Guest list • Hiring • Human resources • Illness and injury • Image • International Association of Administrative Professionals • Interviews • Layoff • Networking • Nonverbal communication • Office • Office management • Office politics • Office positions • Office relationships • Professional development • Project management • Promotion • Sexual harassment • Supervision • Teamwork • Telecommuting • Temporaries • Time management • Training assistants and coworkers • Visitors

Address • Analog transmission • Area codes • Broadcast • Cable • Cellular communication • Common carrier • Digital transmission • E-mail • E-mail communication • E-mail etiquette • Fax transmission • Federal Communications Commission (FCC) • Foreign exchange line • Incoming mail • Integrated Services Digital Network (ISDN) • International dialing codes • International time • Interoffice communication • Leased line • Local area network (LAN) • Mail record • Metropolitan area network (MAN) • Microwave communication • Network • Optical character recognition (OCR) • Outgoing mail • Paging • Polling • Private delivery services • Radio communication • Satellite communication • Telecommunications • Telemarketing • Telephone calls • Telephone etiquette • Telephone exchange • Telephone lists • Telephone services • Telephony • United States Postal Service • Voice mail • Voice mail etiquette • Wide area network (WAN) • Wireless communication

Alphabetic filing system • Alphabetizing • Alphabetizing rules • ARMA International • Charge-out system • Chronological filing system • Color coding • Cross-reference • Document imaging • Document management system • Electronic filing system • File folders • File labels • Filename • Filing procedures • Follow-up system • Forms management • Full-text retrieval • Geographic filing system • Indexing • Keyword retrieval • Magnetic media storage • Metadata • Microforms • Micrographics • Numeric filing system • Optical media storage • Organizers • Records management • Records retention • Records security • Reports management • Subject filing system • Vital records

Adjourned meeting • Adjournment • Agenda • Annual meeting • Appointment • Audioconference • Called meeting • Call of directors' meeting • Call of stockholders' meeting • Committee • Computer conference • Conference • Conflict resolution • Consensus • Directors' meeting • Facilitator • Focus group • Incorporators' meeting • Index to minutes • Loaded conference • Meeting • Meeting file • Meetings held by proxy • Minutes • Minutes book or file • Motion • Notice of meeting • Parliamentary procedure • Presentations • Proxy • Proxy committee • Quorum • Regular meeting • Robert's Rules of Order • Room arrangement • Roundtable meeting • Scheduling • Seminar • Sine die • Special meeting • Staff meeting • Stockholders' meeting • Videoconference

Airline clubs • Air travel • American Society of Travel Agents (ASTA) • Automobile travel • Baggage • Customs • E-ticket • Expense report • Frequent flyer number • Health certificates and immunizations • Hotels • International driving permit • International English • International travel • Itinerary • Passport • Railroad travel • Smart card • Timetable • Tourist card • Translators and interpreters • Travel agency • Travel appointment schedule • Travel equipment and supplies • Traveler's checks • Travel etiquette • Traveling with an employer • Travel policy • Travel security • Visa

Access • Bandwidth • Baud rate • Bit • Bookmark • Browser • Bulletin board system (BBS) • Byte • Channel • Chat room • Client • Client-server model •

Patent • President • Professional corporation (PC) • Professional limited liability company (PLLC) • Promoters • Proprietorship, sole • Public corporation • Public utility corporation • Pyramiding • Quasipublic corporation • Records, corporate • Registered office • Reorganization • Reservation of corporate name • Resident agent • Secretary (corporate) • Seniority • Service mark • Silent partner • Sole practitioner • State of incorporation • Stock • Stock corporation • Stockholder • Subchapter S corporation • Subsidiary • Syndicate • Trademark • Transfer agent • Treasurer • Union shop • Vice president • Voting trust

Acceleration clause • Acknowledgment • Administrative Procedures Act • Affidavit • American Digest System • American Jurisprudence • American Law Reports • Amicus curiae • Answer • Antitrust laws • Appeal • Assessment • Assignment • Attachment • Attestation • Bailment • Bankruptcy • Blue sky laws • Bonding • Boycott • Breach of contract • Breach of warranty • Brief • Bulk sales law • Caveat emptor • Certiorari • Chose in action • Citations to legal authorities • Class action • Commerce clause • Common law • Complaint • Consent decree • Constructive receipt • Contract • Cooling-off period • Corpus Juris • Courts • Covenants • Databases, legal • Default • Defendant • Derivative action • Disability benefit laws • Disaffirm • Discharge of contract • Docket • Eminent domain • Environmental laws • Estoppel • Execution • Fair employment practices • Federal Trade Commission (FTC) • Fraud • Garnishment • Guaranty • Holder in due course • Indemnification of directors and officers • Indemnity • Injunction • Interstate commerce, intrastate commerce • Interstate Commerce Commission (ICC) • Judgment • Jurat • Labor laws • Libel and slander • Lien • Liquidated damages • Model Business Corporation Act • Monopoly • Monopoly price • National Labor Relations Act (Wagner Act of 1935) • National Labor Relations Board (NLRB) • National Reporter System • Negotiable instrument • Nonnegotiable instrument • Notarize • Notary public • Novation • Official reports • Open-housing law • Option • Personal property • Piercing the corporate veil • Plaintiff • Power of attorney • Preemptive rights • Pricing practices • Principal • Protest • Quasi • Ratification • Regulation of business • Representative action • Right-to-know laws • Right-to-work laws • Sale • Seal • Service of process • Social Security Act • Statute of frauds • Statute of limitations • Statutory law • Stipulation • Subpoena • Summons • Testimonium clause • Tort • Trespass • Trust • Trust deed • Unfair employment practice • Uniform Commercial Code (UCC) • Uniform Partnership Act and Uniform Limited Partnership Act • United States court system • Usury • Void, voidable • Wage–Hour Law • Waiver • Warranty • Without recourse • Worker's compensation laws • Writ

Accounting • Accounting records • Accounts • Accounts payable • Accounts receivable • Accrual accounting • Accrued assets • Accrued expenses • Accrued income • Accrued liabilities • Adjusted gross income • Adjusting entries • Alternative minimum tax • Assessment • Assets • Audit • Auditor • Bad-debt losses • Balance sheet • Basis • Books of final entry • Books of original entry • Book value • Capital • Capital assets • Capital expenditures • Capital gain and loss • Capitalization • Capital stock • Cash • Cash account • Cash accounting • Cash disbursements journal • Cash journal • Cash receipts journal • Certified public accountant (CPA) • Chart of accounts • Closing entries • Control account • Cost accounting • Credits, tax • Current assets • Current liabilities • Current ratio • Debit and credit • Deductions/adjustments • Deferred-compensation agreement • Deficit • Depletion • Depreciation • Direct tax • Double-entry accounting • Equity capital • Estimated tax • Excise tax • Exclusion • Financial statement • Fiscal period • Fixed assets • Fixed costs • Footing • Franchise tax • Funded debt • Goodwill • Gross income • Gross revenue • Holding period for securities • Income • Income statement • Income tax • Individual retirement program • Information return • Intangible assets • Interest • Journal • Ledger • Liabilities • Merit rating • Natural business year • Net assets • Net income • Net working capital • Net worth • Notes payable • Notes receivable • Obsolescence • Operating expenses • Overhead • Owner's equity • Paid-in capital • Paid-up capital • Payroll • Payroll taxes • Petty cash • Posting • Prepaid expenses • Profit • Profit and loss • Property tax • Quick assets • Replacements • Retained earnings • Revenue • Sales and use tax • Self-employment tax • Social security tax • Spreadsheet • Stamp tax • State income tax • Statement of activities • Statement of cash flows • State unemployment insurance tax • Taxable income • Trial balance • Variable costs • Wasting asset • Withholding • Withholding deposits • Working capital • Working papers • Work sheet • Write-off

13. Investments and Finance   447

Amortization • Annuity • Assessment • At the opening • Bank note • Bank reserves • Basis point • Bears • Beta • Bid and asked prices • Big board • Blue chip stock • Bond • Bond discount and bond premium • Broad market • Broker • Bulls • Carrying charge • Certificate of deposit (CD) • Clearinghouse • Closing price • Commercial bank • Commission • Commodity • Commodity exchange • Commodity Exchange Act • Commodity Futures Trading Commission • Cost-plus pricing • Databases, financial • Day order • Debenture • Debt, partial payment of • Discount • Discount, cash • Discount rate, bank • Dishonor • Dividend • Earnest money or binder • Endorsement • Equity • Exchange-rate risk • Ex-dividend • Face value • Factor • Federal Deposit Insurance Corporation (FDIC) • Federal Reserve Act • Fidelity bond • Financial leverage • Float • Foreign exchange • Fractional share • GTC order • Hedging • Industrials • Interest • Interest-rate risk • LIBOR • Limit order • Listed securities • Long sale • Margin • Market order • Money market • Mutual fund • Note • Odd lot • Over-the-counter (OTC) market • Par value stock • Pledge • Point • Portfolio • Price–earnings ratio • Prime rate • Puts and calls • Qualified stock option • Qualifying shares • Redemption • Redis-

Preface

Have you noticed that successful office professionals thrive in a high-performance workplace? Perhaps you're one of them. If so, you know that they love the challenge and are delighted with the new technologies that transform a mundane environment into an efficient, productive operation.

They're mentally focused, too, and ready for the next round of change, including:

Voice recognition that lets us talk to our office machines (and get a response)

Biometric devices that can verify our identities from facial features, fingerprints, voice patterns, and handwriting

A *cashless society* that functions via smart cards and on-line transactions

Those few examples only hint at the virtual business world that promises to sweep across civilized societies as rapidly as the Internet did, once it was available to individuals at every economic, social, and professional level.

Have you also noticed that business journalists are enthusiastically touting the new workplace? As they point out, not only are the responsibilities of office professionals changing (that's always been true), but also, entirely new positions, such as the following, are being created:

The *mentoring director,* who shortens training time by teaming company veterans with new employees

The *telecommuting coordinator,* who helps telecommuters and other remote workers establish virtual offices and function effectively via an electronic lifeline with their main offices

To many office professionals, such new functions don't represent specialized positions but are simply part of their present responsibilities, along with a host of other duties created by the new technologies.

With a whirlwind of change all around us, the inevitable concern is how to prepare for the future workplace—or even the current workplace—and do so quickly (we're reminded daily that "the future is now").

This sixth edition addresses the issue of preparation directly in entries such as PROFESSIONAL DEVELOPMENT (Chapter 1) and indirectly in other entries. In general, all entries involve matters that office professionals must know to function proficiently in today's workplace while preparing for tomorrow's.

Technoconsultants believe that in regard to new technologies, we haven't seen anything yet. For example, they predict that turn-of-the-century procedures such as surfing the Web will vanish. We'll simply *tell* our computers what we want and, in an instant, it will appear on our computer screens. The computer will do the behind-the-scenes exploring for us while we go about other business.

Today's wonders will therefore become tomorrow's drudgery. Yet the practical side in all of us tells us to beware. Although technology wizards have almost convinced us—*almost*—that we won't have to know anything or (eventually) do anything except bark commands at a computer, is it really going to be that simple?

No, our practical selves tell us that the prospect of not having to know anything or learn anything beyond the new machines and technologies isn't on any known horizon. The reality is that we still have to know much more, such as:

How to communicate effectively with coworkers, customers, and others

How to maintain records, regardless of their form

How to handle finances, with or without cash

How to deal with legal problems, which may even increase as a result of the new technologies

How to protect ourselves and our property with the right insurance

And how to handle countless other business matters

Such things will likely always be with us, so the sixth edition approaches professional life from both sides—the technological and the practical. It incorporates the new technologies and even emphasizes them, but it also provides practical information in the other important areas of daily office activity.

More than 1,200 entries are arranged alphabetically within the 15 chapters, and more than 600 items are listed in the reference section. In addition, an index at the end of the book includes hundreds of related topics and subtopics.

The chapters are arranged in four parts:

PART ONE: THE ELECTRONIC OFFICE

Chapter 1. Office Responsibilities and Relationships

Chapter 2: Message Transmission and Delivery

Chapter 3: Information Management

Chapter 4: Conferences and Meetings

Chapter 5: Domestic and International Travel

Chapter 6: The Internet

PART TWO: THE *HOW-TO-SAY-IT*™ STYLE GUIDE

Chapter 7: Business English

Chapter 8: Correspondence

Chapter 9: Document Creation and Production

PART THREE: ESSENTIAL BUSINESS OPERATIONS

Chapter 10: Management and Organization

Chapter 11: Business Law

Chapter 12: Accounting and Taxes

Chapter 13: Investments and Finance

Chapter 14: Insurance

Chapter 15: Real Estate

PART FOUR: HELPFUL REFERENCE AIDS

Abbreviations

Forms of Address

Foreign Currency

The Metric System

If some of you who have the previous edition think that certain chapter titles seem different, you're right. This edition has an all-new chapter focusing on the Internet (Chapter 6) and another on information management (Chapter 3). Other chapters, such as Chapters 1 and 9, have a different emphasis in this edition, as well as numerous new entries.

Some of the other chapters (meetings, travel, business law, and so on) have the same focus but have been completely rewritten to reflect current practices and procedures, as well as the new technologies that affect those subjects.

The following are a few examples of the many new entries that have been added to the sixth edition:

BAD-NEWS MESSAGES (Chapter 8)

COMPUTER CONFERENCE (Chapter 4)

COMPUTER LOAN ORIGINATION (Chapter 15)

DOCUMENT MANAGEMENT SYSTEM (Chapter 3)

E-TICKET (Chapter 5)

EXCHANGE-RATE RISK (Chapter 13)

HYPERTEXT MARKUP LANGUAGE (HTML) (Chapter 6)

JARGON (Chapter 7)

PRINT-ON-DEMAND PUBLISHING (Chapter 9)

TELECOMMUTING (Chapter 1)

WIRELESS COMMUNICATION (Chapter 2)

Other important entries from the previous edition, including the following, have been thoroughly updated:

BROKER (Chapter 13)

CITATIONS TO LEGAL AUTHORITIES (Chapter 11)

DEDUCTIBLE (Chapter 14)

E-MAIL (Chapter 2)

ESCROW (Chapter 15)

ETIQUETTE (Chapter 1)

FORMAT (Chapter 8)

FORMS OF ADDRESS (Part Four)

INTERNATIONAL TRAVEL (Chapter 5)

MINUTES (Chapter 4)

RECORDS MANAGEMENT (Chapter 3)

TRADEMARK (Chapter 10)

The heavy use of examples and illustrations and the extensive cross-referencing of the previous edition have been retained in the sixth edition.

The two preceding lists give you a preview of the way in which cross-references are styled:

When a cross-reference refers to an *entry in the same chapter,* it's stated in capital and small capital letters, without any mention of the chapter number. Therefore, if an entry in Chapter 8 (Correspondence) has a cross-reference to letters of apology within that chapter, it appears as APOLOGIES.

When a cross-reference refers to an *entry in another chapter,* the chapter number is included. Therefore, if an entry in Chapter 8 has a cross-reference to nonverbal forms of communication, such as body language, in the first chapter, it appears as Chapter 1/NONVERBAL COMMUNICATIONS.

When a cross-reference refers you to a *subsection of another entry,* the subsection is stated in italic type, as in INCOMING MAIL, *Checking the e-mail.*

When a cross-reference directs you to a *different chapter,* but not a specific entry, it appears in all capital letters, as in Chapter 9/DOCUMENT CREATION AND PRODUCTION.

The index includes numerous topics that are not readily evident from an entry head or cross-reference.

Because the book covers so many topics requiring specialized knowledge, numerous authorities, including the 12 members of the sixth edition's Advisory Board, reviewed entries and contributed extensively to the work. See ACKNOWLEDGMENTS for a list of the board members and a description of their contributions.

Our goal was to provide a twenty-first-century edition that would give you the knowledge and confidence needed not only to *survive* in a rapidly changing business environment but also to *thrive* in a challenging, high-performance workplace.

Toward that end, information was drawn from hundreds of reliable sources, meticulously dissected and evaluated by the experts, and carefully crafted into easy-to-read, encyclopedic–dictionary entries.

Whether you're a veteran or a newcomer, we therefore hope that both your career and your daily office activities will be significantly enhanced and energized by this powerful collection of information.

Acknowledgments

Many individuals and organizations made important contributions to this sixth edition, providing a variety of up-to-the-minute information and valuable suggestions. My thanks go to all of them, especially to the 12 members of the Advisory Board, listed here.

The board members, who were selected because of their expertise in specific areas, remained on call throughout the revision process to answer questions, send information, and correct and update chapters. Their contributions have made the sixth edition the most complete and accurate of all editions to date.

Lin Grensing Pophal did an extensive prereview of all entries in the previous edition and also corrected, updated, and wrote new entries for the sixth edition's chapter on conferences and meetings.

Susan Fenner provided reference material for various chapters and did a detailed postreview of all entries in eight chapters of Parts One and Two of the sixth edition.

Nancy Von Spreckelsen reviewed and provided suggestions for all sixth-edition entries pertaining to e-mail preparation and transmission and those concerning the education and training of assistants and other coworkers.

Anne Vaccarest reviewed and provided suggestions for all sixth-edition entries pertaining to document creation and report writing, word processing, and desktop publishing.

Tina Coleman reviewed, corrected, updated, and wrote new entries for the chapter on domestic and international travel.

Judith Grisham provided massive research material on more than two dozen key topics covered in the book, including several hundred current newspaper and magazine articles and columns, as well as other vital information.

Other board members reviewed, corrected, updated, and wrote new entries for the technical chapters in Part Three (see the table of contents for chapter numbers and titles): Carolyn Baldwin and Pam O'Hanlon, management and law; Jim Spear, accounting and taxes; Gary Tallman, investments and finance; Bob Verhoef, insurance; and Jean McCormack, real estate.

Advisory Board Members

CAROLYN W. BALDWIN, ESQ., Baldwin, Callen, Hogan & Kidd, PLLC, 101 North State Street, Concord, NH 03301

TINA COLEMAN, Writer; Contributing Editor and Management Columnist, Business Travel Executive Magazine, 1107 Allston Road, Havertown, PA 19083

SUSAN FENNER, Ph.D., Manager, Education and Professional Development, International Association of Administrative Professionals, 10502 NW Ambassador Drive, Kansas City, MO 64195-0404

JUDITH GRISHAM, Laboratory Administrator, Harvard University, Cambridge, MA 02138

JEAN B. MCCORMACK, Real Estate Consultant, 945 Yavapai Drive, Prescott, AZ 86303

PAMELA O'HANLON, Office Manager/Paralegal, Baldwin, Callen, Hogan & Kidd, PLLC, 101 North State Street, Concord, NH 03301

LIN GRENSING POPHAL, Business Journalist, 17889 50th Avenue, Chippewa Falls, WI 54729

JAMES R. SPEAR, CPA, 49 Bell Rock Plaza, Sedona, AZ 86351

GARY TALLMAN, Professor of Finance, Northern Arizona University, Box 15066, Flagstaff, AZ 86011

ANNE VACCAREST, RSM, Director of Communications, Sisters of Mercy of the Americas, New Hampshire Regional Community, Windham, NH 03087

R. W. (BOB) VERHOEF, CPCU, CLU, Insurance Broker, Verhoef Insurance Agency, 355 West Alosta Avenue, Glendora, CA 91740

NANCY VON SPRECKELSEN, Employee Relations Manager, State of Florida, District One Personnel Office, Pensacola, FL 32505

PART ONE

THE ELECTRONIC OFFICE

CHAPTER ONE

Office Responsibilities and Relationships

ASSISTANTS. Full-time, part-time, or temporary employees (see TEMPORARIES) hired specifically to help others perform their duties, especially to help those who handle administrative, supervisory, and managerial functions. See also OFFICE MANAGEMENT; SUPERVISION.

Some office professionals are responsible for selecting, training, and supervising their own assistants, especially in small firms. In larger organizations, a HUMAN RESOURCES department may process all requests for additional help.

See also FIRING; HIRING; LAYOFF; TRAINING ASSISTANTS AND COWORKERS.

The assignment of duties to an assistant depends on his or her position in an OFFICE. For example, an employer may assign certain tasks to entry-level assistants and others to executive assistants and administrative personnel. In such cases, the senior employees should assign to the entry-level members only those duties that can be done between the assignments from the executive.

Depending on the type of office and your employer's needs, an assistant's duties may include the following:

1. Opening and routing postal mail
2. Making photocopies
3. Filing information
4. Preparing routine correspondence, such as follow-up messages
5. Locating information from print and electronic sources (research)

6. Handling miscellaneous errands
7. Organizing office supplies

As assistants become more proficient in the duties first assigned to them, you may give them more responsibility. For example, you may ask them to begin marking paper material for filing, writing letters other than routine messages, handling telephone calls, and keeping the schedules and appointment calendars current.

CAREER PLANNING.   See PROFESSIONAL DEVELOPMENT.

CERTIFIED PROFESSIONAL SECRETARY® (CPS®).   A professional rating provided by the INTERNATIONAL ASSOCIATION OF ADMINISTRATIVE PROFESSIONALS (IAAP).

To be certified by the IAAP, applicants must pass a one-day, three-part exam covering finance, business law, economics, office technology, office administration, business communication, behavioral science in business, human resources management, and organization and management.

The IAAP is also developing other certifications for administrative professionals.

Information is available from the IAAP at 10502 Northwest Ambassador Drive, Kansas City, Missouri 64195; through its magazine *OfficePRO;* and at its Web site. See also Chapter 6/WEB SITE.

ETHICS.   The moral principles and values that define professional standards of conduct. In an OFFICE, an employer sets the ethical standards for the employees.

Each employee also should understand the difference between appropriate and inappropriate and legal and illegal behavior. In short, each person must know the difference between right and wrong.

Unethical behavior among employees.   Although some things are clearly right or wrong, unethical behavior takes many forms. It ranges from occasionally pilfering company supplies to regularly using company telephones for personal calls. Or it may involve outright lies, such as telling customers something that isn't true.

In other cases, it may involve something very serious, such as revealing confidential company information to outsiders or sexually harassing a coworker. See also SEXUAL HARASSMENT.

Employees may behave unethically because they feel pressured to do so by their employers or other coworkers. Or they may simply decide on their own to take advantage of others or use company resources for personal needs.

In the long run, it is in one's best interest to perform honestly and ethically in all matters and strictly avoid temptations or pressures to do otherwise. In fact, if a company *requires* unethical or illegal behavior as a condition of employment, an employee should immediately seek another, more reputable place of employment.

Company policy. To prevent unethical lapses among certain individuals or more serious companywide problems, employers should define *ethical behavior* in their company manuals, and top executives should set a positive example for all employees.

Company policy should include a statement of consequences for inappropriate or illegal behavior. This discussion should include dismissal (see Firing) for serious or repeated offenses.

However, since problems are inevitable in any organization, an employer should also instruct employees on how to deal with various pressures or temptations and where to go in the company for help if it's needed.

ETIQUETTE. The tenets of courteous, respectful behavior toward others, commonly summarized simply as good manners. In an Office, common sense suggests many of the basic rules of etiquette:

1. Use the customary polite greetings and partings of "Good morning" or "Good afternoon" (*not* "Hi") and "Good night" (*not* "See you") to your employer, clients, and other business associates.

2. Acknowledge the greeting "How are you?" with a *brief* reply such as "Fine, thank you; how are *you?*"

3. See Visitors for tips on dealing with those who visit the office, including how to introduce people properly.

4. Give newcomers a friendly reception, introduce them to coworkers, and offer assistance as they begin their duties. But if you're the newcomer, use restraint at first, and avoid being overly friendly or trying too hard to impress others.

5. Use first names if that's the practice in your office. But when in doubt, use a person's title, such as *Mr.* or *Ms.,* or, when applicable, a professional title,

such as *Dr.* or *Professor.* Wait for a supervisor or executive to invite you to use his or her first name.

6. Use proper table manners in the company cafeteria, and comply with company policy about having refreshments at your desk. Even if it's allowed, don't let the practice interfere with your work.

7. Never attend to personal grooming at your desk or in any public area, such as in the cafeteria or a meeting room.

8. Be punctual in arriving for work, appointments, or any other occasion.

9. Avoid gossip at all times. It can be serious and harmful and is always a breach of etiquette.

10. See OFFICE RELATIONSHIPS for tips on dealing with the problems of coworkers.

11. Avoid both borrowing from and lending to coworkers. If you must borrow from someone, however, repay the person promptly. If someone is late in repaying you, tactfully remind the person, but don't complain about it to others.

12. Thank people for any kindness, assistance, or other effort on their part, no matter how small. If you don't see them to thank them in person, send a thank you note. (A written note is always appropriate even when you see someone regularly.)

13. Listen carefully to others, and don't interrupt or finish the sentences of a slow speaker.

14. Know the difference between being *assertive,* or making your position known, and being *aggressive,* or rudely and forcefully imposing your views on others.

15. Beware of personal touching or making common American gestures to people from other countries. For example, the curved finger (zero sign), meaning okay in the United States, is an obscene gesture in some countries.

For tips on using proper etiquette in other situations, see Chapter 2/E-MAIL ETIQUETTE; TELEPHONE ETIQUETTE; VOICE MAIL ETIQUETTE; Chapter 5/TRAVEL ETIQUETTE; Chapter 6/NETIQUETTE.

FIRING. The permanent dismissal of an employee because of unacceptable behavior or poor work performance, as opposed to a temporary or permanent LAYOFF for other reasons, such as poor economic conditions. Office personnel who are responsible for hiring ASSISTANTS may also be responsible for firing them.

Steps to avoid dismissal. In most cases, an employee is given an opportunity to avoid dismissal by changing behavior or improving performance. Some companies follow a three-step approach:

1. Tell the person that his or her performance needs improvement and how this can be accomplished.

2. If the employee doesn't respond satisfactorily, tell him or her that you expect to see improvement by a certain date.

3. If that, too, doesn't prompt the necessary results, give a new deadline for improvement, stating that the employee will be fired if sufficient improvement has still not occurred by the specified date.

How to handle the dismissal. Before discussing termination, keep detailed records on the employee and the steps you've taken to encourage improvement. Also, check with the appropriate legal authority in your firm to be certain that the grounds for termination are valid.

If dismissal is necessary, select a neutral location (if possible), but avoid a location that is usually open to others who may overhear your discussion. Avoid your own OFFICE, too, because there you can't logically get up and leave to signal the end of the discussion.

A relatively brief 15- to 20-minute session is usually best for both parties to maintain a professional demeanor and avoid long, emotional exchanges.

Give the person a specific exit date according to company policy, and explain as gently and courteously as possible the reason why dismissal is necessary.

Some companies always advise employees of their dismissal on a Monday or Tuesday, rather than a Thursday or Friday, so that the employee can immediately begin a new job search rather than have to wait and worry about it over the weekend.

Others, who do not want a troublesome employee to have time to do anything disruptive or destructive, may decide that a Friday dismissal is necessary.

Avoid meaningless or insincere comments, such as "We'll still be friends" or "Let's have lunch sometime." Simply wish the employee success in finding a more suitable and rewarding position.

GIFTS. The presents that coworkers exchange in-house or that an executive may send to clients, business associates, or others outside the company.

Executives who give gifts may ask for your advice in making an appropriate selection. They may also want you to remind them about upcoming dates for which a gift may be required (make all such notations on your calendar).

Some employees maintain a list of all gifts that their employers have given each year and to whom the gifts were given. This helps the executive avoid duplication in future years. Some executives give so many gifts that it is difficult to remember what was previously given to whom.

If your employer wants to give a spouse or companion flowers or jewelry for a certain month and needs to know the appropriate flower or gemstone, you can find out the names from local florists or jewelry stores. Lists are also available over the Internet. See also Chapter 6/INTERNET; WEB SITE.

International gift giving. For both ideas and restrictions in international gift giving, consult a book of etiquette or a guide to international customs. Business, social, and religious practices differ from country to country, and it is especially important to check whether a particular gift—type, cost, color, and so on— would please or offend someone.

For example, one should never give liquor to someone in the Arab world, and knives imply cutting off a relationship in Latin America.

In some cases, it may be inappropriate to give any gift. In Western Europe, for example, any gift is considered crass at the first meeting.

Money presents. If your employer gives money on holidays to various employees or service personnel, such as elevator operators or door attendants, keep a list of the amount given and to whom. This information will be useful in future years.

If the amount of money is small, such as $20, use crisp new bills. For a larger amount, the executive should write a check. In both cases, insert the money in an envelope with an appropriate greeting card or message.

GUEST LIST. A list of persons invited to an entertainment function. A guest list may be useful for future events, when one wants or needs to know who attended similar functions in the past.

If you also want to recall who accepted or declined invitations on prior occasions, prepare the lists in alphabetical order, double-spaced, with three columns. Head the first column *Name,* the second column *Accepts,* and the third column *Regrets.*

Each day after the mail is received, record the replies and regrets on the alphabetical lists, and attach a numerical summary to the guest list:

March 11, 200X

Number invited	100
Acceptances	30
Regrets	5
No reply	65

Since the numbers change daily, give the executive issuing the invitations a fresh printout each day showing the exact status of the invitation list as of that date.

HIRING.   The process of contracting with someone for a part-time, full-time, or temporary position (see TEMPORARIES) in the company. Senior office personnel may be responsible for the hiring and FIRING of entry-level ASSISTANTS. They may also recommend to their employers the PROMOTION of deserving assistants.

Depending on the number of steps in the hiring process for which you are responsible, you may take any or all of the following steps:

Evaluate the need for an assistant

Present the case to your employer

Develop a job description

Write ads for newspapers, Web sites (see Chapter 6/WEB SITE), or other sources

Examine applicants' resumes and check the references they provide

INTERVIEW applicants and test them for job skills, such as software applications

Evaluate their personalities, attitudes, and other such personal traits in terms of the requirements of the position and their compatibility with coworkers

Assess their work habits, ethics, ambition, interpersonal and communications skills, judgment, and other pertinent characteristics

Select the most suitable applicant

Establish (according to company policy) the hours of work, the hourly rate or salary, and other factors pertaining to the specific position

See also TRAINING ASSISTANTS AND COWORKERS.

HUMAN RESOURCES. The employees comprising the workforce of a company and all functions associated with the management of those employees. Whereas a large organization may have a human resources department with a manager or director, a small firm may have neither.

When there is no human resources OFFICE or department, the owner–manager may perform all human resources functions. In some cases, an office manager may do the HIRING, FIRING, and training of employees. See also TRAINING ASSISTANTS AND COWORKERS.

The responsible person is concerned with preparing job descriptions, recruiting personnel, conducting INTERVIEWS, selecting the best candidates, and hiring them, as well as keeping the necessary employee records during the process and thereafter.

Preliminary functions. Two of the main preliminary functions are preparing job descriptions and recruiting candidates to match those descriptions.

1. A *job description* is a list of duties and qualifications for the job, such as the skills and personal characteristics required for each duty.

2. *Recruitment* involves looking for job candidates in one or more of the following places:

Commercial employment agencies.

Public employment agencies.

Placement offices in schools and colleges.

Employment bureaus in charitable and social organizations.

Internet recruitment sites. See also Chapter 6/INTERNET; WEB SITE.

Calls from applicants, applications on file, and unsolicited letters.

Newspaper advertisements placed by the applicant or the employer.

Applicants recommended by employees or friends.

Selection process. Candidates may respond almost immediately to recruitment strategies, and a two-step selection process may follow soon after.

1. An *interview* is usually the first step in the selection process. Depending on the available job, you would evaluate various qualities in the preliminary interview, including appearance, attitude, communication skills, accuracy, educational background, and previous experience.

The employment application provides sources that you can call or write to verify the applicant's statements. If the candidate seems promising, you may invite him or her back for one or more additional interviews.

Several kinds of preemployment tests may be used. (See HIRING.) These tests are known by many names, but all are intended to determine the applicant's present abilities, aptitude for doing a certain job, general intelligence, and personality characteristics.

In some organizations, drug testing may also be required for certain positions.

2. In making a final *selection,* the interview, application, test results, and many other factors should be considered. The objective is to choose the candidate most likely to meet the criteria of the available position and fit well in the general company atmosphere.

Record keeping. A variety of forms are needed both before and after the selection of an applicant. Many forms manufacturers maintain advisory services to help employers design efficient human resources forms.

These forms usually include an employment application, a form verifying application statements, and a payroll data sheet. (See Chapter 12/PAYROLL.) The use of additional forms depends on the size and type of business.

See also ILLNESS AND INJURY; LAYOFF; OFFICE POLITICS; OFFICE RELATIONSHIPS; PROMOTION; SEXUAL HARASSMENT; TEAMWORK.

ILLNESS AND INJURY. Health conditions and accidents that affect an employee's work performance. Companies have their own policies in regard to sick leave and continuation of wages in cases of illness and injury. However, all are required to comply with worker's compensation insurance laws.

See also Chapter 11/WORKER'S COMPENSATION LAWS; Chapter 14/WORKER'S COMPENSATION INSURANCE.

Other nonlegal considerations involve the OFFICE procedures that coworkers should follow when the job and welfare of another employee is affected by illness or injury.

What to do in case of illness or injury. General rules of ETIQUETTE and commonsense thoughtfulness, if not company policy, require that employees immediately offer to help when a coworker cannot perform his or her usual duties because of sickness or accident.

If the person who is ill or injured is in the hospital or confined at home, get-well cards, flowers, and telephone wishes are thoughtful responses.

Those employees who are somewhat familiar with the absent coworker's duties may offer to take over certain aspects of the work. Most people worry about losing their jobs in such situations, so others should make every effort to assure the person that the work will be covered while he or she is recovering.

What to do in case of death. If an illness or accident results in the death of a coworker, one should immediately send a sympathy message to the family. Those who were friends with the individual may also convey offers of assistance to the family and may send flowers or donations, as the family prefers.

In the case of the death of an executive in the firm, the individual's staff may help in making funeral arrangements and acknowledging flowers and cards. Some may also prepare an obituary notice for the newspapers or television.

An obituary should include the following: the executive's name and address; age; date, place, and cause of death (if the family requests it); the names of relatives and survivors; and details about the funeral.

It also usually includes information about the person's educational background, his or her job title and company affiliation, significant career information or special awards or honors, and other pertinent information.

An obituary may additionally state if donations instead of flowers will be accepted.

IMAGE. The representation of yourself that you project to others. Since image is a major component in career success, office personnel will greatly benefit from taking positive steps to mold and enhance their professional images.

Many characteristics affect image, one of the most important being appearance. Regardless of the emphasis on formality or informality in your company or OFFICE, the clothes you wear to work, including accessories, should be more conservative and businesslike than those you wear for leisure activities.

The same guideline applies to other aspects of grooming, such as hair style and nail care.

Other factors also play a part in developing a professional image:

The care with which you communicate (correct grammar, tone, enunciation, and so on)

The dignity with which you conduct yourself in controversial or stressful situations

The way that you interact with clients and coworkers (friendly but not overly personal, helpful, attentive, and so on)

Your level of self-esteem or self-respect

The image that you project and the way that you respond to others and to various situations largely determine how you will be perceived and what will be expected of you. Especially, the first impression that you convey will likely be the one that remains in the mind of the receiver.

Because image involves so many factors, it rarely helps to develop one or two aspects and neglect the others. For example, initially projecting a professional image won't compensate in the long run for inadequate job skills or knowledge.

However, the reverse is also true: Superior job skills and extensive education and training won't compensate for an unprofessional appearance and attitude.

See also NONVERBAL COMMUNICATION; OFFICE POLITICS; PROFESSIONAL DEVELOPMENT.

INTERNATIONAL ASSOCIATION OF ADMINISTRATIVE PROFESSIONALS. A nonprofit membership association providing information and services for administrative support staff. Founded in 1942 and formerly known as the Professional Secretaries International (PSI), the International Association of Administrative Professionals (IAAP) has more than 40,000 members and 700 chapters worldwide.

The IAAP represents all administrative professionals and offers opportunities for professional growth through programs, publications, and other activities.

It certifies those who qualify for the CERTIFIED PROFESSIONAL SECRETARY® (CPS®) rating, publishes the magazine *OfficePRO,* tracks OFFICE trends, sets standards for the profession, and holds seminars and conferences for members and other interested persons.

Information is available at the IAAP headquarters (10502 Northwest Ambassador Drive, Kansas City, Missouri 64195) and at its Web site.

INTERVIEWS. The preliminary meetings between an employer and a job applicant. Office personnel who are responsible for HIRING their own ASSISTANTS will screen applicants and arrange and conduct interviews with the candidates.

Usually, these interviews are held face to face, although initial telephone interviews also provide a good screening device. Other options are also available, as described in the forthcoming section *Multimedia interviews.*

Although a principal objective in an interview is to *collect* information about the applicant, it is also important to *provide* information that the person should know and satisfactorily answer his or her questions.

Preliminary tasks. Before advertising the availability of a position, prepare the following:

1. A detailed job description, including job duties, responsibilities, salary or salary range, and to whom the person will report

2. A list of the education, skills, experience, knowledge, and so on that are needed for the job

3. A statement about the degree of independent thinking and performance that will be required

4. A list of any personal characteristics that are desired

The interview. Include the following steps in planning and conducting an interview:

1. Set the interview length, such as 30 minutes or, with tests, an hour or more, and prepare a written plan or agenda to help you stay within the allotted time.

2. Set a mutually convenient time, preferably in the morning or early afternoon (but not the first thing in the morning or the last thing in the afternoon).

3. Make certain that the applicant is comfortable, and try to put the person at ease.

4. Encourage the applicant to volunteer information and indicate his or her relative interest in the different skills and duties that will be required.

5. Prepare a list of specific questions that you want to ask (your company many have a standard application form, but this list is a necessary addition), and take notes throughout the interview.

6. Include a period for skills tests, if applicable. (Use commercially available tests, when possible.)

7. Explain the salary, benefits, and other matters if the person appears to be a good prospect, unless you want to ask him or her back for another interview to discuss those matters then.

8. Give the applicant an opportunity to ask questions before you end the interview, and observe what the questions say about the person's attitude and level of interest.

9. Thank the person for coming, and state when you'll make a decision and how you'll notify the applicant.

10. Draft a summary of the results of the interview, and give your employer a printout along with any recommendations or comments that you have (after all interviews are completed).

People who frequently conduct interviews become adept at guiding the discussion and asking the right questions. Sometimes this involves repeating a question, stating it in different ways, until the candidate supplies sufficient information.

Experienced interviewers sometimes ask a candidate to elaborate on certain topics merely to judge how well the person can focus his or her thoughts and communicate information. The more a candidate talks, the better you can judge interest and enthusiasm.

Interviewers also watch for nonverbal signs that sometimes tell as much as what a candidate says. (See NONVERBAL COMMUNICATION.) For example, does the candidate have annoying physical gestures, does the person avoid eye contact, does he or she appear bored or disinterested, and so on.

If you are inexperienced in interviewing, consider purchasing a book on the subject that describes in detail matters such as what kinds of questions to ask for different types of work and how to ask probing questions in a friendly manner.

Multimedia interviews. New technologies are available for interviewers to supplement the traditional face-to-face meeting. In addition to using resume-scanning services and Internet-based job clearinghouses, one may use video interviews.

Job candidates enter their electronic profiles in a network database and record answers to common questions, such as "What is your most noteworthy achievement?"

The network attempts to match a candidate's skills with a company's needs. Companies that have the network's software can then call up appropriate prerecorded videos and watch and listen to the candidate's performance. If it looks promising, the company can request an on-site, personal interview.

LAYOFF. Discontinued employment, temporarily or permanently, through no fault of the employee. A layoff differs from FIRING, which is a permanent dismissal, usually because of unsatisfactory conduct or performance.

Companies may decide to lay off employees for different reasons, but the decision is often made for financial or technological reasons, particularly the former.

For example, an organization may want to increase profits by reducing labor costs. It may also want to increase efficiency by replacing HUMAN RESOURCES with technological resources, such as replacing people doing data input with data forms that can be scanned into the computer.

Employees who are victims of company layoffs can apply for unemployment compensation, although it may be weeks before the first check arrives. They also may be able to keep their health insurance for up to 18 months if they pay the premiums.

Most employees immediately seek other jobs following a layoff. In the meantime, though, they may be able to find part-time or temporary employment, or they may be able to stay on with their employer as a freelancer or independent consultant.

NETWORKING.   The process of exchanging information or services with others through personal contact or an electronic connection. Networking is a reciprocal process, and those who want to benefit from the process must understand that it is important to *give* information as well as receive it.

The process of networking.   Those who are serious about networking frequently set aside time each week to telephone others, to exchange e-mail, to meet someone for lunch, or in some way to make an exchange.

They may even prepare an agenda or list of questions or points of discussion. But they will also be prepared to listen and let others initiate topics, because a basic principle of networking is that it's a two-way exchange.

Although many office professionals establish connections with others for the specific purpose of exchanging information, others may be using networks regularly to exchange information without even realizing that what they're doing is known as *networking*.

Types of network.   Different types of networks appeal to different people. Some may prefer a traditional voice exchange, in person or by telephone. Others may use their computers to network, perhaps through an Internet discussion group or by e-mail exchanges.

See also Chapter 2/E-MAIL; Chapter 6/CHAT ROOM; MAILING LIST; NEWSGROUP.

Those who want to become part of an existing professional network or set up a new one should immediately view each contact as a prospective source of information. An exchange of business cards often sets the networking process in motion.

Prospective networkers and ready-made networks are available through associations, such as the INTERNATIONAL ASSOCIATION OF ADMINISTRATIVE PROFESSIONALS; through local, state, or national schools and colleges; and through one's own company or similar organizations.

However, not all networks are large or formal. The relationship with a congenial coworker or a mentor is an example of an informal, two-person network.

NONVERBAL COMMUNICATION.   Sending messages or signals by some means other than words, such as through dress or body language.

How people communicate without words.   Most people do not realize that they are conveying information to others through their facial expressions, such as frowning; their physical mannerisms, such as rapid hand movements while talking; or their physical grooming and clothing, such as choice of hair style or type of clothes.

However, most people easily pick up information or cues from others based on what they see. For example, job applicants tell interviewers (see INTERVIEWS) a great deal about themselves through nonverbal cues, such as fidgeting, looking bored, or crossing their legs and arms defensively.

Forms of nonverbal communication.   Body language is considered the most important form of nonverbal communication. For example, leaning forward may communicate interest or friendliness; leaning backward, aloofness.

Other forms of nonverbal communication, such as facial expressions, are also revealing. Smiling at appropriate moments, for example, is engaging. But smiling continually can be annoying to others and also conveys powerlessness.

Physical mannerisms, such as gesturing, also reveal a lot about a person. Crossing one's arms high across the chest, for example, may signal dissatisfaction or a closed mental attitude. Playing with one's hair can have sexual connotations.

International differences.   The physical signals that people send don't necessarily mean the same thing in all countries. Direct eye contact, for instance, is acceptable and even important in the United States. But in other places, such as in Asian countries, it's a sign of disrespect.

Employees who have frequent contacts with others would benefit from studying books or tapes discussing and demonstrating nonverbal communication, especially material on body language.

In the case of contacts with people in other countries, it is mandatory to learn which cues are taboo in the other country to avoid seriously offending someone.

OFFICE.   The permanent or temporary place that a professional person uses to conduct business. This place may be located in the facilities of a company, in the house of a telecommuter (see TELECOMMUTING), or in both locations.

For the business traveler, the place used to conduct business may be a hotel room, an airport lounge, or a vehicle.

A traveler's mobile office may include a cell phone (see Chapter 2/CELLULAR COMMUNICATION), a portable fax machine (see Chapter 2/FAX TRANSMISSION), a notebook or laptop computer, and various other small devices, such as a handheld calendar–organizer.

OFFICE MANAGEMENT.   The overall management, employee SUPERVISION, and coordination of activities in a business setting. Office management may involve any or all of these steps:

1. The supervision of all support activities and the personnel who perform them

2. The supervision of mail processing (paper mail and e-mail) and message transmission, telecommunications activities, fax transmission, word processing, record keeping, filing and records management, and any other activities handled in the particular OFFICE

3. The purchase or rental of all office equipment and furniture, such as chairs, desks, filing equipment, and word processing equipment, including maintenance contracts and leases

4. The design of the physical layout—lighting, furniture arrangement, and so on

5. The coordination of functions with other offices, departments, and external organizations

6. The planning function, including both short-term scheduling of time and activities and long-range planning for the handling of special programs and projects

7. The quality-control activities, such as establishing standards and monitoring work to see that it meets the basic requirements in appearance, accuracy, and so on

OFFICE POLITICS.   The artful actions, practices, and processes that employees sometimes use to accomplish what they need or want in a professional or business OFFICE.

The strategies and tactics that office personnel use to further their careers and meet their objectives may be forthright and ethical or manipulative and ruthless. Every person or situation is different. In most cases, however, the need to play office politics is fueled by competition.

Competition in the office. Fair, ethical competition (see ETHICS) is healthy in most instances, and you can justifiably improve your position in many ways. For example, you may take on extra duties, make useful suggestions, and generally work harder to benefit your employer.

Irrational, unethical behavior, on the other hand, is damaging to the people who are involved. You may see this type of behavior in overly ambitious employees who sometimes bend rules and strain principles without concern for the consequences to themselves and others.

If the competition in your office is clearly unethical, don't feel pressured to compete in the same way. Instead, continue to perform your duties honestly and responsibly. However, there's nothing wrong with taking positive steps, such as promoting your own ideas, to enhance your position.

The politics of survival. Creating a positive IMAGE is essential not only to cope effectively with office politics but also to succeed in your career. Certain basic steps will help to give you a firm footing in any day-to-day combat with rivals:

1. Avoid office gossip and personal criticism.
2. Be friendly, sincere, and positive in your dealings with everyone.
3. State your position clearly but not aggressively.
4. Understand who is in charge, and respect the wishes and decisions of your employer.
5. Be a good listener, and give people time to make their points.
6. Don't give away all your ideas and strategies in your discussions.
7. Be helpful when asked, but don't insist on giving unwanted help.
8. Practice common courtesy, and show respect for the feelings of others at all times.
9. Keep your employer and coworkers informed of your own activities when someone working with you is behaving unfairly to be certain that you aren't associated with the other person's questionable actions.

10. Document your actions and accomplishments, sending memos to your employer from time to time to ensure that someone doesn't claim credit for something you did or blame you for something you didn't do.

See also HUMAN RESOURCES; OFFICE RELATIONSHIPS; SEXUAL HARASSMENT; TEAMWORK.

OFFICE POSITIONS. The jobs commonly available to managers and office support staff. Over the years, surveys have indicated a changing climate in business and professional OFFICES reflected by the change in duties and job titles.

Responsibilities. Businesses expect office professionals to use new technologies, such as the Internet (see Chapter 6/INTERNET) and optical scanning, as well as to assume more responsibilities in other areas.

Additional responsibilities include conducting INTERVIEWS, HIRING new employees, and dealing with business associates in other organizations. However, the traditional competencies in business English, written communication, research, and record keeping remain highly important.

Job titles. The change in job titles, especially a decline in the use of *secretary,* has accompanied the trend toward increasing skills and responsibilities.

Among the most common titles are *administrative assistant, executive assistant, executive secretary, administrative secretary,* and *secretary* (general or specialized, such as *medical secretary*), as well as the traditional titles of *office manager* (see OFFICE MANAGEMENT), *supervisor* (see SUPERVISION), and *receptionist.*

OFFICE RELATIONSHIPS. The personal interactions among employees who regularly work in the same OFFICE or offices of a company.

Under ideal conditions, office personnel work cooperatively in a friendly, congenial atmosphere to further the interests of their employers. In doing so, they also further their own career interests and are rewarded with salary increases, PROMOTIONS, and commendations.

However, conditions are rarely, if ever, ideal, and employees must make a deliberate effort to develop effective working relationships. They must be aware of the many factors that affect office relationships and the consequences of their decisions and actions.

For further information, see ETHICS; ETIQUETTE; FIRING; ILLNESS AND INJURY; IMAGE; NONVERBAL COMMUNICATION; OFFICE POLITICS; SEXUAL HARASSMENT; TEAMWORK.

Handling conflicts.   Being a good listener combined with polished communication skills, including tact and diplomacy, will help you avoid or diffuse many conflicts. But some cannot be avoided, and in fact, it may be best to deal with disagreements rather than let them fester.

In some cases, you may be able to use a conflict positively to clarify your position (and that of others) and to advance your ideas.

Since hostile arguments are counterproductive and since it is usually necessary to continue working with an adversary, a friendly, positive approach to a disagreement is mandatory:

1. Listen thoughtfully and fully to complaints or opposing views.

2. Ask questions if you don't understand someone's disagreement with you.

3. Frequently use the person's name in your comments.

4. Thank the person for explaining his or her position to you.

5. Use calming phrases such as "My approach is a little different" or "My understanding is that," rather than blunt or inflammatory responses such as "That's absurd" or "That doesn't make sense."

6. Emphasize areas of agreement before focusing on areas of disagreement.

7. Suggest a compromise if that would be a realistic solution.

8. Take a first-things-first approach by defusing an explosive situation before you work on a solution or reconciliation.

9. Admit it when you're wrong.

10. Acknowledge points about which your opponent is right.

11. When you can't agree on a decision or action, pleasantly suggest that you'll look forward to other occasions when your views will be the same.

12. When an opponent rejects your conciliatory gestures, gracefully accept that which cannot be changed—without abandoning your views or decisions— but strictly refuse to be drawn into aggressive verbal combat.

13. When you're expected to make a decision and are convinced that your view is correct, go ahead and put your decision into effect.

14. If something is a matter of concern to your employer, let him or her render the final decision.

Dealing with problems of others. If a coworker with a personal problem asks for your help or is in a situation where it seems necessary to offer assistance, you will doubtless feel compelled to offer help and comfort. However, one never really helps another by covering for his or her errors or problems.

If someone has a drinking problem, for example, that affects his or her work, you should not play doctor or psychologist or help the person to cover it up. Rather, if asked for help, you might suggest that the person find professional guidance and recommend nearby sources.

If the person with a problem is your employer and you are asked to offer suggestions, do the same thing—recommend qualified professional assistance.

PROFESSIONAL DEVELOPMENT. The employment, education, and training that employees undertake to prepare themselves for advancement in their careers. All of these activities are important for professional growth.

Employment. Firsthand experience is invaluable. Newcomers to the workforce who know only that they want to have a career in a certain industry or profession, such as telecommunications, might begin by finding an office position with a local firm, such as the local telephone company. In time, they would likely be ready to advance within that company or move on to a larger firm with more opportunities.

Education. Office personnel need to undertake two types of education to advance in their careers: formal education and independent study. Employed persons can find the formal education at a local college that offers weekend or night courses. Often, such an opportunity is offered as an employee benefit.

Many companies support on-line learning, rather than campus classes. Employees in such companies may take Web-based courses at home or at work during slack periods.

Independent study can be done alone, unsupervised, through a self-disciplined schedule of reading and research. Books, magazines, newspapers, tapes, and the Internet are obvious sources of information. Other efforts, such as NETWORKING and computer-based training or tutorials, are also highly useful.

Those who want to achieve the CERTIFIED PROFESSIONAL SECRETARY® (CPS®) rating should contact the INTERNATIONAL ASSOCIATION OF ADMINISTRATIVE PROFESSIONALS in Kansas City, Missouri, for instructions and study guidelines.

Training. In addition to routine, on-the-job orientation and training that all new employees receive, in-house training sessions (seminars, workshops, and so on) are available in many companies.

For example, employees may be able to enroll in a word processing, communications, or other training program held on site or at a nearby location.

Sometimes a company program is held in the evenings or on Saturdays. In some cases, employees may be excused from their duties during the workday to attend a particular company training session.

Some sessions may be conducted by computer through closed-circuit television or by software tutorials, videotapes, or other self-teaching methods.

PROJECT MANAGEMENT. The process of defining, organizing, and scheduling tasks to ensure the satisfactory completion of a project by a specified date.

Senior office personnel are accustomed not only to working independently without SUPERVISION but also to planning, coordinating, and managing various projects, such as the publication of a departmental newsletter or the arrangements for monthly staff meetings.

Larger projects may require the use of project-management aids, such as scheduling software or commercial project-management programs. An example of such programs is the *Program Evaluation and Review Technique (PERT),* which helps managers to determine how long a large project will take and to prepare for problems in reaching completion.

Another example is the *Gantt chart,* used for smaller projects. It illustrates the progress of each scheduled task so that managers can quickly recognize areas that are behind schedule.

Other aids are electronic calendars and schedules, as well as special project-management software. Like the Gantt chart and PERT, such software enables managers to monitor deadlines and recognize problems in advance. Since the information is entered and maintained electronically, it can easily be modified at any time.

PROMOTION. The movement of an employee from one position to another involving greater responsibility and, often, a higher salary, such as the promotion of an administrative assistant to the position of office manager.

Office personnel who are pursuing a career in a particular company or field can take specific steps aimed at being promoted:

1. Cultivate a professional IMAGE that commands admiration and respect and will make a positive impact on your employer.

2. Frequently offer to do more than the work assigned to you, and don't hesitate to stay late or arrive early to do it.

3. Keep your employer informed of your new ideas, special projects, and accomplishments.

4. Search for ways to handle your work more efficiently, and make your OFFICE more productive.

5. Be flexible and dependable so that your employer will know that he or she can always count on you.

6. Regularly work at improving your job skills.

7. Become a more polished communicator in your dealings with clients, coworkers, and your employer.

8. Take the initiative in handling and completing tasks.

9. Aim for nothing less than complete accuracy in all that you do.

10. Be thoughtful and respectful to others.

11. Practice better TIME MANAGEMENT, and don't allow coworkers to distract you.

12. Dress in a conservative, businesslike manner.

See also ETHICS; HIRING; IMAGE; NONVERBAL COMMUNICATION; OFFICE POLITICS; OFFICE RELATIONSHIPS; TEAMWORK.

SEXUAL HARASSMENT. A form of sex discrimination consisting of unwelcome sexual advances, requests for sexual favors, or other verbal or physical conduct of a sexual nature, when the following is evident:

1. An individual's submission to the conduct is explicitly or implicitly made a term or condition of the person's employment.

2. An individual's submission to or rejection of the conduct is used by the harasser as the basis for making employment decisions that affect the individual.

3. The harasser's conduct substantially interferes with an individual's work performance or creates an intimidating, hostile, or offensive work environment.

The Equal Employment Opportunity Commission (EEOC) encourages employers to take steps to prevent sexual harassment, such as publishing for employees a description of the sanctions that harassers will face and explaining to employees how to proceed if sexual harassment occurs.

Victims should immediately report incidents of harassment, and employers should promptly investigate them and take appropriate action to end the harassment, discipline the harasser, and protect the victim from retaliation or recurrence.

If you believe that you have a legitimate complaint, take the following steps:

1. Keep a written record (time, date, place) of unwanted actions or remarks, the name of the harasser, and your efforts to discourage the actions or remarks.

2. Either confront the harasser in person, firmly stating that the behavior is offensive, or write to the harasser stating the same, as well as what action you will take if the harassment does not stop. (Keep a copy of this and any other letters, and keep copies of evidence, such as offensive jokes posted on a bulletin board.)

3. If reporting the incidents to your supervisor or other designated company official is ineffective, contact the nearest EEOC office, and file a complaint. (Check a telephone directory or the Internet for locations.) Since employers are responsible for any occurrence of sexual harassment, they may not legally fire or demote you for filing such complaints.

SUPERVISION. The act, process, or occupation of monitoring, directing, and assisting others in your charge. For some office personnel, the supervisory function is only one aspect of their positions. For example, an administrative secretary may supervise an ASSISTANT but also handle many other nonsupervisory duties.

Other personnel are hired specifically as full-time supervisors to oversee a number of employees in an OFFICE, a department, or the entire company.

Regular supervisory activities. A supervisor is often responsible for the HIRING, FIRING, LAYOFF, and PROMOTION of employees.

In hiring employees, the supervisor will recruit, INTERVIEW, hire, and train full-time and part-time candidates, as well as TEMPORARIES. See also TRAINING ASSISTANTS AND COWORKERS.

Supervisors also commonly conduct job evaluations (comparing a job to other jobs in the company for payroll purposes) and may handle merit ratings (a method of rating the performance of employees).

Those who undertake supervision need to be skilled in communication. To avoid adversely affecting an employee's morale, instructions must be stated clearly and criticism must be given constructively and sensitively.

Special supervisory procedures are needed for those who work with telecommuters. (See TELECOMMUTING.) Usually, a company requires home-based employees to sign an agreement that summarizes expectations, and the supervisor then monitors and enforces the terms of that agreement.

Problem cases. Supervisors also must deal with SEXUAL HARASSMENT, absenteeism, and a variety of discipline or performance problems.

Any actions concerning performance or discipline problems must be consistent with company policy but usually involve one to two warnings to the employee, including a final written warning that states the consequences if the problem persists.

If an employee does not respond after the final warning, the supervisor may suspend or fire the person. With certain problems, however, such as alcohol abuse, the supervisor may send the employee home. But if the problem continues, the supervisor may eventually recommend dismissal.

In unusual or volatile cases, the supervisor may be required to consult someone in a higher management position before taking action. See also OFFICE RELATIONSHIPS; TEAMWORK; TELECOMMUTING; TRAINING ASSISTANTS AND COWORKERS.

TEAMWORK.   Work performed by two or more persons with the intent that the collective effort will benefit the entire OFFICE, department, or organization, rather than the interests of a single individual.

To become a team player, one must develop a cooperative attitude and open communication, with an easy give-and-take approach. Both successes and failures must be shared by all team members, and solutions to problems are typically developed through member contributions.

Participants must be loyal and supportive of one another and always maintain confidences. Responsibilities may not be the same for each member, but whether one has a management or support function, each person should be treated fairly and respectfully.

Working for more than one person.   When you work for more than one person, it's important to treat the combination as part of the team, serving the same company.

For those working in a support role, such as an executive assistant, adaptability and flexibility are key factors in making the arrangement work, because it's necessary to adjust to the different paces, demands, and attitudes of each person.

In particular, you must avoid favoritism. When scheduling conflicts occur, for example, it's helpful to discuss the matter with each person. Meanwhile, to accommodate the needs of each person, you must be adept at scheduling work and managing your time, as well as have strong organizational and planning skills.

If one person works in an outside office, such as a home-based office (see TELECOMMUTING), you may be expected to assume greater responsibility in handling telephone calls and office visits and in processing paper and electronic mail. If you have any doubts, ask the person to clarify his or her expectations.

Working with other offices or departments. You may find occasions when you need the assistance and cooperation of other departments. In a team spirit, therefore, you should also offer to be helpful to others when the situation is reversed.

However, the same type of conflicts may occur in working with other departments as occur in working for more than one person. For example, two people may need something at the same time.

To cope with such problems, you should develop and maintain good relations with your principal contact in each department so that you can explain when requests from more than one source appear at the same time.

Most people are reasonable when an assignment is not an emergency and will help you to schedule both jobs appropriately and resolve any scheduling conflicts.

See also ETIQUETTE; OFFICE POLITICS; OFFICE RELATIONSHIPS; SUPERVISION; TIME MANAGEMENT; TRAINING ASSISTANTS AND COWORKERS.

TELECOMMUTING. Working from a home-based, or virtual, OFFICE that is electronically connected to the company office.

Some employees telecommute on a regular basis, with only periodic visits to their companies for meetings and conferences. Others telecommute only occasionally, such as one day a month, or part time, such as 20 hours a week.

Whereas some job analysts believe that telecommuting can improve employee morale and increase productivity, others believe that the isolation encourages employee dissatisfaction, boredom, and lack of discipline.

Regardless of the advantages or disadvantages, the practice is expanding. Yet no standards exist concerning who funds the home-office setup (employee or employer), how work will be monitored, or when it will be done.

How a telecommuter works. Companies generally have a contract with the telecommuter that is similar to an agreement with an outside consultant. This contract will detail days and hours worked, assignments, delivery of work to the company offices, and so on.

Most communication is handled by telephone, computer, and fax and by making use of suitable technologies such as voice mail and e-mail.

Usually, a telecommuter is expected to contact the company offices once a week and deliver assignments according to a specified schedule. The telecommuter must also attend all regularly scheduled meetings with his or her employer or other coworkers.

In turn, the employer or another company representative may meet periodically at the telecommuter's home office.

Office requirements. The home office must be suitable for the intended use. Typically, this means that the room or area must be private and closed off from the rest of the house. It also must be organized and furnished with appropriate furniture and equipment.

Especially, a home office must be conducive to producing the required work, and it must provide a suitable atmosphere for the telecommuter to conduct his or her business efficiently and professionally.

TEMPORARIES. Those who serve as employees for a limited time, such as a person hired to process registrations for an upcoming conference.

Companies that need temporary help have the option of sending work out (*outsourcing*) or hiring additional employees.

When companies decide to hire temporary help, they generally follow many of the same procedures used in locating permanent help: recruiting, interviewing, contracting, training, supervising, and so on. (The recruitment step may be simplified if the company uses a temporary-help agency.)

In many cases, office personnel handle each of these steps. See also HIRING; INTERVIEWS; SUPERVISION; TRAINING ASSISTANTS AND COWORKERS.

Integration with the regular staff. To be certain that the full-time or regularly employed staff understands and values a temporary worker, the supervisor should explain the reason the person was hired and how the staff can help the effort succeed.

To ensure successful integration of temporaries with the regular staff, trainers and supervisors must prepare a suitable workspace for them and immediately take steps to make them part of the team. See also TEAMWORK.

However, because temporaries are new both to the company and to the team, they usually need additional direction and assistance. Although the immediate supervisor usually provides this, other members of the staff should be encouraged to help.

The staff should make a temporary employee feel as welcome as any other newcomer and should be as helpful as they would be to a permanent employee.

For the temporary worker, the position often represents a good way to find a permanent part- or full-time position.

If a temporary employee does not meet an employer's expectations, it will be necessary to dismiss the person, if he or she is an independent worker, or notify the agency that made the arrangements.

Postproject supervisory duties. After a temporary worker leaves, the supervisor should assess the person's work in terms of stated goals and prepare a performance evaluation for the project manager or other authority. In general, the report should objectively evaluate the person's job skills, attitude, and other pertinent qualities.

This performance evaluation will also reflect on the supervisor's management skills. For example, if the report is unfavorable, it will suggest that the supervisor did not do an adequate job of training and directing the person. Nevertheless, the report must be accurate.

TIME MANAGEMENT. The process of controlling how you spend your time to encourage greater efficiency and productivity at work. Managing one's time better is usually dependent on developing better work habits.

The following practices are intended to encourage better work habits and thereby contribute to a more effective use of your time:

1. Set priorities, and organize your work schedule according to those priorities.

2. Establish goals, and write down everything that you want to accomplish.

3. Use electronic and conventional calendars, pocket planners, or any other form of reminder to help you follow the schedule and meet deadlines.

4. Delegate routine work to ASSISTANTS whenever possible to create more free time to handle important matters that only you can do.

5. Discourage unnecessary time-consuming intrusions and interruptions by coworkers during the workday.

6. Improve communications, such as instructions to assistants, to prevent misunderstandings and backtracking.

7. Group similar activities, such as filing or handling errands, to save time and energy.

8. Regularly look for ways to streamline your work and eliminate unnecessary steps.

9. Use moments when you are waiting for someone or something to plan future work.

10. Avoid procrastination by starting the day with something you like to do.

11. Schedule difficult tasks for times of the day when you do your best work.

12. Return phone calls during less demanding times (or during your lunch period when people in other time zones may be at their desks).

13. Work at your most effective pace, not so rapidly that you quickly tire and are unable to perform satisfactorily after that.

14. Don't spend needless time overdoing a task or handling a piece of paper more times than necessary.

15. Know your time and work capacity so that you don't take on more than you can realistically and effectively handle (just say no).

16. Develop timesaving habits, such as reducing clutter and improving the organization of your files and other materials.

17. Use timesaving equipment or devices, as well as special features, such as automatic telephone redial or stored fax transmissions.

18. Use timesaving procedural devices, such as color-coded file folders.

19. Make your electronic and paper files (and filenames) consistent to facilitate filing and finding.

20. Store stock phrases and form letters in your computer to avoid retyping standard messages each time.

21. Set up style sheets for similar documents to avoid reformatting each new document.

22. Create macros to save computer time in repetitive key strokes.

23. Don't use a keyboard command when using a mouse is faster and vice versa.

24. Arrange your equipment and files for easy, quick access, and take other steps to create a pleasant, quiet, work-conducive environment.

25. Observe others, and adopt the practices of coworkers who are successful time managers.

26. Include stretch breaks during work and leisure activities each day after work or at other appropriate times to ensure that you're refreshed when you return to work.

TRAINING ASSISTANTS AND COWORKERS. The process of instructing part-time and full-time personnel, as well as TEMPORARIES, in the practices and procedures of the OFFICE and the specific duties that they must undertake.

Once an employee or temporary is hired, the job orientation and training should begin immediately. In addition to making the person feel welcome and comfortable, training should include careful instruction and explanation of the person's duties, presented at a pace the trainee can digest.

Practice sessions should be set up in which actual tasks are first completed under your direct supervision, often with step-by-step explanations as work proceeds. It will become evident when direct supervision can be relaxed.

However, even after an employee is functioning independently—with the exception of occasional questions—you should check his or her work from time to time for errors and general quality, as well as evaluate the person for efficiency and overall performance.

If further guidance or discipline is necessary, don't hesitate to provide it. However, remain alert to dissatisfaction or low employee morale, and encourage open communication that will prevent such problems.

It's especially important to provide ongoing motivation. An employee who has no incentive to do better probably will not.

Handle constructive criticism sensitively. For example, instead of saying "You made three errors in this letter, so you'll have to do it over," say "With a little more practice, I think that the letters will be error-free. Let's try this one again—I circled the three typos I noticed."

The following list offers practical training guidelines that can be used in many offices. Since situations vary, however, adjust the examples as appropriate for your needs, and add other steps to fit your situation. See also OFFICE RELATIONSHIPS; SUPERVISION.

1. Prepare a checklist of steps that you want to follow during training, and next to each item, record the date that your instruction is completed.

2. Review the conditions and terms of the trainee's employment, job duties, and procedures for handling miscellaneous matters, such as sick leave, requests for time off, and breaks during working hours.

3. Take the trainee on a tour of your company plant or offices, pointing out different products, specialized language, and so on.

4. Give the trainee a directory of officers, department heads, and key employees.

5. Explain and demonstrate the use of office telecommunications equipment, such as your voice mail system. See also Chapter 2/VOICE MAIL.

6. Explain how to handle incoming calls or place outgoing calls (procedure, telephone etiquette, cost considerations, and so on). See also Chapter 2/TELEPHONE CALLS; TELEPHONE ETIQUETTE.

7. Explain and demonstrate the operation of fax or multifunction machines and computer equipment (peripherals, software, storage media, and so on). See also Chapter 2/E-MAIL; FAX TRANSMISSION; Chapter 3/MAGNETIC MEDIA STORAGE; OPTICAL MEDIA STORAGE.

8. Explain and demonstrate the use of the Internet (for fact finding, use of e-mail, and so on). See also Chapter 6/INTERNET.

9. Explain and demonstrate the operation of reproduction and photocopy equipment (when to use each, difference in cost, and so on).

10. Demonstrate the care and maintenance of all equipment (computer/word processors, faxes, reproduction equipment, copiers, scanners, multifunction machines, and so on) and associated supplies (software, storage tapes and diskettes, and so on), including hotlines for help or telephone numbers for servicing and repair.

11. Explain restrictions on the personal use of company equipment and supplies. See also ETHICS.

12. Instruct the trainee in conventional and electronic filing procedures (explain systems; handling of paper, diskettes, and so on; how to mark paper documents for filing; and how to use the central filing department, if any). See also Chapter 3/ALPHABETIC FILING SYSTEM; ELECTRONIC FILING SYSTEM; NUMERIC FILING SYSTEM.

13. Instruct the trainee on steps in processing incoming paper and electronic mail (opening paper mail, dating it, routing it, making any required paper copies of e-mail, and so on). See also Chapter 2/INCOMING MAIL.

14. Instruct the trainee on steps in processing outgoing paper and electronic mail (folding and inserting paper mail and enclosures, class of mail to use, how to transmit e-mail and send faxes, and so on). See also Chapter 2/OUTGOING MAIL.

15. Explain how to use in-house or external courier services and private delivery services. See also Chapter 2/PRIVATE DELIVERY SERVICES.

16. Show the trainee where supplies are stored, how to requisition additional supplies from a purchasing department, and how to make catalog or on-line purchases.

17. List the approved supplies, and discuss spending limits and the authorization policy (approval that is necessary before making purchases).

18. Show the trainee each type of stationery, and explain how each is used (type of correspondence, number of copies to make, format specifications, and so on). See also Chapter 8/STATIONERY.

19. Show the trainee samples of each form, such as a packing slip; explain what it is used for; and demonstrate how to complete it. See also Chapter 8/FORMS.

20. Instruct the trainee on how to prepare and send paper letters and memos and e-mail (samples of each type, writing style, format, number of copies needed, use of equipment to transmit messages, and so on). See also Chapter 2/E-MAIL COMMUNICATION; Chapter 8/LETTERS; MEMOS.

21. Instruct the trainee on preparing reports, using a sample report as a guide (format, style, whether prepared by word processing or desktop publishing software, and so on). See also Chapter 9/DESKTOP PUBLISHING; REPORT; WORD PROCESSING.

22. Instruct the trainee on how to use computer preparation for special formatting needs (tables, lists, figures, graphics, and so on). See also Chapter 9/GRAPHICS; ILLUSTRATIONS; RESEARCH (see discussion of outline); TABLES.

23. Instruct the trainee on the use of other software applications, such as accounting software, scheduling software, and spreadsheet software (what each is used for, how to use it, and so on). See also Chapter 4/SCHEDULING; Chapter 12/ACCOUNTING; SPREADSHEET.

24. Instruct the trainee on how to improve his or her spelling, punctuation, and capitalization (sensitively and constructively pointing out errors in the trainee's work, explaining how to use an appropriate published style guide or an in-house style manual, and so on). See also Chapter 7/CAPITALIZATION; PUNCTUATION; Chapter 9/STYLEBOOK.

25. Instruct the trainee on how to improve his or her grammar (also sensitively and constructively pointing out errors in the trainee's work, explaining the applicable rules of grammar, and so on). See also Chapter 7/GRAMMAR.

26. Guide the trainee in improving other work (again, sensitively and constructively pointing out problems in the trainee's work, explaining how to overcome them, and so on), including computer correction procedures.

27. Give the trainee a procedures manual to supplement individual instruction on specific tasks, procedures, and related equipment and supplies.

VISITORS. Those who come to an OFFICE for scheduled or unscheduled appointments (see Chapter 4/APPOINTMENT), including employees, clients, business associates, and members of the general public.

Office personnel who greet and assist visitors must draw on many personal qualities, including poise, tact, good judgment, and an understanding of proper ETIQUETTE.

When an employee is the first representative of the company that a visitor encounters, the IMAGE that the employee projects reflects on the entire organization.

Employers commonly expect a receptionist or other member of the staff to take certain steps when a visitor arrives. Therefore, you may take one or more of the following steps:

1. Ask the person for his or her name, company affiliation, and purpose of the visit.

2. Make the visitor's contact with the firm pleasant by being friendly and helpful.

3. Greet visitors appropriately ("Good morning/Good afternoon," *not* "Hi"), and ask how you can be of help if the person doesn't have an appointment. (Let the visitor make the first gesture toward shaking hands.)

4. Decide which visitors your employer will welcome, which he or she wants to avoid, which should be seen by someone else, and which you should deal with.

5. Make polite explanations to anyone your employer will not see, without antagonizing the visitor, and ask if the person would like to leave any literature for your employer.

If your desk is at the office entrance or in a conspicuous location, it isn't necessary to rise every time a visitor arrives, unless the person is someone of considerable importance or much older.

As soon as visitors arrive for an appointment, show them where to place their hats, coats, briefcases, and other articles. If the location is behind your desk or not easily accessible to others, offer to take their articles and hang up their coats.

When people have to wait, show them where to sit. If they have to wait a long time, offer them a newspaper or magazine, or keep copies available in the waiting room.

Continue your work, rather than initiate a conversation with a visitor. But if someone wants to ask questions or make comments, respond courteously.

Introducing a visitor. Mention the names of visitors and their employers when bringing them into an executive's office.

State the name of the person being honored first: "Bishop Davis, this is Mr. Orlando." If the executive's position is of higher rank, mention his or her name first: "Mr. Orlando, this is Jamie Stevens from the Mail Department."

Telephone calls for the visitor. When a call comes in for a visitor, ask the caller if he or she can leave a message. If so, type the message on a piece of paper and sign your name with the date and time, giving the message to the visitor when he or she is leaving.

Otherwise, go into the room and say, "Pardon me for interrupting, Ms. Jansen, but Mr. Shipley is on the phone and wants to speak with you. Do you want to take it here or outside?"

When several people are in a conference, type the message on a piece of paper and hand it to the person being called. The visitor can then quietly leave the conference to take the call outside if he or she wishes.

Problem visitors. When an executive does not want to see someone, tell the visitor that you're sorry but that you aren't authorized to interrupt your employer or schedule any appointments. Suggest that the person write a letter instead or leave literature that you can pass along to your employer.

When a visitor's behavior or comments are threatening, discreetly ring for security (if possible) or quietly step into the executive's office and explain the situation. (Follow your company's policy.)

Refreshments. If visitors arrive while you're having refreshments at your desk and the desk is near the waiting area, it's appropriate to offer them something too. If someone is already waiting in your office, postpone having your own refreshments.

Seeing a caller out. As visitors prepare to leave, hand them their coats and other articles if you placed them in an inaccessible place when they arrived.

If your company is small, it's usually sufficient merely to say "Good-bye" (with a smile) as they leave. If the building is large, however, ask if they need directions to, or help in finding, the elevator or parking lot or if you may call a taxi for them.

CHAPTER TWO

Message Transmission and Delivery

ADDRESS. A location designation for a person, organization, device, or data. An address may consist of numbers, letters, symbols, or a combination of them.

For example, each one of several connected computers must have its own designation, or address, so that messages can be sent specifically to that computer. Therefore, you need an address to send E-MAIL from one computer to another.

When a block of data is transferred or stored electronically, a code, or address is added to direct the block to its destination or a location where it can be found if someone wants to retrieve it. In a NETWORK, therefore, an address provides a link to a site where you can find certain information.

ANALOG TRANSMISSION. A means of transmitting information through a system or with a device in which the data input or output are represented by a continuously changing variable, such as current or voltage.

Early computers were analog, although today, most electronic devices use DIGITAL TRANSMISSION.

AREA CODES. The numerical code used in telephone numbers to designate a particular state or, in states that have more than one area code, a certain area within the state. See also TELEPHONE EXCHANGE.

Your telephone directory will have either a map of area codes covering the United States, Canada, and certain other locations; an alphabetical listing of major cities and the associated codes; or both.

Some directories also include a reverse list arranged numerically so that you can find the location when you know only the area code. Many directories also have a list of INTERNATIONAL DIALING CODES.

Numerous Web sites (see Chapter 6/WEB SITE) also have lists of area codes and recent or scheduled changes. Select lists that have been recently updated.

As population increases, new area codes are continually being added. In fact, long-distance carriers frequently publish a notice that because of the increase in CELLULAR COMMUNICATION, FAX TRANSMISSION, and other TELECOMMUNICATIONS activities, area codes are subject to change at any time.

Check a current Web site, or call the appropriate number for assistance given in the front of your telephone directory if you believe that codes you need to use may have changed.

BEEPER. See PAGING.

BROADCAST. The transmission of the same message to more than one person at the same time or, in FAX TRANSMISSION, consecutively. For example, a sales manager may want to send an agenda for an upcoming sales meeting to *all* sales representatives.

BULLETIN BOARD SYSTEM. See E-MAIL.

CABLE. The material, such as wires, or other media, such as fiber optics, used to connect communications systems.

Fiber optic cables have long, tiny glass or silica fibers that carry pulses of light, and the cables have less signal loss than traditional coaxial cable.

In addition, they're more fragile, which makes them more difficult to tap into, thereby providing greater security for sensitive or confidential data. The data also can be transmitted at billions of bits per second. See also Chapter 6/BAUD RATE; BIT.

Metal cables can carry either power or communications signals. Fiber optic cables can transport only communications signals.

CELLULAR COMMUNICATION. The wireless transmission of voice and data using radio frequencies (traditional mobile technology) or telephone signals (the newer cell phone technology).

Cellular operation. Cellular technology uses geographic cells connected to a series of cellular transmission towers. The towers receive and transmit signals, switching them as necessary to the nearest central office to maintain continuous transmission.

Therefore, when someone who is using a cell phone in a car drives from one area to another, a new cell picks up the transmission so that it is not interrupted (a process known as *roaming*).

In the area covered by a user's cellular carrier, calls are considered local. As a user moves outside that area, the cell phone's roaming light indicates that the user has left his or her phone's local area. Usage charges outside the local area are usually higher.

Certain limitations of roaming will be eliminated when multiple frequencies are included in all cell phones. Toward that end, the International Telecommunications Union is unifying wireless standards worldwide so that users can roam around the globe without ever having to change phones.

Cellular features. Of the several hundred million subscribers worldwide, about three-fourths use digital cell phones. In general, digital networks offer better voice quality and privacy features.

The greater frequency bands of digital cell phones also allow users to talk to others anywhere in the world. Some phones also incorporate other technologies, such as E-MAIL, Internet access, and FAX TRANSMISSION.

Many cell phones have features like those of an office telephone, such as preprogrammed numbers, voice-message capability, and outputs for use with a laptop computer. Some can be converted to a speakerphone for hands-free operation while one is driving.

A voice-recognition feature also contributes to hands-free operation. Users can preprogram the phone with frequently dialed numbers and call a selected number with a single voice command.

However, using a cell phone while driving or even while walking in a crowded area is not recommended. It can lead to collisions with vehicles or people and, in any case, may be annoying to others.

See also SATELLITE COMMUNICATION; TELEPHONE CALLS; TELEPHONE ETIQUETTE; TELEPHONE SERVICES.

COMMON CARRIER. A private or governmental organization, such as a telephone company or railroad, that provides voice, data, and other TELECOMMUNICATIONS services or transport services to the public in a given area.

Long-distance telephone companies, or carriers, are known as *interexchange carriers*. The list of these carriers has grown since the Regional Bell Operating Companies (RBOCs) were granted the right to provide long-distance as well as local services.

Common carriers are usually regulated by local, state, or federal agencies. The Common Carrier Bureau (CCB) administers the policies of the FEDERAL COMMUNICATIONS COMMISSION (FCC) that apply to carriers of local and long-distance TELEPHONE SERVICES.

COMPUTER CONFERENCE. See Chapter 4/COMPUTER CONFERENCE.

CONFERENCE CALL. See Chapter 4/AUDIOCONFERENCE.

DIGITAL TRANSMISSION. A means of transmitting information through a system or with a device in which the data input or output is encoded as discrete (separate) on–off pulses.

In modern computers, the input or output is represented by the digits 0 and 1. Early analog computers (see ANALOG TRANSMISSION) handled information in continuously variable quantities rather than in discrete digital representations.

E-MAIL. The abbreviated form for electronic mail, a form of message transmission handled by computers. In general, a sender prepares a message by computer and transmits it (usually over the telephone lines), along with any attachment, such as a report already stored in the computer, to a receiving computer in another location.

See also E-MAIL COMMUNICATION for preparation guidelines and E-MAIL ETIQUETTE for rules of common courtesy.

Depending on your system, you not only can deliver an e-mail to an e-mail address but also may be able to deliver it to a fax machine or a Telex machine (Teleprinter Exchange Service) on a teleprinter network.

In addition, some organizations offer a service whereby an e-mail can be sent to and printed out at their establishment. The printout can then be delivered to a street address (by postal mail or courier service) or picked up by the recipient. This service is useful when a recipient doesn't have e-mail.

E-mail transmission. A NETWORK e-mail ADDRESS is registered with the service provider (see Chapter 6/INTERNET SERVICE PROVIDER [ISP]) through which you have access to other users.

A service provider enables you to connect your equipment to the regular telephone lines and, through the use of a modem (see Chapter 6/MODEM), send messages to and receive them from others who are also connected to the network.

Usually, when you instruct the computer to send a message through a large public network, it goes either to the recipient's computer, if it is turned on, or to a host computer of the recipient's service provider.

A host computer will hold a message until the recipient turns on his or her computer. At that time, the host forwards the waiting message to the recipient's computer.

A modem will convert a computer's DIGITAL TRANSMISSION signals to the ANALOG TRANSMISSION signals of the telephone lines and back again. However, a new INTEGRATED SERVICES DIGITAL NETWORK (ISDN) standard makes this conversion unnecessary. See also WIRELESS COMMUNICATION.

An incoming message is displayed on the recipient's display screen. Depending on the e-mail system, it can then be read, printed, saved, or deleted, as desired. Some systems automatically delete messages after a certain time.

A *bulletin board system* (see Chapter 6/BULLETIN BOARD SYSTEM [BBS]) is a primarily local system providing a site for a variety of programs, including e-mail. Messages are posted there until the recipient is ready to read them.

In many systems, passwords may be used for privacy and security. Nevertheless, private use is ensured only to the extent that one can protect a password from others who may have learned how to crack codes and breach the security.

Other security measures for sensitive material include using *encryption,* or sending the message in a coded form. You may also route your message through an *anonymous remailer service.*

Integrated systems. Some systems unite e-mail with other technologies. For example, one service enables users to access e-mail messages over the telephone as voice messages, without the use of a PC.

With *e-mail by phone,* users can call from any location worldwide to access messages sent as standard computer e-mail to their e-mail addresses. After they dial a personalized number, the message is read to them in voice.

Listeners may also respond by voice over the telephone, rather than transmit a reply from their computers.

Another system unites voice mail and fax through e-mail. It enables users to have fax and voice mail messages sent to their e-mail address and saved as file attachments. Although the message service is free, users must purchase additional software to handle the voice mail conversions.

E-mail for travelers.   Internet e-mail (see Chapter 6/INTERNET E-MAIL) is often preferred over other commercial e-mail software systems, even though the other systems may have more features, such as graphics and greater editing capability.

An important advantage is that it can usually be sent to and received from any computer worldwide, provided the other computer is also connected to the Internet (see Chapter 6/INTERNET) and is equipped with a browsing program. See also Chapter 6/BROWSER.

Public-access Internet places can be found worldwide. For example, *cybercafes* (Internet cafes), located in many countries, sell Internet access along with cappuccino. Also, better hotels usually have high-speed Internet hookups in guestrooms.

E-MAIL COMMUNICATION.   The preparation, transmission, and receipt of messages by computer; the procedures followed in preparing, sending, and receiving E-MAIL messages. See also E-MAIL ETIQUETTE; Chapter 6/INTERNET E-MAIL; INTRANET E-MAIL.

E-mail preparation.   The memo format (see Chapter 8/MEMOS) is used for e-mail, and the e-mail software that you use will provide a template with guidewords, such as *To, From,* and *Subject* (others may be added).

The template automatically appears on screen when you instruct the computer that you're ready to compose a message. You may then fill in the correct information after each guideword and compose the message, or body, in the space provided beneath the template.

The body should be written in the same style as the body of a paper memo, although various guidelines apply, especially to an electronic version. See the forthcoming list, and see also the tips in E-MAIL ETIQUETTE.

E-mail messages are usually prepared in plain text, without graphics. However, some systems can also handle the transfer of files with graphics.

Special usage guidelines.   Follow these e-mail communication guidelines in addition to observing the rules of proper e-mail etiquette:

1. Use the same care that you would use in preparing postal mail concerning neatness, conciseness, accuracy, clarity, and correct grammar, spelling, and punctuation.

2. Treat your e-mail message as public information to avoid potential litigation prompted by a moment of carelessness in saying too much or saying the wrong thing.

3. Use your company's system for business purposes only, not for personal messages, soliciting personal business, or other unethical practices.

4. Use passwords, coded messages (*encryption*), or any other security measure available in your company to maintain privacy and confidentiality in messages that you send and receive. See also Chapter 6/ENCRYPTION.

5. Do not leave an e-mail message on screen when you leave your desk or your office.

6. Save well-written messages for future reference, the same as you might save postal letters for a model letters file.

7. Use a recognizable name in your e-mail address, not something irrelevant such as *xyz@serviceprovider.com*.

8. Check the mail several times a day, and respond promptly to all legitimate messages (not junk mail), the same as you would do with paper mail.

9. Send copies only to people to whom you would send copies if it were paper mail.

10. Compose your messages off-line to allow more time to review, edit, correct, and proofread them before transmission.

11. Use an effective subject line to save the reader time in digesting the message.

12. Confine each e-mail to a single subject to keep messages as short as possible (but not terse), preferably no more than one computer screen.

13. Include the sender's original message in your reply if your software will allow you to do this.

14. Use the *unsend* option, if available, to take back or cancel a message you shouldn't have sent before it reaches the recipient.

15. Keep a message history log, if this feature is available on your software, if you need to monitor what happens to a message.

16. Check the appropriate box to receive a receipt, if this feature is available and you want to know if someone has opened your message.

17. Do not send attachments that are copyrighted.

18. Send large attachments by paper mail if it would take the recipient a long time to download (copy) them, or use one of the Internet's electronic document delivery services designed especially to transmit exceptionally large files.

19. Find out whether a recipient's system can accept your attachment or whether it has a different standard (software is available to decode attachments that you can't open or that appear as gibberish).

41

20. Beware of opening attachments that someone else sends to you since they may contain a virus (copy them onto a disk where your antiviral software can first scan them).

21. Use filtering software to increase efficiency by categorizing messages by name, subject, and key word.

22. Attach a *signature file* with your telephone and fax numbers and your postal mailing address, if the recipient would find this information useful.

23. Don't respond to junk mail or try to unsubscribe, since *spammers* (those who mail to all possible addresses) may use your response to confirm your e-mail address (investigate whether you can create a filter that will delete all such mail in the future).

24. Check whether messages that you delete—the ones you sent and the ones you received—are actually backed up somewhere and are therefore still in existence.

25. Delete any history file of Web sites, or list of favorites, that you recently visited since marketers may use it in spamming. See also Chapter 6/BOOKMARK; SPAMMING; WEB SITE.

26. Save your messages in your in box or in a message log, or move them to the appropriate folder, according to office practices.

See also INCOMING MAIL for steps to follow in processing all forms of incoming messages.

E-MAIL ETIQUETTE. Common courtesy and proper protocol in preparing, sending, and receiving E-MAIL and attachments. See also Chapter 6/NETIQUETTE and the preparation guidelines in E-MAIL COMMUNICATION.

1. Use e-mail only for appropriate business messages or informal social messages but not for formal messages, such as a formal invitation, and not for sensitive messages, such as a sympathy message or a letter firing someone (use the regular mail, a telephone call, or a personal visit).

2. If you are only testing your e-mail, not sending a realistic message, inform the recipients by putting the word *Test* in the subject line so that they won't waste time reading the message.

3. Don't send information that a recipient may not want. If you're uncertain, consider sending it to a bulletin board where readers may read it if and when they wish.

4. Be considerate of the recipient's time by keeping your messages brief.

5. Use conversational abbreviations, such as *BTW* for "by the way," and *emoticons* (symbols for emotion), such as *;-)* for "winking," only in informal personal mail, never in business mail.

6. Avoid all capital letters, which appear as shouting.

7. Be especially careful not to humiliate the recipient by saying something critical or embarrassing to the person that might be seen by others who have access to his or her e-mail.

8. Don't criticize one person to another since the other person may unintentionally forward your message to the subject of your criticism, or you may unintentionally press the wrong key and send your remarks to the wrong person.

9. Don't compose a message when you're angry or send a hostile message in response to something you perceive as a breach of computer etiquette (known as *flaming*).

10. Send a polite response when you're the one who is being criticized for your e-mail content or etiquette.

See also Telephone etiquette; Voice mail etiquette.

EXCHANGE. See Telephone exchange.

FAX TRANSMISSION. The process of sending exact copies of text or graphics to one or more persons (consecutively) over the telephone lines; the document being sent.

By scanning a document, a fax (short for facsimile) machine creates binary signals that are converted to analog signals by a built-in modem, which enables the signals to travel over the telephone lines. (In a binary system, every value is represented as either 0 or 1.)

See also Analog transmission; Ditigal transmission; Chapter 6/Bit; Modem.

When a fax is sent from one independent fax machine to another, the receiving machine's modem converts the signals back to binary form, and its printer prints a copy of the document.

PC fax board. Whereas an independent fax machine has no keyboard or editing capability, a computer, which does have such capability, can be equipped with a *PC fax board*. This enables it to function as a fax machine as well as a computer. Therefore, messages can both be prepared on and faxed from the computer.

A PC fax board also converts a computer's binary data into analog signals for transmission over the telephone lines. Both text and graphics can be handled with a computer containing a PC fax board, the same as with a standalone fax machine.

If a separate, or independent, fax machine is used, a message must be prepared manually or with other equipment, such as by computer, and then physically brought to the fax machine for transmission.

Internet faxing. Using the Internet for faxing to other countries (see Chapter 6/INTERNET; INTERNET FAX), you can bypass the Public Switch Telephone Network and avoid long-distance telephone charges, paying only the usual service provider's charges. See also Chapter 6/INTERNET SERVICE PROVIDER (ISP).

Some machines are specifically designed to use the Internet, although usually, they can also function as a traditional fax machine.

Faxes can be sent over the Internet to either an independent fax machine or an e-mail address. However, in either case, Internet transmission is slower, so it may take several hours instead of several minutes for a message to reach the recipient.

Special features. Fax machines have numerous special features and capabilities, such as sending multiple transmissions (see BROADCAST) and POLLING. Multifunction machines can handle even more tasks, such as scanning material into the computer.

Small, wireless fax devices (see WIRELESS COMMUNICATION) are available for on-the-road convenience while one is traveling. One model combines fax transmission capability with a calendar, calculator, notepad, and telephone book. The device also has a keyboard for preparing messages to be sent.

A popular innovation is *fax-on-demand,* a digital voice-and-fax document-delivery system. This type of system enables users to telephone an organization, such as the Internal Revenue Service; request information; and immediately receive the requested material by fax.

FEDERAL COMMUNICATIONS COMMISSION (FCC). An independent governmental body whose members are appointed by the president and are charged with regulating COMMON CARRIERS engaged in interstate or foreign communications. The FCC grants licenses and regulates rates.

The Common Carrier Bureau (CCB) administers the FCC's policies concerning local and long-distance telephone companies.

Although profane language and lottery-type offers are not permitted by radio transmission, the FCC generally does not have censorship powers in matters involving TELECOMMUNICATIONS transmissions.

FOREIGN EXCHANGE LINE. Sometimes known as an *FX line*. A communications line provided by a COMMON CARRIER that terminates in one central office but is assigned the number used by a remote central office. See also LEASED LINE.

INCOMING MAIL. All forms of electronic, postal, private delivery, or other mail received in an office. See VOICE MAIL for information about incoming voice messages. See also E-MAIL; FAX TRANSMISSION; PRIVATE DELIVERY SERVICES; UNITED STATES POSTAL SERVICE.

Although incoming e-mail can be viewed on a computer screen and then filed or deleted, some executives want to have a paper copy printed and handled the same as postal mail. Follow your employer's preference. See also MAIL RECORD.

Checking the e-mail. To avoid having messages pile up, check your system's e-mail *in box* regularly, at least three times a day, such as the first thing in the morning, around noon, and later in the afternoon.

If your employer does not retrieve his or her own e-mail messages, print out those that you collect for your employer or other executives (except for junk mail or other items that you delete). Organize them in order of priority, and add them to the incoming paper mail.

If you receive an e-mail in error, forward it to the appropriate persons or return it to the sender, with an attached note explaining that you received it in error.

Reply to all messages promptly, but if you can't immediately reply to something, print out a copy, and add it to your pending paper file. Then send the person a brief message giving a date when you will respond.

File e-mail messages that you may want to refer to later even if they don't require a response. But delete messages that are of no interest and require no response.

Sorting the mail. If you open and sort the mail in your office, organize the e-mail printouts, fax copies, and unopened postal mail in four piles: (1) correspondence, (2) bills and statements, (3) advertisements and circulars, and (4) newspapers and periodicals. Further separate personal from business items and outside mail from interoffice material.

Opening the paper mail. Carefully slit open the sealed correspondence first, and then open the packages, saving the address labels if a letter isn't enclosed.

Attach any enclosures to the appropriate letters, and also attach the envelope if a letter doesn't include a return address.

Write "Not at This Address" on the envelopes of postal mail delivered to you in error. Note that only First Class Mail can be returned to the sender without applying additional postage.

Don't open letters marked *Personal* or *Confidential* unless your employer has asked you to do so.

Routing the mail. Sort e-mail printouts, fax copies, and postal letters and memos into three groups: (1) those requiring your employer's attention, (2) those requiring someone else's attention, and (3) those requiring your attention.

When possible, put e-mail printouts and paper mail on your employer's desk before he or she arrives. If a file or previous correspondence relating to a current letter will facilitate action, attach the incoming letter to that file or correspondence.

If your employer wants the mail annotated, jot appropriate comments in the margins, underscore key phrases, and so on. (Use a yellow marking pen, a non-reproducible blue pencil, or self-sticking, removable notes, as your office requires.)

If several people should see certain correspondence, write the name of each on a routing slip, and number the names in the order in which each person should receive the mail. Then attach the slip to the correspondence, and forward it to the first person on the slip designated to receive it. See Figure 1.

Handling newspapers and periodicals. Put publications your employer likes to read in folders labeled *Newspapers and Periodicals*, and place them on his or her desk. Send the rest of the publications to other people who need them, or organize them on the shelves for reference.

Handling advertisements and notices. Advertisements, bulletins, and so on are often useful as a free source of information on new products, services, meetings, and other items. Therefore, save them until they've been examined.

Handling bills and statements. Items requiring payment are usually held until a certain time of the month. It's not necessary to open them until the other mail has been opened and disposed of.

See also OUTGOING MAIL.

INTEGRATED SERVICES DIGITAL NETWORK (ISDN). An international TELECOMMUNICATIONS standard intended to cover the integration of voice and

INCOMING MAIL: FIGURE 1: Routing Slip

		Read by	*Date*
	*Date:*_____		
	PLEASE INITIAL, DATE, AND ROUTE IN ORDER NUMBERED		
2	A. Ashton, Sales Department	A.A.	3/7
1	T. Hartwell, Training Department	*(initials)*	2/6
4	M. Smith, Training Department	*(initials)*	3/10
3	R. Weiler, Business Office	*(initials)*	2/8
5	File Department		

data as well as other aspects of communications. The ISDN makes it possible for channels to handle digitized voice, data, and even video all at the same time.

The ISDN uses digital links (see Digital transmission) from beginning to end, without the need for a modem (see Chapter 6/Modem) to convert signals from digital to analog and back again. By contrast, traditional networks include analog signals (see Analog transmission) between the users and their exchanges.

With the ISDN, information can be transmitted much faster than would be possible on standard telephone lines. Although the ISDN can be added to most standard lines, the network facilities, or connection, to the local telephone office must be compatible with ISDN technology.

Interexchange carrier. See Common carrier.

INTERNATIONAL DIALING CODES. The international access, country, and city codes preceding a local telephone number that must be used in dialing a location in another country.

Contact your long-distance carrier for instructions on placing direct-dial calls, which usually require the international access code, the country code, the city code, and the local number, as in *011-591-2-555-0700* for a number in La Paz, Bolivia.

A few places, such as the Dominican Republic and the Virgin Islands, can be reached directly from the United States by dialing 1 plus the city code followed by the local number.

If you can't dial direct to an area, call your carrier's operator for assistance in placing the call.

Many telephone directories have lists of international dialing codes, and numerous Web sites (see Chapter 6/Web site) also have lists of international dialing codes. Since codes change frequently, be certain to use the most recent list.

INTERNATIONAL TIME. The time of day in any of the 24 time zones of the world. Each zone is 15 degrees longitude wide, and the starting point for measuring degrees for the various zones is the *prime meridian* (the longitudinal meridian passing through Greenwich, England).

The 12th zone is divided in half by the 180th meridian, known as the *International Date Line.* East of that line, the date is advanced one day. West of it, the date is set back one day.

Coordinated Universal Time (UTC), traditionally known as Greenwich Mean Time (GMT), is the standard time of the prime meridian. It is defined by a formula that relates UTC to mean sidereal time in Greenwich, England.

Time chart. Figure 1 lists the times for selected areas around the world. The listings for the time at the prime meridian are given in the middle row of the chart. The two jagged lines in the chart are included to separate the movement of time from P.M. to A.M., or from one day to the next.

To use the chart, find a starting point in the United States, such as New York City, Chicago, or San Francisco. Then find another city of interest to you or one near to it.

For example, you may want to use Chicago as your reference and find out the corresponding time in Rio de Janeiro. According to the chart, when it is 6 P.M. in Chicago, it is 9 P.M. in Rio.

The chart therefore indicates that you should *add* three hours to Chicago standard time whenever you want to know the corresponding time in Rio. (Add or subtract an hour, as appropriate, for daylight savings time.)

INTERNATIONAL TIME: FIGURE 1: Time Differentials Worldwide

Location	0100	0200	0300	0400	0500	0600	0700	0800	0900	1000	1100	1200	1300	1400	1500	1600	1700	1800	1900	2000	2100	2200	2300	2400
Aleutian Islands / Tutuila, Samoa	2:00pm	3:00pm	4:00pm	5:00pm	6:00pm	7:00pm	8:00pm	9:00pm	10:00pm	11:00pm	MIDNIGHT	1:00am	2:00am	3:00am	4:00am	5:00am	6:00am	7:00am	8:00am	9:00am	10:00am	11:00am	NOON	1:00pm
Hawaiian Islands / Alaska	3:00pm	4:00pm	5:00pm	6:00pm	7:00pm	8:00pm	9:00pm	10:00pm	11:00pm	Medianoche	1:00am	2:00am	3:00am	4:00am	5:00am	6:00am	7:00am	8:00am	9:00am	10:00am	11:00am	Mediodia	1:00pm	2:00pm
Tahiti	4:00pm	5:00pm	6:00pm	7:00pm	8:00pm	9:00pm	10:00pm	11:00pm	MINUIT	1:00am	2:00am	3:00am	4:00am	5:00am	6:00am	7:00am	8:00am	9:00am	10:00am	11:00am	MIDI	1:00pm	2:00pm	3:00pm
San Francisco & Pacific Coast	5:00pm	6:00pm	7:00pm	8:00pm	9:00pm	10:00pm	11:00pm	MIDNIGHT	1:00am	2:00am	3:00am	4:00am	5:00am	6:00am	7:00am	8:00am	9:00am	10:00am	11:00am	NOON	1:00pm	2:00pm	3:00pm	4:00pm
Chicago, Central America (except Panama) Mexico, Winnipeg	7:00pm	8:00pm	9:00pm	10:00pm	11:00pm	Medianoche	1:00am	2:00am	3:00am	4:00am	5:00am	6:00am	7:00am	8:00am	9:00am	10:00am	11:00am	Mediodia	1:00pm	2:00pm	3:00pm	4:00pm	5:00pm	6:00pm
Bogota, Havana, Lima, Montreal, Bermuda New York, Panama	8:00pm	9:00pm	10:00pm	11:00pm	MINUIT	1:00am	2:00am	3:00am	4:00am	5:00am	6:00am	7:00am	8:00am	9:00am	10:00am	11:00am	MIDI	1:00pm	2:00pm	3:00pm	4:00pm	5:00pm	6:00pm	7:00pm
Buenos Aires Santiago, Puerto Rico Lapaz, Asuncion	9:00pm	10:00pm	11:00pm	MIDNIGHT	1:00am	2:00am	3:00am	4:00am	5:00am	6:00am	7:00am	8:00am	9:00am	10:00am	11:00am	NOON	1:00pm	2:00pm	3:00pm	4:00pm	5:00pm	6:00pm	7:00pm	8:00pm
Rio, Santos Sao Paulo	10:00pm	11:00pm	Medianoche	1:00am	2:00am	3:00am	4:00am	5:00am	6:00am	7:00am	8:00am	9:00am	10:00am	11:00am	Mediodia	1:00pm	2:00pm	3:00pm	4:00pm	5:00pm	6:00pm	7:00pm	8:00pm	9:00pm
Iceland	MINUIT	1:00am	2:00am	3:00am	4:00am	5:00am	6:00am	7:00am	8:00am	9:00am	10:00am	11:00am	MIDI	1:00pm	2:00pm	3:00pm	4:00pm	5:00pm	6:00pm	7:00pm	8:00pm	9:00pm	10:00pm	11:00pm
Algiers, Lisbon London, Paris Madrid	1:00am	2:00am	3:00am	4:00am	5:00am	6:00am	7:00am	8:00am	9:00am	10:00am	11:00am	NOON	1:00pm	2:00pm	3:00pm	4:00pm	5:00pm	6:00pm	7:00pm	8:00pm	9:00pm	10:00pm	11:00pm	MIDNIGHT
G.M.T.	0100	0200	0300	0400	0500	0600	0700	0800	0900	1000	1100	1200	1300	1400	1500	1600	1700	1800	1900	2000	2100	2200	2300	2400
Bengasi, Berlin, Oslo Rome, Tunis, Tripoli Warsaw, Stockholm	2:00am	3:00am	4:00am	5:00am	6:00am	7:00am	8:00am	9:00am	10:00am	11:00am	Mediodia	1:00pm	2:00pm	3:00pm	4:00pm	5:00pm	6:00pm	7:00pm	8:00pm	9:00pm	10:00pm	11:00pm	Medianoche	1:00am
Cairo, Capetown Istanbul, Moscow	3:00am	4:00am	5:00am	6:00am	7:00am	8:00am	9:00am	10:00am	11:00am	MIDI	1:00pm	2:00pm	3:00pm	4:00pm	5:00pm	6:00pm	7:00pm	8:00pm	9:00pm	10:00pm	11:00pm	MINUIT	1:00am	2:00am
Ethiopia, Iraq Madagascar	4:00am	5:00am	6:00am	7:00am	8:00am	9:00am	10:00am	11:00am	NOON	1:00pm	2:00pm	3:00pm	4:00pm	5:00pm	6:00pm	7:00pm	8:00pm	9:00pm	10:00pm	11:00pm	MIDNIGHT	1:00am	2:00am	3:00am
Bombay, Ceylon New Delhi	6:30am	7:30am	8:30am	9:30am	10:30am	11:30am	12:30pm	1:30pm	2:30pm	3:30pm	4:30pm	5:30pm	6:30pm	7:30pm	8:30pm	9:30pm	10:30pm	11:30pm	12:30am	1:30am	2:30am	3:30am	4:30am	5:30am
Chungking Changtu, Kunming	8:00am	9:00am	10:00am	11:00am	Mediodia	1:00pm	2:00pm	3:00pm	4:00pm	5:00pm	6:00pm	7:00pm	8:00pm	9:00pm	10:00pm	11:00pm	Medianoche	1:00am	2:00am	3:00am	4:00am	5:00am	6:00am	7:00am
Celebes, Hong Kong Manila, Shanghai	9:00am	10:00am	11:00am	MIDI	1:00pm	2:00pm	3:00pm	4:00pm	5:00pm	6:00pm	7:00pm	8:00pm	9:00pm	10:00pm	11:00pm	MINUIT	1:00am	2:00am	3:00am	4:00am	5:00am	6:00am	7:00am	8:00am
Korea, Japan Adelaide	10:00am	11:00am	NOON	1:00pm	2:00pm	3:00pm	4:00pm	5:00pm	6:00pm	7:00pm	8:00pm	9:00pm	10:00pm	11:00pm	MIDNIGHT	1:00am	2:00am	3:00am	4:00am	5:00am	6:00am	7:00am	8:00am	9:00am
Brisbane, Guam Melbourne, New Guinea Sydney	11:00am	Mediodia	1:00pm	2:00pm	3:00pm	4:00pm	5:00pm	6:00pm	7:00pm	8:00pm	9:00pm	10:00pm	11:00pm	Medianoche	1:00am	2:00am	3:00am	4:00am	5:00am	6:00am	7:00am	8:00am	9:00am	10:00am
Solomon Islands New Caledonia	MIDI	1:00pm	2:00pm	3:00pm	4:00pm	5:00pm	6:00pm	7:00pm	8:00pm	9:00pm	10:00pm	11:00pm	MINUIT	1:00am	2:00am	3:00am	4:00am	5:00am	6:00am	7:00am	8:00am	9:00am	10:00am	11:00am
Wellington Auckland	12:30pm	1:30pm	2:30pm	3:30pm	4:30pm	5:30pm	6:30pm	7:30pm	8:30pm	9:30pm	10:30pm	11:30pm	12:30am	1:30am	2:30am	3:30am	4:30am	5:30am	6:30am	7:30am	8:30am	9:30am	10:30am	11:30am

Web sites. You can also use international time Web sites (see Chapter 6/WEB SITE) to determine time in other locations around the world. At one site, for example, if you enter the closest major U.S. city and the time there that you want to convert, the site will give you the corresponding time in selected cities around the world.

INTERNET. See Chapter 6/INTERNET.

INTEROFFICE COMMUNICATION. Electronic or paper communication between persons in different offices of the same organization.

Traditionally, interoffice communication (or correspondence) has referred to in-house paper messages in a memo format. (See Chapter 8/MEMOS.) Although the term has been expanded to include electronic as well as paper messages, it still refers to *internal* rather than external communication.

INTRANET. See Chapter 6/INTRANET.

LEASED LINE. A private TELECOMMUNICATIONS line reserved by a customer for its exclusive use in transmitting voice, data, or graphics to another location.

For example, a high-volume user or a company in need of extensive security may want its own line for transmission between the home office and an office in another state or country. A private line is then leased from a COMMON CARRIER much in the same way that a computer might be leased from an equipment vendor.

See also FOREIGN EXCHANGE LINE.

LOCAL AREA NETWORK (LAN). A NETWORK of computers located in a limited area, such as in an office building or throughout the buildings on a college campus, that are physically connected to one another, such as by CABLE.

Usually, one or a few computers represent the central server (see Chapter 6/SERVER) to which others are connected. The link enables all machines to share information as well as devices, such as a common printer.

Home LANs, which offer some of the same features (such as file and printer sharing), can be used by telecommuters in their home offices. See also Chapter 1/TELECOMMUTING.

Compare with METROPOLITAN AREA NETWORK (MAN); WIDE AREA NETWORK (WAN).

MAIL RECORD. A record of all electronic or postal mail sent out of the office (other than routine mailings, such as bills and statements).

CHAPTER 2 • MESSAGE TRANSMISSION AND DELIVERY

When an employer needs this type of record and tracking information for legal or other reasons, the record is useful for verifying the disposition of mail. It can also be used for future follow-ups.

If such a record would be helpful but none exists at present, you can devise a suitable form with appropriate headings for columns where you would record daily information. If you intend to maintain the record manually, you can also print or photocopy a supply of the forms as needed.

If you prefer, however, you can maintain the record by computer and store the forms in your electronic files. See Figure 1 for an example of a simple form that can be handwritten or computer generated, as preferred.

METROPOLITAN AREA NETWORK (MAN). A TELECOMMUNICATIONS network within the limits of a metropolitan area, such as a city and its suburbs. Therefore, it is larger than a LOCAL AREA NETWORK (LAN) but smaller than a WIDE AREA NETWORK (WAN).

MANs are usually created when data transmission activity exceeds and extends beyond what a more limited LAN can handle.

MICROWAVE COMMUNICATION. Data and voice communications that are transmitted on straight-line, short-length, high-frequency electromagnetic waves.

Since microwave transmissions travel in straight lines, the towers that are constructed to relay microwave signals across the country must be in proximity of each other (a form of communication known as *line-of-sight transmission*). Usually, they are no more than 30 miles apart.

NETIQUETTE. See E-MAIL ETIQUETTE; Chapter 6/NETIQUETTE.

NETWORK. A collection of any number of points that are connected by communications channels, such as a telephone network or a computer network. The size may vary from a single LOCAL AREA NETWORK (LAN) to a WIDE AREA NETWORK (WAN). The Internet (see Chapter 6/INTERNET), on the other hand, consists of not one but many networks worldwide.

A computer network, for example, connects individual sites, or workstations, enabling users to share data, software, and equipment.

However, individuals may also set up a formal or informal human network, or association, of people who may meet from time to time to discuss matters of mutual interest and to share information. An association such as the INTERNATIONAL

MAIL RECORD: FIGURE 1: Daily Mail Record

	MAIL RECORD				
Date	*Description*	*To*	*By*	*Action*	*Follow-up*
3/5	Wilshire contract draft	L. Snow	Fax	Approval	3/8
	Jennings request for appointment	M. Ellis	E-mail	Reply	---
	Co. brochure	K. Corte	USPS	---	---
3/6	Speaker invitation	G. Steiner	USPS	---	3/12

ASSOCIATION OF ADMINISTRATIVE PROFESSIONALS (IAAP) is an example of a formal network of people who share a common interest.

OPTICAL CHARACTER RECOGNITION (OCR). The identification of printed and, more recently, handwritten characters through the use of light-sensitive equipment to facilitate mail delivery. The UNITED STATES POSTAL SERVICE, for example, uses OCR devices to read addresses for rapid mail sorting. See also Chapter 8/ENVELOPES.

OUTGOING MAIL. All forms of postal, private delivery, electronic, voice, or other mail sent out of an office. See E-MAIL; FAX TRANSMISSION; PRIVATE DELIVERY SERVICES; UNITED STATES POSTAL SERVICE; VOICE MAIL.

Checking the e-mail. Many people do not print out drafts of e-mail for proofreading and evaluation but rather compose the messages on screen and immediately send them.

Senders who do this should take time to reread each message carefully and make the necessary or desirable corrections and revisions before transmission.

See E-MAIL, E-MAIL COMMUNICATION, and E-MAIL ETIQUETTE for guidelines in handling incoming and outgoing e-mail. See also Chapter 6/INTERNET E-MAIL; INTRANET E-MAIL; NETIQUETTE.

The same guidelines apply to attachments, whether they are e-mail attachments or very large files sent separately through an electronic Internet document delivery service. (See Chapter 6/INTERNET.) Proofreading is always mandatory.

Signing outgoing letters. Messages sent by e-mail are formatted as memos (see Chapter 8/MEMOS) and therefore need not be signed. However, many persons nevertheless type their names at the end of a message or create a macro that provides for fast entry of their names.

Since postal letters are signed manually, they require special attention. For example, when you give letters to someone to be signed, those that the person dictated should be separated from those that someone else wrote.

Assembling the mail. Whereas e-mail and fax transmissions are sent from machine to machine electronically (although a paper confirmation copy of e-mail or the original of a fax transmission may be sent later), postal letters must be folded and inserted in envelopes.

First, however, one should check each letter for the following:

1. Has the letter been signed?

2. Are all enclosures included?

3. Are the inside address and the envelope address the same?

4. Did the person dictating the letter make any revisions or corrections on it that must be edited in before mailing it?

Folding letters. Any letters to be sent by the UNITED STATES POSTAL SERVICE that are written on full-size letterheads for insertion in No. 9 or No. 10 envelopes should be folded as follows:

One fold from the bottom, about one-third of the way up

A second fold from the bottom to within 1/16 inch of the top

The folded letter is then ready for insertion in a No. 9 or No. 10 envelope with the top edge up.

Letters written on half-size letterhead should be folded as follows:

One fold from right to left, about one-third of the way across

A second fold from left to right, leaving about $1/16$ inch between the edges at the right

The folded letter is then ready to be inserted in a small envelope with the right edge up.

Letters are usually inserted in envelopes with the top edge up and without turning them over so that a letter is facing the reader right side up when it is pulled from the envelope. However, if you use a paper clip, put the letter in upside down so that the clip is away from the postage area where it might damage a postal machine.

Handling enclosures.   If an enclosure consists of two or more sheets, staple them together, but don't fasten them to the letter itself. Then fold the letter and the enclosures separately, and slip the enclosures inside the last fold of the letter.

If an enclosure is too large for a No. 9 or No. 10 envelope, use a larger envelope, and place the material inside without folding it. If desired, use a combination envelope, with the enclosures in the large envelope and the letter in a smaller envelope affixed to the larger one.

Staple small enclosures together and place them in the folds of the letter, or staple them to the front of the letter in the upper left corner, with the smallest enclosure on top. Tape enclosures such as coins to a card or put them in a small envelope, which can then be handled in the same way as other small enclosures.

PAGING.   Using a one-way communications device to send a message to someone who is not by his or her telephone but rather is in another location.

A variety of paging systems is available, ranging from a loudspeaker arrangement to a tiny pocket beeper. For example, a loudspeaker announcement might ask a person visiting a mall or an airport to pick up a courtesy phone or to go to a certain area.

If you know that someone carries a beeper, you can reach the person by calling the beeper's number. The beeper will then vibrate or emit an audible sound and will display your number. This tells the receiver to call you as soon as he or she can find a telephone. Some beepers also are able to display a short message.

PAL.   See Chapter 5/Air travel, *Planning the trip*.

Personal access link (PAL).   See Chapter 5/Air travel, *Planning the trip*.

Polling.   The process by which a machine, such as a computer or fax machine, sends messages to all the terminals connected to it on a single multi-point line.

Computer polling.   With the appropriate software, a computer may *poll* (ask) each terminal, one after another, if it has anything to send or if it has any data for the computer.

The computer therefore checks the status of each terminal and selects the one that may transmit at a particular moment. To avoid data jams in a multi-point system, the computer must continuously poll the terminals connected to it.

Fax polling.   The term *polling* is also applied in Fax transmission when a fax is programmed to poll various remote machines to collect data from each one.

For example, a fax in a central office may poll machines in remote offices to pick up each remote machine's accumulated sales orders for the day.

Postal Service.   See United States Postal Service.

Private delivery services.   Companies that provide local, national, and international delivery of letters, packages, and other material to the public. Such firms often transport the articles by both air and ground transportation.

In addition to the companies that are dedicated exclusively to message and package delivery, other organizations, such as bus lines, airlines, and taxis, sometimes provide letter and package delivery as a supplementary service.

Types of service offered.   Some companies also offer other forms of message delivery, such as E-mail and Fax transmission. For details, call the various companies (consult your yellow pages), or visit their Web sites. See also Chapter 6/Web site.

Delivery-service Web sites offer a variety of information and instructions ranging from tracking information to rate calculators to pickup requests.

Rates, size and weight restrictions, delivery networks, and services in general vary from one company to another. Delivery time for transport also may vary from within an hour locally to overnight, two-day, or longer service elsewhere.

Pickup and delivery service is commonly available for documents and parcels, and most companies maintain offices locally or in certain cities where you may deliver your letters or packages in person.

Contract mail services also serve as stations for various private delivery companies and provide packing, mailing, and other services, including electronic transmission, for a fee.

Time and cost considerations. Since fast-delivery services, such as overnight express for packages, are more expensive than regular service, senders should consider the urgency for delivery. This is particularly true when a weekend or holiday intervenes.

For example, a letter that might take several days by UNITED STATES POSTAL SERVICE mail does not need a more expensive overnight express service if it is sent on a Friday and would have to wait at the destination until the receiver's office opened again on Monday.

RADIO COMMUNICATION. The transmission of data, video, and voice by means of electromagnetic radio waves. Radio waves are widely used for both local and long-distance transmissions.

Through a process known as *modulation,* radio waves are able to add data, video, or voice signals to a uniform carrier. This enables communication by means such as a cell phone (see CELLULAR COMMUNICATIONS) or a pager. See PAGING.

Radio waves are also used for public television broadcasts and are commonly used for off-shore communications, such as transmissions to and from ships at sea.

SATELLITE COMMUNICATION. The transmission of data, video, and voice signals to and from remote earth stations by orbiting satellites. A satellite, therefore, provides a transmission channel for rapid communication over very long distances, such as between countries on different continents.

Satellite transmission. To transmit information, a satellite must be equipped with antennae that can receive radio signals from one earth station and can resend those signals to another earth station.

With a worldwide system of satellites, signals may be sent from station to station or satellite to satellite. For example, a signal may be sent from one earth station to a satellite, back to a different earth station, and on to a different satellite, and so on, repeatedly, until a far destination is reached.

Each signal between an earth station and a satellite is delayed about 275 milliseconds. An example is the delay that we see in television programs when a speaker in one country questions someone in another country and the latter person appears to wait a moment before replying.

Satellite service. Although inexpensive hand-held satellite communicators (similar to cell phones) are not yet widely available, some organizations make use of satellite transmissions (often at a premium rate). Some cruise ships, for example, that are beyond the reach of cell phones offer satellite-based E-MAIL.

Satellite telephone service, although more expensive than CELLULAR COMMUNICATION, is nevertheless expected to be a strong competitor in time or even to replace cellular service.

Whereas the more limited cell phone can be used only in areas that have transmission facilities available, a satellite phone can be used at any time, anywhere on earth, since signals are bounced off an orbiting satellite and do not require a constructed facility on the ground.

T-CARRIER. See Chapter 6/T-CARRIER.

TELECOMMUNICATIONS. The communication (transmission or reception) of data, voice, and other signals over a distance to or from one or more sites or between two or more sites.

See also ANALOG TRANSMISSION; CELLULAR COMMUNICATION; COMMON CARRIER; DIGITAL TRANSMISSION; E-MAIL; FAX TRANSMISSION; MICROWAVE COMMUNICATION; RADIO COMMUNICATION; SATELLITE COMMUNICATION; TELEPHONE CALLS; TELEPHONE SERVICES; VOICE MAIL; WIRELESS COMMUNICATION.

TELECONFERENCE. See Chapter 4/AUDIOCONFERENCE; COMPUTER CONFERENCE; VIDEOCONFERENCE.

TELEMARKETING. A form of marketing, or selling, goods and services through the use of TELECOMMUNICATIONS technology, primarily the telephone. The process may involve live voice contacts or automated outbound dialers and recorded messages.

To separate legitimate from fraudulent telemarketing practices, follow these guidelines:

1. Don't give in to high-pressure sales tactics, such as the refusal to take no for an answer.

2. Don't agree to make an immediate decision over the telephone.

3. Request that detailed written information be sent to you or to your accountant or attorney by mail before agreeing to buy or invest in anything.

4. Ignore testimonials that you can't verify.

5. Refuse any free offer or gift that also requires you to buy something else.

6. Don't deal with any organization that will not provide written references, such as a bank, that you can check out.

7. Ask for the names of state or federal agencies that regulate the telemarketer and with which the telemarketer is registered.

8. Ask for written information about what recourse you will have if what you buy is unsatisfactory.

9. Don't provide credit card information or other financial details over the telephone unless you have confirmed that the telemarketer is legitimate and you have agreed to make a purchase.

10. Avoid committing to any purchase or investment that is described as without risk.

11. Follow the adage that if something sounds too good to be true, it probably is.

12. Report telemarketers that use questionable sales practices to the Better Business Bureau or your state attorney general's office.

13. Disconnect computer-generated, automated-delivery calls by hanging up.

14. Write to the Direct Marketing Association, Telephone Preference Service, P.O. Box 9014, Farmingdale, New York 11735, to ask to have your name removed from telemarketing lists.

15. Apply the preceding guidelines to calls that you initiate with a company that engages in telemarketing.

TELEPHONE CALLS. Calls placed or received by desk, portable, cellular, satellite, or other telephone. See also CELLULAR COMMUNICATION; SATELLITE COMMUNICATION.

It also includes computer calls made possible with the technology of *audio compression.* As you speak, your voice is digitized, broken down into packets for travel over the Internet (see Chapter 6/INTERNET), and reassembled into sound at the destination.

The long-distance telephone company and associated long-distance charges are excluded with this type of computer call since it is treated like a local call, the same as an e-mail message. See also the description of a voice-response message system in VOICE MAIL.

Types of calls. Most telephone calls are direct-dialed *station-to-station calls* in which you're willing to speak with anyone who answers. If you want to speak only with a specific person and don't want to pay for the call if that person isn't there, you can place a *person-to-person call* through the operator at a higher rate.

To make a *collect call* or charge the call to a third number, follow the instructions in your telephone directory or those given by the telephone company.

International direct-distance dialing (IDDD) is available from most cities in the United States to numerous countries around the world. See INTERNATIONAL DIALING CODES.

Various telephone features and accessories contribute to more efficient and easier calling, as described in TELEPHONE SERVICES.

Telephone cards. A popular calling aid is the *telephone calling card*. Traditional cards, provided by telephone companies, can be used to charge a call to your own telephone number, no matter whose telephone you're using to place the call. Some companies also allow VISA and MasterCard to be used like calling cards.

A *prepaid phone card* is a variation of the traditional telephone calling card. Whereas you can usually get a traditional calling card at no cost, you must purchase a prepaid phone card from a retail or other establishment selling such cards.

Depending on the amount you pay, a card will allow you to make calls for a certain number of minutes or up to a designated face value. Follow the instructions stated on the card or on any literature that accompanies it.

An *international calling card,* available from interexchange carriers (see COMMON CARRIER), generally has more features than a regular calling card. It may also include services such as voice-message store and forward, language translation, FAX TRANSMISSION, and conference calling (multiple simultaneous connections).

Another option is the *call-back card.* You first dial a local number in the city you're visiting, which connects you to a computerized telephone network.

Through this network, your call is then routed to its destination in the United States, like an e-mail message, thereby bypassing the long-distance carriers and associated charges.

See also TELEPHONE ETIQUETTE for guidelines on proper conduct in placing and receiving calls.

TELEPHONE ETIQUETTE. The use of common courtesy in incoming and outgoing TELEPHONE CALLS handled by desk, portable, cellular, satellite, and other telephones. See also CELLULAR COMMUNICATION; SATELLITE COMMUNICATION.

Although the basic rules of etiquette have existed since businesses started using telephones, lapses in practicing common courtesy are still all too common. One telecommunications firm estimates that nearly 70 percent of customers stop doing business with a company because of the way they are treated on the telephone.

Follow these guidelines to create the best possible impression with your incoming and outgoing calls:

1. Answer the telephone on the second ring when possible (the first ring is unsettling to callers, and by the fourth ring, callers are becoming anxious).

2. Use a friendly greeting, and identify yourself when someone calls: "Good morning, Purchasing Department. This is Kathy speaking."

3. Ask for a caller's name if the person doesn't give it (verify the spelling and pronunciation if you have any doubts).

4. Identify yourself immediately when you place a call (name, title or department, company, and so on).

5. Apologize if you dial a wrong number.

6. Use a pleasant, professional, low speaking voice, and speak slowly enough to enunciate clearly (don't chew or eat as you speak), whether speaking to someone directly or leaving a machine message.

7. Get to the point of your call quickly, and don't talk too long.

8. Listen patiently and carefully without interrupting, even if the caller is a very slow speaker.

9. Don't use a speakerphone, except when prearranged for participants gathered in a room for a meeting, and in those cases, give the participants the names of others who will be listening.

10. Answer the telephone as usual even when someone is in the office (excuse yourself to the office visitor as you pick up the call).

11. Return calls during business hours and within 48 hours of receiving a message.

12. Speak with a smile, which usually affects one's speaking voice and encourages a friendlier tone.

13. Respond politely in appropriate places with *please, thank you,* and other courteous comments.

14. Turn down the radio volume and other distracting noise when you're speaking on the telephone.

15. Don't hesitate to ask people with difficult-to-follow accents to repeat or spell anything you didn't understand.

16. Don't confuse people with company jargon that they may not know. See also Chapter 7/JARGON.

17. Be sympathetic and helpful with irate callers, but don't tolerate serious threats or other such abuse (state that you have to hang up or, if appropriate, just hang up and immediately report the call to your supervisor).

18. Never be critical of someone else when you're speaking with a caller.

19. Apologize if you've made an error, but don't apologize inappropriately, such as simply because someone the caller is trying to reach works in a different office.

20. Provide necessary business information, but never volunteer unnecessary private information, such as "Ms. Adams is away from the office this week *because she's having back surgery.*"

21. Interrupt meetings for urgent calls to your employer, but take messages for calls that are not urgent.

22. Cut a call short if necessary, and do so with a polite explanation, such as "Excuse me, Mr. Breaux. I'm sorry to cut this short, but I have someone waiting in my office. May I call you back?"

23. Screen calls if your employer requires this (asking the names of callers and possibly company affiliations and reasons for a call).

24. Avoid the appearance of screening by first stating that your employer is not available; then ask if the call can be returned, who is calling, and so on. (If your employer might want to take the call, say that you'll check to see if he or she can be interrupted.)

25. Try to handle as many calls as possible yourself before taking a message for your employer or transferring the call to someone else.

26. Suggest that a caller write a letter if the person refuses to give his or her name and you have strict instructions never to put through such calls.

27. Arrange for someone else to answer your phone if you're away from your desk and don't have voice mail or call forwarding.

28. Ask permission before putting someone on hold, and thereafter, check in every 20 seconds.

29. Tell a caller where to call back if the call is cut off while you're transferring it.

30. Explain if you're using a cell phone or other device with unique characteristics or potential problems (for example, arrange to get back in touch if you're disconnected).

31. Speak quietly in public places when using a cell phone or public telephone, and avoid using a cell phone while driving in traffic or walking in crowded areas.

32. Take appropriate security precautions with cell phones and other devices that may not have guaranteed privacy (don't reveal credit card numbers, last names, private company information, and so on).

33. Close conversations with a courteous remark, such as "Thanks for calling, Mr. Hammond. Good-bye." (Omit the name if you're using a cell phone or other unsecured device.)

34. Allow callers to hang up first, and if you're the one hanging up first, gently return the receiver to its hook.

See also E-MAIL ETIQUETTE; VOICE MAIL ETIQUETTE.

TELEPHONE EXCHANGE.   One or more central offices or switching centers that administer TELECOMMUNICATIONS services, route calls within a business, and connect users to the outside lines (see TELEPHONE SERVICES); a geographic area served by a COMMON CARRIER (the first three digits of a local number designate the exchange: *555*-8021).

TELEPHONE LISTS.   Small, custom-devised lists, or directories, of frequently called numbers. Most employees are given a directory of company personnel that includes the people they and their employers often call in-house. An office may also have a list of customers and prospects.

In addition, a third list of service numbers and the numbers of family members is helpful. This additional list should include telephone, fax, cell phone, beeper, and other numbers, as well as e-mail addresses:

Business

Airlines

Building manager/
    superintendent

Bus lines

Car-rental agencies

Emergency

Equipment hotlines

Fire department

Internet service provider

Local telephone company

Long-distance telephone
    company

Messenger service

Office-machine repair service

Office suppliers

Police/office security

Post office and contract facilities

Private delivery services

Railroads

Shuttle service

Software hotlines

Taxis

Time of day

Travel agencies

Weather

Personal

Banks

Dentist

Doctors

Emergency

Family (residence/businesses)

Fire department

Florist

Friends frequently called

Garage/service station

Investment broker

Miscellaneous services (dry
    cleaner, tailor, and so on)

Organizations to which one
    belongs

Police

Restaurants that are frequented

Schools that children attend

Stores that are frequented

Theater ticket agency

TELEPHONE SERVICES. The services provided by COMMON CARRIERS to users who transmit on-site and off-site voice, data, and other signals over the telephone lines.

Telephone systems. Two common business systems are the pushbutton, or key, system and the exchange system. However, the distinction between the two is disappearing as both systems provide many of the same features.

1. *Pushbutton, or key, system.* In this system, common among small and medium-size companies, desk telephones are usually interconnected among various offices as well as connected to outside lines. A user may be able to access several lines, each of which has a separate button on the telephone.

2. *Telephone exchange.* A TELEPHONE EXCHANGE, which is common in larger organizations, can usually accommodate many more telephones than a push-button, or key, system can.

Both exchanges and other systems transmit not only voice but also other information, such as data and computer images. The information is sent as an ANALOG TRANSMISSION or a DIGITAL TRANSMISSION, depending on the equipment.

A *private branch exchange (PBX)* is a manual telephone switchboard operated by the user's attendant and located in the user's facilities. It connects telephones within the facilities and also connects them to the public telephone network.

Although a PBX operator answers and connects incoming calls, users can place their own internal or outgoing calls.

A *private automatic branch exchange (PABX)* is a more recent version of the PBX that may or may not require an attendant. The PABX is a private, automatic, dial-system exchange located and operated in the user's facilities.

Like the PBX, the PABX allows calls to be placed to or received from the public telephone network.

A *computerized branch exchange (CBX)* is an electronic PBX that uses computerized switching.

A *personal computer-private branch exchange (PC-PBX),* also known as a *telecommunications server* or *communications server,* is a general-purpose, desktop PC with software that enables it to function similar to other PBXs.

The various forms of PBX all refer to an on-site system on the user's premises. An example of an off-site system is the *Central Office Exchange Service (CENTREX).*

CENTREX is provided by a telephone company that assigns a portion of its central office to switch calls to and from stations located at user sites. Like a PBX, it connects the telephones in a user's company and provides a variety of features.

Accessories and features.   With most telephone systems, you can select a variety of accessories and features, depending on your office needs. For example:

1. A *buzzer button,* which signals someone to take a call
2. A *hold button,* which temporarily holds a call
3. *Automatic speed dialing,* which permits certain numbers to be called merely by pushing a button or dialing an abbreviated code
4. *Call forwarding,* or routing capability, which allows calls to be transferred automatically from one telephone to another

5. A *message feature,* such as a light that signals when someone has a call or message waiting

6. Lightweight *headsets,* which free one's hands to do other work while talking on the phone

7. *Dial safeguards,* which prevent unauthorized persons from making outside calls

8. *Call sequences,* which indicate the next call in line, process unanswered calls after a certain number of rings, and monitor incoming traffic to alert management when more operators are needed

9. A *speakerphone,* which channels sound through a speaker so that one or more persons within a certain distance can talk without using the telephone receiver

10. A *picturephone,* or *videophone,* which has a tiny screen on which you can see the person with whom you're speaking

11. *Call waiting,* which signals you when another call is coming in while you're on the phone

12. *Caller ID,* which displays the number or name (or both) of the caller in certain areas, when such identification has not been blocked by the caller

13. A *message service,* which records your incoming calls when you can't answer or your line is busy

14. *Call rejection,* or *call block,* which blocks unwanted calls

15. *Continuous redial,* which keeps dialing a number while you handle other calls

16. *Last call return,* which redials the last call that you made

17. *Priority call,* which uses a distinctive ring when certain people are calling

18. *Instant three-way calling,* which provides an immediate connection and lets you talk to two other people in different locations at the same time

19. *Wide area telephone service (WATS),* inbound or outbound, which lets customers dial an 800 or 888 number (inbound calls) at no charge and allows businesses to make a large number of calls to a designated area at lower cost (outbound calls)

See also CELLULAR COMMUNICATION; PAGING; SATELLITE COMMUNICATION; VOICE MAIL; Chapter 4/AUDIOCONFERENCE; COMPUTER CONFERENCE; VIDEOCONFERENCE.

TELEPHONY. Pronounced *tell-eff-ah-knee.* The translation of data, voice, video, and other signals into electrical impulses able to travel between users at distant locations; the integration of the telephone and the computer; voice communications. See also TELECOMMUNICATIONS.

TIME ZONE. See INTERNATIONAL TIME.

UNITED STATES POSTAL SERVICE. An independent body of the executive branch of government established as a successor to the Post Office Department in 1971 by the Postal Reorganization Act.

The United States Postal Service (USPS) regularly publishes two large manuals, the *Domestic Mail Manual (DMM)* and the *International Mail Manual (IMM)*, which are available by subscription from the Superintendent of Documents in Washington, D.C.

The two publications describe the many USPS domestic and international services, rules, regulations, and rates.

The USPS also publishes various other material, such as its CD-ROM *Postal Explorer,* which includes the DMM and the IMM as well as numerous other guides.

Domestic postal service. The four classes of domestic mail are Express Mail (a USPS trademark), First Class Mail (a USPS trademark), periodicals, and standard mail.

Express Mail provides expedited delivery for mailable matter subject to certain standards. Options are Express Mail Next Day/Second Day, Express Mail Custom Designed Service, Express Mail Military Service, and Express Mail Same Day Airport Service.

First Class Mail is anything wholly or partially in handwriting or type, including postcards, letters and sealed parcels, and priority mail.

Periodicals consist of magazines, newspapers, and other publications formed of printed sheets and issued at least four times a year at regular intervals from a known office of publication.

Standard mail is matter that weighs 16 ounces or more but not more than 70 pounds. *Subclass A* (regular, nonprofit, enhanced carrier route, and nonprofit enhanced carrier route standard mail) includes circulars, printed matter, catalogs, pamphlets, newsletters, direct mail, and merchandise. *Subclass B* is bound printed matter, library mail, parcel post, and special standard mail.

Domestic mail also has numerous special services that are available to mailers, all of which are described in the DMM.

Examples are *business reply mail,* which allows permit holders to pay postage for mail received from customers who were sent business reply material; *certified mail,* which provides the sender with a mailing receipt (but no insurance); and *registered mail,* which provides the most secure service offered by the USPS, including mailing receipt and insurance.

Consult your local post office or a current issue of the DMM for information about other services, as well as about many other available options, such as mailing permits, ZIP + 4 addressing, and barcoding. See also Chapter 8/ENVELOPES.

International mail.   The three classes of international mail are Postal Union mail, parcel post, and Express Mail International Service.

Postal Union mail is governed by the regulations of the Universal Postal Union and includes *LC mail* (letters, letter packages, post and postal cards, and aerogrammes) and *AO (other articles) mail* (regular printed matter, books and sheet music, publishers' periodicals, matter for the blind, and small packets).

Parcel post (also called *CP mail*) includes one classification generally equivalent to domestic standard mail (B): zone-rated parcel post.

Express Mail International Service is expedited mail to and from other countries under agreements with specific countries. It includes Custom-Designed and On-Demand Service.

Like domestic mail, international mail has a variety of special services, all of which are described in the IMM. Many are the same as those provided in domestic mail.

Examples are *insurance,* which provides coverage against loss, rifling, or damage to parcel post; *recall/change of address,* which allows a sender to recall an item or change its address after it has been mailed; and *restricted delivery,* which limits who may receive an item, as allowed by the destination country.

Consult your local post office or a current issue of the IMM for information about other services, as well as about many other available options and requirements, such as the use of customs declaration forms and the prohibition of mailing certain articles out of the country.

VIDEOCONFERENCE.   See Chapter 4/VIDEOCONFERENCE.

VOICE MAIL.   An electronic system that stores and transfers voice messages. Like E-MAIL, voice mail can be accessed from almost any telephone worldwide.

Businesses can buy a voice mail system or rent mailboxes from a service provider or the local telephone company. However, providers often do not include all the features that a purchased system might have, such as the following:

1. An *automated attendant,* which offers callers a menu from which they can select the desired choice, office, or individual and press the required telephone key to put their selection into effect

2. *Unified messaging,* which converts information received from another medium and allows you to respond in voice to a print message

3. *Fax on demand,* which allows customers to follow voice prompts to select the information they want and then signal the system to fax the selection to them

4. *Remote access,* which allows you to call in from a remote location and retrieve messages, change your greeting, and access other parts of the system

5. *Call forwarding,* which routes calls to pagers (see PAGING), cell phones (see CELLULAR COMMUNICATION), and other locations

6. *Call screening,* which is a form of caller ID that displays the caller's name or announces it

Security measures, such as passwords, are needed to protect the system from hackers who might alter your messages or send damaging messages to others. Even when passwords are used, however, they must be changed regularly and issued only to authorized personnel.

Voice mail systems represent the core of technology's *virtual assistants.* These advanced electronic devices use voice-recognition techniques to dial phones, screen calls, and even locate users who are away from the office.

An outgrowth of voice recognition is the voice-response message system, an interactive voice-response recognition system that enables two-way telephone conversations between people and computers.

With voice response, callers speak normally to the system and receive voice responses from it.

See VOICE MAIL ETIQUETTE for guidelines on recording appropriate greetings and messages and on using proper etiquette in all aspects of voice mail.

VOICE MAIL ETIQUETTE. The rules of courtesy and proper conduct applied both to outgoing voice mail announcements or greetings and to incoming messages. The words and tone of a voice mail user will project an image of the user just as much as a telephone call or a letter will create a positive or negative impression.

The following guidelines will help users leave more courteous, effective messages:

1. Use your own voice for your greeting or announcement; adopt a pleasing, friendly tone; and speak slowly and clearly.

2. Include your name and title or department in your greeting.

3. Change your greeting daily, or even throughout the day as needed, and mention the date: "It's Friday, September 6, and I'll be out of the office until 1 P.M., Eastern daylight time. If you'll leave your name, number, and message, I'll return your call by 5 P.M."

4. Tell callers if they need to do anything other than wait for the tone to leave their messages or if they need to be aware of something such as how much time they have to speak.

5. Tell callers whom they may call immediately, and how to reach them, if they can't wait for you to return their calls: "Press star 8 if you need to speak to someone in our Customer Service Department right away."

6. Keep the messages you leave on someone else's voice mail to about 30 seconds, and speak slowly and clearly in a pleasant, friendly tone.

7. Identify yourself right away when you leave a message, including your name, title or department, company, and telephone number (spell out anything unfamiliar), with the date and time of your call.

8. Make your message interesting to encourage a response: "I just heard about a new development in the Adler case that will directly affect our marketing plans."

9. State when the person may call you back: "You can reach me until 4 o'clock this afternoon or anytime tomorrow. If this isn't convenient, let me know when I may reach you."

10. Limit the choices that you offer callers in an automated system menu to no more than four.

11. Don't make callers go through numerous menus before reaching the information they need.

12. Check your incoming voice messages throughout the day, every couple hours, if possible.

13. Don't allow the convenience of voice mail to cause you to avoid or even discontinue personal contacts and conversations.

WATS. See TELEPHONE SERVICES.

WIDE AREA NETWORK (WAN). A TELECOMMUNICATIONS network that covers a broad geographic area, such as several states, the entire country, or even various other countries throughout the world. Compare with LOCAL AREA NETWORK (LAN); METROPOLITAN AREA NETWORK (MAN).

When the connected sites of a wide area NETWORK are located worldwide, the connection may of necessity involve wireless RADIO COMMUNICATION or SATELLITE COMMUNICATION, as well as the regular telephone lines. See also WIRELESS COMMUNICATION.

WIDE AREA TELEPHONE SERVICE (WATS). See TELEPHONE SERVICES.

WIRELESS COMMUNICATION. Any form of long-distance communication between different sites or stations that does not require a connection by CABLE or wire.

For example, the use of SATELLITE COMMUNICATION or MICROWAVE COMMUNICATION eliminates the need for communicating computers to use the telephone lines and a modem (see Chapter 6/MODEM) to exchange information. See also CELLULAR COMMUNICATION; RADIO COMMUNICATION.

Wireless communication is a rapidly developing technology that is expected eventually to encompass most electronic forms of communication (e-mail, fax, and so on).

Two-way PAGING and the short messaging service (SMS) are examples of widely used wireless forms, both of which are available by subscription.

The SMSs are used to send e-mail, make reservations, and send other brief messages (up to 300 characters).

Many wireless service providers support Internet-based e-mail (see E-MAIL; Chapter 6/INTERNET E-MAIL), and some two-way paging services enable users to access Internet information.

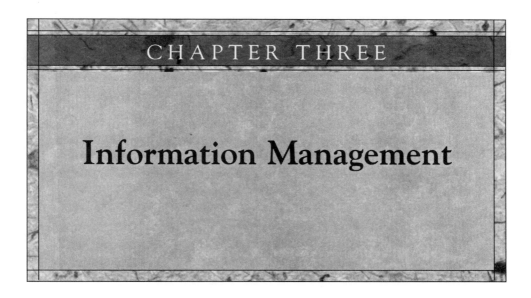

CHAPTER THREE

Information Management

ALPHABETIC FILING SYSTEM. A system of filing material alphabetically, letter by letter or word by word.

See also ALPHABETIZING; CHRONOLOGICAL FILING SYSTEM; ELECTRONIC FILING SYSTEM; GEOGRAPHIC FILING SYSTEM; NUMERIC FILING SYSTEM; SUBJECT FILING SYSTEM.

Method of alphabetizing. A letter-by-letter system of alphabetizing is common with certain material, such as dictionary entries. In filing systems, though, a word-by-word system of organizing FILENAMES is often used. See the examples in ALPHABETIZING RULES.

When material is stored both manually and electronically, paper and computer filenames should be as consistent as possible to facilitate retrieval and to avoid maintaining separate indexes. For example, if a computer filename is *Alfred R. Peterson Sr.,* one should use the same full name in the paper files.

Also, the same method of alphabetizing—word by word or letter by letter—should be used in both the electronic and the paper files.

Alphabetic name file. An easy method of filing is to classify material by name, when that is appropriate, and to file the material alphabetically. An advantage of this type of filing system, compared with a numeric system, for example, is that a cross-index is unnecessary.

To set up an alphabetic name filing system, follow these general steps:

1. Open a separate paper FILE FOLDER or computer file for each name as soon as sufficient material exists (such as about ten items).

2. Arrange the individual items in each paper name folder by date, with the most recent date first. Use the organization scheme of your file-management software for the computer files.

3. Open a miscellaneous paper folder for each letter of the alphabet, and place it after the last folder of each letter group.

4. File material there (alphabetically rather than by date) when there is no other appropriate name folder for an item.

5. If correspondence with the same person or firm is voluminous, separate it in some way, such as by project or date, and open separate paper folders with subheadings corresponding to the projects or dates.

6. Use different colored labels in paper filing, or some other means of distinction, for people who have the same name.

7. Use a symbol or some other designation in computer filing to distinguish the people who have the same name.

See ALPHABETIZING and ALPHABETIZING RULES for guidelines on alphabetizing names and other words that include punctuation, titles, numbers, prefixes, suffixes, and so on.

For a detailed discussion of alphabetic filing, see the material published by ARMA INTERNATIONAL.

ALPHABETIZING.   The procedure of arranging material according to one of the basic methods of alphabetizing, letter by letter or word by word.

Letter-by-letter alphabetizing is common in certain types of indexes and publications, such as in an encyclopedia. The separate words that make up a name or heading are treated as though they are a single unit, as in *MeetingAgenda,* without spaces between them, usually up to the first comma, colon, or period.

Word-by-word alphabetizing is common in filing systems. In this case, each word is usually treated as a separate unit, and everything must be put in order unit by unit, or word by word, with spaces between each unit or word, as in *Meeting Agenda.*

In word-by-word alphabetizing, you would usually disregard an ampersand; the articles *a, an,* and *the;* and any prepositions, such as *of,* or conjunctions, such as *and*. But see also ALPHABETIZING RULES, *Letters used as words* and *Articles, prepositions, and conjunctions in foreign languages.*

The difference between letter-by-letter and word-by-word alphabetizing affects which item is placed before another, as in the following examples:

Letter by Letter

Alphabeticalfiling

Alphabeticfiling

Word by Word

Alphabetic filing
Alphabetical filing

Other guidelines apply to *both* letter-by-letter and word-by-word alphabetizing:

1. Put numbers written as numbers, rather than as words, before alphabetic characters.
2. File material under the most common name, and treat other alternatives as CROSS-REFERENCES.
3. When a word ends in *s* or apostrophe *s,* treat it as part of the word's spelling: *Women's = Womens.*
4. When computerized and paper systems are used together, first adopt filing rules that the automated system can handle, and then simplify or modify the paper system accordingly so that the two are as consistent as possible.

See the various examples in ALPHABETIZING RULES for guidelines that will encourage consistency and facilitate retrieval in an alphabetic filing system. For detailed information about alphabetizing rules, see the pertinent publications of ARMA INTERNATIONAL.

ALPHABETIZING RULES. The rules that govern the procedure of arranging file material alphabetically. For rapid retrieval and to avoid misfiles and other difficulties, an office or organization must have ALPHABETIZING rules that are followed consistently by all personnel.

It's possible to set up virtually any type of system, from a simple alphabetic arrangement to a complex alphanumeric system. See also ALPHABETIC FILING SYSTEM; NUMERIC FILING SYSTEM.

The following suggested rules for basic word-by-word, or unit-by-unit, alphabetizing may be modified as desired to fit the needs of your organization. However, consistency in applying whatever rules are adopted is mandatory.

Personal names.   Put the last name first, the first name or initial next, and any additional names or initials last. Some foreign names, such as Asian names, may already be written with the family name first:

Name

Yam Mun Hoh

Steven Yam

Michael H. Lubrigile

Alphabetize as

Lubrigile Michael H

Yam Hoh Mun

Yam Steven

Company names.   Use the official order of the written name, even when it includes a personal name:

Name

Robert A. Morris Ltd.

Robert A. Morris & Sons

R. L. Jones, Inc.

The Craft Company, Inc.

Alphabetize as

Craft Company Incorporated The

R L Jones Incorporated

Robert A Morris Limited

Robert A Morris[&] Sons

When the first alphabetizing unit of two or more names is the same, alphabetize according to the second one, followed by the third one, and so on:

Name

John Lewis Harper

Adam O. Harper

John K. Harper

Alphabetize as

Harper Adam O

Harper John K

Harper John Lewis

When two or more names are of unequal length but contain some of the same letters or words, as in *Davis* and *Davison,* and when they are spelled the same up to and including the last full word of the shorter name, put the shorter name first:

Name

Annette R. Davis

A. Davis

A. Davison

Annette Davis

Alphabetize as

Davis A

Davis Annette

Davis Annette R

Davison A

Letters used as words. The individual letters of an initialism, such as *NBC*, or an acronym, such as *PAL* (see Chapter 7/ABBREVIATIONS), are treated as a single word, or unit.

An article, preposition, or conjunction, which is usually disregarded, is retained and considered as one of the units *if* it is joined to another word by a hyphen:

Name

A and M Drugstore

AA Club

Arnold's Deli

ABC Cleaners

Astor Insurance Co.

AWACS

A-and-J Advertising

Alphabetize as

A and J Advertising

A[and] M Drugstore

AA Club

ABC Cleaners

Arnolds Deli

Astor Insurance Company

AWACS

Hyphenated personal names. Treat the words of a person's hyphenated name as a single unit:

Name

Jean-Carrie Fleming

Wendy Beale-Parker

Alphabetize as

BealeParker Wendy

Fleming JeanCarrie

Hyphenated company names. Treat each part of a hyphenated company name as a separate word:

Name

Downers-Grove Boat Dock

Miles-Sloane & Co.

Down-Stairs Art Gallery

Winston M. Miles, Inc.

Mile-High Tower

Mary Benton-Miles Fashions

Alphabetize as

Down Stairs Art Gallery

Downers Grove Boat Dock

Mary Benton Miles Fashions

Mile High Tower

Miles Sloane[&] Company

Winston M Miles Incorporated

Abbreviations and numbers in organization names. Alphabetize abbreviations, such as *Chas.* and *St.,* as if they were spelled out, and place numbers before names. Add a CROSS-REFERENCE from the abbreviation or figure if it would be useful:

Name

Walter Snow Landscaping

Jas. Anderson Workouts

3M

St. Peter's Cathedral

Wm. Snow Accounting

Alphabetize as

3M

James Anderson Workouts

Jas Anderson Workouts
   (SEE James Anderson Workouts)

Saint Peters Cathedral

St Peters Cathedral
   (SEE Saint Peters Cathedral)

Walter Snow Landscaping

William Snow Accounting

Wm Snow Accounting
   (SEE William Snow Accounting)

Compound firm names. Treat each part of a two-word compound as a separate word unless the first part is a prefix. Then treat the two words as one unit:

Name

Newport Boat Dock

Last Chance Hotel

Newark Stationers

J. M. South Jewelers

South West Shipping, Inc.

New Port Rentals

Las Vegas Guides

New York Transit

Southwest Distributors

Alphabetize as

J M South Jewelers

Last Chance Hotel

LasVegas Guides

New Port Rentals

New York Transit

Newark Stationers

Newport Boat Dock

South West Shipping Incorporated

Southwest Distributors

Personal names with suffixes. Treat suffixes, such as *Jr.,* as separate units, and put them in *numerical* order, retaining the abbreviated form. *Sr.* should precede *Jr.,* *I* should precede *II,* and numbers should precede the alphabetic equivalent:

Name

John McKay, Jr.
John McKay III
John McKay, Sr.
John McKay II

Alphabetize as

McKay John Sr
McKay John II
McKay John Jr
McKay John III

Personal names with prefixes. Treat a prefix, such as *D', De, Del, De La, Di, Fitz, L', Las, Los, M', Mc, Mac, O', San, Santa, Ten, Van, van Der, von,* and *von Der* (capitalization may vary), and the rest of the name as one unit.

If there are a large number of a certain prefix, such as *Mc,* you may collect those names as a separate group and put them in front of the other names. If there are only a few, however, incorporate them with the others:

Name

A. D. De La Mare
J. Damata
E. M. Ten Eyck
A. C. De Lamare
P. D'Amato
J. M. McIntyre
Robert A. Mead

Alphabetize as

Damata J
DAmato P

DeLamare A C

DeLaMare A D

McIntyre J M

Mead Robert A

TenEyck E M

Articles, prepositions, and conjunctions in foreign languages. Consider an article, such as *the,* in a name in a foreign language as part of the word that immediately follows it.

Retain prepositions, such as *of,* and conjunctions, such as *and*, and treat them as separate words:

Name

Le Monde

Société des Auteurs, Musiciens et Compositeurs

C. H. Deramer Ltd.

Société des Auteurs et Peintres

Alphabetize as

C H Deramer Limited

LeMonde

Societe des Auteurs et Peintres

Societe des Auteurs Musiciens et Compositeurs

Names with numbers. Place names beginning with numbers before those beginning with words. If you also want to include the spelled-out version, CROSS-REFERENCE from it to the numerical version, and include any other cross-references that would be helpful.

If the words in a spelled-out version of a number are joined by hyphens, such as *forty-nine,* treat the combination as one word.

Certain listings, however, such as several numbered branches or chapters of an organization, should be arranged alphabetically first, by the introductory word, and then numerically:

Name

4 Paws Grooming

5th Street Bakers

Branch No. 2, Chicago

Branch No. 1, Milwaukee

The 21 Club

Alphabetize as

4 Paws Grooming

5th Street Bakers

21 Club[The]

Branch No 1 Milwaukee

Branch No 2 Chicago

Government offices.   Put the names of government offices under the name of the main governing body, with the names of departments, bureaus, and so on as subdvisions:

Name

United States Government
   Department of the Treasury
      Bureau of Accounts

State of Mississippi
   Department of Education
      Division of Rural Education

County of Suffolk
   County Clerk

Memphis, Tennessee
   City Planning Commission

Alphabetize as

Memphis Tennessee
   City Planning Commission

Mississippi State[of]
   Education Department[of]
      Rural Education Division[of]
Suffolk County[of]
   County Clerk
United States Government
   Treasury Department[of]
      Accounts Bureau[of]

Titles with names. Disregard titles in filing unless they are needed to distinguish between two or more identical names. Then add them in parentheses at the end of the name, or make them the last unit. If the title is included, file it as written, in full or abbreviated, but without punctuation.

If the name of an individual contains only a title and a first name, without a last name, treat the title as the first word. When someone regularly uses a nickname as a first name, treat the nickname as the person's given first name:

Name

Babe Ruth
Madame Celeste
Count Henri Dizonni
Dr. J. C. Astor
Mrs. Lois Chandler
Sister Mary Bennett
A. R. Astor, D.D.S.
Col. Jeffrey Sloane
Tim Greene, CPA
Brother John

Alphabetize as

Astor A R DDS
Astor J C Dr
Bennett Mary Sister
Brother John
Chandler Lois Mrs

Dizonni Henri Count

Greene Timothy CPA

Madame Celeste

Ruth Babe

Sloane Jeffrey Col

Titles with organization names. If an organization name contains a title, consider the title as the first word:

Name

Queen Anne's Tea Shop

Sir Benjamin Hook's Seafood

Lord Bentley's Apparel

Alphabetize as

Lord Bentleys Apparel

Queen Annes Tea Shop

Sir Benjamin Hooks Seafood

Married women. Use the last name that a married woman prefers, maiden or married, and add a cross-reference to or from the other spouse's name, if needed. Include the personal title *Mrs.* in parentheses or as the last filing unit, if needed:

Name

Mary L. Jenson
  (Mrs. Albert S. Jenson)

Ada R. Browne
  (Mrs. Robert E. Browne)

Alphabetize as

Brown Ada R (Mrs)
  (SEE ALSO Browne Robert E)

Jenson Mary L (Mrs)
  (SEE ALSO Jenson Albert S)

ARMA INTERNATIONAL.   A professional organization for persons engaged in information and RECORDS MANAGEMENT.

ARMA International, the Association of Records Managers and Administrators, Inc., sets the standards for filing practices and procedures and publishes a variety of information about the different filing systems and storage technologies.

For further information, contact ARMA International at 4200 Somerset Drive, Suite 215, Prairie Village, Kansas 66208, or visit its Web site. See also Chapter 6/WEB SITE.

CD-ROM STORAGE.   See OPTICAL MEDIA STORAGE.

CHARGE-OUT SYSTEM.   A method of keeping track of FILE FOLDERS and other records that are removed from a file area. Such a system is necessary when several persons use the same files.

Companies may have different procedures for handling this process, as well as restrictions on the length of time that someone may keep a file.

Charge-out procedure.   Certain information must be recorded whenever a document or folder is removed from its storage area. Whether the information is recorded manually or by computer, it must include the FILENAME or other description of the item, date removed, due (return) date, and name and department of the borrower.

When something is out longer than company policy permits, the person who handles the charge-out system must follow up by telephone, fax, e-mail, or other form of reminder. Software programs are available for recording information and printing out reminder notices that can be sent to borrowers.

When files and records have a bar-code label affixed to them, the file's current location can readily be tracked by computer to the borrower. (A *bar code* is a printed pattern of bars, spaces, and sometimes numerals that can be scanned into computer memory.)

Charge-out forms.   An *out folder* is a distinctively colored folder that is inserted in the paper files in the place that a regular file folder occupied before it was checked out.

Until the regular folder is returned, charge-out information can be recorded on the front of the out folder or on a printed form affixed to it. In addition, new papers can be temporarily filed in the out folder until the regular folder is returned.

An *out guide* is a stiff, distinctively colored, folder-size insert placed in the position that a regular file folder occupied before it was checked out. Like an out folder, it may have a form printed on it or affixed to it for recording charge-out data.

An *out card* is an index card where charge-out information is recorded. It may be inserted in a pocket on an out guide or folder, or it may be placed along with other out cards in a separate charge-out file, such as an alphabetic card file or a tickler file used for follow-ups. See also FOLLOW-UP SYSTEM.

CHRONOLOGICAL FILING SYSTEM. A system of filing material in chronological order, or by date. A chronological file is used in addition to other systems. See also ALPHABETIC FILING SYSTEM; GEOGRAPHIC FILING SYSTEM; NUMERIC FILING SYSTEM; SUBJECT FILING SYSTEM.

Outgoing correspondence and other materials are filed in a chronological file by date, with the most recent date first.

A chronological file is useful in FOLLOW-UP SYSTEMS, where you need to assign a date for checking on something. It's also useful in finding something when you recall the date but not the subject, when you want to study events of a certain period, or when an executive wants to know what happened while he or she was away.

The disadvantage of the system is that it requires a duplication of effort since it must be maintained in addition to the main files.

COLOR CODING. A paper filing technique that uses color as the key to organization and identification to enable quick retrieval and refiling and to make it easy to spot misfiles.

Common uses of color. Color coding is suitable for a variety of uses, such as for paper FILE LABELS, for flexible disk labels (see MAGNETIC MEDIA STORAGE), and in MICROGRAPHICS coding.

With some files, such as terminal digit files (see NUMERIC FILING SYSTEM), color coding is especially important. In a numeric system, for example, a different color may be used for each digit from 0 to 9. However, usually, no more than four digits are color coded to avoid having so much color that nothing stands out.

In an ALPHABETIC FILING SYSTEM, each letter may have a different color. Again, to avoid having an excess of color create an adverse effect, only the first two letters of the last name may be color coded.

Office suppliers carry a variety of color-coded paper, labels, folders, and other supplies. With the right software, you can print your own colored file labels.

Other uses of color. Some offices also use different colored paper copies for different purposes. For example, white copies may be intended for the correspondence files and yellow copies for the accounting files.

Color can also be applied numerically (black = 10, red = 20, and so on) or by subject (black = insurance, red = real estate, and so on).

Some offices use color to make evaluations as well (black = a promising prospect, red = a previous customer, and so on).

You can devise your own system or contact a manufacturer of filing equipment and supplies that has complete systems already designed.

CROSS-REFERENCE. In file systems and indexes, a reference to other items in the file or index (see INDEXING) that contain pertinent information.

For example, if a file is opened under the name *John J. Jones,* and the subject is also known as *J. J. Jones,* a cross-reference may be added for the name *J. J. Jones,* referring the user to *John J. Jones.*

> J. J. Jones
>   (SEE John J. Jones)

In the paper files, cross-references may be made on cross-reference sheets, file folders, or guides inserted among the other papers or folders. See also the definition of *guide* in FILE FOLDER, *Color coding.*

In an index, the cross-reference would be inserted among the other listed items. Usually, the cross-reference sheet or the cross-reference FILE LABEL or guide label is in a color other than white to signal to users that it's a cross-reference.

Cross-reference sheets commonly include other information, such as the name or subject of a record, the date, and a description of the contents.

See the examples of cross-references in ALPHABETIZING RULES, *Abbreviations and numbers in organization names* and *Married women.* See also Chapter 9/CROSS-REFERENCE.

DOCUMENT IMAGING. A technology that transfers the image on a paper document to another medium, such as microfilm, for storage. See also MICROFORMS; MICROGRAPHICS.

Electronic imaging. When an image is transferred to a computer-readable medium, such as a CD-ROM (see OPTICAL MEDIA STORAGE), the process is known as *electronic document imaging (EDI)*.

To process paper images for storage in a computer-readable form, a document must be scanned and the images digitized. Once the images are in digital form, they can be stored on a magnetic disk, optical disk, or other computer-readable storage media. See also MAGNETIC MEDIA STORAGE; OPTICAL MEDIA STORAGE.

Advantages of EDI. An electronic imaging system provides a compact form of storage and enables rapid retrieval of information as well as simultaneous access by multiple users. In addition, files can be expanded and updated regularly, and they can be easily transferred from one person to another.

An EDI system also allows for various forms of input, such as by scanning paper documents onto microfilm, making entries from a keyboard, or using another means of electronic transfer. With compatible computer indexing, the stored documents can later be easily located and retrieved.

Micrographics. See MICROGRAPHICS for an example of an older form of document imaging. This type of storage uses film to record images in reduced size. It is primarily used when documents must be retained for a long time and need not be retrieved on a regular basis.

DOCUMENT MANAGEMENT SYSTEM. An electronic system that provides a document profile, or index, that is "attached" to each stored document so that it can be easily retrieved. Various software is available for managing different types of document formats, from text documents to spreadsheets to video images.

The profile that must be attached to each document provides a coded form of index terms so that documents can be located by keywords. See FULL-TEXT RETRIEVAL; KEYWORD RETRIEVAL.

ELECTRONIC DOCUMENT IMAGING. See DOCUMENT IMAGING.

ELECTRONIC FILING SYSTEM. A system of filing that uses computer technologies, devices, and media for purposes of storage and retrieval.

The two principal forms of storage in an electronic filing system are magnetic and optical storage. See also MAGNETIC MEDIA STORAGE; OPTICAL MEDIA STORAGE.

Magnetic media include hard disks, flexible disks, and tapes. Optical media include optical disks, tapes, and memory cards. Among the optical disk formats are the CD-ROM (compact disk–read only memory), WORM (write once–read many times), CD-DA (compact disk–digital audio), and CD-R (compact disk–recordable).

Computer-output microfilm (COM), in flat or roll format, combines the use of computers with MICROGRAPHICS to record images on microfilm for permanent storage. See also MICROFORMS.

See FILING PROCEDURES for additional information on INDEXING, label preparation for disks and containers, and other electronic filing procedures.

FILE FOLDERS. The heavy paper or plastic folders or envelopes used to hold loose papers in a file cabinet or other storage container. The weight of such folders may range from lightweight manila folders to very heavy pressboard folders.

Folder tabs. File folders are available with top or side tabs to which an identification label (see FILE LABELS) may be attached. The top tabs may be a third cut, half cut, fifth cut, two-fifths cut, or full (straight) cut. Side tabs are usually full cut.

Other features. Folders may have various other features as well. For example, they may be acid-free for use with historical or other papers requiring careful preservation. Some may have printed information on the front or on the tabs; others may have fill-in blanks where information can be recorded.

Some folders may have creases and folds to allow for expansion (*bellows folders*) as more papers are added. Others may have a reinforced bottom to support heavy material. Hanging folders are designed to rest on a frame in a file drawer so that they will remain upright even when full.

Labeling. Folders must be labeled with the appropriate FILENAME to facilitate filing and finding. The filename, or other information written on the file label, must be consistent with the selected filing system.

See also ALPHABETIC FILING SYSTEM; CHRONOLOGICAL FILING SYSTEM; GEOGRAPHIC FILING SYSTEM; NUMERIC FILING SYSTEM; SUBJECT FILING SYSTEM.

Color coding. Color may be used for identification and as a retrieval aid either on the folders or on the labels that are affixed to the folder tabs. COLOR CODING may also be used for open-shelf, drawer, and container labels, as well as for *guides* (folder-size heavy inserts that identify a section, or category, of folders filed behind a guide).

FILE LABELS. The self-adhesive or regular strips of identification affixed to paper FILE FOLDERS and guides, flexible disks, and other media and containers. See also MAGNETIC MEDIA STORAGE; OPTICAL MEDIA STORAGE.

Colored or plain labels (see COLOR CODING) are available in sheets or rolls and may be printed out by computer.

Filenames. In paper storage, labels for drawers and other containers should identify the general contents, whereas labels for folders should have the filename selected for a folder's documents. If possible, folder filenames should match the corresponding electronic filenames.

Usually, a general *miscellaneous* folder and label are needed for material that doesn't fit anywhere else. (Open a new file folder with a specific filename when ten items have accumulated for a particular subject.)

Labels for the file guides that are inserted in front of general sections, divisions, or categories of folders should identify those groups.

Labeling style. Use all capital letters, or capitalize important words, with no punctuation. On a drawer or container label, center the words, numbers, or other identifying information. On a folder or disk label, begin the filename two spaces from the left edge close to the top of a plain label or close to the bottom of any color bar.

Key the name on a side folder label both directly above and directly below the color bar separator. This enables users to read from both sides.

FILENAME. The word, number, symbol, code, or other designation given to a paper or computer file before storage so that it can later be retrieved.

When documents are stored simultaneously in both paper and electronic files, the filenames should be consistent to provide easy matching and to facilitate location in either system.

When both types of files are involved, the computer files should be named first, since certain restrictions apply in electronic filing. The same name should then be used in the paper files.

Filename guidelines.   The naming of electronic files must follow the require-ments of your software. For example, the following guidelines apply in one sys-tem (others may differ):

1. Up to 255 characters (but a short, descriptive filename would be better)
2. A designation including letters, numbers, most punctuation, and spaces, in either lowercase or all capital letters
3. A designation that begins with a letter or number, as preferred
4. No characters such as \ / : * ? " < > |

You usually select a filename when you begin work on a document or when you save it for the first time. For example, you might name a communica-tions skills test as *CStest*. If it's the second of several such tests, you might name it *CStest2*.

At any time, you can rename a filename by using the *save as* feature of your software. If you do that, delete the identical file with the original name when you no longer need it.

Filename extensions.   Current programs no longer require the addition of a three-letter extension, such as *Hallrpt.doc* (document), in a filename. Those who find the extension useful, however, may continue to include it.

See also FILE FOLDERS; FILE LABELS.

FILING PROCEDURES.   The steps taken in preparing material for filing or stor-age and sending it to a selected location.

Manual filing.   Follow these steps in preparing paper material for filing:

1. Be certain that the material has been cleared, or released, for filing.
2. Separate the papers into categories, such as in-house correspondence, out-side correspondence, reports, and purchase orders.
3. Arrange individual items alphabetically or code them numerically accord-ing to the file system being used, and write the code on the document (or on an attached self-sticking note).
4. Mark keywords, if that will help relate a document to a specific filename, using a yellow marker, nonreproducible blue pencil, or self-sticking, remov-able notes, according to office policy.
5. Remove staples and paper clips, if necessary.

6. Mend torn papers.

7. Fill out any CROSS-REFERENCE sheets that will be needed.

8. Use file trays or racks for sorting if the file load is substantial.

9. Prepare any new FILE FOLDER labels or containers labels that are needed. See also FILE LABELS; FILENAME.

10. Prepare any new guide labels that are needed.

11. Insert the coded documents into the appropriate folders.

Electronic filing. Fewer steps are required in electronic filing since the computer automatically handles the task of sending files to storage and enters and organizes filenames in the software's document management program. However, follow these steps in preparing material for electronic filing:

1. Follow the instructions of your software in naming documents for storage on a hard disk, flexible disk, or other media.

2. Set up a directory or general computer "folder," as well as any subdirectory, in which a particular document will be stored on your hard disk.

3. File attachments with the related document or in another location, as appropriate.

4. Enter the filename and other required data on any indexes that you maintain.

5. Add any necessary CROSS-REFERENCES to your filename index. See also the examples in ALPHABETIZING RULES.

6. Regularly print out and distribute the revised indexes to coworkers.

7. Prepare any new labels that are needed for flexible disks and their containers, with filenames that match those of the hard disk.

8. Prepare any required new guide labels for the flexible disk container.

9. Follow the same labeling and indexing steps for other storage media, such as OPTICAL MEDIA STORAGE.

10. Periodically transfer inactive files from your hard disk to flexible disks or other archival storage, according to company policy.

11. Save files in a format or medium that will not soon be obsolete, and include copies of the software used to create the material.

FOLLOW-UP SYSTEM. A system of filing material to alert one to follow up on unanswered correspondence and other pending items by a certain date.

Material for follow-up. The following items are examples of material that might be placed in a follow-up file:

1. Matters referred to other executives or department heads for information or comment
2. Correspondence or memos awaiting an answer
3. Orders for future delivery
4. Items that come up for periodic consideration, such as tax matters and contract renewals
5. Promises to be carried out in the future
6. Regular receivables for which there is no invoice, such as a rental payment

Follow-up programs and equipment. Computer software programs are available for follow-up and reminder purposes. Many are multifunction programs that enable users to prepare schedules, create calendars and address lists, prepare daily reminder or follow-up alarms, and so on. See also ORGANIZERS.

The principal equipment used in a manual follow-up system is a file drawer and FILE FOLDERS: 12 folders labeled January through December, 31 folders labeled 1 through 31, and 1 folder marked "Future Years."

If follow-up activity is heavy, you may need two sets of daily folders—one for the current month and one for the next month.

To make it easy to find a particular folder, use separators or guides (see FILE FOLDERS) marked 1 through 31 and January through December.

Arrangement of folders. Put the daily folders in numerical order in the front of the drawer, and file the follow-up material for the current month in these folders.

Put the folder labeled with the current month at the back of the monthly folders, ready for any material to be followed up in that month next year.

Put the folders for the upcoming months back of the daily folder for the current month.

If your office has only a small amount of correspondence or other matters needing follow-up, you may not need this type of follow-up system. Instead, you may simply mark copies of material with a follow-up date and file the items chronologically in a folder, with the earliest marked follow-up date in front.

How to use a follow-up system. If you want to keep a document that may need follow-up in the regular files, place a *notation* about it in the appropriate folder (daily or monthly, as described previously).

As an alternative, make an extra copy of correspondence requiring follow-up, mark the date for follow-up on it, and put it in the appropriate folder. Keep the original or main copy in the regular files.

Place material that should be followed up in the current month in the appropriate daily folder. At the end of each day, as you empty that day's folder, move it back of the general folder for the upcoming month.

If you have material to be followed up farther in the future, such as in another month, put it in the proper *monthly* folder.

On the first of each new month, transfer material waiting in that month's monthly folder into the 31 individual daily folders. Move the current month's general monthly folder, which is now empty, to the back of all other monthly folders.

To avoid putting material into daily folders for Saturday, Sunday, or holidays, temporarily reverse those folders for that month so that no label will show.

FORMS MANAGEMENT.   An aspect of information management concerned with the control of paper and electronic forms, such as a requisition form, to ensure their proper design and use.

Although many software programs with already designed forms are available, businesses frequently design their own forms or redesign standard commercial forms to fit their requirements.

Forms management has these objectives:

1. The elimination of forms that are no longer used and those that duplicate other existing forms
2. The determination of whether new forms are really needed
3. The redesign of inefficient or otherwise ineffective forms
4. The best identification system, such as a simple consecutive numbering system or a number-plus-code system to indicate the function of each form
5. The determination of whether single or multipart forms are needed
6. The determination of the number of copies of a particular form that will be needed for a designated period
7. The selection of the best medium for duplicating, using, and storing a form

See also RECORDS MANAGEMENT; REPORTS MANAGEMENT.

FULL-TEXT RETRIEVAL.   Sometimes called *free text searching*. A form of document retrieval that uses an inverted index to locate each document that contains the word or words given in the search parameter. See also INDEXING.

In *full-text indexing,* the computer creates an alphabetical index of all words in a document and their location. (Some systems ignore words such as *the* and *but*.) To retrieve information, then, a user instructs the computer to search for all documents that contain certain words.

Full-text retrieval is useful when users don't know precisely what they want. However, it is a slower method than KEYWORD RETRIEVAL. Also, it doesn't have as much precision, because it must rely only on the exact words used in a document and ignores other words with similar or related meanings.

To compensate, therefore, some full-text systems include a form of keyword searching that includes words and phrases with related meanings. For example, when a system has keyword capability, someone searching for *newsletters* could specify *newsletters* but also turn up useful related items such as *bulletins*.

GEOGRAPHIC FILING SYSTEM.   A system of filing material by geographic location, such as first by country, then by state, next by city or town, and last by company or individual.

Although this type of system is not widely used, it's suitable for activities such as sales that are handled and evaluated in terms of area or location.

The files are first arranged alphabetically by geographic area and then alphabetically by company, individual, and so on within each geographic area.

A geographic file requires a cross-index, such as an alphabetic name index. See also ALPHABETIC FILING SYSTEM; NUMERIC FILING SYSTEM; SUBJECT FILING SYSTEM.

GUIDES.   See FILE FOLDERS.

INDEXING.   The process of identifying records or pieces of information within a record so that they can later be retrieved.

Various commercial organizations provide computerized indexing services, and companies that are equipped to handle such work can prepare their indexes in-house.

Firms that want to automate all their stored records must be certain that any software package they select to do this or any internally designed system will be able to handle the volume of records that they have.

Manual systems, commonly set up on cards or sheets of paper, are usually suitable only for small offices with limited records.

Paper files.   In preparing an index for the paper files, the records are classified according to the filing system, such as an ALPHABETIC FILING SYSTEM or a NUMERIC FILING SYSTEM.

A *filing segment* is then developed for each record. This segment includes the full name of the subject and the number or other identifier being used for filing.

A *master index* consists of all file segments developed for all records. For example, the master index for an alphabetic file would list all subjects alphabetically.

A *relative index* would list all words or combinations of words that might be used to request a particular record.

Electronic files. Businesses also need similar types of indexes when they have numerous removable magnetic or optical disks and tapes stored apart from the computer. See also MAGNETIC MEDIA STORAGE; OPTICAL MEDIA STORAGE.

However, operating systems provide their own form of index, or organization, for searching and retrieving files. Therefore, as a start, you can print out the information on each file automatically kept by the computer's file-management program and keep it in a binder for quick manual reference.

Use the various features of your programs to create directories and subdirectories for your files and to assign FILENAMES that will be useful in locating records. If you want to prepare a more detailed, expanded index, it should be based on this information.

Indexes are also needed for other kinds of storage, such as storage on MICROFORMS.

See also Chapter 9/ INDEX for information about preparing an index for a document such as a handbook.

KEYWORD RETRIEVAL. A form of document retrieval that uses an index of field data, with key terms, to locate documents that have information related to the search parameter. A *field* is a location in a record where a particular type of data is stored.

Field-based forms of retrieval are faster and more accurate than FULL-TEXT RETRIEVAL, which depends solely on the specific words used in a document. However, because of this, some search and retrieval systems combine the full-text and keyword methods. See also INDEXING.

MAGNETIC MEDIA STORAGE. A widely used technology for storing computer information that consists of a magnetic surface on which an electromagnetic read–write head records the information.

In *magnetic disk* storage, a platter-shaped magnetic disk is divided into rings, or tracks, where the computer-processable information is stored. In *magnetic tape* storage, the information is recorded on a long strip of polyester film.

CHAPTER 3 • INFORMATION MANAGEMENT

Magnetic disk storage. A fixed *hard disk drive* is a very high storage capacity, very high performance device consisting of one or more magnetic disk platters and a read–write mechanism sealed together in a module.

A *hard disk cartridge drive* is a moderately high (and improving) storage capacity and high-performance device consisting of a read–write mechanism and removable recording media.

A *flexible disk*, also called a *floppy disk* or *diskette,* is a small platter that is inserted in and removed from a floppy disk drive. The adjective *flexible* is a remnant of earlier times when small, removable disks were made of a bendable material. Today, however, the 3.5-inch versions are very rigid and durable.

A flexible disk often has much less storage capacity and lower performance than a fixed hard disk, although increasingly higher-capacity versions are being offered in a double-sided, high-density format. In fact, as technology advances, storage capacity and level of performance are increasing for both fixed and removable disks.

The flexible disks, which are stored apart from the computer, are widely used for multiple copies of software programs. Blank disks are commonly used as backup protection for data kept on a hard disk, in case the hard disk should fail (*crash*) or operator error should cause the loss of its data.

Magnetic tape storage. Like flexible disks, *magnetic tapes* are widely used for long-term storage and for backup protection of information stored on a computer's hard disk. Magnetic tapes are also used for software distribution in conjunction with large mainframe computers and minicomputers.

A variety of formats is available, including large reels, compact cartridges and cassettes, and digital audiotape. Continuous loops have traditionally been used in voice recordings and multiuser dictation systems.

A peripheral drive is needed for a computer to record and read information stored on a magnetic tape. See also MICROFORMS; MICROGRAPHICS; OPTICAL MEDIA STORAGE.

METADATA. Data that describe other data. For example, the name, subject, and size of a data file are the metadata describing that file. The author, publisher, subject, and copyright date of a document are the metadata describing that document.

Metadata, therefore, are necessary to define, organize, and manage massive amounts of information.

MICROFORMS. The various film formats, such as microfilm, microfiche, superfiche, and ultrafiche, on which images may be stored in DOCUMENT IMAGING.

Microfilm consists of film in a roll. *Microfiche* is a sheet of microfilm. *Superfiche* and *ultrafiche* are microfiches with much smaller images and therefore more information per sheet.

Advantages and disadvantages of film.   Although other forms of document imaging, such as electronic imaging, have lessened the interest in microforms, they are still used in certain organizations for long-term, permanent, space-saving storage.

A major advantage is that microfilm is a highly durable, noncombustible storage medium with a life expectancy of hundreds of years. Traditionally, its greatest appeal, however, has been its enormous space-saving characteristic.

A major disadvantage is that files on film cannot be easily revised or updated. New information or documents must be recorded on additional rolls or sheets of film, which increases the time required for search and retrieval. Therefore, microfilm is primarily suitable for long-term storage when frequent access will not be needed.

The use of microfilm.   The first step in transferring files to reduced form on microfilm is to photograph the original documents and process the film for storage or subsequent use. Often this is done by an outside service bureau. See also MICROGRAPHICS.

After the filmed documents are reduced and stored on the film, they can be enlarged to full size again and viewed on the screen of a microfilm reader. A reader–printer will also print out a paper copy. Normally, users work with a *copy*, rather than the original film, which should be stored in a secure, climate-controlled environment.

Depending on company policy and legal requirements, the paper documents that are transferred to microfilm storage may eventually be destroyed and only the film retained. See also RECORDS RETENTION.

MICROGRAPHICS.   The technology of recording images on a MICROFORM format; the industry concerned with the production and processing of microforms.

Preparation and use.   Since microforms are produced in film format, the process of capturing, reducing, and recording images on film requires the use of appropriate camera equipment and the preparation of the film for subsequent use.

Organizations that use microforms for long-term storage usually contract with an outside service bureau to handle the filming and processing. In such cases, businesses should be certain that the service organization processes film consistent with the standards developed by the American National Standards Institute.

The *original* film must be stored in a secure, climate-controlled area (and checked periodically for deterioration) and a *copy* used for data access and viewing.

Even if a business uses a service bureau for the camera work and film processing, it will still have to buy or lease other equipment. For example, it will need a film reader (which enlarges the microimages to a size suitable for viewing and reading) and a printer (usually a combination printer–reader) to make paper copies of documents when needed.

Computer retrieval. If you use a computer-prepared index to the information stored on the film, you will also want a reader that interfaces with your computer to enable computer-assisted retrieval (CAR) of the stored information.

With CAR, you would insert the film in the reader, select an item from the index, and wait for the computer to advance the film automatically to the location of the selected information.

Compare micrographics with electronic DOCUMENT IMAGING, which allows not only storage in space-saving, reduced form but also permits rapid search and retrieval along with the manipulation, or alteration, of stored information at any time.

NUMERIC FILING SYSTEM. A system of filing material by number or a combination of numbers and letters. See also ALPHABETIC FILING SYSTEM; CHRONOLOGICAL FILING SYSTEM; GEOGRAPHIC FILING SYSTEM; SUBJECT FILING SYSTEM.

With a numeric system, numbers are used to identify FILE FOLDERS or computer files and are arranged in a certain sequence.

The numbers may be those that are already printed on the records or documents, such as the numbers on insurance policies, or they may be unrelated numbers that are assigned to the material as it is being prepared for filing. See INDEXING.

This system is an indirect method of filing because it must be used with a cross-index, such as an alphabetical list of names, that shows what each number stands for.

The advantages of a numeric system are the rapidity and accuracy of refiling and the opportunity for indefinite expansion. A numeric system also provides greater protection from unauthorized access of confidential files.

CROSS-REFERENCES are added to an alphabetic cross-index, rather than to the files.

A variety of numeric systems are used, ranging from a simple consecutive system to a more complex system combining numbers and letters.

Consecutive number file. Also called a *serial, sequential,* or *straight numeric system.* With this system, the files are arranged in ascending order (*1, 2, 3,* and so on). The system is often used for prenumbered items, such as invoices.

Although the simplicity of the system is appealing, a major disadvantage is that all recently added numbers pile up at the end.

Middle-digit file. With this system, a number such as *345678* is divided into three groups. The middle digits, *56,* are the primary digits, and material is filed first by those digits, then by the secondary digits on the left, *34,* and last by the tertiary digits on the right, *78.*

The drawer or shelf would be labeled as *56* and the file guide *34 56.* The folders in drawer *56* that are filed after guide *34 56* are numbered *34 56 00, 34 56 01,* and so on up to *34 56 99.*

This system is sometimes used as the next step when something more extensive than a simple consecutive file is needed. A disadvantage, however, is that users may have trouble reading from the middle digit, rather than from left to right.

Terminal-digit file. With this system, a number such as *345678* is also divided into at least three units. In this case, *78* is the primary group; *56,* the secondary group; and *34,* the tertiary group.

The drawer or shelf is labeled *78* and the file guide *56 78.* The folders in drawer *78* that are filed after guide *56 78* are numbered *00 56 78, 01 56 78,* and so on up to *99 56 78.*

This type of system has less congestion since sequentially numbered files are distributed throughout, but you may have to access many different locations to retrieve a group of consecutively numbered files. Also, people used to reading from left to right may have trouble beginning with the last two digits.

Decimal file. This system is based on the Dewey Decimal System used in some public libraries and highly specialized businesses, such as a public utility company.

All records are classified under ten or fewer principal headings, or divisions, which are numbered *000* to *900*. Each of those divisions may be divided into nine or fewer subdivisions, such as *210, 220, 230*, and so on up to *290*.

Those subdivisions may be further subdivided as *211, 212, 213*, and so on. If still further division is needed, decimals may be used, as in *211.1, 211.2, 211.3*, and so on. In a very large system, more decimal places could be added, as in *211.111.1, 211.111.2, 211.111.3*, and so on.

Although expansion is unlimited with a decimal system, the main subject classification is still limited to ten headings and nine subheadings.

Duplex-numeric file. This system uses numbers that are divided into two groups of digits by a space or punctuation, such as a hyphen or period, as in *20-1*. Files are arranged consecutively by the first part of the number and then by the other part.

GEOGRAPHIC FILING SYSTEMS or SUBJECT FILING SYSTEMS might use this type of file. For example, *20* might refer to a main division, such as *Records Management*; *21* to a subdivision, such as *Filing Systems*; and *21-1* to a further subdivision, such as *Numeric Filing System*.

Block numeric file. This system assigns a block of numbers to each major function or area of activity, such as *Finance, 200-400*, and *Sales, 600-900*.

Subdivisions are added in the same way that they are added in a duplex-numeric system. The number *200-1*, for example, might describe *Budgets*, and *650-7* might describe *Field Offices*.

Although the system provides for decentralization of material, which may not be desirable in all cases, the files can be expanded indefinitely. In general, it is a more complex system than some of the others just described and involves considerable time to set up and maintain.

Alphanumeric file. This system combines numbers and letters with a decimal system. Primary names or subjects are first arranged alphabetically. Then a number is assigned to each.

In simplified form, if *Records Management* is a main division filed alphabetically along with other main divisions, a secondary subdivision might be *1 Filing Systems*, and a further subdivision of it might be *1-1 Numeric Filing*.

An alphanumeric system can be devised in many ways and requires expert knowledge and planning to select the best arrangement that works efficiently. In most cases, an alphanumeric system will allow for indefinite expansion.

For a detailed discussion of numeric filing, see the material on that subject published by ARMA INTERNATIONAL.

OPTICAL MEDIA STORAGE. A method of storage that uses laser-generated light to record and read information.

Optical disks. Like MAGNETIC MEDIA STORAGE products, *optical disks* are available in both a read–write format, such as a blank WORM (write once–read many times), and a read–only format, such as a prerecorded CD-ROM (compact disk–read only memory).

Although a write-once WORM format is not rewritable, other read–write formats are erasable and resuable. Even the *write-once* description of WORM means only that new data cannot be written, or recorded, over the old data. But as long as space is available, new information may be added.

Blank read–write and prerecorded read-only disks are available in large and small sizes, such as the large, high storage capacity optical disks used for long-term storage and the smaller blank disks used to record material for on-line storage, backup, and archiving.

The prerecorded optical disks, about the size of a flexible magnetic disk, are also commonly used for multiple copies of databases and software.

CD-ROMs, for example, are widely used for systems and applications software programs, such as an operating system program, and for storing large data collections, such as an encyclopedia.

The read–write formats are available in platters, or disks; tapes; and cards. Like magnetic media, the optical media are operated by a read–write drive. Also, like a magnetic disk, an optical disk's recording surface is divided into tracks.

In contrast to magnetic media, however, the optical media have higher recording densities and can therefore store much more information.

Optical tapes and cards. Although optical disks are the most widely used form of optical media, other forms also exist. *Optical tape* is a ribbonlike tape with an optical recording surface. In addition to large capacity optical tapes, there are cartridges, cassettes, and digital linear tapes.

An *optical memory card,* also called an *optical card* or *optical digital data card,* is a rectangular storage medium resembling a credit card. It is available in both read–write and read-only formats.

ORGANIZERS. Calendars, address books, and other personal information managers (PIMs) that enable one to schedule tasks and record and quickly retrieve notes, reminders, appointments, names and addresses, and other information.

Types of organizers. The three main types of organizers are the traditional print books, such as daytimers; electronic devices ranging in size from that of a small electronic calculator to a laptop computer; and Web-based organizer services.

Typically, the electronic organizers are handheld devices that combine the various features associated with task scheduling in one unit. Web-based calendars and organizers (see Chapter 6/WORLD WIDE WEB [WWW]) offer an alternative to the PIMs and generally include the same features.

Web organizers. Most Web-based services are free and merely involve downloading (see Chapter 6/DOWNLOAD) address books, calendars, and other material.

Some services include a variety of other features, such as e-mail, including encryption (see Chapter 6/ENCRYPTION) and other security measures. However, in many cases, privacy remains a major concern for users.

Some of the Web sites (see Chapter 6/WEB SITE) that offer the calendars and organizers also provide listings of news and events, such as movie releases, and offer chat groups. See also Chapter 6/CHAT ROOM; MAILING LIST; NEWSGROUP.

PERSONAL INFORMATION MANAGER (PIM). See ORGANIZERS.

RECORDS MANAGEMENT. The control of the various forms of recorded information, including the development of policies to govern the creation, use, and storage of all records, as well as the eventual destruction of certain records.

Many decisions must be made in the overall process of records management:

1. How will the records be produced?

2. What filing systems will be used for active files? See also ALPHABETIC FILING SYSTEM; CHRONOLOGICAL FILING SYSTEM; ELECTRONIC FILING SYSTEM; GEOGRAPHIC FILING SYSTEM; NUMERIC FILING SYSTEM; SUBJECT FILING SYSTEM.

3. What process will be used to transfer and store inactive or seldom-used files? See also DOCUMENT IMAGING; DOCUMENT MANAGEMENT SYSTEM; MAGNETIC MEDIA STORAGE; MICROGRAPHICS; OPTICAL MEDIA STORAGE.

4. What methods of retrieval are required? See also FULL-TEXT RETRIEVAL; INDEXING; KEYWORD RETRIEVAL.

5. What type of retention schedule is needed? See also RECORDS RETENTION.

6. Which company policies affect management decisions?

7. What types of safeguards are needed for VITAL RECORDS and to protect confidential records from unauthorized access? See also RECORDS SECURITY.

8. What steps must be taken to protect archival records from natural hazards and physical deterioration? See also RECORDS SECURITY.

9. How will responsibility for each function be assigned?

10. What types of controls must be implemented at each stage, from creation to ultimate disposal?

Off-site services. Records management is commonly handled in-house, but some firms prefer to outsource the entire function to an off-site firm specializing in such services.

Even when outsourcing is preferred, in-house management must still determine policies involving legal and financial matters. The issue of confidentiality must also be considered in decisions involving outsourcing.

Records management software. Depending on the *records management software* that your company has selected, you may be able to manage all forms of information with it. This would include the various paper and computer files and documents, magnetic and optical media, MICROFORMS, and even containers, such as boxes.

When bar codes (see the description in CHARGE-OUT SYSTEM) are affixed to items, the material can be tracked to and from storage areas, as well as to any borrower who may have removed it.

Document management software is also used in records management. Its purpose is to manage information that is stored electronically in the form of documents. See also DOCUMENT MANAGEMENT SYSTEM; FORMS MANAGEMENT; FULL-TEXT RETRIEVAL; INDEXING; KEYWORD RETRIEVAL; REPORTS MANAGEMENT.

RECORDS RETENTION. The storage of records according to a schedule that is based on company policy, federal and state regulations, and other requirements. Because of the legal and financial restrictions that apply to business records, a retention schedule should be approved by an attorney and a certified public accountant.

Records retention programs. Software is available to create, apply, and maintain a retention schedule. Such programs usually classify records with common retention attributes or disposition requirements.

Various codes are assigned to records in software applications. For example, the categories that are established in records retention are called the *record series,* and individual records within a series are each assigned a code.

Retention codes may also be assigned to records with similar retention periods, and codes may be used for the creation date, termination date, permanency of the record, and so on.

Records retention schedule. Although an attorney and accountant should approve any schedule that is developed, the following items and periods are a few examples of business classifications and common retention periods listed in a typical schedule:

Accounts payable	3 years
Bank statements	6 years
Blueprints	30 years
Employee records	Permanent
General ledgers	Permanent
Leases	6 years
Tax returns	Permanent
Vehicle maintenance	4 years
Work orders	5 years

Documents should never be destroyed without authorization, and employees who work with files should regularly refer to the retention schedule.

When destruction is authorized, the elimination of obsolete or nonessential material reduces the storage burden and associated costs and clears the index of unnecessary items.

Periodic reviews. After a schedule has been approved, it should immediately be implemented throughout the company. Depending on company policy, the various offices or departments may be expected to evaluate their records from time to time and conduct a quarterly, semiannual, or annual file purge.

Those responsible for the retention schedule must review and update it at least once a year, eliminating obsolete categories, adding new ones, changing retention periods as the law or company policy changes, and so on.

RECORDS SECURITY. The policies and procedures concerning the safeguarding of files, documents, and other material.

A variety of hazards may affect the files and records of a company: natural hazards, such as fire or mildew; criminal activities, such as theft, vandalism, and computer viruses; and certain intentional or unintentional abuses, such as environmental contamination and carelessness in protecting confidential material.

Managers who recognize the importance of records security will build it into the RECORDS MANAGEMENT procedure at every stage, including the records-creation, active-use, archival, and destruction stages. See also RECORDS RETENTION.

The following are examples of questions that must be answered to ensure adequate records security:

1. Who should have access to active and archival files and records?

2. What steps are required to ensure that files and records are not left unattended or unsecured at any time?

3. Who will be allowed to remove active or archival files and records? See also CHARGE-OUT SYSTEM.

4. How will access to information be supervised and controlled?

5. Are procedures established to provide duplicates of paper documents and backup copies of electronic documents and to store them in secure locations?

6. Are procedures established to prevent the contamination or destruction of files and records from hazards such as computer viruses, fire, and pollutants?

7. What steps have been taken to ensure that intentionally deleted electronic material cannot be recovered by unauthorized users?

8. How will files and records be stored? See also DOCUMENT IMAGING; MAGNETIC MEDIA STORAGE; MICROGRAPHICS; OPTICAL MEDIA STORAGE; and the various entries pertaining to paper filing systems, such as ALPHABETIC FILING SYSTEM, NUMERIC FILING SYSTEM, and SUBJECT FILING SYSTEM.

9. How will files and records be transported to a records storage room or area?

10. Who will have access to the storage room or area?

11. What kind of climate or other control is required in this room or area?

12. Who will authorize the retention or destruction of paper and electronic records?

13. How and where will material scheduled for destruction be disposed of?

See also VITAL RECORDS.

REMINDER SYSTEM.   See FOLLOW-UP SYSTEM.

REPORTS MANAGEMENT. The control of reports from creation to archival storage or destruction. See also Chapter 9/REPORT.

Businesses regularly generate massive amounts of information in the form of reports. These reports range from simple, one-paragraph memos to book-size documents with hundreds of pages.

The number of manual and electronic reports of all sizes has burgeoned to the extent that control of the production and disposition of such material has become a serious problem in many organizations.

The increasing overload of business reports has prompted the need for a strict program of reports management. Many businesses therefore are implementing a program that includes the following steps:

1. Consider whether the various reports, both the nonroutine reports and those that are issued regularly, are essential.

2. Eliminate any report that duplicates information already available in another form, such as in a database.

3. Eliminate any other report that is no longer mandatory or important.

4. Combine similar reports from two or more sources into a single report.

5. Evaluate reports of two or more pages for unnecessary data that could be eliminated or condensed to reduce the size of a report.

6. Send copies of reports only to those who absolutely must have them.

7. Do not produce and store extra copies of a report—just in case someone later might ask for a copy. (Make a duplicate when a copy is requested.)

8. Schedule periodic reports for publication less often whenever possible.

9. Consider issuing smaller reports in electronic format only, without printing paper copies.

Those who would like to develop a reports management program should coordinate efforts with the records management office.

RETRIEVAL. See FULL-TEXT RETRIEVAL; KEYWORD RETRIEVAL.

SUBJECT FILING SYSTEM. A system of filing whereby material is classified by subject, with individual files arranged alphabetically or numerically under a main subject heading.

The classification of records is determined by common features, such as by topics, names, publication titles, dates, or numbers.

An advantage of subject filing is that topics are easier to remember than, say, numbers. Also, files pertaining to a certain topic are conveniently grouped and stored together in one location.

However, a cross-index may be necessary in some cases, such as when the individual FILE FOLDERS within a particular subject classification are coded with numbers or symbols.

Coding systems.   Two main types of codes may be added to FILE LABELS and to the labels of storage equipment or containers: alphabetic or numeric. The numeric code may be alphanumeric, decimal numeric, duplex numeric, or block numeric. See also ALPHABETIC FILING SYSTEM; NUMERIC FILING SYSTEM.

In an *alphabetic coding system*, a two- to six-letter code is added to each subject, as in *BDG BUDGET*. In a simple alphabetic system, the individual files are then arranged in straight alphabetic order by subject.

In an *alphanumeric coding system,* a combination letter–number code might be added to each subdivision, as in *SLS SALES, SLS-01 EQUIPMENT SALES, SLS-01-01 COPIERS,* and so on.

In a *decimal-numeric coding system,* one or more decimal points might be used for the subdivisions, as in *402 MANAGEMENT, 402.1 BOARD OF DIREC-TORS, 402.1.1 TRAVEL EXPENSE,* and so on.

In a *duplex-numeric coding system,* numbers and hyphens might be used for the subdivisions, as in *30 PUBLICATIONS, 30-1 PRINTING, 30-1-1 BROCHURES,* and so on.

In a *block-numeric coding system,* blocks of numbers would be assigned to a particular subject, such as *TRANSPORTATION 300-700.*

Index.   The type of index that is used depends on the type of subject filing system. For example, if a system consists of numeric files collected under certain subject headings, such as the names of office products, the index would have to list all office-product names alphabetically and include a cross-reference to the number assigned to each name.

Basic subject filing systems.   Three basic subject filing systems are the dictionary, encyclopedic, and structured-functional systems.

In a *dictionary subject filing system,* all records are arranged alphabetically by subject, without subdivisions.

In an *encyclopedic subject filing system,* the main subjects are arranged alphabetically, and the individual files within major subject groups are also arranged alphabetically, from general to specific.

A collection of records, therefore, is first organized and alphabtized by general, or broad, subject and then subdivided within each general area into more specific topics, similar to the breakdown of topics in an outline developed to prepare a report.

In a *structured-functional filing system,* records are organized by the general function of each unit in an organization, such as *TRAINING* (level 1), and then subdivided into increasingly more specific aspects of the main function, as in *WRITTEN COMMUNICATION* (level 2) and *REPORTS* (level 3).

For a detailed description of subject filing, see the material on that subject published by ARMA INTERNATIONAL.

See also ALPHABETIC FILING SYSTEM; ALPHABETIZING; CHRONOLOGICAL FILING SYSTEM; ELECTRONIC FILING SYSTEM; FILENAME; GEOGRAPHIC FILING SYSTEM; INDEXING; NUMERIC FILING SYSTEM.

TICKLER FILE. See FOLLOW-UP SYSTEM.

VITAL RECORDS. Irreplaceable records, such as a patent or a deed; any records that would be necessary for a business to be able to resume operations after a disaster.

Because the destruction of vital records can cost an organization a great deal in direct recovery costs and in lost or delayed business, all organizations should have a program that will provide for the protection of vital records.

For example, a *disaster recovery program* should include not only the steps to take after a disaster has occurred but also the steps needed to protect vital records from destruction. This program should include appropriate measures for older paper records as well as for newer electronic records.

Making backup copies and storing them off-site is essential, but other steps may also be needed, such as better security and improved fire safety standards both on-site and off-site.

Implementing a program. A sound program begins with a definition of vital records in terms of the particular business.

For example, some records, such as a pending patent, would be essential to all businesses. Other records, such as a five-year-old policy manual, might not be crucial to a business that just replaced the old manual with a new version.

The next step following the definition process is to take an accurate inventory of all records and find those that fit the approved definition.

An organization must then decide how to protect the listed records. Management often decides on more than one strategy to increase the chances that the vital records will survive a disaster.

Protecting the original from theft, deterioration, and destruction is a key part of any vital records program. In addition, a company may make duplicate paper copies and back up the electronic copies.

All copies may then be dispersed to different locations, with copies stored at more than one site.

Vital records schedule.   Vital records are often listed on the RECORDS RETENTION schedule as permanent or long-term records, although something, such as a license, that changes frequently may still be considered vital during the (relative shorter) period when it is in force.

A separate vital records schedule is needed even though retention periods for vital records are included in the main records retention schedule. This is necessary because a vital records schedule also includes other essential information.

For example, a vital records schedule should include the following information:

The name and, if helpful, a description, of the record

The date of the record

Any coded information used in filing

Its security classification, if any (who may have access to it and so on)

The location of the original

The location of copies (duplicate originals and other copies)

A schedule for partial deposits of incomplete records (until a record is completed)

The retention period for each item

Off-site facilities.   Some organizations do not have branch offices or available sites far enough apart to ensure that at least one will escape a natural disaster or other hazard. In such cases, an organization may choose to disperse duplicate originals and other copies to commercial storage facilities.

Those who use outside facilities should be certain that each one is in a different part of the country and that the facility has appropriate climate control and provides reliable security protection.

CHAPTER FOUR

Conferences and Meetings

ADJOURNED MEETING. The continuation of a MEETING that was originally postponed (adjourned) because a QUORUM was not present or for some other reason that prevented action from being concluded until a later date.

If the necessary quorum fails to attend a STOCKHOLDERS' MEETING, for example, the meeting must adjourn to another time, in the manner fixed by the statutes, certificate of incorporation, or bylaws. (See ADJOURNMENT; Chapter 10/BYLAWS; CERTIFICATE OF INCORPORATION; Chapter 11/STATUTORY LAW.) This is the only legal action that can be taken.

ADJOURNMENT. The act of postponing a MEETING until another time (see ADJOURNED MEETING) or indefinitely. The adjournment may be to a certain day or SINE DIE (without naming a day and finally terminating the meeting), or it may be subject to the call of the chair.

The MOTION to adjourn specifies which form of adjournment will be taken, and if none is specified, the adjournment is final and puts an end to all unfinished business. Such business, however, can be introduced again at another meeting as if it had not been brought up previously.

In a COMMITTEE, a motion "to rise" has the same effect as an adjournment in an assembly, or full body.

A *recess* is an adjournment for a limited time, such as a 30-minute refreshment break.

AGENDA. Sometimes called *order of business.* A list, plan, outline, or digest of matters to be discussed or transacted at a MEETING.

The agenda may be prepared several days or more before a meeting. Confidential matters, however, should be omitted and presented at the meeting at some suitable time, even though this will change the order of the agenda.

Before preparing and distributing an agenda, some leaders write to those who will be attending the meeting to request items that might be included.

Preparation guidelines. Many word processing programs include templates for setting up an agenda. (See Chapter 9/TEMPLATE; WORD PROCESSING.) Follow the practice in your office concerning the number of drafts to prepare (at least one, and more if the agenda is revised several times).

Center each line of the heading:

ABC CORPORATION

Directors' Meeting

November 9, 200X

Summarize the meeting time, the location, and the presiding officer and his or her telephone or other number or address in a paragraph below the heading:

Regular Meeting, 10:00 A.M.–12:00 noon, Corporation Headquarters, 1000 West Avenue, Suite 200, Hanover, Pennsylvania 17333, Benjamin Schurte, presiding (717-555-0900, ext. 2121).

After the opening heading and first paragraph, list the agenda topics in an appropriate order as described in the next section.

Order of topics. Unless an order is prescribed by the bylaws (see Chapter 10/BYLAWS), the business to be transacted need not follow any particular order. A logical order of business, however, expedites the conduct of the meeting.

The following order might be used at an annual STOCKHOLDERS' MEETING, and the agenda would list these items in the same order and elaborate on them as needed:

Stockholders' Meeting Agenda

1. Call to order by [*name of presiding officer*].

2. Election of the chair and the appointment of a temporary secretary, if necessary.

3. Presentation of proof that the meeting was properly called.

4. Presentation and examination of proxies. See also PROXY.

5. Announcement of whether a QUORUM is present.

6. Reading (if required) and approval of the MINUTES of the previous meeting by [*name of secretary*].

7. Presentation of list of stockholders.

8. Reports of officers and committees [*identify each*].

9. Ratification of directors' and executive committee acts.

10. Appointment of inspectors of election.

11. Opening of polls.

12. Election of directors.

13. Closing of polls.

14. Report of inspectors.

15. Declaration of election of directors.

16. New business [*identify items if known*].

17. ADJOURNMENT.

The order of business in a DIRECTORS' MEETING would omit some of the formal steps taken in a stockholders' meeting. It might, for example, include the following items:

Directors' Meeting Agenda

1. Call to order by [*name of presiding officer*]

2. Announcement of a quorum present

3. Reading (if required) and approval of previous meeting's minutes by [*name of secretary*]

4. Treasurer's report

5. Reports of other officers [*identify*]

6. Reports of committees [*identify*]

7. Old business [*identify items*]

8. New business [*identify items known in advance*]

9. Nominations and election of officers

10. COMMITTEE appointments

11. Announcements

12. ADJOURNMENT

The order of business at a weekly staff meeting would be less formal than that of either a stockholders' or directors' meeting. The following list includes examples of items that might be in the agenda for an informal weekly or monthly staff meeting:

Staff Meeting Agenda

1. Approval of previous minutes [*if any*]
2. Matters arising from previous minutes [*if any*]
3. Announcements
4. Report from Human Resources Development and Management Committee (*or any other committee*)
5. Proposed new courses for management-development-program curriculum (*or any other such related proposals or announcements*)
6. Approval of 200X operating budget
7. Other business
8. Date, time, and location of next meeting

Supplementary material. Exhibits and supporting papers, statements, reports, and so on that contain information necessary to supply the groundwork for discussion are usually attached to an agenda and distributed several days before the meeting.

Some organizations like to provide a binder with tabs for each director. The wording on each tab should correspond to an item on the agenda or should designate general areas of business. Copies of all pertinent papers, reports, statements, or other material are then placed behind the proper tabs.

ANNUAL MEETING. In corporation affairs, the yearly MEETING of stockholders for the election of directors. See also STOCKHOLDERS' MEETING.

In certain other organizations, such as an association, the annual meeting may refer to the combined annual meeting and CONFERENCE, with lectures, workshops, and so on.

APPOINTMENT. A prearranged MEETING, frequently between two or three people and usually held in a business or professional office for a specific purpose. The date, time, and purpose of all business appointments should be entered on a computerized or paper calendar or schedule or in a desk appointment book.

Each morning, an assistant should place on his or her employer's desk a computer printout or other schedule of appointments, stating where and with whom each appointment is to be held, the purpose of it, and any additional pertinent information.

At the time of each appointment, the assistant should also provide any material that will be needed for the meeting.

See also Chapter 5/TRAVEL APPOINTMENT SCHEDULE for an example of a schedule to use when an executive travels.

For model letters requesting appointments and for replies to such letters, refer to Chapter 8/APPOINTMENTS.

AUDIOCONFERENCE.   Also called *conference call*. A MEETING in which participants in different locations speak to and hear each other by way of special telephone connections.

Although audioconferencing once required the assistance of a long-distance operator, many telephone systems now include audioconferencing as a feature. Long-distance carriers regularly offer audioconferencing with a variety of options and pricing.

Audioconferences are most successful for short discussions. In many cases, one to two days of travel time would be impractical for a 30-minute or 1-hour meeting.

However, as with any meeting, participants should be notified of the audioconference in advance to avoid delays or absences when the connection is made. See also AGENDA.

BYLAWS.   See Chapter 10/BYLAWS.

CALLED MEETING.   A synonym for a corporation's SPECIAL MEETING, or special-purpose MEETING, as distinguished from its routinely scheduled REGULAR MEETINGS. See also STOCKHOLDERS' MEETING.

CALL OF DIRECTORS' MEETING.   A command or request to assemble a MEETING of the board of directors of a corporation. See also Chapter 10/BOARD OF DIRECTORS.

Who issues the call.   The bylaws (see Chapter 10/BYLAWS) usually indicate who has the authority to issue calls for a DIRECTORS' MEETING, although sometimes this is covered by statute.

The authorized person must call the meeting, but if the designated officer does not send the notices, another officer may do so.

The chairman of the board usually calls a meeting, or in the chair's absence, the president may do so. Meetings may also be called by the written direction of a specified number of directors.

Form of the call. The manner of calling directors' meetings is controlled by the certificate of incorporation (see Chapter 10/CERTIFICATE OF INCORPORATION) and the bylaws, not by an agreement among corporate stockholders or organizational members.

In the absence of other provisions in the statutes or the bylaws of the organization, the meeting need not be called in any particular manner. If all directors receive proper notice (see NOTICE OF MEETING), the meeting will be valid.

A notice may be in the form of a letter, memo, or card. Depending on the number required, one could print copies by computer or, for large quantities, use offset printing.

Preparation of the call. The following form is an example of a formal call that may be prepared on business letterhead:

Call of Special Directors' Meeting

_____, 200X

To the Directors of _____Corporation:

The undersigned, President of the _____ Corporation, hereby calls a special meeting of the Board of Directors of said Corporation, to be held at the office of the Corporation, _____ [*street*], _____ [*city*], _____ [*state*], on the _____ day of _____, 200X, at _____ o'clock in the _____[*morning, afternoon*], for the purpose of _____ [*summarize purpose*].

_____
President

CALL OF STOCKHOLDERS' MEETING. A command or request to assemble a MEETING of the stockholders of a corporation. See also Chapter 10/STOCKHOLDER.

Who issues the call. The bylaws (see Chapter 10/BYLAWS) generally indicate who may call regular and special meetings of stockholders. Occasionally, the provisions governing the calling of meetings are found in the certificate of incorporation. See also Chapter 10/CERTIFICATE OF INCORPORATION.

In many states, the manner of calling meetings is fixed by statute. If there is a conflict between the bylaws and the statutes about who shall make the call, the statutes control.

If neither the bylaws nor the statutes designate who shall call STOCKHOLDERS' MEETINGS, the directors, acting as a board, should do so, and they may call a meeting whenever necessary. See also Chapter 10/BOARD OF DIRECTORS.

Follow the provisions of the certificate of incorporation or the bylaws concerning the number of days of advance notice required to call a meeting. If no formal requirements exist, send a call or notice in sufficient time for out-of-town attendees to make travel and hotel arrangements.

Form of the call.   A call ordinarily consists of written direction to the corporate secretary or other officer authorized to notify the stockholders. Usually, the call is signed by the president or other authorized officer.

In some instances, a copy of the call is posted on a bulletin board in the main office of the corporation. (See NOTICE OF MEETING.) However, the call and notice of a meeting should not be combined.

Preparation of the call.   When time permits, reply slips may be enclosed for participants to use in acknowledging the call or notice and indicating whether they will attend.

Other material also may be enclosed, such as a preliminary AGENDA and various reports. In addition, the mailing may include a request for agenda topics.

The following form is an example of a formal call that may be prepared on business letterhead:

Call of Stockholders' Annual Meeting

To Secretary of Corporation:

The regular annual meeting of stockholders of the _____ Corporation is hereby called for _____ [*day of week*], the _____ day of _____, 200X, at _____ o'clock in the _____[*morning, afternoon*], to be held at the principal office of the Corporation at _____ [*street*], _____ [*city*], _____ [*state*], for the following purposes: [*summarize purposes*].

You are hereby directed, as Secretary of said Corporation, to give proper notice of said meeting to the stockholders of said Corporation, as prescribed by the bylaws thereof.

_____
President

Dated _____, 200X

CHAT ROOM. See Chapter 6/CHAT ROOM.

COMMITTEE. A group of people charged with a specific purpose that meets regularly to accomplish its goals.

Types of committees. The committee may be a standing committee, select committee, or committee of the whole:

1. A *standing committee* is appointed for a particular session or for some definite time.
2. A *select committee* is appointed for a specific purpose.
3. A *committee of the whole* consists of the entire body.

A committee is usually established to accomplish a task or objective that can't easily or practically be done through the entire organization. The membership of the committee should include representatives whose interests the committee is designed to serve.

The size of a committee will vary depending on its specific function and character. When committees become too large, smaller groups (*subcommittees*) may be appointed to address specific subtopics or issues.

Subcommittees meet apart from the larger committee and report back to the larger group at regularly scheduled times.

Two common committees of a board of directors are the executive committee, the most important committee, and the finance committee, which sometimes includes a budgeting subcommittee. See also Chapter 10/EXECUTIVE COMMITTEE; FINANCE COMMITTEE.

Organizations also set up other committees to handle miscellaneous aspects of business operations, such as a temporary task force to plan a building project or a semipermanent standing committee to deal with marketing operations.

Operating procedure. The committee chair, appointed at the time the committee is formed or elected thereafter by the committee members, must be a capable leader. The chair calls the meetings and leads the activities in them.

Formal committees, such as those that report to a board of directors, commonly follow the rules of PARLIAMENTARY PROCEDURE described in ROBERT'S RULES OF ORDER.

Smaller, informal committees usually operate in a less structured manner. In either case, however, it's necessary to maintain order and keep accurate records of committee activities.

COMPUTER CONFERENCE. An electronic MEETING in which two or more people communicate in a synchronous (simultaneous, or real time) or asynchronous (not at the same time) manner.

Computer conferencing technology enables participants in remote locations to send messages and to share, review, and edit computer documents together on screen. The documents that the participants work on may be from various computer applications, such as word processing and spreadsheets.

With the required telephone lines for data and voice communication, users can simultaneously work on screen and discuss the document with voice communication. With a camera attachment, users can add a VIDEOCONFERENCE feature to the meeting.

Since any message sent by a participant is available immediately to all participants, computer conferencing can be used in a variety of applications, including educational courses and training programs.

Preparations for a computer conference, like those for any other meeting, involve determining which participants will be available, sending notices and confirmations, and making technical arrangements with the appropriate in-house department or outside service.

CONFERENCE. A MEETING for discussion and exchange of opinions and ideas. As few as two people may hold a conference, or as many as thousands may gather for a common purpose. Conferences among the executives and professional staff of a company are essential to modern business management.

Although conferences are useful, they can be time consuming and expensive and may not be essential in all cases.

To eliminate time-wasting conferences and associated COMMITTEES, some organizations appoint a conference manager or corporation meeting planner. In general, this person must approve all major, off-site conferences.

Most companies prefer informal conferences in which executives feel free to speak out. See also ROUNDTABLE MEETING.

Conferences are also held among the top executives of various companies. These leaders often spend between 20 and 30 days a year at conferences designed for exchanging information and ideas.

These conferences, sometimes called *conventions* when exhibits and other features are present, are arranged and sponsored by associations such as the American Management Association, and a registration fee is commonly charged.

See also ANNUAL MEETING; AUDIOCONFERENCE; COMPUTER CONFERENCE; DIRECTORS' MEETING; MEETING; SEMINAR; STAFF MEETING; STOCKHOLDERS' MEETING; VIDEOCONFERENCE.

Conference preparations. The conference manager or meeting planner may be in charge of conference preparations or at least some aspect of planning activities. His or her assistant may be involved in sending speakers' invitations and making arrangements for meeting rooms, meals, registration, programs and mailing lists, special events, and equipment rentals.

1. *Room reservations.* After the conference site and hotel, motel, or convention center have been selected, the facility will designate a representative to work with the conference planners in reserving meeting rooms of adequate size, with proper acoustics, and able to accommodate equipment that speakers may need.

2. *Speakers.* Invitations to speak at a conference are generally extended by letter or by a combination of letter and telephone call from the person in charge of these arrangements. Standby speakers are common since someone inevitably drops out at the last minute.

Even when speakers aren't compensated, it's customary to give each one a small gift, conference memento, or honorarium.

3. *Meals.* The facility where the conference will be held will designate a representative to work with the planning committee in selecting menus and estimating the number of meals required and the size of room for service.

Usually, a certain number must be guaranteed and paid for even if fewer persons arrive for each meal. Therefore, closely estimating attendance at meals is very important to control costs.

4. *Registration.* This is the area of activity in which office personnel are most often involved. After registration forms are printed and mailed, the actual registrations begin arriving by postal mail, telephone, fax, and e-mail. Some registrations may be handled at the sponsor's Web site. See also Chapter 6/WEB SITE.

The staff must keep careful records of both the registrations and the checks or credit card charges that accompany them. All registrations must be acknowledged and refunds sent for cancellations.

5. *Programs and mailing lists.* The program committee must collect enough information on speakers, sessions, and other conference activities to prepare a program brochure or booklet. If in-house desktop publishing is not available, the work must be sent to an outside printer.

This work must be done in time for the mailing to reach recipients four to six weeks in advance, or earlier, so that they can make travel plans, request company travel funds, and so on.

6. *Special events.* Many conferences include special events, such as a tour, especially if spouses attend. These events require other arrangements, and preconference publicity should also include information about special events.

7. *Equipment rental.* Invitations to speakers often include a form for them to complete and return that specifies their equipment needs. Most facilities provide Internet access (see Chapter 6/INTERNET) and all necessary hookups.

If other equipment is needed that the facility does not provide, it must be rented elsewhere, with arrangements for delivery and pickup made in advance.

Other office duties. Note all important deadlines (printing, mailing, and so on) on the computer schedule and calendar and on both your own desk calendar and that of your employer.

Add the names of registrants to any mailing list that you maintain for future conference mailings.

Make up a detailed checklist of things that you and your employer want to do before the conference, another of things to take along to the conference, one of things to do at the conference, and another of things to do after the conference.

CONFLICT RESOLUTION. A process by which individuals with differing opinions are encouraged to express their views, listen actively to the views of others, and work together to a mutually acceptable solution.

In conflict resolution, an impartial third party, or FACILITATOR, intervenes in a dispute or disagreement between two or more individuals.

The role of the facilitator is to remove obstacles to communication, encourage open participation, help the parties explore various options, and, ultimately, achieve a satisfactory resolution of the issue.

CONSENSUS. Agreement in principle among a group of individuals. Reaching a consensus means that all parties involved in a decision explicitly agree to abide by that decision.

Consensus generally follows a great deal of discussion in which participants bring forth and discuss information and share viewpoints about an issue. Differences of opinion are openly discussed with a goal of reaching agreement on a single outcome.

Consensus is both a process and an outcome. Although achieving consensus does not necessarily mean that everyone enthusiastically supports a decision, it does mean that the group agrees to support that decision.

Building consensus among a group of individuals is a key task of meeting FACILITATORS.

CONVENTION. See CONFERENCE.

DIRECTORS' MEETING. Formal MEETING or assembly of the individual directors of a corporation for the purpose of transacting the business of the corporation. See also Chapter 10/BOARD OF DIRECTORS.

The board of directors, acting as a body, has sole authority to manage the corporation in matters not reserved for action by stockholders.

Kinds of directors' meetings. Meetings may be either regular or special. (See REGULAR MEETING; SPECIAL MEETING.) The only difference is in the notice. If there is no evidence that the meeting was regular, it will be presumed to have been special.

Call of directors' meetings. See CALL OF DIRECTORS' MEETING; REGULAR MEETING; SPECIAL MEETING.

Time and place of directors' meetings. The meetings should be held at the time and place designated in the NOTICE OF MEETING, which should not conflict with the requirements of the state statutes, certificate of incorporation, or bylaws. See also Chapter 10/BYLAWS; CERTIFICATE OF INCORPORATION.

Meeting preparations. The corporate secretary, who usually is responsible for the preparations, ordinarily takes the following steps:

1. Gathers data to be presented at the meeting.
2. Sends a notice of the meeting to the directors. See also NOTICE OF MEETING.
3. Writes the meeting AGENDA.
4. Arranges for payment of attendance fees to directors, when required, by requisitioning the required funds from the corporation treasurer.
5. Makes preparations for recording of the MINUTES of the meeting.

Preliminary approval of business. In some organizations, prospective business must have the unanimous approval of all officers, meeting as an executive COMMITTEE. (See Chapter 10/EXECUTIVE COMMITTEE.) In other cases, executives meet in advance to discuss matters to be brought before the board.

In some large corporations, special committees are appointed to confer with the officer or department head who advocates the consideration of a certain question by the board of directors.

Usually, formal meetings of executives or officers to discuss proposed resolutions are not held. Rather, the president or the chairman of the board discusses them informally with the interested officers.

Meeting conduct. In small corporations, board meetings are usually conducted informally. In larger corporations, however, meetings may be more formal. The president usually presides at meetings of the directors, unless some other provision is made by the bylaws.

A QUORUM is necessary for the directors to transact business. Votes may be taken informally, such as by a call for *yes* and *no* answers or by a show of hands. They may also be taken electronically when not prohibited by the certificate of incorporation, bylaws, or statutes.

The order of business varies among organizations, but a typical order for a directors' meeting is described in AGENDA.

DOCUMENT CONFERENCE. See COMPUTER CONFERENCE.

FACILITATOR. The individual responsible for leading and maintaining order at a MEETING. A meeting facilitator may be the chair of the group or an individual otherwise uninvolved in the meeting's activities.

Like a chair, the facilitator has many duties, including the following: calling the meeting to order, generating discussion, encouraging involvement among all participants, managing conflict, reaching CONSENSUS on issues brought before the group, and adhering to the meeting AGENDA.

However, most facilitators consider their main responsibility to be keeping the meeting focused and on track and ensuring the participation of all attendees.

A facilitator should remain neutral and not seek to influence the discussion or its outcome. Rather, the person should encourage equal participation by all sides to an issue and, without bias, move the group toward the goals of the meeting.

FIRST MEETING OF STOCKHOLDERS. See INCORPORATORS' MEETING.

FOCUS GROUP. A group of people who are selected, based on certain characteristics, to meet for a controlled, moderated discussion on a specific topic. A focus group typically represents a qualitative form of market research.

A series of questions is posed by a trained moderator, who guides the discussion according to a prescribed plan that has been developed in consultation with management or clients. The session is frequently audio- or videotaped.

Following the MEETING, the moderator usually prepares a written report to management or the clients based on the discussion and its outcome.

As is the case with any CONFERENCE, the assistant may help organize a focus group and is likely to be involved in these steps:

1. Contacting participants
2. Sending invitations or notices
3. Securing an appropriate meeting site and arranging for any required equipment
4. Arranging for refreshment breaks and any desired food services
5. Arranging for travel expenses or other payment to participants
6. Preparing postmeeting reports

Focus groups reveal the feelings that a group has about a topic, issue, or product and are widely used in market research and new product development.

INCORPORATORS' MEETING. The formal organizational MEETING of an organization's incorporators. The purpose of the meeting is to comply with state statutes or laws governing the completion of the organization of a corporation. The meeting must be held in the state of incorporation. See also Chapter 10/INCORPORATORS.

INDEX TO MINUTES. An alphabetically arranged system of references, by keyword (see Chapter 3/KEYWORD RETRIEVAL) and page, to the contents of meeting MINUTES. See also Chapter 3/INDEXING; Chapter 9/INDEX.

Use of an index. Large corporations usually have their minutes carefully indexed so that information about any business transacted at a formal MEETING, however remote in time, may be located quickly and easily.

Some corporations do not index the minutes of DIRECTORS' MEETINGS but keep a complete index of the minutes of the executive COMMITTEE. See also Chapter 10/EXECUTIVE COMMITTEE.

Preparation of an index. The index is usually prepared and maintained by computer, with additions edited in and a revised copy printed after each meeting. However, card indexes or looseleaf binder indexes may also be used.

Using headings in the minutes facilitates preparation. Often, these headings are the same as the topics listed on the AGENDA. The index contains subject matter taken from the headings and a reference to the page on which the heading appears.

If your company prefers a more detailed index, include a number with the headings appearing on each page, and refer to that number in the index, rather than to the page (or refer to both). List the numbers consecutively through the minutes of all meetings.

If you use indexing software to prepare the index, follow the instructions of your particular program.

Usually, state the topic heading first, followed by the date and location. Use cross-references (see Chapter 3/CROSS-REFERENCE) if topics might be described in more than one way, and include any numerical designation or code used in your company's system:

Construction proposal:

    May 7, 200X, DTS.6, p. 3
    Oct. 4, 200X, DTS.41, p. 9

It helps to index the minutes as soon as you finish preparing them for two reasons: Others may want to locate a particular topic, and the index will then be ready for them. Also, the subjects in the index will be fresh in your mind immediately after preparing the minutes, which may prove useful in selecting topics and cross-references.

LOADED CONFERENCE. A CONFERENCE that is held after the executive calling it has talked informally with the conferees and thus assured himself or herself that they are in agreement about some matter to be resolved.

This type of time-wasting formal conference is called to protect the executive from criticism if the action decided on is not successful.

MEETING. A gathering or assembly of persons, such as a STAFF MEETING, a corporation's STOCKHOLDERS' MEETING, or a COMMITTEE meeting, usually for the purpose of discussing and deciding a particular matter or matters.

At least two kinds of meetings must be held by every corporation organized for profit: (1) stockholders' meetings, often called simply *corporate meetings,* and (2) DIRECTORS' MEETINGS.

Meetings of committees, such as an executive committee or a finance committee, may also be held, particularly in large corporations. See also Chapter 10/EXECUTIVE COMMITTEE; FINANCE COMMITTEE.

MEETING CONDUCT. See PARLIAMENTARY PROCEDURE.

MEETING FILE. The *permanent* file of essential material needed for all corporate MEETINGS. In many organizations, office personnel help prepare and maintain this file.

Include the following information in a *meeting file*: a copy of the corporation laws of the state in which the corporation is organized; a copy of the corporation's certificate of incorporation and bylaws (see Chapter 10/BYLAWS; CERTIFICATE OF INCORPORATION), with amendments; and other documents of a similar nature and importance that may be needed at a meeting.

Also include other data that are accumulated as preparations for a particular meeting are being made. After the meeting has taken place, however, remove the papers pertaining to it, and retain only the documents mentioned as necessary for *all* meetings.

Meeting folder. Similar to a meeting file, a *meeting folder* is a *temporary* folder in which you keep notes and material to be used at a forthcoming meeting. The particular meeting to which it applies should be written on the cover.

Keep the following material in the meeting folder: all documents and papers pertaining to matters to be discussed at the meeting; a copy of the call, such as a CALL OF DIRECTORS' MEETING; the NOTICE OF MEETING; a report to the cashier about the directors' fees; a skeleton of the MINUTES; any proxies (see PROXY) or other business received at the corporate secretary's office before the meeting; and a memo for mailing extracts of the minutes.

Prepare a similar folder for any executive who will be attending the meeting. If several folders are needed, use different-colored labels or in some way mark them so that the attendee can quickly and easily find material during the meeting.

Envelope file of memos. An envelope-file method of collecting material is similar to the meeting-folder method in that you keep in the envelope any material that will be referred to at the meeting.

It's different, however, in that the face of the envelope constitutes a page for making entries of material received. It also furnishes a list that the corporate secretary can use in preparing a schedule of business to be taken up at the meeting.

MEETINGS HELD BY PROXY. MEETINGS of stockholders that must be held at the principal office of the corporation in the state in which it is organized when the corporation is represented in that state only by a resident agent. (See Chapter 10/RESIDENT AGENT.) The meetings of the stockholders then may be held entirely by PROXY and conducted by the resident agent.

The minutes are prepared *in advance* of the meeting, with the names of the persons who are present as proxies being temporarily omitted so that they can be inserted *after* the meeting has been held.

Ordinarily, the minutes are prepared by a corporation service company and examined and approved by the corporation's attorney. See also Chapter 10/CORPORATION SERVICE COMPANY.

MINUTES. Generally, the official record of proceedings at a MEETING; specifically, the official record of the proceedings at a meeting *of an organized body,* such as the stockholders or directors of a corporation. See also DIRECTORS' MEETING; STOCKHOLDERS' MEETING.

The corporate secretary is responsible for the minutes of all corporate meetings. However, office personnel may be asked to take notes during the meeting in addition to making a recorded version.

Since minutes are legal evidence of action taken, they should be clear, concise, and unambiguous.

Preparations for taking minutes. This is usually the responsibility of the corporate secretary, although office personnel often assist with some or all of these steps:

1. Prepare an advance statement of the order of business, or an AGENDA.

2. For a DIRECTORS' MEETING, give a copy of the agenda to each director and the presiding officer, or if desired, send it along with the NOTICE OF MEETING.

3. If important matters are to be considered, indicate on the agenda the names of those who are to present the business to the meeting.

4. Have available all books, papers, contracts, and reports that are likely to be discussed or requested at the meeting.

5. Draft any MOTION or resolution of business to come before the meeting if the subject is to be voted on by the directors or stockholders.

6. If payment is to be made immediately to the directors for attendance at the meeting, remind the corporate secretary to have the necessary funds available.

7. Bring a form to the meeting for entering resolutions and other motions. See Figure 1 for an example.

MINUTES: FIGURE 1: Form for Recording Resolutions and Other Motions

---

MEETING OF BOARD OF DIRECTORS
[DATE]

[ ] Annual   [ ] Special   Form of Notice: _____

Hour: _____   Waiver: _____

No. present: _____   Necessary for Quorum: _____

Chair: _____   Secretary: _____

RESOLUTIONS AND MOTIONS:

1. _____

Proposed by: Seconded by:

2. _____

Proposed by: Seconded by:

3. _____

Proposed by: Seconded by:

4. _____

Proposed by: Seconded by:

Adjournment: _____

Fees: _____

Signed: _____
                    Secretary

---

8. Quickly compile a seating chart just before the meeting is called to order to help you recognize persons who are speaking.

Format of minutes. After a meeting has been held, prepare the minutes in a formal or informal format, as required by your organization. Minutes of directors' and stockholders' meetings should follow the form required by the corporation. Use previous copies in the files as models.

Both formal and informal minutes should follow the order of business at the meeting and should contain essential facts and figures. The subject matter should consist of a clear, accurate, and complete report of all business transacted, such as decisions made and actions requiring follow-up.

Depending on your instructions, you may omit the name of a proposer or seconder of a motion, unless names are required for legal purposes. See also CONSENSUS.

In most cases, it's not necessary that the names of those voting for or against a proposition be recorded. But if a special request is made to record dissenting votes of a minority, you should do so. See also MINUTES BOOK OR FILE.

Preparation of minutes. Use the following guidelines for preparing formal minutes unless you have other instructions from your employer. (See Figure 2 for an example of informal minutes.) Also, check whether your word processing program has a template that can be used in setting up meeting minutes:

1. Center the heading, and capitalize important words or use all capitals.

2. Start paragraphs flush left, or indent them 1/2 to 1 inch.

3. Indent the names of attendees and absentees, or similar lists, an additional 1/2 inch, if desired.

4. Double- or single-space most minutes, as desired. Double-space the text of formal minutes unless instructed otherwise.

5. Leave an extra space between each paragraph if the text of informal minutes is single-spaced.

6. Indent resolutions an additional 1/2 inch, if desired.

7. Capitalize words such as *Board of Directors* or *Corporation* when referring to the board or to the corporation whose minutes are being written.

8. Capitalize important words in text headings, or write them in all capitals.

9. Position the text headings in the margin to the left of the associated text paragraphs, or place them directly above the related text paragraphs, flush with the left margin of the text.

MINUTES: FIGURE 2: Minutes of Meeting

Senior Support Staff
Shared Resources Group

MINUTES
1:30 p.m., December 15, 200X
Conference Room A

Present: Alice Samuels, Benjamin Dean, Cecilia Jeffries, David Kendall, Edmund Shoales. **Absent:** Dee Ferguson, Thomas Garnett, Henry Kessler.

CALL TO ORDER
Cecilia Jeffries called the meeting to order at 1:35 p.m.

MINUTES
The minutes of November 17 were reviewed and approved.

SSSSR 200X – SUBCOMMITTEE REPORTS
Fund-raising: Benjamin Dean reported that ten individuals had been contacted to donate items; five accepted, and five are pending.

Publicity: According to David Kendall, the subcommittee information regarding SSSSR 200X will be publicized in the next issue of the *Employee News.*

Program: Alice Samuels reported that the subcommittee will distribute letters to confirm speakers in January. After confirmations are received, the program will be completed. Only two time slots are left to fill as of the meeting date.

REQUEST TO INFORMATION SYSTEMS COUNCIL
The chair requested that a proposal be submitted to the Council at the January 19 meeting. The proposal should include details on software user groups, the development of a user listserv, and details on database training.

ADJOURNMENT
The meeting adjourned at 2:45 p.m.

Edmund Shoales, Secretary

---

10. Summarize the content of the minutes in the headings.

11. When the words *WHEREAS* and *RESOLVED* are used in formal resolutions, write them in all capitals, and begin the word *That* with a capital letter: *RESOLVED That.*

12. Write sums of money, when mentioned in a resolution, first in words and then followed by figures in parentheses.

Making corrections in the minutes. Both the original and the revised versions of corrected minutes must be maintained, with the revised version clearly identified as a revision of the original minutes of a certain date. Also, a note should be added to the original version referring the reader to the revised version that follows.

The minutes of a meeting are usually approved at the next meeting, and the chair may informally direct the correction of simple errors.

If an error can be corrected immediately, the correction should be made at the meeting in pen and ink and the minutes, as changed, offered for approval. If an error involves a more extensive revision of the minutes, the correction of the minutes of a previous meeting are reported in the minutes of the current meeting.

If a formal statement of adoption is required, the following form may be used:

Adoption of Previous Meeting Minutes as Corrected

RESOLVED That the minutes of the meeting of _____, held on the _____ day of _____, 200X, are hereby adopted and approved in their entirety, except that the words _____ be eliminated from the resolution _____ [*specify subject matter of resolution for identification*] contained therein.

See also INDEX TO MINUTES; MINUTES BOOK OR FILE.

MINUTES BOOK OR FILE. A record book or computer file in which the corporate secretary keeps all MINUTES of every MEETING and other pertinent material pertaining to the meetings or to the organization in general.

Separation of minutes. Usually, the minutes of STOCKHOLDERS' MEETINGS and DIRECTORS' MEETINGS are kept in separate books or files. Small companies, however, sometimes use one book or file for both, dividing it into two distinct parts.

Some small corporations have a single book or file containing minutes of both directors' and stockholders' meetings run in consecutive order, without separation of one class of meeting from another. This is helpful when joint meetings are held because the stockholders and directors are identical.

Arrangement of content. The first pages usually contain a copy of the certificate of incorporation of the corporation. (See Chapter 10/CERTIFICATE OF

INCORPORATION.) If minutes are filed in a book, leave room after the certificate to insert amendments.

Following the amendments, beginning at the top of a right-hand page, are the bylaws of the corporation. (See Chapter 10/BYLAWS.) Again, in a book, leave room to insert new bylaws or amendments.

Occasionally, when amendments are brief, you can insert them directly on the bylaws pages.

Place the minutes of the first meeting after the bylaws. (See INCORPORATORS' MEETING.) Always begin the minutes of each meeting on a new page.

MOTION.   Formal proposal or recommendation made at a MEETING for the consideration and action of those present. A motion must be made in accordance with the requirements of the rules of PARLIAMENTARY PROCEDURE or other method of transacting business adopted by the group.

Most matters of business that come before a meeting are introduced by a motion recommending that the participants express an opinion, take certain action, or order that certain action be taken.

A motion, in other words, is a proposal in which the expression *I move* is equivalent to the statement *I propose*.

Figure 1 lists all important motions as classified in *Robert's Rules of Order.* There are four principal types of motions:

1. *Principal,* or *main, motions,* which are motions about an issue that has been brought before the group: "I move that the reorganization plan be adopted."

2. *Subsidiary,* or *secondary, motions,* such as those applied to other motions for the purpose of disposing of them: "I move that the motion to adopt the reorganization plan be tabled."

3. *Incidental motions,* or those that arise out of other questions: "I move to withdraw the motion to adopt the reorganization plan."

4. *Privileged motions,* or those taking precedence over all other questions: "I move that we return to the order of business."

An assembled group adopts a resolution by making, seconding, and voting on a motion to adopt it: "I move that the following resolution be adopted: . . ."

Although not all motions involve a resolution, when someone makes a motion to adopt a resolution, it's important to record the resolution precisely. For an example of a convenient form to use in recording resolutions during a meeting, see MINUTES, Figure 1.

MOTION: FIGURE 1: Rules for Motions

Explanation: The left column of the table lists the various motions alphabetically. The seven column headings are the main rules that apply to motions. An asterisk [*] in one of the seven columns means that the rule described in the column head applies to the adjacent motion in the left column. A note number means that the rule only partially applies, and the extent to which it applies is described in the note itself. For example, "Lay on the Table." Asterisks in two columns show that it's undebatable and can't be amended. Note 5 indicates that an affirmative vote on this motion can't be reconsidered. The other four columns are blank, meaning that the motion does *not* "open the main question to debate," does *not* "require a two-thirds vote," *does* "need to be seconded," and is *not* "in order when another member has the floor."

Notes

1. Every motion in this column has the effect of suspending some rule or established right of deliberative assemblies and, therefore, requires a two-thirds vote, unless a special rule to the contrary is adopted.

2. Undebatable if made when another question is before the assembly.

3. An amendment may be made either (a) by adding or (b) by striking out words or paragraphs or (c) by striking out certain words and inserting others or (d) by substituting a different motion on the same subject or (e) by dividing the question into two or more questions as specified by the mover so as to get a separate vote on any particular point(s).

4. An appeal is undebatable only when relating to indecorum or to transgressions of the rules of speaking or to the priority of business or when made while the Previous Question is pending. When an Appeal is debatable, only one speech from each member is permitted. On a tie vote the decision of the chair is sustained.

5. An affirmative vote on this motion can't be reconsidered.

6. The objection can be made only when the question is first introduced, before debate.

7. Allows but limited debate upon the propriety of the postponement.

8. The Previous Question, if adopted, cuts off debate and brings the assembly to a vote on the pending question only, except where the pending motion is an amendment or a motion to Commit, when it also applies to the question to be amended or committed.

9. Can be moved and entered on the record when another person has the floor but can't interrupt business then before the assembly; must be made on the day or the day after the original vote was taken and by one who voted with the prevailing side.

Motion	Undebatable	Opens main question to debate	Cannot be amended	Cannot be reconsidered	Requires a two-thirds vote	Does not require to be seconded	In order when another has the floor
Adjourn	*		*			*	
Adjourn, Fix the Time to Which to	2						
Amend (n. 3)							
Amend an Amendment			*				
Amend the Rules				*			
Appeal, relating to indecorum etc. (n.4)	*		*			*	
Appeal, all other cases		*	*				
Call to Order	*		*			*	*
Close Debate, motion to	*			*			
Commit or Refer		*					
Extend the Limits of Debate, motion to	*			*			
Fix the Time to Which to Adjourn	2						
Leave to Continue Speaking after Indecorum	*		*				
Lay on the Table	*		*	5			
Limit Debate, motion to	*				*		
Objection to Consideration of a Question (n.6)	*		*		*	*	*
Orders of the Day, motion for the	*		*			*	*
Postpone to a Certain Time	7						
Postpone Indefinitely	*	*	*				
Previous Question (n.8)	*		*		*		
Priority of Business, questions relating to	*						
Privilege, Questions of							
Reading Papers	*		*			*	*
Reconsider a Debatable Question		*	*	*			9
Reconsider an Undebatable Question	*		*	*			9
Refer (same as Commit)			*				
Rescind			*				
Rise (in Committee: Adjourn)	*		*	*			
Special Order, to make a				*			
Substitute (same as Amend)							
Suspend the Rules	*		*	*	*		
Take from the Table	*		*	5			
Take up a Question Out of Its Proper Order	*		*		*		
Withdrawal of a Motion	*		*				

Note: For further information on the use of these motions, consult a recent edition of *Robert's Rules of Order.*

NOTICE OF MEETING. An informal MEETING notice that may be prepared as a letter, memo, or printed form and sent by telephone, fax, e-mail, or postal mail.

For a small meeting, you may prepare the notice by computer and print individual copies. For a large meeting, you will likely have the notice prepared in large quantities by some method such as offset printing.

Whether or not an organization requires that a notice follow a specific format and wording, it should nevertheless be specific about time, place, date, and purpose of the meeting.

Staff meeting. The notice of a STAFF MEETING is usually informal. You may announce it by word of mouth or telephone or send it by fax, e-mail, or interoffice mail delivery. You may also post a brief notice on an office or departmental bulletin board:

> *Notice of Finance Department Staff Meeting*
>
> A meeting of members of the Finance Department will be held at _____ [*time*] on _____ [*date*] at _____
> _____ [*location*] to discuss _____
> [*insert brief description of purpose*].

> See also the memo-list example in Chapter 8/ANNOUNCEMENTS.

Directors' meeting. Follow the provisions of the bylaws (see Chapter 10/BYLAWS) in sending notices to directors. However, even if notice of a regular meeting is not required by the bylaws, it's always a good idea to notify the directors of each meeting.

Unless you have other instructions, prepare the notice of a DIRECTORS' MEETING on the corporation's letterhead and send it under the name of the corporate secretary. Specify the date, place, and hour at which the meeting is to be held, the same as you would do in any meeting notice.

Stockholders' meeting. The bylaws will indicate how and when notices of STOCKHOLDERS' MEETINGS, both regular and special, must be sent, and the corporate secretary should follow those provisions.

Notices should be mailed to the stockholders a certain number of days before the meeting, as specified in the bylaws.

The notice of a stockholders' meeting may be in the form of an announcement card or letter sent in a *sealed* envelope. Like any notice, it should specify the date, place, and hour at which the meeting is to be held and, in the case of a SPECIAL MEETING, the purpose of the meeting. See PROXY, Figure 1, for an example of a notice combined with a proxy.

PARLIAMENTARY PROCEDURE. Formal rules of conduct governing the holding of MEETINGS and the transaction of business, usually based on the rules developed and followed by the British Parliament.

If a corporation's bylaws (see Chapter 10/BYLAWS) require its meetings to be conducted according to the rules prescribed by a certain manual of parliamentary procedure, the requirement is binding on all members of the corporation.

Most ordinary organizations follow rules that are similar to those used in the U.S. House of Representatives. See MOTION, Figure 1; ROBERT'S RULES OF ORDER.

Introducing business. Participants may introduce business at a meeting by making a motion or presenting a communication, such as a report. Before making a motion, an individual needs to obtain the right to speak, referred to as "obtaining the floor."

In a formal setting, a participant should rise to address the presiding officer or committee chair. The presiding officer or chair would, in turn, recognize the individual formally by stating: "The chair recognizes Ms. X."

Once an individual has been recognized and has the floor, he or she may make a MOTION ("I move to . . ." or "I make a motion to . . .") and then should sit down.

Another participant may then state, without rising, "I second the motion to . . ." However, if no one seconds the motion, the chair may ask: "Does anyone want to second the motion to . . . ?"

Once a motion has been seconded, the chair should say, "It has been moved and seconded that . . . Are you ready for the question [ready to vote]?" At this point, the group may debate the motion.

Before speaking during debate, participants must again obtain the floor. At any time, debate may be closed by order of the group through a two-thirds vote or by order of the chair if no one wants the floor to continue the debate.

Voting. Once it appears that the debate has ended, the chair will ask if the group is ready to vote. If no one rises or speaks, the chair may immediately put the matter to a vote.

Various forms can be used to put a motion to a vote. For example, it's common for the chair to state: "It has been moved and seconded that . . . Those in favor of the motion say aye. [*Pause for yes vote*] Those opposed say no."

A show of hands or other indication of Consensus may be used in less formal settings.

A majority of votes cast is generally sufficient to adopt a motion. Once the vote has been taken, the chair should announce the results: "The motion is carried, and the resolution is adopted," or "The no's have it, and the motion is not carried."

See also Motion, Figure 1; Robert's Rules of Order.

PRESENTATIONS.   Programs or forms of delivering information to an assembled group. Presentations may range from an informal discussion, such as the impromptu description of an idea given at a Staff meeting, to a formal program, such as the polished presentation of an ad campaign prepared for an important client.

All presentations, however, should contain the following elements: an introduction, a body, and a conclusion. The challenge for the presenter is to determine the most effective way to convey the information.

Preliminary considerations.   Office personnel may help their employers prepare a presentation. Before anyone makes the presentation, however, the following questions should be answered to determine the most effective type of presentation:

1. What is the topic to be presented, and what specific aspects should be covered?
2. How long should the presentation be?
3. What format should the presentation have (lecture, informational presentation, group discussion, and so on)?
4. When and where will the presentation take place?
5. How many people will attend?
6. What are the characteristics of the audience? (Who are they, and what is their background and level of knowledge about the subject?)
7. Will other presenters be involved, and if so, what topics will they cover?
8. What are the physical characteristics of the room (seating arrangement, podium, and so on)? See also Room arrangement.
9. What equipment will be needed (anything from a simple flip chart to video-conferencing equipment)? See also Videoconference.

Available technologies.   A wide range of technologies is available to facilitate the presentation process. For example, there are individual aids, such as color charts and graphs, videotapes, and visual slides, as well as complete presentation software that enables presenters to prepare a total presentation program.

Services are also available to provide partial assistance in some area or to develop a complete program. Some companies will develop multimedia Web-based presentations (see Chapter 6/WORLD WIDE WEB [WWW]), sometimes called *e-conferences.*

Presentation aids. The benefits of using various presentation aids, such as handouts, is that they may add interest to the presentation, serve as additional reinforcement that will help the audience remember what was discussed, and help to clarify confusing material.

However, unless a prospective aid is used effectively, it may hamper the presentation. Therefore, such material or devices should be used only when they enhance the presentation and do not distract from it.

PROXY. Authority to vote at a MEETING given by an absent stockholder, director, or other organizational member. The term is also applied to the person or persons holding the authority.

Requirements. Although the statutory provisions concerning voting by proxy vary among organizations and from state to state, the usual provisions for stockholders are as follows:

1. That the proxy shall be in writing
2. That the person giving it may revoke it at any time
3. That it will expire after a certain number of months or years from its date unless the stockholder executing the proxy indicates the length of time it is to continue in force
4. That the term of the proxy shall be limited to a definite period

The usual procedure after a stockholder fills out and returns a proxy is to check the proxy signature with the name on the stock certificate to be certain that they match.

Since a STOCKHOLDERS' MEETING usually cannot be held unless a QUORUM (a designated portion of the stock) exists, it's important to get proxies when the stockholders are widely scattered and many will not attend.

The Securities and Exchange Commission (SEC) regulates the solicitation of proxies in respect to registered securities. See also MEETINGS HELD BY PROXY; PROXY COMMITTEE; Chapter 13/SECURITIES AND EXCHANGE COMMISSION (SEC).

Proxy form. A proxy for a stockholders' meeting need not be in any particular form, as long as it meets statutory requirements and the requirements of the SEC. Also, it need not be witnessed, although a witness can prove the authenticity of the signature.

The form for proxies used for other types of meetings also varies. Figure 1 illustrates a combined notice and proxy form that might be used for an annual meeting.

PROXY COMMITTEE. A COMMITTEE appointed by the management of a corporation to represent and vote at MEETINGS for stockholders who authorize it to do so.

The PROXY committee votes for the directors whom management itself has nominated. Thus management selects and elects the directors and,

PROXY: FIGURE 1: Proxy Form with Notice

NOTICE

You are hereby notified that the Annual Meeting of the stockholders of [*company*] will be held in [*location*] on [*date*] at [*time*]. If you do not expect to attend, please sign this proxy card and mail it promptly. No postage is required.

PROXY

I hereby constitute [*name*], [*name*], and [*name*], who are officers or directors of the Company, or a majority of such of them as actually are present, to act for me in my stead and as my proxy at the Annual Meeting of the stockholders of [*company*], to be held in [*location*] on [*date*] at [*time*], and at any adjournment thereof, with full power and authority to act for me in my behalf, with all powers that I, the undersigned, would possess if I were personally present.

Effective Date:_____

Signed:
    Stockholder:_____
    City_____ State_____ ZIP Code _____

PLEASE BE CERTAIN THAT YOU HAVE ADDED YOUR ADDRESS AND SIGNATURE BEFORE MAILING. NO POSTAGE IS REQUIRED.

because of the apathy of stockholders, is able to perpetuate its control of the corporation.

However, any opposing interest may form its own proxy committee, send out its own proxy forms, and solicit proxies for itself.

QUORUM. The number of persons who must legally be present at a MEETING to transact corporate business or the business of any assembled group of persons.

Requirements. When the membership of a group or body consists of a definite number of persons as required by law, such as a board of directors or the United States Senate, a majority (more than half) are required to make a quorum, unless the controlling law expressly states that another number constitutes a quorum.

At common law (see Chapter 11/COMMON LAW), when the membership consists of an indefinite number of persons (the law requires no definite number), such as the stockholders of a corporation, any number constitutes a quorum.

However, the bylaws, and frequently the state statutes or the certificate of incorporation, customarily make an express provision concerning a quorum. See also Chapter 10/BYLAWS; CERTIFICATE OF INCORPORATION.

Shares of stock. In a STOCKHOLDERS' MEETING, the designated quorum usually relates to the amount of stock represented at the meeting and not to the number of stockholders.

A quorum, as specified in the statutes, certificate of incorporation, or bylaws, must be present not only to begin a meeting but to transact business during the meeting. Thus if during a meeting a number of stockholders depart, leaving less than a quorum present, the meeting must be discontinued by ADJOURNMENT.

RECESS. See ADJOURNMENT.

REGULAR MEETING. Also called *general meeting* or *stated meeting*. A routine, periodically scheduled MEETING for the transaction of ordinary business, such as the ANNUAL MEETING of stockholders to elect directors. Compare with SPECIAL MEETING.

The time or schedule of such meetings for corporations is usually fixed by the bylaws. See also STOCKHOLDERS' MEETING; Chapter 10/BYLAWS.

ROBERT'S RULES OF ORDER. A classic manual describing parliamentary procedure. The book is available in many bookstores and in most libraries. Various Web sites (see Chapter 6/WEB SITE) also discuss the rules of parliamentary procedure.

The text of *Robert's Rules of Order* covers methods of organizing and conducting MEETINGS, responsibilities of officers and COMMITTEES, and procedures in regard to motions. See also MOTION, Figure 1.

ROOM ARRANGEMENT. The way in which a MEETING room is set up to afford optimum participation by all attendees.

Room arrangements include consideration of heating and cooling, lighting and ventilation, as well as the arrangement of chairs, tables, the podium, and visual aids.

Visual aids should be placed to allow for maximum viewing from all seats. Tables should be used only when practical, such as when participants will need a writing surface or when meals will be served.

The type of meeting and the needs of participants should dictate the selection of a particular style. The following are common types of room arrangement:

Banquet style. Long rows of horizontal tables are set up, with chairs on both sides of the long ends of the tables. The tables are often set perpendicular to a head table for speakers or dignitaries. This style accommodates large to very large groups (100–500, or more, participants).

Classroom style. Tables face toward a central point, with chairs only on one side so that all participants face forward. The tables may be horizontal to the front of the room or arranged diagonally to ensure optimum viewing of the speaker, visual aids, and so on. This style is appropriate for medium to large groups (25–500 participants).

Conference style. Tables are arranged in square, rectangular, or "U" shapes, with chairs on all sides so that participants face each other. This style is conducive to group discussion and is the most appropriate for small meetings (2–25 participants).

Roundtable style. Small tables are set up throughout the room, with chairs on all sides. Or chairs only may be used, without tables, placed in a circle. (See ROUNDTABLE MEETING.) The informal arrangement promotes discussion and interaction, and it may include meal service. This style can be used for medium to very large groups (25–500, or more, participants).

Theater style.   Chairs, with no tables, are arranged in rows so that all participants face the speakers at the front of the room. Horizontal and vertical aisles, similar to that in a movie theater, allow for access to seating. This style is appropriate for medium to very large groups (25–500, or more, participants).

ROUNDTABLE MEETING.   Also called *open-space meeting*. A usually voluntary gathering of individuals for the discussion of topics of special concern to the participants. See also ROOM ARRANGEMENT, *Roundtable style.*

Roundtables are generally informal sessions, with no AGENDAS, that allow for open discussion and debate among participants. Although formal agendas are often not used or desired, the sessions are usually moderated or directed by someone acting as a chair or FACILITATOR.

The term *roundtable meeting* derives from the common arrangement of chairs in a circle, with no tables. The intent is to signify equality among the participants and to encourage face-to-face discussion and free exchanges.

SCHEDULING.   The process of establishing or defining the time, place, and location for a MEETING or a CONFERENCE.

For STOCKHOLDERS' MEETINGS and DIRECTORS' MEETINGS, the corporate secretary prepares an advance list of meetings to be held during the year so that preparations for each particular meeting may begin in time.

If no definite time has been fixed by the bylaws or by resolution for all meetings that will be held, the schedule may be made up on the basis of tentative dates. See also Chapter 10/BYLAWS.

Other meetings, such as STAFF MEETINGS, may or may not be scheduled for an entire year. Special-purpose meetings may be scheduled only as and when needed.

Preparing the schedule.   Special computer software may be used for preparing and updating the schedule of meetings. If scheduling software is not used, a suitable form, such as the one illustrated in Figure 1, can be devised to fit a particular company's program.

Consult your office copy of the bylaws for the required dates of meetings. Your employer can give you any meeting dates not specified in the bylaws.

Insert the dates in the appropriate monthly column on your schedule. Information for other columns pertaining to place and notice requirements can also be taken from the bylaws.

SCHEDULING: FIGURE 1: Schedule of Meetings

CHART OF MEETINGS FOR THE YEAR

Company	Meeting	Specified Date as per Bylaws	Jan	Feb	Mar	Apr	May	June	July	Aug	Sep	Oct	Nov	Dec	Time	Place Specified		Notice Required	Business Spec'd	Called By	Remarks
																Bylaws	Call				
....Co. Inc. / Ch. of Bd. ...... / Pres. .... / Secy.	Stockholders' Annual / Directors' Annual / Directors' Regular / Directors' Special / Stockholders' Special																				
......Corp. / Ch. of Bd. ...... / Pres. .... / Secy.	Stockholders' Annual / Directors' Annual / Directors' Regular / Directors' Special / Stockholders' Special																				

141

Fill in the information about business to be discussed, who calls the meeting, and remarks at the time each meeting is called.

Scheduling Sunday or holiday meetings. Since the date set for REGULAR MEETINGS may occasionally fall on a Sunday or holiday, corporation bylaws usually have a provision for such a contingency, or a resolution can be adopted to deal with it.

In the absence of a statute or bylaw prohibiting a meeting on a holiday, the meeting cannot be held without notice on any day other than that appointed in the bylaws. Thus an action at a meeting held without notice the day after the regular date, which was a holiday, is void.

A meeting of directors on Sunday is valid if it's affirmed at a weekday meeting. When agreements and contracts entered into on Sunday are void under the statutes, a board of directors cannot amend or rescind a legal contract at a Sunday meeting.

SEMINAR. A MEETING of individuals with similar professional interests for the purpose of exchanging and discussing information.

Unlike trade or professional CONFERENCES, seminars usually have fewer attendees, do not include the more extensive activities and events of a conference (such as product displays), and may not last as long.

SINE DIE. Without day; without a specified day being assigned for a future MEETING or hearing.

SPECIAL MEETING. Also known as a CALLED MEETING. A corporate MEETING that is not one regularly scheduled pursuant to the corporate bylaws (see Chapter 10/BYLAWS) or statutory provisions; any meeting that is not an ANNUAL MEETING or a REGULAR MEETING; a nonroutine, special-purpose meeting.

In general, unless all stockholders are present in person or by PROXY, only the special business for which the meeting was called may be transacted at a special meeting (unless all consent to the transaction of the business).

See also DIRECTORS' MEETING; NOTICE OF MEETING; STOCKHOLDERS' MEETING.

STAFF MEETING. A regular or occasional MEETING with trainees, assistants, and other coworkers to deal with specific projects or general office practices.

Preparation for meeting. Staff meetings may be brief and relatively informal, but they will nevertheless benefit from adequate preparation by both those conducting and those attending the meeting.

The person calling the meeting should send the others an AGENDA or give them a general idea of the topics to be discussed.

The members attending the meeting should review the preliminary information and prepare notes to help them contribute to the discussion. They should bring these notes to the meeting along with pencil, paper, and any other relevant material.

The person calling the meeting should also notify the others of the date, place, and time of the meeting. (See NOTICE OF MEETING.) In small offices, the notice and follow-up reminders may be given in person or by telephone or e-mail rather than in writing.

The person choosing a time and location will need to consider the patterns of business activity peculiar to the individual office. Often such meetings will be scheduled early in the day or during the lunch hour so that normal office activity will not be interrupted.

Office personnel should arrange to have their incoming calls handled and visitors greeted while they are attending the meeting.

Meeting procedure. Formal procedural rules are usually not required for informal staff meetings. An informal check that all members are present is sufficient for the meeting to begin.

The person conducting the meeting should initiate and facilitate the discussion. The FACILITATOR should list topics in a logical order and guide the discussion according to that order, preventing unnecessary digressions. Members, however, should each have an opportunity to speak.

MINUTES are usually not required, but everyone should take notes in regard to decisions reached and assignments made. The person conducting the meeting should keep a prepared summary of activity for future reference, especially in regard to decisions and assignments.

Rather than taking formal votes on issues, members may simply agree on solutions or decisions. (See CONSENSUS.) At the end of the meeting, the person in charge should summarize the discussion orally for the participants.

STOCKHOLDERS' MEETING. A gathering or MEETING of stockholders for the purpose of joint exercise by them of the rights guaranteed to them by statutes, the corporation's certificate of incorporation, or its bylaws. See also Chapter 10/BYLAWS; CERTIFICATE OF INCORPORATION.

A valid meeting cannot be held unless the amount of stock necessary to constitute a QUORUM is represented. See also MINUTES; Chapter 10/CUMULATIVE VOTING; VOTING TRUST.

Kinds of stockholders' meetings. The meetings of stockholders are either REGULAR MEETINGS or SPECIAL MEETINGS. At a regular meeting, a corporation may not transact any *extraordinary* business without having given proper notice to the stockholders. But it may transact any *ordinary* business that may come up.

At a general meeting, a corporation also may not transact any business that the statutes require to be transacted at a special meeting.

Call of meeting. See CALL OF STOCKHOLDERS' MEETING.

Time and place of meetings. Usually, for a meeting to be legal, it must be held at the time and place designated in the bylaws or the certificate of incorporation. See also the forthcoming discussion in *Omission of stockholders' meeting.*

Both annual and special meetings must be held within the state of incorporation unless otherwise provided by statute. If neither the statutes nor the certificate of incorporation specifically require this, action taken at a meeting outside the state will be valid if all stockholders participate.

When a corporation is chartered in more than one state, a meeting in any one of them is valid for all of them.

Preparation for meetings. The corporate secretary often keeps a checklist of preparations for a stockholders' meeting in the MEETING FILE. However, office personnel may maintain the list in a follow-up file and bring each item to the corporate secretary's attention on the days when some action must be taken.

Conduct of the meeting. In the absence of express regulation by statutes or bylaws, accepted usage and custom largely control stockholders' meetings, including those for the election of directors. See also AGENDA; MOTION; PARLIAMENTARY PROCEDURE; ROBERT'S RULES OF ORDER.

Omission of stockholders' meeting. The statutes of many states indicate what will happen if no meeting takes place. Generally, if an annual meeting is not held at the time specified for it, the directors may call a meeting within a reasonable time thereafter.

Also, if a meeting has not been held at the regular time, the directors should call it whenever it is demanded by a stockholder. Meetings that cannot be held because a QUORUM is not present may be adjourned and held at the adjourned hour without subsequent notice. See also ADJOURNED MEETING.

Voting. Every owner of capital stock (see Chapter 10/Capital stock; Chapter 13/Stock) has the right to vote the stock at all meetings of stockholders unless the right is denied by the statutes, the certificate of incorporation, or agreement under which the owner holds his or her shares.

Usually, each stockholder is entitled to one vote for each share of stock owned. Absent stockholders may vote by Proxy. See also Chapter 10/Cumulative voting.

Adjournment. Meetings may be adjourned to a specific day or adjourned Sine die (without naming a day and finally terminating the meeting), or they may be adjourned subject to the call of the chair.

The Motion to adjourn specifies which form of Adjournment will be taken, and if none is specified, the adjournment is final. See also Adjourned meeting.

Teleconference. See Audioconference; Computer conference; Videoconference.

To rise. See Adjournment.

Videoconference. A live connection of two or more people in remote locations using video technology to allow communication between the participants.

The special features of videoconferencing enable participants gathered in a room with video cameras, microphones, speakers, and other equipment to see and hear each other and to share documents in their various locations.

Because the visual feature of videoconferencing has the character of an in-person Meeting, participants can enjoy a similar sense of personal exchange. Without having to travel to an off-site location, they can therefore save money on travel expenses while still having frequent interaction.

Kinds of videoconferences. The following are the three main types of videoconferencing:

> *Desktop videoconferencing* involves video-telephone calls between individuals in remote locations. Participants use special computer software and hardware, in conjunction with a specially installed camera and the telephone lines, to see and hear each other.

> *Group videoconferencing* allows small groups of people that are separated geographically to meet with each other through the use of video and sound equipment installed in each meeting room.

Large-audience videoconferencing is used with large groups in a conference setting equipped with video and sound equipment capable of high-quality broadcast transmission. With it, speakers in remote locations can make presentations before a large assembly, and multinational organizations can hold sales conferences with many people in remote locations.

Videoconference arrangements. Large companies may have in-house video-conferencing equipment, whereas smaller firms usually lease equipment or contract with a videoconferencing service to use their facilities.

Technical arrangements for this type of meeting are more complex than those for an in-person gathering, and the skills and knowledge of specialists are usually needed. Other arrangements may be similar to those that are necessary for other kinds of meetings.

For example, it may be necessary to do the following: determine the availability of participants, set a time and date, prepare an AGENDA and send notices (see NOTICE OF MEETING), inspect the meeting room, arrange for delivery of PRESENTATION materials and equipment, take the MINUTES, and provide postmeeting transcripts or tapes.

Videoconferencing presents many challenges for businesses, particularly those who want to conference with customers and suppliers. Videoconferencing services can answer many questions that arrangers might have. (Consult your yellow pages, and check available Web sites. See also Chapter 6/WEB SITE.)

WAIVER OF NOTICE. See Chapter 11/WAIVER.

CHAPTER FIVE

Domestic
and International Travel

AIRLINE CLUBS.   Organizations that offer services to travelers. Major airlines often offer memberships in such clubs. See also AIR TRAVEL.

Members are provided with information, special lounges at airports, conference rooms with telephones and business equipment, and travel discounts. Other benefits and amenities often include beverages, television, check-cashing privileges, and reciprocal agreements with other airline clubs.

Club memberships are available for an annual fee or, in some cases, may be purchased with frequent traveler miles. See also FREQUENT FLYER NUMBER.

AIR TRAVEL.   Travel by commercial passenger planes, air shuttles, and private aircraft.

Planning the trip.   When planning a business trip by air, a business traveler is interested in these facts:

1. Airlines that can be used
2. Flight schedules
3. Airport parking and shuttle information
4. Airport amenities, such as personal access links (PALs)—pay phones that support e-mail and Internet access

5. In-flight dining and amenities such as telephone, power ports for laptop computers, and movies

6. Cost

7. BAGGAGE facilities

See also ITINERARY; TRAVEL SECURITY.

Information sources. A variety of travel-planning resources are available to corporate travel arrangers:

1. *Travel agents.* See TRAVEL AGENCY.

2. *Printed and electronic materials.* The best-known resource is the *Official Airline Guide,* which includes domestic and international flight schedules and other pertinent information in printed, on-line, and CD-ROM versions (available to subscribers).

3. *Toll-free and on-line resources.* You can get up-to-the-minute information from your corporate travel office or a travel agency, by calling an airline's reservations desk, or by visiting one of the many reservations Web sites. (See Chapter 6/WEB SITE.) Travel-planning software and subscriber databases are also available.

4. *Airline timetables.* Printed schedules that provide general flight schedule and route information are available at airports and airline ticket offices.

Reservations. Businesspeople usually make plane reservations through a company travel department or a TRAVEL AGENCY that has a computerized link to all airlines and can supply up-to-the-minute information.

They may also make reservations via an Internet travel-reservations service or, in some cases, a company's intranet. See also Chapter 6/INTERNET; INTRANET; WEB SITE.

Another option is to telephone the reservations desk at the desired airline and charge the fare to a major credit card, debit card, or Universal Air Travel Plan card (issued by individual carriers).

You'll need the following information to make a reservation:

1. Point of origin and destination

2. Preferred dates for departure and return

3. Preferred times for departure and return

4. Preferred airline and the flight number, if known

5. Preferred class of service desired (first, business, coach)

6. Special needs (such as a wheelchair or meals that meet specific dietary restrictions)

A travel agent will follow through on reservations for the entire trip. If part of the trip is to be made by train, car, or shuttle, for example, a representative or agent will also make those arrangements.

When booking travel directly with an airline, you may be referred to the airline's package desk or to outside vendors to book segments or accommodations other than, or in addition to, air travel. Always request confirmation numbers if they are not automatically provided.

Travel agencies and airlines will usually mail or deliver tickets when time permits and will fax an itinerary immediately on request. Otherwise, someone must pick up the tickets from the airline's ticket office, at the airport ticket counter or gate when an E-TICKET is purchased, or at the travel agency.

Confirmation of reservation. Travelers may confirm reservations in advance by telephone (usually, 24 hours in advance for domestic flights, 48 hours for international flights). In most cases, confirmation is not required but is highly recommended, particularly for INTERNATIONAL TRAVEL.

Travelers also may call the airline on the day of departure to learn about delays or other problems that may affect other travel segments or business plans.

Cancellation of reservation. Travelers should promptly cancel any space that is not going to be used. A reservation must be canceled by a certain date or time for the traveler to receive a refund.

When you cancel a reservation by telephone, it's important to document the name of the reservations agent and the time of the call should any questions arise later about refund eligibility. When you cancel by e-mail or over the Internet, a cancellation number is automatically assigned.

AMERICAN SOCIETY OF TRAVEL AGENTS (ASTA). An association providing information and services for travel agent members who meet ASTA's standards. See also TRAVEL AGENCY.

APPOINTMENT SCHEDULE. See TRAVEL APPOINTMENT SCHEDULE.

AUTOMOBILE TRAVEL. Travel by rental car, limousine, or private vehicle. You can make car-rental reservations—domestic and foreign—in advance either through a company travel department, a TRAVEL AGENCY, at a car-rental Web site (see Chapter 6/WEB SITE), or directly with car-rental agencies.

Usually, you'll need the following information to arrange for a rental car:

1. Pick-up and drop-off locations
2. The traveler's preference for make and size of car
3. Method of payment
4. Dates and times a car is needed and flight information
5. Any discount-program membership information or numbers
6. Driver's license information

Most car-rental agencies provide a computer printout of directions to local destinations.

Additional insurance needs.   When renting a car in other countries, a traveler should consider purchasing the same amount of insurance coverage that is carried on the traveler's personal vehicle, even if the host country requires less. U.S. auto insurance usually does not provide coverage in other countries.

Auto clubs.   Those who frequently travel by automobile will find it advantageous to be a member of an auto club, such as the American Automobile Association (AAA), which has a travel service available to plan any trip a member wants to take.

Some insurance companies, gasoline companies, and other organizations also offer auto club and travel services.

Members may contact the nearest branch of an auto club (check the telephone directory) to have routings forwarded to them, or they may contact the club in person by visiting the nearest branch.

Some clubs maintain Web sites (see Chapter 6/WEB SITE) where you can find or request information.

An auto club usually assists its members in some or all of these ways:

1. Advises them what routes to use, where to stop, and what to see.
2. Prepares a special route map.
3. Provides up-to-the-minute information on weather and highway conditions.
4. Assists in selecting and securing motel and HOTEL accommodations in advance of the trip.
5. Provides emergency road service.
6. Provides bail and arrest bonds.

7. Provides accident insurance.

8. Offers an auto-theft reward. See TRAVEL SECURITY.

9. Offers discounts on car-rental and other travel services.

Members of some clubs also receive a number of maps, travel guides, and directories covering outstanding points of interest.

Cancellation of reservation.   A traveler may cancel reservations by calling the travel agent, car-rental agency, or other organization or by visiting the Web site through which the arrangements were made.

The reservations should be canceled promptly whenever plans change. Guaranteed reservations must be canceled within a specific time before scheduled pick-up to receive a full refund. Always obtain a cancellation number at the time of making the cancellation.

BAGGAGE.   Suitcases, equipment cases, trunks, and other personal belongings of a traveler.

Persons planning a business trip, especially if traveling by plane (see AIR TRAVEL), are interested in knowing the number of bags and total pounds of baggage that can be checked without additional charge, as well as the limitations on dimensions of the baggage.

Information about allowable baggage is available in flight schedules and timetables, at the airline or railway information office, at the airline's Web site (see Chapter 6/WEB SITE), or through a TRAVEL AGENCY.

Labels.   Each piece of baggage should carry an identification label. For security, use labels that cover the address so that onlookers can't see it. Also, use a business card rather than your home address, and put the card *inside* the baggage in case the outer tag is lost. See also TRAVEL SECURITY.

Keep a supply of identification labels, available at ticket and baggage counters, in the office.

Sensitive items.   Check with the airline regarding sensitive baggage (film, cassettes, computer diskettes, and so on), how to package certain items, and how to transport them aboard so that they are not damaged by X-ray machines.

CORPORATE TRAVEL DEPARTMENT. See TRAVEL AGENCY, *Company travel department.*

CUSTOMS.   The federal agency that monitors and may collect duties or tolls on articles purchased in other countries.

Purchases.   Anyone going to another country should know in advance what the United States customs laws and regulations are with regard to purchases made in another country and brought into the United States.

Check with your travel agent regarding items for which receipts or proof of purchase is required to bring them into the United States without charge.

A travel agent will usually supply this information, as well as details about customs requirements in countries to be visited. Customs information is also available over the Internet. See also Chapter 6/INTERNET; WEB SITE.

Information.   Whether or not someone uses a travel service, it's advisable to send for available customs information. If the traveler is going to visit Western Hemisphere nations, send for booklets such as *Know Before You Go, GSP and the Traveler, Customs Hints for Non-Residents,* and *Customs Hints for Returning U.S. Residents.*

These booklets, available from the U.S. Treasury Department, Bureau of Customs, Washington, D.C., furnish travelers with general information about customs laws and regulations.

Other useful material, available from the Superintendent of Documents in Washington, D.C., includes *Your Trip Abroad* and *Health Information for International Travel.*

E-TICKET.   An electronic, or paperless, airline ticket. Travelers can purchase such tickets through a TRAVEL AGENCY or corporate travel office, at a travel-reservations Web site (see Chapter 6/WEB SITE), or by calling an airline reservations desk.

When a traveler purchases an e-ticket, an ITINERARY and receipt are generated and sent to the purchaser.

Rather than presenting a paper ticket at curbside or gate check-in, e-ticket holders are usually required to verify their identity. Often this involves showing a government-issued photo ID and the credit card used to purchase the e-ticket.

ETIQUETTE.   See TRAVEL ETIQUETTE.

EXPENSE REPORT.   A report that businesspeople who travel compile to document and report their travel and entertainment expenses, whether or not they receive advance funds or request reimbursement later.

Some companies have their own expense-reporting forms, expense-reporting software, or expense-reporting link to a company intranet. (See Chapter 6/INTRANET.) Otherwise, one can purchase standard forms in an office-supply store.

Office personnel can help their employers prepare an expense report by taking these steps:

1. Organizing cash receipts, credit card receipts, and personal notes into the categories listed on the form being used (meals, HOTELS, and so on)

2. Double-checking names, dates, and so on

3. Listing items for which receipts may be missing

4. Listing the expenses in each category on the report form in proper order and adding them to arrive at a total for each

5. Preparing a rough draft to be approved by the traveler

Since Internal Revenue Service (IRS) rules and regulations concerning travel and entertainment allowances vary from year to year, check with an accountant, or request current information from the IRS.

FOREIGN CURRENCY. See INTERNATIONAL TRAVEL, *Foreign currency*. See also Part Four/FOREIGN CURRENCY for a list of monetary units in the major countries of the world.

FREQUENT FLYER NUMBER. An account number assigned to a traveler who becomes a member of an airline's frequent traveler program.

Frequent flyer miles are awarded based on travel purchases, frequency of travel, and other purchases made through vendors participating in the airline's frequent flyer program.

The frequent flyer miles that are awarded may be used to purchase travel or upgrades from the airline and from participating program partners.

HEALTH CERTIFICATES AND IMMUNIZATIONS. The health safeguards and requirements of other countries that a traveler must comply with before entering and traveling in each country.

For example, a country may require international certificates of vaccination against yellow fever and cholera. Vaccinations against some diseases, such as typhoid, are not required but are recommended for travel to areas where there is a risk of exposure. In addition, a traveler's regular inoculations should be up to date.

Information on required and recommended immunizations is available from local and state health departments, from the Centers for Disease Control and Prevention in Atlanta or at its Web site (see Chapter 6/WEB SITE), and from the embassies or consulates of the countries to be visited.

Before beginning a trip, ask your health insurer whether your coverage applies in other countries. If not, consider purchasing a temporary health policy that provides such coverage.

HOTELS. For purposes of this entry, any lodging facility, such as a hotel, motel, resort, lodge, or inn.

Information. In addition to travel agencies, some credit and charge-card companies, associations, and hotel–motel chains provide a nationwide information and reservation service.

Detailed information about hotels is available in the latest editions of the *Hotel and Travel Index, Official Hotel and Resort Guide,* and *The Hotel/Motel Red Book.* Other guides, travel books, and maps can be found in libraries and bookstores, and most hotel chains and many properties have established Web sites.

Further information is available through local hotel associations and the Chamber of Commerce in the city of destination.

Reservations. The following information is needed to make a hotel reservation:

1. The name of the person for whom the reservation is to be made
2. The date of arrival and date of departure
3. The type of accommodations required

You can make a reservation through a company travel department or TRAVEL AGENCY, directly by telephone, by postal mail, or at a travel-reservations Web site (see Chapter 6/WEB SITE), depending on how soon it is needed.

Common hotel accommodations are single bedroom and bath, double bedroom and bath, and a suite consisting of a sitting room and one or more bedrooms and baths.

The arrangement, however, may vary in other countries. In Europe, for example, it is common to have two twin beds in a "double."

A reservations request should include the preferred location of a room and information about required amenities, such as computer/modem hookups and smoking or nonsmoking, and desired conveniences, such as express check-in or check-out. See also TRAVEL SECURITY.

Ask about available meal plans, and request specific information about what each plan includes. Although general terms, such as *Continental Breakfast, American Plan,* and *European Plan,* suggest specific inclusions and exclusions, each may vary in different countries.

If you expect to arrive after the time a reservation is usually held, specify *late arrival.* A *guaranteed reservation* means that the room will be held regardless of arrival times. However, you must pay for it even if you fail to arrive as planned.

Check with the hotel regarding policies governing the cancellation of a guaranteed reservation.

When requesting rate information, travelers should provide membership information if they belong to any hotel awards or guest programs or if they belong to an organization such as the American Automobile Association (AAA) that offers members negotiated rates.

For other possible savings, ask whether the hotel offers discounted mid-week or corporate rates.

Confirmation of reservation. If time permits, request written confirmation of the reservation. Attach the confirmation to the copy of the ITINERARY that the traveler takes along on the trip, and add the confirmation number to the itinerary.

Cancellation of reservation. If you must cancel a hotel reservation, notify the hotel immediately by telephone, or use the hotel's Web site. (See Chapter 6/WEB SITE.) Always obtain a cancellation number.

INTERNATIONAL DRIVING PERMIT. The driver's license that allows travelers to drive vehicles in other countries.

To obtain an international driving permit, visit your local American Automobile Association (AAA) office to fill out an application. You will need to provide a valid U.S. driver's license and two passport-size photos (most AAA offices can take your photo).

Drivers must be 18 years of age or older. For additional details and the current fee, contact the AAA or a TRAVEL AGENCY.

INTERNATIONAL ENGLISH. The most widely used language of commercial and international affairs around the world.

Local varieties. Because English is used as a first or second language in most major countries, it has been subject to local influences in each country, and many varieties exist. Traditionally, the English of England was the world standard, but the North American, Australian, and New Zealand varieties are now also widely accepted.

Need for clarity.   Regardless of the variety of English used in another country, it is important to use precise, clear word choices since the people who do not speak it fluently will tend to translate everything literally.

Using precise English is important whether a traveler is speaking or writing through a translator or interpreter (see TRANSLATORS AND INTERPRETERS) or through a foreign host who uses English as a second or third language.

American English speakers and writers, therefore, must avoid the use of acronyms, idioms, jargon, and slang (see Chapter 7/ABBREVIATIONS; IDIOM; JARGON) and use clear enunciation to avoid potentially embarrassing or costly misunderstandings.

INTERNATIONAL TRAVEL.   Travel to a country or region outside the United States and its territories. Travelers may make arrangements through a corporate travel department or the company's designated TRAVEL AGENCY.

Agencies offer complete services in all matters pertaining to travel throughout the world and use computers to retrieve up-to-the-minute schedules and fares. In addition, they have circulars and booklets describing other countries and regions within those countries. See also TRAVEL SECURITY.

Travel agents who arrange a trip need to know the following:

1. Number in the party: names, ages, citizenships, and genders of the travelers
2. Points of origin and destinations
3. Location and duration of desired stops in each country
4. Desired dates and times of departure and return
5. Desired modes and class of travel, types of accommodations, and any special amenities required

When a traveler's ITINERARY is uncertain, a travel agent will, based on the information and locations you provide, research potential accommodations and methods of transportation.

Preparations.   For business travel in other countries, some or all of these steps will be necessary:

1. Ask the travel agent or the consulates about any special requirements for commercial travelers.

2. Check the U.S. Bureau of Consular Affairs Web site (see Chapter 6/WEB SITE) and the various government publications for information that can be ordered on-line and for information about notifying government offices about one's travel plans and itinerary.

3. Request letters of introduction from banks, businesses, individuals, and so on to their foreign offices. Such introductions are very helpful to a traveler.

4. Get a letter of authority, addressed "To Whom It May Concern," from the person authorizing the traveler to represent the firm. This is especially valuable in dealing with immigration or customs authorities.

5. Compile a name and address list of consular offices and of officers and executives in firms to be visited.

6. Prepare a folder of pertinent data for each firm or person to be visited, including material on previous and pending transactions.

7. Write letters (for the traveler's signature) to the firms that he or she will visit to provide travel, HOTEL, or other information concerning the traveler's ITINERARY.

8. If the company subscribes to a credit service, such as Dun & Bradstreet, get a card from it authorizing the holder to call on its foreign offices for credit information.

Before departure. Well before travel begins, complete the following steps:

1. Provide the traveler with a checklist (review and update it just before departure) and timetable that includes information about securing a PASSPORT, required VISAS, HEALTH CERTIFICATES AND IMMUNIZATIONS, and an INTERNATIONAL DRIVING PERMIT (if corporate policy allows employees to drive in other countries).

2. Include on the checklist a debriefing on security issues, alternate transportation in-country, and possible health risks.

3. Check with a local library or bookstore, a travel agency, and over the Internet (see Chapter 6/INTERNET; WEB SITE) for current information on each country to be visited.

4. Assemble data on trade conditions, political aspects including security matters, geography, climate, customs, culture, religion, holidays, work days and

hours, and so on. Contact the State Department, its Citizens Emergency Center, or its Web site for up-to-the-minute travel advisories.

5. Include addresses of hospitals and physicians the traveler can contact if needed, and consider additional health insurance, travel insurance, BAGGAGE insurance, and even special coverages, such as for kidnapping, depending on the destination.

6. Encourage travelers to speak with colleagues who have previously traveled to the destination countries.

7. If travelers will be taking along various items, find out if restrictions apply upon entering or leaving the country.

8. Be certain that travelers carry a list of telephone numbers from home, including business numbers, the travel agency, personal physician, and so on.

9. Keep extra copies of a traveler's itinerary and agenda (see TRAVEL APPOINT-MENT SCHEDULE) on file at the home office.

10. Supply travelers with destination information and directions written in the language of native taxi drivers.

11. Have business cards printed on the reverse side in the language of the country to be visited.

12. For other information, contact the pertinent embassies. Numbers and addresses are available in the Washington, D.C., telephone directory or through Information.

See also TRAVEL APPOINTMENT SCHEDULE; TRAVEL EQUIPMENT AND SUPPLIES.

Foreign currency.   Since banks offer better rates of exchange than do hotels and other sources, some travelers, before leaving the United States, purchase small amounts of foreign currency to use while traveling.

In many cases, ATM cards may be used in other countries to withdraw funds from a U.S. bank account in the currency of the host nation. Check with your bank about fees and locations.

To check current exchange rates, call the international department of your firm's bank just before departure, or consult financial newspapers or financial Web sites. See also TRAVELER'S CHECKS; Chapter 6/WEB SITE.

Telecommunications.   A variety of methods are available for businesspersons traveling in other countries to communicate with the home office. Long-distance carriers offer international calling cards and a variety of calling plans for direct-dial and operator-assisted service.

While telephoning in another country, travelers can ask the operator to connect them with a translator or interpreter. (See Translators and interpreters.) However, they should ask the operator about rates and surcharges for such calls.

Many Internet service providers (see Chapter 6/Internet service provider [ISP]) have local access numbers in numerous cities around the world or 800 dial-up numbers. These numbers enable those with personal computers to stay in touch inexpensively via e-mail and, in some cases, real-time instant messaging.

Other communication options include prepaid telephone cards, postal mail, fax, and any other form of message transmission available in the other country. See also Chapter 2/Telephone calls; United States Postal Service; Chapter 6/Fax transmission.

For those traveling without a computer, a pocket-size e-mail organizer (used with a monthly subscription service) may be helpful. The small device lets travelers send and retrieve e-mail or fax messages from any telephone worldwide, without the need for a computer or Internet access.

INTERPRETER.   See Translators and interpreters.

ITINERARY.   The outline or schedule of a traveler's route or journey. The itinerary of a business trip provides the following information:

1. Point of departure
2. Points of arrival
3. Name of railway or airline and seat assignments, if prearranged
4. Date and time of departure from each point
5. Date and time of arrival at each point
6. Train or flight number, class of service, and confirmation numbers
7. Hotels at which the traveler will be staying, type of accommodation booked, and confirmation number
8. Car-rental, shuttle, and similar arrangements

The corporate travel department or Travel agency that books the travel will provide a complete itinerary. Make four copies or more copies as needed.

Give the traveler one to be left with his or her family, file another copy in the office, and give the traveler two to take along (each carried in a separate place in case of loss or theft). Give additional copies to anyone else in the organization who may need the information.

MOTELS.   See HOTELS.

PAL.   See AIR TRAVEL, *Planning the trip.*

PASSPORT.   The formal document that a government issues to a traveler to enable the person to exit and reenter the country.

One may apply for a U.S. passport at any of several thousand locations nationwide, including many federal, state, and probate courts; many post offices; some libraries; and some county and municipal offices.

A TRAVEL AGENCY also will furnish information about the most expedient method of obtaining a passport in your area. Passports may be renewed by mail under certain circumstances.

Passport forms are available at facilities that accept the applications and at any passport agency. They may also be downloaded from the Internet (see Chapter 6/DOWNLOAD; INTERNET; WEB SITE).

When possible, application should be made several months in advance of a trip. If VISAS will be needed, allow even more time.

If you are applying for a U.S. passport for the first time, if your previous passport was lost or stolen, or if it was issued more than 12 years ago and has expired, you'll need to apply in person.

You'll be required to provide proof of U.S. citizenship, proof of identity, two passport photos, the application fee, and your social security number.

PERSONAL ACCESS LINK (PAL).   See AIR TRAVEL, *Planning the trip.*

RAILROAD TRAVEL.   In the United States, passenger travel by Amtrak trains.

Planning the trip.   When planning a business trip by train, a traveler is interested in the following information:

1. Time schedules
2. Accommodations—sleeping and dining facilities
3. Cost
4. BAGGAGE requirements and facilities
5. Available business amenities, such as power ports for computers and telephones

Information.   The following sources have important information:

1. *The Official Railway Guide.* This publication, available by subscription or single copy, contains all the schedules or timetables of Amtrak and other passenger railroads in Canada and Mexico. It has sample fares, a description of the accommodations on each train, and other pertinent information.

2. *Timetables.* Printed schedules are available at railroad stations and any TRAVEL AGENCY. For up-to-the-minute information, consult a travel agent, telephone the railroad, or visit its Web site (see Chapter 6/WEB SITE), where you can view routes and schedules, plan trips, and make reservations.

3. *Travel agency.* A travel agency will handle reservations on railroads, look up all schedules, and provide you with a complete ITINERARY.

Accommodations. The usual sleeping accommodations are as follows:

1. *Bedroom.* A private bedroom usually contains lower and upper berths, with the lower berth serving as a sofa for daytime use. Toilet facilities are in the same room in some bedrooms.

2. *Roomette.* A private roomette is intended primarily for single occupancy, often with a bed folding into the wall and containing a sofa seat for daytime use. Toilet facilities are usually in the same room.

Special cars are sometimes available for handicapped persons. Tell your travel agent about any such special needs.

Reservations. The procedure for making train reservations is similar to that for obtaining plane reservations. (See AIR TRAVEL.) Knowing precisely what you want before you telephone the railroad will help the representative provide specific information.

Give complete and clear information on the point of departure and destination, time, train number or name, and the accommodations desired.

For long-distance travel, trains are limited, and you may not have a choice of time. When the exact reservations that you want are not available, ask the travel agent or railroad agent to suggest something that is available.

A travel agent or railroad agent will also provide information about special services, such as taking one's car along or availability of express service between certain cities.

Although a travel agent will make all necessary reservations for you, a railway, unlike the airlines, will not make reservations for the entire trip if the trip is broken by plane travel.

However, Amtrak has a tour desk at its toll-free number (check your telephone directory) to help you with hotels, car rentals, and bus connections.

Cancellation of reservations. At the time reservations are made, inquire about refunds on unused tickets and cancellation procedures and requirements. When canceling a reservation, be sure to get a cancellation number.

RESERVATIONS. See AIR TRAVEL; AUTOMOBILE TRAVEL; HOTELS; RAILROAD TRAVEL.

SHUTTLE SERVICE. See AIR TRAVEL.

SMART CARD. A memory card on which information is stored and retrieved by inserting it into a special device that is attached to a personal computer.

For travelers, such cards can store E-TICKET information, frequent traveler information, travel preferences, and so on. They can also facilitate HOTEL check-in and check-out as well as airline ticketing and boarding procedures and car-rental pick-up and drop-off.

TIMETABLE. A schedule showing the times of arrival and departure of trains or planes, indicating the equipment and accommodations on each, and containing general travel information.

TOURIST CARD. A card purchased when entering a country for which a VISA is required but has not previously been obtained.

Travelers are required to complete an application, pay a fee, and present identification to receive a tourist card, which is good for only one entry into the host nation.

TRANSLATORS AND INTERPRETERS. Persons who speak one or more languages and are hired to provide assistance to business travelers who are not fluent in the language of a host nation.

Travelers from large corporations often take along someone from the company who can provide the necessary translation and interpretation, rather than rely on an unknown person or service in the host country.

For translator or interpreter service while telephoning, travelers may ask the operator to connect them with someone providing this service. See also INTERNATIONAL TRAVEL, *Telecommunications*.

Even when accompanied by a translator or interpreter, a businessperson should also have available foreign-language dictionaries and a pocket electronic translator (some devices provide synthesized voice translations).

TRAVEL AGENCY. An agency usually offering complete service in all matters pertaining to travel. Many business concerns that do not have a company travel department use an agency to make all travel reservations for domestic and foreign trips.

A company may open an account with an agency and be billed once a month, thus avoiding the nuisance of paying for numerous reservations throughout the month. Travelers may also make reservations by personal credit card or with a company's credit or charge card.

Selecting an agency. The AMERICAN SOCIETY OF TRAVEL AGENTS (ASTA) has members throughout the United States and Canada. The members may be recognized by the ASTA emblem, which they are permitted to display if they are in good standing.

You can find the name of a nearby ASTA member agency in the telephone directory yellow pages, by writing to the executive offices of the association in New York City, or by visiting its Web site. See also Chapter 6/WEB SITE.

Although there are many reliable agents who are not members of ASTA, the code of ethics of this association is high, and its members are dependable and efficient.

Before contracting with an agency, follow these steps:

1. Check whether it is a member of a national organization with a grievance committee.
2. Check whether fees or service charges are assessed.
3. Check whether it offers packages and other cost-cutting features.
4. Ask for and check references with other clients of the agency.
5. Contact your local Better Business Bureau for information pertaining to the agency.
6. Check into the agency's billing and reporting capabilities and use of current technologies.

What the travel service will do. Although services vary depending on the agency, the following are some of the things that many travel agents will do:

1. Prepare and submit a tentative ITINERARY, which can be changed or adjusted.

2. Make all travel, car-rental, and HOTEL reservations and sightseeing arrangements for the entire trip.

3. Make certain that required amenities are available.

4. Tell you which documents are necessary, such as PASSPORT, VISAS, and health certificates (see HEALTH CERTIFICATES AND IMMUNIZATIONS), and how to get them.

5. Advise how and where to exchange dollars for a small amount of currency of the country to be visited (to be used for tips, taxi fares, and so on).

6. Help the traveler arrange for any necessary insurance.

7. Advise about all regulations, such as restrictions on currency and CUSTOMS requirements.

8. Arrange for TRANSLATORS AND INTERPRETERS at the destination if someone from within the company does not assume this duty. (A member of the firm being visited may meet the traveler.)

9. Suggest money-saving travel rates, such as excursion or group rates.

10. Arrange for interesting side trips to points of interest or special events in the particular area where the traveler will be.

11. Prepare bills and generate reports for expense-tracking purposes.

12. Address travel-related inquiries and problems before, during, and after travel is completed.

Company travel department. Large firms often have their own travel department that functions like an outside travel agency, providing the same services for employees. Some of these departments act as a branch of an outside travel agency.

Firms that have the appropriate software can be linked through travel agencies directly with airline reservation systems, allowing them to make and change reservations, print tickets and ITINERARIES, make seat selections, and produce in-house reports.

TRAVEL APPOINTMENT SCHEDULE. Schedule of a traveler's appointments while on a business trip.

The schedule should show the time and place of the appointment; the name, affiliation, and telephone number of the person with whom one has the appointment; and any additional useful information. See Figure 1.

TRAVEL DEPARTMENT. See TRAVEL AGENCY, *Company travel department.*

TRAVEL APPOINTMENT SCHEDULE: FIGURE 1

CITY/STATE	DATE/TIME	APPOINTMENT	REMARKS
Boston, MA	5/7 – 3:30 p	Bob Williams Williams-McGregor 125 South St, Suite 5 617-555-3485	
	5/8 – 10:00 a	Ellen Brown Brown & Brown 348 South St., 4th Fl. 617-555-1257	
	1 p	Dave Norris at Copley's Bar & Grill 344 South St. 617-555-2300	Lunch
Washington, D.C.	5/9 – 11:00 a	Sen. Mike Howe Senate Office Bldg. Room 906 202-555-4884	

TRAVEL EQUIPMENT AND SUPPLIES. The equipment and supplies that business travelers take along to use in their work.

The list may include some or all of the following items:

Pen, pencils, and erasers

Stationery, note pads, envelopes, mailing labels, mailing cartons, and business cards

Paper clips, scissors, rubber bands, adhesive, cellophane tape, pins, bottle opener, rubber stamps and stamp pad, ruler, first-aid supplies

Address book (with telephone, fax, and e-mail numbers), pertinent files and extra file folders, checkbook, cash, expense forms

Calendar, mail schedules, lists of religious and national holidays for each country

Portable equipment (computer, fax, calculator, translator, and so on), with Internet access numbers, and cables, diskettes, electrical adaptors, and other supplies

Travel guides, transportation and hotel information, and miscellaneous country information

Office personnel usually help collect and organize these supplies, reminding the traveler of any item that is missing or unavailable.

TRAVELER'S CHECKS. The drafts purchased from a bank, and sometimes through machines at airports, that are widely accepted worldwide and can be cashed or used to make purchases while traveling.

These checks are available in various denominations. There are several issuers of traveler's checks, such as American Express.

The traveler will have to sign the checks in the presence of the bank's representative. If the account is particularly valuable, however, the bank's representative may come to the office.

Make and keep copies of traveler's checks in case they are lost or stolen. See also TRAVEL SECURITY.

TRAVEL ETIQUETTE. The rules of proper conduct that travelers should observe.

To avoid making unintentional blunders in another country, check libraries, bookstores, and the Internet (see Chapter 6/INTERNET; WEB SITE) for books and articles on etiquette and protocol.

Rules of etiquette vary greatly from one country to another and from one region of the world to another, depending on the area's business and social customs and religious requirements.

Books, travel guides, newsletters, government reports, and articles on various countries and regions are available, many of which provide tips on travel etiquette.

It's important for a businessperson to study the customs of the countries he or she will visit before leaving home to avoid doing or saying something offensive to the host.

For example, in India, pointing with the finger is rude; Indians point with the chin. In New Zealand, chewing gum or using a toothpick in public is considered rude. In Taiwan, gifts of cutting tools, such as knives or scissors, suggest the severing of friendships.

TRAVELING WITH AN EMPLOYER. The practice in some companies of having an assistant accompany the employer to process work that cannot wait and must be handled at each stopover.

When you travel with your employer, you may spend the day collecting information, taking notes at meetings, making new travel plans, and so on.

Most major HOTELS provide rental computers and other equipment, or you may take along your own equipment or use that in a branch office you are visiting.

When you are with your employer, he or she will handle the tipping and payments for meals. Otherwise, keep receipts for all legitimate business-related expenses so that you can be reimbursed later.

After work, your employer will probably be entertaining clients, and you may be on your own. If you attend business meetings, dress in normal business attire. For evening events, dress as you would for any other social-business event your company might hold.

If you are in a foreign country, respect the customs and etiquette (see TRAVEL ETIQUETTE) that apply.

TRAVEL POLICY. The rules and regulations of a business governing corporate travel, usually part of a general policy manual.

A company's travel policy sets forth the rules that corporate travel planners and business travelers must follow to be in compliance with corporate policies and procedures.

Travel policies often specify things such as reporting requirements, allowable expenses and expense reporting procedures, permitted classes of service for transportation and accommodations, procedures for making reservations, and the use of particular vendors with whom a company has negotiated special fares and rates.

TRAVEL SECURITY. Precautions that travelers take to prevent theft and other illegal acts and to ensure their safety should they become ill while traveling.

Before departure. Photocopy airline tickets, PASSPORTS, the ITINERARY, and other documents containing numbers.

Keep one copy on file at the office, give another to the traveler to leave with family or a friend, and give two additional copies to the traveler—one to have with him or her at all times (apart from the original) and the second to leave in the hotel safe.

For international travel, check with the State Department for the latest travel advisories in other countries. Designate someone from the company or an affiliated company who will be located near the traveler's destination and will be available to help if needed.

Security firms can provide security briefings to companies with whom they have contracted. Such briefings may be critical to a traveler's safety, particularly for an inexperienced traveler.

In the hotel. Insist on a room located above the first floor, to prevent ground-level access, but below the eighth floor, so that fire equipment can reach the traveler if necessary. Also, ask for a room near the elevator.

Personally carry room keys and PASSPORTS at all times, and ask to have the room made up while one is at breakfast. After that, put the Do Not Disturb sign on the door and leave the television on low volume to give the impression that the room is occupied.

Verify any deliveries or unexpected visitors, such as maintenance personnel, with the front desk before opening the door. Use all locks on the doors, and if desired, purchase additional security equipment, such as door alarms or braces.

Put all valuables in the hotel's safe, and meet visitors in the lobby rather than in the guest room.

Leaving the hotel. Ask front desk employees about safe and unsafe areas to walk, and avoid dark streets and parks.

Using a car. Avoid "gypsy" taxis that pick up more than one person per vehicle. If a taxi does not have a meter, agree on the fare before entering the vehicle.

When driving a rental car, remove any markings or stickers that identify the car as a rental.

Park only in well-lit areas, and keep the vehicle locked at all times. Check the back seat to be certain that no one is in the car before entering.

When parking in an attended garage or parking lot, always keep the trunk keys with you.

In all cases, never travel alone after dark.

On the street. Never wear expensive or expensive-looking jewelry.

Women should wear coats, when practical, and keep purses beneath the coats. Men should wear money belts or at least use only the front pockets. Wrap a wallet with a rubber band to make it difficult for a pickpocket to remove the wallet from a pocket.

Don't wear cameras with straps around your neck, carry bags and briefcases close to your body, and avoid walking near a curb, where thieves can grab items and escape by car or motorcycle.

Avoid expensive designer luggage, and never leave possessions unattended. Use combination locks and luggage tags that conceal your name and the corporate logo.

Be wary of distractions intended to divert your attention from a pickpocket or other thief.

Handling money. Do not carry more than $200 in cash, and use discretion in handing out money to small children appearing as beggars.

Do not flash money or use ATMs or telephone credit cards when someone is standing nearby and watching. Stand directly in front of the machine or telephone when punching in numbers.

Whenever possible, prepay hotel and other travel costs, and routinely destroy charge slips and carbons or store them in a safe place.

Regularly check the sequence of your TRAVELER'S CHECKS since some thieves steal only a few, hoping that you won't notice.

Insurance needs. Be certain that your insurance covers travel losses, and if you are robbed, call the police immediately. This is especially important in other countries where it is difficult or impossible to file a claim after leaving the country.

Medical considerations. When carrying medications, pack two sets in separate carry-on bags, never in checked luggage. Be certain that bringing specific medications into another country is not in violation of local or national laws.

Before leaving, obtain a list of English-speaking doctors in the destination cities. For information, call the International Association for Medical Assistance to Travelers in Lewiston, New York.

Consider purchasing a medical evacuation insurance policy to cover transport back to the United States should you become ill while traveling in other countries.

In all cases. Don't discuss travel plans or accept food or drink from strangers. Have a list of pertinent telephone numbers readily available in the event of an emergency.

VISA. An endorsement on a PASSPORT indicating that it has been examined and that the traveler may enter a specific country on a certain date for a designated purpose.

After the traveler gets a passport, the next step is to get visas for the countries that require them. A Travel agency will indicate whether a visa is required. The traveler can also inquire at the consulates of the countries in which he or she is interested or check governmental Web sites (see Chapter 6/Web site) for entry requirements.

Generally, the passport must be presented at the consulate and a visa form filled out. Sometimes a personal appearance by the applicant is required.

The various countries have a number of special requirements for visas, such as additional photographs, police and health certificates, vaccinations, and inoculations. Usually, there is a visa fee.

The length of time required for processing a visa varies with the country.

For additional information, such as the addresses of overseas consular offices, consult a directory such as the *Congressional Directory* or *Key Officers of Foreign Service Posts*. This publication is sold through the U.S. Government Printing Office in Washington, D.C., and is available over the Internet. See also Chapter 6/Internet; Web site.

CHAPTER SIX

The Internet

ACCESS. To obtain entry to an application, system, or component so that you can use it. Users commonly gain access to the resources of the INTERNET through a dial-up connection with an INTERNET SERVICE PROVIDER (ISP) or an ON-LINE SERVICE.

ADDRESS. See INTERNET PROTOCOL (IP); Chapter 2/ADDRESS.

APPLET. See JAVA.

BANDWIDTH. A measure of the capacity that a NETWORK has for transmitting data over a particular line for a specified period.

In analog transmission (see Chapter 2/ANALOG TRANSMISSION), the bandwidth is measured in cycles per second, or hertz (Hz), which is the difference between the highest and the lowest frequencies.

In digital transmission (see Chapter 2/DIGITAL TRANSMISSION), the bandwidth is measured in BITS per second (bps).

Graphics, video, and other nontextual information require greater bandwidth than do straight text and numbers. In digital transmission, the larger the bandwidth, the faster that information can be transmitted.

BAUD RATE. The speed at which a MODEM transmits data. Although at slower speeds the baud rate and the rate in BITS per second (bps) are the same, the two are technically different.

Baud rate refers to the number of signal changes that occur in a second. In high-speed transmission, one such event may encode more than one bit. Therefore, at higher speeds, the transmission rate of a modem is more accurately described in bits per second.

BBS.   See BULLETIN BOARD SYSTEM (BBS).

BIT.   An abbreviation of **binary digit.** The smallest unit of information that a computer can handle. A bit is a single digit, either 0 or 1 (sometimes referred to as *on* or *off*), in a binary number, such as *0111 1010.*

By itself, a bit carries little information, but combined in larger numbers, bits become BYTES and may express greater amounts of information, such as a letter, digit, or other character.

Transmission by modem is commonly measured in bits per second (bps). Compare with BAUD RATE.

BOOKMARK.   A marker inserted in a document or on a page so that you can later return to the marked location.

Bookmarks are used in Web browsing programs (see BROWSER; WORLD WIDE WEB [WWW]) so that you can easily and quickly point and click with a mouse on location names. This immediately brings the information you select on screen and eliminates the need to insert addresses or scroll through numerous screens of information.

A *bookmark file* (also known by other names, such as *favorites* and *hotlist,* depending on the browser being used) is a list of preferred WEB SITE addresses that you can set up. Thereafter, you can go directly to one of the listed sites simply by clicking on it.

BROWSER.   A CLIENT software program that enables you to use your computer to look at different WORLD WIDE WEB (WWW) resources.

With a browser, such as Netscape Navigator or Microsoft Internet Explorer, you can DOWNLOAD pictures and text, view them on screen, navigate (see NAVIGATION) from one page to another, and print any information that you select. See also PLUG-IN.

The first World Wide Web browser, *Mosaic,* is credited with initiating the popularity of the Web. Originally distributed as FREEWARE, it is now also sold commercially under other brand names.

BULLETIN BOARD SYSTEM (BBS). A remote system, which you can ACCESS with your computer, that serves as a central information and message-exchange resource for users.

A BBS offers various information services. It lets you read messages left by others for you and allows you to post your messages to them. Since messages are posted publicly, private comments should not be included.

A BBS also lets you exchange files and DOWNLOAD or UPLOAD various FREEWARE and SHAREWARE.

A particular BBS is usually geared to users who have a common interest, such as travel. Compare with MAILING LIST; NEWSGROUP.

BYTE. An abbreviation for **binary term**. In computer terminology, a measurement of storage capacity, or a unit of data, generally equal to a sequence of eight BITS. One byte may represent a letter, digit, character, or punctuation mark.

Computer memory is commonly stated in kilobytes (1,024 bytes), megabytes (1,048,576 bytes), or gigabytes (1,073,741,824 bytes).

In INTERNET terminology, a unit of data that consists of exactly eight bits is called an *octet*.

CHANNEL. A path through which information passes between two devices; a particular place where computer users meet electronically to hold a discussion. See also CHAT ROOM; INTERNET RELAY CHAT (IRC); MAILING LIST; NEWSGROUP.

A communications channel may carry data, sound, or video as either an analog or digital transmission. See also Chapter 2/ANALOG TRANSMISSION; DIGITAL TRANSMISSION.

CHAT ROOM. An electronic connection that enables two or more people to hold keyboard discussions over the INTERNET (see INTERNET RELAY CHAT [IRC]) or through an ON-LINE SERVICE.

Users talk by sending conversational-style comments back and forth, and the comments are displayed immediately on each person's screen.

Users can thus hold live, simultaneous keyboard conversations with people worldwide. See also MAILING LIST; NEWSGROUP.

CLIENT. A software program that lets you contact another, shared computer (the SERVER) on a NETWORK to obtain information. An example of a client program is GOPHER, which can be used to contact gopher servers worldwide. See also CLIENT-SERVER MODEL.

CLIENT-SERVER MODEL. A concept of NETWORK organization in which a user's computer is equipped with CLIENT software that can be used to contact a SERVER program to obtain information.

CYBERSPACE. A *virtual reality* (artificial, computer-generated) NETWORK described by author William Gibson in his novel *Neuromancer* and now applied to any interactive, computer-generated environment in which connected computers exchange messages and information.

If you search for and obtain information over the INTERNET, for example, you are working in cyberspace.

DNS. See DOMAIN NAME SERVER (DNS).

DOMAIN NAME. A name, or address, used in electronic communication that consists of different subdivisions separated by dots. See also INTERNET PROTOCOL (IP); Chapter 2/ADDRESS.

The first part gives the name of the person or organization using the domain name. The last part identifies the type of entity that owns the address, such as an educational institution (as in *.edu* for education) or a geographical location (as in *.fr* for France).

All computers on a particular NETWORK use the same ending part of the domain name, as in *djones.net, thill.net,* and *progers.net.* See also DOMAIN NAME SERVER (DNS).

DOMAIN NAME SERVER (DNS). A central computer on the INTERNET that translates a DOMAIN NAME, such as *dolsonco.com*, to a corresponding INTERNET PROTOCOL (IP) address, or number. An IP address consists of a four-part number, such as *146.19.2.1.*

The DNS also translates IP addresses back into domain names. This back-and-forth translation process makes it possible to deliver information to, and receive information from, destinations that you specify.

DOWNLOAD. To transfer material, such as files, software, and graphics, from another, remote computer on a NETWORK to your computer, usually by means of a MODEM and the telephone lines. Compare with UPLOAD.

Because so many resources are available through the INTERNET, one of the most common activities is downloading files.

Most files are downloaded from a HOST computer with the help of the Internet's FILE TRANSFER PROTOCOL (FTP), which enables error-free transmission of material. See also CLIENT; SERVER.

E-MAIL.   See INTERNET E-MAIL; INTRANET E-MAIL; Chapter 2/E-MAIL; E-MAIL COMMUNICATION; E-MAIL ETIQUETTE.

EMOTICONS.   An abbreviation of **emot**ion **icons**, also known as *smileys*. A combination of punctuation marks used in personal electronic messages (see INTERNET E-MAIL; Chapter 2/E-MAIL; E-MAIL COMMUNICATION; E-MAIL ETIQUETTE) to represent facial expressions or emotion, such as *:–)* for smile, that may not be obvious from words alone.

Often, the symbol is best viewed by tilting your head to the left. Some non-smiley symbols, however, such as <*g*> for **grin**, use a letter of the alphabet rather than punctuation marks to indicate a particular emotion.

Emoticons should be used only in personal messages. The words in a business message should be unambiguous and should not require symbols to explain any underlying meaning. If the words alone are not clear, a comment should be reworded.

ENCRYPTION.   The process of converting, or encoding, data into *ciphertext*, which is a coded version that appears to be gibberish to all except the recipient, who has the key to decode it.

Encryption is used in electronic transmissions that are confidential, potentially offensive, or generally unsuitable for someone other than the intended recipient to read.

ETHERNET.   A widely used local area network PROTOCOL (see NETWORK; Chapter 2/LOCAL AREA NETWORK [LAN]), or standard, created by Xerox in 1976 that can be used with most computers and can be linked to the INTERNET.

An upgraded form of the original Ethernet was later adopted by the American Standards Institute (ANSI) and the Internet Standards Organization (ISO).

Since the Ethernet networking scheme works with most computers, it is often used by colleges, universities, and other organizations that have a variety of locally connected computers.

In an Ethernet network, data pass between a SERVER and a CLIENT computer on the network according to the CLIENT-SERVER MODEL.

EXTRANET. A limited-access INTRANET that uses INTERNET technology to exchange public information, such as with customers and suppliers, while protecting private data; part of an in-house WEB SITE that outsiders can ACCESS only with a company-supplied password.

For example, a brokerage firm may use an extranet to let customers trade stocks on-line. A large corporation may encourage customers to use its extranet to order products on-line.

Although a business may want to provide outside communication with customers and suppliers, it will not want them to have access to private company data and files used in the interoffice NETWORK. In such cases, FIREWALL software can be installed to block outsiders from accessing the private material.

To set up an extranet, a company must link its WEB SITE to the database it wants to share with customers and suppliers, install a password system, and instruct employees and authorized outsiders how to use it. Compare with INTERNET; INTRANET.

FAQ. See FREQUENTLY ASKED QUESTIONS (FAQS).

FAVORITES. See BOOKMARK.

FILE TRANSFER PROTOCOL (FTP). An INTERNET standard, or PROTOCOL, that makes it possible to transfer files error-free from your computer to another computer on a NETWORK.

An FTP uses the CLIENT-SERVER MODEL. This means that your local CLIENT program accesses a corresponding SERVER on a remote HOST (computer). The FTP can copy one or many files between hosts.

With FTP, you can ACCESS remote files in one of two ways: use a password and a valid account number to gain entry to a file or use an *anonymous FTP.*

Certain Internet sites will give anyone access to their data files and applications. In those cases, you can usually state "anonymous" instead of an account number and use your e-mail address instead of a password.

The various FTPs have different names. *ZMODEM,* for example, is one of the most popular FTPs used to transfer large files over the Internet.

FILTER. A software program that transfers data to fit a different output pattern, such as saving a Word Perfect word processing document as a Microsoft Word document; a program that screens incoming data and blocks or deletes unwanted portions.

For example, a screen might detect and dispose of junk e-mail. (See SPAMMING.) If you receive large amounts of such messages, contact your e-mail system administrator for information on setting up a filter.

FIREWALL. An electronic security system in the form of a shield installed between an external INTERNET connection and an organization's internal NETWORK as a means of controlling outside ACCESS to the network. See also EXTRANET; INTRANET.

An ON-LINE SERVICE, for example, may use a firewall to prevent intruders, or nonsubscribers, from accessing its databases or from improperly using the service as a means of connecting to the Internet.

Firewall software routes all communications through an outside monitor, known as a *proxy server,* that determines which files or messages may properly pass through to the organization's internal network.

FLAME. An argumentative, hostile, or otherwise offensive e-mail message (see Chapter 2/E-MAIL ETIQUETTE) or discussion-group posting that is sent in response to an incoming e-mail message or discussion-group posting.

Flames are often generated over the INTERNET in a USENET or other NEWSGROUP, in a MAILING LIST, or through a BULLETIN BOARD SYSTEM (BBS).

Flames are unacceptable in any setting and can do considerable damage in business. Businesspeople should therefore strictly avoid participating in any such unfriendly exchanges. The messages create an unprofessional image of the sender and reflect unfavorably on the sender's organization.

FREEWARE. Free software that is often distributed through INTERNET user groups. A developer may want to offer a program to evaluate user reception and interest or may merely want to have the satisfaction of distributing his or her creation.

Freeware developers usually retain all rights to their programs, which means that users may not copy or distribute them further without permission. Compare with SHAREWARE.

FREQUENTLY ASKED QUESTIONS (FAQs). Common questions on certain subjects that are listed and answered on the INTERNET and in other places.

A NEWSGROUP (see also USENET), for example, may post FAQs about its group. A WIDE AREA INFORMATION SERVER (WAIS) site may have FAQs that tell users how to search the site.

Organizations and individuals that provide FAQs often do so to avoid having to answer the same questions repeatedly. Although the information provided is useful, especially to beginners, there is no guarantee that it is accurate or reliable.

FTP.   See FILE TRANSFER PROTOCOL (FTP).

GATEWAY.   An INTERNET device that converts information from one PROTOCOL to another or translates data from one kind of NETWORK to another.

For example, when you transmit an e-mail message (see INTERNET E-MAIL; Chapter 2/E-MAIL), it may have to pass through a series of networks on the Internet, each of which uses a different e-mail format. Gateways will convert one format to another as the message reaches each network on the path to its destination.

GOPHER.   An INTERNET tool that lets you browse and retrieve resources world-wide. A project of the University of Minnesota, gopher performs by using the CLIENT-SERVER MODEL.

Accessing gopher.   You would use gopher CLIENT software on your computer to contact and request information from various gopher SERVERS on the Internet. The servers would find the information you want and send it to your computer.

You can also ACCESS gopher servers via the WORLD WIDE WEB (WWW) with a BROWSER, such as Netscape Navigator or Microsoft Internet Explorer, that can function like a gopher client. ON-LINE SERVICES have built-in gopher clients too.

If you don't have gopher client software, a Web browser, or an on-line service subscription, you can use the TELNET command or program to reach a public gopher on the Internet. Regardless of the method you use to reach a gopher server, the process of finding and sending information is the same.

Gopher organization.   Gophers are typically organized in a menu fashion, and you can choose items of interest from menus, submenus, sub-submenus, and so on. The Internet has many gophers, and universities commonly create them for students to use.

Although thousands of gopher servers still exist on the Internet, the tool has been generally replaced by the use of HYPERTEXT.

HIT.   1. In WORLD WIDE WEB (WWW) terminology, an individual request from a Web BROWSER for a certain item from a Web SERVER. A single hit therefore represents

ACCESS to a particular part of a Web page (see WEB SITE) or the retrieval of an item or document that was accessed.

A single Web page may receive as many hits as it has files to DOWNLOAD. Therefore, if a page includes six graphics, seven hits would have occurred if someone accessed that page.

2. In database terminology, a found record. Therefore, if you located 14 files, there would have been 14 hits.

HOME PAGE.   The main page of an individual's or organization's WEB SITE; the introductory page of a group of pages that together make up a single site; the opening page that a BROWSER displays when you start up the browsing program.

A home page usually introduces a site and describes the information that can be found on the other pages (if any). It may include an index or table of contents to the information on the other pages.

HOST.   A main computer on a NETWORK that makes information and services available to other computers on the network; a shared network computer to which other computers are connected.

A Web SERVER, for example, is a host that shares information with other computers on the INTERNET.

HTML.   See HYPERTEXT MARKUP LANGUAGE (HTML).

HTTP.   See HYPERTEXT TRANSFER PROTOCOL (HTTP).

HYPERLINK.   Also called *hypertext link*. A connection to other pages in a WEB SITE or to other documents on the INTERNET; a connection between one element in a HYPERTEXT document and another element in the same document or in another hypertext document or file. The element may be a word, graphic, or icon.

Usually, you activate a link by using a mouse to click on an element that is highlighted as a link. For example, a linked element might appear in a different color.

If you use a Web BROWSER to find and visit Web sites, you will find elements on the various Web pages that can be clicked on with a mouse to open another page or file for viewing. The element that you click on is the *link* to another element, page, or document. See also HYPERMEDIA.

HYPERMEDIA. A HYPERTEXT system that can display multimedia; the multimedia, such as graphics, sound, video, and animation, that are available for viewing and listening to in a nonlinear association (not in logical or sequential order).

Since the association between hypermedia elements is nonlinear, you can move from one to another in any order, without having to progress one at a time, from one to the next. See also HYPERLINK.

HYPERTEXT. Text that contains a HYPERLINK to another file or document or to another part of the same file or document.

The text that represents the link is sometimes displayed in a different color than the surrounding text. By clicking with a mouse on it, you can automatically move to another location or open a file or document that is linked to the highlighted text.

Hypertext therefore lets you work in a nonlinear fashion. For example, you need not move in sequence from one paragraph or page to the next but rather can skip paragraphs, pages, or even entire documents and jump to a completely different location.

With hypertext, therefore, a researcher could immediately pursue additional information on a topic regardless of where it was located. See also HYPERMEDIA.

HYPERTEXT LINK. See HYPERLINK.

HYPERTEXT MARKUP LANGUAGE (HTML). The standard format used in WORLD WIDE WEB (WWW) and other electronic documents. A newer standard, *HTML+,* is intended to provide better support for documents containing multimedia.

The address of a document that is written in the HTML format ends with the small letters *.html,* as in *http://pro.com/pro.html.*

A document prepared with HTML can display HYPERLINKS that enable you to jump to other Web elements, pages, documents, or resources by clicking with a mouse on the linked item.

Commands, called *tags,* which are hidden in a Web document when it is written, tell a Web BROWSER how to display text, graphics, and so on and how to provide the links you'll need to jump to other material.

The process of adding HTML tags to original text is called *tagging.* A document that is written with very complex HTML tagging will take longer to DOWNLOAD than one with simpler instructions.

HYPERTEXT TRANSFER PROTOCOL (HTTP). The main PROTOCOL for moving files and documents over the INTERNET. The HTTP uses the CLIENT-SERVER

MODEL and therefore requires the use of a CLIENT program and an HTTP SERVER for delivery of information.

By using a Web BROWSER, you can find and read documents formatted and delivered by HTTP. The use of the protocol's initials in a Web address tells the browser that a particular document is HTTP compatible.

The protocol's initials must appear *first* in every Web address assigned to an HTTP-compatible document. Small letters followed by a colon and two slashes (*http://*) are used.

A newer standard, Hypertext Transfer Protocol Next Generation (HTTP-NG), is intended to expand performance and offer other features, such as security, along with file delivery.

ICON. A small graphical image displayed on screen that can be clicked on with a mouse to initiate some action, eliminating the need to enter words or commands with the keyboard.

The image of a printer, for example, could be clicked on to begin printing a document. The image for a Web BROWSER could be clicked on to open that program. WEB SITES also may use icons for HYPERLINKS and other purposes.

INTEGRATED SERVICES DIGITAL NETWORK (ISDN). See Chapter 2/INTEGRATED SERVICES DIGITAL NETWORK (ISDN).

INTERNET. A worldwide connection of thousands of individual, often dissimilar, NETWORKS that communicate by using the TRANSMISSION CONTROL PROTOCOL (TCP) and the INTERNET PROTOCOL (IP), together known as TCP/IP.

Development of the Internet. Originally developed in 1969 for use by the U.S. military services, the Internet was initially expanded to include educational and research organizations. Later, its resources were made available to all individuals and businesses.

Efforts are underway to improve the functioning of the Internet. For example, more DOMAIN NAMES will be added, with more than one agency responsible for registering them.

Also, Internet 2, or the Next Generation Internet, is intended to upgrade the original Internet, especially to allow very high speed Internet access.

Internet administration. Because the Internet consists of thousands of independent networks, private and public, it has no centralized form of management. Each network manages itself.

However, cooperating groups have developed standards that serve everyone's interests in that they make it possible for diverse networks or organizations in remote locations to exchange information and services.

In addition, a nonprofit organization, the Internet Society, actively supports standardization and other cooperative efforts that improve communications.

Another organization, the World Wide Web Consortium (W3C) develops standards for the WORLD WIDE WEB (WWW), and the National Science Foundation (NSF) administers NSFNET, one of the Internet's so called *backbones* (a wide-ranging, high-speed network).

INTERNET ADDRESS.   See DOMAIN NAME; DOMAIN NAME SERVER (DNS); INTERNET PROTOCOL (IP); Chapter 2/ADDRESS.

INTERNET E-MAIL. Electronic messages sent from one INTERNET e-mail address to another. See also DOMAIN NAME; DOMAIN NAME SERVER (DNS); INTERNET PROTOCOL (IP); NETIQUETTE; Chapter 2/ADDRESS; E-MAIL; E-MAIL COMMUNICATION; E-MAIL ETIQUETTE.

Transmission protocols.   When an e-mail message is sent over the Internet, it is first divided by the TRANSMISSION CONTROL PROTOCOL (TCP) into packets that are sent to the correct destination by the INTERNET PROTOCOL (IP).

The various packets go to a *router,* which decides if the message is going to someone on the same NETWORK or on a different one. If a message is going to another network, such as an INTRANET, it may have to pass through a company shield, or FIREWALL.

Gateways.   A GATEWAY at each network receiving the packets reconstructs them into the format required by the next network until it is finally reconstructed into the full e-mail message that is delivered to the recipient.

Gateways therefore make it possible for millions of users to exchange e-mail with other users on networks that may use different formats.

INTERNET FAX. A fax message sent over the INTERNET to a fax or e-mail address, bypassing the usual long-distance part of a traditional fax-to-fax connection sent over long distances via the Public Switched Telephone Network (PSTN).

Internet faxing is possible with Internet-enabled fax machines, fax boards, and fax software. External devices are also available to convert a traditional fax machine into an Internet-enabled machine.

Transmission procedure. An Internet fax transmission begins and ends as a *local* PSTN call. In between the entry and exit points, the fax is routed through the Internet to its destination. Therefore, long-distance telephone charges are eliminated, although a business must still pay a monthly Internet ACCESS fee.

The procedure for sending an Internet fax is similar to that for sending a regular fax. You enter the recipient's fax number on the fax machine's keypad and press the Send/Start button.

Store-and-forward Internet faxing, like e-mail transmissions, may not be as immediate as faxing a paper copy over the PSTN. *Real-time Internet faxing,* which does provide immediate transmission, involves using a special device at both ends or, for transmission, using a real-time fax PROTOCOL on a fax SERVER.

Sending a fax to an e-mail address requires the use of a viewer found in BROWERS such as Netscape Navigator and Microsoft Internet Explorer.

Fax services. Various services are available to handle Internet fax-to-fax transmissions or e-mail-to-fax/fax-to-e-mail transmissions. Usually, a service organization charges an activation fee and a monthly service fee to provide a person or company with Internet fax capability.

INTERNET PROTOCOL (IP). A packet-switching PROTOCOL, or standard, that makes certain a message is sent through the various NETWORKS of the INTERNET to the correct destination network.

TCP/IP. The IP works in cooperation with the TRANSMISSION CONTROL PROTOCOL (TCP), which handles the deconstruction of a message into packets that can be routed through the Internet and reassembled into the full message at the destination. Together, the two protocols are commonly referred to as *TCP/IP.*

Since the Internet uses a packet-switching form of operation, a message must be divided into packets for transmission. After the TCP has handled the deconstruction work, the IP routes the individual packets along the most efficient path.

IP address. The address of a computer on the TCP/IP network is known as the *Internet Protocol address,* or the *Internet Protocol number (IP address/number).* It is also sometimes called a *dotted quad.*

An IP address consists of four groups of up to three digits, each separated by periods, or dots, as in *109.217.333.14.* In Internet transmissions, a HOST computer converts the DOMAIN NAME that you enter to a corresponding IP address.

INTERNET PROTOCOL ADDRESS. See INTERNET PROTOCOL (IP).

INTERNET PROTOCOL NUMBER. See INTERNET PROTOCOL (IP).

INTERNET RELAY CHAT (IRC). A multiuser system that provides an opportunity for users worldwide to have live, real-time computer keyboard exchanges over the INTERNET.

IRC topics. Different Internet Relay Chat CHANNELS are dedicated to different topics, and any comment that you type will be read by all others using the same channel. Private channels are also available for private conference calls. See also Chapter 4/AUDIOCONFERENCE.

To read the comments of others, you can scroll through the list of them on screen. At any time, you can respond to a comment simply by keying and sending what you want to say, just as you might do with an e-mail message. However, in this case, everyone connected to the particular IRC discussion will be able to read your comment.

See also CHAT ROOM; MAILING LIST; NEWSGROUP.

The information-exchange process. The IRC uses the CLIENT-SERVER MODEL, so you need the appropriate CLIENT software to participate in a particular discussion group. Your client software will send and receive messages from the particular SERVER that is hosting a chat on the topic or discussion that you have joined.

A principal function of a server is to send the messages you key to other servers that people around the world are using.

INTERNET SERVICE PROVIDER (ISP). Also known as *access provider* and *service provider.* A service organization that, usually for a monthly fee, will connect your computer to the INTERNET.

An ISP may be a large corporation offering ACCESS in many locations or a small company providing access to residents of a particular town or city. The company usually provides the Internet connection and an e-mail address and may provide a BROWSER for use in visiting WEB SITES on the WORLD WIDE WEB (WWW).

Generally, to use Internet resources through an ISP, your computer dials the ISP's number, which connects you to the ISP's main computer, and it in turn passes information back and forth between you and the Internet sources that you select.

You can also arrange a connection to the Internet by other means, such as through an INTRANET or ON-LINE SERVICE, which offers other services in addition to Internet access.

INTRANET. The private, internal NETWORK that an organization establishes for employees to share information, software, and resources, such as a printer; a private, in-house WEB SITE that employees can ACCESS for information and INTERNET-style chats.

If an intranet is also connected to the outside Internet, as it usually is, suppliers, customers, and others that have company-supplied passwords can visit selected parts of the internal site. A company usually installs FIREWALL software to block outside ACCESS to its private information.

An intranet is usually connected to and uses applications associated with the Internet. For example, the intranet may provide e-mail (see INTRANET E-MAIL; Chapter 2/E-MAIL), Web BROWSERS, and other applications.

INTRANET E-MAIL. A private, internal e-mail system set up for employees in a company but patterned after INTERNET E-MAIL. See also Chapter 2/E-MAIL.

In an INTRANET e-mail system, mail is routed within the intranet to and from employees who may also send e-mail to and from outside destinations on the INTERNET.

However, e-mail to and from an outside NETWORK must pass through any FIREWALL that the company has installed to prevent intruders from having ACCESS to private company data.

Intranet e-mail transmissions are not necessarily instantaneous. Delivery time will depend on the amount of traffic existing at any time on the internal system.

JAVA. Also capitalized as *JAVA*. A programming language that allows applications programs to be downloaded (see DOWNLOAD) from the INTERNET and run on any computer.

A small Java program that runs inside a Java-enabled Web BROWSER, such as Netscape Navigator or Microsoft Internet Explorer, is called an *applet*. An example of a single-task applet is an interest-rate calculator offered along with other material on a larger WEB SITE.

To use Java, you would visit a HOME PAGE, or site, that has a Java applet. Before sending the applet to you, a Web SERVER will verify that the program does not have a VIRUS. As soon as the applet is determined to be safe, the server will immediately send it to your computer.

KEYWORD. The word or words that you give to a computer or a SEARCH ENGINE that is performing a search function for you. The more precise the word or words that you enter, the more successful the search will be. See also METASEARCH SITE.

For example, if you are using one of the search engines of your Web BROWSER to find information about jewelry stones, you might begin by inserting the word *gemstones* in the box or space designated by your browser for entering keywords.

If you are only interested in a particular type of stone, specify that type, such as *jade*. If you are only interested in a particular style, also specify *cabochon* (rounded) or *faceted* (flat). Sometimes you will have to experiment with different combinations of words to locate the information you want.

In many databases and word processing applications, you can attach keywords to documents and files or to information within them to make later retrieval easier and faster. See also Chapter 3/FULL-TEXT RETRIEVAL; KEYWORD RETRIEVAL.

LINK. See HYPERLINK.

LISTSERV. See MAILING LIST.

LOG OFF. Also referred to as *log out*. The steps that you take on your computer to end a session with another computer, a NETWORK, an INTERNET SERVICE PROVIDER (ISP), an ON-LINE SERVICE, a discussion group, or any other activity. Compare with LOG ON.

LOG ON. Also referred to as *log in*. The steps that you take on your computer to gain ACCESS to another computer, a NETWORK, an INTERNET SERVICE PROVIDER (ISP), an ON-LINE SERVICE, a discussion group, or any other activity. Compare with LOG OFF.

MAILING LIST. Also referred to as *maillist* and *listserv*. A discussion form of INTERNET e-mail (see Chapter 2/E-MAIL) among people who are interested in the same topic.

In *moderated mailing lists,* messages are screened by a list administrator for duplicates and unrelated messages that should be deleted. In *unmoderated mailing lists,* all mail is sent to everyone on the list without having been screened.

List subscriptions. You may be able to join an Internet mailing list by sending an e-mail message, with your address (see Chapter 2/ADDRESS), to the mailing list administrator.

When you want to subscribe to a list, your request is forwarded to a computer known as a *list server,* which automatically enters your subscription. To unsubscribe, you would send your request to the same place.

In general, to either subscribe or unsubscribe, follow the instructions provided by the particular list.

Listserv. Although Listserv® is a registered trademark of L-Soft international,® Inc., the term is used generically to refer to any list server or a common form of mailing list. A mailing list, or listserv, manages lists, processes subscriptions, and distributes messages.

Excessive e-mail activity. Mailing lists, like CHAT ROOMS, INTERNET RELAY CHAT (IRC), and NEWSGROUPS, provide an easy way to exchange information on topics of interest. However, they can substantially increase your load of e-mail.

If belonging to a mailing list has made your e-mail load unmanageable, use the unsubscribe feature of the list to have your name removed, or send a request to the list administrator.

METASEARCH SITE. A multiple-search WEB SITE, such as ProFusion, that will ACCESS multiple SEARCH ENGINES and directories when you enter a KEYWORD or query.

Because of the expanded search efforts that occur when multiple search engines are accessed, using a metasearch site is sometimes slower than using individual search engines, one at a time.

MODEM. An abbreviation of **mod**ulator-**dem**odular. An internal or external device used with a computer or fax machine that converts digital signals to analog signals for transmission over the regular telephone lines.

At the destination, the analog signals are converted back to digital form. See also BAUD RATE.

A *cable modem,* used to connect a television set to the INTERNET, offers very high speed ACCESS to the Internet. Cable modems use existing coaxial cable, rather than the telephone lines, that has been installed for television viewing.

MOSAIC. See BROWSER.

NAVIGATION. The process of moving around the INTERNET or using a BROWSER to move from site to site on the WORLD WIDE WEB (WWW).

NETIQUETTE. An abbreviation of Inter**net** et**iquette**. The rules of courtesy that apply to Internet communications. The same rules of courtesy required for all forms of e-mail, including messages sent in local area networks and other non-Internet NETWORKS, such as INTRANETS, apply to INTERNET e-mail.

See the list of guidelines in Chapter 2/E-MAIL ETIQUETTE. See also FLAME.

NETWORK. See Chapter 2/NETWORK. See also EXTRANET; INTERNET; INTRANET; Chapter 2/LOCAL AREA NETWORK (LAN); METROPOLITAN AREA NETWORK (MAN); WIDE AREA NETWORK (WAN).

NEWSGROUP. A public INTERNET discussion group, available with USENET software, through which one can have keyboard discussions with other users worldwide.

Thousands of newsgroups are available, each devoted to a particular subject, such as sports or movies.

You can subscribe to a newsgroup by filling in the information requested on screen, and you can unsubscribe in the same way, similar to the way that you would subscribe and unsubscribe to a MAILING LIST discussion group.

Identification of groups. Newsgroups are designated by abbreviations separated by periods. For example, in the *recreation* category, there is a subcategory *arts* and a sub-subcategory *books: rec.arts.books.*

Particular discussions in a newsgroup, such as a discussion in the *rec.arts.books* group about a new book, are known as *threads.* Since countless people may be participating in a newsgroup at any time, many threads may be occurring simultaneously.

Processing messages. After being connected to a group, it is helpful to read any available FREQUENTLY ASKED QUESTIONS (FAQs) before submitting a question:

In a *moderated newsgroup,* any question or comment that you key and send will first go to a person serving as moderator, who will check to ensure that your message is appropriate for the group.

In an *unmoderated newsgroup,* your question or comment will be posted immediately for others to read, without being checked by anyone.

When you send a message in a newsgroup, a Usenet SERVER passes it on to other sites that also carry the discussion group.

OCTET.   See BYTE.

ON-LINE SERVICE.   Also called *on-line information service*. A computer service such as America Online (AOL) that, usually for a subscription fee, connects users to the INTERNET and provides a variety of other services and resources, such as ACCESS to various information databases, news reports, and discussion groups.

An on-line service therefore differs from an INTERNET SERVICE PROVIDER (ISP), which usually offers only an Internet connection.

On-line service resources.   Depending on the service, you may be able to use your own software to access certain resources, or you may be required to use software provided by the on-line service.

In all cases, only subscribers may use the software or resources of the on-line service. Nonsubscribers are blocked from access by the service's FIREWALL software.

If you send e-mail (see INTERNET E-MAIL) through an on-line service, the initials of the service are included in the address, as in *pjenson@aol.com* for America Online.

Internet-based services.   Although on-line services have traditionally used their own software to connect you to various internal and external resources, many of them expect eventually to be fully Internet based.

Services that are Internet based will use Internet technology, such as the TRANSMISSION CONTROL PROTOCOL (TCP) and the INTERNET PROTOCOL (IP) for the transfer of information from computer to computer.

PASSWORD.   A secret word or code adopted by one person or selected persons in an office or organization to prevent others from accessing (see ACCESS) the system and the user's private data.

Selection of a code.   Since some people are skilled at cracking codes, the password must not be something obvious, such as a birth date or telephone number. As an added security precaution, it should also be changed from time to time in case a would-be intruder is close to learning the code.

A code should consist of an unrecognizable combination of letters, numbers, and punctuation but should nevertheless be pronounceable. This will make it easier to remember, which is important since the holder should destroy any written form of the code.

Use of a code. To LOG ON to a system requiring passwords, you must enter your password and wait for the computer to match it against a list of authorized codes, including your code. As soon as the computer finds a match, you'll be connected immediately.

PLUG-IN. Sometimes called *add-on*. A small piece of software that can be added to the memory of other software to introduce a new feature that the main software doesn't have.

For example, a plug-in may enhance the graphic capability of a word processing program, or it may enable Web BROWSER software to ACCESS more files, such as those written in a format previously unrecognized by the browser.

POINT-TO-POINT PROTOCOL (PPP). A data-link PROTOCOL for dial-up telecommunications that provides a way to connect your computer directly to the INTERNET.

The PPP is a successor to the Serial Line Internet Protocol (SLIP), a data link that also enabled a computer to be connected to a NETWORK.

The PPP provides greater security than the SLIP, as well as superior data handling and error correction. For example, if packets of data get garbled during transmission over the telephone lines, the PPP will retransmit them.

PROTOCOL. A description of the rules, or standards, that two computers in a NETWORK follow in exchanging messages with minimal errors or message distortion.

A protocol therefore may describe how digital data are sent from one machine to another in a local area network (see Chapter 2/LOCAL AREA NETWORK [LAN]), or it may describe how a file is sent from one machine to another through many networks on the INTERNET.

See also INTERNET PROTOCOL (IP); POINT-TO-POINT PROTOCOL (PPP); TRANSMISSION CONTROL PROTOCOL (TCP).

SEARCH ENGINE. Also called *Web crawler* or *spider.* A massive software program that enables you to search through it by supplying KEYWORDS that identify the information you want. Popular examples of WORLD WIDE WEB (WWW) search engines are Alta Vista, Excite, and Lycos.

Organization format. Set up in a database format, a search engine uses an algorithm, or step-by-step procedure, to search for the KEYWORDS that you enter.

Some search programs are structured like an *index*, with categories and subcategories, reviewed by a human staff. One of the popular Web indexes is Yahoo!, which also lets you search through it by providing keywords. You're then given links to documents that fit those words.

Data accumulation. Each search engine has its own procedure for continually finding and adding new information. For example, some may index every word in every document they find, whereas others may index only certain keywords or the first 100 keywords.

Hence some search engines may be more thorough and may serve your needs better than others. However, even the largest search engines do not check the entire Web when you enter a request. Moreover, the major search engines have indexed only a portion of the Web's content.

Small search engines. Individual WEB SITES sometimes have their own, usually much smaller, search engines. An employment site, for example, may have a job-search feature that scans employment listings and reports to you those that fit your specifications.

SERIAL LINE INTERNET PROTOCOL (SLIP). See POINT-TO-POINT PROTOCOL (PPP).

SERVER. On the INTERNET or other NETWORK, the software, or the HOST computer that it is used on, that receives and responds to a request or command from a CLIENT. See also ACCESS.

A single server may be running several different server programs at the same time.

Using your computer and its CLIENT software, you may enter a request for a particular file. Your computer sends that request to a server, which receives and reads the request and then sends the requested information back to your computer.

This process illustrates the CLIENT-SERVER MODEL of information delivery. It allows many clients in many different locations to access the same information stored on a server.

SERVICE PROVIDER.   See INTERNET SERVICE PROVIDER (ISP).

SHAREWARE.   Copyrighted software that users may first try and, if desired, may then keep by making a (usually) voluntary donation to the author. Shareware is widely available over the INTERNET. Compare with FREEWARE.

SITE.   See WEB SITE.

SMILEY.   See EMOTICONS.

SPAMMING.   The use of e-mail addresses on a NETWORK, such as those in a NEWSGROUP or MAILING LIST, to distribute unsolicited and usually unwanted information, such as a sales message, simultaneously. The material is the electronic equivalent of postal junk mail.

 The message is called the *spam,* and those who receive it are said to have been *spammed.*

SPIDER.   See SEARCH ENGINE.

T-CARRIER.   A high BANDWIDTH, leased telephone line that can transmit voice and sometimes text and images. Successive T-carriers are numbered, as in *T-1* (or *T1*), *T-2, T-3,* and *T-4.* In general, each successive number represents a higher speed and more voice channels.

 For example, the T-1 carrier originally provided the fastest speed used to connect data NETWORKS to the INTERNET. The improved T-3, however, can also carry full-motion video, and the T-4, with the fastest transmission rate, provides more than 4,000 voice channels compared with 24 on the T-1.

TCP.   See TRANSMISSION CONTROL PROTOCOL (TCP).

TELNET.   An INTERNET resource that allows a user's computer at one site to ACCESS a remote HOST (shared computer) at another site as though the user's computer were directly connected to the host.

 Telnet, one of the Internet's older technologies, follows the CLIENT-SERVER MODEL in which your CLIENT software enables you to use the resources of a distant SERVER, or host.

To LOG ON to the host, you must know the host's Internet address. (See DOMAIN NAME; DOMAIN NAME SERVER [DNS]; INTERNET PROTOCOL [IP].) You must also give the host your address so that information you request can be sent to you.

After logging on, you can select information that interests you from a menu provided by the host.

Compare with other Internet tools, such as GOPHER and the WIDE AREA INFORMATION SERVER (WAIS).

TRANSMISSION CONTROL PROTOCOL (TCP).   A PROTOCOL used in INTERNET communications to divide a message into packets suitable for transmission and to ensure the integrity of NETWORK data transmissions.

TCP/IP cooperation.   Whereas the INTERNET PROTOCOL (IP) makes certain that information is sent to the correct destination, the TCP deconstructs the information before it's sent and reconstructs it at the destination.

Both protocols are necessary to enable all computers and networks worldwide to share information on the Internet. Together, they're referred to as TCP/IP.

Packet creation and routing.   The TCP is necessary because the Internet has a switched-packet network arrangement, which means that information must be reduced to pieces small enough for transmission.

These pieces, or packets, are created according to TCP standards. During transmission, a series of switches, called *routers,* pass along each individual packet according to IP standards.

Since each packet may move along a different route, the various packets making up a single transmission may arrive out of order. The TCP must then reassemble them in proper order.

If even one packet has been corrupted during transmission, however, the TCP will ask for that packet to be transmitted again, before finishing the reassembly.

TRANSMISSION CONTROL PROTOCOL/INTERNET PROTOCOL (TCP/IP).
See INTERNET PROTOCOL (IP); TRANSMISSION CONTROL PROTOCOL (TCP).

UNIFORM RESOURCE LOCATOR (URL).   Also called *Universal Resource Locator (URL).* The address, or identifier, for a page on the WORLD WIDE WEB (WWW).

A URL provides a variety of information. It specifies where a HOST computer is located, the location of a designated WEB SITE on that host, the name of a particular Web page, and the type of document or file.

For example, in the URL *http://www.abco.com/internetdata/books.html,* you can determine the following information:

1. The initials *http* and *www* refer to a HYPERTEXT document using the HYPERTEXT TRANSFER PROTOCOL (HTTP) on the World Wide Web.

2. The host is a company called (or abbreviated as) *abco.*

3. The description *.com* indicates a commercial business.

4. The directory is *internetdata* (if there were subdirectories, they would follow the directory name separated by slashes).

5. The filename is *books.html,* which is written in HYPERTEXT MARKUP LANGUAGE (HTML).

Given a URL, a Web BROWSER knows which document you want and where it is located on the designated host computer of the Internet.

UNIVERSAL RESOURCE LOCATOR.   See UNIFORM RESOURCE LOCATOR (URL).

UPLOAD.   To transfer material, such as files, software, and graphics, from your computer to another, remote computer on a NETWORK, usually by means of a MODEM and the telephone lines. Compare with DOWNLOAD.

URL.   See UNIFORM RESOURCE LOCATOR (URL).

USENET.   Also capitalized as *USENET.* A massive worldwide discussion forum for news, e-mail, and NEWSGROUPS.

Usenet functions like a BULLETIN BOARD SYSTEM (BBS) in that it collects and posts discussion topics to the thousands of INTERNET newsgroups found on numerous HOST computers around the world.

Since Usenet SERVERS are connected to one another, messages posted on one server also appear on the others. However, a systems administrator at each server decides which newsgroups the particular server will carry.

INTERNET SERVICE PROVIDERS (ISPs) and ON-LINE SERVICES provide ACCESS to Usenet newsgroups.

Although Usenet is now part of the Internet, it existed before the Internet was open to all interested users. Since its inception, the Massachusetts Institute of Technology has maintained a user list consisting of the names and e-mail addresses of all who have posted Usenet messages.

See NEWSGROUP for additional information on the structure and functioning of the different Usenet discussion groups.

VIRTUAL REALITY.   See CYBERSPACE.

VIRUS.   A malicious program designed to invade a computer and disrupt electronic systems or destroy data by spreading the damaging effects through a user's other files once the program with the virus is downloaded (see DOWNLOAD) into memory or the infected program is run.

Although many manufacturers regularly update their software to include the detection of recent viruses, other, newer, potentially more damaging viruses continue to appear.

Therefore, users must use caution in exchanging files or software with others, in downloading files or software from unknown or suspicious sources, and in using unsolicited files or programs that are distributed in the mails.

Viruses and antiviral programs.   The most damaging types of viruses may delete data files or programs and even destroy everything on a hard disk:

A *Trojan horse* is a program that appears to be useful but is really a virus.

A *worm* is a program that infects an entire NETWORK, which in turn can rapidly infect other networks through multiple remote exchanges among users.

Users have various means of detecting and removing viruses:

Antiviral software is a program designed to detect a virus in your computer.

A *scanner* is a program that searches for viruses and alerts you when one is detected.

An *eradicating program* is designed to disinfect or remove a virus.

Spread of viruses.   Viruses may be spread by internal or external sources, such as by exchanging files via e-mail, opening attachments to e-mail, or downloading infected files over the INTERNET.

Since e-mail exchanges far outnumber others, such as software exchanges, ongoing caution is necessary. To prevent the spread of a virus in an attached file or document, immediately copy the attachment to a disk—before opening it—where antiviral software can scan it.

WAIS. See WIDE AREA INFORMATION SERVER (WAIS).

WEB CRAWLER. See SEARCH ENGINE.

WEB PAGE. See WEB SITE.

WEB SITE. Sometimes used interchangeably with *Web page,* although a site may have many pages. A location on the WORLD WIDE WEB (WWW) that provides information and HYPERLINKS to other Web sites or to other pages within a single site.

Web pages. Web sites consist of one or more pages, starting with the HOME PAGE, which is the introductory page that describes what the site offers.

The pages of a Web site are created with a markup language known as HYPERTEXT MARKUP LANGUAGE (HTML). An HTML is needed to tell your Web BROWSER how to display information and link one page to another or to other INTERNET resources.

Web site structure. The following are the three main forms of Web site organization, or structure:

1. A *tree structure* organizes information in an outline, or pyramid, fashion.
2. A *linear structure* connects pages sequentially, one after another.
3. A *random structure* has no defined order of pages or information.

Locating a Web site. Once a Web site is created and posted, visitors can reach it by entering the exact UNIFORM RESOURCE LOCATOR (URL) or by giving a SEARCH ENGINE a KEYWORD or words to use in searching for the site.

After being connected to a site, it's up to the user to determine if the information given there is reliable. If the sponsor is unknown, users should check other factors, such as when the site was last updated, whether the terminology used is appropriate, and whether the site offers a satisfactory privacy policy.

Creating a Web site. Various options are available to anyone who wants to create a Web site. Skilled designers can prepare their own site or prepare the pages with Web page design software. Many choose to hire an outside design service to prepare the pages.

Experts advise creators to follow certain basic guidelines in preparing a Web site:

1. Keep it short and simple (known as the KISS principle).

2. Be consistent in writing style and typefaces and in the use of graphics and color.

3. Be conservative in your initial choice of graphics and photos: The more complex they are, the longer it will take to *draw,* or DOWNLOAD, them, and some visitors to the site may not want to wait.

4. Use easy-to-follow, contrasting text and background colors, and select colors that computer monitors can easily create.

5. Limit the amount of text that a viewer must read, use subheads freely in the text, use extra space between text paragraphs, and keep lines to 60 or fewer characters.

6. Have a professional translator prepare material for an audience using another language.

7. Consider offering a way for viewers who have slow MODEMS to switch to a text-only mode and skip the graphics.

8. If you're selling a product or service, include an easy-to-use *shopping cart* feature, such as a place where visitors can click with a mouse next to each item they want to order.

9. Encourage customers to ask questions—by e-mail, fax, or telephone—and be prepared to respond promptly.

WHOIS. A combination of *who* and *is.* A program that provides a limited INTERNET directory service for locating someone's e-mail address, telephone number, and other information:

> A *whois client* is a CLIENT program through which users ACCESS a whois database.

A *whois server* is a SERVER program through which a server provides the names, e-mail addresses, and other information to the clients requesting them.

The whois database is monitored by the Network Information Center (NIC).

WIDE AREA INFORMATION SERVER (WAIS).   A powerful full-text search-and-retrieval tool that enables users to search for and retrieve documents from numerous INTERNET resources by entering a KEYWORD or words. See also Chapter 3/FULL-TEXT RETRIEVAL.

The data must be available in a WAIS-readable database. If it is, WAIS will search through the content of the files, not just the document titles.

WAIS uses the CLIENT-SERVER MODEL in which requests go from a CLIENT computer to a remote SERVER, which locates and displays the requested information on the user's screen.

WORLD WIDE WEB (WWW).   Also called *the Web* and *W3*. A massive system of nonlinear HYPERTEXT documents, or Web pages (see WEB SITE), connected across the INTERNET.

Development of the Web.   The Web, the fastest growing part of the Internet, was developed at CERN, a Swiss research lab, in 1989 and spread to individual and commercial users in the 1990s.

The World Wide Web Consortium, consisting of educational and commercial organizations, oversees research and promotes standards in areas of activity associated with the Web.

Using the Web.   A vast array of information is available on the Web to those who have a Web BROWSER and know a site's UNIFORM RESOURCE LOCATOR (URL) or know how to use a SEARCH ENGINE or METASEARCH SITE.

Web pages are written in HYPERTEXT MARKUP LANGUAGE (HTML) and are identified by the URLs.

The process of exploring different sites is known as NAVIGATION. You can also ACCESS various Internet tools, such as TELNET and USENET, from the Web.

The various WEB SITES represent a doorway to vast databases that users can access and from which they can retrieve information to view on screen or print out on paper.

They can use the Web to do things as diverse as preview a new movie, buy stock, read the daily newspaper, check for recent job openings, and shop at a on-line mall.

To use the Web, which operates on a CLIENT-SERVER MODEL, you start your CLIENT software, which displays the opening HOME PAGE of your browser. From there, you can move to any of the Web's countless offerings.

Companies are increasingly using the Web to conduct research, make travel arrangements, and hold electronic meetings. They're also using the Web for routine tasks, such as purchasing supplies, tracking shipments, comparing rates, and ordering package pickup.

ZMODEM. See FILE TRANSFER PROTOCOL (FTP).

PART TWO

THE
HOW-TO-SAY-IT™
STYLE GUIDE

CHAPTER SEVEN

Business English

ABBREVIATIONS.   Short versions of words and phrases. The three main types of abbreviation are shortened words, acronyms, and initialisms.

1. A *shortened word* omits some letters in the middle, as in *gov't* (government), or at the end, as in *admin.* (administration).

2. An *acronym* consists of the initial letters of the main words in a name or phrase and is pronounced like a word, as in *PERT* (Program Evaluation and Review Technique).

3. An *initialism* also consists of the initial letters of the main words in a name or phrase but is pronounced letter by letter rather than as a word, as in *eer* or *EER* (energy efficiency ratio).

In general correspondence and text, acronyms and initialisms should be spelled out on first use and the abbreviation placed in parentheses immediately after the spelled-out version: sequential access method *(SAM).*

In correspondence and general text, abbreviations of common, nontechnical words, such as *mgr.* for *manager,* should be avoided. However, abbreviations of specialized or technical terminology, such as *dBu* for *decibel unit,* are often used in tables, footnotes, fill-in forms, and technical text.

Authorities differ in matters of CAPITALIZATION and PUNCTUATION of abbreviations, such as whether the abbreviation for alternating current should be capitalized as *AC* or written with small letters as *ac*. Regardless of the preferred style, an abbreviation should be treated consistently throughout a work.

See also Part Four/ABBREVIATIONS for additional examples.

ABILITY, CAPACITY. NOUNS that are often used interchangeably in business to mean the power to do something. However, the distinction in their primary meanings should be observed in strict usage:

Ability primarily refers to the mental or physical power to do something, such as the *ability* to manage.

Capacity primarily refers to legal competency, such as someone's mental *capacity* to stand trial, or to storage potential or physical measurement of content, such as a *capacity* of 2 gallons. Secondarily, it refers to the power to learn or understand, such as a *capacity* for math.

ACCENTS. See DIACRITICAL MARKS.

ACRONYM. See ABBREVIATIONS.

ACTIVE VOICE. See VOICE.

ADAPT, ADOPT. VERBS that have different meanings but are incorrectly used interchangeably to mean accept or apply to:

Adapt means to adjust or modify for a purpose, such as a plumber's effort to *adapt* a pipe to fit a connection.

Adopt means to take by choice or to accept formally, as in an organization's vote to *adopt* a member's proposal.

ADJECTIVE. One of the eight PARTS OF SPEECH; a word that modifies a NOUN (*large* building) or PRONOUN: She is *intelligent*.

Comparison. Adjectives can be used to make comparisons by adding *–er* or *-est* to a word (*tall, taller, tallest*), to mean more or most, or by putting the words *more* or *most* or *less* or *least* before an adjective: *more tall, most tall*.

Some adjectives have irregular forms and make comparisons by using a different word, as in *good, well, better, best,* and *bad, worse, worst.* Others, such as *fatal* or *final,* should not be compared: not *more fatal* or *less final.*

The three degrees of comparison of adjectives are the positive (*old*), comparative (*older* or *more old*), and superlative: *oldest* or *most old.* The *comparative degree* is used to compare two things (the *older* of two computers) and the *superlative degree* to compare three or more: the *oldest* of the five computers.

Compound adjective.   See COMPOUND TERM.

Adjective clause.   A CLAUSE may function as an adjective and modify a noun or pronoun: The speech *that he gave* [clause modifies the noun *speech*] was well received.

ADVERB.   One of the eight PARTS OF SPEECH; a word that modifies a VERB, an ADJECTIVE, and occasionally a NOUN or PRONOUN.

Comparison.   Like adjectives, adverbs can be made comparative or superlative by adding *–er* or *–est* (*slow, slower, slowest*) or by placing *more* or *most* or *less* or *least* before the adverb: *more slow, most slow.*

In some cases, an entirely different word is required to make the comparison: *well* (positive), *better* (comparative), *best* (superlative).

Confusion of adjectives and adverbs.   A common error is the misuse of an adjective, such as *real,* to modify another adjective, such as *good:* He submitted a *really* [not *real*] good [adjective] report to the president. (Since *good* is an adjective, it must be modified by an adverb [*really*], not by an adjective [*real*].)

Frequently, a verb is used to link the SUBJECT of a sentence to a word that follows the verb and specifies a quality or condition of the subject. That word should be an adjective: The report [subject] sounded [verb] *strange* [not *strangely*]. (*Strange* modifies the noun *report* [the subject], not the verb *sounded,* and therefore the adjective form is required.)

When the word following a verb does *not* qualify the SUBJECT but rather qualifies the action of the verb, it should be an adverb: His laugh [subject] sounded [verb] *hollowly* through the room. (*Hollowly* refers to the verb *sounded,* not to the noun *laugh,* and therefore the adverb form is required.)

An *–ly* ending can be added to some adjectives, such as *loud,* to create an adverb, such as *loudly:* The siren sounded *loudly* [adverb modifying the verb *sounded*].

However, some words already ending in *–ly* are adjectives, not adverbs: He wrote a *timely* report. (*Timely* is an adjective modifying the noun *report.*)

Adverbial clause. Adverbs may also take the form of a dependent CLAUSE that modifies a verb, adjective, or another adverb in the main clause: She was thrilled *because management decided to increase the bonuses this year* [adverbial clause that modifies the adjective *thrilled*].

ADVERSE, AVERSE. ADJECTIVES that have distinct meanings but are often incorrectly used interchangeably to mean opposing:

Adverse means in opposition, harmful, or unfavorable, as an *adverse* opinion.

Averse means having a dislike for or being disinclined to, as in being *averse* to loud parties.

AFFECT, EFFECT. VERBS (*affect, effect*) and a NOUN (*effect*) with different meanings that are widely confused in their verb forms:

Affect means to influence or move emotionally: The new policy will *affect* the morale of all employees.

Effect means to cause or bring about: The new policy will *effect* lower absenteeism.

As a noun, *effect* means a result or consequence: The *effect* of the new policy will be lower absenteeism.

AGREEMENT. In GRAMMAR, a correspondence between words or elements in a sentence. For example, a VERB should always agree with its SUBJECT in number: *One* [singular subject] of them *is handling* [singular verb] registrations.

ALL TOGETHER, ALTOGETHER. A two-word PHRASE *(all together)* and an ADVERB *(altogether)* that are commonly confused because of their similar spelling:

All together means all in one place or acting together. It should be used only if other words can logically intervene: They were *all together* at the rally [They *all* were *together* at the rally].

Altogether means entirely or wholly: They were not *altogether* pleased with atendance at the rally.

AMONG, BETWEEN. PREPOSITIONS that are widely used interchangeably, although in strict usage, writers observe the following distinction:

Among means surrounded by or in association with and is generally used when three or more people or things are involved: agreement *among* the participants.

Between means jointly engaging or shared by and is generally used when two people or things are involved or when more than two are considered individually: The solid agreement *between* Joe and Helen and the strong disagreement *between* Phil, Roger, and Karen puzzled everyone.

ANGLICIZED FOREIGN WORDS. Words from another language that have been assimilated into the English language.

An Anglicized foreign word, such as *a la carte,* is usually set in roman type (see Chapter 9/ROMAN TYPE) in general text, without DIACRITICAL MARKS: *They ordered* a la carte *at the restaurant.*

Foreign terms that are not fully assimilated into the English language, such as *académie,* should be written in italics (see Chapter 9/ITALICS) and should include any accents that are common in the country of origin.

ANTECEDENT. See PRONOUN.

APOSTROPHE ('). A mark of PUNCTUATION that is used as follows:

1. To indicate a contraction or omission of letters: *it's* (it is).
2. To form the plural of letters, figures, and symbols (*q's, 5's*), except when the figure does not require an apostrophe for clarity: *1990s.*
3. To indicate the POSSESSIVE case of a NOUN: *car's* engine.
4. To indicate the plural of a word referred to as a word, without regard to its meaning: There are three *and's* in the sentence.
5. To indicate that a letter or word is being referred to as a letter or word: *A's; no's.*
6. To denote the plural or some other form of an abbreviation (*Sc.D.'s*), except when the abbreviation does not require an apostrophe for clarity: *YWCAs.*

APPOSITIVE. A NOUN or noun PHRASE that follows and further identifies or explains another noun or noun phrase.

Punctuation of appositives. If an appositive is necessary to identify a word or phrase, it should *not* be set off by COMMAS: The artist *John Howe* [necessary to indicate *which* artist] will have his first show at the gallery.

If the appositive gives additional information that isn't essential to the meaning of the sentence and can therefore be deleted, it *should* be set off with commas: Mr. Brown, *the president of our company,* is in Europe.

Spouses. The rule for the names of spouses is that they are *always* set off with commas: Her husband, *Bill,* is running for city council. (She has only one husband, so the name *Bill* can be deleted and the sentence will still make sense.)

Children. The rule for the names of children is that they should *not* be set off with commas if there are two or more, because the names are essential to indicate which one: My son *Ron* is a businessperson, but my son *Adam* is still in school.

AUXILIARY VERB. See VERB.

A WHILE, AWHILE. A two-word NOUN phrase (*a while*) and an ADVERB (*awhile*) that are often confused because of their similar spelling:

A while refers to a period or interval and may be preceded by *for:* The one machine was idle [for] *a while,* but the others ran continuously.

Awhile means for a short period and should *not* be preceded by *for:* Let's work *awhile* [not *for awhile*] before going to lunch.

BARELY, HARDLY, SCARCELY. Adverbs that are generally used interchangeably to mean by a small margin but have subtle differences that are observed in strict usage:

Barely means narrowly: She *barely* qualified for the team.

Hardly means with difficulty: They could *hardly* stay awake during the meeting.

Scarcely means by a margin so narrow as to be unbelievable: He could *scarcely* believe that they survived the competition.

BRACKETS [ ].   A mark of PUNCTUATION that is used as follows:

1. To enclose a parenthetical comment within another parenthetical comment: The company manufactures metal frames for outdoor play equipment (swings *[including adult gliders]*, seesaws, and rings).

2. To enclose mathematical expressions that also include parentheses or braces: $a[(x + y)z]$.

3. To enclose the expression *sic*, meaning thus or in this manner, to indicate an error in quoted material: The company close [*sic*] its doors.

4. To enclose instructions to a typesetter or other comments on a manuscript page indicating that the material should not be typeset: *[Insert Figure 3 about here]*.

CAN, MAY.   VERBS that are both loosely used to express ability or probability (It's an unfortunate problem that *can/may* occur from time to time) but differ in precise usage:

Can primarily denotes the ability or the power to do something: We *can* [are able to] ship the goods next week.

May primarily expresses permission or likelihood: We *may* [are likely to] receive the revised instructions by Friday, and you *may* [have permission to] initiate the project anytime after that.

CAPITAL, CAPITOL.   NOUNS that have similar meanings in reference to a place of governmental activity but differ in precise usage:

Capital refers to a city that is the seat of a government and also has various other meanings pertaining to wealth and business assets.

Capitol refers to a building in which the U.S. Congress meets or a building in which a state legislature meets. The word should be capitalized in reference to the U.S. Capitol.

CAPITALIZATION.   The proper use of initial capitals in titles, names, ABBREVIATIONS, and certain other items. Although the preferred capitalization style may vary from one organization to another, the following rules are widely accepted:

1. Capitalize abbreviations of academic degrees and titles (*Ph.D.*), initials in names (*I. D.* Brown), and single-letter abbreviations: *F* for Fahrenheit.

2. In business, use small letters for *a.m.* and *p.m.* (but small capitals—A.M./P.M.—in publishing) and common abbreviations: *fob* (free on board).

3. Capitalize official titles of specific acts, codes, and laws (*Securities Exchange Act*) but not general terms: the *act;* the *securities act.*

4. Capitalize the words in amounts of money (*Four Hundred Sixty-five Dollars*) in certain legal copy, such as a formal contract, but not in general text: *four hundred sixty-five dollars.*

5. Capitalize the full names of the military services (*United States Army*) but not general or abbreviated references: the *army.*

6. Capitalize titles before a proper name (*Judge* Roberts) but not general references: the *judge.*

7. Capitalize geographical regions or divisions (the *East*) but not general directions: toward the *east.*

8. Capitalize words such as *government, federal, city,* and *district* only when part of a full name or title (New York *State*) but not in general references: the *state* of New York.

9. Capitalize important events (the *Olympics*), holidays (*Thanksgiving*), and historical terms: *World War II.*

10. Capitalize each part of a hyphenated word in a title if it would be capitalized when used alone (*Anglo-Saxon*), but use small letters for the second word if both together are considered one word: The *Self-employed* in America.

11. Capitalize the title of an organization (*Iowa State University*) but not general references to it: the *university.*

12. Capitalize personal and professional titles that precede a name (*Governor* Jones) but not those following a name or used in general references: H. R. Jones, *governor;* the *governor.*

13. Capitalize the names of political parties but not the word *party:* Democratic *party.*

14. Capitalize political party *–ist* designations (*Communists*) but not *–ism* derivatives: *communism.*

15. Capitalize references to the U.S. Supreme Court (the *Court*) and the U.S. Constitution (the *Constitution*) but not other general references to a court or constitution: the trial *court;* the state *constitution.*

16. Capitalize the names of ethnic groups (*Fleming*), planets (*Mars*), registered trademarks (*Dacron*), and the principal words in music, drama, and art: *Beethoven's Fifth Symphony.*

Consult a current stylebook (see Chapter 9/Stylebook) for additional examples.

Clause. A group of words in a sentence that includes a Subject and a Predicate: The manager made the arrangements *when he* [subject] *was in Toledo* [predicate]. For a description of essential and nonessential clauses, see That, which.

Cliche. A trite and often vague or wordy expression that has become stale through overuse:

Bottom line

Die is cast

Feel-good factor

Light at the end of the tunnel

Nip in the bud

Pay through the nose

Writing is on the wall

Although many cliches are based on the wisdom of previous generations and cultures, businesspeople should use precise, clear language. This is especially important in international communication, since readers in other countries tend to translate everything literally.

Collective noun. A Noun that is singular in form but refers to a group or class of people or things.

The noun is singular if it refers to the group as a whole: The *committee* [as a unit] is acting according to its instructions.

The noun is plural if it refers to the individual persons or things in the group: The *committee* [individual members] are acting according to their beliefs.

Colon (:). A mark of Punctuation that is used as follows:

1. After the salutation in a traditional letter: *Dear Mr. Bennett:*.
2. Between the hour and minutes in clock time: *4:15*.
3. Between the numbers in a ratio: *5:1*.
4. After the words that introduce a displayed list: *Follow these guidelines:*.
5. After the city or city and state in book citations: *Chicago: The College Press, 2000.*
6. After the date in periodical citations: *(June 1999): 4-16.*
7. Between closely associated comments or sentences: Mr. Maxwell *disagrees: He* would prefer that we close the plant.

COMMA (,).   A mark of PUNCTUATION that is used as follows:

1. To set off a nonrestrictive APPOSITIVE: Our president, *Mrs. Clark,* is out of town.
2. To separate the names of cities and states: *Princeton, New Jersey.*
3. To separate the independent CLAUSES of a compound sentence: He had to work *late, but* it was important to finish the report.
4. To separate the day of the month from the year: *January 14, 2000.*
5. To set off a nonrestrictive clause that adds an additional thought but is not essential to the meaning of a sentence: The answer, *which most of us realize,* is to increase productivity.
6. To indicate that one or more easily understood words have been omitted: He arrived late; the *others, early.*
7. To separate an introductory word from the rest of the sentence: *Nevertheless,* we agreed.
8. To separate a name and the ABBREVIATION *Inc.* (ABC Services, *Inc.*), a name and a title (John Morris, *Esq.*), and so on.
9. To set off parenthetical words or PHRASES: It might increase the risk, *however,* so that possibility must be considered.
10. To separate words and phrases in a series, including the last two members of the series connected by a CONJUNCTION: *coat, hat, and gloves.*

COMPARE, CONTRAST.   VERBS that are generally used interchangeably to make comparisons but have subtle differences in meaning:

Compare is used to indicate similarity or, less often, difference between people or things. When examining *like* things, use *compare with:* If you *compare* voter turnout this year *with* that of last year, you'll find a significant decline.

When examining *unlike* things, use *compare to:* We might *compare* pre-employment test scores *to* on-the-job training results, but I'm not sure there would be a meaningful correlation.

Contrast is used to show *only* differences and often is followed by *with:* Today's offices *contrast* markedly *with* those of the 1970s.

As a NOUN, *contrast* is often followed by *to:* E-mail saves several steps, such as envelope addressing, in *contrast to* traditional postal mail, which needs an envelope or mailing-label address.

COMPLACENT, COMPLAISANT. ADJECTIVES that have distinct meanings but are sometimes used incorrectly because of misspellings:

Complacent means self-satisfied or unconcerned: Jim tends to be *complacent* in the midst of turmoil and rarely worries about anything.

Complaisant means wanting to please or being politely deferential: Bob tends to be *complaisant* around anyone who might help his career.

COMPOSE, COMPRISE. VERBS that are commonly confused in referring to the parts or the whole of something:

Compose means to make up by combining (the parts make up the whole): Three divisions [the parts] *compose* the company [the whole].

Comprise means to include or contain (the whole includes the parts): The company [the whole] *comprises* three divisions [the parts].

COMPOUND TERM. Two or more words written together (*businessperson*), joined by a HYPHEN (*editor-in-chief*), or written separately (*attorney general*) to express a single idea.

Authorities differ about whether the words in certain compounds should be written together, separately, or with a hyphen. However, the following guidelines are widely accepted:

1. Hyphenate two or more words *temporarily* used together as an ADJECTIVE before a NOUN: *short-term* loan.

2. Don't hyphenate compound adjectives that follow a noun: He is *well informed*.

3. Don't hyphenate well-known compounds that have a commonly accepted meaning: *public relations* consultant.

4. Don't hyphenate color variations used as an adjective: *light gray* paint.

5. Hyphenate fractions when the numerator and the denominator are both one-word forms: *one-third; one-hundredth.*

6. Hyphenate two or more words to indicate that the person or thing shares in the qualities of both: *writer-editor.*

7. Don't use a hyphen to connect an ADVERB ending in *–ly* and a past PARTICIPLE: *closely held* stock.

8. Don't hyphenate titles (*rear admiral, chief of staff*), except coined compounds and those with *ex-* or *–elect: ex-*president, president-*elect.*

9. Hyphenate most compounds formed with the prefix *self-: self-*educated.

10. Don't hyphenate compounds formed with prefixes such as *inter-, non-, semi-,* and *sub-* (*sub*standard), unless used with a proper noun: *non-*American.

11. To form a plural, add *s* to the most important word: *attorneys* general, judge *advocates.*

12. When both words are of equal importance, make both plural: *men employ-ees.*

13. When no word in a compound is of more importance, make the last word plural: pick-me-*ups.*

Consult a current dictionary or stylebook (see Chapter 9/STYLEBOOK) for the proper style of writing other compounds.

CONJUNCTION.   One of the eight PARTS OF SPEECH; a word that connects CLAUSES, PHRASES, or sentences: They opened the new offices on Tuesday *and* closed them on Friday. There are three main types of conjunctions:

Coordinate, or *coordinating, conjunctions,* such as *and, but, for, or,* and *while* connect words, clauses, and phrases of equal rank: He *and* I agree.

Correlative conjunctions, such as *neither . . . nor* and *whereas . . . therefore,* are coordinating conjunctions used in pairs: The package contains the instructions *not only* for the new software *but also* for the new office configuration.

Subordinate, or *subordinating, conjunctions,* such as *although, since,* and *unless,* connect subordinate elements, such as a dependent clause, with a main clause in a sentence: She called me [main clause] *after* [subordinating conjunction] *she heard about the layoffs* [subordinate, or dependent, clause].

CONTINUAL, CONTINUOUS. ADJECTIVES widely used interchangeably to mean continuing but having an important distinction in precise usage:

Continual means occurring repeatedly at close intervals: the *continual* beep during fax transmission.

Continuous means without pause or interruption: the *continuous* operation of the printing press.

The distinction between something repeated at intervals, *with* a pause between, and something that continues *without* a pause is often significant in a technical context.

The same distinction applies to the ADVERBS *continually* and *continuously.*

CREDIBLE, CREDITABLE, CREDULOUS. ADJECTIVES that all refer to the act of believing but with important variations in meaning:

Credible means believable: He is not a *credible* witness; no one believes him.

Creditable may also mean believable but primarily means praiseworthy: Her summation of the case was *creditable;* everyone was impressed.

Credulous means gullible or believing too easily: The readers are *credulous* if they believe every word in the editorial.

DANGLING PARTICIPLE. See PARTICIPLE.

DASH (—). A mark of PUNCTUATION that is used as follows:

1. To indicate an abrupt change in thought: Tom Dobson wrote the last report—*or was it Sarah Meyers?*

2. To set off parenthetical comments when PARENTHESES are not used: A new policy—*not yet announced*—will significantly change the way we handle purchasing.

3. To separate words repeated for emphasis: I believe the decision to downsize is *a mistake—a mistake* that will not be beneficial and may be detrimental.

4. To set off introductory words referred to in the main CLAUSE that follows: We have *paper, pens, and erasers—everything* that the attendees will need.

Most word processing programs set a dash, typed as two HYPHENS, as a solid line. In publishing, the line is referred to as an *em dash*. See Chapter 9/EM DASH.

DEPOSITARY, DEPOSITORY. NOUNS that are both related to the deposit of something for safekeeping but differ in their primary meanings:

Depositary primarily refers to the person or authority entrusted with something for safekeeping: The *depositary* is Neville Caruthers. Secondarily, it refers to the place where something is deposited or stored.

Depository applies *only* to the place where something is stored or deposited for safekeeping: The old Henderson building is the *depository* for the Historical Society's archival documents.

DIACRITICAL MARKS. Also called *diacritics*. The marks, or accents, that indicate a change in phonetic value from the same element when unmarked. The following diacritics are used in other languages. See also ANGLICIZED FOREIGN WORDS.

Acute accent (é)

Grave accent (ù)

Breve (ĕ)

Hacek (č)

Diaresis (ï)

Circumflex (ô)

Tilde (ñ)

Macron (ā)

Cedilla (ç)

DIAGONAL (/). Also called *slash, solidus,* and *virgule,* not to be confused with the backslash (\) on computer keyboards. A mark that is used as follows:

1. In fractions: *9/16.*

2. In identification numbers: *21967/5R.*

3. In abbreviations: *B/E*.

4. To mean per: *rev./sec.*

5. In dates, instead of a HYPHEN: *1998/99*.

6. Between lines of poetry run into the text: *The winter comes / The seasons change.*

7. To indicate NOUNS of equal weight when a hyphen is not used: *owner/operator.*

Usually, there should be no space before or after a diagonal. However, when it is used to separate lines of poetry, a space should be inserted on each side of the line, as indicated in item 6 of the preceding list.

DUE TO. An ADJECTIVE meaning owing to or caused by. As an adjective, it should modify a NOUN or PRONOUN: The setback [noun] was *due to* [caused by] poor leadership.

Some authorities prefer *because of* at the beginning of a sentence: *Because of* the unexpected increase in attendance, the program was held over for another day.

EACH. A word commonly used as a PRONOUN (*each* of them) or ADJECTIVE: *each* person.

When *each* is the SUBJECT in a sentence, it takes a singular VERB (*each is*) and pronoun: *Each* department filed *its* report.

However, when it immediately follows and refers to a plural NOUN or pronoun, the verb should also be plural: Stockholders *each have* one vote.

The number of a subsequent noun or pronoun depends on whether *each* comes before or after the verb:

Use the plural when *each* precedes the verb: The employees *each* have [verb] *their* own assignments.

Use the singular when *each* follows the verb: The employees are [verb] responsible *each* for *his or her* own assignment.

ELLIPSIS POINTS (. . . .) See Chapter 9/ELLIPSIS POINTS.

EMINENT, IMMINENT. ADJECTIVES that have different meanings but are sometimes misused because of misspellings:

Eminent means prominent or distinguished and is applied to persons: *eminent* senator.

Imminent means impending, threatening, or close at hand and is applied to events: The storm is *imminent*.

EUPHEMISM.   An inoffensive or agreeable substitute for an offensive expression or for one that may suggest something disagreeable or unpleasant.

Euphemisms may sometimes be preferred over a more specific term because they are more acceptable, or less harsh, to readers and listeners. However, they are undesirable when they mislead others or when they are so mild and vague that they are also imprecise or inaccurate.

The following are examples of euphemisms, some of which describe a situation imprecisely:

Episode (a disaster or the threat of one)

Flexible (willing to abandon principles)

Irregularity (fraud)

Misspeak (lie)

Negative growth (a decline)

Relieve from job (fire)

Sanitize (destroy evidence)

Managed news (slanted information)

EXCLAMATION POINT (!).   A mark of PUNCTUATION that is used at the end of an exclamatory sentence, a PHRASE, or a single word that expresses strong emotion, satire, or irony:

What a wonderful show!

Stop!

How lovely—I tore my shirt!

To be effective, this mark should be used sparingly in domestic material and should not be used at all in international correspondence. Readers in other countries, who tend to translate everything literally, may not understand the intended meaning.

FOREIGN TERMS.   See ANGLICIZED FOREIGN WORDS.

FORMER. An ADJECTIVE meaning preceding or foregoing. It may be used to designate the first of two persons or things: We kept a record of *regular* and *temporary enrollees*. The *former* are mostly company employees.

The word should not be used to designate the first of three or more: We put the *bails, clasps,* and *pendants* on sale. The *bails* [not the *former*] sold out the first day.

Compare with LATTER.

FUTURE PERFECT TENSE. See FUTURE TENSE.

FUTURE TENSE. The TENSE, or form of a VERB, indicating that something will occur *after* the present, in the future. The *future tense* is formed by combining *will* or *shall* with the main verb: I *will return* his call after lunch.

The *future perfect tense* indicates that something will have been completed at a future time. It is formed by combining *will have* or *shall have* with a past PARTICIPLE form of a verb: I *will have finished* writing the report by the time the meeting begins tomorrow.

GERUND. A VERBAL ending in *–ing* and used as a NOUN: *Reading* is a pleasure, not a chore, for her.

When two or more words include a gerund, the combination is known as a *gerund phrase* (see PHRASE): *Reading to her children* is a pleasure, not a chore, for her.

Use the POSSESSIVE form of a noun or PRONOUN before a gerund: *Mike's* [possessive] *working* [gerund] is affecting his grades.

Gerunds are sometimes confused with present PARTICIPLES, which also end in *–ing* but function as ADJECTIVES: His job requires a great deal of *editing* [gerund used as noun], so he needs to work harder on his *editing* skills [participle used as adjective to modify *skills*].

GOOD, WELL. An ADJECTIVE (*good*) and ADVERB (*well*) that are widely used interchangeably in informal conversation. As an adjective, *good* is often imprecise (a *good* film), and a more specific term is preferable: a *terrifying* film.

Well also may be used as an adjective, usually in regard to someone's health: She is not *well*. However, it's most often used as an ADVERB to mean ably: The new stock performed *well* today.

GRAMMAR. The study of words and their use in a sentence; the system of rules that define the structure of a language. See also PARTS OF SPEECH and other specific entries in this chapter.

GUARANTEE, GUARANTY. NOUNS used generally to refer to a promise to assume responsibility for something: The contract stated the company's *guarantee/guaranty* that the work would be completed by January 2.

Guarantee may also be used as a VERB: The manufacturer *will guarantee* the product for one year.

Less commonly, *guaranty* may refer to the thing given as security, or collateral, for a debt: The truck is his *guaranty* for the loan.

In general, *guarantee* is the more widely used of the two terms.

HYPHEN (-). A mark of PUNCTUATION that is used as follows:

1. To connect the parts of a COMPOUND TERM: *fast-moving* train; *3-by-5-inch* cards; *four- to five-step* procedure (suspended hyphen).

2. To divide a long word at the end of a line: *communica- / tion.*

3. To indicate a span of time: *1998-99.*

4. Between a prefix and a proper NOUN: *Pre*-Hispanic.

5. Between a prefix and a common noun to indicate a different meaning from the same word when no hyphen is used: *re*-form (to form again); *reform* (to change or make better).

6. Between a PREFIX and a common noun when the prefix ends with a vowel and the noun begins with the same vowel, causing the resulting word to be hard to read without a hyphen: *anti*intellectual; *anti*-intellectual.

7. To indicate nouns of equal rank: *buyer-seller.*

8. To indicate a temporary compound preceding a noun: *well-known* product.

IDIOM. Words that have a different meaning than that indicated by their literal interpretation; an expression in the language of a particular people or area having a meaning that cannot be understood from its elements.

Because a literal interpretation may cause confusion, idioms such as the following should be strictly avoided in international communication:

Get the feel of

Give the benefit of the doubt

Hope against hope

Make a clean breast of

Pay lip service to

See it through

Tilt at windmills

INFINITIVE.   A VERBAL that functions as a NOUN or VERB and, sometimes, as an ADJECTIVE or ADVERB. It is often preceded by *to:* His objective is to *win* [noun].

If practical, do not split an infinitive by placing a word or words between *to* and the verb: *To compete* [verb] successfully [not *to* successfully *compete*], we must improve our skills.

Split infinitives, however, are preferable to awkward wording: Efforts *to* firmly *unite* party members were a failure [*not* Efforts *to unite* firmly party members were a failure].

INITIALISM.   See ABBREVIATIONS.

INTERJECTION.   One of the eight PARTS OF SPEECH used by itself, rather than as an element in a CLAUSE, PHRASE, or sentence, to express strong feeling: Wow!

INTRANSITIVE VERB.   See VERB.

IRREGULAR VERB.   See VERB.

ITALICS.   See Chapter 9/ITALICS.

JARGON.   The specialized or technical language of a particular group or activity; obscure, pretentious language.

Although business or technical jargon may help members of a group communicate more effectively, it may confuse others and hinder communication when directed to people outside the group.

Therefore, most jargon such as the following should be used cautiously and replaced with clearer, more widely understood language when writing or speaking with outsiders:

Freeware (software offered at no charge by the developer to determine interest in it or merely for personal satisfaction)

Hyphenates (those who are identified by two or more racial or ethnic groups, such as *Mexican-Americans*)

Nonperforming assets (bad debts)

Protocol (rules that govern the flow of information within and between machines and components)

Word engineering (altering or falsifying information to control what others learn about something)

Workout (a means of accommodating a debtor, often by lengthening the payment period or reducing the interest rate)

LATTER. An ADJECTIVE referring to a subsequent time or relating to the end. It may be used to designate the second of two persons or things: Here are the keys and the assembly list. You can throw away the *latter* when you're finished.

The word should not be used to refer to the last of three or more things: Here are the keys, cleaning tools, and assembly list. You can throw away the *list* [not the *latter*] when you're finished.

Compare with FORMER.

LAY, LIE. VERBS that are frequently confused, especially in the PAST TENSE:

The transitive VERB *lay,* which requires an object, means to put or set down, to place, or to deposit. The principal parts of *lay* are *lay, laid,* and *have/has/had laid:* She lay (*laid/has laid*) the file [object] on the desk.

The intransitive verb *lie,* which does not need an object, means to recline or to be in a certain position or location. The principal parts of *lie* are *lie, lay,* and *have/has/had laid:* He *lies/lay/has lain* on the beach for hours.

Since the PRESENT TENSE of *lay* is *lay* and the Past TENSE of *lie* is also *lay,* those two forms are most often confused. However, the basic definitions indicate the difference: He *laid* [past tense of *lay,* meaning put] the book [object] on the table, and it *lay* [past tense of *lie,* meaning to be in a certain position or location] there for hours.

MISPLACED PARTICIPLE. See PARTICIPLE.

NOUN.   A PART OF SPEECH that denotes a person, place, or thing. It may be preceded by the articles *a* or *the:* a *building;* the *suggestion.*

Most nouns can be made plural (*letters*) and can show possession: the *manager's* letters.

A noun may appear almost anywhere in a sentence: The *president* of the *corporation, Madeline Stowe,* called the *meeting* for *noon* on *Thursday.*

If a word denotes a particular person, place, or thing, it is a *proper noun:* the *Mississippi River.* If it denotes a general class or group or any person, place, or thing, it is a *common noun:* the *river.*

ORAL, VERBAL.   ADJECTIVES that describe spoken or written words. *Oral* refers *only* to spoken words. *Verbal* relates to either spoken or written words and primarily indicates communication by *words* rather than by ideas, actions, music, or some other means.

To prevent confusion, avoid using *verbal* in reference to something communicated by mouth or in writing. Use it only if you need to make clear that something is being communicated with words rather than by another means: The first message was *verbal,* but the second was *pictorial.*

To describe something communicated as a document, use words such as *written* or *printed* or another specific description, rather than *verbal:* He made an *oral* commitment yesterday and followed up with a *written* [not *verbal*] contract.

PARENTHESES ( ).   A mark of PUNCTUATION that is used as follows:

1. To enclose brief, additional parenthetical or explanatory expressions within a sentence: This shipment should arrive on time *(before March).*
2. To enclose complete sentences that represent additional parenthetical or explanatory commentary within a paragraph: The merger occurred in 1999. *(This is documented in William Jones's recent text.)*
3. To enclose numbers or letters preceding listed items: You have a choice of *(a)* monarch stationery or *(b)* standard business letterhead.
4. To enclose figures in a formal document when they follow the amount in words: One Hundred Dollars *($100).*
5. To enclose material in mathematical expressions: $3 (x + y)$.

Compare with BRACKETS.

PARTICIPLE.   A VERB form (see VERBAL) that functions as an ADJECTIVE. It may be a present, past, or perfect participle:

The discovery is *exciting* [present participle].

The sales manager, *surprised* [past participle] by the product's success, decided to revise the advertising schedule.

Having finished [perfect participle] the agenda, he quickly e-mailed a copy to the other directors.

Participles should not be confused with *gerunds*, which also end in *–ing* but function as a NOUN. See GERUND for a comparison.

Dangling participle. A participle or participial PHRASE is *dangling* when it does not correctly modify a definite NOUN or PRONOUN in a sentence: When *writing* [participle] this book, an *attempt* [noun that *writing* incorrectly modifies] was made to organize the material to best advantage. (The *attempt* was not *writing* the book.)

The sentence should be reworded so that *writing* modifies an appropriate noun or pronoun: When *writing* [participle] this book, the *author* [noun that *writing* appropriately modifies] attempted to organize the material to best advantage.

Misplaced participle. A participle is *misplaced* when it is placed in a sentence where it seems to modify the wrong word or words, thereby creating a foolish statement: I saw the *file cabinet* [words that *walking* appears to modify] *walking* [participle] up the stairs. (The *file cabinet* was not *walking* up the stairs.)

To correct the problem, rearrange the words so that the participle clearly refers to an appropriate noun or pronoun: *Walking* [participle] up the stairs, *I* [an appropriate pronoun for *walking* to modify] saw the file cabinet.

PARTS OF SPEECH. The traditional classification of words that have certain uses, or functions, in CLAUSES, PHRASES, and sentences.

For definitions and examples, see ADJECTIVE; ADVERB; CONJUNCTION; INTERJECTION; NOUN; PREPOSITION; PRONOUN; VERB.

PASSIVE VOICE. See VOICE.

PAST TENSE. The TENSE, or form of a VERB, indicating that something occurred in the past: The company *declared* bankruptcy.

The *past perfect tense* indicates the earlier of two past actions. It is formed by combining *had* with the past PARTICIPLE form of the main verb: James *arrived* [past tense] after Lori *had arrived* [past perfect tense: the earlier of the two past actions].

PERIOD (.). A mark of PUNCTUATION that is used as follows:

1. To end a sentence: *We should keep complete records.*
2. With certain abbreviations: *Sc.D.* (but *nat'l; NBC*).
3. After initials in a name: *G. M. Hill* (but *Mr. X*).
4. After letters or numbers in lists or outlines: *B.*
5. To indicate omitted material: *I have the original contract . . . signed yesterday.* See also Chapter 9/ELLIPSIS POINTS.

PHRASE. Two or more words, without both a SUBJECT and a PREDICATE, that is used as a PART OF SPEECH.

For example, when a group of words includes a GERUND, the combination is known as a *gerund phrase*. In the following example, the phrase functions as the SUBJECT of the sentence: *Talking about his problems* [gerund phrase] has helped him to relax.

PORTMANTEAU WORD. Also called *blend word*. An expression consisting of two or more separate words, or parts of them, combined to form a single term. Because these terms may be unfamiliar to many readers, particularly in other countries, they should be used judiciously or avoided entirely:

Anglistics (Anglo + linguistics)

Breviloquence (brevity + eloquence)

Fadical (fad + radical)

Immateur (immature + amateur)

Innoventure (innovative + venture)

Repristination (reprise + restoratioin)

See also JARGON.

POSSESSIVE. The form of a word indicating possession or ownership: the *computer's* hard drive.

Compound nouns and proper names. Usually, you should form the possessive by adding *'s* to the word nearest the object possessed: attorney *general's* argument; John Brown, *Jr.'s* office; Jim Mason of *Consolidated's* staff; notary *public's* seal.

Use an "of PHRASE" to form the plural possessives of a compound NOUN: arguments *of* attorneys general; seals *of* notaries public. See also the forthcoming discussion in *Of phrase.*

Awkward or sibilant sounds.   Drop the *s* and add only an apostrophe to form the possessive when the use of both would cause a hissing or awkward sound: for *conscience'* sake.

Words ending in s.   Form the singular possessive of words already ending in *s* by adding *'s,* but form the plural possessive by adding only the apostrophe: Harold *Jones's* car; the *Joneses'* car; Mss. *Smiths'* reception; *bus's* motor.

Use the apostrophe without an *s* in poetic or biblical expressions: *Achilles'* heel.

Words ending in ss.   Form the possessive in most cases by adding an apostrophe and *s* if a new syllable is formed in the pronunciation of the possessive: the *witness's* testimony; my *boss's* office.

Of phrase.   You may also use an "of phrase" to show possession. When the thing possessed is a specific number or group belonging to the possessor, the *'s* is used, thus forming a double possessive: That remark *of the commentator's* [a specific remark] aroused interest.

When the thing possessed is not restricted to or limited to a specific number or group, the *'s* is not used: The remarks *of the commentators* [generally speaking] aroused interest. See also the preceding discussion in *Compound nouns and proper names.*

Appositives and explanatory words.   Whenever possible, avoid appositives or explanatory words with the possessive case (rewrite the sentence if necessary). However, if the object possessed must be named, the word nearest the object takes the possessive: His *guardian's, Roy Nelson's,* control of the money is mandatory.

When this is not essential, change the construction of the sentence: Control of the money by *his guardian, Roy Nelson,* is mandatory.

Inanimate objects.   In some cases, the possessive case may be used with inanimate objects: one *day's* vacation; two *weeks'* pay; five *dollars'* worth. Many of such expressions also form compound ADJECTIVES and therefore can be hyphenated instead of written as possessives: a *one-day* vacation.

PRACTICABLE, PRACTICAL.   ADJECTIVES that generally mean useful or usable but, in strict usage, have slight differences in meaning:

Practicable specifically means feasible or capable of being put into practice and can be used *only* in reference to things: The plan is *practicable* [can be carried out].

Practical specifically means useful or successful in actual practice and may be used in reference to either persons or things: The course offers *practical* [useful] instruction.

PREDICATE.   The part of a sentence that makes a statement about the SUBJECT and includes a VERB: The office [subject] *will be closed* [verb] *from December 25 until January 2* [predicate].

PREFIX.   An affix, such as *anti-, non-, post-,* or *semi-,* that is placed before a word or the main part of a word to form another word: *semiconscious.*
  Follow these guidelines in writing prefixes:

1. Don't double the last letter of a prefix when it's different from the first letter of the root: *dis*appear.
2. Keep the last letter of the prefix even when the root begins with the same letter: *mis*statements.
3. Write most words with a prefix closed (no HYPHEN), except as described in the forthcoming examples: *anti*climax.

To prevent misreading, however, use a hyphen in these cases:

1. When the prefix begins with an *i* or an *a* and the root begins with the same letter: *ultra*-active (not *ultra*active); *anti*-intellectual (not *anti*intellectual).
2. For those few words using the prefix *re* to distinguish them from words of the same spelling but with different meanings: to *re*-form (form again) the group; to *reform* (correct) behavior in the group.
3. Before proper NOUNS: *pro*-Democrat; *mid*-February.
4. For family terms using the prefix *great-:* her *great*-grandfather.
5. When the word *self* is used as a prefix: *self*-addressed.

Compare with SUFFIX.

PRESENT PERFECT TENSE.   See PRESENT TENSE.

PRESENT TENSE.   The TENSE, or form of a VERB, indicating that something currently exists or is occurring now: He told me that the company's headquarters *is* in New York.

The present tense is also used idiomatically to express future action: Congress *adjourns* [will adjourn] next week.

Use a *progressive form*, not the simple present, to express action *in progress:* When I write in the morning, as I *am writing* now, I'm more alert than I am in the evening.

The *present perfect tense* indicates action *completed* at the present time and is formed by combining *have* or *has* with the past PARTICIPLE form of the main verb: The speaker *has concluded* [completed at the present time] his remarks.

PRINCIPAL, PRINCIPLE.   A NOUN (*principal; principle*) and an ADJECTIVE (*principal*) that have different meanings but are commonly confused:

As a noun, *principal* has a variety of meanings, such as the head or main person (the *principal* in the negotiations) and a sum of money: the mortgage *principal* and interest.

As an adjective, *principal* means chief or most important: the *principal* [most important] factor in his decision.

The noun *principle* means a fundamental or general truth or a rule: the *principle* of justice for all.

PROGRESSIVE TENSE.   See PRESENT TENSE.

PRONOUN.   One of the eight PARTS OF SPEECH; a word, such as *they,* that is used in place of a NOUN. The noun for which a pronoun stands is called its *antecedent.*

A pronoun must agree with its antecedent in number: The firm [antecedent] *has* demonstrated that *it* [pronoun] *is* [not *they are*] qualified to look after the interests of *its* [not *their*] clients.

PUNCTUATION.   Standardized marks or signs placed in written material to clarify meaning, separate units, and guide readers through a sentence. See the individual entries in this chapter.

Punctuation in moderation adds emphasis and stress to a writer's words, but it is not a panacea for a poorly constructed sentence. Usually, sentences that are difficult to punctuate or that require numerous COMMAS are weak and should be reworded.

More punctuation, skillfully and accurately inserted, should be used in international communication than in domestic writing. Punctuation will help readers and translators understand material that is not presented in their native language and will help them avoid misreading the material.

QUESTION MARK (?).   A mark of PUNCTUATION that is used after interrogatory sentences: *Is the fax ready?*

Indirect questions.   A question mark should be placed *only* after a direct question but not after an indirect question for which no answer is expected: *Will you please return the signed copy as soon as possible* [request to which no answer is expected].

Series of questions.   In a series of questions included within one sentence, a question mark may be placed at the end of the sentence or, for emphasis, after each question. In that case, begin each question with a capital letter: Should we abandon *our principles? Our honor? Our respect?*

Within quoted material.   When used with quoted material, a question mark comes before or after the QUOTATION MARKS, depending on whether the entire question is quoted. If the full question is also the full quotation, the punctuation should be placed inside the concluding quotation marks: *"How much can we improve the quality of life?"*

If only part of the question involves quoted words, the question mark should be placed outside the concluding quotation marks: How much can we improve the *"quality of life"?*

QUOTATION MARKS ('', "").   Marks of PUNCTUATION that are used to enclose one or more words; the titles of articles, chapters, television and radio episodes, short poems and songs, and unpublished works; and, in certain disciplines, words used in a special sense.

For guidelines about the proper use of single and double quotation marks and the placement of other punctuation inside or outside the marks, see Chapter 9/QUOTATION MARKS.

REACTION, REPLY, RESPONSE.   Generally, NOUNS that are used interchangeably to mean a response, although subtle differences are recognized in precise usage:

Reaction is a response to *stimuli:* adverse *reaction* to the flu vaccination.

Reply is an oral or written response to something: a *reply* to the letter sent by fax.

Response is any type of reply, answer, attitude, or action that is prompted by something: a negative *response* to the proposal.

REDUNDANCY.   Unnecessary use of words or superfluous repetition. Although speakers and writers may intentionally repeat something for emphasis or to draw attention to their words, needless and unintentional excess must be avoided.

Certain words, for example, mean essentially the same thing and therefore are unnecessarily repetitive:

Red *in color*

Deeds and actions

Final conclusion

The month of April

Small *in size*

Spell out *in detail*

Some letters in ABBREVIATIONS refer to a word that may be unnecessarily repeated after the abbreviation. In *HIV virus,* for example, the *V* in *HIV* stands for *virus.* Therefore, adding the word *virus* after the initials is unnecessary and repetitious.

In other cases, writing may simply be unnecessarily wordy. *"I'd be interested in knowing* what you think," for example, could be more succinctly stated as *"Let me know* what you think."

REGULAR VERB.   See VERB.

SEMICOLON (;). A mark of PUNCTUATION that is used as follows:

1. To indicate a break in thought more pronounced than a COMMA indicates and less pronounced than a PERIOD indicates.

2. To separate the parts of a compound sentence when the CONJUNCTION between the parts is omitted: The invoice is more than 90 days past *due; we'll* have to begin collection procedures shortly.

3. To separate a CLAUSE or sentence introduced by an ADVERB that functions like a conjunction: The mayor called an emergency meeting; *consequently,* the shutdown was avoided.

4. To separate two or more clauses that are punctuated by commas: She completed the *correspondence, filing, and billing;* processed the outgoing postal mail; and picked up the *stationery, copy paper, and diskettes.*

5. To separate listed items (unless they are brief) or items with other punctuation: The following action was taken: *(1)* amendment of the standing rules, bylaws, and rules of order*; (2)* adoption of new resolutions, reworded to be consistent with the new policy*; and (3)* replacement of two directors who are retiring.

SHALL, WILL. Auxiliary Verbs that are used with a main verb to form the Future tense (*will* determine) or are used with *have* and the past Participle of a verb to form the future perfect tense: *will have* determined.

Shall and *will* also are combined with a verb ending in –*ing* to create a progressive form: *will be* determining.

Traditionally, *shall* has been used in the first person (I *shall*) and *will* in the second and third persons (you/he/she/they *will*) to indicate simple futurity. In contemporary usage, *will* is used in all cases: I/you/he/she/they *will.*

The Past tense of *shall* is *should,* and the past tense of *will* is *would. Should* is commonly used to indicate obligation: We *should* [ought to] exercise daily before work.

Would is commonly used to indicate customary action: Usually, we *would* exercise daily before work.

SLASH. See Diagonal (/).

SPLIT INFINITIVE. See Infinitive.

SUBJECT. The part of a sentence about which something is said or that indicates its topic.

The subject must be, or must include, a Noun or the equivalent, such as a Pronoun. The specific topic or word about which something is said is the *simple* subject: The company's *employees and friends* celebrated its 35th anniversary today.

The entire group of words that together express the topic of the sentence, including words that modify the noun or pronoun, is the *complete* subject: *The company's employees and friends* celebrated its 35th anniversary today.

Compare with Predicate.

SUFFIX. An affix, such as *–wide,* that is placed at the end of a word or the main part of a word: nation*wide.*

The rules for using suffixes are so complex and have so many exceptions that they are of questionable value. Users should therefore consult a current dictionary when in doubt about the proper spelling of a word with a suffix.

The following are examples of common suffixes:

-able/service*able*

-ance/extravag*ance*

-cede/pre*cede*

-ence/neglig*ence*

-ible/deduc*ible*

-ite/suburban*ite*

-ize/union*ize*

-or/react*or*

-ous/advantage*ous*

Compare with PREFIX.

TENSE. The form of a VERB that indicates when something occurs. For examples, see FUTURE TENSE; PAST TENSE; PRESENT TENSE.

THAT, WHICH. PRONOUNS that are used to refer to persons, animals, or things. Whereas *that* is used to refer to either persons, animals, or things, *which* is properly used to refer *only* to animals or things:

That is used to introduce essential CLAUSES without which the meaning of a sentence would be unclear.

Which is used to introduce nonessential clauses that can be eliminated without affecting the logic or completeness of the sentence.

An essential clause should *not* be set off by COMMAS: He has the qualities *that prompt admiration.* (The sentence wouldn't make sense without the clause.)

A nonessential clause *should* be set off by commas to signal that the material set apart can be deleted: Michael's account of the accident, *which I sent to you yesterday,* will explain the damage. (The sentence makes sense with or without the clause.)

TRANSITIVE VERB. See VERB.

VERB. One of the eight PARTS OF SPEECH; a word that expresses action (*take*) or state of being (*is*). A verb is indispensable in a sentence and is the only part of speech that can stand alone to express meaning: *Come.*

Transitive and intransitive verbs. Verbs may be either transitive or intransitive. The action of a *transitive verb* goes from a doer to a receiver or from a subject to an object: She *opened* [transitive verb] the *window* [object].

The action of an *intransitive verb* either does not include an object or is limited to the subject, or the verb shows no action: He *is* [intransitive verb showing no action] a skilled machinist.

Main or auxiliary verb. Verbs are either main, or principal, verbs or auxiliary verbs, depending on their use. A verb PHRASE uses the main verb combined with an auxiliary verb: *will* [auxiliary verb] *write* [main verb].

Common auxiliaries are *be, can, do, have, may, must, shall, will,* and *ought.* Sometimes more than one occur together: You *should have seen* the show.

Regular and irregular verbs. Most verbs form the PAST TENSE and the past PARTICIPLE by adding *–ed* to the PRESENT TENSE: *look* (present), *looked* (past), *have/has/had looked* (past participle).

Other verbs are irregular, and no rule exists for forming the past tense or the past participle: *give* (present), *gave* (past), *have/has/had given* (past participle).

VERBAL. VERBS that are used as various PARTS OF SPEECH. The following are the three types of verbals:

1. GERUND, used as a NOUN
2. INFINITIVE, often preceded by *to* and used as a noun or verb and sometimes as an ADJECTIVE or ADVERB
3. PARTICIPLE, used as an adjective

See the individual entries for examples.

VIABLE, WORKABLE. ADJECTIVES often used interchangeably to mean practicable, although their primary meanings differ (see also PRACTICABLE, PRACTICAL):

Viable primarily means capable of existing biologically: a *viable* life form.

Workable primarily means capable of being handled or put into operation: a *workable* plan.

Not only do the primary meanings of the two terms differ, but also when *viable* is substituted for *workable*, it tends to sound pretentious. Businesspeople should therefore apply each term according to its primary meaning and not treat the two as synonyms.

VOICE.   The quality of a VERB that shows when the SUBJECT of a sentence is acting (*active voice*) or is being acted on (*passive voice*):

> The active voice is more direct and forceful: The manager *accepted* the proposal.
>
> The passive voice is the weaker of the two: The proposal *was accepted* by the manager.

Although the active voice is usually preferred in most types of business writing, the passive voice may be helpful in some cases to avoid an accusatory or overly critical tone: A few errors *were made* [not *You made* a few errors].

When practical, avoid mixing the voices within a sentence or successive sentences: The *jurors deliberated* for 48 hours before *the judge discharged* them [not The *jurors deliberated* for 48 hours before *they were discharged* by the judge].

WHILE.   As a CONJUNCTION, a word meaning during the time that or as long as: He waited *while* [during the time that] she completed the letter.

While should be used *only* in this sense and not as a substitute for connectives such as *although, whereas,* or *but.* For example, *although* means regardless or even though: *Although* [not *while*] some persons complained, the motion passed easily.

To say that "*While* some persons complained, the motion passed easily" suggests that the motion passed precisely at the same time that (while) the people were voicing their complaints, which probably was not the case. To avoid such ambiguity or inaccuracy, confine the use of *while* to situations properly related to time.

WHO, WHOM.   PRONOUNS that are often incorrectly used interchangeably.

Traditionally, *who* has been used in the nominative case, such as in the SUBJECT of a CLAUSE or sentence: The woman *who* [subject of clause] *spoke* [verb of clause] *at the meeting* had just returned from Europe.

When a clause with a subject intervenes between the main subject and verb of a sentence, it's important to determine which is the main subject: *Who* [main subject of sentence] do you believe [intervening clause] *will be promoted* [main verb]. (*Who,* not *whom,* is used as the subject.)

Whom is used in the objective case, such as the object of a verb or PREPOSITION: The woman *whom* [object of *met*] we *met* [verb] is in charge of research. (To test this usage, reverse the words: We *met whom* [not *who*]?)

As the object of a preposition, *whom* usually immediately follows the preposition, and the correct usage may therefore be easier to determine: By [preposition] *whom* [object of preposition] were you contacted? (However, you may again reverse the words if further clarity is needed: You were contacted *by whom* [not *who*]?)

WORD DIVISION.   The proper division of a multisyllable word at the end of a line. It may be helpful to divide a very long word at the end of a line to make the lines on a page more equal and thereby to improve the appearance of the text.

However, avoid having divided words in two or more successive lines. Also, avoid dividing the last word in a paragraph or on a page. (An exception occurs in legal documents where the last word may be intentionally divided if it is necessary to indicate in that way that the document continues on another page.)

The correct division of a word usually depends on the breakdown of the word into syllables (consult a current dictionary for examples). The following rules apply:

1. Don't divide a word such as *through* that is pronounced as one syllable.

2. Don't divide a four-letter word such as *into.*

3. Don't separate one-letter syllables, such as the *a* in *alone,* from the rest of the word.

4. When possible, divide a word that has a one-letter syllable within the word *after* the single letter: *prolifera- / tion,* not *prolifer- / ation.*

5. Don't carry over to the next line a two-letter syllable unless a punctuation mark follows the two letters so that at least three characters are carried to the second line: *call- / er.* (The period after -er would create three characters for the second line.)

6. Always leave at least three characters, including the HYPHEN used in division, on the top line: *re-* / *form.*

7. Don't confuse the *a* and *i* in the suffixes *–able* and *–ible* with a single syllable. Divide words with such suffixes *before*, not *within*, the suffix: *appli-* / *cable*, not *applica-* / *ble.*

8. When the final consonant in a word is doubled before a suffix or verb ending, keep the second consonant with the letters following it: *occur-* / *ring,* not *occurr-* / *ing.*

9. Don't carry over to the next line a single or double consonant in the root word: *divid-* / *ing*, not *divi-* / *ding.*

10. When two consonants occur within a word, divide the word between them: *expres-* / *sive*, not *express-* / *ive.*

11. Avoid dividing a compound hyphenated word, except where the hyphen falls naturally: *ex-* / *senator,* not *ex-sena-* / *tor.*

12. Don't divide abbreviations, contractions, or acronyms: *PERT,* not *PE-* / *RT.*

13. Avoid dividing numbers, but if it's necessary to break them, divide on a COMMA, and retain the comma on the first line: *2,302,-* / *700,000,* not *2,30-* / *2,700,000.*

14. Divide dates between the day and the year, not between the month and the day: *May 2,* / *2000*, not *May* / *2, 2000.*

15. Avoid dividing proper names, but if it's necessary, divide between the first name or initials and the last name: *E. R.* / *Taylor,* not *E.* / *R. Taylor.*

16. Avoid separating professional designations, degrees, and so on from a name, but if it's necessary, divide between the name and the initials or designation, not within the initials or designation: *James Thompson,* / *Ph.D.,* not *James Thompson,* Ph.- / *D.*

CHAPTER EIGHT

Correspondence

ACCEPTANCES. Messages written to accept an offer or INVITATION, such as an invitation to help organize a new project.

Informal acceptances to associates may be sent by e-mail (see MEMOS; Chapter 2/E-MAIL), but formal acceptances sent to customers, public officials, and others outside the company are usually prepared on business letterhead.

Both e-mail and paper acceptances, usually brief, should express appreciation and enthusiasm:

Thanks very much for inviting me to serve on the Planning Committee for the Better Burlington Project. I'd be happy to join your group and look forward to meeting with you and Steve Norton next week.

ACKNOWLEDGMENTS. Messages that recognize or confirm something. Depending on the intended recipient and what is being acknowledged, the message may be formal or informal.

For example, the brief acknowledgment of an associate's report is commonly sent by e-mail. The formal acknowledgment of a legal document or a financial offer is often prepared on business letterhead and sent in a sealed envelope.

Simple acknowledgment. Office personnel compose routine acknowledgments in their employers' absence. This type of brief message should be written in a friendly tone and sent promptly:

Thanks for asking Ms. Adams about her plans for a conference booth. Although she's away from the office now, we expect her to return to Washington the second week of June. I'll let her know about your query as soon as she returns.

We're sorry to keep you waiting, but if I can help in the meantime, please let me know.

Acknowledgment that also provides information. This type of message, commonly prepared by the office staff, goes a step farther. It also supplies important information:

Your letter asking Bill Watts to address the Business Club on April 10 arrived the day after he left town on business.

I talked to him this morning, and he said that since he'll be out of town on the 10th, he won't be able to attend your meeting. But he hopes that you'll find a spot for him at a future meeting and, in the meantime, sends his thanks for thinking of him.

ADDRESS, FORMS OF. The proper way to write a person's name and address in correspondence, including personal and professional titles, mailing address, and salutation.

Part Four/FORMS OF ADDRESS gives the correct form of INSIDE ADDRESS and SALUTATION to use in LETTERS to persons holding official or honorary positions.

The following guidelines apply to business messages written in a letter FORMAT. See MEMOS for a description of paper memos and e-mail messages, which don't include an inside address or salutation.

Titles. When a person has a professional title, such as *Dr.,* use it in the INSIDE ADDRESS. Otherwise, use *Mr.* or *Ms.* (in business, use *Mrs.* only if the woman uses this title in her signature line or in some other way indicates that she prefers it).

Follow the practice in your office concerning the use of first names in the salutation:

Dr./Ms. Jennifer Cantrell
Autosharp Manufacturing, Inc.
[Address]

Dear Jennifer/Dear Dr./Ms. Cantrell:

Esquire is seldom used in the United States, except occasionally by attorneys. In those cases, it may be used for either men or women and should be abbreviated (*Esq.*) and placed after the name, with no title preceding the name:

Walter Hiam, Esq.
Hiam and Samuelson
[Address]

Dear Walter/Dear Mr. Hiam:

Man and woman together.   Use the full names of each person, whether or not they are married, and stack the names, with the higher-ranking person first (alphabetically if both have equal rank):

Mr. Henry Page, President
Ms. Annette Colter, Vice President
[Address]

Dear Hank and Annette/Dear Mr. Page and Ms. Colter:

Gender unknown.   If you're unable to determine an addressee's gender, begin with the person's first name or initials but no title:

V. R. Schroeder
Crestview Developers
[Address]

Dear V. R. Schroeder:

Name unknown.   If you don't know a person's name, use a job title, or if that's also unknown, address the letter to the company (see the forthcoming company example):

Human Resources Manager
Bixby Aereonautics
[Address]

Dear Human Resources Manager:

Company.   If a departmental name is available, include it, and address the letter to the manager of the department, as illustrated in the previous example.

If only the firm name is known, omit the salutation, or use *Ladies and Gentlemen:*

The Catalog Shoppe
[Address]

Ladies and Gentlemen:

Social-business usage. See INVITATIONS.

ADJUSTMENTS. Messages that correct or alter something that is inaccurate, unacceptable, or undesirable. A customer, for example, may want a refund or credit upon returning defective merchandise.

These messages are usually prepared on business letterhead. Responses may also be prepared on business letterhead, although those pertaining to financial adjustments are frequently noted directly on the person's statement, without a separate letter.

The tone of an adjustment message should be clear and reasonable, whether one is requesting an adjustment or responding to a request for one:

The June statement of Robert Walker's account 14825 contains an incorrect charge of $68.95 on May 15 for two cases of copy paper.

Mr. Walker charged two cases of copy paper for $68.95 on May 10 and again on May 20 but made no charges on May 15. The four cases he bought before and after the 15th were properly charged to his company account.

I have deducted $68.95 from the total amount of the statement and am enclosing our check number 067339 for the remainder, $50.80.

Thank you.

See also REFUSALS for an example of a letter that says no to a request.

ANNOUNCEMENTS. Messages that notify others or make a statement about something. An announcement may involve a major event or a relatively minor activity.

For example, a business may announce the development of an important new product or policy, or someone may simply announce the date of the next staff meeting. The latter type of announcement is commonly composed by the office staff.

Announcements may take any suitable form, from a newspaper notice to a brief letter or e-mail message to a printed card.

A formal announcement may resemble an INVITATION, as illustrated in Figure 1. An informal meeting announcement to coworkers may be sent as an e-mail message:

TO: Production Staff
SCHEDULED MEETING: February 6
TIME: 10:30 a.m.
PLACE: Second-floor cafeteria

If you have items for the agenda, please let me know by February 1. Also, let me know if you can't attend (Ext. 6614). Else I'll see you then.

APOLOGIES.   Messages that express regret about an event or situation, sometimes with an admission of error or with an explanation or defense.

Any situation that requires an apology also requires a conciliatory tone:

ANNOUNCEMENTS: FIGURE 1

Matthew, Deitrich, and Helmsley

Management Consultants

announce the opening

of their new offices

at 901 Biltmore Avenue, NW, Suite 5

Concord, CA 94529

Tuesday, July 24, 200X

Tim, I'm sorry that I wasn't able to give my presentation at yesterday's meeting.

As I mentioned when I called, it was impossible for me to attend, and I regret that my family emergency didn't allow you enough time to find a substitute.

Thanks much for covering for me.

The reply to an apology should also be conciliatory:

Don't worry about the meeting, Marie. We're pleased that your son is out of danger.

Ellen Stowe filled in for you with an impromptu description of her new plan to track late payers who move frequently. It all worked out fine.

However, we missed you, and everyone is looking forward to hearing your remarks at another meeting. I'll review the schedule for the rest of the year and will call you later this month to discuss a possible slot.

APPOINTMENTS. Messages that arrange meetings (see Chapter 4/MEETING) between two or more persons. Office personnel compose many of these messages, including those that ask for an appointment and those that grant one.

This type of message is usually brief, although it must carefully state the key facts of time and day, place, and purpose:

Ned Brown will be in Memphis on Tuesday, March 22 from 1 to 3 p.m., and he'd like to talk to you about the recent decision in the McNally case and how it affects overseas marketing.

Please let me know if you'll be available for a meeting at 2 o'clock on the 22nd. If that's not convenient, would another day or time be better?

Thanks very much.

The reply should restate the key facts of time and day, place, and purpose:

Susan has said that she'll be happy to meet with Ned in her office on Tuesday, March 22, at 2 o'clock to discuss the *McNally* decision. Tell him that she's looking forward to his visit.

See also REFUSALS for an example of a message that must say no.

APPRECIATION MESSAGES. GOODWILL messages that express gratitude for something that someone has done or said. For example, a message may thank someone for hospitality or assistance.

The tone should be genuine and friendly but never so effusive that the person's sincerity is not believable:

Liz, I attribute our recent increase in sales to your diligent and creative work on the ad campaign. You're a real asset to the company.

It was great to work with you, and I'm looking forward to planning next year's promotion.

ATTACHMENTS. Additional documents or other material, such as a report prepared in a word processing program (see Chapter 9/WORD PROCESSING), and included with an e-mail message. See also MEMOS; Chapter 2/E-MAIL.

Depending on the software being used, you may be able to attach either a straight text file or both text and graphics. (See Chapter 9/GRAPHICS.) The program may have an attachment icon (symbol) or button that, when clicked on with a mouse, will activate a list from which you can select the file to be sent.

An incoming e-mail message usually displays an attachment notice or icon to signal the recipient that a document has been included. By clicking on the words or the icon, the attachment will appear on screen for reading. It can also be saved in another file or folder or can be deleted.

ATTENTION LINE. The designation of a person (or department) in the INSIDE ADDRESS of a traditional LETTER, other than the addressee, who should receive and act on a message if the addressee is absent; the designation of a person who, if available, should act on a message addressed generally to a firm.

For example, a message may be addressed generally to a firm or department with a person named in the attention line. If that person is there, he or she will read the message. Otherwise, someone else in the firm or department will handle it.

Place the attention line against the left margin in the inside address on the first line if the letter is addressed generally to a firm or department. Omit titles, such as *Ms.* or *Mr.,* and begin with the word *Attention:*

Attention Joseph Bell
Barston Industries
[Address]

Place the attention line immediately after the addressee's name if the letter is addressed to a person:

Ms. Vivian Schummer
Attention Nora Deitrich
Barston Industries
[Address]

BAD-NEWS MESSAGES. A message with information that may affect the recipient adversely. Bad-news messages commonly involve orders, requests, credit, employment, and other matters that have a direct impact on a person's interests, needs, or welfare.

Because this type of information may involve private matters or reflect on someone personally, it's usually sent by postal mail in a sealed envelope. When a serious problem is involved, it may be more appropriate to meet in person rather than discuss the matter by mail.

Since bad-news messages may cause the recipient disappointment, embarrassment, or harm, they must be worded sensitively.

The sender frequently uses *buffers*—gentle openings that provide a cushion before the bad news is presented. Examples are compliments, thanks, and summaries of the circumstances necessitating the bad news.

The first paragraph in the following letter is a buffer in the form of a thank you:

> Thanks, Bill, for providing such a thorough analysis of our accounting practices and the need for departmental reorganization.

> As much as we appreciate your detailed study and would like to act on your recommendations, the budget for the next fiscal year is firm. We therefore won't be able to undertake such an extensive overhaul at this time.

> I know that you spent considerable time preparing the proposal, and we intend to reopen the matter next year during our annual budget review (September 1-November 1, 200X).

> If you have any interim measures to suggest that would not affect the budget, please let me know. Your ideas are always useful, Bill, and we hope you'll generate many more.

BODY. The part of a message that consists of the commentary. In a LETTER format, it usually has three main parts: (1) an opening sentence or paragraph introducing the purpose of the message, (2) the discussion paragraph or paragraphs, and (3) a final sentence or paragraph that closes the discussion, sometimes with a suggestion or request.

Begin the body as follows:

1. Two lines below the SALUTATION or SUBJECT in the block and traditional letter FORMATS

2. Three lines below the INSIDE ADDRESS or subject in the simplified-block letter format

3. Two or three lines below the guidewords (*To, From,* and so on), or headings, in a traditional MEMO or e-mail format

Single-space the paragraphs, with a blank space between them. Begin each paragraph against the left margin or indented, as preferred.

BUSINESS CARDS. Small cards of introduction providing the holder's name; company; street address; telephone, fax, and other numbers; e-mail address; and sometimes various other information, such as a company logo, slogan, advertising message, or Web site. See also Chapter 6/WEB SITE.

Format and style. A business card is usually about 3½ by 2 inches. Foldover styles may be 4 inches, folded in half to the same size as a single card.

The card stock used for business cards may have a shiny (coated) or matte finish. Most cards are white, off-white, or a pastel color, although more eye-catching colors may be preferred in certain businesses.

No rules exist concerning what may or may not be printed on a card or how the data should be arranged. For example, a card for an executive might have the person's name in the middle and his or her job title and firm name in the lower left corner. The street address, e-mail address, and various numbers might be placed in the lower right corner.

Staff members might have the firm name in the center and the person's name, title, and department in the lower left corner. The addresses and numbers might be placed in the lower right corner

Printers have numerous examples of different card stock, type styles, ink colors, and arrangements of data, and software is available to print your own cards.

Cards for international use. Businesspeople who distribute cards in other countries should have the information that appears on one side of the card translated into the recipient's language and printed on the other side.

Certain changes may be necessary for clarity in international use. For example, it's best to avoid abbreviations and spell out words such as *Parkway* and *Suite,* as well as compass directions such as *Northwest.* Telephone and fax numbers should include the complete international code. See also Chapter 2/INTERNATIONAL DIALING CODES.

COLLECTIONS. Messages sent to motivate people to pay past-due amounts. Although these letters are frequently prepared by specialists, the office staff should be familiar with the appropriate tone and pattern.

Most collection letters are developed as a series, from the first casual reminders that a payment is past due to the final demand for payment preceding legal action. The usual strategy in collection is to give the debtor a chance to pay before the creditor takes more serious action to collect.

Because these letters involve private financial matters, and because the sender may want a signed receipt, they are usually sent by sealed postal mail.

Before the formal series of letters is sent, office personnel may routinely send one or several invoices or notices. Printed forms or form letters may be used for such reminders:

> Just a friendly reminder that we would very much appreciate your payment of $97.50 for the five copies of our conference proceedings that you purchased on October 9.

> If your check is already in the mail, please disregard this notice and accept our thanks. If it is not, won't you take a moment to mail it today?

COMMERCIAL CARDS. Standard cards with printed messages available in greeting-card, stationery, and office-supply stores. A wide selection of card styles and messages is also available over the Internet (see Chapter 6/INTERNET; WEB SITE), and software is available for creating printed cards in-house.

Some cards are especially designed for business use, such as for HOLIDAY WISHES from the company. When many cards must be sent, a printed message and printed signature may be the only practical option.

In other cases, however, it's important to personalize a message. This can be done simply by writing a few words beneath the printed message or at least personally signing your name beneath the printed company name.

Some situations, such as thanking a colleague for a special gift or thanking an important customer for patronage, require more personal attention than the printed message on a card conveys. Such messages should be composed individually, printed on executive-size paper or regular business letterhead, and personally signed.

COMPLAINTS. Messages in which someone objects to something, such as a defective product, poor service, or improper behavior.

One should never compose a message of complaint while angry. The most effective complaints are clear, rational, and reasonable. Therefore, it's helpful to set aside the draft for a day (or more) and reread it before sending it.

Complaints are preferably sent by sealed postal mail, both to avoid accidentally transmitting an e-mail message before it's ready and to avoid embarrassing the recipient with an on-screen complaint that others might see:

I've completed a preliminary review of departmental travel activities during the past six months and notice that your travel costs are running ahead of related sales for the *Business Aids* series.

Let's meet next week to discuss the problem and perhaps develop a new strategy. Call me at extension 9191, and we'll set up an appointment. In the meantime, let's cancel all sales trips until a new plan is in place.

Thanks, Paul.

COMPLIMENTARY CLOSE. The closing phrase in a traditional LETTER that expresses the regard of the writer for the addressee.

The complimentary close will vary with the formality and tone of the letter, depending on how well the parties know each other. In this respect, the close should be consistent with the SALUTATION.

In domestic correspondence, both the close and the salutation are usually casual and friendly. In INTERNATIONAL MESSAGES, more formality is necessary since recipients in other countries tend to be much more reserved.

Place the close two lines below the last line of the BODY of the message in one of the following positions:

1. Against the left margin in the block letter FORMAT
2. Beginning at the center of the page (or slightly to the right of center) in the traditional format

Omit the close in the simplified-block letter format.

Common business closes are *Sincerely, Regards,* and *Best regards.* Examples of formal alternatives are *Sincerely yours* and *Yours very truly.*

CONFIDENTIAL NOTATION. See PERSONAL OR CONFIDENTIAL NOTATION.

CONGRATULATIONS. GOODWILL messages that recognize and commend someone for having accomplished something special or having attained a noteworthy status.

This type of message might be sent to someone who receives a professional or civic honor or a promotion, makes a speech, writes an article or book, retires from business, renders an outstanding community service, celebrates a business anniversary, and so on.

The message should be brief, be expressed naturally, and sound enthusiastic. To emphasize its personal character, such messages are often signed and sent as postal mail:

I was really pleased to read about your election as mayor of Albany, and I want to congratulate both you and your community.

I know that you'll bring the same outstanding abilities to this important position as those that helped make your business such a success.

All the best, Jim, in your exciting and challenging new position.

CONTINUATION PAGE.   Any page after the first page of a message. Whereas the computer automatically identifies and numbers successive pages of an e-mail message (see MEMOS; Chapter 2/E-MAIL), you need to insert the desired heading or page number on traditional LETTERS and MEMOS.

Use the same type of paper for a continuation page that you use for the letterhead (first) page of the message. Some companies have the firm name or name and address printed on continuation sheets, and any heading that you add is then placed two to three lines below the printed information.

The heading that you insert should contain the name of the addressee, the date of the message, and the page number. This information may be stacked or written on one line:

Henry Smith, July 7, 200X, page 2

Henry Smith
July 7, 200X
Page 2 [*or* two]

Carry at least two lines from the BODY on the first page over to the continuation page.

COPY NOTATION.   A notation used in correspondence to identify persons other than the addressee who will receive a copy of the message.

In traditional LETTERS and MEMOS, place the notation against the left margin, below the REFERENCE INITIALS, FILENAME, ENCLOSURE NOTATION, and DELIVERY NOTATION.

In e-mail messages (see MEMOS; Chapter 2/E-MAIL), fill in the names of the copy recipients after the appropriate initials, such as *cc* and *bc,* in the e-mail template (heading). See also Chapter 9/TEMPLATE.

Common notations are *c* or *Copy* (any type of copy), *cc* (a computer copy; any type of copy), *ec* (a paper copy of an e-mail message), *fc* (a fax copy), or *pc* (a photocopy):

cc: J. A. Williams
fc: B. T. Zimmerman

The blind-copy notation *bc,* which is seldom used, indicates that the addressee does not know that the bc recipient is receiving a copy. Therefore, it should appear *only* on the copy going to the bc recipient, *not* on the original sent to the addressee or on any copies going to others:

bc: J. A. Williams

See also DISTRIBUTION LIST.

CREDIT MESSAGES. Messages that request credit or that grant or deny credit. Many credit matters are handled routinely by FORMS, such as credit card application forms, and REFUSALS may be handled with a form LETTER.

Many nonroutine credit matters may be processed by telephone or over the Internet. (See Chapter 6/INTERNET.) For nonroutine matters or individual situations, a specially composed letter is necessary.

Because credit is usually a private financial concern, a letter involving a credit matter is commonly sent by postal mail in a sealed envelope:

> Our training department is interested in purchasing binders and pocket folders suitable for company orientation and training classes.

> We currently spend from $300 to $500 a month on such material. Would you be able to extend your usual credit terms to our department for amounts in that range?

> I'm enclosing the name of our bank and other suppliers who are presently extending credit to us. If you need additional information for us to establish an account with you, please let me know.

DATE. The day, month, and year listed beneath the letterhead address in a LETTER format or entered after the guideword *Date* in a MEMO format. In an e-mail message (see MEMOS; Chapter 2/E-MAIL), the software automatically inserts the date.

Position the date as follows in a letter:

1. In the block and simplified-block FORMATS, against the left margin two or more lines (depending on the length of the letter) below the printed letterhead data

2. In the traditional format, beginning at the center of the page (or slightly right of the center), two or more lines below the printed letterhead data

The proper style in general business correspondence is *October 4, 200X.* Companies in other countries, the military, and, less commonly, other organizations use the style *4 October 200X.*

All numerals, such as *10/4/0X,* should not be used since it's uncertain how recipients may read the numbers. In many countries, for example, *10/4/0X* means April 10, 200X.

DELIVERY NOTATION. A notation sometimes used on correspondence to indicate a particular class or treatment of mail or a particular form of transmission.

In LETTERS and MEMOS, place a notation such as *By Federal Express* or *By fax* two lines beneath the REFERENCE INITIALS, FILENAME, and ENCLOSURE NOTATION. (Also put it on the ENVELOPE in postal mail when a special service, such as *Registered Mail,* is included.)

DISTRIBUTION LIST. A list of the people on an e-mail mailing list or the recipients of an e-mail message. See also MEMOS; Chapter 2/E-MAIL.

Rather than reenter a long list of names each time a message is sent to the same people, you may use an *alias,* or designated name, to direct an e-mail message to a group of people on a network.

Alternatively, you can enter the names of all recipients after the *cc* and *bc* guidewords on the e-mail template. See also COPY NOTATION; Chapter 9/TEMPLATE.

E-MAIL. See MEMOS, Figure 2; Chapter 2/E-MAIL; E-MAIL COMMUNICATION; E-MAIL ETIQUETTE.

E-MAIL ETIQUETTE. See Chapter 2/E-MAIL ETIQUETTE; Chapter 6/NETIQUETTE.

EMOTICONS. See Chapter 6/EMOTICONS.

ENCLOSURE NOTATION. The notation used in a LETTER or MEMO format to indicate that the communication includes one or more enclosures.

Place the notation, usually abbreviated as *Enc.* or *Encs.,* against the left margin, one or two lines beneath the REFERENCE INITIALS and FILENAME.

Indicate the number of enclosures, or identify the enclosures immediately after the abbreviation:

Encs. 3

Enc.: Policy 36-4698-M (to be returned)

Encs.: Check
     Brochure

ENVELOPES. The various paper mailing containers, most commonly identified in correspondence as No. 10 (about 4⅛ by 9⅛ inches) envelopes or No. 9 (about 3⅞ by 8⅞ inches) envelopes. The No. 10 size is the most common. See also STATIONERY.

The items in the address on an envelope are usually the same as those in the INSIDE ADDRESS. Follow the current requirements of the U.S. Postal Service (see Chapter 2/UNITED STATES POSTAL Service) for preparing the address. See also Figures 1 and 2.

The Postal Service requirements are also generally acceptable to private delivery services. Private services, however, often provide their own mailing containers and print a mailing label with the address that you supply. Consult the particular company for details.

For the No. 10 or No. 9 envelopes used in postal mail, leave a bottom margin of at least ⅝ inch and left and right margins of at least 1 inch. Recent software will automatically place the address in the correct location.

The traditional format is the basic arrangement and style that has been used in postal mail for decades. The optical-character-reader (OCR) format was developed by the U.S. Postal Service for rapid mail sorting.

ENVELOPES: FIGURE 1
Traditional Envelope Format

Writing Consultants, Inc.
500 Stateside Parkway, Suite 25
Austin, TX 78712

REGISTERED

Mr. Paul Anderson
The Business School
12 Harrington Place
Greenpoint, NJ 07201

ENVELOPES: FIGURE 2
OCR Envelope Format

Writing Consultants, Inc.
500 Stateside Parkway, Suite 25
Austin, TX 78712

ATTN MR JV DAVID
WEST INDUSTRIES
22 E 62 ST RM 1400
MILWAUKEE WI 12345

Depending on the postal equipment being used, the address block must appear within the specified boundaries of 5/8 inch for the bottom and 1 inch for the left and right margins for OCR sorting. The address data should be prepared using regular capitalization or all capital letters, with approved postal abbreviations, and omitting all punctuation:

ATTN MR JV DAVIS
WEST INDUSTRIES
22 E 62 ST RM 1400
MILWAUKEE WI 12345

More recent postal equipment, however, can scan even handwritten addresses. For current addressing information, consult your local post office or the latest issue of the U.S. Postal Service's *Domestic Mail Manual* or *International Mail Manual.*

FILENAME NOTATION. A notation used on correspondence to designate the name given to a message for purposes of storage and retrieval.

Place the notation below the REFERENCE INITIALS:

vmadis.ltr

If you include the recipient's filename (or other reference), place it below your filename, and add *Our file/ref.* and *Your file/ref.* for clarity:

Our file: vmadis.ltr
Your file: parsons.doc

FOLLOW-UPS. Messages requesting a response to unanswered correspondence or other communication. If unacknowledged material in a follow-up file is not answered by a specified date, send a follow-up message. See also Chapter 3/Follow-up system.

Follow-up messages should identify the original communication or event or include a copy of the original message (if it was detailed) and request a prompt reply:

> Have you had a moment to consider our request to use some of your marketing ideas in our *Real Estate Guide*, with proper credit to you? In case our original request didn't reach you, I'm enclosing a copy of it.

> We'd like to include this information in the next issue of the guide but will need your reply by our deadline, December 15. I'd therefore appreciate hearing from you by that date.

> Thanks very much.

FORMAT. The shape and size of a document and the general arrangement of its elements; the physical arrangement of the parts of a document on the page.

In correspondence, the positions of the parts of a message are largely governed by current practice, although alternatives are available.

Three common LETTER formats used in business are the *block* (also called *full-block*), *traditional* (also called *modified-block*), and *simplified-block formats*. For examples, see LETTERS, Figures 1–3.

Two common MEMO formats are the *traditional* and *e-mail formats*. The two are very similar, with only minor differences. For examples, see MEMOS, Figures 1 and 2.

Two common ENVELOPE formats are the *traditional* and *optical-character-reader (OCR) formats*. For examples, see ENVELOPES, Figures 1 and 2.

See also Chapter 9/FORMAT.

FORMS. Standard messages, fill-in documents, and stock phrases, clauses, and paragraphs used in repetitive situations. Because the entire message need not be prepared from scratch, forms can save time and money.

For correspondence, standard messages can be stored in the computer and printed individually as needed. New facts can also be edited into a stored form and a copy printed as needed.

With merge features, it's possible to incorporate into a standard message the individual names from a mailing list, as well as other personalized information, such as products that a customer previously purchased, so that each message appears original.

Since many LETTERS, MEMOS, and other communications can be turned into generic forms, office professionals may find it useful to begin collecting samples of repetitive messages, such as meeting notices or APPOINTMENT confirmations, in a forms file.

If a company doesn't already have standard messages to use in repetitive matters, forms can be created and organized for later retrieval.

GOODWILL MESSAGES. Thoughtful messages that are intended to generate feelings of support and approval and to create a favorable impression of the writer and his or her company. See, for example, APPRECIATION MESSAGES; CONGRATULATIONS.

HOLIDAY WISHES. Brief messages that convey warm wishes to clients, customers, and others on special holidays, such as Thanksgiving, Christmas, Hanukkah, Kwanzaa, and New Year's Day.

Messages are traditionally printed on business letterhead or smaller-size executive STATIONERY or may be added to COMMERCIAL CARDS. Greetings can also be selected from samples available over the Internet. See also Chapter 6/INTERNET; WEB SITE.

Unless numerous cards are being sent, traditional commercial cards should be personally signed beneath the printed company name.

Although some Web sites (see Chapter 6/WEB SITE) offer large selections of electronic greetings, companies may prefer to send clients, customers, and other important contacts a more personal and traditional greeting.

Traditional messages often express appreciation for the recipient's support, patronage, friendship, confidence, cooperation, and so on:

> The winter holidays remind me of the many things for which we're grateful at Concord Plastics. At the top of the list is our association with loyal customers like you.

> It's always a pleasure to work with you, Marilyn, and all of us at Concord are looking forward to a New Year of continued service to your company.

> Very best wishes to you and your associates for a wonderful holiday season.

INFORMATIONAL MESSAGES. Messages that request, provide, or acknowledge information. See also ACKNOWLEDGMENTS; REQUESTS.

Office professionals write many requests and acknowledgments and provide routine information, particularly when their employers are absent:

> Thanks for asking Ms. Cole about our Model ABC office copier. Although she's presently away from the office, I wanted to let you know that this machine is currently in stock and is available for $1,560.

> I'm enclosing a brochure that may answer a few of your questions, and I know that Ms. Cole will be happy to answer further questions after she returns on Monday, September 20.

> In the meantime, you might like to visit one of our showrooms at the addressees listed on the enclosed brochure.

INSIDE ADDRESS. The name and address of the addressee in a LETTER format. The inside address is omitted from a traditional memo and an e-mail message. See also MEMOS; Chapter 2/E-MAIL.

Generally, the information in the inside address and that in the address block on an ENVELOPE should be the same. The address on the envelope, however, may be written in all capital letters, without punctuation, and with various words abbreviated. See ENVELOPES, Figure 2.

With most word processing programs (see Chapter 9/WORD PROCESSING), you can create a macro for the inside address (or inside address and SALUTATION) of any person you write to frequently, thereby eliminating the need to reenter the information each time.

Place the inside address against the left margin two or more lines below the DATE, and follow these basic guidelines:

1. Precede a person's name with a title, such as *Mr., Ms.,* or *Dr.* (*Ms.,* however, is seldom used in other countries).

2. Place a short business title, such as *Editor,* after the name and a long title, such as *Vice President of Marketing and Sales,* on the next line.

3. Place abbreviations indicating scholastic degrees *after* a name.

4. Use only the abbreviations of the highest degree held by the person. Place the one pertaining to the person's profession first if there are two or more equally high degrees.

5. For attorneys and other persons who use *Esq.* (*Esquire*), place the abbreviation after the name, and omit any title before the name.

For examples of the inside address in letters to persons holding official or honorary titles, see Part Four/FORMS OF ADDRESS.

Use traditional capitalization and punctuation in the inside address:

Ms. Linda Johnson
McDaniels & Associates
1341 West Avenue
New York, NY 10011

In international addresses, place the country name on the last line by itself:

Mr. Neville Hurst
Crandall's Outlet Stores Ltd.
50 Garden Lane
London WIP 6HQ
ENGLAND

INTERNATIONAL MESSAGES. LETTERS, e-mails (see MEMOS; Chapter 2/E-MAIL), and other messages sent outside the United States to residents of other countries.

Although the same FORMAT may be used for domestic and international correspondence, different rules apply to the composition of an international message:

1. Avoid idioms, jargon, and other language that, when translated literally, may be unclear to an international reader. See also Chapter 7/IDIOM; JARGON.

2. Punctuate more heavily to help guide international readers through each sentence.

3. Use short words, sentences, and paragraphs that will be easier to translate.

4. Spell out an abbreviation on first use, and enclose the abbreviated version in parentheses immediately after the spelled-out version.

5. Be strictly consistent in punctuation, capitalization, spelling, and other usage matters to avoid confusing the reader with unexplained changes.

6. Avoid using people's first names, unless asked to do so, and use greater formality than you would use with a domestic reader.

7. Use the personal and professional titles common in the particular country, such as *Señorita* (*Miss*) and *Señora* (*Mrs.*).

8. Do not address an international reader as *Ms.*, which is rarely used outside the United States.

9. Follow the style of the other country in the order of family names, as in *Mr. Yam Mun Hoh, Dear Mr. Yam.*

10. Avoid controversial topics, such as politics, or other topics that may be forbidden, such as sex.

11. Respect the practices of other countries, such as not conducting business in the first letter and the preference for referring to a person's company (*your company*) rather than the individual (*you*).

12. When English is not the language used for business in the other country, have your letter translated into the recipient's language.

See also Chapter 5/INTERNATIONAL ENGLISH; INTERNATIONAL TRAVEL.

INTEROFFICE COMMUNICATION. See MEMOS.

INTRODUCTIONS. Messages that introduce one person to another or that acquaint someone with a product, service, organization, idea, or other item.

Although an introduction may be prepared traditionally or electronically, a paper copy is sometimes given to the subject to deliver in person. For example, a job seeker may want to have copies of an introduction letter to hand out to prospective employers.

A general SALUTATION should be used when the recipient is unknown. *To Whom It May Concern* is a common greeting in such cases, although some writers prefer something friendlier, such as *Dear Reader.*

An introduction is written in the spirit of asking a favor. When a person is being introduced, the message should include the name of the subject, the reason for the introduction, other relevant details, and a statement to the effect that any courtesy shown to the subject will be appreciated:

It's a pleasure to introduce Maxine Bell, CPS, to you as a possible candidate for a supervisory or administrative position with your firm. She'll soon be contacting you to request an interview.

Maxine is presently employed at the Middleton Paper Mill as a supervisor. We previously worked together before I left to move to the West Coast. During the five years of our association, she was the perfect employee—responsible, highly capable, and a thoroughly delightful person to know.

I'd appreciate any consideration that you can extend to her. Thanks very much.

INVITATIONS. Formal or informal messages requesting someone's presence at, or participation in, an event. Informal invitations, such as an invitation to address a group, are usually prepared in a LETTER format on business letterhead and sent by postal mail.

Very informal invitations, such as a request sent to a friend to join you for lunch, may be issued by telephone, e-mail (see MEMOS; Chapter 2/E-MAIL), or any other suitable method.

Formal invitations, such as an invitation to attend a company's 25th anniversary party, are commonly printed (or engraved) on heavy white or off-white paper in a traditional invitation format. In this format, each line is centered, except for the concluding *R.s.v.p.* (please reply) line, which begins at the left margin. See Figure 1.

INVITATIONS: FIGURE 1: Company Invitation

Harrison L. Olmstead II

President and General Manager

of

Bentley Distributors Incorporated

cordially invites you to

cocktails

to celebrate the company's tenth year of service

Saturday, September 16

5 to 7 p.m.

1800 Skyview Drive

Scottsdale, Arizona

R.s.v.p card enclosed

Formal business invitations follow essentially the same guidelines used for social invitations:

1. State the day of the event but not the year.

2. State the time in numerals, such as *7 p.m.*, in general company invitations, such as an invitation to an open house.

3. State the time in words, such as *at half after* [or *past*] *seven o'clock*, for socially oriented formal events, such as a private dinner for a few executives or clients.

4. Abbreviate *Mr., Ms., Mrs., Dr., Jr., Sr.*, and so on in general company invitations, the same as in other business correspondence, but spell out *senior* and *junior* in socially oriented formal events.

The trend is toward informality in business invitations, with the exception of private social events hosted by high-ranking officials or executives.

Fill-in reply cards are usually included, unless an event is open to the public and no replies are expected. See Figure 2.

Although both invitations and reply cards can be created in-house with the appropriate equipment and software, outside printers commonly handle this task. They have numerous samples with various styles of wording, arrangement of data, typefaces, and so on.

INVITATIONS: FIGURE 2: Reply Card

M_____

Accepts _____   Regrets _____

Saturday, September 16
Bentley Distributors Incorporated

Etiquette books also have samples and discuss in detail the requirements for invitations to dinners, lunches, receptions, balls, and various other business and social activities.

LETTERS. Traditionally styled messages that include an INSIDE ADDRESS, SALUTATION, COMPLIMENTARY CLOSE, and SIGNATURE line in the block and traditional FORMATS and an inside address and signature line in the simplified-block format. Compare with MEMOS.

Letters are printed on paper and are delivered by postal mail or private delivery service or are transmitted by fax. See also Chapter 2/FAX TRANSMISSION; PRIVATE DELIVERY SERVICES; UNITED STATES POSTAL SERVICE.

For sample letters, see ACCEPTANCES; ACKNOWLEDGMENTS; ADJUSTMENTS; ANNOUNCEMENTS; APOLOGIES; APPOINTMENTS; APPRECIATION MESSAGES; BAD-NEWS MESSAGES; COLLECTIONS; COMPLAINTS; CONGRATULATIONS; CREDIT MESSAGES; FOLLOW-UPS; HOLIDAY WISHES; INFORMATIONAL MESSAGES; INTRODUCTIONS; INVITATIONS; REFUSALS; REMINDERS; REQUESTS; SALES PROMOTION MESSAGES; SYMPATHY MESSAGES; THANK YOU'S; TRANSMITTALS.

See also ENVELOPES; FORMS; GOODWILL MESSAGES; INTERNATIONAL MESSAGES; STATIONERY.

Parts of a letter. The basic parts of a letter, usually appearing in the following order, are the DATE, PERSONAL OR CONFIDENTIAL NOTATION, INSIDE ADDRESS, SALUTATION, SUBJECT, BODY, COMPLIMENTARY CLOSE, SIGNATURE, REFERENCE INITIALS, FILENAME, ENCLOSURE NOTATION, DELIVERY NOTATION, COPY NOTATION, and POSTSCRIPT.

Letter formats. Three common formats used in business are the *block letter format* (see Figure 1), the *simplified-block letter format* (see Figure 2), and the *traditional letter format* (see Figure 3).

The block format is one of the most widely used business styles, although the traditional style is still preferred in some conservative organizations, such as banks and law firms. Some writers also prefer the traditional style for SOCIAL–BUSINESS LETTERS, such as letters to persons in the community concerning a company social event.

The International Association of Administrative Professionals uses the simplified-block format, in which the SALUTATION and COMPLIMENTARY CLOSE are omitted. See also Chapter 1/INTERNATIONAL ASSOCIATION OF ADMINISTRATION PROFESSIONALS.

MEMOS. Informal messages that substitute a heading of guidewords with fill-in information for the INSIDE ADDRESS, SALUTATION, COMPLIMENTARY CLOSE, and SIGNATURE LINE used in a letter format.

LETTERS: FIGURE 1: Block Letter Format

July 16, 200X

Ms. Sheila Jones
The Business School
12 Harrington Place
Greenpoint, NJ 07201

Dear Ms. Jones:

BLOCK LETTER FORMAT

As you requested, this is an example of the block format, used in many businesses.

The letter has no indentions, and when the person who writes it is also the signer, his or her reference initials are not needed.

Please let us know, Ms. Jones, if we can help you in any other way. We appreciate your interest.

Sincerely,

Martha Scott
Correspondence Chief

hc

jones.ltr

Memos were originally designed as a less formal means of interoffice communication. In time, the use of the memo FORMAT widened to include outside associates and regular customers and clients. The modern e-mail message (see MEMOS; Chapter 2/E-MAIL) is styled after the traditional memo.

LETTERS: FIGURE 2: Simplified-Block Letter Format

July 16, 200X

Ms. Rosiland Warner
The Business School
12 Harrington Place
Greenpoint, NJ 07210

SIMPLIFIED-BLOCK LETTER FORMAT

Here's an example of the simplified-block letter format that
you inquired about, Ms. Warner. This style omits the salutation
and complimentary close and leaves extra space above and below
the subject and above the signature.

Please let us know, Ms. Warner, if you have any other
questions. We appreciate your interest.

Martha Scott
Correspondence Chief

hc

c: Ben Shaw

P.S. More about formats is available at our Web site:
www.writingconsultants.com. MS

Memos may be printed on memo letterhead, regular business letterhead, or
special-size memo paper, as preferred. Commercial forms, such as multiple-copy
sets and fast-message forms that provide a place for the recipient to reply, are
also widely used.

LETTERS: FIGURE 3: Traditional Letter Format

July 16, 200X

Mr. Paul Anderson
The Business School
12 Harrington Place
Greenpoint, NJ 07201

Dear Mr. Anderson:

TRADITIONAL LETTER FORMAT

Thanks for requesting an example of a traditional letter format. This letter is prepared in that style.

The traditional format is the same as the block format, with two exceptions: Each paragraph is indented, and the date, closing, and signature data begin at the center of the page.

Please let us know, Mr. Anderson, if we can offer any other information. We appreciate your interest in our models.

Sincerely,

Martha Scott
Correspondence Chief

hc

Enc.: List of Guidelines

By Global Overnight Express

Parts of a memo.   The main parts of a memo are the template (see Chapter 9/TEMPLATE), or heading, consisting of the guidewords and spaces where you fill in the appropriate data, followed by the Body, Reference initials, Filename, Enclosure notation, Delivery notation, Copy notation, and Postscript.

The body in a traditional memo format is composed the same as the body in a Letter format. For examples, see Acceptances; Acknowledgments; Adjustments; Announcements; Appointments; Appreciation messages; Follow-ups; Informational messages; Introductions; Reminders; Requests; Transmittals.

E-mail messages, which are read on a computer screen, should be more succinct. For special guidelines that apply to e-mail, see Chapter 2/E-mail; E-mail communication; E-mail etiquette.

Memo formats. Two common formats are the *traditional memo format* (see Figure 1) and the *e-mail format* (see Figure 2).

Both formats begin with standard guidewords, such as *Date, To, From,* and *Subject,* and others may be added as needed. In a traditional memo, the information must be inserted after each word. In an e-mail message, the software automatically inserts the date and time as well as the recipient's name, if it's already in an address file.

The e-mail template also includes guidewords for "carbon" copies and blind copies. (See Copy notation.) In a traditional memo, these notations are inserted *after* the body of the memo.

OCR addressing. See Envelopes.

Personal or confidential notation. A notation placed on a Letter and the Envelope when no one but the addressee is supposed to open and read the letter.

Place the word *Personal* or *Confidential* against the left margin two to four lines beneath the Date. On the envelope, place it a couple lines beneath the return address.

Postscript. An additional thought unrelated to the subject of a Letter or Memo, but not something that one merely forgot to include in the letter Body.

Begin the postscript with the initials *P.S.* (or *PS*), and place it two lines below the last notation of the letter or memo. See the example in Letters, Figure 2. Indent the left margin if you also indent the paragraphs in the body, such as in the traditional letter Format.

Avoid having more than one postscript, but if two are essential, begin the second with *P.P.S.* (or *PPS*).

MEMOS: FIGURE 1: Traditional Memo Format

TO: Bernard Stein

DATE: May 11, 200X

FROM: Martha Scott

SUBJECT: Traditional Memo

You asked about formatting traditional memos, Bernie: As you can see from this example, the body and all notations are handled the same as in a block, simplified-block, or traditional letter.

However, memos have no salutation, complimentary close, signature line, or inside address. Nevertheless, some writers like to leave an extra space after the body and sign their initials.

Hope this answers your questions, Bernie.

MS

hc

stein.memo

Enc.: Format Manual

By fax

c: Roy Williamson, Jr.

P.S. I'll see you at the board meeting on Friday. MS

Add the initials of the person writing the letter at the end of the postscript, with no concluding period:

P.S. I hope that your report is coming along nicely. I'm looking forward to reading it. JMC

MEMOS: FIGURE 2: E-Mail Format

From: Martha Scott <mscott@wcinc.org>
To: Lillian Schiller <lschiller@cyberline.com>
Date: Monday, May 01, 200X 11:50 AM
Subject: E-Mail Format

I agree, Lillian: Although it's easy to format traditional memos with word processing software, the automatic setup of e-mail is even more appealing.

The templates are so clear that even beginners should have no problem filling in the information. Users can also add more guidewords and, with many programs, can automatically insert a detailed signature block at the end of the message, such as the one that appears at the end of this e-mail.

I hope that we can pursue this discussion further on June 5 at the business communicators' meeting. In the meantime, Lillian, thanks so much for your prompt response to my inquiry. It was a big help.

****

Martha Scott, Correspondence Chief
Writing Consultants, Inc.
500 Stateside Parkway, Suite 25
Austin, TX 78712
Tel: 512.555.2190
Fax: 512.555.2191

REFERENCE INITIALS. The first of the concluding notations in a LETTER or traditional MEMO format indicating who wrote or dictated the message and who transcribed or prepared the printed copy.

If the person composing and signing the message are the same, his or her initials are usually omitted, and only the initials of the person preparing the final computer copy (if someone else) are given.

Place the initials against the left margin two lines below the SIGNATURE in a letter or below the last line of the BODY in a memo:

rt	The same person who writes the letter signs it, and only the initials of the computer operator, if any, are needed.
SRD:rt	The same person composes and signs the letter, another prepares the computer copy, and the company requires both to be listed (less common).
HRL:SRD:rt	One person dictates the message, another signs it, a third prepares the final copy, and the company requires that all three be identified (used only in special occasions).

REFUSALS. Messages that say no. Because of the sensitive nature of many refusals, such as a refusal to grant CREDIT or a refusal to promote someone, these messages are often sent by postal mail in a sealed envelope:

I was happy to see the progress report that you sent me last week, Kelly. I can see that you've done an excellent job during your first six months with our firm.

Although I'm certainly impressed with your record and am pleased that you're eager to make further contributions, company policy prevents me from considering a salary increase for you until the end of your first year of employment.

In March 200X, therefore, our review board will automatically evaluate your record and will let you know the results, as well as any decisions about a salary increase. I'm forwarding your progress report to the board so that it will be in your file when the review takes place.

In the meantime, Kelly, I'll be happy to answer any questions you have and hope that you'll continue to enjoy your association with Wexler Associates as much as we enjoy having you here.

REMINDERS. Usually brief messages that call someone's attention to an approaching deadline or event or to some other matter. Reminders may be sent simply as a precaution to be certain that the recipient won't forget something, or they may be sent because the recipient has already forgotten or is likely to forget.

Office professionals compose and send many of these messages by postal mail, fax, or e-mail.

When deadlines or specific dates are involved, as they often are, the reminder should restate key facts or enclose a copy of an earlier communication with full details:

> John, I hope that you're still planning to attend our August 23 committee meeting. Since it's only a week away, I'd like to get an early head count to be certain that we'll have a quorum.
>
> Please telephone me at extension 2151 or e-mail me to confirm that you'll be there.
>
> Thanks.

REQUESTS.   Messages that ask for something, such as assistance or information. Although many requests are brief, those that involve persuasion, such as a request to head a fund-raising campaign or donate to a charity, should have more detail.

Routine requests are commonly prepared by the office staff. In-house requests and those to services and suppliers may be prepared in a traditional MEMO format. Other requests may be sent as an e-mail message (see MEMOS; Chapter 2/E-mail) or as a paper LETTER. Some may be standard messages (see FORMS) with individual, personal facts inserted:

> As a valued member for many years, Ms. Pennington, we're naturally concerned about your recent decision to discontinue your membership.
>
> However, from past experience, we know that circumstances change, and we're always eager to tailor our membership benefits to the changing needs of our members. Therefore, we'd appreciate it if you would take a few minutes to answer the following question and return this letter in the enclosed postage-paid envelope.
>
> I discontinued my membership for the following reasons:
>
> ( ) Cost   ( ) No longer working in this field   ( ) Retired   ( ) Other

---

> Let us hear from you, Ms. Pennington, and we'll do our best to serve your needs and interests more fully in the future.

SALES PROMOTION MESSAGES.   Messages that stimulate interest in and acceptance of a product, service, organization, idea, program, or something else.

Most sales promotion letters are prepared by specialists, often as part of a larger marketing or advertising plan.

The message may be a standard response, with individual facts merged to give the communication a personal character:

> We're happy to send you the new Office Aids catalog that you requested, Mr. Shaw. The self-adhesive labels that you asked about are described on page 11.
>
> These labels are still available in a continuous strip for fast computer addressing, and **a new feature has been added:** You may have your company's name and address imprinted in your choice of bold black, brilliant blue, or bright red.
>
> If you like, **we'll even add your company logo** to ensure quick recognition by your customers. What better way to cash in on your good name?
>
> For a limited time, label imprinting is being offered to special customers like you for **half price!** That's right—for any order you place within the next 30 days, you may **deduct a full 50 percent from the cost of imprinting!** Just follow the easy instructions on the enclosed order blank.
>
> Mail or fax your order to us at 800-555-7701 within 30 days. Or call us *toll-free* at 800-555-7702.
>
> We look forward to hearing from you!

SALUTATION. A greeting to the recipient of a message. A salutation is used in the block and traditional LETTER formats but is omitted in the simplified-block letter FORMAT.

Place the salutation two lines below the INSIDE ADDRESS against the left margin. Capitalize each main word, and end the salutation with a colon.

The following examples are common forms for businesspeople. See also Part Four/FORMS OF ADDRESS for the proper forms to be used with officials:

1. Follow the practices in your office concerning the use of first names.

2. When first names are not used and the addressee has a scholastic title, such as *Dr.,* use it instead of a personal title, such as *Mr.* or *Ms.*

3. Don't use *Ms.* in salutations to people in other countries (use the country's equivalent of *Miss* or *Mrs.*). See also INTERNATIONAL MESSAGES.

4. Spell out religious, military, and most professional titles, such as *Sister, Colonel,* and *Professor.*

5. Omit the salutation, or use *Ladies and Gentlemen* in letters that are addressed generally to a firm, rather than to an individual or a department.

6. Use a departmental manager's title, such as *Dear Education Manager,* when a letter addressed generally to a firm also identifies the department.

7. Use a collective term, such as *Dear Friends* or *Dear Employee,* in a letter sent to a group of men and women.

8. Use the individual names when only a few people are involved: *Dear Dr. Snow, Ms. Randall, and Mr. Thomas.*

9. Repeat the titles with the names when two women have the same title: *Dear Ms. Carstairs and Ms. Dashell.*

10. Use *Mss.* with the individual names for three or more women who have the same title: *Dear Mss. Porter, Findley, Hall, and Watts.*

11. Repeat the titles with the names when two men have the same title: *Dear Mr. Foster and Mr. Gianelli.*

12. Use *Messrs.* with individual names for three or more men who have the same title, as in *Dear Messrs. Foster, Gianelli, Barston, and Rogers.*

13. Use all names and respective titles when both men and women are included, listing the names by employment rank or, if rank is the same, in alphabetical order: *Dear Dr. Lawson and Ms. Carter; Dear Ms. Carter and Mr. Lawson.*

14. Use a job title when both name and gender are unknown but the position is known: *Dear Finance Editor.*

15. Use the person's first name or initials when the gender is unknown: *Dear K. B. Thompson.*

SIGNATURE. The part of a LETTER that consists of the writer's name and, sometimes, business title, as well as the person's handwritten signature.

Place the writer's name about four lines below the COMPLIMENTARY CLOSE in the block and traditional FORMATS and about five lines below the letter BODY in the simplified-block format. See the examples in LETTERS, Figures 1–3.

If the person's name is already listed as part of the letterhead data, it's usually omitted from the signature line at the end of the letter, and only the handwritten signature is added.

The name of the company may also be included in a signature line to formal documents or in a letter representing an official company statement, such as an auditor's statement.

Place the company name two lines below the complimentary close and the writer's name about four lines below the firm name:

Sincerely yours,

FARNSWORTH ACCOUNTING SERVICES

Donald Whitaker

Donald Whitaker, CPA
General Manager

In domestic correspondence, place the titles *Mr.* and *Ms.* in parentheses before a name only if the person's gender is unclear from the name alone:

R. R. Phillips

(Mr.) R. R. Phillips
Vice President, Sales

However, include *Ms.* in parentheses before your name in international correspondence since readers in other countries don't use this title and will address you as *Miss* or *Mrs.* if you don't specify *Ms.* When you omit the title in the signature line of regular domestic correspondence, it's assumed that you use the title *Ms.:*

Eleanor Davis

Eleanor Davis

When you sign another's name to a letter, place your initials immediately below the handwritten signature, or put your initials in parentheses after the name:

Miriam R. Jones (tk)

Miriam R. Jones
President

When you sign a letter in your own name and your supervisor's name is part of your job title, omit the supervisor's first name or initials, and use only his or her personal or professional title (unless someone else in the firm has the same last name):

Elizabeth Mason

Elizabeth Mason
Assistant to Mr. Nelson

SOCIAL–BUSINESS LETTERS. Messages pertaining to company social occasions, such as an invitation to a company-sponsored dinner, or messages generated by a company for nonbusiness situations, such as a SYMPATHY message to an employee's family.

Social–business messages may be ANNOUNCEMENTS, APPRECIATION MESSAGES, CONGRATULATIONS, GOODWILL MESSAGES, HOLIDAY WISHES, INVITATIONS, SYMPATHY MESSAGES, or THANK YOU'S.

STATIONERY. The letterhead and envelopes used for business messages, including LETTERS and MEMOS.

Paper. Business messages are often printed on 20- or 24-pound, white or off-white bond paper. Higher-ranking executives may use a 25, 50, 75, or 100 percent cotton-content paper or a high-grade sulfite bond. Higher-grade papers may also be *watermarked,* or impressed with a translucent mark or design.

For regular office use, many businesses choose recycled papers, many of which can't be distinguished from nonrecycled products.

Paper is also classified according to intended use, such as for laser printers or fax machines. Multifunction paper, suitable for printers, copiers, and plain-paper faxes, is also common.

Sizes. Standard letterhead is 8½ by 11 inches. When folded twice, it will fit into a standard No. 10 ENVELOPE (about 4⅛ by 9⅛ inches) or a slightly smaller No. 9 envelope (about 3⅞ by 8⅞ inches).

Smaller envelopes, such as the No. 6¾ (about 3⅝ by 6½ inches), are used for notes, invoices, and other small-size material.

Executive-size paper, sometimes called *Monarch* (about 7¼ by 10½ inches), may be used for SOCIAL-BUSINESS LETTERS, such as a SYMPATHY MESSAGE or THANK YOU letter. It can be folded twice to fit into a small matching Monarch envelope.

Printing. Because of the high cost of engraving stationery, most business stationery is printed (see Chapter 9/OFFSET PRINTING), sometimes by a process called *thermography,* which creates raised letters.

Paper and printing for continuation pages, or second sheets, should match the letterhead sheets and envelopes.

A different design may be used for memo letterhead, but often the same stationery is used for both letters and memos. However, some companies design memo paper that includes the guidewords *Date, To, From, Subject,* and so on printed just beneath the company name and address data.

Large companies that have in-house desktop publishing (see Chapter 9/DESKTOP PUBLISHING) and printing capabilities may design and print their own stationery. Those that use outside printing services will find that printers have numerous examples of letterheads, envelopes, and BUSINESS CARDS.

SUBJECT.   The topic of a message, indicated in a subject line at the beginning of a LETTER or following the *Subject* guideword in a traditional MEMO or e-mail message. See also MEMOS; Chapter 2/E-MAIL.

Place the subject against the left margin two lines *beneath* the SALUTATION in a block or traditional letter and three lines below the INSIDE ADDRESS in a simplified-block letter.

In a business letter, the subject is considered part of the body. In legal correspondence, the words *In re* are commonly used to introduce the subject, and the subject line is placed two lines *above* the salutation.

The word *Subject* is one of the guidewords in the template (see Chapter 9/TEMPLATE) of an e-mail message and often is printed in the heading of a traditional memo (but may be omitted). In a letter, however, the word *Subject* is often omitted from the subject line.

No punctuation follows *In re* in legal writing, but when the word *Subject* is included in a traditional letter, a colon should follow it.

Capitalize the important words in a subject line, or write the entire line in all capital letters.

Although single-subject messages are preferred, especially in e-mail, if more than one subject is included, use a more general subject line to cover all of the subjects:

JOB-TRAINING BROCHURE [single subject]

JOB ORIENTATION AND TRAINING [multiple subjects]

See the enclosed examples of a subject line in LETTERS, Figures 1 to 3, and MEMOS, Figures 1 and 2.

SYMPATHY MESSAGES.   Brief messages of condolence or acknowledgments of such messages, written upon death, personal injury or illness, or material loss or damage.

Because of the personal nature of such situations, the messages are often sent on executive-size stationery used for SOCIAL-BUSINESS LETTERS.

Personal sympathy messages should be handwritten, sometimes as a note added to a COMMERCIAL CARD. Messages sent on behalf of a company are commonly computer generated. However, if desired, executives may also handwrite a personal message on executive stationery.

> Upon my return to the city this morning, I was saddened to learn of the sudden death of your wife.

> You have my deepest sympathy, Ken, and I hope that you'll call on your friends and coworkers at Holt Building Supply if we can offer any assistance during this difficult time.

TEMPLATES. See Chapter 9/TEMPLATE.

THANK YOU'S. Messages giving thanks for a gift, assistance, an idea, or anything else that warrants an expression of appreciation.

Whether a thank you message should be sent as a handwritten message, a computer-generated message on business stationery, an e-mail message, a COMMERCIAL CARD, or an Internet card depends on the circumstances.

Traditionally, a special gift from a friend was always acknowledged in handwriting or by a handwritten note added to a commercial card. Some computer users ignore this traditional rule and acknowledge gifts by e-mail or select a card and message from an Internet collection. See also Chapter 6/INTERNET; WEB SITE.

A thank you to a client, customer, or business associate for a business matter is usually prepared on business letterhead. A thank you for a routine matter, such as acknowledging the receipt of information, may be sent by e-mail or printed on business STATIONERY.

Anything that merits a thank you should be acknowledged promptly, preferably within two to three days unless one is out of town or otherwise unable to respond that quickly. In such cases, however, an assistant or someone else in the office should temporarily acknowledge (see ACKNOWLEDGMENTS) the gift or other matter:

> Many thanks, Ann, for all your help while I was out of the country last month. Without your capable assistance at the office, I couldn't have been away that long.
>
> I know the extra work must have put a strain on your own workload, and I really appreciate your special effort. I just hope that some day I can reciprocate.
>
> Sincerest thanks.

TITLES. See INSIDE ADDRESS; Part Four/FORMS OF ADDRESS.

TRANSMITTALS. Messages that accompany something, such as a report, being sent to the recipient. A transmittal is usually brief and may be sent as a traditional MEMO or LETTER or in the form of an e-mail with an ATTACHMENT.

The message should describe the enclosure or attachment and serve as a record. It may explain or comment on various aspects of the transmitted item or may simply identify it:

> Liz, here's a copy of our June 14 minutes for your files.
>
> If you have any questions, let me know.

CHAPTER NINE

Document Creation and Production

APPENDIX. (*pl.* appendixes, appendices) Supplementary material added at the end of a book, article, REPORT, or other document that is not essential but adds information or interest.

Place appendixes just before the NOTES, GLOSSARY, and BIBLIOGRAPHY in a book-length document. In multiauthor works, put them at the end of each author's chapter.

When a work has more than one appendix, number or letter them in sequence:

Appendix 1, Appendix 2, Appendix 3

Appendix A, Appendix B, Appendix C

Appendixes may also have subject titles similar to chapter titles. In that case, place the appendix number first on a line by itself, or put it just before the title on the same line, as preferred:

Appendix 1
Style Guide

Appendix 1: Style Guide

Include the number or letter of the appendix in the numbering of appendix TABLES and ILLUSTRATIONS:

Table 1.1, Table 1.2, Table 1.3

Figure A.1, Figure A.2, Figure A.3

Number the appendix pages in ARABIC NUMERALS, the same as the text pages, continuing in sequence after the last chapter of the work.

ARABIC NUMERALS. The NUMBERS *0* through *9* that are used for PAGE NUMBERS in the main body of a document. Compare with ROMAN NUMERALS, which are used in the FRONT MATTER.

AUTHOR–DATE CITATIONS. Also called *name–date citations*. In-text citations consisting of an author's name and the date of the work, rather than the SUPERSCRIPT numbers used in a NOTES system.

The name and date of a citation corresponds to the name and date given in the complete source, which is provided in an alphabetical REFERENCE LIST located at the end of each chapter or at the end of the document.

Place an author–date citation in parentheses at the end of a text quotation, sentence, or EXTRACT:

> Employees who telecommute must have a well-equipped home office suitable for conducting business (Johnson 2001).

If a paragraph has successive references to different pages in the same source, give the author and date the first time but only the page thereafter:

> Employees who telecommute must have a well-equipped home office suitable for conducting business (Johnson 2001, 17). Other family members should not use the same space for personal activities (p. 107).

These additional guidelines apply to the style of writing author–date citations:

1. Omit the abbreviations for *editor (ed.), compiler (comp.),* and so on in the in-text citation, but include them in the full reference list.
2. Use *et al.* (and others) for successive names when there are more than three authors: *McDaniels et al. 1999.*
3. Include the last name of the second author when two or more of the first authors' last names are the same and when their works were published in the same year: *McDaniels, Hill, et al. 1999; McDaniels, Jones, et al. 1999.*
4. When no author's name is given, use the sponsoring organization's or publisher's name: *Cyberconsultants 2001.*

5. Place page numbers and references to illustrations after the date: *Barnes 1998, 261, Table 3.*

6. When a volume number is included, place it *before* the page number, and insert a colon (but no space) between the two elements: *Morris 1999, 2:44-150.*

7. Include the abbreviation for *volume (vol.)* before the volume number if no page is given, to ensure that readers won't think that it's a page number: *Morris 1999, vol. 2.*

8. Place a comma between successive references to different dates for the same author: *Norris 1997, 1999, 2000.*

9. Use semicolons between the dates if page numbers are included: *Norris 1997, 364; 1999, 12–59; 2000, iv.*

10. When an author has several works, all with the same date, include small letters after the years to distinguish them: *Parsons 1999a, 1999b, 1999c.*

11. Separate references to different authors with a semicolon, whether or not page numbers are included: *Thomas 1996; Watson 2000, 14–78.*

BACK MATTER. The portion of a book or other large document where concluding materials are gathered.

The back matter consists of material related to the text body, such as the APPENDIX, ENDNOTES, GLOSSARY, BIBLIOGRAPHY or REFERENCE LIST, and INDEX.

Pages are numbered in ARABIC NUMERALS, continuing in sequence after the last chapter.

BIBLIOGRAPHY. A descriptive list of publications and other materials or events, usually alphabetized by author, that gives the reader a source of additional information about a subject discussed in the text.

Place the bibliography in the BACK MATTER, before the list of contributors, if any, and the INDEX. In a multiauthor book, place each author's bibliography at the end of his or her chapter.

Bibliography sources. A bibliography may be limited to the sources used by the author, often called *Works Cited,* or it may consist of both cited works and additional, useful sources. One that includes selected sources, but not all sources listed in the NOTES, is called a *Selected,* or *Select, Bibliography.*

Although the FOOTNOTES, ENDNOTES, or other notes may not contain full source data, each entry in a bibliography must be complete.

Format and style. Most bibliographies are styled as alphabetical lists, but in some scholarly works, they're styled as essays, with the sources incorporated into the essay's discussion paragraphs.

The typical FORMAT for an alphabetical entry is called *flush and hang,* with all lines after the first in each entry indented. See the forthcoming examples.

When an author has successive entries, use a 3-EM dash in place of the person's name for all entries after the first.

In most nonscientific business material, write the titles of books and other documents in ITALICS and the titles of articles and chapters in ROMAN TYPE, enclosed in QUOTATION MARKS.

Common forms. The following are examples of common bibliography forms (consult a STYLEBOOK for additional examples):

Kelly, Pierce C., and Norris B. Brisco. *Retailing,* 3d ed. Madison, Wisc.: Madison Publishing Co., 1998.

Hamilton, Earl J. "Prices and Wages Under John Law's System." *New Journal of Economics* 1, no. 51 (November 2000): 42–47.

King, John Jr. "The Middle East Crisis." Ph.D. dissertation, New York University, 1997.

———. "Monetary Skill." In *High Finance.* Edited by J. William Crawley, pp. 64–81. Chicago: College Press, 1994.

"Wright Company Shuts Doors." URL: http://www.wright.com/newsletr/ jun8-99.html.

BINDING. See OFFSET PRINTING.

BLUEPRINT. Also called *blues* and *blueline.* A proof on sensitized paper made from the photographic negatives of text and ILLUSTRATIONS used in OFFSET PRINTING. The printed material on a blueprint appears blue after processing.

Other proofs made from negatives, in which the printed material appears in a different color, are called *vandykes, brownlines* or *brownprints,* and *silver prints.*

In checking blueprints or any other type of proof, verify that:

1. No pages are missing or out of order
2. Facing pages are the same length
3. Illustrations appear in the proper position on the proper page

4. Errors appearing in the earlier PAGE PROOF stage have been corrected on the blueprint

5. There are no unwanted scratches or other blemishes on the pages

6. All other problems have been resolved

BOLDFACE. A heavy TYPEFACE, used principally for titles and HEADINGS, text CROSS-REFERENCES, and any other material that needs to be emphasized.
This is boldface (bf) type.
To instruct a TYPESETTING or DESKTOP PUBLISHING operator to set something in boldface in a MANUSCRIPT, draw a wavy line under the word or words.

CAPTION. The title or headline used with an ILLUSTRATION. A caption may consist of a word or words but not a complete sentence:

Systems of Chronology

Figure 1: Systems of Chronology

Fig. 1. Systems of Chronology

The terms *caption* and LEGEND are sometimes used interchangeably, but they're not the same. A *caption* is strictly a title or HEADING, whereas a *legend* is a descriptive explanation or comment.

A caption is often placed below an illustration when an explanation, or legend, follows it.

During the proofreading stage (see BLUEPRINT; PAGE PROOFS; PROOF-READERS' MARKS), read captions and legends for accuracy along with the text of the document.

If a negative proof, such as a blueprint, is provided, verify that captions and legends have each been placed with the correct illustrations and that all appear in proper order.

CHART. Often used interchangeably with *graph* and *diagram*. A representation of data in pictorial form.

Graph-drawing software enables you to create various charts or graphs. Some WORD PROCESSING programs also have graph-drawing features for preparing common types of illustrations.

1. A *line graph* or *chart* shows the relationship between different sets of NUMBERS, which are plotted on a grid with points connected by a line.

2. A *bar graph* or *chart* shows values or quantities by using thick vertical or horizontal bars of different lengths.

3. A *picture graph* or *chart* is a bar graph or chart that uses picture symbols for items or values instead of thick bars.

4. A *pie graph* or *chart* shows portions of a whole through the use of pie-shaped wedges.

See also CAPTION; ILLUSTRATIONS; LEGEND.

CONTENTS. See TABLE OF CONTENTS.

COPY. MANUSCRIPT to be sent to a publisher, TYPESETTING or DESKTOP PUBLISHING department, or printer; the text of an advertisement; any written material intended for further processing.

COPYEDITING. Preparing a MANUSCRIPT for TYPESETTING or DESKTOP PUBLISHING and printing. See also OFFSET PRINTING.

Copyediting often involves rewriting, revising, styling, and polishing the COPY, as well as verifying the facts, accuracy of grammar, consistency of style, and consistency and accuracy of spelling and punctuation. It may also include TYPEMARKING.

Mechanical editing refers to the correction of technical errors, omissions, and inconsistencies in grammar, spelling, punctuation, capitalization, and formatting (see FORMAT) and in the treatment of words, NUMBERS, citations (see AUTHOR–DATE CITATIONS; FOOTNOTES; NOTES), ILLUSTRATIONS, and other such matters.

Substantive editing, which may be handled by another editor, refers to the major reorganization, revision, and rewriting that is necessary to improve the content and presentation of a document.

Copyeditors should use standard PROOFREADERS' MARKS and write directly on the manuscript pages. Office personnel who only occasionally copyedit business material may find it helpful to devise a checklist of problems to look for.

COPYRIGHT. The legal right to exclusive publication and use of an original literary, dramatic, artistic, or musical work.

A work for which copyright has expired, or one not properly registered or otherwise protected, is said to be in the *public domain* and is subject to appropriation, or use, by anyone, without permission.

Forms and information on the process of, and fees for, registering various material are available from the Copyright Office at the Library of Congress in Washington, D.C., or at its Web site. See also Chapter 6/WEB SITE.

Period of protection.   Works published after January 1, 1978, that are properly registered are protected for the author's life plus 70 years, and jointly produced works are protected for 70 years from the death of the last living author.

Most registered works created before January 1, 1978, are protected for 95 years. (Consult the Copyright Office for exceptions.)

The Digital Millennium Copyright Act extends copyright protection to works that appear on-line. It also provides that devices designed to circumvent copyright on the Internet (see Chapter 6/INTERNET), such as by deactivating a protective measure in an electronic work, shall be banned.

Copyright notice.   Although a printed or on-line work does not have to carry a copyright notice, using the notice may discourage infringement and may be helpful in case of a lawsuit.

The following are examples of appropriate notices. The addition of the words *All rights reserved* is required for protection under the Buenos Aires Convention:

©2000 Marin Routledge

©2000 Marin Routledge. All rights reserved.

Copyright 2000 by Marin Routledge. All rights reserved.

Copr. 2000 by Marin Routledge. All rights reserved.

©1970 by Marin Routledge. © renewed 1998 by Marin Routledge. All rights reserved.

Place a copyright notice on the copyright page in the FRONT MATTER of a printed book, following the TITLE PAGE.

In an electronic work, put it at the bottom of the home page (see Chapter 6/HOME PAGE; WEB SITE), at the end of each division of a site, or at the end of the last Web page of the site. Since some visitors may not see all divisions of a Web site, it's helpful to repeat the notice at the end of each one.

Photocopying copyrighted material.   Although copyright law does not have clear-cut rules about photocopying material from a copyrighted source, use of a copyrighted work for purposes such as criticism, comment, news reporting, teaching, scholarship, or research is not considered an infringement of copyright.

However, systematic reproduction and distribution of single or multiple copies and spontaneous copying for classroom use must not exceed the number of students in a course, and the amount copied must be brief.

Written permission of the copyrighted owner is necessary to include material from a copyrighted source in another document. Even when permission is unnecessary, such as for using material from works in the public domain, one should credit the source of any material that is used.

CROPPING.   The process of indicating the portion of a photograph (see HALFTONE) or piece of art to be reproduced. Cropping requires an understanding of balance and composition in deciding what detail to keep and what to crop out.

For help in cropping and scaling, consult the printing establishment that will print the document. Members of the printer's camera or art department may be able to provide useful instruction.

Cropping procedure.   To mark the area to be retained on a glossy photograph or ILLUSTRATION, use a grease pencil to insert the crop marks since they can be easily removed.

With nonglossy material, you may want to mark the area to be retained on an acetate overlay. However, if you press down on the overlay with a pen or pencil, it may leave creases that will damage the surface of the material.

To indicate the area that you want to use, place small marks in the four margins to depict the outer limits of the selected area. The camera operator will focus only on the area within the crop marks and will exclude anything outside those boundaries.

Scaling procedure.   When a photograph or illustration must be reduced, the finished dimensions have to be computed in a process known as *scaling.*

Dimensions of width and depth must be proportional. For example, if a photograph must be reduced to a square size of 3 by 3 inches, the original must be cropped proportionally, marking off a square area of, say, 7 by 7 or 6 by 6 inches (but not 7 by 4 or 8 by 6 inches).

Various cropping and scaling aids are available, such as a handheld electronic dimension calculator that can be used to compute proportional scaling.

CROSS-REFERENCE.   In document preparation, a reference to another part of a document that contains additional, related information. See also Chapter 3/CROSS-REFERENCE.

The style of writing cross-references depends on the preferences of the organization preparing the document. In all cases, the cross-reference should be distinguished from the other text.

The cross-reference may therefore be stated in ITALICS or BOLDFACE. It may also be written in small capital letters or in a combination of capital and small capital letters (*caps and small caps*). The latter style is used in this book.

The most common wording of cross-references begins with *See* (a direct reference to other necessary material), *See also* (a reference to additional, useful material), and *Compare* (a reference to something noteworthy that is similar or different).

Such introductory words may or may not be italicized, as preferred:

See DATABASE MANAGEMENT.

See also INFORMATION MANAGEMENT SERVICES, Figure 2.

Compare with Chapter 20: INDUSTRIAL RATIOS.

A cross-reference in the middle of a sentence is often enclosed in parentheses. Between sentences or at the end of the last sentence in a paragraph, it may or may not be enclosed in parentheses, as preferred.

Cross-references may appear anywhere in the text or ILLUSTRATIONS of a document, as well as in the PREFACE or in BACK MATTER material, such as in an INDEX. See the example in that entry.

DATABASE.   A usually large electronic collection of information organized in a way that will facilitate rapid search and retrieval.

Although the terms *database* and *databank* are used interchangeably, the former is primarily a collection used by a person or organization, and the latter is primarily a wider collection, such as a library.

An electronic database enables businesses to locate quickly the information needed to perform different operations, and it provides extensive information for those engaged in RESEARCH and educational activities.

A database may have almost any orientation desired. For example, it may be organization-specific, such as a collection of customer names, addresses, and other information used by the sales department of a company.

It may also be subject-specific, such as a collection of financial information available to the public on the Internet. (See Chapter 6/INTERNET; WEB SITE.) For examples, see Chapter 11/DATABASES, LEGAL; Chapter 13/DATABASES, FINANCIAL.

DEFAULT.   The choice made by a software program when a user does not select an alternative.

For example, your WORD PROCESSING program may be preset always to provide 10-POINT type in a Times Roman TYPEFACE unless you temporarily enter another choice or permanently change the default setting.

DESKTOP PUBLISHING. The use of a computer and special software to create documents that can be printed by laser printer or by some other printing method, such as OFFSET PRINTING. See also TYPESETTING.

Desktop publishing software. MANUSCRIPTS and disk copies intended for desktop publishing are generally prepared with WORD PROCESSING software, sometimes in conjunction with drawing and painting software or other programs.

Different elements may need to be coded, or tagged, on the disk copy, as in *AT* for the appendix title.

The original text and illustrations are then transferred to a *page-makeup program,* commonly referred to as the *desktop publishing software.* This software usually has both word processing and layout capabilities, enabling operators to show text and GRAPHICS on screen in page format.

Because the final, printed copy is the same as the on-screen version, users commonly use the expression *WYSIWYG* (pronounced *whiz-ee-wig*): What you see is what you get.

Printing. A full-service desktop publishing department may include a desktop or larger color printer that is also connected to the company's computer network. High-volume printers using laser technology may function as part of desktop publishing in three ways:

1. As traditional long-run printers (see OFFSET PRINTING) connected to a large, shared computer

2. As high-volume document printers able to produce multiple copies in varying quantities, or runs

3. As print-on-demand printers (see PRINT-ON-DEMAND PUBLISHING) able to produce large documents in very short-run quantities

E-BOOK. An electronic copy of a book that can be distributed anywhere over the World Wide Web (see Chapter 6/WORLD WIDE WEB [WWW]) and read by e-book customers on screen. Compare with PRINT-ON-DEMAND PUBLISHING.

Publication and distribution. An e-book may be published after a hardcover print version has first appeared, although some books may be published only in electronic form. Those published only in electronic form eliminate the costs of print production, warehousing, shipping, and physical handling.

E-books may be distributed either directly from a publisher or through an e-book distribution system. In the latter case, the publisher sends a copy of the book to an e-book vendor, who installs it in a central DATABASE. From there, electronic copies are created and sold to e-book customers.

Reading devices. With the appropriate reader software, you can read an e-book on a notebook or desktop computer screen, just as you could view a CD-ROM or other information disk or tape. See also Chapter 3/MAGNETIC MEDIA STORAGE; OPTICAL MEDIA STORAGE.

Also available are small, handheld reader devices that are operated with rechargeable batteries. These portable e-book readers have features that enable you to browse, mark text, and link passages.

Some portable readers have built-in modems that can download a book of several hundred pages in mere minutes and also enable you to download other electronic material, such as a daily newspaper or various business files. See also Chapter 6/DOWNLOAD; HYPERLINK; MODEM.

EDITING. See COPYEDITING.

ELLIPSIS POINTS. A series of spaced periods (. . .) used in QUOTED MATERIAL to indicate the omission of words, sentences, or paragraphs.

One of two methods may be used. With one system, three periods are used to show *any* omission, regardless of where it is located in the quoted material.

A more common method is to use three periods for omissions *within* a sentence or *at the end of* a sentence fragment and four periods for omissions *between* sentences and paragraphs.

A space is usually inserted between the successive points, but there should be no space between the last quoted word of a sentence and the first of four periods placed immediately after it. This rule is easy to remember since there never is a space between the last word of a sentence and the concluding period.

If any paragraph other than the first one omits the first sentence of that paragraph, place three periods before the opening word.

In business material, capitalize the first word of a sentence following four periods, even if that word is not the first word of the sentence:

> Businesses regularly publicize their activities, such as . . . the opening of a new division. . . .

> . . . An organization's product or service and various newswor-
> thy events may be reported . . . through articles, press releases . . . ,
> letters, . . . and any other suitable form of communication. . . .

See also EXTRACT.

EM DASH. A solid line—as in this example—used to set off words from the rest of the sentence. Compare with EN DASH.

One *em* is equal to the POINT size of the type being used. In a 10-point type size, therefore, a 1-em paragraph indention would also be a 10-point indention.

Most WORD PROCESSING software presents a dash as a solid line. Otherwise, it can be typed in a MANUSCRIPT as two hyphens.

To instruct a TYPESETTING or DESKTOP PUBLISHING operator that you want two hyphens set as an em dash, write a capital letter *M* over the two hyphens, or write the numeral *1* over the two hyphens and a capital *M* below the two hyphens.

EN DASH. A solid line, one-half the length of an EM DASH (slightly wider than a hyphen), used in place of a hyphen in certain cases. Compare with EM DASH.

In printed material, an en dash is used between nouns of equal weight (*owner–operator*), between the first part of a three-part compound adjective when two of the words are written open (*ex–mayor Watson*), and between inclusive PAGE NUMBERS (*121–64*). See also NUMBERS for examples of abbreviating inclusive page numbers.

You can type an en dash in a MANUSCRIPT as a hyphen and instruct the TYPESETTING or DESKTOP PUBLISHING operator that you want the hyphen set as an en dash. To do that, write a capital letter *N* over the hyphen, or write the numberal *1* over the hyphen and a capital *N* below the hyphen.

ENDNOTES. The NOTES in a book or other large document that are collected in the BACK MATTER just before the BIBLIOGRAPHY or REFERENCE LIST.

Either number all endnotes consecutively throughout a document, or, in a document with chapters, group them under HEADINGS consisting of chapter numbers and titles, and start over with note 1 in each chapter.

Use the same form for end-of-book and end-of-chapter notes. See NOTES for examples of the arrangement of data.

EXTRACT. QUOTED MATERIAL or other excerpts taken from a larger work and set apart from the regular text. Usually, an extract is indented from the main text and is sometimes set in a smaller size or a different TYPEFACE.

Set quotations of eight or more lines as extracts, and omit the beginning and ending quotation marks. However, enclose other quoted words *within* the extract in quotation marks:

> Don't justify (set with a straight right edge) a legal document. Indent displayed material, such as lists and extracts, about 1/2 inch more than the main body of the material.
>
> According to Richard Samuels, "You may, but need not, indent the right margin an extra half inch."
>
> In addition, never end a paragraph with the last line of the page. Carry at least one or two lines to the next page. This is especially important in documents such as wills as a means to check against the omission of pages (Dawson 1999, 34).

See Ellipsis points for an example of an extract with omitted material.

FOOTER.   See Running head.

FOOTNOTES.   Notes that are placed at the foot of the text pages where corresponding numbers, letters, or symbols appear in the text.

Footnote content.   A footnote may consist of various information. For example, it may be the published source of a quotation in the text or an acknowledgment of assistance. Or it may be additional commentary related to the text discussion.

End-of-page footnotes are less common than end-of-chapter notes sections or a collection of Endnotes at the conclusion of a document. However, when a work has only a few notes, and when a writer primarily wants to provide additional commentary in the notes, bottom-of-page footnotes may be preferred.

When a work has both end-of-page discussion footnotes and end-of-chapter (or document) notes sections with straight source notes, number the source notes, and letter the discussion footnotes (*a, b, c,* and so on). You may also use symbols (*, #, §, and so on) for the end-of-page footnotes.

Footnote preparation.   Like a numbered note in a notes section, a footnote must have a corresponding Superscript reference in the text, preferably at the end of a sentence, rather than in the middle:

Only one solution is offered.[a]

Begin each footnote that applies to a particular text citation with the *same* letter used in the text. Whereas the text letter is always written as a superscript, the footnote letter may be written either as a superscript or on-line, as preferred:

> a. Although Henderson implies that other alternatives exist, he believes strongly that the best solution—in his mind, the *only* solu-tion—is to reconfigure the network.

In a MANUSCRIPT prepared for TYPESETTING or DESKTOP PUBLISHING, list the footnotes on separate sheets of paper, and place the sheets at the end of each chapter or at the end of the manuscript (before the BIBLIOGRAPHY). During com-position, the computer operator will insert the appropriate footnotes at the bot-toms of the text pages.

See NOTES for examples of the arrangement of data.

FOREWORD. An introductory statement in a book, immediately preceding the PREFACE in the FRONT MATTER, usually written by a prominent person or an author-ity on the book's subject.

A foreword may be one or several pages long and should comment on the book's content, presentation, the author's qualifications, or other matter related to the material.

Set PAGE NUMBERS in small ROMAN NUMERALS, the same as other pages in the front matter. Place the name of the person writing the foreword two or more lines below the text, against the right margin. If desired, add the person's title and company affiliation on the next line or lines in a smaller type size.

FORMAT. The arrangement of the elements of a document on a page. (See Chapter 8/FORMAT for examples of letter and memo formats.) Format includes anything that affects the appearance of the finished page:

1. The trim size (outer dimensions) of the page
2. The TYPEFACE and size of type for different elements
3. The spacing between lines of type (traditionally called *leading*)
4. The number of columns on a page
5. The treatment of characters (BOLDFACE, ITALICS, capital letters, small capital letters, and so on)
6. The use of borders and shading
7. The amount of paragraph indention
8. The positions of PAGE NUMBERS and RUNNING HEADS

9. The treatment of EXTRACTS, lists, and other special elements
10. The typeface, size, and position of HEADINGS

Most WORD PROCESSING programs have TEMPLATES (preset formats) and auto format features for use when you don't have a particular format in mind.

FRONT MATTER.   Also called *preliminaries.* The first major division in a book, which may include some or all of the following parts, usually in the order listed here:

1. Half title page (book title only)
2. Series title page (when a work is one of several books in a series: series title, volume, and sometimes series editor and titles of the other books)
3. List of contributors (if not placed in the BACK MATTER)
4. TITLE PAGE (title plus author and publisher)
5. COPYRIGHT notice
6. Dedication
7. Epigraph (quotation in the front of a book or on chapter opening pages)
8. TABLE OF CONTENTS
9. List of ILLUSTRATIONS
10. List of TABLES
11. FOREWORD
12. PREFACE
13. Acknowledgments (of assistance or contributions to book, if not part of the preface)
14. Introduction (if not the first chapter in the main body of the book)
15. List of abbreviations (used in the text)
16. Chronology (a listing in a book with numerous dates and associated names and events)

Use small ROMAN NUMERALS (*v, vi, vii,* and so on) for PAGE NUMBERS, beginning with the contents page.

For example, if a book has a half title page (*p. i*), blank page (*p. ii*), title page (*p. iii*), and copyright page (*p. iv*) preceding the table of contents, you would place a roman numeral *v* on the contents opening page. However, although page numbers *i* through *iv* would be counted, the numbers should not be printed on those pages.

GLOSSARY. A usually alphabetical collection of special terms mentioned in a work or pertaining to the subject of a work, with brief definitions:

> **Amplifier** An electronic device used to increase the electrical strength of a signal.

Place the glossary in the BACK MATTER of a document, after the ENDNOTES and before the BIBLIOGRAPHY (if any).

Number the pages in ARABIC NUMERALS, the same as those in the rest of the text, continuing consecutively from the last page of the endnotes.

GRAPHICS. The pictorial representation of data, such as a picture or graph; the words, symbols, or devices used to represent sound or convey meaning; the use of computer devices to produce pictorial representations.

Graphics software is available as some form of graph-drawing software or art/painting software. Both forms enable you to create pictorial representations on screen.

Large WORD PROCESSING programs have a variety of graphics that you can add to a document, including clip art (standard art pieces) and various pictorial symbols, such as the drawing of a car. With a word-art feature, you can change the shape and appearance of letters or words.

A particular program may not include the material you want, but if you have a scanner, you can scan outside material into your computer. Or there may be a symbol or picture that you can import from another document already stored in your computer.

HALF-TITLE PAGE. See TITLE PAGE.

HALFTONE. A photograph or other continuous-tone piece of art (as opposed to LINE ART) that is broken up into dots of various sizes by photographing it through a special halftone screen in preparation for making a printing plate. See also CROPPING; OFFSET PRINTING.

When an item is printed, the dots merge to again give the appearance of a continuous tone on paper. See also ILLUSTRATIONS for information about the numbering and positioning of halftones in printed documents.

HEADER. See RUNNING HEAD.

HEADINGS. The titles and subtitles used to introduce text and other material in a book, REPORT, or other document.

Treat the headings for topics of equal importance the same, and give them equal emphasis. For example, you may use a one- or two-word description for all first- and second-level headings and complete sentences for all run-in, third-level headings.

You can also make headings parallel through the consistent use of centering, capital letters, ITALICS, BOLDFACE, or other such techniques for each level of heading.

If your WORD PROCESSING software doesn't have an auto format feature that will automatically set up the headings, or if you prefer to custom format your documents, you can develop a suitable pattern and follow it consistently.

For example, you may want both displayed headings and those run in with the text set in a bold type but with different placement and styles of capitalization for each level:

FIRST-LEVEL HEADING (*centered on line alone, with space above and below*)

Second-Level Heading (*flush left on line alone, with space above and below*)

Third-Level Heading. (*run in with text paragraphs, with space above*)

Fourth-level heading. (*run in with text paragraphs, with space above*)

Leave at least two blank lines between a centered heading and the text above it and at least one blank line between the heading and the text below it. Leave at least one or two blank lines above and one below a second-level heading.

If you expect to use the same FORMAT in future documents, save it as a TEMPLATE. To conserve keyboard time, you can also create macros to reduce the number of keystrokes needed for repetitive work.

ILLUSTRATIONS. Any photographs, artwork, or other illustrative material, other than TABLES, used to explain or enhance the text discussion.

Line art, printed with the text, does not require special processing. HALFTONES, however, must be photographed through a halftone screen before printing.

Place both line art and halftones as close as possible to the text to which each figure is related, and refer to each illustration in the text, as in *See Figure 4.*

Numbering guidelines. Number figures consecutively throughout a document, or use double enumeration and start over with number 1 in each chapter: Figure 1.1, Figure 1.2, Figure 2.1, Figure 2.2, and so on.

Leave photographs or reproductions of special art, such as a painting, unnumbered, if desired. However, before you submit them with a MANUSCRIPT, lightly number the pieces on the back sides, and circle a note referring to them in the margins of the manuscript pages to show the printer where to place each one.

There may not be room for a printed PAGE NUMBER or RUNNING HEAD on pages with full-size illustrations. Nevertheless, count the pages in the consecutive numbering of the text.

Checking illustrations on proofs. The actual halftones will not appear on PAGE PROOFS. Rather, blank spaces (*holes*) or ruled boxes (*windows*) will show where illustrations should be inserted later. However, the halftones will appear on a BLUEPRINT (negative proof) or final press proof (if any).

Negative proofs and press proofs are used to verify that the illustrations have been processed as cropped (see CROPPING), that they are right side up, that they appear in the correct order and position, and that they appear with the correct CAPTIONS and LEGENDS.

Preparing a list of illustrations. When a document has numerous illustrations, it may be helpful to the readers to include a *list of illustrations* in the FRONT MATTER, following the TABLE OF CONTENTS.

Use a FORMAT similar to that of a contents page, with figure numbers and titles listed in the left column and page numbers in the right column. See NUMBERS for guidelines on abbreviating inclusive numbers.

INDEX. A detailed alphabetical list of the contents of a book, REPORT, or other document, with the pages where each item can be found. An index is usually the last item in a book, although occasionally, a special index may be placed in the FRONT MATTER.

Different types of indexes may appear in the same document. For example, there may be a *name index* (persons), a *title index* (publications), and a general *subject index*. Some documents may need special indexes, such as a *geographical index* in an atlas.

You can prepare an index manually or with special indexing software. To prepare it with indexing software, follow the instructions of the particular program. To prepare it without specialized software, follow these steps after you receive PAGE PROOFS from a TYPESETTING or DESKTOP PUBLISHING department:

1. *Select key words and phrases.* Underline key terms on each page of proof. Each occurrence of the same item will represent another page number on the completed index:

statistics

capitalization of, 93, 184–89

in word division, 76, 102, 344

sources of, 166, 184–85

To help you visualize what type of words and phrases to underline, study the indexes in published books.

2. *Record the items.* Transfer the underlined words to a computer list, and have the computer sort them in alphabetical order. (If you prefer, enter the words on 3- by 5-inch cards, and manually alphabetize the cards.)

3. *Edit the list of items.* Identify all major items, such as *statistics,* and subitems, such as *capitalization of,* and reorganize the subitems under appropriate main items.

Delete any repetition that occurs. For example, you may see something repeated several times, such as this:

sources of, 166

sources of, 184

sources of, 185

Combine such items as *sources of, 166, 184–85.*

Beware of compound words that should *not* be divided, such as the following:

stock

broker

certificate

Since the word *stockbroker* should not be broken, two separate entries are required, *stockbroker* and *stock certificate.*

Begin the first word of each entry with a small letter, unless your employer prefers a different style or unless the word is a proper noun that must be capitalized. The capitalization and punctuation style and the format used depend on the designer's plan for a particular document.

Insert CROSS-REFERENCES where it would be helpful:

point (measurement), 4, 11, 92. *See also* size

printing. *See* offset printing

ITALICS. A type style characterized by slanted letters, *as in these words.* Italic type is used principally for emphasis and side HEADINGS, to indicate unfamiliar foreign words, and in the titles of certain published material.

The following are examples of *titles* that should be printed in italics:

Computer Dictionary (book)

Time (magazine)

the *Wall Street Journal* (newspaper)

Men in Black (film)

Star Trek: Voyager (television series)

The Ancient Mariner (long poem)

Swan Lake (long musical/ballet composition)

Rodin's *The Thinker* (sculpture)

Brown v. Nuncio (legal case)

The following are examples of *names* that should be printed in italics:

Spirit of Saint Louis (aircraft)

Voyager 2 (spacecraft)

USS *Enterprise* (ship)

Sputnik II (satellite)

Canis (genus name for dog)

To instruct a typesetter to set certain MANUSCRIPT material in italics, draw a single straight line under the word or words.

LAYOUT. A designer's manual or computer rendering of a work to be printed, showing, page by page, the margins, blocks or columns of type, ILLUSTRATIONS, HEADINGS, CAPTIONS, and so on, with each element drawn to exact size.

Every item, even PAGE NUMBERS and credit lines (see NOTES), must be carefully identified for size, with the specifications handwritten on the layout.

A layout should include all preliminary pages (see FRONT MATTER); a typical chapter opening page; at least two facing pages of text that illustrate HEADINGS, EXTRACTS, FOOTNOTES, PAGE NUMBERS, and other elements; and a sample page from each section of the BACK MATTER: APPENDIX, NOTES, GLOSSARY, BIBLIOGRAPHY or REFERENCE LIST, and INDEX.

LEGEND. A description or explanation of an ILLUSTRATION. Although the term is sometimes used interchangeably with CAPTION, the latter refers to the title or HEADING of an illustration.

An illustration may have both a legend and a caption or either of them alone. A legend is usually set beneath an illustration, whereas the caption may be above or below it. When both are given, they are often set beneath the figure.

Place the caption and legend on separate lines, with the caption on top, or put them on the same line, with the caption first:

Fig. 23. Credit Statement: A sample monthly report that summarizes purchases and payments and indicates the amount due.

During proofreading (see BLUEPRINT; PAGE PROOFS; PROOFREADERS' MARKS), read the captions and legends for accuracy along with the text of a document.

If a negative proof, such as a blueprint, is provided, verify that the captions and legends have each been placed with the correct illustrations and that all appear in the proper order.

LINE ART.   ILLUSTRATIONS that have only solid blacks and whites, such as a hand- or computer-drawn diagram, as opposed to continuous-tone HALFTONES.

Line art and text type can both be photographed directly, unlike a photograph, which must be photographed through a special halftone screen.

Line art may be prepared in a variety of ways, such as by computer, pen and ink, or brush and ink.

Such drawings usually print well on all types of paper, although very fine lines may look sharper and cleaner on a smooth paper. When there is any doubt, consult a printer.

LOWERCASE.   Abbreviated in MANUSCRIPT instructions as *lc*. Consisting of small letters of the alphabet, as opposed to capital, or UPPERCASE, letters. *To lowercase* a letter is to change it from a capital to a small letter.

MANUSCRIPT.   Also called COPY. Written material, usually prepared by WORD PROCESSING or other programs, to be sent to a TYPESETTING or DESKTOP PUBLISHING department.

Dead copy, or *dead manuscript,* is manuscript that has been set and printed as PAGE PROOFS and, therefore, for which no further revision will be made on the manuscript pages. Alterations at that point will be made on the proofs.

Manuscript preparation.   Follow these general guidelines in preparing the manuscript, but also observe any special requirements of the desktop publishing or typesetting department:

1. Print the copy on 8½- by 11-inch, white bond paper.

2. Keep the length of each line at 6 or fewer inches.

3. Use double spacing throughout, including in supplementary or displayed material, such as in FOOTNOTES and EXTRACTS.

4. Leave the right edge of the type uneven (*unjustified*), or *ragged right*.

5. Use standard paragraph indentions (½ inch on most word processing programs).

6. Position HEADINGS where you want them to be on the final printed page, and use a consistent style for each level of heading.

7. Use only one side of each sheet.

8. Put footnotes on separate sheets rather than at the bottoms of the manuscript pages.

9. If the text mentions a figure, TABLE, or other supplementary material, handwrite and circle a reference to it, such as *Photo 4,* in the margin next to the text where it is first mentioned.

10. Type extracts the same as the main text, double-spaced, but indent the left margin an additional half inch.

11. Identify special or unusual material, such as an *exercise* that may need special formatting, by circling a designation in the margin where the material begins.

12. Insert PAGE NUMBERS at the bottom of pages or in the upper right corners.

See also BACK MATTER; BIBLIOGRAPHY; FRONT MATTER; NOTES; REFERENCE LIST; REPORT; TABLE OF CONTENTS.

Checking manuscript. Use your computer grammar- and spell-checker, and read the manuscript several times, looking for errors and omissions. Each error corrected in the manuscript stage will save the time and expense of resetting a line or more in the typesetting or desktop publishing stage.

In addition, follow these guidelines:

1. Be consistent in spelling, abbreviating, capitalizing, and punctuating.

2. Keep a written list (*style sheet*) of your selected style, such as the style of writing compounds (open, closed, or hyphenated), and note the PAGE NUMBER where an item first occurs.

3. Make last-minute pen-and-ink corrections by crossing out the incorrect word and writing the correction above it (not in the margins, which should

be used only for circled instructions to the typesetter, desktop publishing operator, or printer).

4. Edit in lengthy corrections with your computer, and print a revised copy.

5. Circle notations that are intended as instructions to the typesetter, desktop publishing operator, or printer, not material to be set.

6. To indicate a new paragraph, insert a paragraph sign; to combine two paragraphs, draw a line from the end of one to the beginning of the next.

7. To separate two words typed as one, draw a vertical line between them.

8. To make deletions, use a heavy pencil, and neatly and heavily cross out what you don't want.

9. To retain material already crossed out, insert a row of dots beneath the material, and circle *stet* (let it stand) in the margin beside it.

10. Check that page numbers have been inserted and that the pages are still numbered consecutively after all corrections have been made.

11. Examine the pages for the following: use of parallel headings (both in wording and in FORMAT), smooth paragraph transitions, correct sentence structure, consistency in writing style, appropriateness of word choice, use of active versus passive voice, redundancies, use of cliches and other unprofessional language, and references that may be considered discriminatory.

12. Check the entire manuscript for general accuracy, consistency, clarity, completeness, and readability.

NAME–DATE CITATIONS.   See AUTHOR–DATE–CITATIONS.

NEGATIVE PROOF.   See BLUEPRINT.

NOTES.   Comments, explanations, and sources of information that support and supplement the text of a document.

Notes may be organized as bottom-of-page FOOTNOTES, end-of-chapter notes sections, or end-of-document ENDNOTES (placed just before the BIBLIOGRAPHY).

Note numbers.   Footnotes that are lettered or introduced with symbols should have corresponding letters or symbols at appropriate places in the text. Similarly, numbered notes used in chapter notes sections or endnotes should have corresponding *numbers* in the text.

Number the notes consecutively throughout the document, or begin over with number 1 in each chapter. Number or letter notes to TABLES and ILLUSTRATIONS separately, and place those notes beneath the body of the tables or figures.

Place the corresponding numbers in the text, written as SUPERSCRIPTS, *after* punctuation marks, preferably at the end of a sentence:

In standard dictionaries, alternative spellings are given for certain terms, with the preferred spelling listed first.[3]

Move numbers after titles and HEADINGS into the text below. Place any *unnumbered note,* or *credit line,* stating permission to reprint a section, chapter, or other part at the foot of the page where the material begins.

Abbreviations in notes. Certain abbreviations are common in notes, such as *ibid.,* which refers to the immediately preceding entry. To refer to another previous entry, but not the immediately preceding one, use a *shortened reference* consisting of the author's last name, a short version of the title (if it's long), and the PAGE NUMBER.

Use *idem* to refer to the immediately preceding author *in the same note.* Use the expressions *See also* and *Compare* or *Compare with* (sometimes abbreviated as *Cf.*) before a source when you want to direct readers to that additional source of information.

Common note forms. The following are examples of common note forms (consult a STYLEBOOK for additional examples):

1. Pierce C. Kelly and Norris B. Brisco, *Retailing,* 3d ed. (Madison, Wisc.: Madison Publishing Co., 1998), 421–27.

2. Ibid., 433.

3. Earl J. Hamilton, "Prices and Wages Under John Law's System," *New Journal of Economics* 1, no. 5 (November 2000): 45.

4. Kelly and Brisco, *Retailing,* 426.

5. John King, Jr., "The Middle East Crisis" (Ph.D. diss., New York University, 1997); idem, *International Politics* (Cincinnati: Pickshaw Printers, 1998), ix–x. See also Kelly and Brisco, *Retailing,* 427.

6. John King, Jr., "Monetary Skill," in *High Finance,* ed. J. William Crawley (Chicago: College Press, 1994), 66–70.

7. "Wright Company Shuts Doors," URL: http://www.wright.com/newsletr/jun8-99.html.

8. Ibid. Compare with Hamilton, "Prices and Wages," 45.

NUMBERS. The figures or words used to represent countable items in a MANUSCRIPT or printed document. The two common styles for writing numbers are the technical and nontechnical styles.

Technical style. Spell out numbers *one* through *nine* or *ten* (as preferred), and use figures for everything else. If large numbers appear in the same paragraph, use figures for everything, even for numbers below *nine* or *ten*, in the same category in that paragraph:

> His office has four computers

> His office has *4* computers, but the company, run by *eight* men and women, owns *17* computers and rents several others.

Nontechnical style. Spell out numbers *one* through *ninety-nine* and large round numbers, such as *two hundred.* If large uneven numbers appear in the same paragraph, use figures for everything, even for numbers below *ninety-nine,* in the same category in that paragraph:

> His office has *fourteen* computers.

> His office has *14* computers, but the company, consisting of *three hundred* employees, owns *165* computers and leases many others.

In both types of writing, some items may always be given in figures, such as metric measurements and degrees of temperature: *2 mm* (or *2 millimeters*); *40°C* (or *40 degrees Celsius*).

Inclusive numbers. In certain cases, one or more digits may be dropped in writing inclusive numbers as figures.

PAGE NUMBERS of three or more digits, for example, are commonly abbreviated, unless the result might not be clear if any digits were dropped, such as when the first number ends in two or more zeros or when numbers designate a change in centuries:

1–29	795–96
65–70	900–1022
83–171	901–2
100–102	1008–9
105–9	1376–477
155–59	1999–2000
713–844	2000–2001

OFFSET PRINTING. Also called *offset lithography.* A common form of printing that makes an impression with a thin metal plate containing images of the material to be printed.

The traditional procedure has been to photograph the matter to be reproduced, prepare a negative, and transfer the images to a plate. In some printing operations, however, electronic images are transferred directly onto the plates, without first creating a negative:

> A *plate proof* is an impression created on paper from the plate, to be used for final checking before printing begins.

> A *press proof* is a limited initial run of the printing job, also for purposes of making a final check of the material before the rest of the copies are printed.

The impression on a plate never comes in direct contact with the paper. It is inked, and the inked impression is transferred to a *rubber blanket,* which in turn comes in contact with the paper.

Presses of varying sizes are used for very small to very large runs. Small, sheet-fed presses, for example, can handle small to medium runs. Larger Web presses, which print on big rolls of paper, are used for very large runs.

Full-service printers offer the three basic phases of the printing process:

1. *Prepress phase.* The printer (a) will prepare a design or transfer a designer's computer file to film or plates and (b) will scan in illustrations with a drum scanner able to provide high resolution in color.

2. *Printing phase.* The printer (a) will transfer images from a DESKTOP PUBLISHING file directly onto film, which in turn is used to make a metal plate, and (b) will print any desired quantity, including very high quantities requiring a large Web press.

3. *Binding.* The printer will cut, fold, and bind the material by an appropriate method, such as stitching, spiral binding, or gluing.

OUTLINE. See RESEARCH.

PAGE MAKEUP. See DESKTOP PUBLISHING.

PAGE NUMBERS. Also called *folios.* The consecutive NUMBERS of a document placed in the top or bottom margins of the pages. Bottom-of-page numbers are referred to as *drop folios.* See also RUNNING HEAD.

Page numbers in the FRONT MATTER are set in small ROMAN NUMERALS. Those in the main body of the document and in the BACK MATTER are set in ARABIC NUMERALS.

Front matter pages.   Certain front matter pages are counted in the numbering of pages but should not have a number printed on them: the half title page, TITLE PAGE, series title page, COPYRIGHT page, and any blank pages.

Text pages.   The first page of the main body is number 1. This page may be a *second* half title page, a part page (introducing a group of chapters), the first page of an introduction, or the first page of Chapter 1.

The numbers should not be printed on a second half title page, a part page, or the blank page following it. Therefore, if a book had an introductory right-hand (*recto*) part page (page 1), followed by a blank left-hand (*verso*) page (page 2), the next page—the opening page of Chapter 1 (page 3)—would be the first page to have a number printed on it.

Some full-page ILLUSTRATIONS in the body of a document may also omit the printed numbers, even though they are counted in the numbering of pages.

Multiple volumes.   Large works that have more than one volume may begin over with number 1 in each volume, or they may continue the numbering of pages in consecutive order from one volume to another.

PAGE PROOFS.   A copy or printout of text that has been set in final pages. A TYPESETTING or DESKTOP PUBLISHING department may provide more than one set of page proofs so that you can mark final corrections on one set and return it while keeping the other set for your files or for other uses, such as in preparing an INDEX.

The proofs sent to a customer are known as the *author's proofs* or *copy.* Those kept by the compositor are known as the *master proofs* or *copy.* See also REPRODUCTION PROOF.

In reading page proofs, check that facing pages are of equal length; that FOOTNOTES, ILLUSTRATIONS, PAGE NUMBERS, RUNNING HEADS, and so on are positioned properly; and that all errors marked on the MANUSCRIPT have been corrected.

Also examine each page for errors that you may have missed in an earlier reading or new errors that the typesetter introduced. But avoid *unnecessary* changes at this stage (known as *author's alterations*), which can be expensive to make and may, over a certain limit, be charged to the customer.

See PROOFREADERS' MARKS, Figure 1, for a list of the standard marks to use in marking corrections on proofs and Figure 2 for an example of a page of corrected proof.

PHOTOGRAPHS.   See HALFTONES.

PICA. A TYPESETTING measurement. One pica equals 12 POINTS, or about 1/6 inch. Thus there are 6 picas in an inch.

In typesetting and printing, the *type page* (the printed area of a page) is indicated in picas. Therefore, the elements on a page, such as the space marked for an ILLUSTRATION, must also be stated in picas.

The type page differs from the *trim size,* which refers to the entire sheet running to each outer edge, including the margins. Also, the trim size is specified in inches rather than picas.

Handheld electronic dimension calculators are available for use in figuring picas, points, centimeters, millimeters, inches, and fractions and for various other production tasks.

POINT. A TYPESETTING measurement. A point is 1/12 of a PICA, or about 1/72 inch. Type size and the space between lines (traditionally called *leading*) are measured in points.

The text of a large document, such as a book or REPORT, is often set in a size of 8 to 10 points. Titles and HEADINGS, however, are commonly set in larger sizes.

Different TYPEFACES of the same point size, such as all 12-point type, may not look the same size. The style or design of a typeface may cause variation in the height and width of the letters.

Handheld electronic dimension calculators are available for use in figuring picas, points, centimeters, millimeters, inches, and fractions and for various other production tasks.

PREFACE. A statement in the FRONT MATTER of a book or other large document that introduces and describes the work, including its purpose and scope. The preface, often placed immediately after the TABLE OF CONTENTS, may range from one to several pages. PAGE NUMBERS are set in small ROMAN NUMERALS.

Acknowledgments of assistance may be included in the preface or placed on a separate Acknowledgments page, especially if they're numerous.

The author's name is often omitted, because it's generally assumed that the author of a document also wrote its preface. (See also FOREWORD.) However, if the name is included, place it a couple lines below the last paragraph, against the right margin.

In a revised edition, a new preface usually replaces the one in the previous edition. If both are included, put the most recent one first.

PRELIMINARIES. See FRONT MATTER.

PRINTING. See DESKTOP PUBLISHING; OFFSET PRINTING; PRINT-ON-DEMAND PUBLISHING.

PRINT-ON-DEMAND PUBLISHING. Also known by other names, such as *on-demand digital publishing* and *customized on-demand publishing*. A publishing technology in which a single book can be stored electronically and printed only when ordered. Compare with E-BOOK.

A print-on-demand service, which maintains electronic sales outlets on the World Wide Web (see Chapter 6/WORLD WIDE WEB [WWW]), will scan a book into its digital library, where it is stored until an order for it is placed. At that time, the book is printed and delivered to the retailer or customer placing the order.

Print-on-demand publishing eliminates the traditional initial print run of thousands of copies and the warehousing of those copies. A book is not printed until ordered, and at that time, only the number of copies ordered is printed, whether it is one copy or thousands of copies.

A single book of several hundred pages can be printed in less than a minute and delivered with any binding option (see OFFSET PRINTING) that a customer selects.

Print-on-demand services emphasize that since a book is stored electronically, rather than in bulky paper form in a warehouse, it need never go out of print.

Usually, the book publisher, rather than the electronic service, sets the price and pays the author royalties, the same as with traditional book publishing.

PROOFREADERS' MARKS. Standard symbols and abbreviations used for marking errors on PAGE PROOFS, BLUEPRINTS, and other proofs.

Figure 1 has a list of standard proofreaders' marks, and Figure 2 illustrates the use of these marks on a page of corrected proof.

The following are general guidelines for marking corrections on the pages:

1. Read a page of proof word for word against the original MANUSCRIPT, watching for errors and omissions and examining each word, mark of punctuation, and other element for accuracy.

2. Place all marks in the margins of the proof, not between the printed lines, next to the line in which the error occurs.

3. For clarity, separate two or more side-by-side corrections with a slash, as in *lc/tr,* and note them in the same order in which the actual errors occur.

4. If the same correction is to be made in two places in the same line, with no intervening correction, write it only once and follow it with two slashes, as in *d//*.

5. When material is to be added to the line, place a caret (^) in the text at the point of insertion, and indicate the material to be added in the margin.

6. When material is to be deleted and nothing added in its place, simply cross out the unwanted characters or words, and place a delete sign in the margin.

7. When material is to be substituted for a deletion, don't use the delete sign, but rather, cross out the unwanted material, and write the substitution for it in the margin.

8. Use ink or pencil of a different color than that of any markings already on the proof.

PROOFREADING. See PROOFREADERS' MARKS.

PROOFS. See BLUEPRINT; PAGE PROOFS; REPRODUCTION PROOF.

PUBLIC DOMAIN. See COPYRIGHT.

QUOTATION MARKS. The marks of punctuation placed around words that are taken from, or quoted from, another source. See also Chapter 7/QUOTATION MARKS.

Run-in quotations. If QUOTED MATERIAL is set the same as, or run in with, the general text of a document, and if it's not set off or indented as an extract, enclose the material in quotation marks.

Use double quotation marks ("/") at the beginning and end of the quoted material and at the beginning of any other paragraphs within a group of quoted paragraphs. Use single quotations marks ('/') for any quoted material *within* the quoted passage:

> Jenson made the following comment about renewals. "The pertinent part of the opinion reads as follows: 'It is the duty of the publisher to take all necessary steps to effect renewals.' "[2]

Extracts. When quoted material is formatted as an indented extract, omit the beginning and ending quotation marks, and enclose any quote *within* the quoted material in *double* marks:

PROOFREADERS' MARKS: FIGURE 1

∧	Make correction indicated in margin.
Stet	Retain crossed-out word or letter; let it stand.
Stet (dotted)	Retain words under which dots appear; write "Stet" in margin.
X	Appears battered; examine.
═	Straighten lines.
✓✓✓	Unevenly spaced; correct spacing.
‖	Line up; i.e., make lines even with other matter.
run in	Make no break in the reading; no paragraph.
no ¶	No paragraph; sometimes written "run in."
Out—see copy	Here is an omission; see copy.
¶	Make a paragraph here.
tr	Transpose words or letters as indicated.
ℓ	Take out matter indicated; delete.
ℓ	Take out character indicated and close up.
ℓc	Line drawn through a cap means lower case.
⊘	Upside down; reverse.
⊃	Close up; no space.
#	Insert a space here.
⊥	Push down this space.
⏄	Indent line one em.
[	Move this to the left.
]	Move this to the right.
⊓	Raise to proper position.
⊔	Lower to proper position.

////	Hair space letters.
wf.	Wrong font; change to proper font.
Qu?	Is this right?
lc	Set in lowercase (small letters).
s.c.	Set in small capitals.
Caps	Set in capitals.
c&sc	Set in caps and small caps.
rom.	Change to roman.
ital.	Change to italic.
≡	Under letter or word means caps.
═	Under letter or word means small caps.
──	Under letter or word means italic.
∿∿	Under letter or word means boldface.
⅄	Insert comma.
⅄	Insert semicolon.
⅃	Insert colon.
⊙	Insert period.
/?/	Insert interrogation mark.
/!/	Insert exclamation mark.
⅄	Insert hyphen.
⋁	Insert apostrophe.
⋁⋁	Insert quotation marks.
⅄	Insert superior letter or figure.
⅄	Insert inferior letter or figure.
[/]	Insert brackets.
(/)	Insert parentheses.
─	One-em dash.
═	Two-em parallel dash.
Ⓢ	Spell out.

PROOFREADERS' MARKS: FIGURE 2: Page of Corrected Proof

HOW TO CORRECT PROOF

s.c. It does not appear that the earliest printers had any method of
///. correcting ✓errors before ✓the ✓form was on the press/ The learned
learned correctors of the first two centuries of printing were not
proof/readers in our sense/ they were rather what we should /erm
not/ office editors. Their labors were∧chiefly to see that the proof corre∧
sponded to the copy, but that the printed page was correct in its
Latinity/that the words were there, and that the sense was right.
They cared but little about orthography, bad letters∧or purely printers'
errors, and when the text seemed to them wrong they consulted fresh
authorities or altered it on their own responsibility. Good proofs∧in
not/# the modern sense, were impossible until professional readers were employed∧
men who had first a printer's education, and then spent many years
in the correction of proof. The orthography of English, which for
the past century has undergone little change, was very fluctuating
until after the publication of Johnson's Dictionary, and capitals, which
have been used with considerable regularity for the past 80 years,
were previously used on the miss or hit plan. The approach to regularity,
so far as we have, may be attributed to the growth of a class of professional
proof readers, and it is to them that we owe the correctness of modern
printing.∧More errors have been found in the Bible than in any other
one work. For many generations it was frequently the case that Bibles
were brought out stealthily, from fear of governmental interference.∧
They were frequently printed from imperfect texts, and were often
modified to meet the views of those who publised them.The story is
related that a certain woman in Germany, who was the wife of a Printer,
and had become disgusted with the continual assertion of the superiority
of man over woman which she had heard, hurried into the composing room
while her husband was at supper and altered a sentence in the Bible, which
he was printing, so that it read∧Narr∧instead of∧Herr∧thus making
the verse read "And he shall be thy fool" instead of "And he shall be thy
lord." The word∧not∧was omitted by Barker, the King's printer in
England in 1632, in printing the seventh commandment∧He was fined
£3,000 on this account.

Jenson made the following comment about renewals:

> The pertinent part of the opinion reads as follows: "It is the duty of the publisher to take all necessary steps to effect renewals."²

QUOTED MATERIAL. Verbatim text taken from one document or source and used in another. Quoted material should be double-spaced in a MANUSCRIPT and single-spaced, the same as the rest of the text, in printed material.

Copyrighted material. To use an exact quote from another, copyrighted source, secure written permission from the COPYRIGHT owner. In your document, include a proper FOOTNOTE or NOTE noting the permission and crediting the source of the quote.

If the copyright owner, or publisher, provides special wording to be used in the permissions note, follow such instructions precisely.

Format. Quoted material of more than eight printed lines is often set as an EXTRACT and indented at least ¹/₂ inch, with an additional indention for the beginning of a paragraph in the quoted passage. Extracts may be indented only on the left side or on both the left and right sides.

If the original version of the passage does not have paragraph indentions, begin each paragraph flush left, and leave a line space between the paragraphs. Also begin a passage flush left if the quoted words are taken from the middle of a paragraph in the original work.

Omit the usual beginning and ending quotation marks required for quoted material when the quotation is set as an extract. If the words are incorporated in a regular paragraph, however, enclose them in quotation marks.

See the examples in ELLIPSIS POINTS and QUOTATION MARKS.

Errors. Quoted material is usually quoted exactly, even with obvious errors (some writers correct minor typos, such as *the* for *them*). To indicate that the error is in the original quote, and that it is not your error, insert [*sic*] in brackets after the word with the error, as in *to you and I* [*sic*].

Italics and boldface. If words in the original appear in ITALICS or BOLDFACE, also use italics and boldface in the MANUSCRIPT.

However, if certain words are *not* in italics or boldface in the original, but you want to use italics to emphasize them, state *Emphasis mine* or *ours* (or *Italics mine* or *ours*) in brackets immediately after the words that you alter.

If another part of the quoted passage already has italics or another form of emphasis, you can distinguish between the two by stating something such as *Emphasis theirs* in brackets after the already existing italics:

> "The Copyright Office does not undertake to pass upon the author's rights, leaving the question to the courts in case of dispute. It simply *records* [Italics theirs] his or her claims and by this recording gives the author certain rights *provided those claims can be substantiated* [Italics ours]."

REFERENCE LIST. A descriptive list of publications and other materials or events, usually alphabetized by author, that gives the reader a source of additional information about a subject discussed in the text.

Place the reference list in the BACK MATTER before the list of contributors, if any, and the INDEX. In a multiauthor book, place each author's reference list at the end of his or her chapter.

Reference list sources. A reference list, sometimes identified by other names, such as "Literature Cited," includes all sources cited in the text as AUTHOR–DATE CITATIONS. Although the text citations do not contain full source data, each entry in the reference list must be complete.

Format and style. Because the text citations refer to the author's name and the date of his or her work, the reference list gives the author's name first, followed by the date of the person's work. This differs from a BIBLIOGRAPHY, in which the date is given at or near the end of an entry.

Also, reference lists sometimes give only the initials of first and middle names, rather than full names as used in a bibliography. However, many readers prefer that a name be stated exactly as it appears on the TITLE PAGE to make it easier to locate the source later or to order a copy of it.

Set the entries in a reference list in a *flush-and-hang* style, the same as in a bibliography, with all lines of an entry after the first line indented. For successive entries by the same author, substitute a 3-EM dash for the name after the first listing.

In nonscientific business material, write the titles of books and other documents in ITALICS and article and chapter titles in ROMAN TYPE, enclosed in quotation marks.

Common forms. The following are examples of common reference-list entries (consult a STYLEBOOK for additional examples):

Kelly, Pierce C., and Norris B. Brisco. 1998. *Retailing,* 3d ed. Madison, Wisc.: Madison Publishing Co.

Hamilton, Earl J. 2000. "Prices and Wages Under John Law's System." *New Journal of Economics* 1, no. 51 (November): 42–47.

King, John Jr. 1997. "The Middle East Crisis." Ph.D. dissertation, New York University.

_____. 1994. "Monetary Skill." In *High Finance.* Edited by J. William Crawley, pp. 64–81. Chicago: College Press.

"Wright Company Shuts Doors." 1999. URL: http://www.wright.com/newsletr/ jun8-99.html.

REPORT. A written presentation of information designed to provide greater understanding of a particular subject or problem.

A report may be periodical, such as a progress report issued monthly, or it may be special, prepared for a specific, nonrecurring occasion or purpose. See also Chapter 3/REPORTS MANAGEMENT; Chapter 10/ANNUAL REPORT.

Parts of a report. All but very short memo reports usually include the following parts, in the order listed:

1. Cover or TITLE PAGE
2. TABLE OF CONTENTS
3. Body, consisting of an introduction, the development of the subject, and, sometimes, conclusions and recommendations
4. Supplementary material, such as TABLES, CHARTS, NOTES, BIBLIOGRAPHY, and APPENDIX

A formal report may also include the following parts:

1. A letter of transmittal addressed to the person receiving the report, following the title page
2. A list of ILLUSTRATIONS, following the table of contents
3. A FOREWORD or an abstract of the report (brief summary), following the list of illustrations
4. An appendix, following the report body

5. A notes section and a bibliography, following the appendix

6. An INDEX, following the bibliography

Some reports may have various other parts, as needed, such as a GLOSSARY, a special map, or a COPYRIGHT PAGE, if the report is being published.

Report preparation. The preparation of most reports involves four main steps:

Organization: Developing the theme, a checklist of things to do, a list of equipment and supplies that will be needed, and so on.

Research: Making a list of sources of information (people, Web sites, printed material, company files, and so on), scheduling appointments, developing an outline of topics to RESEARCH, taking notes, preparing a bibliography, getting releases for photographs and other material, and so on.

Drafting: Converting each item on the topic outline into a sentence, each sentence into a paragraph, and so on; positioning notes, appendixes, illustrations, and other material; and preparing FRONT MATTER and BACK MATTER.

Revision: Verifying facts and figures; rechecking the placement of illustrations and other items; polishing the copy; rearranging the copy as needed; checking grammar, spelling, language, and style consistency; and generally making the material as professional as possible. See also COPYEDITING.

In the absence of other instructions, print a large report on white, 20-pound, $8^{1}/_{2}$- by 11-inch bond paper and a small memo or letter report on business stationery. See also Chapter 8/LETTERS; MEMOS.

Although you may want the printed document to be single-spaced, double-space all drafts and any MANUSCRIPT copy sent to a TYPESETTING or DESKTOP PUBLISHING department.

See APPENDIX and PAGE NUMBERS for guidelines on numbering and titling chapters and appendixes and numbering front matter, text, and back matter pages.

REPRODUCTION PROOF. Also referred to as *repro*. The final proof of typeset material from which a negative is made for OFFSET PRINTING. See also DESKTOP PUBLISHING; TYPESETTING.

Repros consist of white, coated paper that has been carefully prepared to avoid any flaws or blemishes that would be captured by the camera.

They are not sent to the author for checking but are examined by the production department or person in charge of production. Corrections and changes made at this late stage can be costly and should be avoided.

See also BLUEPRINT; PAGE PROOFS.

RESEARCH. The process of finding facts and collecting information; a careful search, inquiry, or examination.

Depending on the information you need, you may consult one or more sources, including the Internet (see Chapter 6/INTERNET; WEB SITE), in-house files and records, outside libraries, in-house and outside DATABASES, clipping services, educational institutions, and persons who are knowledgeable about the topic being researched.

The kind of information that you need will influence your choice of fact-finding methods (interviews, questionnaires, review of on-line material, and so on) and tools (computer, tape recorder, camera, and so on).

Preliminary outline. To save time that would be wasted in an aimless inquiry and to make the research process easier and more productive, writers often prepare a preliminary *outline* to guide their fact finding.

An outline should list each main item or topic being investigated and prospective subtopics under each main heading:

A. Trusts and Guardianships
  1. Trusts
      a. Inter vivos (living) trust
      b. Pourover trust
      c. Testamentary trust
  2. Guardianships
      a. Testamentary guardian of the person
      b. Guardian of the property
      c. Guardian ad litem

Library research. Company, public, and specialized libraries have a wealth of published material. The particular indexing method that the library uses will indicate what is available, and the reference librarian can give additional assistance.

Computer research. If you have a telephone, computer, and modem, you can reach electronic libraries or DATABASES from your own office. You can also review the encyclopedias and other works available on CD-ROM. See also Chapter 3/OPTICAL MEDIA STORAGE.

Some databases are open to anyone for an hourly rate (billed to your credit card) or by monthly subscription. Others are available only through an on-line service. See also Chapter 6/ON-LINE SERVICE.

Some will respond to your inquiries with a list of citations for the topic you want to research, and others will give both citations and abstracts (summaries) of the published works. In some cases, you can download (see Chapter 6/Download) the full text of a work.

Computer-search services (check your yellow pages) and some libraries will provide electronic research for a fee or hourly rate. The organization will need a list of keywords (see Chapter 3/KEYWORD RETRIEVAL; Chapter 6/KEYWORD) to undertake a search.

See also Chapter 6/METASEARCH SITE; SEARCH ENGINE; WEB SITE.

Interviewing. After securing an appointment with an expert on your topic, collect all material that you will need during the interview. Study the topic in advance, and prepare a list of questions to ask.

Take along pen, pencils, paper, a notebook computer (if available), and any other note-taking material that would be helpful. If you want to tape record the session, *ask for permission*, and be certain that the recorder and cassettes are in proper working order.

Also *request permission* to take any pictures you may want, and be certain that your camera and film are ready.

Take along the *release forms* used by your company, or devise your own, which will authorize you to use photographs or quotes in your document. Get the subject's signature on all forms before you leave.

If it is necessary to clarify any points later, follow up with another visit, or contact the person by telephone or e-mail, explaining what you want to verify.

ROMAN NUMERALS. Numerals that are formed with capital and small letters of the alphabet. Compare with ARABIC NUMERALS.

Small roman numerals are used for PAGE NUMBERS in the FRONT MATTER of a large document:

I	i	VI	vi	XI	xi	XVI	xvi
II	ii	VII	vii	XII	xii	XVII	xvii
III	iii	VIII	viii	XIII	xiii	XVIII	xviii
IV	iv	IX	ix	XIV	xiv	XIX	xix
V	v	X	x	XV	xv	XX	xx

ROMAN TYPE. A basic design of type characterized by upright letters, as opposed to the slanted letters in ITALIC type. In reference to type, the word *roman* is written with a small *r.*

Unless copy is marked otherwise, a compositor will set a MANUSCRIPT in roman type.

RUNNING HEAD. Also called *header.* The word or words that run across the top of a page in a document to indicate the material printed on that page. Although running heads are not required in business documents, they are useful to readers who can see at a glance what is covered on each page.

Types of running heads. A running head might consist of the document's title or a chapter title. In a magazine, it might consist of the name of the magazine or the date of issue.

Usually, left-hand (*verso*) pages and right-hand (*recto*) pages have different heads. For example, the verso page might carry the chapter title, and the recto page might have the text subheading applicable to the copy on that page.

Placement of running heads. Running heads are never used on chapter or other opening pages or on any FRONT MATTER display pages, such as the TITLE PAGE.

Sometimes the words in the running head are positioned near the center or inside of the book page, with the PAGE NUMBERS positioned at the outer margins of the page. See the examples of placement in this and other books.

When such titles are placed at the bottom of the pages, they are called *running feet* or *footers.* Most WORD PROCESSING programs will automatically insert a header or footer on each page if you choose that option.

STET. A PROOFREADERS' MARK meaning let it stand, that you want to retain material previously crossed out.

To indicate this to a compositor, place a row of dots beneath the crossed-out words, and write and circle *stet* in the margin.

The material to be retained must still be legible after having been crossed out, or it should be rewritten.

STYLEBOOK. A guide to style (capitalization, punctuation, and so on), the distinctive treatment of words, such as whether to hyphenate a compound term, and NUMBERS, such as *14* versus *fourteen;* documentation style (BIBLIOGRAPHY; NOTES; and so on); the production of printed material; and TYPESETTING and printing.

Stylebooks may be general or specialized, and some businesses develop their own manuals especially for in-house use.

SUBSCRIPT. Also called *inferior figure*. An element set below the normal line of type, as in H_2O. Subscripts are used in technical material, such as in chemical formulas.

SUPERSCRIPT. Also called *superior figure*. An element set above the normal line of type, as in R^2. Superscripts are used in technical material, such as in mathematical copy, and in text material as FOOTNOTE or NOTE designations.

TABLE OF CONTENTS. Often referred to as the *contents page* and titled simply *Contents* in a document. A list of the titles that appear in a work and the beginning PAGE NUMBER, if any, for each title.

Most WORD PROCESSING software will provide automatic formatting in the style you select. (See TEMPLATES.) Although the printed version may be single-spaced, the table of contents in a MANUSCRIPT should be double-spaced.

Depending on the document, you may list only main titles or main titles and one or more levels of HEADINGS, such as the chapter titles and all first- and second-level headings within each chapter. REPORTS commonly have detailed contents pages, whereas a nonfiction book usually lists only the chapter titles:

> 2. An Effective Style
>> Using Action Verbs
>> Editing for Clarity
>> Being Precise
>> Avoiding Cliches

TABLES. Systematic arrangements of data in rows and columns. The data may consist of figures or words and may have any number of columns that can be accommodated on a page.

A table that will not fit vertically on a page may be set up and printed sideways on the page (called *broadside* or *landscape*), with the left column against the bottom margin.

Table titles and numbers. Number the tables consecutively throughout a document, or begin with number 1 in each chapter, usually with double numbering, as in *Table 1.1, Table 1.2, Table 2.1,* and *Table 2.2*.

Place the table number on a line above the title. Place a subtitle on the same line, immediately following the title, or on the line below the title. Enclose it in parentheses when it refers to a value or quantity:

Sales by Country, 1999–2000
(In Millions of Dollars)

Column headings.   The first column head (the *stub*) should always be singular. Additional heads may be singular or plural, as desired:

Name   Age   Marital Status

Use *decked heads* when there are two or more levels of column heads. The upper-level head is called the *spanner head,* and it is separated from the lower-level heads by a *spanner rule:*

Shipments	
Weight	Value

Most WORD PROCESSING programs will automatically create table columns and align figures at the decimal points.

Table notes.   Place the various forms of NOTES beneath the table body, with a source note first (see Figure 1), followed by any general note, and ending with individual numbered or lettered FOOTNOTES.

Avoid placing footnote numbers or letters after table titles. Use a general (unnumbered) note instead, as illustrated in Figure 1.

List of tables.   When a document has numerous tables, it may be helpful to the readers to include a *list of tables* in the FRONT MATTER, following any list of illustrations or, otherwise, the TABLE OF CONTENTS.

FORMAT a list of tables similar to a contents page, with table numbers and titles listed in the left column and page numbers in the right column.

TEMPLATE.   A preset layout on a software program. For example, to create a document, such as meeting minutes, with a WORD PROCESSING program, you can devise your own format or use the program's template, which already includes the formatting.

If you use the formatting that the program provides, all you need to do is add your own information. However, you can usually make modifications to a template to give it a custom look. You can also save as templates any original documents that you formatted yourself.

When you save a document prepared with a template, give it a different name, leaving the original template as is, ready for use with future documents.

TABLES: FIGURE 1

Table 6.1

Decimal, Binary, Octal, and Hexadecimal Numbers

Decimal	Binary	Octal	Hexadecimal
0	000	0	0
1	001	1	1
2	010	2	2
3	011	3	3
4	100	4	4
5	101	5	5
6	110	6	6
7	111	7	7
8	1000	-	8
9	1001	-	9
10	1010	-	A
11	1011	-	B
12	1100	-	C
13	1101	-	D
14	1110	-	E
15	1111	-	F

Source: John P. Winterbaum, "By the Numbers," working paper, Watson Technoconsultants, Inc., Phoenix, Ariz., 2000.

Note: A *decimal system* (the system in common use in the United States) has a base of 10. A *binary system* (used in computer systems) has a base of 2. An *octal system* (sometimes used in computer programming) has a base of 8. A *hexadecimal system* (often used by programmers), based on the number 16, uses the digits *0* through *9* and the letters *A* through *F*.

TITLE PAGE. The first or second page of a large document, consisting of the document title, any edition number, and various other information, such as the name and location of the publisher or sponsoring organization.

Whether or not the title page is the first page depends on whether there is also a *half title page,* which always precedes the title page. A half title page consists only of the document title. In some cases, a second half title page appears just before the first printed page in the body of a document.

Report title page. All formal REPORTS have a title page, which may also serve as the front cover of the document. If the report is enclosed in a binder, the title page is the first page after the cover.

The information on the title page of a report may include the report title; the name, title, and full or abbreviated address of the writer; the date of submission; and the name, title, and full or abbreviated address of the recipient. In some cases, the last item may consist of only the organization's name. See Figure 1.

Style and format. When a title is written on more than one line, divide it at a logical place. However, don't separate adjectives and articles from the words they modify or prepositions from their objects, and don't end a line in a conjunction.

For example, don't divide the title *The Participation of Middle Management in Modern Labor Disputes* between *Middle* and *Management* but rather between *Management* and *in:*

The Participation of Middle Management
in Modern Labor Disputes

Single- or double-space the material on a title page, as preferred. Separate the different items, such as the names of the writer and the recipient, by at least four lines. See Figure 1 for an example of a common FORMAT.

TYPEFACE. The design of a complete set, or *font,* of type, including sizes and character style. Some typefaces are known by the person who designed them, such as *Baskerville.* The text for this book is called ITC Garamond.

Each typeface has a distinctive design that makes it appear heavy or light, condensed or open, formal or informal, modern or traditional.

Part of the distinctive character is created by the style of the ascenders and descenders. An *ascender* is the part of tall LOWERCASE letters, such as *h* and *d,* that extends above the top of the lowercase letter *x* (the *x-height*). A *descender* is the part of lowercase letters, such as *j* and *p,* that extends below the main body.

See also BOLDFACE; ITALICS; ROMAN TYPE; TYPEMARKING.

TYPEMARKING. Marking on a MANUSCRIPT, according to a designer's specifications, the TYPEFACE and size of various elements, position of and spacing around HEADINGS, paragraph indentions, page dimensions, and so on.

The typemarking should include all the instructions that a DESKTOP PUBLISHING or TYPESETTING operator will need to prepare COPY for reproduction.

TITLE PAGE: FIGURE 1

The Participation of Middle Management

in Modern Labor Disputes

Kenneth M. Archer, Director
Research and Development
Avery-Madison Laboratories
Seattle, Washington

January 14, 200X

Marilee J. Worcester, President
The Association of Labor Management
Portland, Oregon

Write and circle the instructions in the margins beside the material in question. For example, *10/12 Times Roman* would mean that you want the copy next to those instructions to be set in a Times Roman typeface with a 10-POINT type size and 12-point line spacing (traditionally called *leading*).

Once a type size and the leading have been established, it's not necessary to repeat those instructions beside every paragraph or even on every page. Therefore, any such instructions written in the margin would indicate a deviation from the established specifications for the document.

TYPESETTING.   The process of setting MANUSCRIPT material in type to be used in printing. This may be done with a DESKTOP PUBLISHING system or by one of the various photocomposition, or phototypesetting, methods.

Photocomposition involves entering the text with a computer-style keyboard, storing and retrieving it by computer, and transferring the images to photosensitive paper or film with special typesetter equipment. The exact procedure may vary, depending on the equipment being used.

For example, one method, called *CRT composition,* uses a cathode-ray tube (CRT) to transfer images to paper or film. A *laser imagesetter* uses a laser beam to project the images onto paper.

UPPERCASE.   Abbreviated in MANUSCRIPT instructions as *uc.* Consisting of capital letters of the alphabet, as opposed to small, or LOWERCASE, letters. *To uppercase* a letter is to change it from a small to a capital letter.

WIDOW.   A very short last line of a paragraph carried over from the previous page or column to the top of the next page or column; a very short line at the end of a page or column; a word ending, such as *–ed,* carried to a line by itself.

Typesetters usually reset a sentence if a short line is carried to the top of the next column or page. However, they may or may not reset the copy to avoid a short word ending set on a line by itself.

WORD PROCESSING.   The use of word processing software to prepare documents of all kinds and sizes, from a letter or memo to a book-size REPORT. See also Chapter 8/LETTERS; MEMOS.

Word processing software.   With most word processing programs, you can create a wide variety of material, including brochures, newsletters, contracts, and even Web pages. See also Chapter 6/WEB SITE.

The software usually offers an automatic formatting and error-correction option, along with other timesaving features, such as TABLE and CHART creation. TEMPLATES, with preset formats, can be used for rapid setup of different documents.

In addition, programs have traditional text-manipulation (editing) and file-management features. They also commonly include grammar checking along with spell checking.

Manual requirements. In spite of all the document-creation aids that are available in modern programs, writers must continue to plan their work, organize the material logically, use proper language in the document, and proofread it manually.

Manual proofreading is essential because software programs will not know if you meant to say one thing but inadvertently said another.

For example, if you said that prices will *fall* when you meant to say *rise,* the computer will accept your error as correct if it is spelled correctly and the usage is grammatically correct.

See also COPYEDITING; DESKTOP PUBLISHING; Chapter 3/DOCUMENT MANAGEMENT SYSTEM; ELECTRONIC FILING SYSTEM; FILENAME; FORMS MANAGEMENT; MAGNETIC MEDIA STORAGE; RECORDS SECURITY.

PART THREE

ESSENTIAL BUSINESS OPERATIONS

CHAPTER TEN

Management and Organization

ACCOUNTING.   See BUDGET; Chapter 12/ACCOUNTING.

AFFILIATED COMPANIES.   Companies that are related through ownership of their STOCK by a common PARENT CORPORATION or through a community of interest. The community of interest may arise through the same person or persons serving as directors (see BOARD OF DIRECTORS) or merely through the influential ownership of the stock of one person or a closely associated group.

AFFIRMATIVE ACTION.   A remedy, established under Title VII of the 1964 Civil Rights Act and some state laws, to correct discriminatory hiring practices.

It may be applied voluntarily or imposed by court order upon a finding of past discriminatory practices of a business, government, or other hiring entity.

An affirmative action program may not set quotas but may give preference to equally qualified persons of a category subject to the past discriminatory practice, such as race, sex, national origin, religion, and, more recently, disability.

See also Chapter 11/LABOR LAWS.

Affirmative action statutes have recently been subject to court challenge or repeal.

AFL–CIO.   A united labor federation resulting from the 1955 merger of the American Federation of Labor and the Congress of Industrial Organizations.

AGENCY.   An agreement between two persons in which one person authorizes another to act for him or her. The one granting the authority is the *principal;* the one authorized to act is the *agent.* An agent has a fiduciary duty to act for the benefit of the principal.

For an agent to act, a *third party* with whom the agent contracts, is necessary. An agency relationship is created when a person gives a power of attorney or a proxy and in other situations. See also Chapter 4/PROXY; Chapter 11/POWER OF ATTORNEY.

An agency may be *general*—the agent has broad powers to represent the principal—or *special*—the agent represents the principal for a specific purpose or for a series of routine tasks. The principal is liable for the acts of an agent within the scope of the agency.

ALIEN CORPORATION.   A business organization incorporated outside the United States and its territories. The state statutes make no distinction between an alien CORPORATION and a FOREIGN CORPORATION, except in those few states that do not recognize alien corporations.

AMERICANS WITH DISABILITIES ACT.   See Chapter 11/LABOR LAWS.

ANNUAL REPORT.   A report containing the audited financial statements of a CORPORATION sent at the close of its fiscal year to its STOCKHOLDERS and others. See also Chapter 12/BALANCE SHEET; FISCAL PERIOD; INCOME STATEMENT.

Usually, an annual report contains a letter from the president or CHAIRMAN OF THE BOARD of the corporation with comments on the year's operations and plans for the future. See also BOARD OF DIRECTORS.

Successful reports aim to build stockholder interest, create better understanding between the company and its employees, and improve industrial and public relations.

States require that corporations file certain information annually, together with filing fees. These filings are less detailed than a published annual report to stockholders.

ANTITRUST LAWS.   See Chapter 11/ANTITRUST LAWS.

ARBITRATION.   A method frequently used to settle disputes whereby a single arbitrator or a panel of arbitrators attempts to settle differences without litigation. The arbitrator's decision is binding on the parties if they have so agreed:

Compulsory arbitration is that required by a governmental agency.

Voluntary arbitration arises by consent of the disputing parties, usually as part of an underlying CONTRACT.

Arbitration is commonly used to settle labor disputes.

ARTICLES OF INCORPORATION.   See CERTIFICATE OF INCORPORATION; CORPORATION.

AUDIT.   See Chapter 12/AUDIT.

BANKRUPTCY.   See Chapter 11/BANKRUPTCY.

BOARD OF DIRECTORS.   A group of individuals elected by STOCKHOLDERS, who, as a body, manage a CORPORATION. See also INTERESTED DIRECTOR; INTERLOCKING DIRECTORATES; OFFICERS OF A CORPORATION.

Qualification.   Any person who is legally competent to contract can be a director, unless the statutes, CERTIFICATE OF INCORPORATION, or BYLAWS provide otherwise.
    The statutes, certificate of incorporation, or bylaws may require that a director own STOCK. Some statutes require that one or more directors reside in the STATE OF INCORPORATION; a few require U.S. citizenship.

Number.   The minimum number, usually three, is generally fixed by statute, and the maximum may also be fixed by statute. The actual number, within statutory limits, is fixed by the certificate of incorporation or bylaws and may be revised by amendment.

Election.   The certificate usually names the first board of directors. Thereafter, the statutes give stockholders the right to elect directors annually.

Term of office.   The bylaws usually set the term of service, and directors continue to hold office until successors are elected.

Resignation.   A director may resign at any time unless prevented by the certificate of incorporation or bylaws or by a statute of the state of incorporation. A director who has contracted to serve a definite period is liable for damages caused by his or her resignation before completion.

Powers. The directors have power to conduct the ordinary business of the corporation without interference by the stockholders, except in matters requiring the stockholders' consent.

Liabilities. Directors must act in good faith and with reasonable care and prudence. But they are not personally liable for losses resulting from accident or mistakes of judgment.

Since directors have a FIDUCIARY responsibility, they must not use their positions of trust and confidence to further private interests. Also, they may incur liabilities under certain federal and state statutes.

Meetings. Generally, directors can bind the corporation by their acts only when a quorum is assembled in a meeting. A director may not vote by proxy or on any matter in which he or she is personally interested. See also Chapter 4/DIRECTORS' MEETING; PROXY; QUORUM.

Compensation. In the absence of a certificate of incorporation or bylaws provision granting compensation, directors are not *legally* entitled to compensation for performing duties or attending meetings. However, those who perform duties beyond the normal scope are entitled to compensation. See also INTERLOCKING DIRECTORATES.

Often, corporations pay no fees to directors who are salaried. Some corporations pay no fees even when all or a few are *not* salaried. In other cases, they do pay fees but only to those who receive no salaries.

Generally, when fees are paid, each director receives a stipulated amount for each meeting. Or a definite sum may be appropriated for each meeting and distributed among those who are present.

See also Chapter 11/INDEMINIFICATION OF DIRECTORS AND OFFICERS.

BONDS. See Chapter 13/BOND.

BOYCOTT. See Chapter 11/BOYCOTT.

BREACH OF CONTRACT. See Chapter 11/BREACH OF CONTRACT.

BREACH OF WARRANTY. See Chapter 11/BREACH OF WARRANTY.

BUDGET.   Generally, a plan that estimates and controls income, expenses, and business activities for a specified period, such as a year; an appropriation for a designated purpose.

Various budgets may be developed to help management plan and control operations, allocate resources, and make long-term investments.

BUSINESS CORPORATION.   A CORPORATION organized for the purpose of doing business and making profits, as distinguished from a CHARITABLE CORPORATION or a NONPROFIT CORPORATION. See also PROFESSIONAL CORPORATION (PC).

For example, a manufacturing corporation is usually a business corporation, whereas a corporation created to open and maintain a summer camp for disabled children is often a nonprofit corporation. Both, however, must be established in accordance with state statutes.

BUSINESS LAW.   See Chapter 11/BUSINESS LAW.

BUSINESS ORGANIZATION, FORMS OF.   See CORPORATION; LIMITED LIABILITY COMPANY; PARTNERSHIP; PROPRIETORSHIP, SOLE.

BYLAWS.   Rules adopted by a Corporation to guide its internal governance and to define the rights and duties of its Stockholders and the rights, powers, and duties of the directors and officers. (See BOARD OF DIRECTORS; OFFICERS OF A CORPORATION.) Bylaws are permanent, except insofar as they may be amended.

Sample bylaws are available in published forms books, in legal-supplies catalogs, and through on-line legal-forms suppliers. Incorporation services can also be found on the Internet. See also Chapter 6/INTERNET; WEB SITE.

Essentials of bylaws.   Most corporate bylaws include the following:

1. Location, date, and hour of stockholders' meetings
2. When notice of the annual meeting must be given
3. Who may call special stockholders' meetings and when notice must be given
4. Number and qualifications of directors and officers
5. Percentage of stock constituting a quorum
6. Location of directors' meetings

7. When regular directors' meetings are to be held and when notice must be given

8. Who may call special directors' meetings and when notice must be given

9. Number of directors constituting a quorum

10. Officers who are to sign/countersign checks and stock certificates

11. Specification of end of fiscal year

12. Provisions for amendment

Amendment of bylaws. The power to adopt and amend the bylaws rests with the stockholders. The board of directors, however, may be authorized to adopt and amend them by the statute under which the corporation is organized, by the corporation's CERTIFICATE OF INCORPORATION, or by resolution of the stockholders.

The bylaws may limit but not extend the powers granted to a corporation in its certificate of incorporation.

See also BOARD OF DIRECTORS; CORPORATE SEAL; OFFICERS OF A CORPORATION; RECORDS, CORPORATE; Chapter 4/STOCKHOLDERS' MEETING; Chapter 13/DIVIDEND; STOCK.

CAPITAL. 1. In business, the actual wealth or total assets of the business in money, tangible property (such as a factory), or intangible property (such as GOODWILL).

A distinction is ordinarily made between *working capital* and *fixed capital.* See Chapter 12/FIXED ASSETS; WORKING CAPITAL.

2. In a strict legal sense, that portion of the consideration received by a CORPORATION upon issuing STOCK that has been set up in its records as capital, in accordance with the laws of the state in which the corporation is organized.

It cannot be impaired by paying dividends or acquiring the corporation's own stock. See also Chapter 13/DIVIDEND.

CAPITAL STOCK. The aggregate ownership interest of a CORPORATION. See also Chapter 12/CAPITAL STOCK; Chapter 13/STOCK.

CAPITAL STRUCTURE. A reference to the kinds of securities that make up the capitalization of a CORPORATION, such as whether capitalization consists of a single class of STOCK, several classes of stock with different characteristics, various issues of bonds (see Chapter 13/BOND), a large or small surplus, and so on. See also Chapter 12/CAPITALIZATION.

Capital structure is used interchangeably with *capitalization,* although it carries a connotation of the various components of the structure, whereas *capitalization* generally refers to the structure as a whole. The term is also used interchangeably with *financial structure.*

Equity securities (corporate stock) and long-term debt securities (bonds) are usually the principal parts of a company's capital structure. To enable the corporation to raise permanent capital with a minimum of effort and cost, these elements must be kept flexible.

Flexibility is affected by the terms of the securities that are outstanding. Therefore, upon the creation of any class of stock or bond issues, considerable attention is given to the characteristics of the securities issued by the corporation.

CARTEL. An association of producers who enter into an agreement to regulate output, divide markets, and establish prices at which they will sell their products.

Although American Corporations have entered into cartel arrangements with corporations in other countries, there are no purely American cartels, because they violate the antitrust laws by fostering monopolistic practices. See also Chapter 11/Antitrust laws; Monopoly.

CEO. An initialism (see Chapter 7/ABBREVIATIONS) for the chief executive officer of a CORPORATION.

CERTIFICATE OF INCORPORATION. Also called *charter, articles of incorporation,* and *articles of association* (in a JOINT STOCK COMPANY). A document that tells what a CORPORATION is authorized to do. Each state's laws provide what must or may be included in the certificate.

Content. Most certificates specify the corporate name, purpose and place of business, duration of the corporation, amount of CAPITAL STOCK and number of shares (see CAPITAL; Chapter 13/STOCK), INCORPORATORS' names and residences, number of directors (see BOARD OF DIRECTORS), and name and address of the RESIDENT AGENT.

Printed forms are available from the appropriate state office, through legal-supplies catalogs, and in legal-forms books. Incorporation services are also available on the Internet. See also Chapter 6/INTERNET; WEB SITE.

Distribution of copies. Most attorneys provide clients with at least three additional copies of the certificate: one for the headquarters office, one for the minutes book (see Chapter 4/MINUTES), and a file copy.

After the copies have been signed, the required number must be sent to the proper state official (some states require that an original copy be filed with each public official).

If the certificate is acceptable, the company will receive a certificate of approval and a receipt for the tax and fees. The office should retain a copy and file the certified copy with the proper local official, if required.

CFO. An initialism (see Chapter 7/ABBREVIATIONS) for the chief financial officer of a CORPORATION.

CHAIRMAN OF THE BOARD. The presiding officer of a corporation's BOARD OF DIRECTORS. He or she is often the senior person in the corporation's leadership and acts as a spokesperson in its public relations. The chairman is sometimes given specific powers, such as the power to call a directors' meeting.

CHARITABLE CORPORATION. Also known as *eleemosynary corporation*. A CORPORATION organized and operated for charitable or nonprofit purposes, such as a public charity, hospital, or school, as distinguished from a BUSINESS CORPORATION, which exists for profit purposes.

Charitable corporations are organized under separate statutes and usually apply for tax-exempt status under the federal Internal Revenue Code.

CHARTER. See CERTIFICATE OF INCORPORATION; CORPORATION.

CLOSED SHOP. A business that hires only workers belonging to the union. Compare with OPEN SHOP; UNION SHOP.

CLOSELY HELD CORPORATION. Sometimes called *close corporation*. A CORPORATION whose CAPITAL STOCK is held by a limited group, in contrast to one whose STOCK is sold to the public generally.

Usually, a closely held corporation is comparatively small, although there are also some that are large.

COLLECTIONS. The function of collecting past-due accounts. Depending on company policy, many offices send their own routine follow-up notices, whereas others seek professional assistance. See also Chapter 3/FOLLOW-UP SYSTEM; Chapter 8/COLLECTIONS; FOLLOW-UPS.

Some organizations rely on attorneys and collection agencies to handle collections. In such cases, an attorney or agent will send a planned series of follow-up notices and letters, often culminating in a lawsuit if payment is not received. Most collections are handled on a contingent-fee basis.

COMMITTEE.   See Chapter 4/COMMITTEE.

CONDITIONAL SALE.   An INSTALLMENT SALE in which the buyer usually gives the seller a promissory note secured by a conditional sale contract or a chattel mortgage. See also Chapter 11/PERSONAL PROPERTY; Chapter 13/NOTE; Chapter 15/MORTGAGE.

Type of contract.   A *conditional sale contract* is a contract for the sale of goods under which the goods are delivered to the buyer while title remains in the seller's name until the goods are paid for in full or the conditions of the contract are fulfilled.

When a chattel mortgage is used, the seller transfers the goods to the buyer who in turn executes a chattel mortgage in favor of the seller. This instrument gives the seller a lien on the goods. See also Chapter 11/LIEN.

If the goods are in the form of equipment, the instrument is often filed or recorded under the terms of the Uniform Commercial Code (UCC). See also Chapter 11/UNIFORM COMMERCIAL CODE (UCC)

Acceleration clause.   The instrument usually includes a provision that if an installment is not paid when due, the entire debt becomes payable at once. This provision is called an *acceleration clause.*

An acceleration clause is essential in any installment contract. (See Chapter 11/ACCELERATION CLAUSE.) Otherwise, the seller would have to sue for the amount of each installment as it became due or would have to wait until the entire debt matured.

CONFERENCES.   See Chapter 4/CONFERENCE.

CONGLOMERATE.   A diversified CORPORATION formed by acquiring and consolidating companies in different industries. See also CONSOLIDATION.

CONSIGNMENT.   A shipment of merchandise from the owner (*consignor*) to another party (*consignee*), who becomes a selling agent of the owner. A consignment is not a sale, because the title to consigned goods remains with the consignor.

A consignment contract must follow certain legal requirements. For example, the consigned goods must be kept apart from other merchandise or must be marked clearly and distinctly as the property of the consignor. Also, the proceeds from any sale must be kept separate from the consignee's general funds.

CONSOLIDATION. A combination of two or more corporations into a new CORPORATION in a manner prescribed by the laws under which the existing corporations are organized.

When a plan for consolidation goes into effect, the constituent corporations go out of existence. Only the new corporation remains, along with the combined rights, privileges, FRANCHISES, properties, and liabilities of the constituents. See also MERGER.

CONSORTIUM. A group of persons or companies that combine their resources to undertake some enterprise. See also SYNDICATE.

CONTRACT. See Chapter 11/CONTRACT.

CONTROLLER (COMPTROLLER). Chief accounting officer of a CORPORATION. Unlike the office of TREASURER, the office of controller is not compulsory under state statutes, and many small and medium-size companies do not have a controller.

The controller, who is usually the head of the accounting division, prepares analyses and interprets business results. He or she is also responsible for tax matters and is in charge of preparing the annual BUDGET for the business.

COOLING-OFF PERIOD. See Chapter 11/COOLING-OFF PERIOD.

CORPORATE ENTITY. The concept of a CORPORATION as a legal person or body, separate and distinct from its STOCKHOLDER-owners. The corporate entity—not the individual stockholders, directors, or officers—contracts, sues, and transacts corporate business in general.

The separate entity of the corporation is disregarded and the individual owners are held liable for the acts of the corporation when it is used for improper purposes. See also Chapter 11/PIERCING THE CORPORATE VEIL.

CORPORATE SEAL. An engraved device used by a CORPORATION to make an impression on its business papers. The seal usually bears the name of the corporation and the year and state of incorporation. See also Chapter 11/SEAL.

A corporation's BYLAWS usually provide that any instrument signed on behalf of the corporation shall be impressed with the corporate seal. An OFFICER OF THE CORPORATION impresses the seal on the instrument when it is signed.

In many cases, the SECRETARY (CORPORATE) must bear witness, or attest, to the fact that the imprint on the paper is indeed the seal of the corporation. When a document states that the seal is to be attested, the following lines are placed on the left-hand side of the page, opposite the signature lines:

ATTEST

_____
Secretary

CORPORATION. An organization formed under a state statute to carry on business in such a way as to make the enterprise distinct and separate from the persons who are interested in it and who control it. It must be organized in strict compliance with the laws of the state in which it is incorporated.

A number of states have adopted statutes based on the Model Business Corporation Act developed (and revised) by the American Bar Association Section of Corporation, Banking and Business Law. See also Chapter 11/MODEL BUSINESS CORPORATION ACT.

Forming a corporation. One or more persons may form a corporation by filing a statement in the office of a designated state official providing required information, by paying initial taxes and filing fees, and by holding required organizational meetings at which various details of organization must be completed.

The statement that must be filed is known as the CERTIFICATE OF INCORPORATION, *Articles of Incorporation*, or corporate *Charter.*

A corporation is referred to as a DOMESTIC CORPORATION in the state in which it is incorporated, as a FOREIGN CORPORATION in any other state, and as an ALIEN CORPORATION if it is incorporated in a country other than the United States and its territories.

Since a corporation owes its existence to the state in which it is organized, no other state need recognize its existence. However, all states permit FOREIGN CORPORATIONS to do business in their states by complying with special state requirements.

Characteristics of a corporation. Certain characteristics have made the corporation a popular form of business organization: easy transferability of ownership, continuity of existence, and limited liability of STOCKHOLDERS. Management is concentrated in the hands of a BOARD OF DIRECTORS elected by the stockholders.

The ownership of the corporation is represented by its CAPITAL STOCK (see Chapter 12/CAPITAL STOCK; Chapter 13/STOCK), which is divided into identical units or groups of identical units called *shares*. These shares are represented by written instruments called *certificates of stock*. See also Chapter 13/STOCK CERTIFICATE.

The owners of the shares are called *stockholders*. Since every stockholder has the right to sell or transfer his or her shares, the corporation enjoys continuous succession and is not disturbed by death, insanity, or bankruptcy (see Chapter 11/BANKRUPTCY) of individual stockholders or by change of ownership.

An owner of fully paid stock ordinarily has no liability to creditors. However, in case of the corporation's insolvency, an owner of stock that has not been fully paid is liable, as far as is necessary to satisfy creditors, for the amount required to make his or her stock fully paid.

Common forms. The following are common forms of corporations:

Public corporations, as well as government-owned corporations, are subdivisions of a state, such as cities and tax districts. See also PUBLIC CORPORATION.

Publicly held corporations sell stock to the public, and the Securities and Exchange Commission regulates the sale. See also Chapter 13/SECURITIES AND EXCHANGE COMMISSION.

Corporations not for profit, such as religious groups, do not have capital stock or pay dividends.

Corporations for profit, which do have stock and do pay dividends, include MONEYED CORPORATIONS, such as banks; public service corporations, such as utility companies (see PUBLIC UTILITY CORPORATION); and private BUSINESS CORPORATIONS, such as machine tool companies.

For other forms, see CHARITABLE CORPORATION; CLOSELY HELD CORPORATION; LIMITED LIABILITY COMPANY; PROFESSIONAL CORPORATION (PC); SUBCHAPTER S CORPORATION.

CORPORATION SERVICE COMPANY. A company that performs for CORPORATIONS certain services that the corporations themselves would find prohibitively expensive or inconvenient to perform.

For example, a corporation service company may incorporate a business in states other than those in which the CORPORATION resides. It may also obtain, establish, and maintain a RESIDENT AGENT and a REGISTERED OFFICE, where needed.

CUMULATIVE VOTING. A system of voting for the directors of a CORPORATION under which each STOCKHOLDER is entitled to a number of votes equal to the number of shares he or she owns multiplied by the number of directors to be elected. See also BOARD OF DIRECTORS.

The stockholder may cast all votes for one candidate (cumulate them) or distribute the votes among the candidates in any way desired. Cumulative voting therefore enables minority stockholders to elect one or more directors.

The right to cumulative voting cannot be claimed unless provided for by statute, by the corporation's CERTIFICATE OF INCORPORATION or BYLAWS, or by contract among all stockholders, provided the agreement is not otherwise illegal.

DATABASE. See Chapter 9/DATABASE; Chapter 11/DATABASES, LEGAL; Chapter 13/DATABASES, FINANCIAL.

DE FACTO CORPORATION. A CORPORATION that has not met some of the state's requirements of a legal corporation but continues to function as one *in good faith*. Thus it exists *in fact* but not, as a DE JURE CORPORATION, *in law*.

DE JURE CORPORATION. A CORPORATION that has met all legal requirements governing incorporating procedure. Thus a de jure corporation exists *in law* as well as *in fact*, unlike a DE FACTO CORPORATION, which exists in fact only.

DIRECTORS. See BOARD OF DIRECTORS.

DOCUMENT MANAGEMENT. See Chapter 3/DOCUMENT MANAGEMENT SYSTEM.

DOMESTIC CORPORATION. In a particular state, a CORPORATION organized under the laws of that state. In that same state, a corporation organized under the laws of a different state would be considered a FOREIGN CORPORATION.

DUMMY INCORPORATORS. Individuals to whom shares of STOCK in a new CORPORATION are issued to qualify them nominally as INCORPORATORS of the corporation, even though they have no real interest in it.

Dummy incorporators are used to meet the requirement of state statutes that incorporators be residents of the state or to avoid immediately identifying the persons actually forming the new corporation.

DUN & BRADSTREET.   An organization providing credit, financial, marketing, and other information and services, including Moody's Investors Service, with a database covering more than 40 million businesses. Dun & Bradstreet *ratings,* for example, show a firm's credit standing and its estimated financial strength.

For Internet users, the organization has a number of sites providing general information, with more detailed information available to subscribers. See also Chapter 6/INTERNET; WEB SITE.

E-COMMERCE.   Business conducted electronically, such as Web-based sales over the Internet. See also Chapter 6/INTERNET; WEB SITE; WORLD WIDE WEB (WWW).

By the late 1990s, the number of Web users had reached about 60 million, and Web-site sales represented a billion-dollar market.

ECONOMY OF SCALE.   The decrease in the per-item cost of producing a commodity or service as output is increased.

ELEEMOSYNARY CORPORATION.   See CHARITABLE CORPORATION.

EQUAL-OPPORTUNITY EMPLOYER.   An employer that does not discriminate in hiring and other employment practices because of race, color, sex, religion, or nationality. See also Chapter 11/FAIR EMPLOYMENT PRACTICES.

ERGONOMICS.   An applied science that studies the relationship or interaction between people and their work environment to improve performance and increase productivity.

ETHICS.   See Chapter 1/ETHICS.

EXECUTIVE COMMITTEE.   A committee (see Chapter 4/COMMITTEE) appointed by the BOARD OF DIRECTORS of a CORPORATION to exercise many of the board's powers between board meetings. The executive committee meets more often than the board does.

In many large corporations, members of the executive committee work at the offices of the corporation and are paid a regular salary. See also FINANCE COMMITTEE; OFFICERS OF A CORPORATION.

FEATHERBEDDING.   Unproductive labor practices in which unnecessary personnel are hired or workers are paid for work they have not done.

FIDUCIARY.   A person or organization that manages money or property or both for another party and that acts in a capacity of trust or confidence. A fiduciary, therefore, has special ethical responsibilities and duties.

FINANCE COMMITTEE.   A committee (see Chapter 4/COMMITTEE) appointed by the BOARD OF DIRECTORS of a CORPORATION to exercise the power of the board between board meetings in matters pertaining to corporate finance.

Finance committee is the name given by some corporations to their EXECUTIVE COMMITTEE, but many corporations have both committees.

FIRING OF EMPLOYEES.   See Chapter 1/FIRING.

FIRST-IN, FIRST-OUT (FIFO).   A method of valuing the INVENTORY of merchandise. This method assumes that the goods first acquired are the goods first sold, in typical grocery-store style. It is the most common method used largely because it conforms most nearly to the physical flow of goods.

By pricing inventory at the cost of the most recent acquisitions equal to the quantity on hand, the FIFO method puts the oldest costs into the cost of sales of the period.

When goods are continually turned over and replaced, as is usual, this method tends to increase inventory values in periods of rising prices, even though there may be no material change in the relative composition or quantity of the entire inventory. Compare with LAST-IN, FIRST-OUT (LIFO).

FOREIGN CORPORATION.   A CORPORATION doing business in a state of the United States other than the one in which it was created or incorporated. A foreign corporation must comply with certain terms and conditions imposed by the state in which it does business.

The state statutes make no distinction between a foreign corporation and an international corporation, or ALIEN CORPORATION. Each is regarded as foreign.

FRANCHISE. A right to sell or rent a company's products, services, or methods of operation and use its name to do business; a right conferred by the government, such as the right to vote or to form a CORPORATION. See also Chapter 12/FRANCHISE TAX.

GENERAL CONTRACTOR. A person or organization that assumes responsibility for an entire project, often hiring other contractors, who work as subcontractors, to perform specific tasks. Compare with INDEPENDENT CONTRACTOR.

GOODWILL. An intangible asset that in business is computed as the difference between a firm's book value and a greater purchase or sale price. See also Chapter 12/GOODWILL.

HOLDING COMPANY. Any company that holds the STOCK of other CORPORATIONS. However, the term is usually restricted to two types of organizations: pure holding companies and mixed holding companies:

> A *pure holding company* is a nonoperating company organized for the purpose of investing its CAPITAL in the stocks of other companies, the affairs of which it undertakes to direct or administer.

> A *mixed holding company* or *holding-operating company* is a holding company that is itself an operating company.

Any company owned or controlled by another to the extent that it is a mere instrument to carry out the orders of the owning company is called a SUBSIDIARY. The owning company itself is usually called the PARENT CORPORATION.

Holding companies may be vulnerable to antitrust prosecution when used as a device to suppress competition or to create a monopoly. See also Chapter 11/ANTITRUST LAWS.

HUMAN RESOURCES. See Chapter 1/HUMAN RESOURCES.

INCORPORATORS. Persons who agree to organize themselves into a corporate body, or CORPORATION, and who perform the acts and execute and file the documents required for incorporation.

Many states require three or more incorporators, with one or more being a state resident. Some states also require that the organizational meeting be held in the state. To meet this requirement, corporations may have DUMMY INCORPORATORS who act for the principals until the organizational meeting.

INDEPENDENT CONTRACTOR.   Someone hired to perform a service who is responsible for the end results of the effort.

One has no control over an independent contractor's methods of performance or other details of work as one would have over an employee's labor. Usually, the person has no employee benefits, and a hirer is not required to withhold income or social security taxes from payments.

Compare with GENERAL CONTRACTOR. See also Chapter 12/WITHHOLDING.

INSTALLMENT SALE.   A written contract of sale calling for payments in equal amounts at stated regular intervals. The term consists of two elements: the *down payment* required at the time of purchase and the *installments,* or unit payments, to be made at regular intervals until final maturity of the debt.

A service charge, or interest, is usually included to meet the extra expense of carrying the deferred account. See also CONDITIONAL SALE.

INSURANCE.   See Chapter 14/INSURANCE, BUSINESS.

INTERESTED DIRECTOR.   A member of a BOARD OF DIRECTORS who has a personal, usually pecuniary, interest in a matter that may be profitable for his or her CORPORATION.

An interested director is usually disqualified from voting on a matter of personal interest since his or her decision or vote may be biased. In fact, if the director does vote and the vote is necessary to carry the matter, the directors' action thereon may be voidable or void. See also Chapter 11/VOID, VOIDABLE.

INTERLOCKING DIRECTORATES.   BOARDS OF DIRECTORS of two or more CORPORATIONS having one or more directors in common. Through this method of control, the will of the dominant STOCKHOLDERS is carried out.

The law does not look favorably on interlocking directorates and closely scrutinizes dealings between corporations that have them.

INTERNET.   See E-COMMERCE; Chapter 6/INTERNET.

INTERSTATE COMMERCE, INTRASTATE COMMERCE.   See Chapter 11/INTERSTATE COMMERCE, INTRASTATE COMMERCE.

INVENTORY. The aggregate of goods awaiting sale in the ordinary course of business (merchandise of a trading concern and the finished goods of a manufacturer), goods in the process of manufacture (work in process), and goods to be consumed directly or indirectly in production (raw materials and supplies).

The aggregate is found by taking a *physical inventory.* This involves counting, listing, and valuing all items that make up the raw materials and supplies, work in process, and finished goods.

Included in the inventory are items in transit (material that has left a supplier's place of business just before an inventory cut-off date but that has not arrived at its destination before inventory taking), goods in warehouses, and goods transferred to a consignee, agent, or elsewhere for sale.

In most modern businesses, the inventory is managed by a computerized system created for a particular type of business.

INVESTMENT COMPANY. An organization that invests in securities of other companies and sells its own shares to the investing public, thus making diversification and professional management possible for the small investor. See also Chapter 13/MUTUAL FUND.

JOB LOT. An odd or miscellaneous assortment of goods for sale; a quantity less than the usual amount sold, such as a partial case of some item.

JOINT STOCK COMPANY. A form of business organization created by an agreement of the parties. The agreement is commonly called *articles of incorporation.*

This type of company is similar to the CORPORATION in that the ownership is represented by transferable certificates, management is in the hands of a board of governors or directors elected by the members (shareholders), and the business continues for its fixed term notwithstanding the death or disability of one or more of the members. See also BOARD OF DIRECTORS.

Unlike the STOCKHOLDERS in a corporation but like the partners in a PARTNERSHIP, each shareholder in a joint stock company is personally liable for the company's debts.

In many states, the laws affecting taxation and regulation of corporations make the definition of a corporation broad enough to include joint stock companies. These states regard a joint stock company organized in another state as a FOREIGN CORPORATION.

In other states, a joint stock company may conduct business in the state without being subject to restrictions imposed on corporations.

JOINT VENTURE. An association of two or more persons or business entities for a given, limited purpose but without the usual powers, duties, and responsibilities that go with a PARTNERSHIP.

For example, if two people buy a specific piece of real estate for resale at a profit, they become parties to a joint venture. But if they enter into an agreement whereby each contributes money and services in establishing and carrying on a real estate business, they become partners in a partnership.

KISS. An acronym for **Keep It Simple, Stupid,** a policy applied by many companies in their meetings, communications, and other business activities. Some companies, for example, in an effort to simplify activities and thereby improve performance, have banned memos longer than one page.

LAST-IN, FIRST-OUT (LIFO). A method of valuing an INVENTORY of merchandise. This method assumes that the units sold are those most recently acquired, whereas the units on hand are those first acquired.

In practice, this assumption is usually a fiction that attempts to accomplish a measurement of economic income. It does this by assuming that the real income to the business, especially in a period of changing prices, is measured by the difference between current cost (or most recent cost) and selling price.

LIFO produces less profit than the FIRST-IN, FIRST-OUT METHOD (FIFO) in periods of rising prices and more profit in periods of declining prices.

LAYOFFS. See Chapter 1/LAYOFF.

LEASING. Using real estate (see Chapter 15/REAL PROPERTY), equipment, or other assets for a specified time by making period payments, usually in the form of rent. Under a *lease-purchase option,* the user may purchase the leased property at the end of the term for a specified amount.

Other lease forms and special terms may also be available, depending on the intent and needs of both owner and user. The owner of the leased property is known as the *lessor;* the user is referred to as the *lessee.*

If the leasing arrangement meets certain criteria, the lease payments may be tax deductible. For details, refer to current federal and state tax laws.

LIMITED LIABILITY COMPANY. A hybrid of the SUBCHAPTER S CORPORATION and the PARTNERSHIP, the limited liability company combines the corporate characteristic of limited liability with the tax advantages and flexibility of a partnership.

LIMITED PARTNERSHIP. A PARTNERSHIP in which one or more limited partners' liability for debts of the firm is limited to the amount of his or her investment in the business. To organize a limited partnership, one usually files a certificate in a public office and publishes a notice in the newspaper.

Limited partners have no voice in the management of the partnership. They merely invest money and receive a certain share of the profits. There must be one or more general partners who manage the business and remain liable for all of its debts.

In a limited partnership, as in a general partnership, the death, insanity, or departure of only one of the general partners dissolves the partnership.

Many statutes pertaining to limited partnerships are codified as the Uniform Limited Partnership Law and must be strictly observed. See Chapter 11/UNIFORM PARTNERSHIP ACT AND UNIFORM LIMITED PARTNERSHIP ACT.

LIQUIDATION. The process of distributing the assets of a dissolved CORPORATION or other business (whether voluntarily or involuntarily dissolved) to its STOCKHOLDERS after corporate debts have been paid; the process of selling the INVENTORY and assets of a business that is closing.

LOCKOUT. The refusal of an employer to permit employees to work, a tactic used in labor (employer–union) disputes.

MANAGEMENT BY OBJECTIVES (MBO). A method of managing whereby goals are established and employees are encouraged to work toward those goals, with periodic meetings to review their progress.

MANAGEMENT GUIDE. An *organization manual* that delineates the functions, responsibilities, authority, and principal relationships of a particular position or series of positions in an organization.

For example, a management guide for the office of treasurer might have principal headings such as "Functions," "Responsibilities and Authority," and "Relationships." Under the "Relationships" heading, relations with various insiders and outsiders, such as departmental managers and insurance companies, would be clarified.

MANAGEMENT INFORMATION SYSTEM (MIS). Also known as *data processing, information processing, information system, information technology, information management,* and *management information service.* A system designed to provide essential management information to department heads and other managers in a company.

A management information system (MIS) uses computers and information technology to provide a business with key information and communication services that will help it improve productivity.

An MIS includes hardware and software designed to acquire, manipulate, store, and present accurate and timely information to the various levels of management in an organization. As a result, the managers can more easily solve problems and make the best possible decisions while carrying out their duties.

MARKDOWN. The retail practice of lowering the price of an article below the original retail price. A reversal of the markdown that does *not* increase the selling price above the original retail is called a *markdown cancellation.* Compare with MARKUP.

MARKUP. The retail practice of raising the selling price above the original price. The markup is the difference between the selling price of an article of merchandise and the cost to the seller.

A deduction from the markup that does *not* decrease the selling price below the original retail is called a *markup cancellation.* See also MARKDOWN.

Markup may be expressed in dollars and cents or as a percentage. The markup percentage may be stated as a percentage of cost price, which is called *markup on cost,* or as a percentage of the sales price, which is called *markup on retail.*

In retailing, markup is generally figured as a percentage of the selling price.

MEETINGS. See Chapter 4/DIRECTORS' MEETING; STOCKHOLDERS' MEETING.

MERCHANDISING, RETAIL. The buying, selling, and control of merchandise. The essence of merchandising is the adjustment of supplies to consumer demand, a practice that requires a thorough and continuing study of consumer market trends.

Advertising and publicity help move the products that are stocked in response to demand. Sales promotion creates demand and may be used to introduce a new item or to increase sales of existing items.

MERGER. The joining of two or more CORPORATIONS to form a new entity; the absorption of one or more corporations by another existing corporation. The existing corporation may retain its identity and take over all the rights, privileges, FRANCHISES, properties, and liabilities of the absorbed companies. See also CONSOLIDATION.

MERIT RATING. Periodic review of an employee's performance for purposes of salary increases, promotion, firing, layoff, or training. See also Chapter 1/FIRING; LAYOFF; PROMOTION.

MODEL BUSINESS CORPORATION ACT. See Chapter 11/MODEL BUSINESS CORPORATION ACT.

MONEYED CORPORATION. Generally, a CORPORATION that deals in money or the lending of money. STOCK CORPORATIONS are classified as moneyed, railroad, transportation, business, and cooperative corporations. A *moneyed corporation* is organized under the Banking Law or Insurance Law.

MONOPOLY PRICE. See Chapter 11/MONOPOLY PRICE.

MUNICIPAL CORPORATION. See PUBLIC CORPORATION.

NONPROFIT CORPORATION. A CORPORATION organized for purposes other than to make profits for its members, such as for religious, educational, or scientific purposes. In some cases, it is considered a CHARITABLE CORPORATION, as distinguished from a BUSINESS CORPORATION. See also NONSTOCK CORPORATION.

NONSTOCK CORPORATION. Any CORPORATION other than a STOCK CORPORATION. Nonstock corporations include membership corporations; religious, educational, and charitable institutions; and some PUBLIC CORPORATIONS.

Usually, special laws are passed to regulate the management of the various nonstock corporations. See also CHARITABLE CORPORATION; NONPROFIT CORPORATION.

OFFICE MANAGEMENT. See Chapter 1/OFFICE MANAGEMENT.

OFFICERS OF A CORPORATION. Statutes in most states specifically require a CORPORATION to have a PRESIDENT, SECRETARY (CORPORATE), and TREASURER, as well as a RESIDENT AGENT for service of process upon the corporation. Some organizations also have one or more VICE PRESIDENTS and other officers.

Requirements of officers. Generally, the CERTIFICATE OF INCORPORATION or BYLAWS specify the qualifications of the officers. In some states, the statutes prescribe certain qualifications, such as that the president must be a director.

One person may hold two or more offices in the same corporation, unless the statutes prohibit certain combinations.

In most states, the BOARD OF DIRECTORS has the power to appoint officers.

Term of office. The term of office is usually fixed by the statute of the state in which the corporation is organized or by the corporation's certificate of incorporation or bylaws. Otherwise, an officer holds office at the pleasure of the corporation or until he or she resigns.

Resignation. An officer may resign at any time, even if elected for a fixed period, unless certain restrictions apply. For example, the officer may be restricted by the corporation's certificate or bylaws, by the laws of the state in which the corporation is organized, or by the terms of his or her contract with the corporation.

Powers and duties. An officer derives his or her power from the state corporation laws, the corporation's certificate and bylaws, and any resolutions of the board or committees appointed by that board. His or her duties may vary widely from one corporation to another.

Liabilities. An officer is not chargeable for loss caused by mistakes or errors of judgment. But he or she is bound by the restrictions in the bylaws and is liable for loss resulting from failure to observe them.

A corporate officer may also incur liabilities under certain federal and state statutes. See also Chapter 11/INDEMNIFICATION OF DIRECTORS AND OFFICERS.

Compensation. An officer is not *legally* entitled to compensation for services unless it is authorized by the certificate of incorporation, the bylaws, a board resolution, or an express or implied agreement with the corporation.

In practice, most officers perform ministerial duties for which they are entitled to compensation unless they agree to serve gratuitously.

OPEN SHOP. A business in which an employer may hire nonunion personnel, although in some cases all employees must join the union within a specified period. Compare with CLOSED SHOP; UNION SHOP.

ORGANIZATION MANUAL. See MANAGEMENT GUIDE.

PARENT CORPORATION. A CORPORATION that owns the majority of the STOCK of another corporation known as its SUBSIDIARY.

PARTNERSHIP. An association of two or more persons who, as co-owners, carry on a business for profit. A partnership is organized by oral or written agreement among the parties. Agreement may also be implied from the acts and representations of the parties.

Partnerships are governed by fairly uniform laws, which are codified in many states by the Uniform Partnership Law. (See Chapter 11/UNIFORM PARTNERSHIP ACT AND UNIFORM LIMITED PARTNERSHIP ACT.) A partnership may carry on business in any state without paying more taxes than residents of the state pay.

Partnership property. All types of CAPITAL produced or acquired by the partnership become partnership property. Real estate is generally acquired in the individual names of the partners or in the name of one partner who holds the property in trust for the partnership.

Profits and losses. In the absence of a specific contract, partners share profits and losses equally. However, the partnership agreement may provide that profits and losses shall be distributed pro rata according to the amount of capital contributed by each partner or in any other ratio to which the partners agree.

Each partner of a general partnership is fully liable personally for all partnership debts regardless of the amount of his or her investment. See also LIMITED PARTNERSHIP.

Salaries. Partners have no right to salaries unless they are agreed on, even though one partner may devote all of his or her time to the business and the other may devote little or none. However, the agreement may provide for the division of profits after allowing each of the partners an agreed-upon salary.

Dissolution of partnership. Partnerships are dissolved without violation of the partnership agreement by one of three acts: (1) One of the members may simply withdraw or die; (2) the partnership may be dissolved by operation of law, such as a change in the law that makes the business illegal; or (3) a court decree may be granted because of the incapacity, insanity, gross misconduct, neglect, or breach of duty of one of the partners.

Accounting records.   The net worth (see Chapter 12/NET WORTH) is represented by a capital account for each partner (in an amount equal to the interest of each). Profits and losses are reflected in the capital accounts in the proportion in which profits are shared and losses are borne.

PATENT.   An exclusive right granted by the federal government to an inventor for a fixed period to make, use, and sell an invention. The person to whom a patent is granted is called the *patentee.*

For example, a person may apply for a patent if he or she perfects a new machine, process, or material or any new and useful improvement of the machine, process, or material. Similarly, a person may apply for a patent if he or she invents, discovers, or reproduces a distinct and new variety of plant.

Businesspeople most often use a design or utility patent:

A *design patent* provides protection to the patentee on the ornamental design of an invention.

A *utility patent,* which is more effective but also more difficult to obtain, provides protection on the function or method of an invention.

Patent rights are issued for 14 to 20 years without renewal. Holding a patent gives the owner the right to stop someone else from using or selling the invention without the owner's permission. Anyone producing a patented product without the owner's consent may be compelled to pay damages.

A patent attorney usually prepares the patent application. However, information and forms are available to anyone from the Assistant Commissioner for Patents in Washington, D.C.

PRESIDENT.   The principal executive officer of a CORPORATION. See also OFFICERS OF A CORPORATION.

In companies using the office of CHAIRMAN OF THE BOARD, the office of president is ordinarily subordinate, but the president is still considered, subject to the control of the chairman, the principal officer in charge of the business. For this reason, all other offices are subordinate to that of the president.

PRICING PRACTICES.   See Chapter 11/PRICING PRACTICES.

PRINCIPAL. See AGENCY.

PROFESSIONAL CORPORATION (PC). Most states permit specified professionals, such as accountants, architects, lawyers, and physicians, to organize as professional CORPORATIONS to render services in their profession. Shares may generally be issued only to members of the particular profession.

PROFESSIONAL LIMITED LIABILITY COMPANY (PLLC). A LIMITED LIABILITY COMPANY organized by specified professionals as authorized by state statute. See also PROFESSIONAL CORPORATION (PC).

PROMOTERS. Persons who undertake to organize and publicize individuals and activities; those who undertake to form a new CORPORATION.

The formation of a new business includes procuring for it the rights and CAPITAL by which it is to carry out the purposes set forth in its CERTIFICATE OF INCORPORATION. Frequently, the promoters become affiliated with the corporation in some official capacity. See also INCORPORATORS.

PROPRIETORSHIP, SOLE. A common form of business organization, along with the CORPORATION, the LIMITED LIABILITY COMPANY, and the PARTNERSHIP. A sole proprietorship differs from the other forms in that ownership of the business is vested in one individual.

Organization. The individual proprietorship is the earliest and simplest form of business organization. No formalities are necessary to establish it. All that an individual need do is to ascertain whether a license is required to conduct the particular business and whether a license fee or tax must be paid to state or local authorities.

Duration. A sole proprietorship is not limited in its duration by law. It is not, however, a stable form of organization since the illness of the owner may interrupt it, and his or her death may terminate it.

Profits and losses. The individual owner is personally liable for all debts of the business to the full extent of his or her property. The owner cannot limit liability to creditors to the amount put into the business. But the individual is not required to pay taxes greater than the other residents of the particular state pay.

All profits are his or hers to reinvest in the business or to dispose of as the owner chooses. The proprietor may raise additional CAPITAL for the business by borrowing from banks and from others, by purchasing goods on credit, and by personally investing additional amounts in the enterprise.

PROXY. See Chapter 4/PROXY.

PUBLIC CORPORATION. A CORPORATION organized by the federal government or a state government to serve as an administrative agency of that government. This includes *municipal corporations,* which are formed by a state government. See also QUASIPUBLIC CORPORATION.

PUBLIC SERVICE CORPORATION. See PUBLIC UTILITY CORPORATION.

PUBLIC UTILITY CORPORATION. A CORPORATION that is engaged in supplying services regarded as public necessities, such as railroad, electric, gas, power, telephone, or water services.

The corporation usually is specially franchised by a federal, state, or municipal authority and is subject to supervision and regulation by a public service commission. It is also known as a *public service corporation* or *company.*

PYRAMIDING. The technique by which a few individuals who control a HOLDING COMPANY gain control over vast properties with relatively small investments in each of a number of interrelated companies. The structure is made up of a holding company at the apex and various levels of intermediate holding and operating companies.

Pyramiding is generally done for speculative profit and not to serve as an improvement in the operations of the individual companies involved.

QUASIPUBLIC CORPORATION. A CORPORATION that is not a PUBLIC CORPORATION organized as an instrument of government administration but one that nevertheless contributes to the safety, comfort, or convenience of a community, such as a telephone company. See also PUBLIC UTILITY CORPORATION.

REAL ESTATE. See Chapter 15/REAL PROPERTY.

RECORDS, CORPORATE. The records that state CORPORATION laws sometimes require a corporation to maintain.

The required records usually include the record of minutes (see Chapter 4/MINUTES), the stock certificate record, and the stock records and transfer records, sometimes described as *stock ledgers*.

Most business organizations maintain such records by computer or in both print and electronic form.

Maintenance requirements. The statutes, which must be strictly followed, indicate who shall have charge of the records and whether or not they must be kept at the corporation's principal office.

Provision for the maintenance of corporate records is also included in the BYLAWS, which follow the requirements of the statute. Generally, the rights of STOCKHOLDERS to inspect the records are covered there.

Custody of the corporate records. Although the minutes, stock records, and so on are the property of the corporation, custody normally resides with the SECRETARY (CORPORATE), or clerk. In the absence of a statutory provision, the stockholders and directors are free to entrust any person with custody of such records.

Under common law (see Chapter 11/COMMON LAW) and under most statutes, the stockholders have a right to inspect the minutes and stock ledgers at a proper and reasonable time.

RECORDS MANAGEMENT. See Chapter 3/RECORDS MANAGEMENT; RECORDS RETENTION; RECORDS SECURITY.

REGISTERED OFFICE. An office of a CORPORATION located in a state in which the corporation is only nominally incorporated or does business. It is maintained to satisfy that state's statutory requirement that the corporation maintain a registered office and RESIDENT AGENT there for service of process, holding of STOCKHOLDERS' meetings, and other purposes.

REGULATION OF BUSINESS. See Chapter 11/REGULATION OF BUSINESS.

REORGANIZATION. In a financial sense, the overall revision of the entire CAPITAL STRUCTURE of a CORPORATION. Reorganization is often forced by creditors and is accomplished through the courts. Often a new corporation is formed to take over the assets of the old, and a new management supplants the old.

The term is common in connection with bankruptcy proceedings. (See Chapter 11/BANKRUPTCY.) For example, reorganization under Chapter 11 of the Bankruptcy Law allows corporations to restructure their obligations.

RESERVATION OF CORPORATE NAME. The steps taken in reserving a name for a new corporation with the appropriate state officials.

A corporate name must use the word *company, association,* or *incorporated* or some other word or abbreviation to indicate that the firm is a CORPORATION. Usually, only a banking institution may use the word *bank* or *trust.*

The appropriate state official, such as the secretary of state, can tell you if your chosen name is already in use or if your chosen name too closely resembles another. In some states, inquiries may be made by telephone, fax, or e-mail.

RESIDENT AGENT. An employee or agent of a CORPORATION, or one obtained through a CORPORATION SERVICE COMPANY, who resides in a state that is only nominally the residence of the corporation incorporated therein.

A resident agent performs for a FOREIGN CORPORATION the services required by that state's statutes to be performed there by the corporation. See also REGISTERED OFFICE.

RETAILING. See MERCHANDISING, RETAIL.

RIGHTS. See Chapter 13/RIGHTS.

RIGHT-TO-WORK LAWS. See Chapter 11/RIGHT-TO-WORK LAWS.

SALE. See Chapter 11/SALE.

S CORPORATION. See SUBCHAPTER S CORPORATION.

SEAL. See CORPORATE SEAL; Chapter 11/SEAL.

SECRETARY (CORPORATE). One of the OFFICERS OF A CORPORATION. The corporate secretary is charged with keeping the minutes of meetings (see Chapter 4/MINUTES), including those of the BOARD OF DIRECTORS, the STOCKHOLDERS, and certain committees. See also Chapter 4/COMMITTEE.

The secretary has charge of the records and is generally authorized to sign, with the PRESIDENT, all contracts, leases, mortgages, bonds, stock certificates, and other such documents and to affix the CORPORATE SEAL. Also, he or she has charge of the stock certificate records, transfer records, and stock ledger.

SENIORITY. Job status based on length of service. The term commonly implies preference in job security, promotions, and other rewards.

SERVICE MARK. A word, phrase, symbol, design, or combination thereof used to distinguish the source of a service. The purpose is to ensure that the service will be readily identified in the market and its origin established. Usually, the mark appears in advertising for the service.

Registration. In general, the same registration and use procedures, as well as the same degree of protection offered, that are described in the entry TRADEMARK apply to a service mark. (A trademark is the same as a service mark except that it distinguishes and identifies the source of a product rather than a service.)

Information and application forms for both types of marks are available from the Assistant Commissioner for Trademarks in Arlington, Virginia.

Registration designation. Until an application is approved, however, the company applying should use an *SM* designation; after approval, the letter *R* in a circle indicates registration:

Fix It While U Wait^{SM}

Fix It While U Wait®

Although the symbols need not be used with the name in running text, such as in a paragraph, the name should be treated as a proper noun (see Chapter 7/NOUN) and capitalized.

SEXUAL HARASSMENT. See Chapter 1/SEXUAL HARASSMENT.

SHARES. See CORPORATION, *Characteristics of a corporation;* Chapter 13/STOCK.

SILENT PARTNER. A partner who has no voice in the management of the business. Except for limited partners (see LIMITED PARTNERSHIP), a silent partner is equally responsible with other partners for debts of the business. See also PARTNERSHIP.

SOLE PRACTITIONER. One who practices a profession independently, as an individual, such as a lawyer or doctor who is not associated with others for the purpose of practicing the particular profession. See also PROPRIETORSHIP, SOLE.

SOLE PROPRIETORSHIP. See PROPRIETORSHIP, SOLE.

STATE OF INCORPORATION. The state in which a CORPORATION is organized. A U.S. corporation is considered a DOMESTIC CORPORATION in the state in which it is incorporated and a FOREIGN CORPORATION in all other states. Outside the United States, it is considered an ALIEN CORPORATION.

STOCK. A term that refers to the aggregate ownership interest in a BUSINESS CORPORATION. Hence it refers to ownership of the CORPORATION, not of the corporation's *assets,* which are in turn owned by the corporation. See also Chapter 13/STOCK; STOCK CERTIFICATE.

STOCK CORPORATION. A CORPORATION that has CAPITAL STOCK (see also Chapter 12/CAPITAL STOCK) divided into shares of STOCK. When it has a surplus, it is authorized by law to distribute to the holders of these shares proportional amounts of its profits in the form of dividends. See also Chapter 13/DIVIDEND; STOCK.

STOCKHOLDER. Owner of one or more shares of STOCK in a CORPORATION. Stockholders do not participate directly in the control of the ordinary affairs of a corporation. Instead, they elect directors to manage the business, thereby exercising indirect control. See also BOARD OF DIRECTORS; Chapter 4/STOCKHOLDERS' MEETING; Chapter 13/STOCK.

Stockholder consent. The Uniform Corporations Act provides for certain amendments to the CERTIFICATE OF INCORPORATION or BYLAWS by directors and shareholders. State statutes or the certificate of incorporation generally requires the consent of all or a portion of the stockholders before certain actions are taken.

These actions include the removal of directors, MERGER or CONSOLIDATION of the corporation with another company, transfer of all assets of the corporation by sale or lease, and voluntary dissolution and LIQUIDATION of the corporation.

Exercise of stockholder rights. Laws of the state in which a corporation is organized, the certificate of incorporation, and the bylaws give the stockholders certain rights and powers that must be exercised at a meeting. However, the validity of action taken at a meeting does not always depend on whether the meeting was formal.

Before an objecting stockholder can succeed in nullifying an action taken at a meeting, he or she must show that his or her rights have been affected by the irregularity.

STOCK LEDGER. See RECORDS, CORPORATE.

SUBCHAPTER S CORPORATION. A small CORPORATION that earns limited money and chooses to be taxed as an ordinary PARTNERSHIP under the federal Internal Revenue Code. Its STOCKHOLDERS thus have limited personal liability and are taxed individually.

SUBSIDIARY. A company that is controlled by another CORPORATION known as a HOLDING COMPANY or a PARENT CORPORATION. The entity that controls the subsidiary owns all or a majority of its STOCK.

SYNDICATE. An association of persons formed to conduct some business transaction, usually financial. Most syndicates are formed temporarily for a specific objective and are terminated when the objective is realized. See also CONSORTIUM.

TAXES. See Chapter 12/ALTERNATIVE MINIMUM TAX; CREDITS, TAX; DEDUCTIONS/ADJUSTMENTS; DEPRECIATION; DIRECT TAX; ESTIMATED TAX; EXCISE TAX; EXCLUSION; FRANCHISE TAX; INCOME TAX; INFORMATION RETURN; PAYROLL TAXES; PROPERTY TAX; SALES AND USE TAX; SELF-EMPLOYMENT TAX; SOCIAL SECURITY TAX; STAMP TAX; STATE INCOME TAX; STATE UNEMPLOYMENT INSURANCE TAX.

TELECOMMUNICATIONS. See Chapter 2/TELECOMMUNICATIONS.

TELECOMMUTING.   See Chapter 1/TELECOMMUTING.

TRADEMARK.   A distinctive mark, symbol, word, phrase, design, or combination thereof used to distinguish the products of a particular manufacturer or merchant. (A SERVICE MARK is the same as a trademark except that it distinguishes and identifies the source of a service.)

The purpose of using a trademark is to ensure that an article will be readily identified in the market and its origin will be well established. Usually, the mark appears on the product or its packaging.

Registration.   Registration of a trademark with the Patent and Trademark Office is not mandatory in that a trademark rightfully belongs to the first person who has used it.

Also, federal registration applies only to the use of trademarks in interstate and foreign commerce. Although federal law now offers wider protection, users may want to seek state registration to ensure protection in intrastate commerce. See also Chapter 11/INTERSTATE COMMERCE, INTRASTATE COMMERCE.

Registration does not automatically protect an owner from litigation. Although the Patent and Trademark Office is empowered to refuse to register an infringing idea, the registered owner nevertheless has to bring suit to restrain another who has unlawfully appropriated the owner's trademark.

Information and application forms are available from the Assistant Commissioner for Trademarks in Arlington, Virginia.

Registration designation.   Until the application is approved, the company may use the *TM* designation. After approval, the letter *R* in a circle indicates registration:

Designmaster™

Designmaster®

Although the symbols need not be used with the name in running text, such as in a paragraph, the name should be treated as a proper noun (see Chapter 7/NOUN) and capitalized.

Trademark rights last as long as a company continues to use the mark with its products. The initial term of trademark registration is ten years, with ten-year renewal terms thereafter. If a mark is no longer used, the registration is terminated.

TRANSFER AGENT. An individual, bank, or trust company that keeps the stock ledger of a CORPORATION and records all transfers of STOCK. (See also Chapter 13/STOCK.) The transfer agent must make certain that the act of transfer is executed properly.

TREASURER. The financial officer of a CORPORATION. The treasurer is the custodian of the corporation's assets and is primarily responsible for financial planning, including the procurement, use, and investment of funds.

The treasurer has the right to sign checks for payment of obligations and to endorse checks, notes, and other obligations payable to the corporation. Also, he or she has custody of the securities owned by the corporation and is usually in charge of the credit and COLLECTIONS department.

There is a lack of uniformity among corporations in the division of administrative duties between the treasurer and the controller. (See CONTROLLER [COMPTROLLER].) In all cases, though, the treasurer is primarily in charge of finance, and the controller is primarily in charge of accounting.

TRUST. See Chapter 11/TRUST.

UNFAIR EMPLOYMENT PRACTICE. See Chapter 11/UNFAIR EMPLOYMENT PRACTICE.

UNIFORM COMMERCIAL CODE (UCC). See Chapter 11/UNIFORM COMMERCIAL CODE (UCC).

UNIFORM PARTNERSHIP ACT AND UNIFORM LIMITED PARTNERSHIP ACT. See Chapter 11/UNIFORM PARTNERSHIP ACT AND UNIFORM LIMITED PARTNERSHIP ACT.

UNION SHOP. A business in which nonunion members may be hired for up to a 30-day trial period, at which time they must join the union or will be discharged. Compare with CLOSED SHOP; OPEN SHOP.

USURY. See Chapter 11/USURY.

VICE PRESIDENT. An OFFICER OF A corporation who performs all the usual duties of the PRESIDENT in his or her absence or disability. There are no basic functions for a vice president, such as those for TREASURER, SECRETARY (CORPORATE), or CONTROLLER (COMPTROLLER).

In large corporations, a vice president is often a department head. Thus there may be as many vice presidents as there are departments, each designated as *vice president in charge of sales, vice president in charge of production,* and so on.

In some companies, the vice presidents are designated as *first vice president, second vice president,* and so on.

VOTING TRUST.   An entity created to concentrate the control of a company in the hands of a few people. However, competing corporations cannot use a voting trust to form a monopoly. See also Chapter 11/MONOPOLY.

Voting trust agreement.   A voting trust is usually organized and operated under a *voting trust agreement.* This agreement is a contract between the STOCKHOLDERS and the *voting trustees,* who manage the CORPORATION.

Under the agreement, the stockholders transfer their STOCK to the trustees. In doing so, they give them the right to vote the stock during the life of the agreement.

All stockholders may become parties to the agreement, which is generally subject to state statutory regulation.

Voting trust certificates.   The trustees issue certificates of beneficial interest, called *voting trust certificates,* to the stockholders, who are entitled to the dividends. See Chapter 13/DIVIDEND.

The trust is usually set up for a definite period. When it is terminated, the certificate holders are notified to exchange their trust certificates for certificates of stock.

WORKING CAPITAL.   See Chapter 12/WORKING CAPITAL.

CHAPTER ELEVEN

Business Law

ACCELERATION CLAUSE. A CONTRACT, promissory note (see Chapter 13/NOTE), or mortgage clause (see Chapter 15/MORTGAGE) that permits a lender to demand the full and unpaid balance owed under specified circumstances, especially DEFAULT.

ACKNOWLEDGMENT. The act by which a person who has signed a legal instrument goes before an authorized officer, such as a NOTARY PUBLIC, and declares that he or she executed the instrument. Compare with AFFIDAVIT.

An authorized officer signs the *certificate of acknowledgment,* which entitles the instrument to be recorded or filed and authorizes it to be given in evidence without further proof of its EXECUTION. See also JURAT.

The six essential parts of an acknowledgment are the venue (place), date, name of person making the acknowledgment, signature of person taking it, date of officer's commission expiration, and the notarial seal. See Figure 1.

In some jurisdictions, officers who are not notaries may attest acknowledgments. The seal and expiration date then may not be required.

ADMINISTRATIVE PROCEDURES ACT. A uniform law, adopted in most states, to govern rule making and the decision and appeal processes of regulatory agencies.

A compatible federal law governs administrative procedures for federal agencies.

ACKNOWLEDGMENT: FIGURE 1
Certificate of Acknowledgment

STATE OF

COUNTY OF

    On this the _____ day of 200X, before me, _____, the

undersigned officer, personally appeared JOHN JONES, known to me or

sufficiently proven to be the person whose name is subscribed to the within

instrument and acknowledged that he executed the same for the purpose

therein contained.

    IN WITNESS WHEREOF, I have hereunto set my hand and official

seal.

_____
Notary Public

My commission expires _____

AFFIDAVIT. A written statement signed and sworn to before some person authorized to take an oath. It may be accepted as proof when no other evidence of a fact is available. The person making the affidavit is the *affiant* or *deponent*.

An affidavit is a complete instrument within itself and is an affirmation that the statements made are true. By contrast, an ACKNOWLEDGMENT is appended to another document. An affidavit is sworn to, but an acknowledgment is not.

Both the person making the affidavit and the officer administering the oath sign it. However, only the officer taking an acknowledgment signs it. Also, an affidavit has a JURAT, whereas an acknowledgment does not.

Affidavits are frequently attached to a legal pleading or a COURT document, such as a Motion for Summary Judgment, to support the facts set forth in the document.

The seven essential parts of an affidavit are the venue (place), name of affiant, averment of oath, statement of facts, affiant's signature, jurat, and NOTARY PUBLIC's signature. See Figure 1.

AFFIDAVIT: FIGURE 1

I, _____, on oath depose and say as follows:

My name is _____, and I live at _____,
_____.

I have read the attached Motion for Summary Judgment. The facts stated therein are true to the best of my knowledge and belief.

_____

(Signed) _____

Date:

STATE OF

COUNTY OF

Appeared before me this _____ day of _____, 200X, the above-named _____, known to me or satisfactorily proven to be the same, and swore that the statements made in the foregoing document are true to the best of his/her knowledge and belief.

_____

Notary Public

My commission expires _____

AMERICAN COURT SYSTEM. See UNITED STATES COURT SYSTEM.

AMERICAN DIGEST SYSTEM. A series of digests covering all reported legal cases in America since 1658. The topics are arranged alphabetically in numerous volumes, and an extensive index makes up several volumes in itself.

It can be found in law libraries and is also available on-line through WEST-LAW. See also DATABASES, LEGAL.

AMERICAN JURISPRUDENCE. A legal encyclopedia, usually cited as *Am. Jur.* It can be found in law libraries and is also available on-line through WESTLAW. See also DATABASES, LEGAL.

AMERICAN LAW REPORTS. A large series of books that report selected cases in full along with a related annotation, or commentary, usually cited as *A.L.R.,* or *ALR.*

It can be found in law libraries and is also available on-line through WEST-LAW. See also DATABASES, LEGAL.

AMERICANS WITH DISABILITIES ACT (ADA). See LABOR LAWS.

AMICUS CURIAE. Latin for "friend of the court." An individual or, more commonly, an organization that is permitted to appear in a lawsuit, usually in the appellate phase, by furnishing an opinion, or filing a BRIEF, presenting a point of view not otherwise represented.

However, that person or organization has no right, or standing, to appear otherwise.

ANSWER. A DEFENDANT's formal written statement of defense, prepared and signed by his or her attorney. An answer is supplied in response to a COMPLAINT and may deny some or all of the complaint's allegations.

ANTITRUST LAWS. Federal and state laws designed to prevent restraint of trade, MONOPOLY, and unfair practices in interstate commerce. (See INTERSTATE COMMERCE, INTRASTATE COMMERCE.) The statutes constitute a patchwork of loopholes plugging and exempting enactments.

The *Sherman Act (Antitrust Act of 1890)* was adopted to protect trade and commerce against unlawful restraints and monopolies.

During the twentieth century, as the nature of U.S. business and commerce evolved, several acts amended the Sherman Act to prevent abuses and close loopholes in the original act. These acts include the *Clayton Act* (1914) and the *Robinson–Patman Act* (1936).

The laws are administered by several regulatory agencies for various types of business, including the following:

The Federal Reserve Board (FRB) (see Chapter 13/FEDERAL RESERVE ACT) for banks and financial institutions

The Federal Communications Commission (FCC) (see Chapter 2/FEDERAL COMMUNICATIONS COMMISSION [FCC]) for broadcasting and telephone

The FEDERAL TRADE COMMISSION (FTC) for other areas of commerce

A few states incorporated in their constitutions declarations of policy regarding monopolies. (See MONOPOLY.) A larger number adopted constitutions with broader provisions to prevent combinations that suppress competition, and some enacted statutes for that purpose.

Today, enforcement of federal antitrust legislation has, as a practical matter, made prosecution under state antitrust laws unusual.

APPEAL. A review procedure entered in a higher COURT to examine the decision of a lower court or of some government official or agency. The higher court examines the record and decides whether a decision was in accordance with applicable law.

ARBITRATION. See Chapter 10/ARBITRATION.

ASSESSMENT. In law, the amount of damages that the successful party in a lawsuit is entitled to; in real estate, the value placed on real property (see Chapter 15/ASSESSED VALUATION; REAL PROPERTY) for purposes of property taxation.

ASSIGNMENT. An act whereby a party (the *assignor*) transfers property, real or personal, or some right or interest in property to another party (the *assignee*). See also PERSONAL PROPERTY; Chapter 15/REAL PROPERTY.

An assignment may be oral or written, unless it involves a CONTRACT required to be written according to the STATUTE OF FRAUDS. It may be a formal document or an endorsement on a contract, and it must effect an immediate transfer to a specific assignee.

Like any contract, an assignment, to be valid, must be executed by a party having legal capacity. Every assignment is a transfer, but not every transfer is an assignment.

ATTACHMENT. The process of seizing or taking into custody. Attachment is a legal proceeding used by a creditor to have the property of a debtor seized under COURT order, pending a determination of the creditor's claim.

An attachment is recorded in the appropriate public records as a notice that a claim has been made, which, if found valid, would affect the value of the property attached. An attachment creates or perfects a LIEN on property.

ATTESTATION. The act of signing a written instrument as witness to the signature of a party, at the party's request, such as witnessing signatures to a CONTRACT or will. See Figure 1.

The witness is called a *subscribing witness,* because he or she signs the instrument as a witness.

A legend or clause that recites the circumstances surrounding the signing of an instrument often precedes the signature of the attesting witnesses. This is called the *attestation clause.* The wording varies from a simple "In the presence of" to the lengthy clause used in some wills.

When a corporate secretary attests to an instrument, he or she impresses the corporate seal upon it. See also Chapter 10/CORPORATE SEAL.

Attestation is the act of the witness, whereas EXECUTION is the act of the party to the instrument.

ATTESTATION: FIGURE 1

IN WITNESS WHEREOF, we the undersigned, have set our hands

to the foregoing instrument on this _____ day of _____, 200X.

Signed and delivered by grantor in the)
presence of:)
)
)
                                                    Grantor

Signed and delivered by grantee in the)
presence of:)
)
)
                                                    Grantee

BAILMENT. The transfer of possession of PERSONAL PROPERTY for some particular purpose upon a CONTRACT that the property will be returned to the person delivering it after the accomplishment of the purpose for which it was delivered.

The person delivering the property is the *bailor*. The person receiving it is the *bailee*.

A bailment may be created by express agreement, or it may be implied by the conduct of the parties or by the law. An essential ingredient is that the parties contemplate return of the property or an accounting in accordance with the terms of agreement.

If the contact requires the bailee to pay a sum of money instead of returning the goods, the obligation is a *debt* and not a bailment.

A conditional sale (see Chapter 10/CONDITIONAL SALE) is therefore distinguished from a bailment in that the purchaser has an obligation to pay the purchase price, at which time he or she acquires title to the property.

BANKRUPTCY. A legal process in which the property of a debtor is taken over by a receiver or trustee in bankruptcy for the benefit of the creditors.

The action is performed under the jurisdiction of the COURTS as prescribed by the federal Bankruptcy Act.

In general, the Bankruptcy Act provides for the relief and rehabilitation of debtors, and the intent is to restore the debtor to a viable entity by reconstituting the debtor's financial and business operations.

Voluntary bankruptcy. This type of bankruptcy is initiated when a debtor files a petition in bankruptcy. The form of the petition is prescribed by the act.

By filing a voluntary petition, a debtor seeks to have assets fairly distributed among all creditors, on the basis of established priorities, and to be free of debt. A person or company is thus able to begin business life anew, free of the discharged debts.

Voluntary bankruptcy is open to all individuals, firms, partnerships, and corporations, except banking, building and loan associations, and insurance, railroad, and municipal corporations. No minimum amount of debt is required.

Involuntary bankruptcy. This type of bankruptcy is initiated when creditors file a petition against an insolvent debtor.

However, the debtor must owe the creditors filing the petition a specified amount more than the value of any LIENS the creditors hold on the debtor's property. Also, the debtor must have committed an act of bankruptcy, such as admitting an inability to pay debts, preceding the filing of the petition.

Involuntary bankruptcy proceedings cannot be brought against a wage earner, farmer, building and loan association, or banking, insurance, railroad, or municipal corporation.

Reorganization, or plans for repayment of debt under court supervison, are also provided for in Chapter 11 (for businesses) and Chapter 13 (for individuals) of the bankruptcy code.

BLUE SKY LAW. A law that regulates and supervises the sales of stock and other activities of investment companies. (See Chapter 13/STOCK.) It is intended to protect the public from fraudulent stock deals.

BONDING. The process by which one entity (often an insurance company) agrees to be responsible for the debt or failure to perform of another upon payment of a premium.

BOYCOTT. An attempt by many persons to injure another by refusing to do business with the object of the boycott. A *secondary boycott,* which is an attempt to injure someone by applying economic pressure to a third party, is illegal.

BREACH OF CONTRACT. The failure or refusal by one of the parties to a CONTRACT, without legal excuse, to perform some act required under the contract.

A contract may also be breached by preventing or obstructing performance by the other party or by *anticipatory breach,* such as the unqualified announcement by a seller, before delivery date, that he or she will not deliver the goods.

A right of action occurs or is complete upon the other party's failure to do the particular thing he or she agreed to do. However, damages may be obtained only for losses that can be shown to have resulted directly from the breach.

BREACH OF DUTY. See TORT.

BREACH OF WARRANTY. Providing a false WARRANTY to a buyer. Several alternatives are available to the buyer in this situation.

The buyer may accept the goods for a reduced price, keep them and seek damages, refuse them and bring action for damages, rescind the CONTRACT before delivery, or return the goods after delivery and recover what has been paid.

BRIEF. A written summary or condensed statement; a written statement filed in COURT by one side in a lawsuit to explain its case; a summary of a published opinion in a case.

A court brief usually contains a fact and law summary and an argument about how the law applies to the facts.

BULK SALES LAW. A law intended to protect creditors from being defrauded when a seller liquidates all or most assets to a single buyer. Bulk transfers are controlled under Article 6 of the UNIFORM COMMERCIAL CODE (UCC) adopted in all states. See also Chapter 10/LIQUIDATION.

CAVEAT EMPTOR. Latin for "Let the buyer beware." A COMMON LAW doctrine that imposes on the buyer the duty of examining what he or she buys. The purchaser must examine, judge, and test the property, whether it is real or personal property. See also PERSONAL PROPERTY; Chapter 15/REAL PROPERTY.

The doctrine is applied when a seller makes no express WARRANTY and is not guilty of fraud.

Exceptions to the doctrine are made in the following circumstances:

1. A fiduciary relation exists between the parties, such as between a PRINCIPAL and an agent. See also Chapter 10/AGENCY.

2. The defects are not obvious, and the buyer has not had an opportunity to make a thorough inspection.

3. The sale was made by sample or by description.

4. The sale was for a specific purpose.

The scope of the doctrine has been narrowed in recent years. Both case and statutory law have enlarged the responsibilities of the seller, with warranties being inferred from the facts and circumstances of a transaction.

The UNIFORM COMMERCIAL CODE (UCC) has expanded the scope and application of *implied warranties* to the sale of goods.

CERTIORARI. Latin for "to make sure." A request that is filed with an appellate COURT asking the court to review a trial court decision. A request for certiorari is not an APPEAL of right, and the appellate court may refuse to accept the case for consideration.

CHATTEL. See PERSONAL PROPERTY.

CHOSE IN ACTION.   A phrase used to describe a right to PERSONAL PROPERTY that is not reduced to physical possession and that requires some form of legal action to acquire or recover possession.

Some of the most important choses in action are CONTRACTS, promissory notes, checks, trade acceptance, stocks, bonds, bank accounts, and the right of legal action to recover money or property. See also Chapter 13/BOND; NOTE; STOCK.

CITATIONS TO LEGAL AUTHORITIES.   References to the sources of legal information. Most citations occur in legal BRIEFS, memorandums of law, and lawyers' opinion letters. References are usually made to constitutions, statutes, and codes; to published COURT decisions; and to texts and periodicals.

The following are examples of common forms of legal citations. For detailed information about the appropriate style in specific cases, consult the latest edition of *The Bluebook: A Uniform System of Citation* (Harvard Law Review, Cambridge, Massachusetts):

> *Constitution:* U.S. Const. art. IV, §2.
>
> *Statutes and codes:* Administrative Procedures Act §6, 5 U.S.C. §555 (1994).
>
> *Cases in official reports and reporters: United States v. Virginia,* 518 U.S. 515 (1996).
>
> *Slip decision: American Express Travel v. David Moskoff,* No. 98-016 (N.H. Sept. 13, 1999).
>
> *Unpublished cases: Rotella v. Wood,* No. 97-11279 (N.D. Tex. July 30, 1998).
>
> *Cases available on database: Rotella v. Wood,* No. 97-11279, LEXIS (N.D. Tex. July 30, 1998).
>
> *Law reviews:* 106 *Yale L.J.* 1849 (1997).

CIVIL RIGHTS ACT.   See FAIR EMPLOYMENT PRACTICES.

CLASS ACTION.   A lawsuit brought by one or more PLAINTIFFS on behalf of other persons who are similarly situated or have suffered a similar wrong. For example, a group of stockholders in a corporation may bring a class action on behalf of all other stockholders who have a similar grievance.

COMMERCE CLAUSE.   The clause in Article 1, Section 8, of the Constitution that gives the federal government the power to regulate commerce among the several states. It is the basis for all federal regulation of business.

The purpose of the clause is to facilitate free trade among the states and to ensure the uniform regulation of commerce free from local pressure and discrimination. See also INTERSTATE COMMERCE, INTRASTATE COMMERCE; REGULATION OF BUSINESS.

COMMON LAW. A system of law, or body of legal rules, developed in England and carried over into the American legal system. It is derived from the decisions of judges based on accepted customs and traditions.

The system is known as the *common law* because it is believed that these rules were generally recognized and in full force throughout England.

Common law, which is continually expanding and changing, is now the basis of the laws in most states. An important exception is Louisiana, where law is based on the civil law derived from the Napoleonic Codes.

Statutes have been enacted to supplement and supersede the common law in many fields. However, common law governs where no statute deals with a specific subject.

Although the common law is written, it is called the *unwritten law* because it is not enacted by legislatures as is STATUTORY LAW.

COMPLAINT. The statement that a PLAINTIFF makes setting forth the grounds on which the plaintiff is suing a DEFENDANT. A complaint asks for damages or other relief.

The complaint is usually the initial document filed in a COURT action. See also ANSWER.

CONSENT DECREE. A decree arrived at by agreement of the parties. Provided the agreement is approved by the COURT, it is entered into the record and is enforceable as a JUDGMENT.

For example, in antitrust cases, the decree ends a controversy between the government and a private firm in a manner acceptable to both sides. The DEFENDANT agrees to changes in operating procedure that will bring its activities into conformity with ANTITRUST LAWS.

Once a court has reviewed and approved a consent decree, the case is settled without the right of APPEAL.

In a consent decree, the defendant neither admits nor denies the allegations made by the plaintiff or the prosecution.

CONSTRUCTIVE RECEIPT. That which in the eyes of the law amounts to an act, although the act itself is not necessarily performed. The law presumes an act to have been performed and applies the term to many situations.

Constructive receipt of income, for example, usually constitutes taxable income. Therefore, at any time during the year, a firm may credit a salesperson's commissions on the firm's records, although the salesperson may not draw on the credit until the following year.

Nevertheless, each commission is *constructively received* in the year in which it is credited, and each amount credited will have to be reported by the salesperson as income *in the year in which it is credited*.

CONTRACT. An agreement, enforceable at law, by which two parties mutually promise to give some particular thing or to do or abstain from doing a particular act.

A contract may be formal or informal. It may be oral or written, sealed or unsealed. However, state statutes, usually designated as the STATUTE OF FRAUDS, require certain agreements to be in writing.

A contract may be *executed* (fully carried out by both parties) or *executory* (yet to be performed). It may be executed by one party and executory by the other. For example, the purchase of merchandise on credit, followed by delivery, is *executed* on the part of the seller but *executory* on the part of the buyer.

Under the UNIFORM COMMERCIAL CODE (UCC), a contract may be *express* (all terms expressed, or stated, in the oral or written agreement) or *implied* (not expressed but implied by law from the actions of the parties). For example, when a person gets on a bus, this action *implies* a contract with the transit company.

Essentials of an enforceable contract. To be enforceable at law, a contract must have four elements: an offer and acceptance, competent parties, legal subject matter, and consideration.

1. *An offer and acceptance must take place.* The *offerer* must make an offer or proposal to do or to refrain from doing a certain thing. The *offeree* must then accept the proposal.

If during the negotiation of a contract one party makes a counteroffer, the offerer will then accept or reject the new terms or price. In general, once an offer is accepted, it cannot be withdrawn or revoked.

2. *The persons seeking to contract must be competent parties.* All persons are presumed to have unlimited power to contract, except infants, insane persons or persons with impaired mental faculties, intoxicated persons, and corporations.

A corporation's ability to contract is limited by its certificate of incorporation and by various statutes. See also Chapter 10/CERTIFICATE OF INCORPORATION.

3. *The subject matter must be legal.* A contract is illegal if it calls for the performance of an act forbidden by law or against public policy. Usurious contracts (see USURY), for example, are generally held to be illegal. Also, federal and state laws make illegal those contracts that restrain trade, fix prices, or result in unfair practices.

4. *Consideration is required.* To make a contract binding, one must give something of value to the person making a promise or the person to whom a promise is made must suffer some detriment. Therefore, *consideration* is the price, motive, or matter inducing the contract.

Contracts under seal.   Placing a SEAL on a contract is required in some states on contracts of major importance. Deeds, mortgages, and other conveyances of real estate are among the contracts requiring a seal in certain states. See also Chapter 15/DEED; MORTGAGE.

Uniform Commercial Code (UCC).   Adopted in all states, the UNIFORM COMMERCIAL CODE governs all contracts dealing with the sale of goods. It defines a *contract* as the total legal obligation that results from the parties' agreements as affected by the code and any other applicable rules of law.

An *agreement* is the bargain of the parties as found in their language or by implication from other circumstances. This includes "course of dealing," "usage of trade," or "course of performance," as provided in the code.

A *bargain* is defined as an agreement of two or more persons to exchange promises or to exchange a promise for a performance.

Recision of contract.   To *rescind* a contract is to abrogate, annul, void, or cancel it. The term is frequently used to refer to the action of one party to a contract.

Types of contracts.   Contracts may take many forms:

A *unilateral contract* is one in which one party promises to do something without receiving any promise, acceptance, or consideration from the other party.

A *bilateral contract* is one in which *each* party has rights and duties.

An *oral contract* is one not in writing and not signed by the parties.

A *cost-plus contract,* often used in government contracts, is one in which a contractor is paid the cost of producing goods or services plus a stated percentage that is the contractor's profit.

An *output contract* is one in which one party promises to deliver an entire production and the other party promises to purchase it.

COOLING-OFF PERIOD.   A period, usually 30 to 90 days, during which a union is barred from striking or an employer is barred from locking out its employees. See also Chapter 10/LOCKOUT.

Provided for under certain state labor laws and the Taft-Hartley Act (see NATIONAL LABOR RELATIONS ACT [WAGNER ACT OF 1935]), the cooling-off period is part of a policy covering management–labor disputes. Its purpose is to encourage peaceful settlement of disputes.

The term is also applied to the right of cancellation imposed on certain transactions by federal and state laws. Examples are home-solicitation sales and loans.

CORPUS JURIS.   A legal encyclopedia that represents a complete statement of the body of American law. The update *Corpus Juris Secundum* is usually cited as *C.J.S.* or *CJS.*

It is found in law-school libraries, large public libraries, and many law-firm libraries and is also available on CD-ROM.

A descriptive word index helps you locate discussions and supporting authorities in the various volumes.

COURTS.   Generally, the places established for transacting judicial business. The word *court* may refer to the law, the persons assembled under authority of the law, the judge, or a specific court of law.

Usually, the parties to an action (lawsuit) are represented by attorneys at law. A party who represents himself or herself, without an attorney, is said to be appearing *pro se* (for himself).

Court proceedings may range from a simple, informal hearing or conference in a judge's chambers, or even by telephone, to a complete, formal trial before a judge or a judge and jury.

Court pleadings.   The series of written statements of the claims and defenses of the parties to a court action are called *pleadings*.

In most states, in a civil legal proceeding, the PLAINTIFF makes a written statement of the facts that caused him or her to bring the suit. The designation of this first pleading may be called a COMPLAINT, *declaration, libel,* or *petition.* In some states, the first pleading in an equity action is designated as a *bill in equity* or *bill of complaint.*

A Summons, or its equivalent, is issued and served on the person against whom an action is brought. The Defendant provides an Answer to the summons and complaint, defending himself or herself by raising legal arguments or by denying the facts stated by the plaintiff.

When the case is submitted to the court for a decision, the judge decides controversies about legal points. A jury, or a judge acting in place of a jury, decides questions of fact.

Court system.   See United States court system.

COVENANTS.   Written agreements between two or more persons promising to do or not to do something. In real estate matters (see Chapter 15/Real property), two common forms are covenants in deed and covenants of title:

> *Covenants in deed* are promises made between parties in the sale of real property. Some deed covenants impose restrictions on the use of real property in a development and apply to all parcels or units in the project. See also Chapter 15/Deed.

> *Covenants of title* are assurances that a deed conveys good and unencumbered title to real property. See also Chapter 15/Title.

DATABASES, LEGAL.   On-line commercial services that offer comprehensive legal information. Although these services can be expensive, they provide an extensive system for doing precision research.

Some services represent a collection of databases rather than a single database. Services like DIALOG, LEXIS/NEXIS, and WESTLAW offer hundreds of specialty databases and thereby provide a gateway to sources such as *Black's Law Dictionary,* various law journals, and a variety of other legal information.

DIALOG has more databases available to on-line searchers than any other similar service. Topics are wide ranging, covering everything from aerospace to child abuse to labor law to zoology. LEXIS/NEXIS and WESTLAW are also two very powerful services that offer hundreds of databases on a wide range of subjects.

Other professional services are available as well, such as AB/net, the American Bar Association's on-line search service. See also Chapter 9/Database; Chapter 13/Databases, financial.

If you want to know which other databases are available for on-line searching, consult a current directory of databases. The WESTLAW service, for example, includes the annual *Directory of On-Line Databases,* which lists several thousand databases.

Also, most states have Web sites (see Chapter 6/WEB SITE) that include state statutes, COURT decisions and rules, legislative activity, agency rules, and so on.

DEFAMATION.   See LIBEL AND SLANDER.

DEFAULT.   A failure to perform what is required by law or duty. For example, a borrower who fails to repay a loan according to the terms of a transaction is in default. When someone is sued and fails to appear in response to a SUMMONS, he or she is in default.

DEFENDANT.   The person or entity against which a lawsuit is brought. In criminal cases, the defendant is often called the *accused.* Compare with PLAINTIFF.

DERIVATIVE ACTION.   A lawsuit by a stockholder of a corporation, often against an officer of the corporation, to compel management to act properly to protect the corporation's interests. See also Chapter 10/CORPORATION; OFFICERS OF A CORPORATION; STOCKHOLDER.

Before a suit can be brought, a complaining stockholder must ask the board of directors to take the desired action, and the board must refuse to do so. See also Chapter 10/BOARD OF DIRECTORS.

DISABILITY BENEFIT LAWS.   Laws enacted in certain states that provide for cash benefits to workers who lose wages because of nonoccupational illness or accident.

These laws are the counterpart of worker's compensation laws, which provide benefits for occupational injuries or illness. See also Chapter 14/WORKER'S COMPENSATION INSURANCE.

An employer may be insured under a state plan or under a voluntary plan approved by the state agency administering the program. Benefits payable under such insurance usually are geared to the average weekly wage of the claimant, with the claimant being paid a fixed percentage thereof.

As in the case of unemployment compensation, disability benefits are paid for a certain period up to a maximum number of weeks. There is usually a waiting period before a claimant is eligible for benefits, the intent being to prevent claims for brief illnesses.

Eligibility for benefits depends on whether the claimant is within the labor market and specifically within that portion of the labor market intended to be protected.

DISAFFIRM.   To repudiate or take back consent once it is given; to refuse to stick by former acts.

DISCHARGE OF CONTRACT.   To end an obligation specified by an agreement; to release the parties from their obligations under a CONTRACT.

Discharge of contract may occur in several ways:

By the performance of, or the carrying out of, the contract terms

By mutual agreement to end the contract

By impossibility of performance because certain assumed factors no longer exist

By operation of law, such as a change in the law

By breach, or failure of one party, thereby discharging the other party of obligations

DISCRIMINATION.   See FAIR EMPLOYMENT PRACTICES.

DOCKET.   A brief, formal record of the proceedings in a COURT of law or the book or file containing such record; the list or calendar of cases scheduled to be heard at a specific term, prepared by the clerk of court.

A docket number is an essential reference on court papers or correspondence dealing with a case before court.

EMINENT DOMAIN.   The power of federal, state, and local governments to appropriate property for public use or the public welfare. The owner is reimbursed according to an appraisal of the fair market value of the property but has the right to sue for a greater amount.

Public service corporations (public utility corporations) also have the power of eminent domain. See also Chapter 10/PUBLIC UTILITY CORPORATION.

ENVIRONMENTAL LAWS.   Federal, state, and local laws and regulations that affect a range of business, governmental, and private activity:

The *National Environmental Policy Act (NEPA)*, adopted in 1979, requires an environmental impact assessment for any project paid for in whole or in part with federal funds or licensed by a federal agency. Many states have adopted state versions of NEPA that may require assessments of projects paid for by the state or private sources.

The *Clean Air Act,* adopted in 1970 and amended in 1990 to meet new concerns (acid rain, ozone depletion, airborne toxins, and so on), regulates emissions from both stationary and mobile sources.

The *Resource Conservation and Recovery Act (RCRA)* and other laws deal with waste and the handling of toxic materials. They regulate the disposal of waste, the cleanup of spills and improperly disposed of materials, and the use of toxic substances in industry and commerce.

The *Federal Water Pollution Control Act (Clean Water Act)* and the *Safe Drinking Water Act,* among others, regulate the discharge of pollution into surface and ground water and the alteration of wetlands and water courses.

ESTOPPEL. A bar raised by law preventing a person from taking a position, denying a fact, or asserting a fact in COURT that is inconsistent with the truth as established by judicial or legislative officers or by his or her own deed or acts, either express or implied:

> *A* sells *B* a house that *A* does not own, giving *B* a COVENANT and warranty deed (see Chapter 15/DEED) in which he warrants that he has title to the house. Later, *A* obtains title from the actual owner and attempts to eject *B* on the ground that *A* is now the true owner and *B* is not.
>
> *A* would be *estopped* from disputing what he formerly warranted, namely, that he was the true owner when he sold the house to *B*.

EXECUTION. A term used in reference to a legal WRIT directing an officer of the law to carry out a JUDGMENT (*execution of judgment*); a term used in reference to the signature to and delivery of a written instrument (*execution of instrument*).

FAIR EMPLOYMENT PRACTICES. Government regulations aimed at preventing discrimination in employment that are embodied in state fair employment practices acts and in the federal Civil Rights Act.

Civil Rights Act.   The purpose of this act, as well as various state acts, is to guard against discrimination because of an individual's race, creed, color, sex, or national origin. The law prohibits asking such questions on employment applications.

The federal government moved to prevent discrimination in employment through the Civil Rights Act of 1964. Under this act, it is unlawful for an employer in an industry affecting commerce and having 15 or more employees to fail or refuse to do certain things, such as refuse to hire an individual because of religion.

It is also unlawful to limit, classify, or segregate an employee in a way that would adversely affect his or her status as an employee on the basis of race, color, religion, sex, or national origin.

Other laws. Other laws have also been adopted to promote fairness in hiring and promotion practices. They include the Equal Pay Act (1963), Age Discrimination in Employment Act (1967), Equal Employment Opportunity Act (1972), and Americans with Disabilities Act (1990). See also LABOR LAWS.

Discrimination is also prohibited by laws governing CONTRACTS covering federal projects or federally funded projects. See also NATIONAL LABOR RELATIONS ACT (WAGNER ACT OF 1935); WAGE–HOUR LAW.

FAIR HOUSING ACT. See OPEN-HOUSING LAW.

FAIR LABOR STANDARDS ACT. See WAGE-HOUR LAW.

FAMILY MEDICAL LEAVE ACT. See LABOR LAWS.

FEDERAL COMMUNICATIONS COMMISSION (FCC). See Chapter 2/FEDERAL COMMUNICATIONS COMMISSION (FCC).

FEDERAL RESERVE ACT. See Chapter 13/FEDERAL RESERVE ACT.

FEDERAL TRADE COMMISSION (FTC). A federal body established by the Federal Trade Commission Act in 1914 to administer and enforce several federal statutes designed to prevent unfair trade practices and methods of competition.

The FTC may conduct investigations and enforce the provisions of the acts it administers, including sections of the Robinson–Patman and Clayton acts that fall within its jurisdiction.

FRANCHISE. See Chapter 10/FRANCHISE.

FRAUD. False representation of some fact that causes injury to the person defrauded. Fraud consists of the following:

1. False and material representation by someone who knows it is false or is ignorant of the truth

2. Intent that the false representation be relied on by someone else in a manner reasonably contemplated

3. Someone's ignorance of the false representation

4. Someone's reasonable reliance on the false information

5. Injury to someone caused by the misrepresentation

There are a number of different types of fraud, including the following:

Legal, or *constructive, fraud* is an act or omission that causes damage to another.

Positive fraud, or *fraud in fact,* is an act or omission with intent to defraud.

Extrinsic fraud is an intentional act whereby one party prevents a losing party from having a fair trial of all issues in a controversy.

Intrinsic fraud is fraudulent representation that influences a judgment about something.

Fraud in the execution arises when a person is induced to sign a document, the nature of which is unknown to the person, through no fault of his own.

Fraud in the factum arises when there is a difference between an instrument actually executed and the one intended to be executed.

Fraud in the inducement occurs when something false intends to and does persuade someone to execute an instrument or make an agreement.

GARNISHMENT. The right of a creditor to compel a third party owing money to, or holding money for, a debtor to pay the money to the creditor instead of to the debtor. The third party against whom the proceedings are brought is called the *garnishee.*

Not only wages and salaries but also TRUST funds, insurance disability payments, and other funds may be garnished.

The laws that govern the right of garnishment differ considerably in the various states. In some states, garnishment is referred to as a *factoring process* or *trustee process.*

GUARANTY. Generally, a promise of responsibility concerning an obligation or goods being sold. The term is used interchangeably with *suretyship* by the COURTS and lawyers as well as by laypersons. However, one may draw a distinction about the degree of liability:

The *surety* is primarily liable upon engagement.

The *guarantor* is secondarily liable and is not chargeable with nonperformance until notice is given.

A *contract of guaranty* or *of suretyship* is a CONTRACT whereby one person agrees to be responsible to another for the payment of a debt or the performance of a duty by a third person. It must be in writing to be enforceable.

The term *guaranty* (or *guarantee*) is often loosely used in the sense of WARRANTY. In a strict legal and commercial sense, it is the essence of a *contract of guaranty* that there should be a principal who is liable directly to perform some act or duty:

A *contract of guaranty* is an agreement by a third party guaranteeing the honest and faithful performance of a contract of sale.

A *contract of warranty* is an agreement in a sales contract guaranteeing the efficient performance of a product for a set time.

HOLDER IN DUE COURSE. The transferee of a NEGOTIABLE INSTRUMENT who acquires the instrument under conditions defined in the UNIFORM COMMERCIAL CODE (UCC) (Article IX as adopted by state legislatures).

INDEMNIFICATION OF DIRECTORS AND OFFICERS. A promise or agreement to protect and secure corporate officers and directors against loss or damage.

Indemnification involves the reimbursement of corporate directors and officers for litigation expense or damages they may be required to pay under a COURT decision. See also Chapter 10/BOARD OF DIRECTORS; OFFICERS OF A CORPORATION.

To address the problem of heavy litigation expenses that directors and officers may face, some states have passed laws that permit corporations to reimburse them for such expenses under specified circumstances.

INDEMNITY. An express or implied CONTRACT to compensate someone for loss, damage, expense, or trouble. The indemnity may be payable to the indemnitee or to someone else authorized to accept payment.

INJUNCTION. A WRIT issued by a COURT of equity restraining a person or corporation from doing or continuing to do something that threatens or causes injury or requiring a DEFENDANT to perform a particular act:

A *prohibitory injunction* restrains the commission or continuance of an act, such as restraining a board of elections from placing a certain candidate's name on the ballot.

A *mandatory injunction* commands acts to be done or undone, such as compelling a property owner to open a road that he or she had fenced off.

A *restraining order* may be granted without notice to the opposite party for the purpose of restraining a defendant until the court has heard an application for a temporary inunction.

A *temporary restraining order (TRO)* is frequently used in domestic relations cases.

A *temporary injunction,* granted before the court has heard a case on its merits, restrains the defendant during the litigation of a case. It is also called a *preliminary injunction,* an *interlocutory injunction,* or an *injunction pendente.*

A *permanent injunction* is granted on the merits of the case. This type of injunction is also called a *final injunction.*

INTERSTATE COMMERCE, INTRASTATE COMMERCE. Terms used in reference to Article I of the Constitution, which gives the federal government the power to regulate commerce among the several states. (See Regulation of business.) However, the Constitution does not define either *commerce* or *interstate commerce.*

See also INTERSTATE COMMERCE COMMISSION (ICC).

Definitions. The COURTS, however, decided that *commerce* means buying and selling, so if the interchange is between states, it is *interstate* commerce. If it is within a state and is not part of an interchange or movement of tangible or intangible commodities (isolated cases of interstate commerce do not count), it is *intrastate* commerce.

Today, the courts avoid giving the term *interstate commerce* a comprehensive definition. However, it comprises general movements of commodities and includes transportation of persons and property, transmission of power, and communication (radio, television, telephone, and telegraph).

Regulation. Under the broad interpretation given the commerce clause, Congress has the power to regulate interstate commerce and local (intrastate) incidents thereof.

In general, a state cannot prohibit foreign corporations (those incorporated in other states) from doing interstate business within its borders but may require certain qualifying conditions.

The federal regulatory laws also differentiate between *intrastate* and *interstate* commerce. The Fair Labor Standards Act (see WAGE–HOUR LAW), for example, regulates labor conditions in industries engaged in commerce and in the production of goods for commerce.

The regulatory laws are not consistent in their definition of *interstate commerce,* although the tendency is toward uniformity. As yet, being engaged in intrastate commerce under one law, and therefore exempt from federal regulation, does not mean that one will be exempt under another law.

INTERSTATE COMMERCE COMMISSION (ICC). An independent commission appointed by the president to regulate water or land transportation—railroads, water carriers, freight forwarders, and motor carriers—engaged in interstate commerce. See INTERSTATE COMMERCE, INTRASTATE COMMERCE.

The commission is an administrative board invested with powers of supervision and investigation.

JUDGMENT. An *adjudication* (judicial decision) by a court, usually after a trial or hearing, of the rights of the parties; the sentence in a criminal case.

Judgments and decrees. Broadly, an adjudication by a COURT of either law or equity is considered a *judgment.* Technically, though, an adjudication by a court of equity is a *decree,* such as a divorce decree.

Court awards. Following a judgment, if a debtor fails or refuses to pay an award of the court, the debtor may direct that a WRIT of EXECUTION be issued by the clerk of the court. Pursuant to its terms, a sheriff may then seize and sell any property of the debtor not exempt by law to satisfy the judgment.

If no property is available, the court may order that periodic payments be made. Or the court may direct that the debtor's wages be garnished. (See GARNISHMENT.) If the debtor fails to obey a court order, he or she may be found in contempt.

If the party against whom a judgment is rendered APPEALS to a higher court, execution of the judgment is *stayed* (put on hold) pending the higher court's decision. Interest on any amount due may be applied during the appeal period.

JURAT. A clause in an official certificate attesting that an AFFIDAVIT, or *deposition* (statement of a witness under oath), was sworn to at a stated time before an authorized officer, such as a NOTARY PUBLIC. It is often referred to as the *sworn-to clause*. However, the term ACKNOWLEDGMENT is more common.

The form of jurat varies slightly in the different states. In a few states, the jurat recites the title of the officer and the state, or state and county, in which he or she is authorized to act. In a few other states, the name of the affiant is repeated in the jurat.

The following form of jurat is the most common:

Subscribed and sworn to before me this _____day of _____, 200X.

_____

Notary Public

The notary signs immediately beneath the jurat and affixes the notarial seal and the expiration date of his or her commission. In some states, the expiration date precedes the signature.

LABOR LAWS. Federal and state laws dealing with the rights and welfare of workers.

Federal laws. The following federal laws are especially important:

The *Fair Labor Standards Act* (1938) establishes the minimum wage.

The *Wagner Act* (1934) deals with the right of workers to unionize and bargain collectively.

The *Taft–Hartley Act* (1947) addresses certain practices of unions that are deemed to be unfair.

The *Occupational Health and Safety Act (OSHA)* (1970) promotes safe working conditions for employees.

The *American with Disabilities Act (ADA)* (1990) forbids discrimination against persons with disabilities and requires that places of public accommodation be accessible to disabled persons.

Title VII of the *Civil Rights Act* (1964), administered by the Equal Employment Opportunities Commission (EEOC), prohibits discrimination in employment on grounds of race, color, sex, religion, and national origin.

The *Family Medical Leave Act* (1993) entitles employees to balance the demands of the workplace with the needs of families, allowing leave for medical reasons, the birth or adoption of a child, and the care of a child, spouse, or parent who has a serious health condition.

State laws.   Each state has adopted a worker's compensation act and employment security act:

Worker's compensation provides for payment of medical expenses and some percentage of lost wages for work-related injuries. See also Chapter 14/Worker's compensation insurance.

Unemployment compensation provides for payments to workers who are laid off or otherwise lose their jobs through no fault of their own.

LIBEL AND SLANDER.   False and malicious statements that tend to damage a person's character or reputation (*defamation*):

Slander is oral, or spoken, defamation of one person by another in the presence of a third party.

Libel is written or printed defamation of one person by another in published form, such as in a newspaper or letter.

LIEN.   An encumbrance imposed on property by which the property is made security for the discharge of an obligation. Common liens are the vendor's lien, mechanic's lien, mortgage lien, and tax lien. An ATTACHMENT is also a lien.

Some liens, particularly those on PERSONAL PROPERTY, must be accompanied by actual possession of the property. A *lienor* (holder of a lien) who gives up or loses possession therefore loses the lien.

Other liens, particularly those on real estate (see Chapter 15/REAL PROPERTY), need not be accompanied by possession. The lienor gives notice of the lien by a public record of it, recorded in the registry of deeds or other public repository.

LIQUIDATED DAMAGES.   The amount specified in a CONTRACT to be paid for a loss resulting from BREACH OF CONTRACT. The amount must be in proportion to the actual loss or the agreement cannot be enforced.

MODEL BUSINESS CORPORATION ACT. A standard statute adopted in most states providing uniform procedures and rules for establishing and governing corporations.

The model act is revised from time to time, and the revisions may or may not be adopted by state legislatures.

MONOPOLY. Under COMMON LAW, an abuse of free commerce whereby one company or group acquires exclusive control over strategic sources of material, means of production, or distribution within a given area and for a particular product or service.

Possessing such sole rights, a monopolist is in a position to dictate prices and terms and to stifle competition until it is exterminated or reduced to insignificance.

Certain types of business have been considered *natural monopolies,* subject to both federal and state regulation. Some, such as telephone and electric power companies, have been opened to competition and are no longer considered natural monopolies.

The common law has consistently condemned complete and partial monopolies in any recognizable guise. Its principles have been clarified and extended through both federal and state statutory law. See also ANTITRUST LAWS; MONOPOLY PRICE; REGULATION OF BUSINESS.

MONOPOLY PRICE. A price charged by a MONOPOLY or, generally, the prices set in markets that are subject to some degree of monopoly control or restraint of trade. See also ANTITRUST LAWS; PRICING PRACTICES; REGULATION OF BUSINESS.

NATIONAL LABOR RELATIONS ACT (WAGNER ACT OF 1935). An act that sought to protect the right of labor to organize and strike, picket, or boycott and defined five labor practices as unfair to employees:

1. Interference with, restraint of, or coercion of employees in the exercise of their rights to collective bargaining and self-organization
2. Prevention or domination of the formation of any labor organization
3. Discrimination in hiring and other employment practices, such as against union members
4. Discrimination against employees who filed charges or testified under the act
5. Refusal to bargain collectively with the employees' representative

In 1947 the act was amended by the Labor–Management Relations Act (Taft–Hartley Act). This act outlawed the closed shop, defined unfair union practices, and established a COOLING-OFF PERIOD. See also FAIR EMPLOYMENT PRACTICES.

The act is administered by the NATIONAL LABOR RELATIONS BOARD (NLRB).

NATIONAL LABOR RELATIONS BOARD (NLRB). A federal agency that administers the NATIONAL LABOR RELATIONS ACT (WAGNER ACT OF 1935).

The board's chief responsibilities are to arrange elections among workers to select the labor organization that will be the bargaining agent of the workers, and to investigate and render decisions on unfair labor practices.

NATIONAL REPORTER SYSTEM. The published opinions of all federal and state COURTS of final appellate jurisdiction. These opinions are first published in weekly pamphlets called *advance sheets* and thereafter in the bound volumes of the National Reporter System.

Current and, to a larger extent, past state and federal COURT opinions are available on CD-ROM and on-line databases. See also DATABASES, LEGAL.

The system not only covers cases from both state and federal courts but also gives a digest for each region.

NEGOTIABLE INSTRUMENT. A written instrument, such as a check, signed by a maker or drawer that contains an unconditional promise or order to pay to the bearer, or holder, a certain sum of money. Compare with NONNEGOTIABLE INSTRUMENT.

Negotiable documents. Documents of title, such as order bills of lading and warehouse receipts, are not strictly negotiable instruments, because they don't contain an order to pay a sum of money.

However, various statutes have given certain documents of title known as *quasinegotiable instruments* the quality of negotiability.

Method of transfer. A negotiable instrument can be passed freely from one person to another without a formal ASSIGNMENT. The transferee then becomes the new holder:

If the instrument is *payable to bearer,* it may be negotiated simply by delivery.

If the instrument is *payable to order,* it is negotiated by endorsement (see also Chapter 13/ENDORSEMENT) of the holder and completed by delivery.

The UNIFORM COMMERCIAL CODE (UCC) (Article 9), which governs negotiable instruments, sets out the manner in which a negotiable instrument shall be transferred. It fixes the rights and duties of the maker, payee, holder, and endorser.

For example, under the law, an endorser of a negotiable instrument vouches for its genuineness. If it is a forgery, the endorser is liable to the HOLDER IN DUE COURSE of the instrument after delivery.

NONNEGOTIABLE INSTRUMENT. A written instrument for which the title cannot be transferred from one holder to another without formal ASSIGNMENT. Compare with NEGOTIABLE INSTRUMENT.

For example, a valid CONTRACT may be nonnegotiable because of its express terms or because it contains or fails to contain matters affecting negotiability.

NOTARIZE. To acknowledge or attest a document as a NOTARY PUBLIC. A notary should observe the following details when notarizing a document:

1. When a corporation is a party to an instrument, the notary should be certain that the corporate seal (see Chapter 10/CORPORATE SEAL) is impressed on the instrument, if required. (Seals are usually required on corporate instruments.)

2. The notary should fill in all blanks on the certificate of ACKNOWLEDGMENT or the JURAT and should be certain that the instrument is fully signed and properly witnessed, if required.

3. The notary should be certain to impress his or her notarial SEAL on the certificate, when required. (Some states don't require the seal on papers acknowledged within the state.)

4. The notary should be certain that rubber stamps make legible imprints. A black stamp is preferable because black ink photocopies more clearly than other inks.

5. If the notary doesn't personally know the party executing the instrument, he or she should require proper identification and should be satisfied that the party has executed the instrument willingly and without duress.

Although it's not required, it's a good idea for a notary to keep a print or electronic record of documents notarized, indicating the person signing, date of signing, county, and title of the document or a description. If questions arise, this record will substantiate whether a notary notarized a particular document.

NOTARY PUBLIC. (*pl.,* notaries public) A commissioned officer of a state whose powers and duties include administering oaths, certifying to the genuineness of documents, and taking ACKNOWLEDGMENTS.

In some states, a notary is authorized to act only in the county in which he or she is commissioned. In other states, the notary is qualified to act throughout the state.

A commission as a notary public is a trust. It confers certain powers on the notary in addition to requiring that he or she perform certain duties. In exercising those powers and duties, a notary should strictly observe the letter of the law.

A notary should never take an acknowledgment without the actual appearance of the individual making it. (See also NOTARIZE.) Nor should a notary ever antedate or postdate a certificate of acknowledgment, which would constitute fraud and deceit.

NOVATION. The substitution of a new CONTRACT, or debtor or obligor, for an existing one. The substitution must be agreed to by all parties:

> *A* sells a car to *B*, who makes a small down payment and agrees to pay the balance in installments. Unable to make the payments, *B* sells the car to *C*, who agrees to make the payments to *A*.

> If *A* agrees to release *B* from the contract and to look to *C* for payment, a novation is created.

OCCUPATIONAL SAFETY AND HEALTH ACT (OSHA). See LABOR LAWS.

OFFICIAL REPORTS. COURT opinions prepared by an appointed reporter for publication by authority of statute. Most states have official reports, although their court opinions are also published in the NATIONAL REPORTER SYSTEM and appear at on-line Web sites. See also Chapter 6/WEB SITE.

OPEN-HOUSING LAW. Also known as the *Fair Housing Act, affirmative marketing,* and *equal opportunity housing.* A law that prohibits discrimination in housing on the basis of race, color, national origin, sex, or religion.

Grounds for rejection of buyers or renters for reasonable cause still exist but must apply to all persons equally.

OPTION. An agreement, usually in *consideration* (see CONTRACT) for the payment of a certain sum of money by the offeree, to hold an offer open for a designated period. The offer then ceases to be an offer. It becomes a *contract of option* and cannot be withdrawn until the option period expires.

Although an option is generally based on a consideration, a few states require no consideration if the contract is in writing. Others recognize an option under seal as binding, because a seal, at COMMON LAW, indicates consideration.

The consideration for an option is not returnable to the optionee if he or she fails to take up the option. However, if the contract so provides, it may be applied to the purchase price if the offer is accepted.

PERSONAL PROPERTY. Sometimes called *personalty.* A right or interest, protected by law, in something that is not land or anything permanently attached to land and is capable of ownership. Compare with Chapter 15/REAL PROPERTY.

Generally, personal property is movable. It may be *tangible* (also called *chattel*), such as money, gold, merchandise, or any movable object susceptible to physical possession. Or it may be *intangible,* such as a CONTRACT or stocks. See also CHOSE IN ACTION.

Products of the soil become personal property when severed from the land. Trees and crops that are sold while attached to the land constitute real property, but when they are severed from it, they constitute personal property.

PIERCING THE CORPORATE VEIL. An expression used by the COURTS to mean that they will disregard the corporate entity because it is being used improperly.

This situation occurs when the corporation is being used for purposes contrary to public policy, for fraud, or in a situation in which the owner uses the corporation to conduct his or her personal affairs. See also Chapter 10/CORPORATE ENTITY.

The result of piercing the corporate veil is that stockholders, directors, or officers may be held personally liable for the acts of the corporation. See also Chapter 10/BOARD OF DIRECTORS; OFFICERS OF THE CORPORATION; STOCKHOLDER.

PLAINTIFF. The person or organization that brings a lawsuit. Compare with DEFENDANT.

PLEADING. See COURTS.

POWER OF ATTORNEY. A written instrument in which the PRINCIPAL (person giving the power) authorizes another to act for him or her. The person appointed is commonly called an *attorney in fact.*

Scope of the power. The instrument may be a blanket authorization, but more commonly, it authorizes the agent (see also Chapter 10/AGENCY) to represent the principal in a specific transaction, such as in the closing of a real estate deal, or to do a certain act continuously, such as to sign checks.

Revocation of the power. A power of attorney may be revoked at the will of the principal, unless it was given to the agent for a consideration. (See also CONTRACT.) The death of the principal constitutes an instantaneous revocation, unless consideration was given for the power.

In special cases in which the principal wants the attorney in fact to act for him or her in the event of disability or death, the principal conveys an *irrevocable power of attorney.* Such instruments often relate to decisions involving medical care when the principal is unable to make his or her own decisions.

PREEMPTIVE RIGHTS. In corporations, the right of a stockholder to buy new stock issues before the shares are offered to outsiders. See also Chapter 10/CORPORATION; STOCK; STOCKHOLDER.

Stockholders may determine if they have preemptive rights by examining the organization's certificate of incorporation. See also Chapter 10/CERTIFICATE OF INCORPORATION.

PRICE FIXING. See PRICING PRACTICES.

PRICING PRACTICES. A reference to the pricing policies and practices that are regulated by the federal government and most states. The following are common examples:

Discounts and price discrimination: The Robinson–Patman Act (see ANTITRUST LAWS) prohibits sellers from charging different prices for the same product if the effect is to injure competition.

Advertising allowances: The allowances must be granted to all customers on proportionately equal terms.

Brokerage payments: The Robinson–Patman Act prohibits an individual seller from making brokerage payments to buyers under the theory that payments should be made only to agents for services rendered. Such payments also must not be used to conceal discriminatory discounts.

Basing-point and zone pricing: Prices that include delivery costs must accurately reflect actual shipping costs. Any pricing that includes delivery costs and tends to injure competition may be prohibited under the Sherman Act (see Antitrust laws) or the Federal Trade Commission Act. See also Federal Trade Commission (FTC).

Sales below cost: No federal legislation forbids such sales. They are open to attack, however, under the Sherman Act and the Federal Trade Commission Act if they are part of a systematic combination to drive competitors out of business.

Price advertising: The Federal Trade Commission will take action if the public interest is threatened by advertising that deludes buyers about prices.

PRINCIPAL.   A person who authorizes an agent (see Chapter 10/Agency) to do certain things for him or her; a person directly involved with committing a crime; a person primarily or ultimately responsible or liable in a legal action.

PROTEST.   A formal certificate attesting the dishonor (see Chapter 13/Dishonor) of a Negotiable instrument after negotiation; loosely, the process of presenting an instrument for payment, demanding payment, and giving notice to the drawer or endorser.

A protest is usually made by a Notary public but may be made by a responsible citizen in the presence of two witnesses.

The certificate must state the following:

The time and place of presentment

The fact that presentment was made and the manner thereof

The cause or reason for protesting the bill

The demand made

The answer given or the fact that the drawee or acceptor could not be found

The protest is attached to the dishonored instrument or a copy of it, and a notice of protest is then sent to the parties who are secondarily liable (drawer and endorser).

Protest is *required* only when a bill of exchange or check drawn in one state (or county) and payable in another is dishonored, but in practice, domestic instruments are often protested.

QUASI.   (Latin) A term used in legal phraseology to indicate that one subject resembles another with which it is compared. Although the one subject resembles the other in certain characteristics, intrinsic and material differences exist.

A *quasi contract,* for example, is an obligation similar to a CONTRACT but does not arise from an agreement between parties. Rather, it arises from some relation between them or from a voluntary act by one of them.

A federal, state, or local regulatory agency acts in a quasijudicial capacity when it makes a determination on an application or decides whether an individual or organization has acted according to its authorizing legislation or rules.

Such decisions may usually be appealed to a higher authority in the agency and ultimately to the COURT.

RATIFICATION. The approval of an act that was not previously binding. Ratification, or affirmance, becomes effective as of the date the act was performed.

For example, a minor may ratify a CONTRACT after he or she reaches majority, and a PRINCIPAL may ratify the unauthorized acts of an agent.

A corporation may ratify the unauthorized acts of its officers. However, it cannot ratify the acts of its incorporators before the corporation was formed. (It was not in existence then and therefore could not possibly have entered into a contract at that time.) Rather, it may *adopt* the acts of the incorporators.

REGULATION OF BUSINESS. The local, state, and federal regulation performed by various regulatory bodies that have been created by law. These regulatory bodies act in diverse fields, ranging from communications to environmental protection:

Communications (see Chapter 2/FEDERAL COMMUNICATIONS COMMISSION [FCC])

Public utilities (state public service commissions)

Finance (see Chapter 13/SECURITIES AND EXCHANGE COMMISSION [SEC])

Railroads (see INTERSTATE COMMERCE COMMISSION [ICC])

Banking (Federal Reserve Board [see Chapter 13/FEDERAL RESERVE ACT] and state banking commissions)

General trade (see FEDERAL TRADE COMMISSION [FTC])

Environmental protection (see ENVIRONMENTAL LAWS)

The laws aim to prevent various types of abuses:

1. Those arising from the action of individuals or groups against the public interest, such as the pure food and drug laws

2. Those caused by firms or individuals acting against each other or in combination against the public, such as ANTITRUST LAWS, including fair trade and unfair practices acts

3. Those caused by employer–employee differences, such as WAGE–HOUR LAWS and collective-bargaining laws

4. Those caused by damage to the environment from activities that pollute the air, surface water, or ground water

The laws are administered by agencies in the executive department of federal and state governments, which adopt rules under their authorizing statutes.

Regulatory bodies, such as the Federal Trade Commission, are part executive in their administration of the law, part judicial in their enforcement, and part legislative in their establishment of rules. See also ADMINISTRATIVE PROCEDURES ACT.

Tax laws also exert a regulatory influence and are sometimes designed to encourage one activity and discourage another.

Licensing agencies, such as those granting licenses to sell liquor or practice a profession, regulate numerous fields.

Franchises (see Chapter 10/FRANCHISE) or certificates of convenience and necessity are used principally in public utility regulation:

A *franchise* is permission to operate in a specified area.

A *certificate* is a permit for expansion or alteration to satisfy the public necessity.

See also ANTITRUST LAWS; BLUE SKY LAWS; INTERSTATE COMMERCE, INTRASTATE COMMERCE; PRICING PRACTICES.

REPRESENTATIVE ACTION. A lawsuit brought by one stockholder to redress injury to many or all stockholders in a corporation. See also Chapter 10/CORPORATION; STOCKHOLDER.

RESCIND. See CONTRACT.

RIGHT-TO-KNOW LAWS. State laws requiring disclosure to employees of information relating to hazardous substances to which workers may be exposed in the workplace.

Sunshine laws mandating public availability of governmental records and proceedings are sometimes called *right-to-know laws* or *freedom-of-information laws.*

Congress has also adopted the Freedom of Information Act, which guarantees access to government records except where national security may be compromised.

RIGHT-TO-WORK LAWS. Laws that prohibit an employer from denying employment to someone because of membership or nonmembership in a union.

SALE. An agreement whereby the seller transfers property to the buyer for a *consideration* (see CONTRACT) called the price. To be enforceable, a sale must have all the elements necessary to the validity of a contract: offer and acceptance, competency of parties, legality of subject matter, and consideration.

The sale of goods is governed by the UNIFORM COMMERCIAL CODE (UCC) adopted by all states. Under the code, a *sale* is defined as the passing of title from the seller to the buyer for a price.

SEAL. An impression on an instrument. Material affixed to an instrument and intended as a seal, or the writing of the word *Seal* or *L.S.* (*locus sigilli:* Latin for "place of the seal") after the signature, are considered a seal.

If an instrument is to be sealed, the testimonium will so indicate. (See TESTIMONIUM CLAUSE; Chapter 10/CORPORATE SEAL.) The process of affixing the seal is referred to as *sealing the instrument,* and the instrument then becomes a *sealed instrument.*

In most jurisdictions, the COMMON LAW rule regarding seals has been modified by judicial decision or statutory enactment. The UNIFORM COMMERCIAL CODE (UCC) provides that the affixing of a seal to a CONTRACT for the sale of goods does not constitute such writing of a sealed instrument.

In many states, the requirement of a seal being affixed to contracts or other instruments has been abolished, and others require a seal only on certain instruments, such as on deeds. See also Chapter 15/DEED.

SERVICE OF PROCESS. As required by law, giving notice of a lawsuit to a DEFENDANT, which makes him or her a party to the suit and compels the person to appear in COURT or suffer JUDGMENT by DEFAULT:

Process is the means of summoning a defendant to appear in court.

Service of process is the act of giving the notice. See also SUMMONS.

Service is generally made personally to the defendant or to his or her agent (*personal service*).

Under some circumstances, service may be made by publication, such as by publishing a notice in a newspaper a required number of times, by leaving the notice at the defendant's last known address (*abode service*), or by certified mail, return receipt.

In some jurisdictions, service may also be accomplished by ATTACHMENT of some property of the defendant found within the jurisdiction. All states have adopted *long-arm statutes,* which designate a method for service of process on out-of-state defendants.

When a defendant is out of state, service is usually made in person on some state official, such as the secretary of state, who is deemed to be the agent of the defendant, and by certified mail to the defendant.

SLANDER.   See LIBEL AND SLANDER.

SOCIAL SECURITY ACT.   A federal act designed primarily to safeguard individuals against some of the major hazards of life arising out of old age, unemployment, disability, and poverty. When someone receiving benefits dies, the survivors may be eligible to receive the benefits.

The act originally included taxing provisions for the payment of social security benefits, which are commonly known as *social security taxes.* These taxing provisions have been superseded by a number of other acts.

The acts that have superseded the taxing provisions of the Social Security Act are the Federal Insurance Contributions Act (FICA), the Self-Employment Contributions Act, and the Federal Unemployment Tax Act. See also Chapter 12/SOCIAL SECURITY TAX; STATE UNEMPLOYMENT INSURANCE TAX.

STATUTE OF FRAUDS.   A COMMON LAW concept formalized by legislation, with variations, in all states.

The statute provides that certain CONTRACTS cannot be enforced unless they are in writing and signed by the party against whom the contract is sought to be enforced. (Consult the statutes in your state for a list of pertinent contracts.)

The writing need not be a formal document signed by both parties. A written note or memorandum of the transaction signed by the party to be bound by the agreement is sufficient.

STATUTE OF LIMITATIONS.   A state statute that limits the time within which legal action may be brought. There are different statutes of limitations for particular kinds of civil action, such as personal injury or BREACH OF CONTRACT, and for criminal prosecution.

The purpose of the limitation is to make it impossible to bring suit many years after a cause of action originates, when witnesses and evidence may no longer be available.

The statutes also disallow prosecution long after a crime has been committed. Some crimes, such as murder, however, are not subject to any statute of limitations.

When a debt is involved, it is possible to interrupt (or *toll*) the running of the statute—to lengthen the period in which action may be brought—by obtaining a payment on the debt or a promise to pay.

A promise to pay a debt that has been barred by the statute of limitations does not require new *consideration*. (See CONTRACT.) However, many states do require such a promise to be in writing.

STATUTORY LAW. Rules formulated into law by legislative action and often implemented by regulatory agencies under rules adopted by them. See also ADMINISTRATIVE PROCEDURES ACT.

The Constitution of the United States and the constitutions of the various states are the fundamental written law. All other law must be in harmony with the constitutions, which define and limit the powers of government.

Congress, state legislatures, and cities and towns find in the constitutions their authority, either express or implied, to enact certain laws. These enactments are the *statutes,* and they constitute the greater part of the written, or statutory, law.

Statutory law supplements and supersedes the COMMON LAW.

STIPULATION. A formal agreement between lawyers or parties on opposite sides of a lawsuit. It is usually in writing and may concern any one of a number of matters.

For example, the agreement may concern COURT procedure, such as an agreement to extend the time in which a pleading is due; may be an agreement to settle a lawsuit; or may refer to certain facts that the parties *stipulate to* so that they do not have to be proven in court.

SUBPOENA. A WRIT, or order, commanding someone to appear and testify in a legal proceeding. Anyone who fails to obey a subpoena without reasonable cause may be subject to contempt of COURT and liable for damages sustained by the aggrieved party.

SUMMONS. A legal notice requiring a person to answer a COMPLAINT within a specified time.

Service of process. The act of serving the summons is commonly referred to as SERVICE OF PROCESS, and a copy of the summons must be left personally with (served upon) the person against whom it is directed.

A corporation is served with process when a copy of the summons is left with an agent of the corporation, as indicated in the records of the secretary of state. See also Chapter 10/REGISTERED OFFICE.

In a few jurisdictions, the summons may be left with an adult member of the defendant's household or with some person at the defendant's place of business. An attorney at law is often authorized by a client to accept service of a summons on his or her behalf.

Return of service. When a summons is served, the process server endorses it, indicating when, where, and on whom served, with an affidavit to that effect. He or she then sends the affidavit to the plaintiff or the plaintiff's attorney, who files it with the COURT. This procedure is called *return of service* or *return of the summons.*

After return of the summons, the court has jurisdiction over the defendant.

TESTIMONIUM CLAUSE. The clause with which a written instrument or document, such as a CONTRACT, deed (see Chapter 15/DEED), or will closes. It immediately precedes the signature.

Purpose of the clause. The testimonium clause is a declaration by the parties to the instrument that their signatures are attached in testimony of the preceding part of the instrument.

It should not be confused with the *witness clause,* or *attestation clause.* (See ATTESTATION.) The testimonium clause relates to those who sign the paper as parties to the instrument.

What the clause indicates. Often, the testimonium clause is a guide to setting up the signature lines. It will indicate which parties are to sign, which officer of the corporation is to sign, whether the instrument is to be sealed, and whether a corporate seal is to be attested.

For example, from the following commonly used form, you know that the corporate president is to sign, that the seal is to be affixed, and that the corporate secretary is to attest the seal:

> IN WITNESS WHEREOF, Wright Corporation has caused its corporate seal to be hereto affixed, and attested by its secretary, and these presents to be signed by its president, this 26th day of October, 200X.

From the following clause, also commonly used, you know that the instrument is *not* to be sealed:

> IN TESTIMONY WHEREOF, the parties hereto have set their hands the day and year first above written.

TORT. A civil wrong or injury inflicted otherwise than by a BREACH OF CONTRACT. Elements of a tort are a wrongful act or a wrongful failure to act that causes an injury to some person or property.

Tort gives the injured party the right to sue for damages resulting from the defendant's breach of some duty.

Persons (including minors) and corporations are liable for torts. Action arises from *breach of duty,* not from breach of contract, as this example illustrates:

> A person visits a department store and may not even intend to make a purchase. The visitor may merely want to examine the merchandise.
>
> During the visit, the person falls on a slippery floor that wasn't clearly marked as such, or perhaps the proprietor leaves a small stool unattended in the aisle, and the visitor falls over it. The visitor may then recover damages from the proprietor for injuries caused by the negligent maintenance of the store premises.

TRESPASS. Unauthorized entry on the property of another; an unlawful and violent interference with the person or property of another.

In COMMON LAW pleading, an *action in trespass* is brought to recover damages sustained by the plaintiff as the immediate result of trespass.

The common law recognizes a distinction between *trespass,* which is a direct injury, and *trespass on the case,* which is an indirect or consequential injury. However, in modern practice, the distinction has lost much of its importance, because an action of TORT comprehends all cases in which a remedy is afforded.

TRUST. A holding of property subject to the duty of applying the property, the income from it, or the proceeds for the benefit of another, as directed by the person creating the trust:

> A trust is created when *A* transfers property to *X,* the trustee, and *X* undertakes to apply the property and income from it for the purposes and in the manner directed by *A.*

The elements of an ordinary trust include the following:

1. The *trustor* (also called *grantor, donor,* or *settlor*), who furnishes the property to be put in trust
2. The *subject matter* or *property* that is put in trust (called the *trust principal, corpus,* or *res*)
3. The *trustee,* who holds the property and administers the trust
4. The *beneficiaries,* for whose benefit the trust exists

A trust may be created by oral declaration, by writing, or by operation of law. It may be established by will (*testamentary trust*) or by trust agreement (*inter vivos* or *living trust*).

A trust may be created for any purpose not in contravention of law or public policy. It is frequently used as a vehicle for transacting business or as part of an estate plan.

A person might put property in trust to pay the income to a spouse for life and then to pay the principal to the children. In this situation, the receiving spouse would be the *income beneficiary* (or *equitable life tenant*), and the children would be the *beneficiaries* or *remaindermen.*

TRUST DEED.   Also called *deed of trust, trust agreement,* or *trust indenture.* A document whereby one person transfers legal ownership of real property to another. See also Chapter 15/MORTGAGE; REAL PROPERTY; TRUST DEED.

An agreement between a corporation and a trustee who serves as guardian of bondholders' interest would set forth the terms and conditions of a bond issue (see Chapter 13/BOND) and the rights, duties, and powers of the parties involved.

UNFAIR COMPETITION.   See ANTITRUST LAWS; MONOPOLY; PRICING PRACTICES.

UNFAIR EMPLOYMENT PRACTICE.   Action by an employer or union that violates a FAIR EMPLOYMENT PRACTICES law or executive order prohibiting discrimination in employment because of race, creed, color, sex, or national origin.

UNIFORM COMMERCIAL CODE (UCC).   A comprehensive body of laws and principles covering commercial transactions.

The UCC has replaced the older Uniform Negotiable Instruments Law in all states and the District of Columbia, the Virgin Islands, and Guam. The UCC, first published in 1952, has been revised several times since.

The code consists of nine articles intended to simplify, clarify, and modernize the law covering commercial transactions and to make the law uniform among the various jurisdictions. See also CONTRACT.

UNIFORM PARTNERSHIP ACT AND UNIFORM LIMITED PARTNERSHIP ACT.
Model acts adopted by many states to govern the establishment, operation, and dissolution of partnerships. See also Chapter 10/PARTNERSHIP.

The acts are revised from time to time, and the revisions may or may not be adopted by the state legislatures.

UNITED STATES COURT SYSTEM.
The COURT system in the United States consisting of the U.S. Supreme Court, 13 circuit courts of appeals, district (trial) courts in each state, and special courts, such as bankruptcy courts and the court of claims.

State courts follow a similar structure, consisting of a senior appellate court (usually called the supreme court), intermediate appellate courts (in many but not all states), and trial courts.

A case is brought and tried before a lower (trial) court. APPEALS from a trial court decision may be taken to an appeals court and ultimately to the highest state appellate court.

In a federal case, appeals may be taken to a circuit court of appeals and ultimately to the U.S. Supreme Court. Only rarely may state law cases be appealed in federal courts.

USURY.
Contracting for or receiving something in excess of the amount of interest (see Chapter 13/INTEREST) allowed by law for the loan or forbearance of money, such as in the sale of goods on credit or under the installment plan. See also Chapter 10/INSTALLMENT SALE.

Consequences of a usurious rate.
In some states, a lender who charges a usurious rate of interest loses the right to collect *any* interest. In a few states, the lender may collect the legal rate. In some states, the lender forfeits both principal and interest.

Service charges, investigation fees, and commissions charged by an agent are not usually considered interest and may be added to the legal rate without constituting usury.

Allowable higher rates.
In some states, the parties to a CONTRACT may agree on a rate of interest higher than the legal rate but within a statutory limit. In a

few states, they may agree on any rate. In some states, loans to corporations, but not to individuals, may be made at more than the legal rate.

Certain types of loans, such as small, personal loans, are not covered by the usury law but are subject to other, special laws.

VOID, VOIDABLE. Terms that both pertain to the loss of legal effect but with an important distinction. That which is *void* is of no legal force or effect; that which is *voidable* may be or is capable of being rendered void.

For example, a gambling or wagering CONTRACT is *void,* whereas a minor's contacts are merely *voidable* at his or her election.

WAGE–HOUR LAW. Also known as the Fair Labor Standards Act. A federal law that establishes a minimum wage and overtime requirements and restricts child labor in companies engaged in interstate commerce. See also INTERSTATE COMMERCE, INTRASTATE COMMERCE.

Coverage of the statute. The law is the major federal statute regulating wages and hours. Although it applies only to interstate commerce, the act has wide coverage, because the COURTS have broadly interpreted *interstate commerce.*

State statutes dealing with wages and hours are not as comprehensive as the Fair Labor Standards Act.

Equal Pay Act (amendment). A 1963 amendment, known as the Equal Pay Act, seeks to eliminate wage differentials based on sex in companies covered by the Fair Labor Standards Act. It deals essentially with three fields: wages, hours of work, and child labor.

For example, the law sets up a minimum hourly wage that varies according to the type of employment and a maximum of 40 hours per week at the regular rate of pay. An employee must be paid time and one-half the regular rate for hours of work over 40.

Regular rate means the hourly rate actually paid for the normal nonovertime workweek. It excludes gifts, bonuses, certain premium payments, payments for vacations and illness, profit sharing and pension payments, and so on.

WAIVER. The surrender, either expressed or implied, of a right to which one is entitled by law.

Samples of waivers can be found in legal-forms books, on the Internet, and in CONTRACT software. See also Chapter 6/INTERNET; WEB SITE.

Waiver of notice is a voluntary and intentional surrender of the right to be notified of an event or fact, such as a meeting. The writing setting forth such surrender is also called a *waiver:*

> The directors of a corporation may waive notice of a meeting before it is held. But in the absence of a permissive statute, the directors who are absent from a meeting, the time and place of which were not fixed, cannot waive the required notice *after* it has been held.

> Stockholders may waive notice of a meeting of stockholders, whether required by statute, the certificate of incorporation, or the bylaws. See also Chapter 10/BYLAWS; CERTIFICATE OF INCORPORATION; STOCKHOLDER.

Waivers may be created in writing or by action.

WARRANTY. Affirmation of a material fact or promise by the seller, which acts as an inducement for the buyer to make a purchase. See also CAVEAT EMPTOR.

Any warranty made by a seller that proves to be false gives the buyer a right of legal action.

Express and implied warranties. A warranty may be *express* (a direct statement made by the seller) or *implied* (one that is indicated by the nature of the CONTRACT). The UNIFORM COMMERCIAL CODE (UCC) has adopted this distinction and has added a class of warranties that are neither but rather consists of warranties of title and those against infringement.

Warranties relate to many things: fitness of the goods sold for a special purpose, merchantability of the goods, title to real property (see Chapter 15/REAL PROPERTY) or PERSONAL PROPERTY, and quiet enjoyment of premises.

All representations made by an applicant for insurance, whether material or not, are deemed warranties.

Warranty also applies to conveyances of real estate wherein a *warranty deed* warrants that the grantor holds good title to the property conveyed. See also Chapter 15/DEED.

Guaranty. The term GUARANTY is loosely used in the sense of warranty. However, the common guaranty of a product is, strictly, a warranty and not a guaranty.

WITHOUT RECOURSE. A phrase used in an endorsement (see also Chapter 13/ENDORSEMENT) that relieves the endorser from assuming liability in the event the maker fails to pay the instrument when due.

WITNESS TO SIGNATURE.   See ATTESTATION.

WORKER'S COMPENSATION LAWS.   Laws passed in most states that provide for compensation to workers injured during employment. Companies pay into an insurance fund to cover such liabilities. See also Chapter 14/WORKER'S COMPENSATION INSURANCE.

Employers are liable even though they take appropriate precautions and even though the employee is negligent. An employee's injury does not have to take place on the employer's property but must be within the scope of employment.

WRIT.   An order issued by a COURT, or judge, in the name of the state to compel a defendant to do something mentioned in the order:

A *writ of error* is a court order commanding judges that the record be examined to correct some alleged error in proceedings.

A *writ of execution* is a court order directing a sheriff to seize and sell a debtor's property to pay a creditor out of the proceeds.

CHAPTER TWELVE

Accounting and Taxes

ACCOUNTING. The process of recording, classifying, summarizing, and reporting transactions in the financial records to show the financial position of a business and the results of operations.

All accounting procedures are directed toward the preparation of an INCOME STATEMENT (profit and loss statement) and a BALANCE SHEET at the close of the accounting period. See also FISCAL PERIOD.

This process includes the entries made in the BOOKS OF ORIGINAL ENTRY, POSTING to LEDGER accounts, making CLOSING ENTRIES and ADJUSTING ENTRIES, and preparing a TRIAL BALANCE. These steps are usually called the *accounting cycle* and are the essence of accounting.

Computer software, such as SPREADSHEET analysis, general LEDGER and accounting packages, database-management systems, and tax packages are used to reduce time-consuming, repetitive work. They enable operators to perform complex calculations with a high degree of accuracy.

JOURNALS and ledgers may be maintained by computer, provided they meet Internal Revenue Service requirements. FINANCIAL STATEMENTS can also be prepared quickly and accurately by computer. See also ACCOUNTING RECORDS; ACCRUAL ACCOUNTING; CASH ACCOUNTING.

ACCOUNTING RECORDS. The records associated with the ACCOUNTING process that a firm maintains. Business accounting records may be kept manually or electronically.

IRS requirements. According to the Internal Revenue Service, an electronic system must include a method of producing legible records that will provide proof of tax liability.

For example, it must print out the general Ledger and any subsidiary ledgers; provide an Audit trail so that invoices, vouchers, and so on are readily available; and provide a way to trace any transaction back to the original source or forward to a final total.

Classes of records. People with large estates and diversified investments usually need three broad classes of records:

1. Records of what the person owns, such as bank accounts, time deposits, stocks, bonds, and real and personal property. See also Chapter 11/Personal property; Chapter 13/Bond; Stock; Chapter 15/Real property.
2. Records that must be kept for Income tax and other tax purposes.
3. Records of living expenses that are *not* deductible under the income tax law, in addition to records for other purposes.

Consult current IRS and state regulations for specific requirements and the related record keeping that is needed for the various types of income and expenses, such as dividends and contributions to individual retirement accounts.

Accounts. Items in Accounting listed as Assets, Liabilities, Owner's equity, Revenue, or Expenses, such as Operating expenses.

For descriptions of specific accounts, see Accounts payable; Cash account; Control account; Notes payable; Notes receivable; Profit and loss.

Accounts payable. 1. An Account in the general Ledger representing the amount owed by the business to its general creditors on open purchases of merchandise. It is a Control account equaling the total of the individual account balances in the accounts payable ledger.

It first appears on the books of account through the purchases Journal when a charge purchase is recorded (see Debit and credit):

Debit Purchases
　Credit Accounts Payable

When the creditor is paid, the entry is made in the Cash disbursements journal:

Debit Accounts Payable
　Credit Cash

This assumes that the amount of cash paid equals the amount owed. However, deductions may be made for items such as cash discounts, returned merchandise, and inferior merchandise that is not returned but for which allowances are made.

The entry recording payment in full of the account then becomes the following:

Debit Accounts Payable
   Credit Purchase Returns
   Credit Purchase Allowances
   Credit Purchase Discounts
   Credit Cash

Accounts Payable is one of the CURRENT LIABILITIES and is included under that heading on the BALANCE SHEET.

2. (*Sing.*) An individual account in the accounts payable ledger.

ACCOUNTING RECORDS for an executive usually do not include an individual Accounts Payable account.

ACCOUNTS RECEIVABLE. 1. An ACCOUNT in the general LEDGER representing the amount due the business from its customers. It is a CONTROL ACCOUNT equaling the total of the individual account balances in the accounts receivable ledger.

It first appears on the books of account through the sales JOURNAL when a charge sale is recorded (see DEBIT AND CREDIT):

Debit Accounts Receivable
   Credit Sales

When the customer pays his or her account, the entry is made in the CASH RECEIPTS JOURNAL:

Debit Cash
   Credit Accounts Receivable

This assumes that the amount of cash received equals the amount due. However, the customer may make deductions for items such as cash discounts, returned merchandise, and inferior merchandise that is not returned but for which allowances are made.

The entry recording the receipt of payment in full of a customer's account then becomes the following:

Debit Cash
Debit Sales Returns

> *Debit* Sales Allowances
> *Debit* Sales Discounts
>   *Credit* Accounts Receivable

Accounts Receivable is one of the CURRENT ASSETS and is included under that heading on the BALANCE SHEET.

2. (*Sing.*) An individual account in the accounts receivable ledger.

ACCOUNTING RECORDS for an executive usually do not include an individual Accounts Receivable account.

ACCRUAL ACCOUNTING. A method of keeping the books of account by which expenses and INCOME are allocated to periods to which they are applicable, regardless of when payment is made or income received. REVENUE is thereby recognized when earned and expenses when incurred. Compare with CASH ACCOUNTING.

ADJUSTING ENTRIES are made in the general JOURNAL to record ACCRUED INCOME, expenses, and other allocations.

ACCOUNTING RECORDS for an executive are generally kept on a cash accounting basis.

ACCRUED ASSETS. The amount of INCOME earned through commissions and interest on bank accounts and NOTES RECEIVABLE but not received at the close of the accounting period. See also FISCAL PERIOD.

The accrued ASSETS are set up on the books at the close of a fiscal period through ADJUSTING ENTRIES. The ACCRUED INCOME is credited to PROFIT AND LOSS for the period.

Accrued assets usually appear on the BALANCE SHEET as ACCOUNTS RECEIVABLE.

ACCRUED EXPENSES. Expenses such as wages, interest on NOTES PAYABLE, taxes, and interest on bonds payable (see INTEREST; Chapter 13/BOND; INTEREST) incurred on or before the close of the accounting period (see FISCAL PERIOD) but not to be paid until some time in the future.

Accrued expenses are recorded in the books of account through ADJUSTING ENTRIES. These expenses are charged against current PROFIT and are generally recorded as an Account Payable on the BALANCE SHEET.

ACCRUED INCOME. INCOME such as commissions and interest on bank accounts and NOTES RECEIVABLE that is earned but not yet collected.

At the close of the FISCAL PERIOD, the accrued income is recorded in the books of account through ADJUSTING ENTRIES. This income is credited to current PROFIT and is generally recorded as an Account Receivable on the BALANCE SHEET.

ACCRUED LIABILITIES. The amount of wages, interest on NOTES PAYABLE, interest on bonds payable (see Chapter 13/BOND; INTEREST), taxes, and so on that is incurred but not yet paid.

The accrued liabilities are recorded in the books of account at the close of a FISCAL PERIOD through ADJUSTING ENTRIES. At that time, the ACCRUED ASSETS and liabilities are charged to PROFIT AND LOSS for the period. Accrued liabilities generally appear on the BALANCE SHEET as CURRENT LIABILITIES.

ADJUSTED GROSS INCOME. For INCOME TAX purposes, GROSS INCOME after various deductions (see DEDUCTIONS/ADJUSTMENTS), such as those for IRA and Keogh plan contributions, self-employed health insurance, one-half of SELF-EMPLOYMENT TAX, student loan interest, and certain losses on sales.

ADJUSTING ENTRIES. An ACCOUNTING term for JOURNAL entries made at the close of a FISCAL PERIOD. The purpose is to record INCOME and expenses in the proper period and make any adjustments or corrections to specific accounts. This ensures that ACCOUNTS on the BALANCE SHEET and INCOME STATEMENT reflect the proper amounts.

Adjusting entries are also made to correct errors discovered when the books of account are audited (see AUDIT) at the close of the fiscal period preliminary to preparing a profit and loss, or income, statement and a balance sheet.

ALTERNATIVE MINIMUM TAX. A special tax enacted to ensure that taxpayers who benefit from special treatment of certain kinds of INCOME or special deductions from certain kinds of expenses will pay at least a minimum amount of tax.

This tax, which exists for both corporate and individual taxpayers, is figured on certain tax benefits known as *tax-preference items*.

ASSESSMENT. The levying of a tax; the additional amount that a taxpayer is required to pay because of a deficiency; the valuation of property to establish a BASIS for PROPERTY TAXES. See also Chapter 15/ASSESSED VALUATION.

ASSETS. Items of value owned by a business or an individual. On a BALANCE SHEET, assets are usually classified and grouped as CURRENT ASSETS, FIXED ASSETS, INTANGIBLE ASSETS, and Other Assets.

The relation of an asset to the business determines its classification. For example, in a business engaged in buying and selling trucks, the trucks are classified as a *Current Asset* (Inventory ACCOUNT). But if the trucks are used for delivery purposes, they are classified as a *Fixed Asset*.

AUDIT. A verification of the reported ASSETS, LIABILITIES, CAPITAL, REVENUE, and Expenses (such as OPERATING EXPENSES) of a business as of a given date and the verification of the recorded financial transactions during the FISCAL PERIOD then ended.

An *internal audit* is performed by a firm's own personnel, whereas an *external audit* is performed by an independent CERTIFIED PUBLIC ACCOUNTANT (CPA) hired from outside the business.

Lending institutions generally require audited FINANCIAL STATEMENTS before making a major lending decision.

During an audit, an AUDITOR examines the ACCOUNTING RECORDS and supporting documents of a firm. Office personnel often assist by locating the necessary materials and seeing that records and files are up to date and in their proper place for immediate access.

AUDITOR. An independent CERTIFIED PUBLIC ACCOUNTANT (CPA) or an ACCOUNTING officer of a corporation who examines the ACCOUNTS to determine if the financial transactions of the company have been properly classified and to report to the board of directors on the financial position and results of operations of the company. See also Chapter 10/ BOARD OF DIRECTORS; CORPORATION.

Most large corporations provide for the office of internal auditor. The internal auditor's functions are performed in many instances by the controller or, in smaller companies, by outside accountants. See also Chapter 10/CONTROLLER (COMPTROLLER).

Corporations that have internal auditors also employ outside accountants to perform independent AUDITS.

BAD-DEBT LOSSES. Losses on ACCOUNTS RECEIVABLE and NOTES RECEIVABLE caused by the failure of customers to pay. Under ordinary circumstances, they should be charged to the PROFIT AND LOSS account of the year in which they are known to be bad.

In most businesses, however, this practice would result in unpredictable and uneven charges to PROFITS. Bad debts vary from year to year, and large losses may occur infrequently.

An ACCOUNTING device is therefore used to apportion the losses evenly over the years. This device consists of making an annual Allowance for Doubtful Accounts by setting aside from Profit each year an estimated amount for expected bad-debt losses. This amount may be determined based on an aging of accounts receivable or as a percentage of credit sales.

Debts written off as bad are charged to the Bad Debts account, which affects the current Profit and Loss account.

The amount of the Allowance for Doubtful Accounts is shown on the BALANCE SHEET as a deduction from the CURRENT ASSET Accounts Receivable.

BALANCE SHEET. A systematic statement of the ASSETS, LIABILITIES, and CAPITAL of a business at a specified date. This FINANCIAL STATEMENT is included in every annual report. See also Chapter 10/ANNUAL REPORT.

Account form. In the *account form* of balance sheet, the assets are listed on the left side of a double sheet, with the liabilities and OWNERS' EQUITY (capital) on the right side.

The arrangement of the ACCOUNTS follows a fundamental ACCOUNTING equation:

Assets = Liabilities + Capital (A = L + C)

The assets and liabilities stated on a balance sheet follow a definite order. On the *assets side,* the usual order is CURRENT ASSETS, investments, FIXED ASSETS, and INTANGIBLE ASSETS and other assets.

On the *liabilities side,* the usual order is CURRENT LIABILITIES, long-term liabilities, and CAPITAL accounts.

Report form. In the *report form* of balance sheet, the current assets are listed first in a single column followed by current liabilities, the total of which is deducted from total current assets to arrive at WORKING CAPITAL.

Other assets are added to the working capital, and other liabilities are deducted from this total to arrive at NET ASSETS.

Preparing the balance sheet. Both sides of an account form of balance sheet should end on the same line of the page. See Figure 1.

When there are only a few accounts, some accountants prefer that all of them be placed on the same page, with *Assets* at the top and *Liabilities* and *Capital* at the bottom.

BALANCE SHEET: FIGURE 1: Account Form

ABC COMPANY, INC. AND SUBSIDIARY COMPANIES
Comparative Balance Sheet, September 30, 200X and 200Y

ASSETS   *LIABILITIES*

CURRENT ASSETS:	200X	200Y	CURRENT LIABILITIES:	200X	200Y
Cash	$ 5,767,825	$ 5,113,776	Trade accounts payable	$ 5,645,278	$ 5,730,155
U.S. gov't securities	741,524	1,465,703	Accrued exp. & other liab.	4,477,096	4,537,961
Accounts rec., less allow.			Fed. & state income taxes	1,885,747	3,602,040
for doubtful accounts	2,249,583	1,956,227	Notes payable	1,350,000	350,000
Inventories of merchandise,			TOTAL CUR. LIAB.	13,358,121	14,220,156
priced at the lower of					
cost or market	22,516,940	23,440,729			
TOTAL CUR. ASSETS	31,275,872	31,976,435			
PREPAID RENT, INS.,			10% NOTE due Aug. 15		
TAXES, ETC.	2,014,423	1,225,080	200X. Accts. ranging		
			from $350,000 to		
INVESTMENTS AND			$500,000 due annually		
OTHER ASSETS:			(current maturity incl.		
Invest. in affiliated &			above)	2,950,000	3,300,000
other comp., at cost	1,604,413	2,042,394			
Est. net recovery of prior					
years' fed. income tax	440,000	440,000			
TOTAL INVEST. AND					
OTHER ASSETS	2,044,413	2,482,394	CAPITAL STOCK		
			AND SURPLUS:		
FIXED ASSETS, at cost:			Common stock, $10		
Land	22,000	37,000	par value--Authorized		
Buildings (owned & leased			1,955,522 shares;		
land)	1,554,101	1,596,100	issued and outstanding		
Equipment	18,591,051	17,699,910	1,292,485 shares	12,924,850	12,924,850
	20,167,152	19,333,010	Retained earnings per		
Less accum. depreciation	8,575,604	8,270,736	accompanying		
			statement	16,693,286	16,301,178
TOTAL FIX. ASSETS	11,591,548	11,062,274			
GOODWILL, LEASEHLDS,					
LH IMPROVEMENTS,			TOTAL CAPITAL		
ETC. at nom. amt.	1	1	AND SURPLUS	29,618,136	29,226,028
	$45,926,257	$46,746,184		$45,926,257	$46,746,184

Even in a single-page arrangement, however, the balance sheet is still in *account* form. For example, it is still in balance according to the equation $A = L + C$.

BASIS. A method of measuring the cost of property for tax purposes. Basis is used to figure DEPRECIATION, amortization (see Chapter 13/AMORTIZATION), DEPLETION, and casualty losses and to determine whether you have a gain or loss on the sale or exchange of a CAPITAL ASSET.

Property that you buy usually has an *original basis* that is equal to its cost. Property received in some other way, such as by gift or inheritance, requires a basis other than cost.

Various events may take place to change the original basis, and these events will increase or decrease the original basis. The resulting change is called the *adjusted basis:*

Basis may be *increased* by the cost of permanent improvements, legal fees, other charges that you must capitalize, and any other capital expenditure, including amounts spent after a casualty loss to restore the damaged property to its original condition.

Basis may be *decreased* by amounts you receive that are a return of CAPITAL, by depreciation, by amortization, and by all other amounts that should be properly charged to a Capital Asset account.

When you cannot use cost as a basis, *fair market value* may be important. The Internal Revenue Service defines this as the price at which the property would change hands between a buyer and a seller, neither being required to buy or sell and both having reasonable knowledge of all necessary facts.

Sales of similar property, on or about the same date, may be helpful in figuring the fair market value of property. See also CAPITAL GAIN AND LOSS.

BOOKS OF FINAL ENTRY. Any conventional or electronic LEDGER to which ACCOUNTING entries are transferred from a JOURNAL. (Compare with BOOKS OF ORIGINAL ENTRY.) The most common book of final entry is the general ledger.

BOOKS OF ORIGINAL ENTRY. Any conventional or electronic JOURNAL in which financial transactions of a business are originally recorded. Compare with BOOKS OF FINAL ENTRY. The most common books of original entry are the cash disbursements and cash receipts journals.

BOOK VALUE. 1. The net amount at which an ASSET is recorded on the books of a company, as distinguished from its market or intrinsic value.

The book value of FIXED ASSETS is usually cost plus additions and improvements less accumulated DEPRECIATION.

2. The book value of common stock (see Chapter 13/STOCK), which is determined by dividing the NET WORTH of a corporation—the excess of ASSETS over LIABILITIES as they appear on the BALANCE SHEET—by the number of shares of common stock outstanding:

> The book value of the shares of a company that has a net worth of $1 million and 10,000 shares of stock outstanding would be $100 per share.

> If the corporation has an issue of preferred stock (see Chapter 13/STOCK) outstanding, in addition to the common stock, the book value of the common stock is determined only *after* taking the following steps: (1) deducting from net worth the liquidation value of the preferred stock and (2) subtracting cumulative preferred dividends in arrears. See also Chapter 13/DIVIDEND.

> Treasury stock should be eliminated from the calculation of net worth before determining the book value of common stock.

CAPITAL. The NET WORTH of a business as shown in the Capital account of a sole proprietor; the sum of the capital ACCOUNTS of the partners in a partnership; the sum of the CAPITAL STOCK, PAID-IN CAPITAL, and RETAINED EARNINGS less Treasury Stock accounts in a corporation. See also Chapter 10/CORPORATION; PARTNERSHIP; PROPRIETORSHIP, SOLE.

CAPITAL ASSETS. ASSETS, such as equipment, that are acquired for long-term use. See also CURRENT ASSETS; FIXED ASSETS.

Under the CAPITAL GAIN AND LOSS provisions of the federal INCOME TAX law, a *capital asset* is any property held by the taxpayer, except the following:

1. Stock in trade or other property, including inventory held for sale to customers.

2. ACCOUNTS RECEIVABLE or NOTES RECEIVABLE received for services in the ordinary course of a trade or business, from the sale of any property described in number 1, or for services performed as an employee.

3. Depreciable property used in a trade or business. See also DEPRECIATION.

4. Copyrights and literary, musical, or artistic compositions and similar property as follows: (a) created by your personal efforts, (b) prepared or pro-

duced for you (in the case of a letter, memo, or similar property), or (c) received from a taxpayer mentioned in (a) or (b) in a way, such as by gift, that entitles you to the BASIS of the previous owner.

5. Federal, state, and municipal obligations issued on or after March 1, 1941, on a discount basis and payable without INTEREST at a fixed maturity date not exceeding one year from the date of issue. See also Chapter 13/INTEREST.

The term *capital asset* includes tangibles, such as shares of stocks and bonds, unless they fall under one of the exceptions just mentioned. See also Chapter 13/BOND; STOCK.

CAPITAL EXPENDITURES. Expenditures for FIXED ASSETS, such as for equipment, land, or buildings. Capital disbursements are charged to one of the ASSETS accounts, unlike other expenses that are charged against the PROFITS of a company.

CAPITAL GAIN AND LOSS. The gain or loss of *income* characterized as CAPITAL, rather than ordinary, with *gains* characterized as long or short term.

Gain or loss on securities transactions. Before a taxable gain or loss, if any, on a securities transaction can be determined, a taxpayer must know the cost or other BASIS of the securities disposed of, the amount realized upon disposal, and the length of time the investment was held before it was disposed of:

The *basis* of an ASSET depends on the manner in which the securities were acquired. It may be the actual cost, the fair market value, or a substituted basis. The basis must be compared with the sales proceeds to determine the gain or loss.

The *amount realized* includes both money and the fair market value of any property received on the sale or other disposition of the securities.

Long-term capital gains or *losses* are gains or losses resulting from the sale or exchange of a security held for more than one year.

The *holding period* for gains or losses is computed by *excluding* the day on which the property was acquired and *including* the day on which it was disposed of.

The *date basis* is determined, in certain securities transactions, by following particular rules that specify when a security was acquired. For securities bought or sold through stock exchange transactions (see Chapter 13/STOCK EXCHANGE), the dates of the trade, rather than the settlement, constitute the dates of acquisition or disposition.

Record of capital gains and losses.   For INCOME TAX purposes, a list must be kept of all securities transactions involving gains and losses. The final schedule of capital gains and losses realized during the year, which must accompany the income tax return, is made up from the record that is kept throughout the year.

CAPITALIZATION.   The total ACCOUNTING value of the CAPITAL STOCK, PAID-IN CAPITAL, and borrowed CAPITAL, which consists of bonds or similar evidence of long-term debt (see Chapter 13/BOND); the total amount of a corporation's securities outstanding in the form of capital stock and long-term bonds.

Capitalization is used interchangeably with *capital structure*. See also Chapter 10/CAPITAL STRUCTURE.

CAPITAL STOCK.   The ACCOUNT set up to reflect the amount received from the sale of stock (see Chapter 13/STOCK) regarded as legal CAPITAL; the aggregate ownership interest of a corporation. See also Chapter 10/CORPORATION.

Capital Stock appears on the credit side of a BALANCE SHEET and is recorded at the par value of the shares issued. See also Chapter 13/FACE VALUE; PAR VALUE STOCK; STOCK.

CASH.   The total individual CASH ACCOUNTS belonging to a company.

CASH ACCOUNT.   An ACCOUNT in the general LEDGER used for the bank accounts owned by a company. A separate Cash account is kept for each bank account.

Debits to the account, entered through the CASH RECEIPTS JOURNAL, represent deposits made to the bank account. Credits, entered through the CASH DISBURSEMENTS JOURNAL, represent checks drawn on the bank account. See also DEBIT AND CREDIT.

This account differs from one commonly called Cash on Hand or PETTY CASH. The latter term refers to cash in the company's cash box or till. Debits and credits to this account have no direct effect on the bank account.

Certain items are often erroneously considered to be cash, notably postdated checks, dishonored checks, IOUs, and postage stamps. See also Chapter 13/DISHONOR.

For ACCOUNTING purposes, nothing should be included under the Cash classification that is not money or an instrument that calls for the payment of money from definite funds on deposit with a bank.

CASH ACCOUNTING. A method of keeping the books of account in which consideration is given to cash receipts and cash disbursements only. INCOME is not considered earned unless received; expenses are not chargeable to PROFIT AND LOSS unless paid. Compare with ACCRUAL ACCOUNTING.

Generally, individuals account for income and expenses on the cash basis, and the ACCOUNTING RECORDS for an executive are usually kept on the cash basis.

For tax purposes, most service businesses (lawyers, doctors, and other professionals) and other businesses that do not deal in inventories also maintain their accounting records on the cash basis.

CASH DISBURSEMENTS JOURNAL. A multicolumn ACCOUNT book or computer record; one of the BOOKS OF ORIGINAL ENTRY in which disbursements of cash, represented by checks drawn on a bank, are recorded.

Figure 1 illustrates sample computer entries in a cash disbursements journal. (*G/L Account* refers to the corresponding account to be posted.)

CASH DISBURSEMENTS JOURNAL: FIGURE 1

ABC COMPANY, INC.
CASH DISBURSEMENTS
CASH IN BANK – CHECKING

AS OF 06/30/0X   PAGE 1

DATE	PAYEE	CHECK NO	G/L ACCT	SUB ACCT	DETAIL	NET AMT
06/30/0X	ACME SUPPLY CO	1100	5000			1,000.00
06/00/0X	NEW YORK TIMES	1101	6000			500.00
06/30/0X	BRANSON OIL CO	1102	6010			100.00
	BATCH TOTAL					1,600.00

If all transactions can be handled by one person, a combination cash disbursements journal and CASH RECEIPTS JOURNAL may be used.

CASH JOURNAL. A multicolumn ACCOUNT book or computer record; one of the BOOKS OF ORIGINAL ENTRY in which all transactions involving cash are entered.

CASH RECEIPTS JOURNAL. A multicolumn ACCOUNT book or computer record; one of the BOOKS OF ORIGINAL ENTRY in which receipts of cash, represented as deposits in a bank account, are recorded.

Figure 1 illustrates sample computer entries in a cash receipts journal. (*G/L Account* refers to the corresponding account to be posted.)

If all transactions can be handled by one person, a combination cash receipts journal and CASH DISBURSEMENTS JOURNAL may be used.

CERTIFIED PUBLIC ACCOUNTANT (CPA). An accountant who has met stringent professional qualifications, such as passing the Uniform CPA Examination of the American Institute of Certified Public Accountants. A CPA is licensed by the state and is the only accounting professional allowed to issue an AUDIT opinion.

CASH RECEIPTS JOURNAL: FIGURE 1

ABC COMPANY, INC.
CASH RECEIPTS
CASH IN BANK – CHECKING

AS OF 06/30/0X   PAGE 1

DATE	PAYOR	G/L ACCT	SUB ACCT	DETAIL	NET AMT
06/30/0X	WIDGET SALES INC	4000			2,000.00
06/00/0X	ACME SALES CO	4000			1,000.00
06/30/0X	JOHN D SMITH	4000			100.00
	BATCH TOTAL				3,100.00

Often, a CPA has also met the requirements of the particular state, such as having a certain number of years of public ACCOUNTING experience.

A *public accountant (PA)* also performs accounting services and is licensed by the state. However, the licensing requirements are much less stringent than are those for a CPA.

CHART OF ACCOUNTS.   A numbered listing of those ACCOUNTS that are used to classify ASSETS, LIABILITIES, CAPITAL, REVENUE, and Expenses, such as OPERATING EXPENSES. See Figure 1.

CIRCULATING CAPITAL.   See WORKING CAPITAL.

CLOSING ENTRIES.   Entries made in the general JOURNAL at the end of an ACCOUNTING period (see FISCAL PERIOD) to transfer all balances of the INCOME and Expense ACCOUNTS to BALANCE SHEET accounts.

This has the effect of clearing all balances in the REVENUE and Expense accounts so that the Revenue and Expense accounts all begin a new accounting period with zero balances, and PROFIT for that year may be determined.

The closing entries first transfer the balances to the PROFIT AND LOSS account, which in turn is closed by closing entries into the CAPITAL accounts of a sole proprietorship or partnership or into the RETAINED EARNINGS account of a corporation. See also Chapter 10/CORPORATION; PARTNERSHIP; PROPRIETORSHIP, SOLE.

Balance sheet amounts are not closed; they are carried forward.

The term also refers to entries that have the effect of balancing an account, a set of accounts, or a LEDGER.

CONSTRUCTIVE RECEIPT.   See Chapter 11/CONSTRUCTIVE RECEIPT.

CONTROL ACCOUNT.   An ACCOUNT in the general LEDGER that summarizes what appears in detail in the corresponding subsidiary ledger.

There is a separate control account for each subsidiary ledger. Thus the ACCOUNTS RECEIVABLE control account shows in summary the totals of all DEBITS AND CREDITS appearing in the customers' accounts in the accounts receivable ledger.

The balance of the control account equals the aggregate of the account balances in the subsidiary ledger.

CHART OF ACCOUNTS: FIGURE 1

ABC COMPANY, INC.
Listing of
General Ledger
Date Printed: 10/09/0X

G/L ACCT NUMBER	ACCT NAME	PAGE 1
	CURRENT ASSETS	
1000	CASH IN BANK	
1001	CASH IN BANK – CHECKING	
1002	CASH IN BANK – SAVINGS	
1300	ACCOUNTS RECEIVABLE	
	FIXED ASSETS	
1500	FURNITURE/FIXTURES	
1501	OFFICE EQUIPMENT	
	CURRENT LIABILITIES	
2000	ACCOUNTS PAYABLE	
2200	FEDERAL PAYROLL TAX	
2210	FICA PAYABLE	
	CAPITAL	
3000	CAPITAL STOCK	
3050	RETAINED EARNINGS	
	INCOME	
4000	SALES REVENUE	
	COST OF SALES	
5000	COST OF SALES	
	EXPENSES	
6000	ADVERTISING	
6010	AUTO EXPENSE	
6020	BAD DEBTS	
6030	COMMISSIONS PAID	
	OTHER EXPENSES	
9999	INCOME TRANSFER	

CONTROLLER (COMPTROLLER). See Chapter 10/CONTROLLER (COMPTROLLER).

COST ACCOUNTING. An ACCOUNTING system that uses specific accounting principles to examine the cost of operating a particular business activity.

Management uses cost accounting to ensure efficient and profitable operations by providing data essential to evaluate costs and performance and to examine the effects of new policies, pricing changes, expansion, and so on.

Cost accounting is most often used in businesses involving manufacturing and is mainly directed at the preparation of reports for internal management decision making. A budget is an example of such a report.

CREDIT. See DEBIT AND CREDIT.

CREDITS, TAX. An expenditure that may, if allowed by the Internal Revenue Service, be applied directly against the taxpayer's INCOME TAX liability.

The following are examples of tax credits: credit for the elderly; child- and dependent-care expenses; federal tax on gas, special fuels, and lubricating oil; taxes paid by a regulated investment company; foreign taxes; and earned income.

Care must be taken to distinguish between deductions and credits. *Deductions* reduce ADJUSTED GROSS INCOME, which is then used to compute TAXABLE INCOME. *Credits* are applied against the tax itself to arrive at the taxpayer's actual liability. See also DEDUCTIONS/ADJUSTMENTS.

CROSS-FOOTING. See FOOTING.

CURRENT ASSETS. ASSETS that, in the course of business, will be realized or converted within the ACCOUNTING cycle (see FISCAL PERIOD), generally one year. For example, ACCOUNTS RECEIVABLE is a Current Asset.

Generally, Accounts Receivable are due in 10, 30, or 60 days. In that time, they will be paid in cash, or if not paid, they may be replaced by NOTES RECEIVABLE.

Inventory, in the ordinary course of business, will be sold within one year (converted into accounts receivable or cash). Hence it, too, is a Current Asset.

Thus the ordinary operations of a business involve the circulation of CAPITAL within the group of Current Assets—from Cash to Inventory to Accounts Receivable to Cash again.

Even when an inventory item takes more than one year to sell (such as a crop that must age several years), the item is considered a Current Asset—hence the term *accounting cycle,* or *operating cycle,* rather than *one year,* in the general definition.

The following are included under the *Current Asset* heading of the BALANCE SHEET: Cash (in banks), Cash on Hand, Accounts Receivable (due within one year), Marketable Securities (that represent the investment of cash available for current operations), Merchandise Inventory, ACCRUED INCOME, and other items. In some cases, PREPAID EXPENSES are also included.

CURRENT CAPITAL. Gross WORKING CAPITAL, or *circulating capital.*

CURRENT LIABILITIES. Debts or obligations that must be satisfied from CURRENT ASSETS or by incurring additional LIABILITIES. Current Liabilities are liquidated within the ACCOUNTING cycle (see FISCAL PERIOD), generally one year. For example, ACCOUNTS PAYABLE is a Current Liability.

Accounts Payable are due in 10, 30, or 60 days. In that specified time, they will be paid in cash, or they may be replaced by NOTES PAYABLE.

Expenses arising currently, such as salaries and rent, are also considered Current Liabilities.

Included under the *Current Liabilities* heading of the BALANCE SHEET are Accounts Payable (due within one year), Notes Payable (due within one year), ACCRUED EXPENSES, Taxes Payable, and other items. Unearned Income may also be included.

CURRENT RATIO. Also called *working-capital ratio.* The ratio of CURRENT ASSETS to CURRENT LIABILITIES.

The current ratio shows the number of dollars of current assets for each dollar of current liabilities. This reveals a company's *liquidity* (the ability of an entity to satisfy current liabilities using current assets).

The following formula can be used to test the sufficiency of a company's WORKING CAPITAL:

$$\frac{\text{Current Assets}}{\text{Current Liabilities}} = \text{Current Ratio or Working Capital Ratio}$$

Companies may use their own current ratio to compare their position with that of a competitor and as a forecasting aid for financial planning. Lenders may also use this ratio to determine the ability of a borrower to repay loans.

DEBIT AND CREDIT. Entries in DOUBLE-ENTRY ACCOUNTING that record additions to or reductions in an ACCOUNT. An entry on the left side of the account is a *debit,* abbreviated *Dr.* An entry on the right side is a *credit,* abbreviated *Cr.*

In general, a *debit* does the following:

Increases ASSET accounts (Cash, ACCOUNTS RECEIVABLE, Furniture and Fixtures, and so on)

Increases Expense accounts (Salaries, Office Supplies, Taxes, and so on)

Decreases CAPITAL accounts

Decreases LIABILITY accounts (NOTES PAYBLE, ACCOUNTS PAYABLE, ACCRUED EXPENSES, and so on)

In general, a *credit* does the following:

Decreases Asset accounts

Increases Capital accounts

Increases INCOME accounts

Increases Liability accounts

As a verb, *debit* means to record a debit, or make a debit entry, and *credit* means to record a credit, or make a credit entry.

DEDUCTIONS/ADJUSTMENTS. Items that reduce the amount of TAXABLE INCOME on a tax return.

Deductions. Items that may be subtracted from ADJUSTED GROSS INCOME to arrive at TAXABLE INCOME. These items materially reduce one's INCOME TAX liability.

Examples of deductions are medical expenses, state income and personal property taxes, and mortgage INTEREST on a personal residence. See also Chapter 13/INTEREST; Chapter 15/MORTGAGE.

Adjustments. Items that may be subtracted from GROSS INCOME to arrive at adjusted gross income.

Examples of adjustments are ordinary and necessary expenses on property held for producing rents and royalties, alimony payments, and payments by employees and self-employed persons to their own retirement plans.

Because deductions/adjustments affect the amount of taxes paid, it is important to keep meticulous records of the various items. This is necessary not only to substantiate the deductions but also to facilitate preparation of the income tax return.

For examples of specific types of deductions/adjustments, see DEPRECIATION; INDIVIDUAL RETIREMENT PROGRAMS; INTEREST; PROPERTY TAX; STAMP TAX.

DEFERRED-COMPENSATION AGREEMENT. A contract for payment to be made in the future in consideration of services rendered in the past. Deferred-compensation plans today constitute an important method of compensating executives.

Under this type of agreement, one is currently paid compensation less than one might otherwise have received, payment of additional compensation being deferred to a future period.

Deferred-compensation agreements are made as a means of obtaining substantial tax savings. Many people want to postpone receipt of INCOME in the hope that lower tax rates will prevail or until retirement or other causes will reduce GROSS INCOME and the applicable tax rates.

However, deferred-compensation plans are also adopted for purposes other than tax reduction. For example, the aim may be to provide a savings plan or to postpone part of one's compensation as a guaranty of continued performance or as a stimulus for greater future effort.

DEFICIT. The amount by which total LIABILITIES and CAPITAL accounts (other than RETAINED EARNINGS) exceed ASSETS. A deficit results in a debit balance in the Retained Earnings account. See also DEBIT AND CREDIT.

DEPLETION. The expiration of the cost of natural resources, such as mineral deposits and timber tracts, caused by their conversion into a salable product:

> During coal mining, the value of the coal properties will decrease through the depletion of the resources. When the coal properties are completely exhausted, they will have to be *written off*. See also WRITE-OFF.
>
> Instead of taking the loss at the beginning (charging the coal properties to PROFIT AND LOSS upon acquisition) or when the coal properties are completely exhausted, the original cost is allocated over the estimated productive life of the properties. This process of allocation is known as *depletion*.

DEPRECIATION. The periodic systematic writing down in value of the cost of buildings, equipment, and other limited-life ASSETS because of wear and tear from use or disuse, obsolescence, accidents, or inadequacy; the spreading out of the original cost of FIXED ASSETS, such as equipment, over its useful life:

Depreciation is loss of value.

Deterioration is loss of substance.

The term *depreciation* is not applied to the exhaustion of WASTING ASSETS, such as mineral deposits and timberlands (see DEPLETION), or to small tools or items of supplies, such as stationery. See also PREPAID EXPENSES.

In general, depreciation assigns to a FISCAL PERIOD a portion of the original cost of the fixed assets.

Depreciation and taxes. If you buy property to use in a trade or business or to earn rent or royalty income and the property has a useful life of more than a year, you may elect to deduct its entire cost in one year, up to statutory limits. Otherwise, you must spread the cost over more than one year and deduct a part of it each year.

If you use property in part for business and in part for personal purposes, you can only depreciate the business part.

The federal INCOME TAX law allows a deduction (see DEDUCTIONS/ADJUST-MENTS) toward GROSS INCOME for exhaustion, wear and tear of property used in a trade or business, or property held for the production of INCOME.

Methods of depreciation. Among the methods of computation traditionally used, the *straight-line method* is the simplest and most widely used method. With it, the taxpayer spreads the cost of the property evenly over the years of its estimated life.

Under the *accelerated depreciation* method, a greater portion of the cost of the property is recovered in the initial years of its useful life. Since land does not wear out, its value is excluded from the cost of real property in computing depreciation. See also Chapter 15/REAL PROPERTY.

Under the *sum-of-the-years-digits method,* a changing fraction is applied to the cost of the asset reduced by the estimated salvage value. The numerator equals the remaining life of the asset in years, and the denominator equals the sum of the numbers representing the years of an asset's life.

With the *production method,* traditionally used primarily for manufacturing equipment, hours of operation or units produced are used to allocate deprecia-tion for assets that have a limited useful life.

The Internal Revenue Service presently requires the use of a depreciation method referred to as *MACRS (Modified Accelerated Cost Recovery System).*

Tables are available that reflect the annual percentage rate that must be applied to the asset's original cost to arrive at the year's depreciation.

However, taxpayers may still elect to use the straight-line method under certain circumstances.

DIRECT TAX.   1. A tax that is collected from someone who is expected to bear the entire tax cost. An *indirect,* or *hidden, tax,* by contrast, is usually hidden in the price of goods and hence borne by others.

The SALES AND USE TAX and admissions tax are examples of a *direct tax.* State gasoline taxes may be *hidden taxes,* depending on how they are levied. A manufacturer's EXCISE TAX is usually an *indirect tax* included in the sales price.

2. A type of tax that is limited by the Constitution. The Sixteenth Amendment, for example, was needed to enable Congress to pass an INCOME TAX law.

DOUBLE-ENTRY ACCOUNTING.   The method of recording business financial transactions by equal DEBITS AND CREDITS. In recording financial transactions in a JOURNAL, two phases of the transaction are recorded in each individual entry.

For example, the purchase of machinery for cash is recorded as follows:

Debit Machinery $5,000
   Credit Cash $5,000

The entries signify the two phases of the transaction.

The debits and credits in journal entries must always equal each other, and these balanced entries, in turn, are posted to a LEDGER. See also POSTING.

Therefore, the aggregate of the debits in all ledger ACCOUNTS must be equal to the aggregate of the credits in these accounts. This is the basic concept of the double-entry method.

EQUITY CAPITAL.   The portion of a firm's CAPITAL that is furnished by stockholders rather than creditors.

ESTIMATED TAX.   A federal tax return WORK SHEET showing INCOME and tax as estimated for the current year.

To keep INCOME TAX payments on a pay-as-you-go basis, the government, in most cases, requires the taxpayer to estimate his or her tax for the current year. The taxpayer then pays this estimated amount in four installments.

Estimated tax payments are required when the taxpayer's total liability is estimated to exceed the amount of tax withheld by an employer. The tax WITHHOLDINGS do not always pay an employee's tax liability in full.

A taxpayer who filed a regular income tax return (Form 1040) for the preceding year should also file a Declaration of Estimated Tax (Form 1040 ES) if certain conditions are met.

A taxpayer must file Form 1040 ES if his or her total estimated tax is above a specified amount for the current year and if the total amount of tax that will be withheld by an employer will be less than the lesser of the following: (1) 90 percent of expected tax liability for the coming year or (2) 100 percent of the tax shown on the preceding year's return. See also GROSS INCOME.

EXCISE TAX. A federal, state, or local tax that is imposed on acts rather than as a DIRECT TAX on property. An excise tax is generally levied on the right to follow a particular occupation or trade, to carry on a business, or to transfer and receive property:

> An *estate tax* is an excise tax on the right of a decedent's estate to transfer property to the heirs.

> An *inheritance tax* is an excise tax levied on the heirs who receive such property.

Some excise taxes, such as the excise tax on cameras, are a percentage of the manufacturer's selling price. Other excise taxes, such as a tax on safe deposit boxes, are borne directly by the consumer but are collected by the seller and remitted by the seller to the government.

State excise taxes include the following: franchise, stock transfer, document recording, death and gift, motor fuel, admissions and amusements, chain store, and tobacco taxes, as well as severance taxes on the use of natural resources, such as timber and minerals.

Federal excise taxes paid are not deductible in computing an individual's tax liability.

EXCLUSION. An item of INCOME that is exempt from tax by the federal government. An example is interest on state and municipal bonds. (See INTEREST; Chapter 13/BOND; INTEREST.) In filing a return, the taxpayer generally is allowed to exclude such items from GROSS INCOME.

Examples of income that is excluded by federal statute are gifts and inheritances, life insurance proceeds, employer-provided child-care benefits, and qualifying scholarships and fellowship grants.

An *exclusion* should not be confused with a *deduction*. See also DEDUCTIONS/ADJUSTMENTS.

EXPENSES. See ACCRUED EXPENSES; CAPITAL EXPENDITURES; FIXED COSTS; OPERATING EXPENSES; OVERHEAD; PREPAID EXPENSES; VARIABLE COSTS.

FINANCIAL STATEMENT. A written presentation of financial data prepared from the ACCOUNTING RECORDS. Common financial statements are the BALANCE SHEET, INCOME STATEMENT, statement of RETAINED earnings, STATEMENT OF CASH FLOWS, and notes to financial statements.

FISCAL PERIOD. Also known as the *accounting period* or *fiscal year.* The period covered during one cycle of business operations, generally one year.

The fiscal period may coincide with the calendar year, in which case the firm is said to be on a *calendar-year basis.* Or it may include 12 successive calendar months, terminating at the end of the same month each year.

The fiscal year also may consist of 13 four-week periods. In that case, the extra day (two days in a leap year) is added to the last week.

Fiscal periods may be monthly, quarterly, semiannual, or annual. PROFIT AND LOSS figures may be prepared for any of these periods. Fiscal periods shorter than one month and longer than one year are infrequent. See also NATURAL BUSINESS YEAR.

FIXED ASSETS. Those ASSETS with a useful life in excess of one year that the business or individual does not intend to dispose of or that could not be disposed of without interfering with the operation of the business.

Such assets usually include land, buildings, equipment, furniture, and fixtures. They are included in the *Fixed Assets* group on a BALANCE SHEET.

FIXED COSTS. Expenses such as rent and salaries that do not change in *total* but are not affected by routine variations in the volume of business on a per-unit basis. Fixed Costs may change by management decision or by changes in operational capacity.

FOOTING. The total of a column in one of the books of account, on a FINANCIAL STATEMENT, on a financial schedule, or on WORKING PAPERS; in computer-generated SPREADSHEETS, or schedules, the total obtained by the computer, checked against the totals obtained by manual calculations.

Footings. The *footings,* or totals, are obtained by adding the entries in each column.

Since a balanced set of books is a basic requirement in ACCOUNTING, the DEBIT AND CREDIT amounts in each entry must be equal, and the total debits must equal the total credits.

Cross-footing. Whenever a financial account or schedule contains debits and credits, each of the columns should be footed, or totaled. Then the sum of the columns standing for debits should be checked against the sum of the columns standing for credits. This procedure is known as *cross-footing.*

FRANCHISE TAX. Also called *qualification tax, corporation fee, license fee,* and *privilege tax.* A CAPITAL STOCK tax imposed on corporations by most of the states.

A *franchise tax* is a tax on the privilege of operating as a corporation and applies to a domestic corporation and a foreign corporation alike. See also Chapter 10/CORPORATION; DOMESTIC CORPORATION; FOREIGN CORPORATION.

A franchise tax is usually levied on either issued CAPITAL STOCK, authorized capital stock, or CAPITAL used in the state levying the tax.

Franchise taxes must be paid before a corporation may do business within the state.

FUNDED DEBT. A debt acquired to purchase ASSETS or pay off a number of short-term debts. Funded debts are usually long-term debts for which a specified schedule of repayments has been made.

GOODWILL. INTANGIBLE ASSETS arising when the amount paid to acquire a business is greater than the BOOK VALUE of the underlying NET ASSETS.

Generally, Goodwill relates to the value of the acquired company's name, reputation, customer lists, and so on.

GROSS INCOME. INCOME before deducting any expenses; an expression used in ACCOUNTING for the income earned by individuals and businesses.

In general, gross income includes gains (see CAPITAL GAIN AND LOSS), income received as salary, fees, PROFITS from business, INTEREST, dividends, and rents. See also Chapter 13/DIVIDEND; INTEREST; Chapter 15/RENT.

Certain deductions are subtracted from gross income to arrive at ADJUSTED GROSS INCOME in the computation of a taxpayer's INCOME TAX. See also DEDUCTIONS/ADJUSTMENTS.

GROSS PROFIT.   See PROFIT.

GROSS REVENUE.   A term used to emphasize the fact that no deduction for cost has been made from REVENUE. See also GROSS INCOME.

HOLDING PERIOD FOR SECURITIES.   The length of time that an investment is held before its sale. See also CAPITAL GAIN AND LOSS.

INCOME.   Money or money's worth received or accrued during an ACCOUNTING period (see FISCAL PERIOD), increasing the total of previously existing ASSETS and arising from sales and rentals of any type of goods or services.

Income is any element, other than additional investment, that increases OWNER'S EQUITY. Thus the money invested by stockholders in additional stock is not income. But income may be the gain from CAPITAL (such as dividends on securities held by a corporation), labor (the manufacture of a product for sale at a profit), or a combination of both. See also Chapter 13/CORPORATION; DIVIDEND; STOCK.

Income also includes gain from the sale or conversion of CAPITAL ASSETS (the sale of an asset at a profit produces income). Thus income includes not only operating PROFITS (or operating income) but also extraneous profits.

Some accountants use the terms *income* and REVENUE interchangeably. Others use the terms to mean different things. When the words *gross* and *net* are used with *income* and *revenue,* the terms again have different meanings. See also GROSS INCOME; NET INCOME.

INCOME AND EXPENSE STATEMENT.   See INCOME STATEMENT.

INCOME STATEMENT.   Also known as *profit and loss statement.* A summary of the INCOME and expenses of a business, in classified form, showing the NET INCOME or loss for a specified period. It generally consists of income, cost of sales, and expenses.

Income statements may be presented in a detailed report form or in a shortened version. When a statement has adjacent columns with corresponding amounts for previous periods, such as a previous year, it is called a *comparative income statement.* Figure 1 illustrates a short form, comparative income statement.

In nonprofit organizations, the income statement is called the STATEMENT OF ACTIVITIES.

INCOME STATEMENT: FIGURE 1: Short Form

ABC COMPANY, INC.
Statement of Income
Years Ending December 31, 200X and 200Y

	200X	200Y
Sales, net of returns and allowances	$132,532	$108,560
Cost of sales	(68,305)	(56,295)
Gross Profit	64,227	52,265
Selling expenses	(26,211)	(23,582)
General and administrative expense	(18,560)	(16,893)
Income from operations	19,456	11,790
Interest expense	(12,082)	(8,563)
Income before income taxes	7,374	3,227
Provision for income taxes, federal and state	(3,687)	(1,613)
Net Income	$ 3,687	$ 1,614

INCOME TAX. A federal, state, or local tax levied on the TAXABLE INCOME of individuals, corporations, and certain trusts.

Payment procedure. Most individuals pay all or a substantial part of their income tax during the year in which they receive their income. The income tax is withheld from their wages (see WITHHOLDING) or is paid in quarterly installments based on a declaration of ESTIMATED TAX, or both.

Under federal law, taxpayers may report INCOME on either the accrual or cash basis, and the accounting period (see FISCAL PERIOD) may be a calendar or fiscal year. See also ACCRUAL ACCOUNTING; CASH ACCOUNTING.

Tax rates are usually based on taxable income, which is ADJUSTED GROSS INCOME less certain allowable DEDUCTIONS/ADJUSTMENTS, including the deduction for exemptions.

Income tax records. Records for income tax purposes include tax information and records relating to the previous three years, as well as the current year.

Previous years' tax records should be kept for a minimum of three years after filing or until all possible statutes of limitations have run out. See also Chapter 11/STATUTE OF LIMITATIONS.

At the beginning of each year, a folder should be set up labeled "Federal Income Tax, 200X, Name of Taxpayer." This should be a general folder for material pertaining to the current year's tax records. See also Accounting records.

An assistant may keep separate files for his or her employer, the employer's spouse, and each member of the employer's family whose tax records are the assistant's responsibility.

INDIVIDUAL RETIREMENT PROGRAM. A program designed to provide retirement benefits for which tax-deductible contributions may be made.

After retirement, funds distributed from the account are taxed as ordinary income. Premature withdrawals from individual retirement programs are subject to severe tax penalties, with limited exceptions.

Retirement programs. The following are the main individual retirement savings programs:

1. *Individual retirement accounts (IRAs)* at a participating bank, federally insured credit union, savings and loan association, or other institution that may act as a trustee or custodian

2. *Individual retirement annuities* or endowment contracts of a life insurance company

3. *Keogh plans* established by self-employed individuals

4. *Self-employed retirement programs (SEPs)* established by self-employed individuals or by employers on behalf of eligible employees

5. *Trust accounts* established by an employer for the benefit of its employees and the employee–owner

Deduction of contributions. In most cases, a contribution to individual retirement savings programs is an *adjustment* to Income. Therefore, you may claim it as a deduction in the year for which the contribution was made. See also Deductions/adjustments.

Certain restrictions on the deductibility of individual retirement account contributions exist if Adjusted gross income exceeds certain amounts.

However, even if a contribution to an individual retirement account is deemed to be nondeductible, a contribution up to a specified amount may still be made if the taxpayer has sufficient earned income. In this case, the income earned on such contributions remains tax deferred.

INFORMATION RETURN. Information required under the Internal Revenue Code to be furnished by persons or organizations that pay certain types of

INCOME to noncorporate taxpayers. The following are the main types of income to be reported on Form 1099:

Payments to nonemployees above a specified amount (if not shown on Form W-2)

Dividends and interest in excess of a specified amount (see INTEREST; Chapter 13/DIVIDEND; INTEREST)

Payments above a specified amount to noncorporate recipients of rents and royalties

Estates, trusts, partnerships, and subchapter S corporations must also file information returns. The information supplied must include details of REVENUES and expenses and distributable shares of NET INCOME or loss.

The government uses the returns to ensure that the person receiving the income includes it on his or her tax return.

INTANGIBLE ASSETS. Those ASSETS of a business that have value but are neither tangible property nor a direct right to tangible property.

Intangible assets include items such as patents, trademarks, copyrights, franchises, licenses, GOODWILL, and leaseholds. See also Chapter 9/COPYRIGHT; Chapter 10/FRANCHISE; PATENT; TRADEMARK; Chapter 15/LEASEHOLD.

Most intangible assets have a limited useful life, such as 7 years for copyrights and 14 years for patents.

The cost expended for such items is written off over the period of years representing the useful life of the asset, the WRITE-OFF being accomplished during a period of 40 years or less by debits to Expense and credits to Accumulated Amortization.

INTEREST. Amounts paid on indebtedness. See also Chapter 13/INTEREST.

Interest on income-producing property. Although interest paid on personal indebtedness, such as on credit card debt, is not tax deductible, interest paid in connection with income-producing property is deductible (see DEDUCTIONS/ADJUSTMENTS) from GROSS INCOME to arrive at ADJUSTED GROSS INCOME.

Mortgage interest. Mortgage interest (see Chapter 15/MORTGAGE) on a taxpayer's principal residence and one other home is deductible to the extent that the mortgage does not exceed the lesser of fair market value of the property or the costs of the home plus improvements.

Interest on mortgage debt incurred before August 17, 1986, is not subject to the limitation concerning purchase price plus improvements.

Interest on additional mortgage indebtedness, up to the property's fair market value, that is incurred for qualified educational or medical expenses can also be deducted.

Interest related to investments. Interest paid to acquire or maintain an investment is allowable as an itemized deduction up to the amount of net investment income.

JOURNAL. Any of the BOOKS OF ORIGINAL ENTRY in which transactions are recorded manually or electronically in chronological order and in a specific manner. Journals are either specialized or general.

General journal. A simple journal that is used when no other specialized journals exist in which to record particular transactions. The general journal is therefore used for transactions that do not occur frequently enough to require a specialized journal.

Specialized journal. Also known as *subsidiary journal*. This type of journal is used to record transactions of a like kind that occur frequently. The most common specialized journals are the sales journal, purchase journal, purchase returns journal, sales return journal, CASH RECEIPTS JOURNAL, CASH DISBURSEMENTS JOURNAL, and PETTY CASH journal.

Transactions not recorded in the specialized journals are recorded in a *general journal*.

In any journal, an entry gives the date of the transaction, ACCOUNT and amount debited, account and amount credited, and an explanation of the item. See also DEBIT AND CREDIT.

Subsidiary journals save time, space, and labor. The use of separate columns for accounts that are frequently debited or credited eliminates entering the name of the accounts to be debited and credited for each entry.

Also, the time involved in POSTING is reduced. Postings from the subsidiary journals are made periodically instead of after each entry as is done with the general journal.

The column totals are posted in a single amount to the proper CONTROL ACCOUNT in the general LEDGER.

LEDGER. A book in which the financial transactions of a business are classified by separate ACCOUNTS, each bearing its own name.

Entries in the ledger are made manually or electronically by POSTING from BOOKS OF ORIGINAL ENTRY. They are therefore called BOOKS OF FINAL ENTRY.

General ledger. The ledger that contains a summary of the accounts that are maintained in a subsidiary or private ledger. The general ledger contains the CONTROL ACCOUNTS for each of the subsidiary and private ledgers.

The balances in the general ledger for ASSET, LIABILITY, and CAPITAL accounts become the basis for data set forth on the BALANCE SHEET.

The balances in the INCOME and Expense accounts become the basis for data set forth in the INCOME STATEMENT. Figure 1 illustrates a computer printout of ledger entries that were posted from CASH RECEIPTS JOURNAL and CASH DISBURSEMENTS JOURNAL transactions.

Subsidiary ledger. A ledger maintained for subsidiary accounts of a homogeneous nature. The balances of the accounts in this ledger equal the total of the balance shown in the control account for the particular subsidiary ledger maintained in the general ledger.

Common subsidiary ledgers are the customers' ledger, creditors' ledger, factory ledger, expense ledger, plant and equipment ledger, and stores ledger.

Private ledger. A separate ledger in which accounts containing confidential data are maintained. Examples are management salaries, withdrawals, loans, capital investment, and items that are required to prepare financial statements.

All accounts in a subsidiary ledger are similar. For example, all accounts in the customers' ledger are ACCOUNTS RECEIVABLE. But each account in the private ledger is different, the only similarity between them being their confidential nature.

A control account called Private Ledger is maintained in the general ledger. However, this account does not reveal the details of the entries in the private ledger.

The treasurer or controller of an organization usually keeps the private ledger.

LIABILITIES. Debts or obligations of a business or individual, the satisfaction of which will require the use of the ASSETS of the business or individual for the benefit of creditors.

LEDGER: FIGURE 1: General Ledger

ABC COMPANY, INC.
General Ledger

AS OF 06/30/0X   PAGE 1

ACCT NO	ACCOUNT NAME	FOLIO	BALANCE FORWARD	CURRENT PERIOD	BALANCE
1001	CASH IN BANK – CHECKING		.00		
	CHECKS FOR PERIOD	CD1		2,150.00-	
	RECEIPTS FOR PERIOD	CR1		3,350.00	
					1,200.00
1002	CASH IN BANK – SAVING		.00		
	CHECKS FOR PERIOD	CD2		.00	
	RECEIPTS FOR PERIOD	CR2		.00	
					.00
1300	ACCOUNTS RECEIVABLE		.00		
	JOHN D SMITH	CR1 06/30/0X		250.00-	
					250.00-
1500	FURNITURE/FIXTURES		.00		
	ACME FURNITURE CO	CD1 #1103		300.00	
					300.00
1501	OFFICE EQUIPMENT		.00		
	E-Z OFFICE SUPPLIES	CD1 #1104		250.00	
					250.00
2000	ACCOUNTS PAYABLE		.00		
	MDSE PURCH SUMMARY	MP		.00	
					.00
3050	RETAINED EARNINGS		.00		
	PERIOD NET INCOME (CR) OR LOSS (DB)			1,500.00-	
					1,500.00-
4000	SALES REVENUE		.00		
	WIDGET SALES INC	CR1 06/30/0X		2,000.00-	
	ACME SUPPLY COMPANY	CR1 06/30/0X		1,000.00-	
	JOHN D SMITH	CR1 06/30/0X		100.00-	
					3,100.00-
5000	COST OF SALES		.00		
	ACME SUPPLY COMPANY	CD1 #1100		1,000.00	
					1,000.00
6000	ADVERTISING		.00		
	NEW YORK TIMES	CD1 #1101		500.00	
					500.00

Liabilities also include future services required for which advance payment has already been received. A legal retainer fee is an example.

Normally, the liabilities appear on the credit side of a BALANCE SHEET and are segregated into CURRENT LIABILITIES (due within one year) and Long-Term Liabilities, such as bonds and mortgages payable, to facilitate the determination of WORKING CAPITAL. See also Chapter 13/BOND; Chapter 15/MORTGAGE.

Contingent Liabilities, such as warranty expense, may be included in FINANCIAL STATEMENT disclosures as a footnote.

MERIT RATING. Also known as *experience rating*. A means of encouraging employers to stabilize employment by increasing or decreasing contribution rates on unemployment insurance tax rates.

To achieve this purpose, most of the state unemployment compensation laws make some provision for a reduction in the STATE UNEMPLOYMENT INSURANCE TAX or contribution rate for those employers that have stabilized their employment.

Under some of the laws, higher rates are imposed on employers that have heavy labor turnovers.

NATURAL BUSINESS YEAR. An ACCOUNTING period, or FISCAL PERIOD, that ends with the close of the month in which the activities of a business are at or near their lowest point.

Since natural business years end at various times, an accountant is able to spread his or her work more evenly throughout the year.

To change from a calendar year to a natural year, a business must apply for permission from the Internal Revenue Service.

NET ASSETS. Also called NET WORTH or *stockholders' equity.* The excess of the BOOK VALUE of ASSETS over LIABILITIES.

NET INCOME. The difference between INCOME derived from sales or services and the expenses associated with them.

NET PROFIT. See PROFIT.

NET WORKING CAPITAL. The excess of CURRENT ASSETS over CURRENT LIABILITIES. See also WORKING CAPITAL.

NET WORTH. For either an individual or business, the BOOK VALUE of ASSETS minus LIABILITIES.

In the case of a sole proprietorship, net worth is reflected in the proprietor's CAPITAL account; in the case of a partnership, in the total of the partners' Capital ACCOUNTS; in the case of a corporation, in the total of the PAID-IN CAPITAL and RETAINED EARNINGS, less any Treasury Stock. See also Chapter 10/CORPORATION; PARTNERSHIP; PROPRIETORSHIP, SOLE.

NOTES PAYABLE. An ACCOUNT in the general LEDGER showing the amount of promissory notes given by the business. See also Chapter 13/NOTE.

Notes payable usually require the payment of INTEREST. See also Chapter 13/INTEREST.

The item is on the LIABILITIES side of the BALANCE SHEET. It may include any of the following:

1. The amount owing on notes to merchandise creditors for supplies or merchandise purchases
2. Notes payable to banks, representing money borrowed from the banks
3. Notes payable for paper sold through note brokers
4. Notes payable to others, representing notes given when a loan is obtained or other obligations are incurred from sources other than the first two mentioned

NOTES RECEIVABLE. An ACCOUNT in the general LEDGER showing the amount of negotiable promissory notes received from customers in payment for goods sold and delivered and from other debtors. See also Chapter 13/NOTE.

Notes receivable usually involve the receipt of INTEREST. See also Chapter 13/INTEREST.

The item is on the ASSETS side of the BALANCE SHEET.

OBSOLESCENCE. The end of the normal useful life of an ASSET due to some factor such as economic changes or new technological developments.

OPERATING EXPENSES. Those expenses incurred in the conduct of ordinary business activity, such as administrative costs and selling expenses.

OPERATING STATEMENT. See INCOME STATEMENT.

OVERHEAD.   Expenses of a business not associated with the direct production of a good or service, such as rent, fuel, and DEPRECIATION on machinery.

Factory overhead is the factory cost to manufacture an item other than direct material and direct labor costs.

Overhead may be classified as either fixed or variable. See also FIXED COSTS; VARIABLE COSTS.

OWNER'S EQUITY.   The value of one's NET WORTH or CAPITAL; the ASSETS remaining after all debts are paid. See also NET ASSETS.

PAID-IN CAPITAL.   The amount received by a corporation from its stockholders, whether in cash, property, or services. See also Chapter 10/CORPORATION; STOCKHOLDER.

A minimum amount of paid-in CAPITAL may be required by state statute before a corporation can begin business.

Paid-in capital is a major BALANCE SHEET item. It is reflected in the CAPITAL STOCK account of the general LEDGER.

PAID-UP CAPITAL.   The aggregate of par value stock and the stated value of no par stock for which the corporation has received full consideration. See also Chapter 13/PAR VALUE STOCK.

PAYROLL.   A manual or electronic record showing gross salary or wages of each employee, various DEDUCTIONS/ADJUSTMENTS, and net amount of pay for a definite payroll period, usually weekly, semimonthly, or monthly.

The deductions are for taxes withheld from wages, employee's contributions to his or her own retirement or savings account, and other deductions.

Statutory requirements.   The payroll department must comply with federal, state, and local laws, including those concerning income tax WITHHOLDING, SOCIAL SECURITY TAX, unemployment tax (see STATE UNEMPLOYMENT INSURANCE TAX), and wages and hours. See also Chapter 11/WAGE–HOUR LAW.

Payroll records.   All federal payroll laws require employers to keep records of certain information concerning their employees. Severe penalties may be imposed for failure to comply.

The records used in the preparation of the payroll at each period may be classified as follows:

1. *Authorization records,* which include notices of new employees added, changes in rate of pay, transfer, leaves of absence, terminations, and overtime authorization.

2. *Time-keeping records,* which are the original entries from which the payroll department can determine employee gross pay for a pay period.

3. *Payroll-preparation records,* which are used in the actual preparation of the payroll. They include the payroll journal, individual earnings records, paychecks or employer's receipts, and a statement of earnings and deductions for the employee's use.

A *payroll journal,* also called a *payroll record, payroll sheet,* or *payroll summary,* is a manual or electronic record for each payroll period that states the amount of compensation paid to each employee.

It is usually in a columnar format that provides for listing an employee's name and social security number, gross pay, tax withholdings, deductions (individually listed), total deductions, net pay, period ending, and check number. A common form also has columns for the regular overtime hours worked and the hourly rate.

PAYROLL TAXES.   Taxes based on a company's gross PAYROLL that the employer must pay; taxes that an employer must withhold from an employee's pay. See also WITHHOLDING.

The employer must *pay* SOCIAL SECURITY TAX (Federal Insurance Contributions Act [FICA]), federal unemployment tax (FUTA), STATE UNEMPLOYMENT INSURANCE TAX (SUTA) in some states, and disability contribution or tax in some states. See also Chapter 11/DISABILITY BENEFIT LAWS.

The employer must *withhold* from the employee's pay federal INCOME TAX, social security tax, medicare tax, state unemployment insurance tax in some states, disability contribution or tax in some states, and state or city income tax in some states.

PETTY CASH.   An amount of cash on hand used for disbursements that are too small to justify the use of checks. Petty cash is usually maintained on the *imprest system,* which operates as follows:

Assume that a firm's experience indicates that it needs about $100 a week for petty disbursements, such as postage stamps or taxi fare. It therefore starts the fund by drawing a check for $100 charged to the Petty Cash ACCOUNT and cashing it at the bank. It then places the $100 cash in a cash drawer in the office.

Disbursements are made from the cash only upon receipt of a properly approved *petty cash voucher,* which describes the exact purpose for which the cash has been withdrawn, by whom, the amount, and the date.

The total of the cash remaining in the drawer and the amount on the vouchers equals the amount of the fund ($100 in this case).

At the end of the week, the vouchers are collected from the drawer, itemized, and canceled. Another check is then drawn in the amount of the canceled vouchers, thereby bringing the fund back to its original amount ($100).

Although this replacement check is made out to Petty Cash, it is entered in the CASH DISBURSEMENTS JOURNAL with charges to the proper expense accounts indicated on the canceled petty cash vouchers.

If petty cash transactions are numerous and involved, a petty cash journal is maintained manually or electronically to itemize the various charges of petty cash disbursements. Checks drawn to Petty Cash for reimbursement then are not itemized in the cash disbursements journal.

POSTING. The procedure of transferring DEBIT AND CREDIT entries from the BOOKS OF ORIGINAL ENTRY to the proper ACCOUNTS in the subsidiary or general LEDGER.

The manual procedure for posting from the CASH JOURNAL to the general ledger is as follows:

1. Foot (see FOOTING) each column in the journal. Then cross-foot the debit columns and the credit columns. Enter the totals in pencil. The totals of the debit and credit columns must equal each other, or an error has occurred. After the totals are correct, enter them in ink.

2. Post the totals from all columns in the cash journal to the corresponding accounts in the general ledger, either to the debit or credit side of the account, as indicated by the journal. Also enter the date of posting and the journal's page number.

3. As each column is posted, draw a double red line beneath it to show that it has been posted. Also, place beneath the column the page number of the ledger where the item is posted.

4. Since the items in the general ledger column of the journal are miscellaneous, they cannot be posted as a whole. Post the individual items to the

respective accounts in the general ledger, showing the date the entry was made and the journal's page number. In the journal, show the page number of the ledger to which each item was posted.

Usually, computer-generated totals are automatically posted to the general ledger. In this case, the totals transferred from the journal must be traced to the general ledger to ensure accurate balance transfer.

PREPAID EXPENSES. Expenses paid for but not associated with the current period. For example, fire insurance premiums are frequently paid three years in advance. Other common prepaid expenses are rent, taxes, commissions, and interest.

One-third of a three-year premium would be chargeable to the first year's PROFIT AND LOSS. The other two-thirds is considered prepaid expenses.

Prepaid expenses usually appear separately on the BALANCE SHEET as CURRENT ASSETS.

PROFIT. Excess of INCOME over the cost of merchandise sold and the expenses of doing business. Accountants distinguish between profits and income:

Profits are derived from the sale of merchandise.

Income is derived from rendering services or from any other source.

Gross profit is the difference between the selling price and the cost of merchandise sold.

Net profit before INCOME TAX is the difference between gross profit and the general and administrative expenses of conducting a business, such as rent, office salaries, and telephone service. Income tax is then deducted to arrive at net profit.

PROFIT AND LOSS. A temporary ACCOUNT in the general LEDGER to which the balances of all accounts reflecting REVENUE, INCOME, PROFIT, expenses, and losses are transferred periodically. The balance of the Profit and Loss account shows the NET INCOME or loss for the period.

It is transferred, or closed out, to the RETAINED EARNINGS account in the case of a corporation and to the CAPITAL account in the case of a sole proprietorship or partnership. See also CLOSING ENTRIES; Chapter 10/CORPORATION; PARTNERSHIP; PROPRIETORSHIP, SOLE.

PROFIT AND LOSS STATEMENT. See INCOME STATEMENT.

PROPERTY TAX. A tax levied by state and local governments on personal property (tangible, intangible, or both), such as automobiles and jewelry, and real property, such as land and improvements. See also Chapter 11/PERSONAL PROPERTY; Chapter 15/REAL PROPERTY; RENT.

Personal property. Most taxes on personal property have been difficult to administer. They are not rigorously enforced, particularly with respect to compelling taxpayers to disclose the exact value and makeup of their personal property.

Personal property taxes are allowed as a deduction (see DEDUCTIONS/ADJUSTMENTS) from ADJUSTED GROSS INCOME on the federal INCOME TAX return.

Taxes on personal property are included in the group of DEDUCTIONS/ADJUSTMENTS that are subtracted from GROSS INCOME to arrive at ADJUSTED GROSS INCOME.

Real property. Frequently, there are several taxes on real property, such as a county tax, village tax, and school district tax. In regard to federal INCOME TAX, real estate taxes fall into two categories: taxes on real property held for the production of income and taxes on real property held for personal use, such as a residence.

Taxes on real property are classified as itemized deductions and are subtracted from adjusted gross income to arrive at TAXABLE INCOME.

QUICK ASSETS. Those CURRENT ASSETS that are quickly convertible into cash. They usually include cash, receivables, and temporary investments in marketable securities.

Inventories are generally omitted, because it takes time to convert them into receivables. However, commodities immediately salable at a quoted price on the open market would be considered quick ASSETS.

REPLACEMENTS. Also called *renewals*. FIXED ASSETS acquired to replace a similar, existing ASSET, with the newly acquired asset possessing the approximate capacity of the asset being replaced.

RETAINED EARNINGS. The accumulated earnings or deficit of a corporation remaining in the business from the date of incorporation. See also Chapter 10/CORPORATION.

Reductions in retained earnings occur through distributions of dividends. (See Chapter 13/DIVIDEND.) Additions occur through closing out the PROFIT AND

LOSS account at the close of the FISCAL PERIOD, when that ACCOUNT shows a PROFIT or a credit balance.

Retained earnings are part of the stockholders' equity and are added to CAPITAL STOCK to determine the NET WORTH of the business.

Appropriations from retained earnings for specific purposes are considered subdivisions of retained earnings, because the appropriated amount can be returned to the Retained Earnings account at any time.

REVENUE. Gross sales of products and GROSS INCOME from services. Accountants commonly apply the term to the principal classes of gross operating INCOME of various business entities.

For example, the first item on the INCOME STATEMENT of a railroad is *operating revenue*, whereas a real estate agent would use the term *commission income*.

SALES AND USE TAX. A tax imposed by state and local governments as a flat rate on sales. *Sales taxes* take the form of retail sales taxes; taxes on gross sales of retailers, wholesalers, and manufacturers; or taxes on the GROSS INCOME from sales of commodities and services.

The *use tax* was devised to counteract avoidance of the sales tax by those who buy in neighboring, nontaxed or reduced-tax jurisdictions. An example is a resident of a state that has a sales and use tax who purchases a car in another state that does not have this tax or in one whose tax rate is lower.

Such buyers avoid their home state's *sales tax* but not its *use tax*. When they register their cars in their home states, they will be billed for the use tax.

Sales and use taxes paid by retailers, wholesalers, or manufacturers usually allow certain exemptions from gross sales before the tax is applied. Sales taxes paid by a retail customer usually start on all sales over a minimum amount, which may be as little as ten cents.

No deduction for sales tax paid on personal purchases is allowed against individual INCOME TAX. See also DEDUCTIONS/ADJUSTMENTS.

SELF-EMPLOYMENT TAX. A federal tax levied on the NET INCOME of self-employed persons for social security and medicare benefits. See also SOCIAL SECURITY TAX.

SOCIAL SECURITY TAX. A tax levied under the Federal Insurance Contributions Act (FICA) on employers and employees in amounts based on wages paid in performance of employment. The tax is commonly referred to as the *social security tax*, because the Social Security Act originally levied it.

Withholdings. Employers withhold the taxes levied on employees from their wage payments. The employers then remit the tax WITHHOLDINGS, as well as the taxes levied on the employers, to the Internal Revenue Service via periodic deposits in an authorized commercial or Federal Reserve Bank.

Depending on the amounts involved, deposits may have to be made as often as every week.

Social security taxes provide for payments to retired people age 65 or older (younger in certain cases), to their dependents and survivors, and to totally and permanently disabled workers between ages 50 and 65. The benefits are technically known as *old age, survivors, and disability insurance.*

The amount of tax deducted from an employee's wages must be reported to the employee. A common practice is to show the deduction on either the pay envelope if wages are paid in cash or on a detachable remittance slip or check stub if wages are paid by check.

The employer must keep a record of the deductions in the PAYROLL records. The employee may not deduct his or her share of the social security tax from ADJUSTED GROSS INCOME.

Wages paid to domestic employees. An employer is required to pay social security taxes on the wages of domestic employees, to withhold the employees' share of the tax, and to file a tax report at the end of each quarter. An employer may also pay the employees' share of the tax, if desired.

Since wages paid to domestic employees are personal expenses, neither the employer nor the employee may deduct the tax from adjusted gross income.

It is therefore unnecessary to keep a record for tax purposes. But a running record should be kept to facilitate preparation of the quarterly tax report that must be filed.

SPREADSHEET. A software application used in handling financial tasks, such as preparing a budget or making a sales forecast. The program organizes data on a grid with rectangular areas called *cells*.

A *cell* appears on screen as the intersection of a row and a column. Each cell is numbered and lettered to indicate the column and row. In Figure 1, Cell D4, for example, refers to column D and row 4.

A user sees the cell as a rectangular space or boxed area where data can be held. There, the user can enter data, edit it, move it, store it, print it, and so on.

If the user enters certain formulas, the computer will perform any necessary calculations and display the results in the appropriate cell. Each time that a number is changed, the formulas are automatically recalculated.

SPREADSHEET: FIGURE 1: Cell

	A NAME	B CAMPAIGN 1	C CAMPAIGN 2	D CAMPAIGN 3	E TOTAL VOTES
1	NAME	CAMPAIGN 1	CAMPAIGN 2	CAMPAIGN 3	TOTAL VOTES
2					
3	BENSON, J	84	86	92	262
4	FIFE, T	916	809	531	2256
5	PARKER, A	211	292	206	709
6	REESE, B	410	421	476	1307
7					
8					

Spreadsheets can also present data in the form of a graph, which can illustrate the relationship of items, or variables, and indicate how a variable changes over time.

STAMP TAX. Also known as *transfer tax.* A tax collected by the states through the sale of stamps that must be affixed to certain documents and securities before they are bought, sold, or transferred.

Most state laws make all parties to a taxable transaction liable for the tax. Although those concerned may agree among themselves about who shall pay the tax, the agreement does not relieve the others from liability.

State stamps are issued by the various state tax commissions, which usually designate certain commercial banks as sales agents for stamps. Records must be available at all times for inspection by the tax authorities.

State stamp taxes paid on the transfer of securities or real property are treated as an increase in the BASIS of the property transferred. Therefore, one should keep separate records of state stamp tax payments. See also CAPITAL GAIN AND LOSS.

The amount of state stamp taxes is generally indicated on the sale confirmation.

STATE INCOME TAX. A state tax on INCOME in those states that levy a personal income tax on residents (as most states do) or on those who are employed in the state (in states that tax income earned by nonresidents).

In most cases, the records maintained for and used in filing the federal INCOME TAX will be used in preparing the state income tax return. But there may be deductions (see DEDUCTIONS/ADJUSTMENTS) permissible in a particular state that are not allowed under federal income tax law.

STATEMENT OF ACTIVITIES. The name given to the INCOME STATEMENT of a nonprofit organization. The statement emphasizes the content of INCOME and expenditures as opposed to a measurement of net PROFIT for profit-oriented entities.

STATEMENT OF CASH FLOWS. Also commonly referred to as the *cash flow statement.* A report of how a business has financed its activities and how the various cash resources have been generated and used.

The cash flow statement traces the flow of cash related to major financial events during a specific reporting period.

The statement evolves from the same data used in preparation of the BALANCE SHEET and INCOME STATEMENT. But it provides unique business insights not gained from examination of those two statements.

For example, one can determine from reading the cash flow statement the cash resources generated from PROFITS, how equipment acquisition was financed, how dividends were able to be paid, or what the cash proceeds were from new stock issuances. See also Chapter 13/DIVIDEND; STOCK.

The statement generally offers valuable information concerning a business's potential ability to meet LIABILITIES or to handle an increased debt load due to expansion.

STATEMENT OF FINANCIAL POSITION. See BALANCE SHEET.

STATE UNEMPLOYMENT INSURANCE TAX. A PAYROLL TAX imposed by state unemployment insurance laws to pay benefits to unemployed persons who meet certain requirements. See also PAYROLL.

The state laws are generally similar, because they all conform to standards specified in the Federal Unemployment Tax Act. Conformance is necessary so that employers will be allowed a credit for the state tax against the federal unemployment tax.

The laws also vary, however, in many important respects. For example, each state law specifies the minimum number of employees that an employer must have to be subject to the law, the types of employment that are exempted, and so forth. The amount of benefits payable also varies from state to state.

All state laws provide for some form of MERIT RATING under which a reduction in the state contribution rate is allowed to employers that have given steady employment.

In most cases, the responsibility for these taxes usually rests with the person who handles the firm's payroll.

TAXABLE INCOME. INCOME after adjustments and deductions (see DEDUCTIONS/ADJUSTMENTS) that is subject to tax by any governmental authority; the amount of income upon which the INCOME TAX is computed.

To arrive at the amount of income subject to federal income tax, certain adjustments are subtracted from GROSS INCOME to arrive at ADJUSTED GROSS INCOME.

Additional deductions are subtracted from adjusted gross income to arrive at taxable income.

TRIAL BALANCE. A listing of the DEBIT AND CREDIT balances of ACCOUNTS in a LEDGER (usually, the general ledger) to prove that the total debit balances equal the total credit balances.

The trial balance is one of the WORKING PAPERS and is used as a basis for preparing a FINANCIAL STATEMENT.

VARIABLE COSTS. Expenses that fluctuate directly with the level of production or in relation to the activities of a business. Examples are direct materials and direct labor.

WASTING ASSET. A natural resource that is subject to DEPLETION, included as an organization's ASSETS.

WITHHOLDING. Making a deduction at the source of INCOME to satisfy the recipient's INCOME TAX liability, as required by federal, state, and local laws. The withholding agent must pay the amount withheld to the proper taxing authority.

Federal law requires employers with one or more employees to withhold from each payment of wages an amount representing a proportionate part of the employee's approximate income tax liability for the year. This assumes that an employee's entire income is from wages.

The law applies to all employees who are paid wages subject to income tax.

The amount to be withheld can be computed by a percentage method or may be determined from specially prepared withholding tables obtainable from the Internal Revenue Service.

WITHHOLDING DEPOSITS. SOCIAL SECURITY TAX and withheld INCOME TAX that must be deposited periodically. (See WITHHOLDING.) These deposits must be made in an authorized commercial bank or in a Federal Reserve Bank on or before the due date for payment.

Special rules have been established for these tax deposits. Each employer is provided with tax-deposit coupons to use in depositing withheld income taxes and social security taxes reported quarterly on Form 941.

The taxes include income taxes, social security and medicare taxes withheld from the pay of employees, as well as the employer's share of the social security and medicare taxes that it must pay for its employees.

Deposits. For social security, medicare, and withheld income tax, each month of the return period is divided into eight deposit periods. At the end of each deposit period, a deposit is required if the tax owed reaches the threshold level defined by the Internal Revenue Service.

State and local withholding. Some states that have income tax laws require employers to withhold income taxes from nonresidents. The laws vary from state to state concerning the amount to be withheld, exemptions from withholding, and time for withholding.

Some cities also require employers to deduct and withhold income tax on salaries and wages.

WORKING CAPITAL. ASSETS available for use in the everyday operations of a business. Accountants use the term to mean CURRENT ASSETS less CURRENT LIABILITIES.

Those current assets that are changed in the ordinary course of business from one form to another, such as from cash to inventories, from inventories to receivables, and from receivables back to cash, are sometimes called *circulating capital.*

Companies without sufficient working capital are forced to borrow to meet their day-to-day needs.

WORKING PAPERS. The schedules, analyses, records, and memos developed in connection with the preparation of a FINANCIAL STATEMENT or in connection with an AUDIT.

WORK SHEET. Any manual or electronic columnar form used to analyze a TRIAL BALANCE and to organize figures for use in preparing a FINANCIAL STATEMENT. See also SPREADSHEET.

The ACCOUNTS on a BALANCE SHEET are listed first, followed by the accounts on an INCOME STATEMENT. Opening balances are written in the first two columns, transactions for the specific ACCOUNTING period (see FISCAL PERIOD) in the next two columns, ADJUSTING ENTRIES in the next two columns, and the final adjusted balances in the last two columns.

WRITE-OFF.   A charge against an ACCOUNT RECEIVABLE or NOTE RECEIVABLE for the amount that has been deemed uncollectable by management. Worthless ASSETS of many kinds, both FIXED ASSETS and INTANGIBLE ASSETS, may be written off to a loss account.

CHAPTER THIRTEEN

Investments and Finance

AMORTIZATION. The process of extinguishing, reducing, or writing off (eliminating) an item or a value.

Extinguishing a debt. The process of making a series of periodic and often equal payments to a creditor at equal intervals of time. Each payment will include INTEREST on the outstanding debt and a repayment of part of the principal.

This method is used mainly in the liquidation of bonded indebtedness, mortgages, and installment loans.

Reduction of book value. The process of gradually reducing the book value of fixed or intangible assets having a limited life by allocating the original cost over the life of the asset. See also Chapter 12/ASSETS; BOOK VALUE; DEPRECIATION; FIXED ASSETS; INTANGIBLE ASSETS.

Write-off. The process of writing off the BOND DISCOUNT AND BOND PREMIUM; the process of writing off prepaid expenses and deferred charges (see Chapter 12/PREPAID EXPENSES); as defined by the U.S. Treasury Department, the rapid write-off or accelerated depreciation of certain facilities in certain circumstances for income tax purposes. See also Chapter 12/WRITE-OFF.

ANNUITY. A stipulated payment made to a named person or persons at stated intervals, either for life or for a certain number of years; also, the contract under which the payments are made. The person receiving the payments is the *annuitant*.

The following terms are used to describe common forms of annuity:

An *immediate annuity* may be purchased for a single premium, with the payments to begin 30 to 60 days after purchase.

A *deferred annuity* may be purchased for a single premium or by paying an annual premium over a period of years, with the annuity payments to begin at the end of a term of years.

An *annuity certain* involves a series of payments made to the annuitant or his or her beneficiary at periodic intervals for a definite number of years only, regardless of any life contingency.

An *annuity certain and life*, commonly referred to as a *year's certain annuity*, provides for payments to continue to a beneficiary if the annuitant should die before a specified number of years.

A *life annuity*, also known as an *ordinary-life, straight-life, regular-life, single-life*, or *maximum-income life annuity*, is in force for the duration of one's life and terminates at one's death.

A *joint annuity* includes two or more persons who are interested in the proceeds under the contract.

A *joint life annuity* is payable to two or more persons while all are alive.

A *joint and survivor annuity* provides for payments to continue as long as any one of two or more designated persons lives.

A *variable*, or *equity*, *annuity* provides for payments to be made to the beneficiary in income units rather than in fixed dollar amounts (the value of the units varies from time to time because the annuitant's reserve is invested in equity rather than in debt securities).

ASSESSMENT. 1. An additional amount that owners of real estate or other investments may be required to pay. For example, if improvements were made to a road, property owners who benefit would be assessed monies on a pro rata basis to pay for the improvement.

2. Values assigned by taxing authorities to taxable holdings, such as real estate and inventories. See also Chapter 11/ASSESSMENT; Chapter 12/ASSESSMENT; Chapter 15/ASSESSED VALUATION.

AT THE MARKET. See LIMIT ORDER; MARKET ORDER.

AT THE OPENING. An expression used in securities trading to mean an order given by an investor to buy or sell securities at the beginning of trading in the security. See also GTC ORDER; LIMIT ORDER; MARKET ORDER; STOCK INDEX; STOP-LOSS ORDER.

BANK NOTE. A noninterest-bearing promissory NOTE issued by a Federal Reserve Bank. (See FEDERAL RESERVE ACT.) It is payable to the bearer on demand and thus serves as money.

BANK RESERVES. The funds that banks keep available to meet regular demands for cash. Such reserves include a bank's supply of cash on hand plus deposits the bank has in other banks.

Banks that are members of the Federal Reserve System (see FEDERAL RESERVE ACT) are legally required to keep a percentage of their deposits in an account with the Federal Reserve.

BASIS POINT. An expression of variations in yield changes of fixed-income securities, especially BONDS:

> 100 basis points = 1 percent, and 1 basis point = 1/100 of 1 percent. Thus the difference between 9.76 percent and 9.79 percent is 3 basis points. The difference between 6.76 percent and 9.76 percent is 300 basis points.

BEARS. A stock market term for investors who believe that security prices are about to decline. (Compare with BULLS.) Someone who holds this view is said to be *bearish*.

BETA. In reference to common STOCK, a measure of risk. As a risk measure, the presumption is that an investor holds a number of different stocks in a PORTFOLIO. Prices of some stocks are increasing while others are decreasing. Thus the value of the total portfolio is more stable than the stocks in it.

The degree to which stocks held in a portfolio offset each other's movements is called *diversifiable risk*. Also, major economic events and trends cause most stocks to increase or decrease in value as a group.

Beta measures the degree to which the return on an individual stock moves with the return expected on stocks in general (also called *nondiversifiable risk*). It is also used in the capital assets pricing model to estimate the return that an investor should require from an investment in that stock.

BID AND ASKED PRICES.   A market expression (see STOCK EXCHANGE) referring to the amount that buyers of a STOCK or other investment are offering to pay (*bid*) and the amount that sellers are asking (*asked*) for an investment. The combined bid and asked prices are known as *quotations.*

The difference between the bid and asked price is the SPREAD. A dealer in a stock or other investment would simultaneously offer both a bid and an asked price, indicating a willingness to buy or sell at the stated prices.

BIG BOARD.   Also capitalized as Big Board. A popular expression referring to the New York Stock Exchange. See also STOCK EXCHANGE.

BLUE CHIP STOCK.   Common STOCK in a well-established corporation that is recognized widely and regarded favorably for its stability and earning power. This stock typically has the ability to pay DIVIDENDS in bad as well as good times.

BOARD OF TRADE.   See COMMODITY EXCHANGE.

BOND.   The written promise of a corporation or government to pay a specified amount of money in the form of principal and INTEREST to the bondholder at specified future dates.

A corporate bond is covered by a deed of trust, or *indenture,* that sets forth the terms under which the loan is made and the bond issued.

The amount of the bond indicated on its face (see FACE VALUE) is the *principal,* payable at maturity. The *coupon rate* is the interest paid on a bond stated as a percentage of its face value.

Differences between stocks and bonds.   Bonds differ from STOCKS in important ways: A bond is evidence of a debt, whereas stock is evidence of ownership. Therefore, a bond pays interest, whereas a stock pays DIVIDENDS. The interest on bonds must be paid before the corporation may pay dividends even to the holders of preferred stock.

Bondholders are creditors and ordinarily do not have voting rights. Therefore, they have no voice in the management of a corporation. STOCKHOLDERS, however, have voting rights and therefore do have a voice in the management.

Common types of bonds and bond features.   Different types of bonds have different features, including the following:

Baby bonds are issued in denominations smaller than the standard $1,000 bond.

Bearer bonds are payable to the holder and are not registered. Therefore, the owner must watch for public announcements to see whether the bond has been redeemed.

Collateral trust bonds are secured entirely by a PLEDGE of other securities. Sometimes leaseholds, rents, franchises, and patents are offered as additional collateral. A pledge enables the trustee to reimburse bondholders if the corporation fails to pay its bond obligation when due.

Convertible bonds give a holder the right to exchange them for another security, usually preferred or common stock, at a fixed price for a specified time, as described in the indenture. This privilege makes a bond more attractive and salable.

Coupon bonds, which are no longer issued, are bearer bonds (payable to anyone who possesses them) that have certificates, or coupons, attached to them. The individual coupons represent the amount of interest due at specific times during the bond's term.

Equipment trust bonds are bonds, NOTES, or certificates secured through the pledge of equipment, especially rolling STOCK, such as railroad cars, trucks, and aircraft.

General mortgage bonds are secured by a blanket mortgage on the property of a company.

Guaranteed bonds are guaranteed as to principal and interest, or both, by a company other than the issuing company. For example, a parent corporation might guarantee the obligation of its subsidiary.

Income and adjustment bonds pay interest only when the company earns it. Income bonds also usually include a provision for accumulation of unpaid interest, commonly up to three previous years, which may accumulate as a claim against the issuing corporation.

Joint bonds, principally used in railroad financing, are a form of guaranteed bond backed by two or more guarantors. For example, the corporation owning a station may issue bonds that are secured by a mortgage *and* guaranteed jointly and severally by all the railroads that run tracks into the station.

Junk bonds, issued by firms with a low credit rating, have a substantial risk of default on interest or principal payments.

Mortgage bonds are secured by a mortgage on real property. (See Chapter 15/MORTGAGE; REAL PROPERTY.) Corporations frequently issue bonds secured by a general mortgage on the corporate assets and on assets to be acquired in the future.

Municipal bonds are issued by a state or municipality. The interest earned is usually exempt from federal, state, and local income taxes.

Redeemable bonds or *callable bonds* have a *call*, or *redemption*, feature that enables a corporation to pay off its bonds before maturity by selling other securities in the market that are less costly.

Registered bonds are made out in the name of the holder and registered in the records of the issuer. The bonds are not negotiable unless the assignment form on the back of the bonds is signed by the registered holder.

Savings bonds are government bonds, issued in different denominations, that promise to pay a certain sum of money at a specified date in the future, with interest at a fixed rate and also payable at specified dates.

Secured bonds are secured by a PLEDGE of assets (plant or equipment), the title to which would be transferred to the bondholder in the event of foreclosure.

Serial bonds have the same date of issue, and a certain portion of the debt becomes due each year. For example, those numbered 1 to 100 will mature in one year, those numbered 101 to 200 in two years, and so on.

Series bonds are issued in series under limited and open-end mortgages. These bonds are issued on different dates, unlike serial bonds, but under the same mortgage. See also TREASURY NOTES, BILLS, AND BONDS; Chapter 15/MORTGAGE.

Sinking-fund bonds impose on the issuing corporation the obligation to set aside a certain sum from earnings periodically to reduce or retire the bond indebtedness. Since a fund is usually turned over to a trustee to be invested in the same issue, it is not actually a fund but a partial extinction of the debt.

Split-coupon bonds have a rate of interest that is both fixed and contingent on earnings. Like income and adjustment bonds, they have been issued as a result of corporate reorganization or debt adjustment, particularly in the fields of real estate and railroad financing.

Zero-coupon bonds pay no interest to the holder (they have a zero coupon rate). At maturity, the holder receives the face value. The return to the holder derives from the fact that the bond is purchased at a price substantially below its face value.

BOND DISCOUNT AND BOND PREMIUM. The difference between the *par value*, or FACE VALUE, of a BOND and the price for which it is sold by the issuer.

If the price is less than par value, the difference is called the *bond discount;* if it is more, the difference is called the *bond premium*.

The bond discount and premium are written off over the life of the bond by a process called AMORTIZATION of bond discount and bond premium.

The terms *discount* and *premium* also apply to the purchase of bonds in the open market. They may be purchased at a discount (for less than the face value) and at a premium (for more than the face value).

A bond purchased at a discount will provide the purchaser a return higher than the coupon rate (a bond purchased at a premium will produce a return below the coupon rate).

BROAD MARKET. A situation in which there is a large supply of and demand for a security or COMMODITY.

BROKER. An agent who brings parties together and assists them in negotiating a contract. He or she usually performs this service for a commission or fee. An agency relationship is established between brokers and the principals who employ them. See also Chapter 10/AGENCY.

In the context of common STOCK, there are two main kinds of brokers:

1. A *full-service broker* will develop a PORTFOLIO for an investor based on the individual's level of risk comfort.

2. A *discount broker* makes no recommendations regarding investments but rather takes only buy or sell requests. Because the services are limited in the latter case, the fees are also lower.

Usually, a broker sends a customer a statement of account at the end of the month. It reports all *completed* transactions on which the broker has made deliveries.

In addition to using a broker, investors may use the Internet (see Chapter 6/INTERNET; WEB SITE) to place purchase and sell orders with brokers, as well as to obtain data on the performance of investments.

The variety and depth of financial information on the Internet has made it a major source of information for many investors.

A typical trade in STOCKS follows this path:

An investor establishes an account with a broker, and the broker is liable for the completion of any trades carried out at the instruction of a client investor. The broker investigates the financial position of each client before carrying out the requested trades for that client.

An investor instructs the broker to purchase or sell stock via telephone, fax, e-mail, or other method. The broker then determines whether the trade is in compliance with securities regulations and uses a secure electronic network in his or her firm to submit the order to the firm's trader on the floor of the STOCK EXCHANGE.

The order is completed, and the trader on the stock exchange confirms the facts of the transaction to the broker who submitted the order, using the same secure electronic network.

The broker then notifies the investor about the particulars of the transaction and confirms it in writing within the next few days. In many instances, the broker can carry out the trade and indicate the price while the investor is waiting on the phone after instructing the broker to proceed.

Trading via the Internet requires that the investor establish an account with a broker. In this case, the broker is one who specializes in rapidly carrying out trades on the stock exchange in response to instructions received from investors over the Internet.

Trading via the Internet has allowed investors to carry out trades faster and at lower commission costs (a typical transaction is completed in under a minute). The broker in this case is carrying out the transaction but is not providing advice about the transactions.

BULLS. A stock market term for the investors who believe that securities prices are about to rise. (Compare with BEARS.) Someone who holds this view is said to be *bullish*.

CALL. See PUTS AND CALLS.

CAPITAL. See Chapter 10/CAPITAL; Chapter 12/CAPITAL.

CARRYING CHARGE. In securities trading, the charge made by a BROKER for carrying a customer's transactions on MARGIN; in retailing, the service charge on installment sales. See also Chapter 10/INSTALLMENT SALE.

CERTIFICATE OF DEPOSIT (CD). A formal statement or certificate indicating that someone has a specified sum of money on deposit.

The amount plus accumulated INTEREST at a designated rate may be withdrawn at the end of a designated period, such as 3, 6, 12, 18, 24, or 36 months. A penalty is imposed when a CD is cashed in before maturity.

A special type of CD (negotiable) is available in multiples of $100,000. The negotiable designation allows the holder to sell the CD to another investor before the maturity date.

CLEARINGHOUSE. A voluntary association of banks formed to speed the delivery of checks to the bank on which they are drawn. The purpose is to provide cash more quickly to those who deposit checks.

Before checks are delivered to the clearinghouse, they are sorted by the member banks according to the banks on which they are drawn. To facilitate sorting, all checks have electronically readable coding indicating the bank and account on which the check is drawn.

CLOSING PRICE. The price at which the last sale of a particular STOCK, BOND, or COMMODITY was effected before the closing of the exchange. See also COMMODITY EXCHANGE; SECURITIES MARKET; STOCK EXCHANGE.

Some listings include closing BID AND ASKED PRICES. This means that after the last transaction for the day, and before the close of the trading day, buyers of the stock were offering to pay the amount reported as *Bid*, and sellers were asking the amount reported as *Asked*.

COLLATERAL. See PLEDGE.

COMMERCIAL BANK. A bank chartered by the state or the controller of currency (national) that accepts demand deposits, provides short-term credit, and offers a variety of other services to customers.

COMMISSION. The amount a fiduciary (see Chapter 10/FIDUCIARY) receives as compensation for services. Commissions are normally a percentage of the principal, the income from the principal, or both.

In securities and commodities trading, a commission is the fee charged by BROKERS.

COMMODITY. A tangible good or product, such as grains, foods, or metals, that is sold or bartered. Commodities are traded on a COMMODITY EXCHANGE or SPOT MARKET.

COMMODITY EXCHANGE. An organized market in which staple commodities, such as wheat, cotton, or sugar, are traded on a *cash basis* or a *futures basis*. The difference between the two types of trading is principally in the form of the sales contract:

Cash, or *spot,* trading calls for immediate delivery.

Futures are standard contracts prescribed by the exchanges for future delivery. They specify grade, amount, price, and delivery date by month and allow the seller to deliver any time during the specified month.

The futures market performs an important function in the process of distribution. It helps to reduce the cost of products to the consumer. Trading in futures through *hedging* also provides an insurance against violent price fluctuations. See the example in HEDGING.

COMMODITY EXCHANGE ACT. An act established to regulate COMMODITY EXCHANGES and dealers trading in commodity futures.

The act created a commission of five members, appointed by the president with the approval of the Senate, known as the COMMODITY FUTURES TRADING COMMISSION.

COMMODITY FUTURES TRADING COMMISSION. A federal commission, established by the Congress in 1974 to regulate the commodity futures and option markets in the United States.

The commission regulates commodities trading, prevents fraud, and sets trading limits to prevent excessive speculation.

COMMON STOCK. See STOCK.

CONDITIONAL SALE. See Chapter 10/CONDITIONAL SALE.

COST-PLUS PRICING. Pricing, or a charge, that includes the cost of providing goods or services plus a fee that represents the seller's profit. Such contracts are common when costs are unknown in advance.

DATABASES, FINANCIAL. On-line information that users, for an hourly rate or monthly subscription fee, or both, can access by computer. The information that is available may cover everything from industry surveys to financial trends to investment data.

One well-known financial service is *Dow Jones News/Retrieval,* which offers financial news, company information, economic data, and publications, such as the *Wall Street Journal.*

Other on-line services and databases, such as *CNNfn.com,* also provide financial information via the Internet. See also Chapter 6/INTERNET; WEB SITE.

DAY ORDER. An order to a BROKER to buy or sell a security or COMMODITY that is good only for the day on which the order is given. If the order is not executed on that day, it is automatically canceled.

DEBENTURE. A BOND issued without security and therefore not protected by any specific lien on property. (See Chapter 11/LIEN.) Debentures are simply the promise of the borrower to pay a certain sum of money at a stipulated time and place, with INTEREST at a fixed rate.

DEBT, PARTIAL PAYMENT OF. An agreement among the involved parties that a debtor who owes a large amount may make equal or unequal payments on the principal at regular or irregular intervals.

The method adopted by the U.S. Supreme Court is the *United States Rule,* which is now a law in most states. Another method, occasionally used by businesspeople, is the *Merchants' Rule.*

In some cases, the term of a loan may affect the method used. For example, the balance due on obligations of one year or less is usually computed by the Merchants' Rule. The balance due on obligations of more than one year is generally computed by the United States Rule.

United States Rule. Under this rule, payments must be applied against accrued INTEREST before any deductions can be made from the principal. Payments that do not equal the accrued interest leave the principal undiminished until other payments are made that are sufficient to cover all accrued interest.

Any excess remaining after the payments exceed the accrued interest is applied on the principal.

Merchants' Rule. Under this rule, the principal draws interest from the date of the loan until the date of final settlement, and such interest is added to the principal. Each payment draws interest from the date of the payment until the date of final settlement. The balance due is the principal plus interest minus the payments plus interest.

DEPRECIATION. See Chapter 12/DEPRECIATION.

DISCOUNT. The difference between the price of a product or security and its sale or redemption value:

A $195 chair that is available at $145 is discounted $50.

A BOND with a FACE VALUE of $1,000 and a current market value of $950 is selling at a $50 discount.

DISCOUNT, CASH. A deduction, commonly ranging from 1 to 10 percent, allowed to customers who pay their bills within a definite time.

Cash discount terms are stated in an invoice as, for example, 2/10 net 30, or 2/10/30. Both forms mean that 2 percent may be deducted from the invoice total if the bill is paid in 10 days. Otherwise, the full amount of the bill must be paid in 30 days.

The following examples illustrate the cost of not taking the cash discount terms:

1% 10 days net 30 days = 18% per annum
2% 10 days net 30 days = 36% per annum
2% 10 days net 60 days = 14% per annum

DISCOUNT RATE, BANK. Also known simply as the *discount*. The INTEREST charge made by a bank on a loan or for converting commercial paper (NOTES, CERTIFICATES OF DEPOSIT [CDs], and negotiable instruments that transfer funds to the holder in the future) into cash before maturity.

The discount is computed as simple interest on the amount due at maturity on a NOTE or draft and is deducted in advance:

1. The amount received from the bank—amount due at maturity less the discount and collection charge—is called the *proceeds*.

2. The number of days from the date the note is discounted to the date of maturity is called the *term of discount*.

3. The period from the date of discount (not including the *day* of discount itself) to and including the date of maturity of the instrument is the *time*, or the number of days counted.

A COMMERCIAL BANK usually charges a discount for the actual or exact number of days in the discount period and computes the discount on the basis of 360 days to the year.

For example, if a note due May 6 is discounted March 6, the bank counts the actual number of days between these dates (61) and computes the discount on the basis of 360 days to the year.

DISHONOR. Refusal to pay a negotiable instrument, such as a check, presented for payment. See also Chapter 11/NEGOTIABLE INSTRUMENT.

Notice of dishonor is usually given to *endorsers* (see ENDORSEMENT) and *drawers* (those who order that the payment be made), who—in addition to the *maker* (the person, or possibly a bank, that makes the payment)—are liable on the instrument.

Notice of dishonor may be given orally or in writing. If it is not given, endorsers and drawers are discharged from liability.

DIVIDEND. The earnings or profit of a corporation that is distributed (paid) to shareholders. Dividends on STOCK represent a distribution of current or accumulated profits of a corporation to STOCKHOLDERS.

Declaration of dividends. Usually, dividends are declared by a formal resolution of the board of directors.

The resolution fixes the rate, or amount, per share; the class of stockholders to whom a dividend is payable; the date set for determining who is entitled to a dividend (see EX-DIVIDEND); the date of payment; and the medium in which the dividend is to be paid.

Payment of dividends. Dividends are usually declared and paid quarterly, semiannually, or annually. They are paid either as a percentage of par value per share in the case of preferred stock or in dollars and cents per share in the case of common stock.

Cash dividends are usually paid by check. But it is inaccurate to refer to *cash dividends* on stock as *stock dividends*. The latter refers to a distribution of additional stock to the stockholders, pro rata according to holdings. A stockholder may refuse the stock but can't demand cash instead (unless an optional dividend is declared).

Cumulative dividends on preferred stock are those that are unpaid as of the date they fall due. Those dividends must typically be paid before any other dividends may be paid on common stock.

The amount of a stock dividend is transferred from surplus to capital stock (see Chapter 12/CAPITAL STOCK), and the stated value of each share remains the same. Compare with STOCK SPLIT.

In most circumstances, stock dividends are not subject to federal income tax.

DOW JONES INDUSTRIAL AVERAGE. See STOCK INDEX.

EARNEST MONEY OR BINDER. The payment that one contracting party (the buyer) gives to another at the time of entering into a contract to bind the sale.

Usually, the binder will be forfeited if the buyer fails to carry out the terms of the contract. But the money is applied to the purchase price if the buyer lives up to the bargain. See also Chapter 11/CONTRACT.

ENDORSEMENT. The signature and any notation that the holder writes on an instrument, such as on the back side of a check, in order to cash, deposit, or transfer it.

Blank endorsement. The writing of one's name alone, without any additional words. The effect is to make the paper payable to the bearer.

However, someone other than the endorser could take the instrument and transfer it to a third party. For example, a thief could take another person's check and, if it had a blank endorsement, could cash it.

Special endorsement. The designation of a particular person to whom an instrument is payable. Thus if a check were endorsed *Pay to Frances Jones* or *Pay to the order of Frances Jones,* followed by the endorser's signature, no one other than Frances Jones could cash it.

Restrictive endorsement. An endorsement that transfers possession of an instrument for a particular purpose:

Pay to National City Bank for collection. Sam Brown.

For deposist only. Sam Brown.

Qualified endorsement. An endorsement that qualifies or limits the liability of the endorser. If someone endorses an instrument *without recourse,* he or she does not assume liability in case the maker fails to pay the instrument when due.

Conditional endorsement. A special endorsement with words added that create a condition that must happen before the special endorsee is entitled to payment. The endorser is liable only if the condition is fulfilled:

> Pay to Greenwood Cotton Growers Association upon delivery of warehouse receipt for 25 standard bales of cotton, strict to middling. Frances Jones.

EQUITY. The value of an owner's interest in property in excess of all claims and liens against it. See also Chapter 11/LIEN.

For example, an owner's equity in his or her home is its present value less the amount of a mortgage. See also Chapter 15/MORTGAGE.

The equity of the STOCKHOLDERS of a business is the net worth of the business, or the value of the assets in excess of the liabilities. See also Chapter 12/ASSETS; LIABILITIES; NET WORTH.

ESCROW. See Chapter 15/ESCROW.

EXCHANGE-RATE RISK. The risk that an unexpected change in currency conversion rates will cause a change in the value of currencies to be received or expended:

> Assume that your firm wants to import wool sweaters from England, and you agree to pay £1,000 for the shipment with the expectation that the conversion rate of dollars to pounds will be $1.50. You therefore expect to pay $1,500 for the shipment.
>
> Before you can make payment, however, the conversion rate changes to $1.60. The dollar price of the shipment will then be $1,600.

EX-DIVIDEND. A STOCK quotation indicating that a buyer will *not* get a DIVIDEND that has been declared but not yet paid.

Dividends are declared payable to STOCKHOLDERS of record on a specific date, called the *record date*. The stock sells ex-dividend usually several days before that date, depending on the delivery rules of the exchange (see SECURITIES MARKET; STOCK EXCHANGE) on which the stock is traded. On the *ex* date, the dividend is reserved for the seller.

FACE VALUE. The nominal value of an instrument, such as a BOND, NOTE, mortgage (see Chapter 15/MORTGAGE), or other security, as set forth in the document itself. See also PAR VALUE STOCK.

FACTOR. A corporation that purchases a firm's account receivables (see Chapter 12/ACCOUNTS RECEIVABLE) outright rather than lend the firm monies with the account receivables used as collateral.

The purchase of account receivables places the risk of nonpayment (by customers who owe the money) on the firm purchasing the receivables (the factor), rather than on the firm selling them. The factor must therefore conduct a careful credit analysis of the customers and be adept at credit and collection efforts.

FEDERAL DEPOSIT INSURANCE CORPORATION (FDIC). A federal organization established by the Banking Act of 1933 to provide insurance for depositors in member banks. Members of the Federal Reserve System are required to join the Federal Deposit Insurance Corporation.

In 1989, a subsidiary of the FDIC was formed to insure deposits in savings and loan associations. See also SAVINGS ASSOCIATION INSURANCE FUND.

Insured deposits include regular commercial, checking, and savings deposits and certain trust funds.

FEDERAL RESERVE ACT. An act that instituted a banking system in the United States known as the Federal Reserve System. Under it, 12 Federal Reserve Banks were established to supply credit to member banks, which in turn distribute credit to their customers.

A Federal Reserve Board governs the Federal Reserve System, with seven members appointed by the president.

The banks are operated under the management of local officers and boards of directors but are subject to the authority of the Board of Governors of the Federal Reserve System.

All national banks in the United States are required to belong to the Federal Reserve System. State banks may belong if they meet the requirements of the act and choose to belong.

FIDELITY BOND. Also called *blanket fidelity bond* or *blanket bond*. Insurance coverage guaranteeing that the insurance company will pay a specified sum in case a bonded person is dishonest.

If employees are *bonded,* an employer is thereby protected against loss for reasons such as embezzlement or larceny. See also SURETY BOND.

FINANCIAL LEVERAGE. The use of fixed-cost sources of funds, such as BONDS, to finance the assets of a firm. INTEREST on the debt used is stated as a fixed percentage of the principal.

If the firm is very profitable, the interest rate on the debt does not change. The return to the common stockholder, however, does change based on how well the firm performs (this is a variable-cost source of funds):

> A firm using financial leverage advantageously may borrow funds at a cost of 8 percent and use those funds in the firm to earn 15 percent. The earnings in excess of the interest due on the funds borrowed can be used to increase the return the common stockholders earn on their investment.
>
> However, this principle also works in reverse. If the return on the invested funds turns out to be 3 percent, earnings that would otherwise have been available to the common stockholders will have to be redirected to pay the interest on the debt. (Creditors have first claim on all earnings of the firm.)

FLOAT.   The period that elapses between the time that a check is written and the time that it is presented to the bank for payment.

A substantial industry has been created around developing systems that allow those who *receive* checks to convert them into spendable cash more quickly and to enable those who *write* checks to slow the conversion of checks to cash.

FOREIGN CURRENCY.   See Part Four/FOREIGN CURRENCY.

FOREIGN EXCHANGE.   The conversion of the money of one country into its equivalent in money of another country. Dollars are converted into pounds sterling, pesos into dollars, and so forth.

The rate at which the currencies are exchangeable at any time is called the *rate of exchange.*

FRACTIONAL SHARE.   Less than a whole share of STOCK. A STOCKHOLDER sometimes becomes entitled to less than a whole share upon the declaration of stock DIVIDENDS.

A fractional share may also result from an increase in stock when RIGHTS to subscribe to additional shares are granted to present stockholders.

Corporations generally avoid issuing fractional shares. Instead, they usually pay to stockholders the cash value of any fractional shares to which they may be entitled.

FUTURES.   See COMMODITY EXCHANGE.

GOOD TILL CANCELED. See GTC ORDER.

GTC ORDER. An order to buy or sell a security at a specific price limit that is *good till canceled*. The order is kept by the BROKER until it is executed or canceled by the person giving it. At the end of the month, the broker may ask a customer to confirm any remaining GTC orders.

HEDGING. Offsetting the obligations under one contract with those of a second contract for the purpose of reducing risk:

> A cotton merchant buys cotton to have an ample supply on hand to fill orders for his cotton mill customers. The merchant may buy several thousand bales without having an immediate outlet for them and therefore runs the risk that the market may decline sharply before the cotton can be resold.
>
> Consequently, the merchant sells a futures contract for cotton on the futures exchange. (See COMMODITY EXCHANGE.) The contract specifies that cotton will be delivered at a future date and at a fixed price.
>
> If the price declines, the cotton will be sold on the spot (cash) market at a loss. (See SPOT MARKET.) The futures contract will have increased in value because the fixed price under that contract is now higher than the cash price. The merchant can in effect sell the futures contract at a profit while selling the actual cotton at a loss.

The procedure described in the preceding example is the standard method used by various industries for protection against price fluctuations in a wide variety of commodities, currencies, and interest-bearing instruments.

INDUSTRIALS. The securities of a company that produces or sells a product or service, such as a manufacturing company or a retail store. Industrials should be distinguished from the securities of other concerns, such as financial institutions and public utility companies.

INSTALLMENT SALE. See Chapter 10/CONDITIONAL SALE; INSTALLMENT SALE.

INTEREST. An amount paid for the use of capital. (See Chapter 12/CAPITAL.) It is usually stated as a percentage of the amount borrowed, such as in a BOND that pays 7 percent interest or a loan that is advanced for 90 days at 12 percent.

In interest calculations, three factors are involved: principal, time, and rate:

1. The *principal* is the sum of money upon which the interest is paid—the sum borrowed, loaned, or invested.
2. The *time* is the number of periods for which the interest is paid.
3. The *rate* is the percentage of the principal per period that is paid as interest. The rate is usually expressed as a certain percentage per year.

Simple and compound interest. The two main kinds of interest are simple interest and compound interest:

1. If the interest is calculated on the original principal only, it is called *simple interest.*
2. If at the end of each period the interest for that period is added to the principal and the interest for the next period is calculated on this new sum, it is called *compound interest.*

State laws govern the rate of interest that can be charged. The legal rate is charged in the absence of a contract between the parties. In a contract, the rate the parties have agreed to cannot exceed the legal rate.

Ordinary and exact interest. Interest may also be classified as ordinary or exact:

1. *Ordinary interest* is simple interest computed on the basis of 360 days to the year, rather than 365 days.
2. *Exact,* or *accurate, interest* is simple interest computed on the basis of 365 days to the year.

Since calculations are much easier on the basis of 360 days to the year, businesses and banks generally compute simple interest using the 360-day method, even when the exact number of days for which interest is due is counted.

Numerous books are available with tables of interest computed for varying periods and at different rates. Various software programs, spreadsheets, and Internet sites (see Chapter 6/INTERNET; WEB SITE) are also available to perform interest calculations.

INTEREST-RATE RISK. The risk that the value of BONDS and other investments that pay a fixed rate of return will change in the current market as the return required by current investors changes. This is true even if an investment, such as U.S. government securities, has no risk of default.

An increase in the current return required by investors will cause the current value in the market of existing bonds to fall. A decrease in the current return required by investors will cause the current value in the market of existing bonds to rise.

LIBOR. Acronym for the **L**ondon **I**nterbank **O**ffered **R**ate. The INTEREST rate at which large international commercial banks lend deposits to one another. This base rate is widely reported in the financial markets and is often used as a base rate to price floating-rate loans to firms.

LIEN. See Chapter 11/LIEN.

LIMIT ORDER. In securities trading, an order to buy or sell securities at a specific price; in commodities trading, an order to buy or sell a contract at a specific price. BROKERS will execute this type of order only within the limits set by the customer.

Unless a specific period is stipulated, limit orders are presumed good only for the day on which they are given.

LISTED SECURITIES. Securities approved for trading by a STOCK EXCHANGE. Before the securities can be listed, the corporation must meet certain requirements and procedures of the exchange.

The New York Stock Exchange does not permit trading on its floor in securities that are not listed by it. But other exchanges sometimes do allow trading in unlisted securities.

Listing does not guarantee a security's worth. However, it does provide a ready market for the buying and selling of a security.

LONG SALE. The sale of securities or commodities that are actually owned by the seller, as opposed to a SHORT SALE, where the seller is not the owner.

MARGIN. 1. In securities trading, the use of borrowed funds by an investor to purchase securities.

The margin is usually expressed as a percentage of the total transaction. The Board of Governors of the Federal Reserve System (see FEDERAL RESERVE ACT) regulates requirements in that it stipulates the *loan value,* or the amount a broker may loan against a transaction:

> *A* buys one hundred shares of XYZ STOCK at $50. With 50 percent margin requirements, *A* need pay only $2,500. Her broker supplies the balance of $2,500 using the securities that were purchased as collateral in borrowing from the bank. (Or the broker may use his own funds.)

> When *A* sells the stock, the loan is repaid. The broker charges *A* INTEREST on the amount borrowed.

> If the market drops and the margin becomes "too thin," the broker calls for additional margin money or securities from the investor (a margin call). If none is forthcoming, the broker sells enough securities to reestablish the required margin on the remaining securities.

> If the losses are in excess of the margin and the investor cannot repay the broker, the broker must bear the loss or take legal action against the investor for repayment.

2. In commodities trading, the percentage of the purchase price of a commodities futures contract that the investor pays a broker to protect parties to the contract from the effects of market fluctuations.

An investor deposits money through a broker, and the broker in turn deposits money with his or her clearinghouse as required by the COMMODITY EXCHANGE.

The profit or loss in the futures contract is determined at the end of each day and is added to or subtracted from the margin account. Brokers may call for additional margin, or investors may withdraw excess margin.

MARKET ORDER. An order given to a BROKER to buy or sell securities *at the market*—at the best price obtainable when the order is received on the trading floor. This is the most common type of order in New York Stock Exchange trading activity.

See also AT THE OPENING; GTC ORDER; LIMIT ORDER; SECURITIES MARKET; STOP-LOSS ORDER.

MONEY MARKET. A market for short-term, low-risk investment, such as Treasury bills. (See TREASURY NOTES, BILLS, AND BONDS.) Most transactions in the money market are in amounts of $1 million or more and are carried out by banks and other financial institutions.

Individual investors participate in the market by investing in a money market mutual fund or by depositing funds in bank accounts whose interest rate is indexed to the money market.

Most banks offer *demand money market accounts.* Money market mutual funds and demand money market accounts are typically set up like INTEREST-earning checking accounts, and checkbooks are provided for the withdrawal of funds. Interest rates earned on the account changes as key interest rates in the money market change.

MUTUAL FUND. An *open-end investment company* that raises money by selling its own STOCK to the public and investing the capital in other securities.

A *closed-end investment company* is not a mutual fund in that it usually sells stock to the public at certain times, just as a corporation does. The stock is then traded in the market based on the value that investors believe it has.

Investors in a mutual fund benefit proportionately from the investment made by the fund. See also Chapter 10/CAPITAL; INVESTMENT COMPANY.

Mutual funds both sell new shares in the fund on a continuous basis as investors demand them and repurchase their shares at the net asset value of the shares.

Net asset value per share is the market value that day of all investments held by the fund divided by the number of shares outstanding of the mutual fund.

Load and no-load funds. Mutual funds may be either load or no-load types:

1. A BROKER typically sells a *load fund,* which indicates that a sales commission is charged on each purchase.

2. A *no-load fund* does not charge a sales commission and is typically sold via direct sales methods by the fund itself.

Management and other fees. All funds charge a management fee for managing the investments made by the fund. Some funds may charge redemption fees or recover marketing costs through annual fees allowed under SECURITIES AND EXCHANGE COMMISSION (SEC) rule 12(b)–l.

NEGOTIABLE INSTRUMENT. See Chapter 11/NEGOTIABLE INSTRUMENT.

NEW YORK STOCK EXCHANGE. See SECURITIES MARKET; STOCK EXCHANGE.

NONNEGOTIABLE INSTRUMENT. See Chapter 11/NONNEGOTIABLE INSTRUMENT.

NOTE. A written promise to pay unconditionally a definite sum of money on demand or at some specified time in the future. An individual, a corporation, or a government may issue notes, which usually require the payment of INTEREST during or at the end of the loan period:

> The *maker* is the person who promises to pay, and he or she therefore signs the note.
>
> The *payee* is the person to whom the note is payable.

If a note is payable to a particular person's order or to the bearer, the note is negotiable. The title may be transferred by ENDORSEMENT and delivery.

To the payee, the instrument is a *note receivable;* to the maker, it is a *note payable.*

ODD LOT. An order for less than the established unit of trading. STOCKS are customarily traded in SECURITIES MARKETS in units of 100 shares, although a few stocks are authorized for trading in units of 10 shares. Both are known as *round lots* or *full lots.*

Odd-lot trading enables a small trader with restricted capital to make a limited investment in each of several stocks. The cost of the BROKER'S commission, however, will be more on both the purchase and sale of odd lots than on round-lot transactions. An odd-lot transaction usually costs 1/8 of a point (12.5 cents per share) more than a round-lot transaction.

OPTIONS. See PUTS AND CALLS; QUALIFIED STOCK OPTION; RESTRICTED STOCK OPTION.

OVER-THE-COUNTER (OCT) MARKET. A market that consists of a large number of dealers and BROKERS throughout the nation who use computers and the telephone lines to buy and sell securities among themselves and with the public, without the use of any exchange facility or trading floor.

Quotations. Quotations on the most active OTC stocks are listed in newspapers and over the Internet. (See Chapter 6/INTERNET; WEB SITE.) Trading is largely subject to the self-governing rules of the National Association of Securities Dealers (NASD), with quotations reported through its automated system, NASDAQ.

Trading. The OTC market is the principal one for federal, state, and municipal BONDS; for the majority of public utility, railroad, industrial, and foreign bonds; and for bank and insurance company STOCKS. Most STOCK EXCHANGE member firms also operate in the over-the-counter market.

Most OTC trading, however, is in the securities of companies that have insufficient earnings, STOCKHOLDERS, or outstanding shares to meet the listing requirements of an organized stock exchange.

The volume of bond trading on exchanges is relatively small compared to that of the dealers who make up the OTC market.

PAR VALUE. See FACE VALUE.

PAR VALUE STOCK. STOCK for which each share has been given a FACE VALUE. The amount is indicated in the certificate of incorporation (see Chapter 10/CERTIFICATE OF INCORPORATION) and on the face of the STOCK CERTIFICATE.

The original intent of par value was to assure buyers that the investment behind each share was equivalent to the value printed on the face of the stock certificate. Today, par value on common stock is arbitrarily set at a low amount, usually $1.

Because of the meaningless nature of par value to investors, some corporations have abandoned the practice of placing a face value on common stock certificates.

PLEDGE. A borrower's placement of personal property with a lender as security for a debt.

The thing of value that is deposited, or pledged, is referred to as *collateral*. Pawned articles and STOCKS and BONDS put up as collateral for a loan are the most common pledges. If the borrower does not repay the loan as required, the lender may sell the collateral to satisfy the debt.

The *pledgor* is the one who gives a pledge, and the *pledgee* is the one who receives it. The pledge itself includes the following:

1. A debt or obligation to be secured
2. The thing pledged
3. The transfer of possession of the property (if actual physical possession is practically impossible, the pledgee may acquire constructive possession)
4. The retention of title by the pledgor
5. The pledgor's right to redeem the pledge
6. A contract, express or implied, covering the transaction

When STOCK is pledged as collateral, the pledgee has the right, and is bound, to collect the DIVIDENDS and apply them to the loan, in the absence of an agreement to the contrary.

In practice, though, the STOCKHOLDER makes an assignment of the stock in blank, and the stock is not transferred on the records of the corporation unless the pledgor defaults. (See Chapter 11/DEFAULT.) The stockholder–pledgor therefore continues to collect the dividends.

POINT.   In STOCK trading, a measure of the change in value, with 1 point equal to $1. Thus an increase of 5 points means that a share of stock has risen $5. In BOND trading, a point refers to BASIS POINTS, or $1/100$ of a percent.

PORTFOLIO.   A list of securities owned by an individual, a company, a bank, or an investment house. A portfolio may consist of a variety of investment vehicles—STOCKS, BONDS, precious metals, real estate (see Chapter 15/REAL PROPERTY), MONEY MARKET funds, and so on.

The portfolio chosen depends on the individual's risk return preference (the desire to earn a return offset by the desire to avoid risk). For example, an investment portfolio may be designed for diversification to spread the risk among a variety of investments. See also SECURITIES RECORD.

PRICE–EARNINGS RATIO.   A ratio computed by dividing the price of a STOCK by its earnings per share. This ratio can be very significant to potential investors.

For example, the price–earnings ratio will be higher for a company that is considered low risk and promises higher earnings in the future.

PRIME RATE.   The INTEREST rate that COMMERCIAL BANKS charge their best customers on short-term commercial loans. Other borrowers are charged a higher rate.

PROMISSORY NOTE.   See NOTE.

PUTS AND CALLS.   Options to buy or sell a certain number of securities at a stipulated price within a stipulated time, usually 30, 60, or 90 days and no more than 9 months. A *long-term equity option,* however, may not expire for up to 39 months:

> A *put* is an option giving an owner the right to sell his or her STOCK at a prearranged price (*strike price*), regardless of the current price in the market.

A *call* is an option that permits the holder the right to purchase stock at a prearranged price (*strike price*).

In each case, the purchaser of the put or the call has the right (option) to sell or buy the stock but not the obligation to do so. The seller of the option is obligated to buy or sell if the purchaser of the option demands it.

The Chicago Board Options Exchange maintains one of the markets for options trading. The puts and calls are traded in units of 100 shares.

Put.　The following example illustrates a *put:*

An investor believes that XYZ stock currently selling at $35 is going to fall. He can buy a 30-day *put* on 100 shares at a strike price of $30, which gives him the right to make the seller of the *put* take the 100 shares at $30 per share.

The purchaser and seller of the *put* determine a nonrefundable payment (premium), which the seller receives immediately for selling the *put*.

The investor may use a *put* to protect himself against a loss on a stock he already owns or as a speculative device. In the latter case, he does not own the stock. If XYZ stock goes below $30 to $27, he can buy the stock at $27 and *put* the stock (require the seller of the *put* to purchase the stock) at $30 per share.

Call.　In the case of a *call*, the investor is concerned with the right to purchase stock at a prearranged price:

An investor believes that XYZ stock currently selling at $35 is bound to rise, but she is not willing to purchase the stock. Instead, she buys a 30-day *call* on 100 shares of XYZ at $40 per share.

If within 30 days the stock goes above $40 to $43, for example, she can demand delivery at $40 from the maker of the option (*call*) and sell the stock at $43, making a profit of $3 per share (less the compensation paid to the maker of the *call*).

The seller of the *call* thought that the stock would not rise beyond $40 within 30 days, that the buyer would therefore not *call* the stock, and that he would earn the amount the buyer paid for the *call*.

Calls are also used as insurance by those making a SHORT SALE. The short seller in this case, who owns a call on the stock he or she has sold short, knows at what price the stock can be acquired should it rise and hence what the maximum loss may be.

Also, an owner of stock may write (sell) a *covered call* on his or her stock, thus fixing the price that he or she will receive for the stock if the call is made. If the call is not made, the premium received by the writer is retained by the writer along with the stock.

Selling a call on a stock that is not owned is known as *selling a naked call*.

PYRAMIDING. See Chapter 10/PYRAMIDING.

QUALIFIED STOCK OPTION. An option to purchase the STOCK of an employer–corporation, given by the employer to an employee. This type of option must meet the requirements of the Internal Revenue Code.

If the option qualifies and the employee observes certain requirements, there is no tax when the option is granted or exercised.

If the employee sells the stock within the prescribed holding period, the difference between the option price and value of the shares on the date of exercise is ordinary income in the year the employee sells it. This amount is limited to the gain on the sale of the shares.

The excess of the amount realized over the amount reported as ordinary income is *capital gain.*

QUALIFYING SHARES. The shares of STOCK given or sold by a corporation to prospective directors or officers to satisfy statutory or certificate of incorporation requirements that directors or officers be shareholders. A director or officer holds the shares only while serving in that capacity.

See also Chapter 10/BOARD OF DIRECTORS; CERTIFICATE OF INCORPORATION; OFFICERS OF A CORPORATION.

QUOTATION. See BID AND ASKED PRICES; STOCK INDEX.

REDEMPTION. A term commonly used in one of two senses: in connection with redeeming a security or in regard to the recovery of property used as a PLEDGE. In other cases, it also may refer to the exchange of securities for cash.

1. In the sense of redeeming a security, common STOCK is never redeemed, but preferred stock may be. See also STOCK for a definition of *redeemable,* or *callable, preferred stock.*

BONDS are frequently subject to redemption. For example, a company may want to call or redeem its bonds before maturity to eliminate or reduce fixed charges, to avoid burdensome terms, as a step in refinancing, to invest idle cash, or to strengthen its credit position.

2. In the sense of recovery of property, the term refers to property given as security for a debt by paying off a NOTE, bond, or mortgage. See also Chapter 15/MORTGAGE.

Equity of redemption is the right of a mortgagor to recover, or redeem, property and obtain legal title to it by paying the amount due in full, with INTEREST.

Upon default (see Chapter 11/DEFAULT), the right to redeem applies not only to the mortgagor but also to any other person having an interest in the property derived directly or indirectly from the mortgagor.

A clause in a mortgage waiving the equity of redemption is void. The equity of redemption is terminated by foreclosure. See also Chapter 15/FORECLOSURE.

Statutory redemption is the right given to a mortgagor by statute in some states to redeem his or her property within a specified time *after* a foreclosure sale. The statutory redemption may be made not only by the mortgagor but also by other persons interested in the property.

In some states, the statutory right of redemption may be waived under the terms of the mortgage when the mortgagor is a corporation. See also Chapter 10/CORPORATION.

REDISCOUNT RATE. The discount rate charged by the Federal Reserve Banks for discounting commercial paper (U.S. government securities and certain other low-risk debts) presented by member banks. In this capacity, the Federal Reserve Banks are bankers' banks.

Each Federal Reserve Bank has the power to set its own rediscount rate, subject to review by the Federal Reserve Board.

At times, the banks use the rediscount rate to control credit, raising the rate to limit borrowing and therefore limit expansion of the economy and lowering the rate to encourage borrowing and therefore encourage expansion of the economy.

RESTRICTED STOCK OPTION. An option given by an employer to an employee allowing the employee to purchase STOCK in the corporation. The option must meet the requirements of the Internal Revenue Code.

Frequently, a corporation grants its employees an option to acquire its stock at reduced prices. Generally, the difference between the amount paid for the stock and its fair market value is taxable compensation.

If the option meets the requirements of the Internal Revenue Code, however, the employee receives favorable treatment. To get this tax benefit, the employee must not dispose of the stock within six months of the date of acquisition or within two years of the date the option was granted.

REVERSE SPLIT. See STOCK SPLIT.

RIGHTS. Certificates distributed by a corporation to existing STOCKHOLDERS, entitling them to subscribe to additional shares of the same issue at a stipulated price and before a fixed date.

Preemptive rights. Stockholders may have *preemptive rights* to purchase their proportionate share of new STOCK being sold to the public as a means of maintaining their relative ownership in the corporation. See also Chapter 11/PREEMPTIVE RIGHTS.

Usually, the rights give shareholders the privilege of purchasing the new stock at less than market price. Thus the rights have a market value.

Ex-rights. When stock-carrying rights are sold, they usually go with the stock until the day of closing of the company's books for such rights. After that time, quotations of the stock on the STOCK EXCHANGE are made *ex-rights*.

The term *ex-rights* means that the stock is bought and sold *without* the rights and that the rights are also bought and sold separately.

SAVINGS ASSOCIATION INSURANCE FUND. A subsidiary of the FEDERAL DEPOSIT INSURANCE CORPORATION (FDIC) formed to insure depositors in state and federal savings and loan associations.

SECURED LOAN. A loan for which a debtor must PLEDGE property of value, which then passes to the creditor in case of the debtor's default. See also Chapter 11/DEFAULT.

SECURITIES AND EXCHANGE COMMISSION (SEC). A federal agency that administers the federal laws regulating the sale of securities to the public. It was created by Congress in 1934 as an independent bipartisan agency.

Basic functions. The SEC has certain functions that may be classified as regulatory, investigative, and quasijudicial. It regulates largely through its authority to compel full and timely disclosure of factual information.

On its own initiative, and as a matter of routine practice, the SEC undertakes to conduct inquiries and also may hold hearings whenever it believes that any person or group subject to the securities acts has violated the law or its regulations.

The SEC often intervenes as a party to civil litigation brought by private persons. It serves at times in the role of *amicus curiae*—friend of the court. In that capacity, it files briefs to aid the court in making its decisions.

Other powers. The SEC has other broad powers and performs a variety of duties. For example, it may withdraw or revoke the registration of a security and may procure restraining orders and injunctions to prevent violations or arrest them in process.

In addition, it may suspend or expel members of a STOCK EXCHANGE or the securities dealers' association, as well as issue warnings and reprimands. It may also invoke criminal sanctions by referring willful violations to the Department of Justice.

The SEC also publishes Accounting Series Releases that provide accounting and reporting guidelines to companies.

SECURITIES MARKET. An organized or unorganized market in which traders buy and sell government and corporate securities daily through BROKERS and dealers.

Organized market. This type of market is represented by STOCK EXCHANGES in cities throughout the country, all of which are patterned after the New York Stock Exchange. The exchanges essentially function like auction markets.

Through an intricate yet smoothly functioning process, they bring together the buyers and sellers of LISTED SECURITIES. In doing this, they form a continuous market that immediately publishes exact prices of all transactions.

Unorganized market. In this type of market, such as the OVER-THE-COUNTER (OTC) MARKET, prices are not determined by an auction process but rather by the negotiation and trading by dealers who buy and sell for their own account.

SECURITIES RECORD. An individual record, maintained by businesspeople, of each security owned. It should include the following information and any other facts needed for income tax purposes:

Type of security

Issuing company

Number of securities

From whom purchased

Date purchased

Held by whom (bond or trust company)

Purchase price

Date sold

Sale price

Date of maturity

Interest received and dates

Dividends received and dates

SHARES.   See STOCK.

SHORT SALE.   The sale of commodities or securities that the seller does not own but expects to purchase after the consummation of the sale.

Short sales are made by those who expect market prices to decline and who hope to profit by buying securities or commodities for less than the price at which they are sold:

> X Company STOCK is currently selling at $50 a share, and John Doe believes that the price will soon drop. So he wants to sell 100 shares short at $50. Since STOCK EXCHANGE rules require delivery within a specified time, his BROKER borrows 100 shares and delivers them to the purchaser.
>
> If X Company stock drops below $50 to $45, Doe will then buy 100 shares and return them, via his broker, to the person from whom he borrowed to make the original delivery, thus completing the transaction. Doe must pay INTEREST on the amount borrowed.
>
> There is no time limit within which Doe must *cover* (return securities to the lender). Hence he has made a profit of $5 per share: He sold stock that cost him $45 for $50 (less commissions and taxes).
>
> If the stock had risen to $55 instead of falling, Doe would have lost $5 per share. He would have sold for $50 what cost him $55. See also the examples in PUTS AND CALLS.

The sale of securities or commodities actually owned by the seller is called a LONG SALE. The rules of the SECURITIES AND EXCHANGE COMMISSION (SEC) stipulate that the sales must be marked *long* or *short*.

SINKING FUND. A fund that consists of amounts set aside at certain periods that will eventually be used to pay off a debt. See also AMORTIZATION.

Municipalities and corporations maintain sinking funds to satisfy BOND issues at maturity. Sinking funds may also be used for purposes other than debt repayment, such as for plant expansion.

SPLIT. See STOCK SPLIT.

SPOT MARKET. A commodities market (see COMMODITY EXCHANGE) in which tangible goods or products, such as grains, foods, or metals, are sold for cash and delivered immediately.

SPREAD. 1. The difference between the price paid by a securities UNDERWRITING group for an issue of securities and the price at which the securities are to be sold to the public:

> An underwriting group buys an issue of BONDS at $99 to be sold to the public at $101. The *spread* is 2 points regardless of whether some bonds remain unsold for a time and later have to be liquidated at $95.

2. A combination of a put and a call (see PUTS AND CALLS) at equal margins from the market price of a STOCK:

> If XYZ stock is selling at $30, a *spread* would consist of a put at 25 (5 points down) and a call at 35 (5 points up).

3. The difference between the BID AND ASKED PRICES of a stock:

> If the bid is 36 and the asked is 37 1/2, the *spread* is 1 1/2 points.

STOCK. The aggregate ownership interest of a business corporation. The term refers to ownership of the *corporation,* not of the corporation's *assets,* which are owned by the corporation. See also Chapter 10/CORPORATION; Chapter 12/ASSETS.

Stock is divided into identical units called *shares* that are represented by written certificates of stock. See also STOCK CERTIFICATE.

Authorized capital stock is the amount of stock that a corporation is empowered to issue by its certificate of incorporation. (See Chapter 10/CERTIFICATE OF INCORPORATION.) It does not change from time to time unless the certificate of incorporation is amended.

Authorized stock, therefore, may be *issued* (sold) or *unissued*. A corporation may want to keep some of the authorized stock as unissued shares in case it needs to sell them later to raise additional capital.

Outstanding stock is issued stock in the hands of STOCKHOLDERS. The DIVIDENDS are calculated and based on outstanding stock.

Sometimes a corporation will obtain, by purchase or gift, some of its own stock. Such stock is called *Treasury stock* and may be used in employee compensation plans or for other purposes.

Common stock.   The two principal classes of stock are common and preferred. All corporations have common stock; some may also have preferred stock. The main characteristic of common stock is that its holders have an unlimited interest in the corporate profits and assets.

Holders of common stock share in dividends after the preferred stockholders' rights to dividends have been satisfied. They also participate in the distribution of assets after all prior debts of the corporation have been paid.

In addition, common stockholders have voting rights that permit them to elect the board of directors. (See Chapter 10/BOARD OF DIRECTORS.) Through their vote, therefore, they indirectly participate in the management of a corporation.

The New York Stock Exchange (see STOCK EXCHANGE) and various government agencies have discouraged the issue of nonvoting common stock. Nevertheless, there are outstanding issues of common stock, one with and one without voting power.

Preferred stock.   This class of stock arose from the need to give investors an ownership security less speculative than that provided by common stock.

A holder of preferred stock usually has the same rights as a holder of common stock, except that he or she will receive a specified share of the profits annually *before* any profits are distributed to common stockholders.

Also, the holder of preferred stock usually has the right to share in a distribution of assets upon corporate dissolution before the holders of common stock may do so. Therefore, the position of preferred stock relative to earnings and assets is stronger than that of common stock but not as strong as that of BONDS.

Frequently, preferred stock is nonvoting or vetoing. See also Chapter 4/ STOCKHOLDERS' MEETING.

There are many types of preferred stock, including the following:

Convertible preferred stock is convertible into some other form of security, such as common stock. However, stock cannot be made convertible into bonds, except at the option of the corporation.

Cumulative preferred stock means that a preferred stockholder will receive any unpaid dividends from previous years *before* any common stock dividends can be paid.

Noncumulative preferred stock means that if dividends have not been declared, those that are omitted in any year do not accumulate and need not be made up.

Nonparticipating preferred stock is entitled only to the fixed or stated rate of dividends.

Participating preferred stock gives stockholders the right to participate in the residual earnings of a corporation after all preferred and initially declared common stock dividends have been paid.

Preferred stock in series, sometimes called *blank stock,* is allowed in some states and gives the board of directors the right to fix preference, restrictions, and limitations for each group at the time of issuance. When they want to sell it, they can therefore give it the attributes that will make it marketable.

Protected preferred stock provides that profits must be conserved by being placed in a special surplus account to pay shortages in preferred stock dividends in the lean years when current profits are insufficient.

Redeemable, or *callable, preferred stock* gives a corporation the right to demand that stockholders surrender their stock and receive cash in payment for it.

Other stock.   The following terms apply to various other types of stock:

Bankers' shares applies to a class of stock that has sole voting power and is held by a small group, commonly the organizers of the corporation and the bankers who financed the issues. Therefore, they are essentially *management shares.*

Deferred stock is stock on which dividends are deferred until a certain date or certain conditions have been met. It is usually created in connection with some form of readjustment of the capitalization.

Founders', or *management, shares* refers to stock given to management personnel at the time of incorporation for services rendered.

Growth stock applies to stock that has the potential for increasing its value substantially over time. It tends to have low dividend yields, low dividend payout RATIOS, high PRICE–EARNINGS RATIOS, and a high percentage of retained earnings.

Guaranteed stock is sometimes incorrectly used as a synonym for preferred stock. But a company cannot *guarantee* dividends on its own stock. The term is correctly used for a stock whose dividends are guaranteed by another corporation, usually a parent.

Promoters' stock also refers to stock given to promoters in part or full payment for services rendered.

Watered stock refers to stock that is issued in excess of the true value of a corporation's assets. The purpose may be to hide heavy earnings or to give promoters a profit.

See also PAR VALUE STOCK; STOCK PURCHASE WARRANT.

STOCK CERTIFICATE. Written evidence of ownership in a corporation. (See Chapter 10/CORPORATION.) The certificate is issued and registered in the records of the corporation in the name of the owner of the shares of STOCK represented by the certificate.

A certificate may represent one share or numerous shares. When ownership of a share is transferred (see TRANSFER OF SECURITIES), the certificate held by the original owner is canceled, another is issued to the new owner, and appropriate changes are made in the records of the corporation.

A certificate has a form on the back for making such transfers or assignments. Whereas a corporation provides a new, original certificate for an original owner, one can transfer ownership by using the transfer-assignment form.

After the shares of stock are transferred in this way, a corporation issues a new certificate to the new owner and cancels the old one. For example, the holder of a 100-share certificate might want to transfer 50 shares and keep the other 50. In that case, the corporation would issue two new certificates of 50 shares each.

STOCK EXCHANGE. An organized form of SECURITIES MARKET in which securities are bought and sold daily through BROKERS and dealers. U.S. exchanges are patterned after the New York Stock Exchange (NYSE), the oldest and largest of the exchanges and the one where the securities of large corporations are usually traded.

Membership. Trading on stock exchanges is conducted by members. Memberships (seats) on the NYSE are limited, and new members must buy their seats from retiring members or the estates of deceased members. Regardless, all members must comply with the rigid qualifications for admission imposed by the exchange.

Members may act as brokers or dealers but never as both in the same transaction. They buy or sell as an agent for public customers and charge a commission for their services. As dealers, they buy and sell for their own account.

Trading.   The New York Stock Exchange does not permit trading on its floor in securities that are not listed by it. However, the American Stock Exchange (AMEX), the second largest exchange in New York City, and other stock exchanges throughout the country permit trading in unlisted securities.

Securities of many small and medium companies, as well as some over-the-counter stocks (see OVER-THE-COUNTER [OTC] MARKETS), are traded on the AMEX. Various securities are also traded on other, smaller exchanges, such as the Pacific Stock Exchange (PSE) in Los Angeles and the Chicago Stock Exchange (CHX).

Other countries also have exchanges that function in a similar manner. Examples are the International Stock Exchange in London and the Tokyo Stock Exchange in Tokyo.

Transactions.   To process a transaction via an exchange, a broker must take numerous steps, including the following:

Someone in Dallas gives an order to a local broker to sell 100 shares of XYZ common (see STOCK) (1) at the market (see LIMIT ORDER; MARKET ORDER) or (2) at $50 per share.

The broker transmits the order electronically to a commission house in New York. The New York office contacts the floor of the exchange (again, electronically) where a clerk receives it and gives it to a floor member or the commission house or to a floor broker.

If the order is to sell at the market, the last bid will be the price at which the transaction is completed. If the order is to sell at $50, the transaction will be completed when a bid is entered at 50.

If the order reaches the floor of the exchange when the price trend is downward, and the last sale was at 49$1/2$, the stock may not be sold that day.

Since all transactions are electronically reported almost instantly throughout the country, the person who gives an order may note the trend and reenter the order at a lower price to dispose of his or her stock.

If the order is not executed and remains with the broker as a GTC ORDER, the seller will have to wait until the trend reverses itself and a bid is entered at 50.

A market order will be executed by the floor member of the commission house. An order to buy or sell at a fixed price is generally entrusted to the specialist to execute.

When a sale is executed, the notice goes back to Dallas within a matter of minutes. The Dallas broker then delivers the stock to the New York commission house and credits the customer's account for the proceeds of the sale.

STOCKHOLDER. Owner of one or more shares of STOCK in a corporation. See also Chapter 10/CORPORATION; STOCKHOLDER.

STOCK INDEX. A measure of changes in the value of securities. Whereas a stock average is an arithmetic mean, an *index* is an average expressed in relation to an established base market value.

Well-known U.S. indexes are the Dow Jones Industrial Average, NYSE (New York Stock Exchange) Composite Index, AMEX (American Stock Exchange) Market Value Index, NASDAQ (National Association of Securities Dealers Automated Quotation) Composite Index, Value Line Composite Index, and Wilshire 5000 Equity Index.

Each one uses its own method of computing the index. The Dow Jones Industrial Average, for example, is based on the prices of 30 BLUE CHIP STOCKS traded on the New York Stock Exchange. (See STOCK EXCHANGE.) It is the most popular U.S. index of the daily market trend in both value and price.

Other countries also have measures of changes in the values of securities. For example, the Nikkei Stock Average is the Dow Jones Industrial Average of the Tokyo market. An example of another index is the FT 100 in London.

When averages are up, the market as a whole is considered optimistic. When they're down, the market is viewed as being in a slump.

STOCK MARKET. See SECURITIES MARKET; STOCK EXCHANGE.

STOCK OR BOND POWER. A power of attorney (see Chapter 11/POWER OF ATTORNEY) given by the owner of securities to someone, usually his or her BROKER, to assign and transfer the securities on the books of the issuing corporation. A printed form of power can be obtained from one's broker.

When a signed power is mailed to a broker, it is usually sent separately from the securities that are to be assigned (unless the broker's name is already filled in on the power). If the securities were accompanied by a signed *blank* power and they fell into the wrong hands, they could then be assigned by that person to someone else.

Sometimes, however, powers are intentionally signed in blank and left with a broker to be used, for example, if the seller is out of the city and a GTC ORDER is executed.

STOCK PURCHASE WARRANT. A certificate attached to preferred or senior issues of STOCK or BONDS that entitles the holder to purchase common stock of a corporation at a certain price and within a prescribed period.

This feature makes the securities to which it is attached attractive to the market at the time of original issuance.

Warrants are usually detachable instruments that may be purchased and sold apart from the security to which they were originally attached. In that case, they may be bought and sold in a SECURITIES MARKET.

If the warrant is nondetachable, however, there can be no market in warrants alone, and the warrant can be exercised only by the presentation of the security to which it is attached.

Provision is usually made to permit the holder of a nondetachable warrant to exercise a portion of the warrant.

STOCK QUOTATION. See BID AND ASKED PRICES.

STOCK SPLIT. Division of shares of capital STOCK into a larger number *without changing the dollar amount* and *without reducing the surplus.* (See Chapter 12/CAPITAL STOCK.) Therefore, the number of shares of outstanding stock is increased, but the total value of the shares remains the same as before the division.

General stock split. The certificate of incorporation (see Chapter 11/CERTIFICATE OF INCORPORATION) must be amended for a corporation to initiate a stock split. Each STOCKHOLDER then receives a certain number of shares for each original share owned:

In a two-for-one stock split, a shareholder with 100 shares worth $50 each ($5,000) will end up with 200 shares worth $25 each ($5,000).

The usual purpose of a split is to lower the price per share to improve marketability. But the holder doesn't receive anything of value from a financial viewpoint. However, splits may have a psychological value, and a reduced market price may also make it easier for a small investor to buy shares.

Reverse stock split. A reverse split reduces the number of shares outstanding. In this case, each stockholder receives one share in exchange for a larger number (one share for four held, for example).

A reverse split has the effect of increasing the price of a stock that is selling at a very low figure.

STOP-LOSS ORDER. A LIMIT ORDER given to a BROKER by an owner of securities who wants to protect himself or herself against a loss. When the market price of the stock falls to the price stipulated in the order, the stock is automatically sold *at the market.*

The broker will try to execute the order at the *stop* price, but there is no guarantee that this can be done. The directors of a STOCK EXCHANGE may limit or halt the placing of stop-loss orders.

STRADDLE. A speculative transaction in COMMODITY trading (see COMMODITY EXCHANGE). It consists of buying a futures contract in one month and selling a contract in another month with the expectation of making a profit on the price differential between the two.

The term also refers to a combination of a put and a call, both at the same price. See also PUTS AND CALLS.

STRAIGHT LOAN. A loan for a definite term of years at a specific INTEREST rate and payable in full at maturity, with no payment of principal in advance of the due date. In real estate (see Chapter 15/REAL PROPERTY), this is known as a *term mortgage* or a *straight mortgage.*

During the period of the loan, the borrower pays interest only on the principal. At maturity, he or she must pay the loan principal, refinance the loan for another term, or have the lender carry the loan as an open or past-due debt.

The straight loan is generally made for a short term—from three to five years—and may be renewable at the end of the term.

SURETY BOND. A promise, or contract, by one party (the *surety*) to pay a debt if the principal, or *obligor,* defaults in performance. (See Chapter 11/DEFAULT.) The person to whom the obligation is owed is the *obligee.*

A surety therefore guarantees the responsibility of a principal. See also FIDELITY BOND; Chapter 11/GUARANTY.

TRANSFER OF SECURITIES. Every STOCKHOLDER of a corporation has the right to transfer STOCK, and every bondholder has the right to transfer BONDS. A bearer bond, however, does not require an assignment. It can be delivered as is since it is negotiable, provided that all unpaid coupons are attached.

Transfer tax. When securities are transferred, the seller usually pays the transfer tax. See also Chapter 12/STAMP TAX.

Assignment. Before a STOCK CERTIFICATE or registered bond is ready for transfer and delivery, it must be assigned by the person whose name appears on its face.

The transfer can be accomplished by filling in the assignment form that is printed on the reverse side of the certificate or bond or by drawing up an entirely separate assignment.

A BROKER can provide a separate form, which should be used if the securities are already in the hands of the broker (or dealer) or if they are to be sent by mail.

Without an assignment directly on the back of the securities, they would not be negotiable, an important precaution in case they should fall into the wrong hands.

TREASURY NOTES, BILLS, AND BONDS. Short-term NOTES, bills, and long-term BONDS that are marketed by the U.S. Treasury to meet its short- and long-term financial requirements.

Although government obligations are traded in a free market (subject to SECURITIES AND EXCHANGE COMMISSION [SEC] regulations), the Federal Reserve Board influences the price of such obligations and attempts to stabilize the market by restricting price fluctuations within a narrow range.

Notes and certificates. Obligations that may run as long as ten years, with a minimum denomination of $1,000. Notes and certificates pay higher rates than do Treasury bills but are subject to the same taxation rules.

Treasury bills. Short-term (less than a year), low-INTEREST obligations that are constantly being refunded. The minimum denomination is $1,000.

Treasury bills are issued at a discount and redeemed at par value (see FACE VALUE) at maturity. The return earned is subject to federal income tax but is exempt from state income tax.

Bonds. Outstanding government savings and coupon bonds. The latter are relatively long term, maturing in 20 to 30 years.

UNDERWRITING. A function performed by the investment banking industry in the formation of new capital for business enterprises or governments through the issuance of securities. The person, firm, or group underwriting a new issue of securities is the *underwriter.*

The process consists of the outright purchase of an entire issue by a purchase group and its sale to the ultimate buyers. The process also includes an agreement by the underwriters to purchase any of the securities not bought by investors to whom the issue has been offered.

UNLISTED SECURITIES. Securities that are not listed on a STOCK EXCHANGE. Unlisted securities are either traded in an OVER-THE-COUNTER (OTC) MARKET or are admitted to unlisted trading privileges on exchanges.

The qualifications for unlisted trading on organized exchanges are far less exacting than for listed trading. Unlisted securities may include new companies or existing companies with financial problems and therefore are often more risky.

USURY. See Chapter 11/USURY.

WARRANT. See STOCK PURCHASE WARRANT.

WASH SALE. A sale for which a loss is not tax deductible. This situation arises when a substantially identical security is purchased within 30 days before or after selling the other security.

The term also applies to the illegal practice of buying and selling large blocks of STOCK simultaneously to create the illusion of active trading. The intent is to generate more purchases, thereby driving up the price.

WHEN ISSUED. Short for "when, as, and if issued." The term describes a transaction that is conditional on delivery. This situation exists when the SECURITIES AND EXCHANGE COMMISSION (SEC) has not finally approved the securities being traded or when the certificates for them are not yet ready for delivery.

YIELD. The annual percentage rate of return on an investment in securities:

An amount of $5 is received annually in Dividends on a Stock that cost $100. The *yield* is said to be 5 percent ($5/$100).

Yields are computed on both stocks and Bonds:

The *stock yield,* as illustrated in the previous example, is calculated by dividing the annual dividends by the price paid for the stock.

The *bond yield* is calculated as a nominal yield, current yield, or yield to maturity.

1. The *nominal yield* of a bond, also called the *coupon yield,* is the yield stated on the face of the bond certificate, such as 8 percent. It does not vary with the market price of the bond.

2. The *current yield* is the annual Interest payment on the bond divided by the current market price of the bond. Although the interest paid on the bond does not change, the current yield will vary from the coupon yield when the market value fluctuates:

A bond with an 8 percent coupon yield (pays $80 per year in interest) is trading in the market for $800. Its *current yield* is 10 percent (80/800).

Because bond prices change as market conditions change, the current yield is calculated to reflect the bondholder's actual return.

3. The *yield to maturity* is calculated using time-value-of-money concepts. It depends on the interest rate of the bond (coupon rate), the amount paid for the bond, the number of years to the maturity date, and the amount to be paid at maturity:

A purchases a bond at 105, paying $1,050. The interest rate is 8 percent.

If *A* holds this bond until maturity, which is ten years, and the principal is $1,000, *A* is going to lose $50 of capital (purchase price $1,050 and redemption price $1,000), or an average of $5 per year.

This capital loss must be considered in calculating the yield to maturity and would reduce *A*'s percentage return on his investment.

On the other hand, if *A* had purchased the bond at 95, paying $950, he would have gained $50, or $5 per year, by holding to maturity, thus increasing the percentage return on his investment.

Yields to maturity are usually determined by using software or calculators programmed for this type of calculation.

CHAPTER FOURTEEN

Insurance

ACCIDENT INSURANCE. Personal insurance providing weekly indemnity for loss of income resulting from an accident. Definite sums are also paid for loss of life or certain bodily injuries resulting from accidents but not from illness.

A variety of accident insurance contracts are issued to business owners and professional people only (commercial policies). Some cover only certain accidents, such as injuries caused by hazards of travel.

Accident insurance also is often issued in conjunction with a health policy. See also HEALTH INSURANCE; WORKER'S COMPENSATION INSURANCE.

ACTUAL CASH VALUE. The sum of money for which damaged or destroyed property could have been sold by the INSURED on the date of the loss; in general, the replacement cost less wear and tear, depreciation, and obsolescence.

However, many factors may affect the actual cash value of a particular loss. See also REPLACEMENT-COST INSURANCE.

Actual cash value should not be confused with the CASH SURRENDER VALUE of a LIFE INSURANCE policy.

ACTUARY. A mathematical, statistical, and accounting specialist who does the computations in connection with rates charged for insurance and DIVIDENDS paid and who also undertakes various statistical studies.

ADJUSTER. Also called *claims representative.* A representative of an INSURANCE COMPANY who determines the amount of loss and the firm's liability when a CLAIM is submitted for settlement:

> *Brokers* or other representatives may handle the adjustment function. See also BROKER.
>
> *Independent adjusters* have their own offices and work for insurers on a fee basis.
>
> *Public adjusters* help INSURED parties deal with the insurer.

All adjusters typically check the validity of coverage, the value of the insured property, the insured party's share of loss, the parties to whom the loss is payable, and related matters.

AGENT. A sales and service representative of an INSURANCE COMPANY who negotiates contracts for the insurer. An agent is usually paid on a commission basis.
Various terms describe the different types of agents, depending on the type or number of policies they sell or the companies they represent:

> An *independent agent* represents many insurance companies and chooses the most appropriate company for the INSURED.
>
> An *exclusive agent* represents only one insurance company but is not an employee of that company.
>
> A *direct writer agent* also represents only one company and is an employee of that company.
>
> A *specializing agent* sells one or a few closely related lines of insurance.
>
> A *general agent* sells all types of insurance. The term also applies to agencies that act as wholesale distributors of insurance policies to other agents or BROKERS.

Usually, the contractual arrangement with the company is the only difference between an independent agent and an insurance broker. Most agents are also brokers.

AIR TRAVEL INSURANCE. See AVIATION INSURANCE.

ALL-RISK INSURANCE. A broad policy that covers loss caused by all perils except those specifically excluded by the terms of the policy. This type of insurance differs from the *named-perils policy,* which covers loss from a specific peril or perils.

APPRAISAL. An evaluation of property undertaken to determine the amount of insurance to be written or loss to be paid. When an insurer and the INSURED cannot agree on the amount of a loss, a policy may provide for an appraisal by a competent and disinterested appraiser.

Appraisers determine the amount of loss, ACTUAL CASH VALUE of property at the time of loss, and so on. If they arrive at different amounts, a neutral umpire may review the various appraisals and make a final determination.

For specific value coverages under some types of policies, the appraisal must be made when the policy is written, not at the time of loss.

ASSIGNED-RISK PLAN. A plan covering RISKS that are usually not acceptable to insurers but for which coverage is required by law. They are used mainly in WORKER'S COMPENSATION INSURANCE and AUTOMOBILE INSURANCE but can also include hard-to-place FIRE INSURANCE and LIABILITY INSURANCE.

To deal with situations of undue risk, state governments have spread the undesirable-risk applications among all insurers, who then provide, at fixed rates, coverage commonly described as *assigned-risk plans.*

Some state legislatures have set up several plans for different liability risks, such as child-care centers and municipalities.

ASSIGNMENT. The transfer of the legal right or interest in an insurance contract to another party.

For example, insurance policies covering property can sometimes be assigned when the property is sold. LIFE INSURANCE policies are often assigned as collateral for loans.

An INSURANCE COMPANY must be informed of any transfer of rights or interests.

ASSURED. See INSURED.

AUTOMOBILE INSURANCE. Various types of coverage for one or more vehicles. Policies may protect the INSURED against any or all of the following:

1. Losses resulting from legal liability for bodily injury (or death) to another person.

2. Losses resulting from legal liability for damage to the property of another.

3. Losses resulting by reason of damage to the insured's car through collision or upset. See also COLLISION INSURANCE.

4. Losses caused by theft of the car.

5. Direct damage to the insured's car caused by fire, lightning, tornado, cyclone, windstorm, hail, earthquake, explosion, and other perils.

6. Legal liability of an employer for losses for which an employee is primarily responsible.

7. Legal liability of garage keepers, service stations, and automobile mechanics for negligence resulting in losses to customers' vehicles. See also GARAGE INSURANCE.

In states that allow *no-fault automobile insurance,* the INSURANCE COMPANY pays for property damage and bodily injury of the insured without regard to fault.

The standard automobile policy definition of the insured extends coverage to certain others in addition to the named insured. It makes the insurance follow the car, with certain exceptions, rather than the named insured.

The terms of the policy are therefore extended to cover the legal liability of any other person using the insured's automobile or any firm or corporation legally responsible for the operation of a covered automobile.

See also COLLISION INSURANCE; DEDUCTIBLE; FLEET INSURANCE; GARAGE INSURANCE; NONOWNED AUTO LIABILITY INSURANCE.

AVIATION INSURANCE. Insurance that provides *liability coverage* for bodily injury or property damage resulting from the ownership, maintenance, or use of aircraft, along with *material damage coverage* for insured aircraft.

Although insurance in the aviation industry is highly specialized, the various forms of coverage are similar to those used in AUTOMOBILE INSURANCE.

For example, loss to an aircraft would be covered by hull insurance. The responsibility to passengers and others would be covered by LIABILITY INSURANCE. WORKER'S COMPENSATION INSURANCE, written for employers, would be of the same character as it is in other types of business.

BENEFICIARY. The person or institution to whom a LIFE INSURANCE policy is made payable in the event of the death of the INSURED.

BINDER. A temporary agreement given by an INSURANCE COMPANY or its AGENT to one who wants insurance coverage. The agreement *binds* the company to pay for a covered loss should the loss occur before the policy is issued or before the insurer gives notice of its election to terminate the agreement.

A binder must be in writing to avoid future lawsuits regarding intent.

BLANKET POLICY. A broad type of coverage commonly used for property insurance and GROUP INSURANCE. See also OPEN FORM INSURANCE.

For example, a blanket FIRE INSURANCE policy may be written to cover any of the following:

1. A building and its contents, without a definite proportion of the insurance being carried on the building or its contents

2. Two or more buildings at different locations, together with the contents, without any definite proportion of the insurance being assigned to any particular location

3. The contents at several locations

BROKER. A representative who solicits and negotiates INSURANCE CONTRACTS and places orders for coverage with insurance companies. In most cases, a broker is an agent of the INSURED rather than the INSURANCE COMPANY. Compare with AGENT.

The broker earns a commission that he or she deducts from the PREMIUM, paying the net to the company. Brokers may also charge a broker's fee in addition to the commissions earned. However, many large international brokers work on a fee basis rather than by commission.

BUSINESS INSURANCE. See INSURANCE, BUSINESS.

BUSINESS-INTERRUPTION INSURANCE. A policy that protects against loss of business income resulting from the interruption of business caused by damage to or destruction of property.

This type of insurance is used to meet payrolls, pay taxes, pay other fixed expenses, and cover lost income not provided for in the policies covering the actual physical damage to business property.

CASH SURRENDER VALUE. The amount of money given to a LIFE INSURANCE policyholder who withdraws or cancels the contract. It is paid in accordance with the no-forfeiture value clause of the policy and is usually less than the amount paid in for PREMIUMS.

The term also refers to the amount that ordinarily can be borrowed on a life insurance policy at a particular time.

CASUALTY INSURANCE. Protection against loss caused by legal liability resulting from negligent acts and omissions that injure a third party or damage a third party's property. In practice, it refers to most insurance except LIFE INSURANCE, MARINE INSURANCE, and certain types of FIRE INSURANCE.

CATASTROPHIC INSURANCE. A form of HEALTH INSURANCE coverage that provides benefits for high-cost (above $100,000) hospital and related expenses arising from major illness or accident.

CLAIM. A formal request for indemnification made by an INSURED to an INSURANCE COMPANY for loss relating to an insured peril. The loss is usually reported to an AGENT or BROKER who in turn reports the claim to the insurance company.

The insurance company may furnish a blank proof-of-loss form to the agent or broker, who will send it to the insured to be completed. When the document is completed, the insured usually returns it to the agent or broker.

Losses are often adjusted with the company's ADJUSTER. Sometimes, however, minor amounts are paid without adjustment after the proof of loss is filed.

CLASS RATING. A method of classifying INSURED parties by identifiable characteristics, such as type of business or type of building.

Rating systems reflect varying loss probabilities so that all of those who are in the same category will pay the same PREMIUM rate.

COINSURANCE. A requirement that the INSURED carry a certain percentage of insurance according to the value of the property insured:

A FIRE INSURANCE policy contains an 80 percent coinsurance clause, and the property covered under the policy has a value of $50,000. The amount of insurance to be carried is $40,000.

However, if the amount of insurance actually carried is *less* than $40,000, the insured is considered to have assumed a proportionate part of the RISK and, in case of a loss, will have to bear a proportionate part of that loss.

If the insured carries $30,000, for instance, he or she will collect only $30,000/40,000$ times the amount of the loss on a partial loss.

COLLISION INSURANCE. AUTOMOBILE INSURANCE that protects the owner from loss as the result of damage to his or her own motor vehicle.

For example, a business firm may incur a substantial loss as the result of accidental collision damage to its motor vehicles. A collision contract protects against direct loss caused by the contact of an INSURED's vehicle with another object or due to upset of the insured's vehicle.

The cost of full-coverage collision insurance has always been high. Consequently, policies with a DEDUCTIBLE clause are widely used.

COMPARATIVE NEGLIGENCE. A principle of law applied in insurance cases in some jurisdictions in which the degree of each person's negligence in an accident is based on the person's contribution to the accident.

Under this principle, each person is liable for his or her portion of damage, and recovery is based on the other party's degree of comparative negligence. Compare with CONTRIBUTORY NEGLIGENCE.

COMPREHENSIVE THEFT AND FIRE INSURANCE. Coverage that is broader than the specified perils of theft, fire, lightning, and transportation.

For example, in AUTOMOBILE INSURANCE, the coverage protects against loss or damage to the INSURED's automobile from any source except collision and certain specific exclusions.

CONCEALMENT. The intentional failure of an INSURED to disclose material facts to an insurer. Such action by an insured or prospective insured party may cause an insurer to avoid providing coverage or to cancel coverage already provided.

CONDITIONS. See INSURANCE CONTRACT.

CONTRIBUTORY NEGLIGENCE. A principle of law applied in insurance cases in some jurisdictions stating that anyone whose negligence contributed to an accident, no matter how small the contribution, is barred from recovery of damages from the other party.

Contributory negligence is based on common law. Compare with COMPARATIVE NEGLIGENCE. See also Chapter 11/COMMON LAW.

CONVERSION PRIVILEGE. The right of a certificateholder to convert GROUP INSURANCE (life or health) to an individual insurance policy, without physical examination, when the INSURED ceases to be a member of the insured group. Usually, the conversion occurs at the person's attained age rate.

State laws require a conversion privilege in INSURANCE CONTRACTS.

Many individual-term policies provide a conversion privilege at little or no additional cost or allow conversion, under certain circumstances, from TERM LIFE INSURANCE to a permanent type of LIFE INSURANCE.

CREDIT LIFE INSURANCE. A policy that provides for the repayment of a loan if the borrower dies before completing the payments. Payment therefore is provided to the creditor (the BENEFICIARY).

Usually, coverage is limited to the amount of the debt and is used with installment purchases such as that for jewelry, furniture, or automobiles.

DECLARATION. See INSURANCE CONTRACT.

DEDUCTIBLE. The amount of each loss that the INSURED agrees to assume before being entitled to indemnification from the insurer. The insurer agrees to pay the remainder up to the full amount provided by the policy.

Through the use of a deductible provision an insured may be able to receive protection against serious losses for which coverage would otherwise be too expensive.

Types of insurance providing deductibles. The deductible clause has had widespread acceptance in the case of automobile COLLISION INSURANCE and is also common in FIRE INSURANCE and MARINE INSURANCE.

Deductibles are sometimes available in general public LIABILITY INSURANCE, too, particularly property-damage liability.

Types of deductibles. A *level* or *straight deductible* may be applied to each commodity involved or to each illness or accident. Or it may be applied to the total losses involved in a specified period.

A *franchise deductible* is based on a percentage of the FACE AMOUNT of insurance. This is not a real deductible, however, since the loss is paid in full if it exceeds the specified franchise deductible.

A deductible may also be available for a specific amount or for a percentage of the loss involved.

The deductible may not apply to certain forms of loss, such as loss by fire under an ALL-RISK INSURANCE contract.

DISABILITY INCOME INSURANCE. Insurance that pays benefits for income lost by an individual because of accidental injury or illness. See also Chapter 11/DISABILITY BENEFIT LAWS.

The insurance may be ACCIDENT INSURANCE, HEALTH INSURANCE, or a combination of the two. WORKER'S COMPENSATION INSURANCE covers disability arising from job-related injuries.

DIVIDEND. The amount of PREMIUM returned to a policyholder with a policy issued on a participating basis. See also PARTICIPATING AND NONPARTICIPATING INSURANCE; Chapter 13/DIVIDEND.

Under some LIFE INSURANCE policies, called *participating policies,* the INSURED is entitled to a share of the divisible surplus of the company in the form of dividends. Such dividends are usually payable annually and are ordinarily declared at the option of the INSURANCE COMPANY's board of directors.

A few companies pay dividends at the termination of a policy contract. If death is the cause of termination, they are called *mortuary,* or *postmortem, dividends.* Otherwise, they are called *maturity dividends* or *special settlement dividends.*

During the life of the contract, a policyholder may have his or her dividends paid in cash, applied as partial payment of the premium due, applied to the purchase of additional insurance (*paid-up additions*), or left with the company to draw interest, subject to withdrawal (*dividend accumulations*).

Dividends may also be returned to the INSURED by property and by LIABILITY INSURANCE companies (usually a MUTUAL INSURANCE COMPANY) as a method of allowing the policyholder to share in the profits.

DOUBLE INDEMNITY RIDER. The payment of double the insured amount if something specified takes place. A person carrying LIFE INSURANCE for $50,000 might have a double indemnity RIDER stating that $100,000 will be payable to the BENEFICIARY if death is accidental.

EMPLOYEE BENEFIT PLANS. See GROUP INSURANCE.

ENDORSEMENT. A form, clause, or agreement added to an insurance policy to modify the basic policy. The endorsement may be written on a printed page of the policy or attached as a supplemental agreement, or RIDER.

Some endorsements *must* be made. For example, a description of insured property must be added to a standard FIRE INSURANCE policy.

Other endorsements *may* be made to waive certain provisions or add certain privileges. For example, an endorsement permitting an insured building to remain unoccupied more than the usual 60 days may be made on a standard fire policy. See also EXTENDED COVERAGE ENDORSEMENT.

ENDOWMENT INSURANCE. A form of LIFE INSURANCE that promises payment of the full FACE AMOUNT of the insurance upon the death of the INSURED within a specified period or upon his or her survival to the end of the specified period.

Endowment insurance PREMIUMS are considerably higher than are premiums for ORDINARY LIFE INSURANCE.

EXCLUSION. See INSURANCE CONTRACT.

EXPERIENCE RATING. See MERIT RATING.

EXTENDED COVERAGE ENDORSEMENT. An ENDORSEMENT added to a FIRE INSURANCE policy that extends coverage to protect against the perils of windstorm and hail, riot and civil commotion, explosion, damage from aircraft and motor vehicles, and smoke.

The coverage may be extended by still other supplementary endorsements to cover other perils, such as vandalism and malicious mischief, collapse, and falling objects.

FACE AMOUNT. The amount of insurance provided under the terms of a specific contract, commonly stated on the face of the policy; the amount of the death benefit in a LIFE INSURANCE policy.

FIRE INSURANCE. A standard contract, prescribed by the laws of each state, that provides coverage against the peril of fire. No other form of contract is written, but the standard form may be modified or extended by ENDORSEMENT.

The standard fire policy insures against direct loss by fire and lightning. Almost any type of loss is covered when fire is the primary cause, whether or not it is the immediate cause:

Direct loss by fire means damage only to the property itself.

Indirect loss involves other damage or loss. For example, a fire may also cause a business to shut down, with a loss of many times the value of the damaged property.

Unless the policy includes an endorsement to the contrary, recovery is possible only for damage to the property actually destroyed. See also BUSINESS-INTERRUPTION INSURANCE; RENT AND RENTAL-VALUE INSURANCE.

Regardless of the FACE VALUE of the policy and of whether a loss is total or partial, an INSURED may recover only to the extent of the ACTUAL CASH VALUE of the property at the time of loss or damage. Proper deductions are also made for depreciation. See also REPLACEMENT-COST INSURANCE.

Some states have a *valued policy law* providing that, in cases of a total loss to the property, the INSURANCE COMPANY must pay the full face amount of the insurance carried. See also COINSURANCE.

FLEET INSURANCE. Coverage for numerous vehicles under a single policy. The fleet plan gives businesses a more flexible form of insurance than would be possible with individual policies.

PREMIUMS are based primarily on vehicle garaging, use, radius of operation, and size of vehicle or gross vehicle weight. Fleet discounts applied to the premium may be available, depending on the number of cars.

Newly acquired cars are automatically covered. However, any changes in the fleet—additions, disposals, and so on—must be reported to the INSURANCE COMPANY.

FLOATER POLICY. Coverage for property that is frequently moved from one location to another. The insurance applies no matter where the property described in the policy may be, except places specifically excluded. See, for example, INLAND MARINE INSURANCE.

GARAGE INSURANCE. Coverage for garage or auto-repair owners and their employees or representatives who may be held liable if customers suffer injury or damage to their vehicles resulting from the operation of the garage.

GOVERNMENT INSURANCE. Also called *social insurance.* Coverage provided through state or federal government agencies, such as with veterans' benefits. In these cases, individuals and organizations rely on the resources of the government operating either alone or in a program of cooperation with the private sector.

This type of insurance is usually compulsory, as with social security programs of life, disability, survivors', and medical benefits and with worker's compensation plans. See also WORKER'S COMPENSATION INSURANCE.

Other associated programs include the Federal Deposit Insurance Corporation (FDIC), Federal Savings and Loan Insurance Corporation (FSLIC), Security Investors Protection Corporation (SIPC), and flood and crop insurance programs.

GROUP INSURANCE.   Coverage for a changing group of individuals by means of a BLANKET POLICY. This type of policy is commonly issued to an employer to cover his or her employees. It is also frequently issued to labor unions on their members.

Under an employer–employee contract, the employer assumes responsibility for the collection and payment of the PREMIUM. State laws require the employer to contribute part of the premium. They also specify the minimum number of individuals that must be covered by the blanket policy.

A general policy is issued to the group, and a certificate evidencing the insurance is issued to each individual.

Insurance available on a group basis includes life, accidental death and dismemberment, accident and sickness, hospitalization, surgical, medical, and permanent disability. Some insurers have also offered group auto and home insurance in recent years.

HEALTH INSURANCE.   Insurance protection covering sickness or injury. Policies include accident, disability, income, and hospitalization. See ACCIDENT INSURANCE; CATASTROPHIC INSURANCE; DISABILITY INCOME INSURANCE; GROUP INSURANCE; HEALTH MAINTENANCE ORGANIZATION (HMO); LONG-TERM CARE INSURANCE; MEDICAID; MEDICARE.

HEALTH MAINTENANCE ORGANIZATION (HMO).   A health or treatment center that provides a wide range of services to HMO participants, who pay PREMIUMS for their services, the same as do those who are covered by conventional insurance companies. This form of coverage is a prepaid group plan that stresses preventive maintenance.

As a member of an HMO, a participant selects a participating HMO physician, often called a *personal care provider* or *personal care physician,* who is responsible for providing or managing all of the participant's health care. See also PREFERRED PROVIDER ORGANIZATION (PPO).

HOMEOWNER'S INSURANCE. A property and liability contract for owners of private, single-family or two-family residences, condominiums, and so on.

Policies commonly cover both the outside and inside structure, including liability, and the personal contents, although separate policies may be obtained for each. Compare with RENTER'S INSURANCE.

A basic policy might cover property (dwelling and contents) and liability, with an ENDORSEMENT for theft and vandalism.

INDEMNITY. See Chapter 11/INDEMNITY.

INLAND MARINE INSURANCE. Coverage for property subject to the hazards of inland marine transportation.

The property includes moveables written on floater forms (see also FLOATER POLICY); goods in transit, such as imports, exports, and domestic shipments; as well as instrumentalities of transportation (bridges, tunnels, piers).

Transportation does not include seagoing ventures. See also OCEAN MARINE INSURANCE.

Many forms of inland marine insurance are ALL-RISK INSURANCE types of contracts. Others are *named-perils policies* covering only listed causes of loss.

INSURABLE INTEREST. The interest that a person has in a subject (person or property) such that he or she would be financially injured by the occurrence of an event insured against.

If an insurable interest is not present, an insurance contract is a mere wager and is not enforceable.

Examples of other relationships giving rise to an insurable interest include the following:

Employer and valued employee

Several partners of a partnership

Creditor and debtor

A corporation and its officers

A wife and her husband

Dependent children

Property and casualty insurance. An insurable interest must exist at the time the loss occurs. Title to the property insured is not necessary, and an owner, lessee, mortgagee, or purchaser each has an insurable interest.

Life insurance. An insurable interest must exist at the time a LIFE INSURANCE policy is written but need not exist at the time death occurs. Every person has an insurable interest in his or her own life and may name anyone as BENEFICIARY.

INSURANCE, BUSINESS. Coverage that protects a business against loss pertaining to the enterprise or the owner's vocation.

Often, a business needs many forms of business insurance:

Property insurance protects the owner or mortgagee of property against actual destruction by fire, windstorm, explosion, and other perils.

Business-interruption insurance protects the business against loss of earnings resulting from an interruption of business operations caused by damage to or destruction of property.

Liability insurance protects the business against loss arising from legal liability for bodily injury and property damage to others.

Fidelity bonds guarantee the business against loss caused by dishonest employees, and *surety bonds* guarantee the faithful performance by others of certain duties or obligations.

Worker's compensation insurance (see WORKER'S COMPENSATION INSURANCE) covers employees for accidental injury and occupational disease developing from and during employment.

No *general* insurance program is suitable for every business. Therefore, various types of coverage are available, including arrest-bond, burglary, consignee, earthquake, flood, glass, hail, landlord's liability, malpractice, negligence liability, officer's and director's liability, power-interruption, records-destruction, safe deposit boxes, title, unoccupied-building, and water-damage insurance.

A trained insurance AGENT or BROKER can analyze the perils facing a particular business and advise the business about the kinds and amounts of coverage that are needed.

INSURANCE COMPANY. A company that writes various kinds of insurance for individuals and organizations. Some companies handle specific kinds of insurance, whereas others deal in most major areas of coverage.

Types of companies. Insurance companies may write one or more kinds of insurance, depending on the company's interests, state laws, and other factors. The following are common arrangements:

Life insurance companies write LIFE INSURANCE, annuities, ACCIDENT INSURANCE, and HEALTH INSURANCE.

Accident and health insurance companies write only accident insurance or both accident and health insurance.

Life and accident companies write both accident and health insurance and life insurance.

Fraternal societies write either life insurance or accident and health insurance.

Fire insurance companies write FIRE INSURANCE and miscellaneous property insurance, such as windstorm, riot, explosion, collision, and water-damage insurance.

Marine insurance companies write MARINE INSURANCE, both OCEAN MARINE INSURANCE and INLAND MARINE INSURANCE.

Fire and marine insurance companies are fire insurance companies that also transact a marine insurance business.

Casualty insurance companies write theft, glass, boiler and machinery, elevator, animal, and personal-injury liability insurance, as well as WORKER'S COMPENSATION INSURANCE and employer's liability and credit insurance. They may also write accident and health insurance, water-damage, and COLLISION INSURANCE.

Casualty and surety companies are CASUALTY INSURANCE companies that also write fidelity and surety bonds.

Surety companies write fidelity bonds and surety bonds. They also sometimes write burglary, robbery, and forgery insurance.

Title insurance companies guarantee the right to real property. See also Chapter 15/REAL PROPERTY.

Multiple-line companies write all lines of insurance.

Previously, state laws prevented companies from writing certain combinations of coverages. For example, a fire insurance company could not write liability coverage and vice versa. However, most of these laws have been repealed.

Method of organization. A company may be organized as a MUTUAL INSURANCE COMPANY or a stock insurance company. The two differ in the manner of organization, ownership, and distribution of profits:

A *mutual insurance company* has policyholders who own the company and share in any profits through DIVIDENDS calculated as a percentage of the PREMIUMS they pay.

A *stock insurance company* sells shares of stock (representing ownership), and the individuals who buy the shares (stockholders) thereby own the company and share in any profits, usually through stock dividends.

A *reciprocal insurer* has subscribers who are insurers as well as the INSURED and are liable for a proportionate share of every RISK pooled except their own. Resembling a mutual company in many ways, this is a kind of unincorporated consumer cooperative insurer.

INSURANCE CONTRACT. An agreement by which one party (insurer), for a consideration known as a PREMIUM, promises to make a certain payment of money on the destruction of something or the injury of someone, which represents a loss to the INSURED. See also INSURABLE INTEREST.

The premium is usually paid in money either in one sum or at different times during the continuance of the RISK.

In FIRE INSURANCE and MARINE INSURANCE, the thing insured is property. In LIFE INSURANCE, HEALTH INSURANCE, or ACCIDENT INSURANCE, it is the life or health of a person.

Contracts have numerous clauses and provisions:

Declarations are the insured's statements concerning matters such as occupation and age.

Agreements concern the definition of perils insured against, losses covered, limits of liability, and other terms of the contract.

Exclusions state what is not covered.

Conditions state what must occur for a claim to be paid.

Renewal certificates are simplified versions of the original contract sent when premiums are due and the policy is continuous.

See also DEDUCTIBLE; DOUBLE INDEMNITY RIDER; ENDORSEMENT.

INSURANCE RECORDS. The records, often maintained by office personnel, concerning various PREMIUMS, coverages, expiration dates, and so on.

Life insurance. One should keep two classes of LIFE INSURANCE records: a manual or computer reminder of PREMIUM dates and a description of the policies. A premium distribution record also may be desirable.

The reminder for premium dates should list the following for each policy:

1. Name of the insured.
2. Name of company issuing the policy.
3. Policy number.
4. Due date of premium.
5. Amount of premium.
6. Date of payment.
7. To whom the premium is payable. Checks should be made out to the company, AGENT, or BROKER who bills the INSURED.
8. Name of the bank account used for a particular check (if more than one bank account is involved).
9. If DIVIDENDS are to be applied as part payment of a premium.
10. Where to mail the check.

Insurance other than life. The records that one might maintain for insurance other than life are determined by the extent of the particular insurance program and therefore may vary widely, depending on the situation. In most cases, though, a reminder of expiration dates must be kept and the following information recorded, regardless of the type of policy:

1. Name of the insured
2. Name of agent
3. Name of company issuing the policy
4. Policy number
5. Type of coverage and expiration date
6. Property covered
7. Due date of premium
8. Amount of premium
9. Date of payment
10. To whom the premium is payable
11. Where to mail the check

Whereas the premium distributions (due dates, payments, and so on) for all general and life policies may be recorded on the same sheet, a separate sheet or record should be kept for each kind of insurance on each piece of property.

INSURED.   The person, partnership, corporation, or association in whose name an insurance policy is written.

LEVEL PREMIUM.   A LIFE INSURANCE premium that remains the same—a fixed amount—through all the years that PREMIUMS are paid. This type of premium is different from a renewable TERM LIFE INSURANCE premium, which increases with the age of the policyholder.

LIABILITY INSURANCE.   Protection against unforeseen financial losses resulting from injury or property damage for which the INSURED is legally liable.

Examples of liability insurance are the *personal liability* section of HOMEOWNER'S INSURANCE and the *bodily-injury or property-damage* (commonly called (BIPD) coverage in AUTOMOBILE INSURANCE.

When the negligence of one party is responsible for a loss suffered by another, the injured party is entitled to recover damages from the party causing the loss.

Theoretically, for an injured party to recover damages, his or her loss must have been caused by negligence of the other party. However, the legal definition and interpretation of *negligence* are very broad. See also COMPARATIVE NEGLIGENCE; CONTRIBUTORY NEGLIGENCE.

Liability may be vicarious, absolute, or contractual:

Vicarious liability (or *contingent liability*) is indirect liability, such as an employer's responsibility for an employee's acts.

Absolute liability (or *strict liability*) means that one is liable for damages regardless of whether one is negligent.

Contractual liability occurs through a written agreement to indemnify someone for damages, such as to satisfy a buyer if a product is damaged or to indemnify a landlord if a leased apartment is damaged.

LIFE INSURANCE.   Individual or group coverage under which the insurer pays the INSURED's heir, or BENEFICIARY, a stated sum upon the death of the insured.

The amount payable to the beneficiary is the FACE AMOUNT of the policy plus any other benefit payable under the terms of the policy minus any outstanding loans.

The common forms of life insurance are WHOLE LIFE INSURANCE, TERM LIFE INSURANCE, and ENDOWMENT INSURANCE. See also LIMITED-PAYMENT INSURANCE; ORDINARY LIFE INSURANCE; SINGLE-PREMIUM INSURANCE; UNIVERSAL LIFE INSURANCE.

LIMITED-PAYMENT INSURANCE. LIFE INSURANCE for which the INSURED makes payments for a definite number of years, after which no more payments are required. The policy remains in force for life and affords the same protection as WHOLE LIFE INSURANCE.

LLOYD'S. Popularly known as *Lloyd's of London.* An insurance association incorporated in 1871 by an act of the British Parliament.

The association consists of several hundred insurance syndicates, each having numerous underwriters and each specializing in a particular RISK. The facility provides support for member activities but is itself not an INSURANCE COMPANY.

Lloyd's is traditionally known for its activity in MARINE INSURANCE, although it is also recognized worldwide for its importance in most other areas (except life).

LOAN INSURANCE. A form of coverage for loans that meets certain governmental requirements in areas such as housing projects. The loans are guaranteed and thus insured by the lenders.

LONG-TERM CARE INSURANCE. Coverage for patients, usually older than age 65, who need extended care in a nursing facility or in their residence because of an illness or injury or simply as a result of old age.

Private long-term care policies are usually purchased apart from and in addition to other health-insurance coverage. MEDICARE will pay a small part of the cost of nursing care.

Individuals who purchase long-term care policies at a young age generally have much lower PREMIUMS than do those who seek coverage when they are older.

The following are the three main types of long-term care for which coverage may be required:

1. Full-time *skilled nursing care,* usually in a nursing facility
2. *Intermediate care,* requiring some skilled nursing care and possibly some rehabilitation services
3. *Custodial care,* in which a patient needs some type of personal daily-living assistance

MARINE INSURANCE. Hull, cargo (freight), and liability contracts for marine interests. Marine insurance, the oldest branch of the insurance business, is subject to marine insurance laws. See also INLAND MARINE INSURANCE; OCEAN MARINE INSURANCE.

MEDICAID. The common name for Title XIX of the Social Security Act pertaining to comprehensive care and services for the needy and low-income people who qualify under the limits set by state law.

As a joint federal–state program, the federal government pays a percentage of administrative costs and payments made under state-administered programs to doctors, hospitals, and other vendors of medical care.

MEDICARE. The common name for hospital insurance and supplementary medical insurance for persons aged 65 and over, as well as for persons who are qualified as disabled, as provided by amendments to the Social Security Act.

Under Title XVIII, Part A, Medicare Basic Hospital Insurance, the federal government automatically pays a percentage of hospital costs, extended-care facility costs, and home health services costs.

Part B of the program, Supplemental Medical Insurance, is voluntary. Participants who pay a monthly PREMIUM receive medical services, supplies (such as artificial limbs), and home health services. Patients need not be hospitalized to receive such services.

MERIT RATING. A form of *experience rating* used to calculate a PREMIUM rate based on the loss experience of an INSURED group.

More complex than CLASS RATING, this system measures how a specific RISK differs from some standard so that the rate for that risk can be adjusted accordingly.

MORTALITY TABLE. A table based on the experience of LIFE INSURANCE companies that shows the probable number of years that any man or woman of a given age may be expected to live. Mortality tables form the basis of calculating the RISK factor in life insurance contracts.

MUTUAL INSURANCE COMPANY. An INSURANCE COMPANY owned by the policyholders. There are no shares of stock or stockholders in this type of company.

Net earnings are distributed to the policyholders in the form of DIVIDENDS calculated as a percentage of the PREMIUMS paid.

NAMED-PERILS POLICY. See ALL-RISK INSURANCE.

NATURAL PREMIUM. A *yearly renewable term premium* in which the amount collected each year is sufficient to pay for that year's coverage.

The PREMIUM is increased each year as the policyholder gets older. See also TERM LIFE INSURANCE.

NONOWNED AUTO LIABILITY INSURANCE. A form of LIABILITY INSURANCE that protects an employer against claims arising out of the operation of an automobile by an employee or others in connection with the employer's business.

In the case of nonowned auto liability insurance, the automobile involved in a claim is not owned, hired, loaned to, or registered in the name of the employer.

This type of insurance is necessary because the law of agency holds the principal responsible for the acts of his or her AGENT.

NONPARTICIPATING INSURANCE. See PARTICIPATING AND NONPARTICIPATING INSURANCE.

NUCLEAR-ENERGY LOSS INSURANCE. Coverage provided by insurers for injury to persons or loss of property caused by nuclear hazard.

OCEAN MARINE INSURANCE. Coverage against the perils of transportation at sea. This type of insurance protects the Insured against loss resulting from damage or destruction of a ship's hull or cargo.

Examples of perils encountered at sea are fire, collision with another ship, and piracy. Compare with INLAND MARINE INSURANCE.

OPEN FORM INSURANCE. Also called *reporting form insurance*. A policy covering property with varying values that contains a provision requiring periodic reports of value. This eliminates the problems of being overinsured or underinsured when inventories vary.

ORDINARY LIFE INSURANCE. Also called *straight life insurance*. A type of WHOLE LIFE INSURANCE for which PREMIUMS are based on the assumption that they will be paid until the death of the INSURED.

The policyholder therefore pays a definite sum every year until death, and the proceeds are payable at death to his or her BENEFICIARY or estate.

In addition, the policy also contains an investment or savings feature, whereby DIVIDENDS may be applied to reduce the premiums or increase the insurance.

OWNERS', LANDLORDS', AND TENANTS' LIABILITY INSURANCE. Protection against legal liability for accidents resulting in bodily injuries, death, or property damage arising out of ownership, occupation, or use of premises.

Coverage is available to owners or tenants of private residences, apartments, office and public buildings, and stores.

The *lessor* (landlord) and *lessee* (tenant) under a lease (see Chapter 15/LEASE) can protect themselves against liability for injuries sustained upon alleged failure to make necessary repairs of leased premises by carrying this form of insurance.

A policy will cover any judgment against the INSURED within the limits of coverage and will obligate the INSURANCE COMPANY to defend the insured even if claims are groundless.

PAID-UP LIFE INSURANCE POLICY. A LIFE INSURANCE policy for which the required PREMIUMS have been fully paid. For example, a ten-payment policy becomes a paid-up policy at the expiration of the ten-year period. A SINGLE-PREMIUM INSURANCE policy becomes a paid-up policy after the single premium is paid.

PARTICIPATING AND NONPARTICIPATING INSURANCE. A classification of insurance that indicates whether or not the policyholder receives DIVIDENDS:

With *participating insurance,* often issued by a MUTUAL INSURANCE COMPANY, the policyholder receives dividends from the INSURANCE COMPANY. The dividends are basically a refund arising from the savings, economies, and efficient management of the company.

With *nonparticipating insurance,* the policyholder does not receive dividends. However, the PREMIUM is often lower for nonparticipating contracts.

Stock companies, rather than mutual companies, generally issue nonparticipating contracts, although some also issue participating policies if the state law does not forbid it. When a *stock* company issues a nonparticipating contract, the *stockholders* rather than the policyholders share in any profits of the company.

PENSION PLAN. A plan maintained by an employer to provide retirement benefits to employees. A percentage of an employee's salary or wages is accumulated in a fund to be released in periodic payments upon the employee's retirement.

Employers sometimes handle GROUP INSURANCE and pension plans together as part of an overall benefits program.

PREFERRED PROVIDER ORGANIZATION (PPO). A particular physician, treatment facility, or other health-care provider that an insurer recommends to an INSURED. Participants pay PREMIUMS for their health coverage the same as do those who have conventional insurance policies.

The PPO is a combination of the traditional fee-based form of medical service and the newer HEALTH MAINTENANCE ORGANIZATION (HMO) system that requires the patient to have an approved personal care provider.

Under the PPO system, insurers negotiate with health-care facilities and physicians for better prices.

PREMIUM. The consideration of money that an insurer receives from an INSURED for the assumption of the liability or RISK or the hazard insured against. For various types of premiums, see LEVEL PREMIUM; NATURAL PREMIUM; SINGLE-PREMIUM INSURANCE.

PROPERTY INSURANCE. See INSURANCE, BUSINESS.

PUBLIC LIABILITY INSURANCE. See LIABILITY INSURANCE.

REINSURANCE. Insurance coverage for the insurer, rather than the INSURED, whereby part or all of an insurer's liability for a contract is transferred to another INSURANCE COMPANY, the *reinsurer.*

An insurance company needs reinsurance to protect itself when it writes a larger amount on a single insured party or in a single region than it can adequately handle should an excessive claim or an excessive group of claims arise.

RENT AND RENTAL-VALUE INSURANCE. Protection against the loss that results when property cannot be used because an insured-against event occurs and the income from it is therefore lost during this time.

Although property-damage policies cover damage to the physical property by fire or other causes, something else may be needed to cover the lost income during the interval that the property cannot be used because repairs are being made.

For example, a policy may be written to cover the rent that a property owner would have to pay for other quarters after his or her own property has become uninhabitable through damage. It may also provide for a tenant whose lease requires continuous rental payments even though the property has been destroyed.

RENTER'S INSURANCE. Also known as *tenant's insurance.* Coverage for the personal contents of a renter's place of residence and for liability.

The coverage includes the tenant's personal belongings and any improvements to the interior structure (including appliances) done or provided by the tenant.

REPLACEMENT-COST INSURANCE. A form of property insurance or an ENDORSEMENT designed to cover the cost of replacing lost property without any deduction for depreciation, as opposed to paying on the basis of ACTUAL CASH VALUE or depreciated value.

REPORTING FORM INSURANCE. See OPEN FORM INSURANCE.

RETIREMENT PLAN. A form of insurance that provides coverage for a specified period or up to a designated age and after that provides one or more payments to the INSURED. See also PENSION PLAN.

ENDOWMENT INSURANCE, for example, is payable at its FACE AMOUNT at the end of the endowment period if the insured is living at that time. A *retirement annuity,* on the other hand, provides a guaranteed number of payments beginning at a specified age.

RIDER. An ENDORSEMENT on an insurance policy.

RISK. The uncertainty about or the chance or possibility of suffering harm or loss if a given contingency occurs. For an individual or business to suffer a loss, some force must act to damage an object or injure a person so that the value of the object or person declines.

Insurance AGENTS and companies make risk-management concepts available to interested persons. They can help one identify and handle loss exposures.

SALVAGE. Generally, what is left of property after it has been damaged by fire or other perils. Salvage applies to property taken over by the insurer as partial reimbursement of the loss paid:

In property insurance, *salvage* is a contract clause generally specifying that the insurer may claim the damaged property after payment for the loss has been made.

In OCEAN MARINE INSURANCE, *salvage* refers to the property saved or the compensation due to those who voluntarily help to save a ship or cargo in danger.

SELF-INSURANCE. The self-retention of RISK. As an alternative to purchasing insurance from an INSURANCE COMPANY, one may elect to set aside one's own funds to pay for a loss that may occur later.

However, since a loss and the associated cost could be formidable, most individuals and businesses prefer to purchase the necessary insurance, or at least part of it, from an insurance company and use their own funds for other purposes.

SINGLE-PREMIUM INSURANCE. A LIFE INSURANCE contract in which the PREMIUM is paid in one sum. A premium of this kind is necessarily very large, but if the INSURED lives to an old age, the single premium is less than the sum that he or she would have paid in annual premiums.

SUBROGATION. The right of an insurer to recover from a third party that has caused injury or accident the amount that the insurer paid to an INSURED party for the insured's claim:

> *A*'s car is insured by an INSURANCE COMPANY against collision. *A*'s car is negligently damaged by *B*. The insurance company pays $2,000 for repairs to *A*'s car. The insurance company is therefore subrogated to *A*'s position and may prosecute the claim for damages against *B*.

SUPPLEMENTAL INSURANCE. Coverage that aims to protect a policyholder after benefits of the basic hospital contract have been used up. It may involve the use of a *corridor deductible,* which refers to the interim period between policies.

During this interim period, the INSURED is required to pay some of his or her expenses before protection from a supplemental insurance policy will begin.

TENANT'S INSURANCE. See RENTER'S INSURANCE.

TERM LIFE INSURANCE. Temporary LIFE INSURANCE obtainable for various periods.

The INSURANCE COMPANY agrees to pay a stipulated sum upon death, provided that death occurs within an agreed-on period, such as 1, 5, 10, 20, or more years. If the insured outlives the period, he or she receives nothing.

At younger ages, this type of policy costs less than any other life plan, but the price increases rapidly with age.

TITLE INSURANCE.   Also known as *title insurance policy, title guaranty policy,* and *guaranty title policy.* A contract by a title INSURANCE COMPANY guaranteeing to compensate the BENEFICIARY for any loss, up to a fixed amount, sustained through defects in title to real property. See also Chapter 15/REAL PROPERTY; TITLE.

A title company issuing its policy of insurance agrees to indemnify the BENEFICIARY against any loss that he or she may sustain by reason of any defects in title not enumerated as *exceptions* in the policy.

These defects may be discoverable defects disclosed by the public records or hidden defects, such as the forgery of a deed (see Chapter 15/DEED) in the chain of title.

Some title insurance also guarantees that the title is marketable, and the title insurance company agrees to defend, at its own expense, any action attacking the title based on a defect in the title insured. See also Chapter 15/MARKETABLE TITLE.

TRANSPORTATION INSURANCE.   See INLAND MARINE INSURANCE; OCEAN MARINE INSURANCE.

UNDERWRITER.   An employee of an INSURANCE COMPANY who evaluates RISKS and determines rates and coverages for them; more broadly, the home office of the insurer that classifies and finally accepts the risks in an INSURANCE CONTRACT.

In LIFE INSURANCE, the term *life underwriter* is sometimes used in referring to a life insurance agent.

UNDERWRITING.   The process of selecting RISKS and classifying the risks by degree of insurability in order to assign appropriate rates; the function of assuming a risk for another in return for a PREMIUM.

Underwriting departments have various selection procedures designed to spread their risk over a sufficient number and type of INSURED parties and to achieve profitable distribution of risks.

UNEMPLOYMENT INSURANCE. A form of unemployment protection that pays a weekly income to unemployed persons for a specified period. Funds are derived by means of a payroll tax.

The amount of funds paid to an unemployed person is based on the earnings of the employee before being laid off. Employers pay into the fund an amount based on an employee's rate of pay. See also WORKER'S COMPENSATION INSURANCE.

UNIVERSAL LIFE INSURANCE. A flexible-premium LIFE INSURANCE policy that accumulates cash value and has an adjustable death benefit. The owner may increase or decrease scheduled PREMIUMS, skip premiums, or make unscheduled premium payments.

Insurance coverage may be increased or decreased without having to buy a new policy. It can be tailored to meet specific needs during a lifetime.

WHOLE LIFE INSURANCE. A form of LIFE INSURANCE with coverage extending over the entire life of the INSURED, at a fixed PREMIUM. The premium may or may not be payable throughout life. See LIMITED-PAYMENT INSURANCE; SINGLE-PREMIUM INSURANCE; TERM LIFE INSURANCE.

WORKER'S COMPENSATION INSURANCE. Coverage that pays benefits to employees (or survivors) who are injured on the job or contract a job-related disease. It covers an employer's liability to his or her employees under worker's compensation laws, which have been enacted in all states.

Generally, these laws provide that every employee is entitled to recover from his or her employer certain prescribed amounts for job-related injury or disease.

Since the amount of payments an employer may be required to make within any one year is subject to wide fluctuation, most employers prefer to transfer to an INSURANCE COMPANY the obligation to compensate the employees. Such a transfer is effected by the purchase of worker's compensation insurance.

The methods that an employer may use to meet the liabilities imposed by the various worker's compensation insurance laws depend on the particular law of the state in which the employer conducts his or her business. In most states, the employer may choose from the following methods:

1. *Insurance in a state fund.*
2. *Insurance with a private insurance company.*

3. *Self-insurance.* SELF-INSURANCE of the worker's compensation RISK, on proof of solvency, is permitted in most of the states.

4. *Partial self-insurance.* Under this system, the employer assumes the liability for all losses under a specified amount. The excess risk is placed with a private insurance company.

See also Chapter 11/DISABILITY BENEFIT LAWS; WORKER'S COMPENSATION LAWS.

CHAPTER FIFTEEN

Real Estate

ABSTRACT COMPANY. See TITLE COMPANY.

ABSTRACT OF TITLE. Evidence of TITLE to REAL PROPERTY. An *abstract* is a condensed history of ownership of a particular tract of land.

Software programs with basic, fill-in abstract or title report forms are available, and these programs contain all the forms necessary for a REAL ESTATE CLOSING.

Contents of the abstract of title. An abstract consists of a summary of the material parts of every recorded instrument affecting the title, such as a lien (see Chapter 11/LIEN) or MORTGAGE. It concludes with the abstracter's certificate disclosing what records the abstracter has or has not examined.

Abstracters do not guarantee clear title to the real estate in question. Because of this and other inadequacies, the abstract of title is becoming obsolete in many places.

Title insurance. Most states are known as either an abstract state or a title insurance state. In a title insurance state, a TITLE COMPANY researches the chain of title and prepares a title report. The report outlines anything of record against the property but does not state the history of ownership.

After researching the chain of title and preparing a report, the title company issues a title insurance policy, which protects the buyer from prior claims against the title. See also Chapter 14/Title insurance.

Adverse possession. The *continuous* occupancy and use of Real property by one without legal Title and without the consent of the owner.

To acquire title by this means, a claimant must prove that he or she was in actual, open, notorious, hostile (against the rights of the owner), and exclusive possession for the statutory period.

The occupancy may result in the person's obtaining title to the land by remaining in possession for a number of years specified by state law. A limitation on the size of the claim is also governed by state law.

Agency. The relationship between a principal and an agent wherein the agent is authorized to represent the principal in transactions. See also Chapter 10/Agency.

In states that have enacted mandatory disclosure laws, real estate agents may be required to disclose whether they are representing the buyer, the seller, or both. Formerly, an agent represented only the seller.

Air rights. The right to the use or control of the air space over property. Such air rights may restrict the surface rights but usually allow the surface to be used for another purpose.

Examples of other rights that an owner may have, by state or local ordinance, Zoning, or Deed restrictions, are view rights and solar rights.

Appraisal. An estimation of the value of real estate based on factual analysis by qualified appraisers as of a specific date. Software programs are available to help appraisers prepare a detailed report.

The following are different approaches to the process of appraisal:

The *cost approach* adds the separately appraised parts of a property to arrive at the final value. Land value will be added to the cost of replacing a structure less depreciation.

The *income approach* uses the estimated future net income from the property as the basis for the appraisal of its present value.

The *market-value approach* compares the sales prices of recently sold similar properties.

APPURTENANCES. The incidental articles, rights, and interests that attach to and pass with the land, such as right-of-way, EASEMENT, and orchards.

ASSESSED VALUATION. The value at which REAL PROPERTY or personal property (see Chapter 11/PERSONAL PROPERTY) is appraised for tax purposes by the appropriate governmental authority. See also Chapter 11/ASSESSMENT; Chapter 13/ASSESSMENT.

BENEFICIARY. The person for whose benefit a TRUST DEED is given. See also Chapter 14/BENEFICIARY.

BINDER. See EARNEST MONEY; Chapter 14/BINDER.

BROKER. See REALTOR® AND REALTOR ASSOCIATE®.

BUYER'S BROKERAGE. See REALTOR® AND REALTOR ASSOCIATE®.

CERTIFICATE OF TITLE. A certification of the ownership of land, based on an examination of the record of title. A certificate of title is not used in all states.

An examiner researches the public records before issuing a certificate of title. However, the certificate is merely the examiner's *opinion* of the validity of the title based on those records. It offers no protection against hidden defects.

Thus an examiner does not guarantee the title but is liable for damages caused by his or her negligence.

For example, if the certificate failed to show a MORTGAGE that was recorded, the examiner would be liable to a buyer who relied on this certificate and purchased the property without knowledge of the mortgage.

Abstract companies, title companies, and lawyers prepare and issue certificates of title. See also ABSTRACT OF TITLE.

A certificate of title should not be confused with the registration of title under the TORRENS SYSTEM or with title insurance policies issued by a TITLE COMPANY. See also Chapter 14/TITLE INSURANCE.

CHATTEL MORTGAGE. See MORTGAGE; Chapter 11/PERSONAL PROPERTY.

CLOSING. See REAL ESTATE CLOSING.

CLOSING STATEMENT. See REAL ESTATE CLOSING.

CLOUD ON THE TITLE. An ENCUMBRANCE or outstanding claim on real estate, which, if valid, would impair or affect the owner's TITLE.

An example of a cloud is a dower interest or a judgment. (A *dower* interest is the interest in real estate that a deceased husband has given to his wife.) Court action or a quit-claim DEED may be necessary to remove a cloud.

COMMISSION. 1. The compensation paid to a real estate broker for services. (See REALTOR® AND REALTOR ASSOCIATE®.) The amount is usually a percentage of the sale price.

2. The *tribunal* charged with the administration and enforcement of real estate license laws.

COMMUNITY PROPERTY. A concept of property ownership in force in some states in which a husband and wife become equal and concurrent co-owners of all REAL PROPERTY and personal property (see Chapter 11/PERSONAL PROPERTY) acquired during marriage by their joint effort:

Property acquired in exchange for separate property is considered *separate property.*

Property acquired in exchange for community property is considered *community property.*

Statutes and judicial decisions have directed the development of the system along different lines in the various states. For example, in some states, only property acquired by the labor of either party is common. In other states, income from separate property is also community property.

COMPUTER LOAN ORIGINATION. The initiation of MORTGAGE loan applications via a computer network that allows real estate brokers, agents, and others to contact major lenders electronically and initiate loan applications in their offices. The person originating the loan may earn a fee.

This procedure has been approved by the Department of Housing and Urban Development (HUD) as being in compliance with the Real Estate Settlement Procedures Act (RESPA) if three conditions are met:

1. Full disclosure of the fee is made.

2. The fee is charged as a dollar amount rather than as a percentage of the loan.

3. Multiple lenders are displayed on the computer screen to give the borrower a basis for comparison.

CONDOMINIUM. Individual ownership of a unit in a multiunit structure, such as an apartment building.

This form of ownership is based on a legal description of the air space the unit actually occupies, combined with joint ownership of areas and facilities used in common.

CONTRACT OF EXCHANGE. A formal contract (see Chapter 11/CONTRACT) entered into between two owners of separate parcels of REAL PROPERTY concerning the transfer of that property.

The contract sets forth in full the terms of the agreement between them for the transfer of their properties to each other.

CONTRACT OF SALE. See PURCHASE AGREEMENT.

CONVEYANCE. The means or medium by which TITLE to REAL PROPERTY is transferred. Voluntary transfer of title during the lifetime of the owner is always accomplished by a written document known as a DEED.

See also Chapter 10/INSTALLMENT SALE; Chapter 11/CONTRACT; SALE.

COVENANTS. See Chapter 11/COVENANTS.

DEED. A formal written agreement by which TITLE to REAL PROPERTY is conveyed from one person to another.

A PURCHASE AGREEMENT is a contract (see Chapter 11/CONTRACT) to convey title, whereas a *deed* is the conveyance itself.

An exception is a TRUST DEED, an instrument that conveys only "naked," or "bare," legal title (title without the right of possession). See also MORTGAGE.

The parties to a deed are the *grantor,* who conveys his or her interest in the property, and the *grantee,* to whom the conveyance is made. The grantor is the seller, and the grantee is usually the buyer. However, a buyer may buy property for a grantee.

Forms of deeds. The following are common forms of deeds:

A *warranty deed* transfers title in FEE SIMPLE and also covenants and warrants (1) that the grantor has the right to transfer the title to the property and (2) that the grantee shall enjoy the premises quietly, forever.

A *bargain and sale deed* conveys title as effectively as a warranty deed, but it does not warrant the title against adverse claims or use of the property.

A *quit-claim deed* obtains a release from someone believed to have an interest in or claim to property, whether real or not.

A *deed of gift* is given in consideration of the "love and affection" that the grantor has for the grantee and passes title as completely as a deed for which there is monetary consideration.

A *statutory deed* is a short form used in some states to save space needed to record deeds. Certain covenants and warranties are made part of the deed by statute rather than being set forth in the deed itself.

A *fiduciary deed* may have a grantor as executor, administrator, trustee, guardian, receiver, or commissioner.

A *sheriff's deed* is one prepared by a sheriff for real estate sold at public sale.

Contents of deed.   A deed must state the following:

1. Execution date.
2. Grantor's full name; marital status; full name of spouse if spouse must join in the CONVEYANCE; whether grantor is an individual, partnership, or corporation; and full description of grantor's office and authority when acting as a representative.
3. Grantee's full name and residence.
4. Property description. See also LAND DESCRIPTION.
5. Type of deed.
6. *Consideration* (price paid for the property or motive for giving it).
7. Recital of any MORTGAGE or other ENCUMBRANCE.
8. *Habendum clause* stating that the grantee is to have the property transferred to him or her.
9. *Covenants* (promises made by grantor and grantee).
10. *Testimonium clause* (closing clause immediately preceding signature).
11. Names and official position of officers signing and acknowledging deed (if grantor is corporation).

Fill-in deed forms, along with other documents used in the sale of property, are available in software programs used by TITLE COMPANIES and lawyers.

Deed restrictions. Covenants (see Chapter 11/COVENANTS), conditions, and other restrictions placed on property beyond the limits enacted by zoning or other governmental rules or regulations.

DEPRECIATION OF PROPERTY. See Chapter 12/DEPRECIATION.

DISCLOSURE. The requirement imposed on sellers, who are obligated by law in some states, to disclose all known material facts about a property to the buyer in a Seller's Property Disclosure Statement (SPDS).

The SPDS, which is completed by the seller, is not intended to be a binding contract. It may contain information about ownership and property, buildings and safety, utilities, environmental matters, waste disposal, lead-based paint hazards, and other conditions and factors.

DOWN PAYMENT. See EARNEST MONEY.

EARNEST MONEY. Evidence of good faith given by a buyer in the form of a deposit of money, down payment, or binder. See also Chapter 14/BINDER.

EASEMENT. The right or privilege to make some use of land belonging to another. An easement may terminate at some future time based on a certain time element or the occurrence of a certain event.

The most common easements are right-of-way, right-of-drainage, right to suspend power lines, and right to lay pipelines beneath the surface:

A *private right-of-way* is generally created by a grant from or an agreement with the owner of land over which the right-of-way exists.

A *public right-of-way* is the right of the public to use public streets, roads, and highways.

An easement may be established in a number of ways:

By *agreement,* which may simply be a commonly held opinion regarding the right and not necessarily a contract

By *prescription,* when adverse use of the land has been open and continuous for a period of time (see ADVERSE POSSESSION) and a court grants the right on the presumption that a written easement was given

By *necessity,* when the right is granted by a court on the basis of the absolute necessity for use of the land, as opposed to mere convenience

EMINENT DOMAIN. See Chapter 11/EMINENT DOMAIN.

ENCUMBRANCE. A claim or charge against property, such as a MORTGAGE, that lowers its value. See also CLOUD ON THE TITLE; Chapter 11/LIEN.

EQUITABLE TITLE. A person's right to obtain absolute ownership of property to which another person has TITLE at law.

EQUITY OF REDEMPTION. See Chapter 13/REDEMPTION.

ESCHEAT. The reversion of property to the county or state, according to state law (1) when a person dies without a will and no heirs are legally entitled to inherit the property or (2) when property has been abandoned.

ESCROW. A deposit of funds and documents, along with written instructions, to a third party called an *escrow agent* (a disinterested, neutral party), who holds the funds or something of value in trust for another.

The documents and funds must be delivered in accordance with written escrow instructions, which may be changed by agreement of the parties. See also EARNEST MONEY.

Escrow instructions are used when a transaction is closed through an escrow. The document specifies the duties of the escrow agent, as well as the obligations and requirements of the parties to the escrow.

ESTATE. The quantity of ownership of REAL PROPERTY. Estates may be categorized in various ways:

Freehold estates include FEE SIMPLE, which gives complete ownership of the property without ENCUMBRANCE or condition.

Less-than-freehold estates are granted for a defined and limited period. See also LEASEHOLD.

Life estates grant ownership of property for the lifetime of an individual.

Conditional fee estates have some limit or condition to the CONVEYANCE of the property, such as a requirement to use it for a specific purpose, as for a church. The property reverts to the grantor upon the cessation of such use.

Estates at will do not require any formal notice before termination. Therefore, they may be terminated at will.

Estates at sufferance exist when a person extends possession of property beyond the expiration of his or her legal term.

ESTATE IN REAL PROPERTY. The right or interest in the use, enjoyment, and disposition of land and improvements attached to it. See also FEE SIMPLE; JOINT TENANCY; TENANCY BY THE ENTIRETY; TENANCY IN COMMON.

FEE SIMPLE. The absolute ownership of REAL PROPERTY. It gives the owner and his or her heirs the unconditional power of disposition and other rights.

FORECLOSURE. The legal process of obtaining possession of mortgaged property upon the failure of the mortgagor to meet his or her obligations under the MORTGAGE or TRUST DEED.

In some states, foreclosure is handled by advertisement and sale, held in accordance with the legal technicalities prescribed by the state statutes. In most states, foreclosure is undertaken by litigation, which shuts out or bars the mortgagor's equity of redemption. See also Chapter 13/REDEMPTION.

Before taking further steps, an attorney must file the required summons, complaint, and LIS PENDENS. See also Chapter 11/COMPLAINT; SUMMONS.

Thereafter, the attorney will apply for receivership, arrange for a hearing before a referee or master, and, finally, arrange for sale of the foreclosed property. The specific steps depend on the case and the jurisdiction.

FREEHOLD ESTATE. Ownership of REAL PROPERTY for an indeterminate time, as opposed to a LEASEHOLD estate, which is property rented for a specific term.

HOMESTEAD. Real estate occupied by the owner as a home at the time of filing the Declaration of Homestead (can only be filed by the head of a household).

In many states, a homestead protects the equity in a property against judgments and from liability in any form for the debts of the owner (excluding property taxes, Mortgages, and mechanic's liens), up to specific limits according to state statutes. See also Chapter 11/Lien; Chapter 12/Property tax.

INSTALLMENT SALE. See Chapter 10/Installment sale.

INTEREST RATE. See Chapter 13/Interest.

JOINT TENANCY. Also called *joint estate.* Undivided interest in property held by two or more persons who acquire the same estate at the same time and by the same Title or source of ownership, each having the same degree of interest (including Right of survivorship), and each having the same right of possession as the others.

The distinguishing characteristic of a joint tenancy is that upon the death of one of the joint tenants, his or her interest automatically passes to the others by survivorship.

However, the courts don't favor joint tenancies and in many jurisdictions permit joint tenants to defeat the right of survivorship by Mortgage or Conveyance.

Some states have passed retroactive statutes making existing undivided interests Tenancy in common, unless a contrary intent plainly appears in the instrument sufficient to negate the presumption of a tenancy in common.

LAND DESCRIPTION. Identification of a tract of land contained and required in Deeds, Mortgages, and assignments of Leases.

To avoid dispute and litigation, land should always be described according to one of the following methods, known as the *record,* or *legal, description:*

Metes and bounds

Rectangular survey system

Recorded plat (lot and block) system

The accepted method depends on the state or locality within a state.

Metes and bounds. A description of land that is characterized by the lines that constitute its boundaries, with terminal points and angles. Boundaries might consist of a natural landmark, such as a river, or an artificial one, such as a railroad.

Metes formerly referred to distance and *bounds* to direction, but those definitions are no longer strictly observed.

Rectangular survey system. A description of land that is characterized by rectangular tracts, located with reference to base lines running east and west and *prime*, or *principal*, *meridians* running north and south.

The tracts are divided into six-mile-square *townships,* which in turn are each divided into 36 sections. See Figures 1 and 2.

The description of five acres of land identified by the section and township system might read as follows:

> The East Half of the Northeast Quarter of the Northeast Quarter of the Northeast Quarter of Section One, Township 39 North, Range 12 East of the Third Prime Meridian.

LAND DESCRIPTION: FIGURE 2: Section of Township

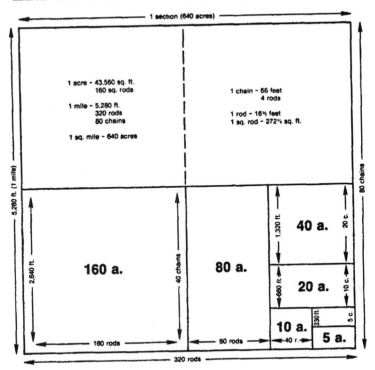

LAND DESCRIPTION: FIGURE 2:
Township Divided into Sections

The recorded plat (lot and block) system. A description of land that is characterized by further division of tracts into streets, blocks, and lots. Maps or plans of these divisions are called *plats.*

A *plat book* is a public record containing maps of land showing the division of the land into streets, blocks, and lots and indicating the measurements of the individual parcels:

> Lot Ten (10), Block Eight (8), Bay Shore Subdivision, as recorded in Volume 5 of Plats, Page 39, records of Blank County, State of Arizona.

Preparation of descriptions. The land, or legal, descriptions to be included in an instrument are usually copied from some earlier document, such as an ABSTRACT OF TITLE, or from a survey. In the absence of other instructions, follow these general guidelines:

1. Single-space descriptions, with a double space between paragraphs.
2. Do not abbreviate *Street, Avenue, Road, Boulevard,* and so on in the text.
3. Write the words *North, Northeast, South, West, Southwest,* and so on with initial capitals, but do not capitalize the words *northerly, northeasterly,* and so on.
4. Capitalize *Quarter, Township, Section, Range,* and the name or number of a *Prime Meridian.*
5. Write courses as follows: *South twenty (20) degrees, thirty-three (33) minutes, forty-five (45) seconds West.*

6. Write distances as follows: *One hundred thirty-three and twenty-nine one hundredths (133.29) feet.*

7. When several courses and distances are given in succession, write each separately, indented and single-spaced, with a double space between them.

8. Do not use figures, symbols, or abbreviations unless necessary because of limited space.

Land, or legal, descriptions are usually available to the public from the county offices records division.

Interested persons can retrieve the information on-line from the county courthouse. Real estate agents and others may have access to the information through their on-line connection with a local multiple listing service (MLS) office.

Records are usually listed by property parcel numbers and cross-referenced by owners' names and addresses.

Computers and microfiche are commonly used for storing the records, and the plat maps also may be scanned into computers for easier maintenance and access.

The *original* plat maps are often retained as individual maps and filed in a suitable folder. Although the term *plat map book* is common, it usually refers simply to a group of plat maps, rather than to a book.

LANDLORD.   See LEASE.

LEASE.   A contract (see Chapter 11/CONTRACT), written or oral, under which the owner of REAL PROPERTY grants the use, possession, and occupancy of the property to another. The owner is called the *landlord,* or *lessor,* and the person leasing is called the *tenant,* or *lessee.*

The contract sets forth in detail the terms and conditions upon which the lessor grants the use and possession of the property to the lessee. In most states, the statutes provide that leases for periods in excess of one year must be in writing to be enforceable.

Office-supply stores and real estate and PROPERTY MANAGEMENT software programs have standard fill-in lease forms. Sample forms may also be found in real estate reference books in libraries and bookstores.

Local real estate multiple listing services (MLSs) and state Realtor® association offices frequently have state-approved printed forms available for purchase by members and state-licensed brokers and agents.

The following are among the various forms of leases:

A *straight lease,* in which the same amount or rent is paid periodically, such as monthly, throughout the lease term.

A *sale and leaseback,* in which the buyer of property leases it back to the seller.

A *graded,* or *step-up, lease,* which calls for prescribed rent increases at designated intervals.

A *lease with option to purchase,* which gives the lessee the right to buy the leased property within a specified time.

A *long-term lease,* which is the lease of land for an extended period, generally 99 years, with an obligation on the part of the tenant to improve and maintain the leased property within a given period. The tenant also pays the property taxes (see Chapter 12/PROPERTY TAX) and periodically pays RENT.

LEASEHOLD. An ESTATE IN REAL PROPERTY granted for a definite number of years under the terms of a LEASE. Compare with FREEHOLD ESTATE.

LIEN. See Chapter 11/LIEN.

LIS PENDENS. The notice filed with the clerk of court that FORECLOSURE of a MORTGAGE is pending.

LISTING. A contract or agreement (see Chapter 11/CONTRACT) under which the owner of REAL PROPERTY employs a broker (see REALTOR® AND REALTOR ASSOCIATE®) to find a buyer who will agree to buy the property at the price and on the terms fixed in the contract:

An *exclusive listing* gives the listing broker the exclusive right to market the property to other brokers (who work as his or her subagents), as well as to the public.

An *exclusive agency listing* is the same as an *exclusive right to sell,* except that the owner, or principal, reserves the right to sell the property himself or herself without being obligated to pay the broker's COMMISSION.

An *open,* or *nonexclusive, listing* allows the owner to employ a broker to negotiate with respect to the property but does not forbid him or her from engaging other brokers for the same purpose or from disposing of the property personally.

The *multiple listing service (MLS)* provides each member with the listings of other brokers, and the broker who initially received the listing gets a percentage of the commission of any other member who may sell the property.

Any fees for the listing of a property in the multiple listing, or *multilist,* service are usually a set amount (not a percentage) and are usually paid by the listing broker.

Real estate offices commonly have software programs that link them with a local MLS office. This enables the office to send and revise its company listings simply by filling in the necessary blanks.

Individual offices also have software programs that enable users to store, revise, and update the status of a listing, such as sales pending, listing expiration, and sales closed. See also ON-LINE INFORMATION.

MARKETABLE TITLE. Also known as *merchantable title.* A TITLE free from defects or flaws that would disturb a buyer's peaceful possession and enjoyment of the property or its market value. A title is not marketable if there is risk of litigation regarding its validity.

A seller is generally required to convey marketable title to a buyer, unless the PURCHASE AGREEMENT provides otherwise. Whether or not a title is marketable depends on the facts of each case and the terms of the agreement.

MECHANIC'S LIEN. See Chapter 11/LIEN.

MORTGAGE. 1. A conditional CONVEYANCE. A mortgage is given by a borrower or debtor (*mortgagor*) to a lender (*mortgagee*) to secure the payment of a debt, with a provision that the conveyance will become void on the payment of the debt by a specified date.

A mortgage may be given on REAL PROPERTY or personal property. (See Chapter 11/PERSONAL PROPERTY.) A mortgage on tangible personal property is referred to as a *chattel mortgage,* whereas a mortgage on real estate is referred to simply as a *mortgage.*

Some mortgages cover both real and personal property, such as a mortgage on a furnished apartment building.

2. The instrument used to make the conveyance. The debt is evidenced by a promissory note. (See Chapter 13/NOTE.) The mortgage is the security instrument that secures payment of the note.

In some states, the debt is evidenced by a bond (see Chapter 13/BOND) instead of a promissory note. Frequently, the bond and mortgage are combined in one instrument, referred to as a *bond and mortgage.*

Forms of mortgage. Many forms of mortgage are available, including the following:

A *conventional mortgage* is essentially a DEED stating that the mortgage will be void when the debt is paid.

A *deed of trust* or a *trust mortgage* conveys land to a third party, who holds it until the debt is paid. See also TRUST DEED.

A *second mortgage* is an additional debt or claim that is subordinate to the first mortgage.

A *purchase money mortgage* is one that is given as partial payment of the purchase price.

An *open-end mortgage* allows one to reborrow up to the amount of the original loan.

A *closed-end mortgage* prevents the property from being used as security for another loan.

An *asssumable mortgage* permits the loan to be transferred to the next buyer without any change in terms.

A *wrap-around mortgage* is used when a seller wants to keep his or her assumable low-interest loan. (See Chapter 13/INTEREST.) The seller continues making payments on the low-interest loan and lends additional funds to the buyer, who pays the seller a higher interest rate on the entire amount owed.

An *adjustable-rate mortgage (ARM),* also called *variable-rate mortgage (VRM),* offers an interest rate that is adjustable throughout the life of the loan based on selected indexes. Payments therefore change accordingly. Most ARMs have caps to protect the parties from excessive changes in the interest rate.

A *reverse mortgage,* also called *reverse equity mortgage* or *reverse annuity mortgage,* provides that a homeowner will receive a series of small payments, to be repaid to the lender in one lump sum at a designated time. Older people who own their own homes may seek this type of mortgage as a means of receiving steady income.

Contents of a mortgage. A mortgage commonly includes the following:

1. A description of the debt.
2. An indication that it is void when paid (*defeasance clause*).
3. A statement of the *consideration* (either the amount of indebtedness or a nominal consideration).
4. An acceleration clause. See Chapter 11/ACCELERATION CLAUSE.
5. A description of the property.
6. A statement of any prepayment privilege.
7. A statement whether the mortgagor may sell part of the land (*partial-release clause*).

Standard conventional mortgage forms are usually prepared by a mortgage broker or the lender and are available on their software programs. When completed, the loan documents become part of the ESCROW.

Title companies usually prepare other types of loan documents for the escrow, such as the TRUST DEED and installment sale agreement (see Chapter 10/INSTALLMENT SALE), also known as the *land contract.* Such forms are available on TITLE COMPANY software programs.

MULTIPLE LISTING SERVICE. See LISTING.

NONCONFORMING USE. The continued use of property that is allowed after a ZONING ORDINANCE has been established prohibiting such use.

ON-LINE INFORMATION. Information about LISTINGS, geographic locations, and other real estate matters available on Web sites (see Chapter 6/WEB SITE) and various software programs.

Web sites. Large companies with nationally franchised real estate offices usually have a Web site that provides information about housing, cost of living, jobs, schools, crime, transportation, arts and recreation, banking services, and climate, as well as a directory of all office locations in a particular area.

Many individually franchised offices and other independently owned offices also have Web sites where their company listings are advertised with pictures of the property and information about price, size, location, and so on.

The National Association of Realtors® has a Web site where real estate agents or company members may set up a Web page for marketing their listings and their services.

Free real estate advertising magazines also have ads that include Web site locations for geographical areas where real estate companies and individual agents display their listings. E-mail addresses and Web sites are usually included in most printed real estate advertising.

Software programs. Real estate office-management software programs supplement the use of the Internet (see Chapter 6/INTERNET) and other on-line sources of information.

Many programs enable users to manage every aspect of real estate office activities, such as sales management, listings, accounting, forms, financial reports, scheduling, personnel, payroll, referrals, and transactions.

OPEN-HOUSING LAW. See Chapter 11/OPEN-HOUSING LAW.

OPINION OF TITLE. See ABSTRACT OF TITLE.

OPTION. See Chapter 11/OPTION.

PARCEL. A specific portion of a tract or plot of land, such as a lot.

PREPAYMENT PENALTY. A charge imposed on a borrower who pays off the loan principal early. The penalty compensates the lender for interest and other charges lost. See also Chapter 13/INTEREST.

PROPERTY MANAGEMENT. The business of operating income properties, such as office buildings. See also LEASE; REAL PROPERTY.

A property manager acts as agent for a property owner and, for a fee, seeks to maximize the income obtainable from the property. This is accomplished by keeping up the facilities, servicing tenants, and attempting to have the property fully rented at all times.

Some states require property management companies to have all financial transactions computerized for auditing purposes.

Property management database programs are available for most functions of the business, such as lease-expiration dates, property-availability lists, maintenance-work-order scheduling and records, tenant ledgers, and rent rolls.

State-approved lease forms are available from local and state Realtor® associations, and standard forms are available from office-supply stores. Samples also may be found in real estate reference books in libraries and bookstores.

Some property management and real estate offices either devise and print their own forms by computer or have them prepared by an attorney.

PROPERTY TAXES.   See Chapter 12/PROPERTY TAX.

PURCHASE AGREEMENT.   Depending on the area, also called *contract of sale, offer to purchase, sales contact, contract of purchase and sale, purchase contract,* and various other terms. A formal written contract (see Chapter 11/CONTRACT) entered into between a seller (VENDOR) and a buyer (VENDEE) of REAL PROPERTY.

Content.   The purchase agreement sets forth in full all terms of the agreement between the parties for the CONVEYANCE of TITLE within a specified time.

The instrument also sets in motion the various investigations of title and ENCUMBRANCES, arrangements for financing, and preparation of instruments to be signed upon closing title. See also REAL ESTATE CLOSING.

It's important that the agreement be prepared carefully to include all terms between the buyer and seller and to state them clearly. If any dispute should arise, the courts will not admit any oral testimony in variance of the written contract.

Forms and copies.   Local boards of Realtors® offices usually have a variety of printed state and local forms available for purchase by members and other state-licensed brokers and agents.

These forms also may be found on software programs, and samples are available in office-supply stores and real estate reference books in libraries and bookstores.

At least four copies of a purchase agreement are needed: an original and duplicate original for the buyer and seller, a copy for the real estate broker (see REALTOR® AND REALTOR ASSOCIATE®), and a copy for the files.

REAL ESTATE CLOSING. The transaction between a seller and a buyer and their representatives in which the formalities of a sale are executed.

Preliminary steps. When a buyer agrees to purchase property, he or she generally pays a deposit (see EARNEST MONEY) and enters into a contract with the seller. See PURCHASE AGREEMENT; Chapter 11/CONTRACT.

The contract designates a certain day, and sometimes an hour, when the DEED and MORTGAGE, if any, shall be delivered and the balance of the purchase price paid.

The initial contract sets in motion the various investigations, as well as the preparation of papers that are signed at the closing. The buyer has the title searched, informs the seller of any ENCUMBRANCES that must be removed before the closing, and makes arrangements for financing.

Closing documents. The documents are prepared by the seller's attorney or by the ESCROW agent of a TITLE COMPANY in some states. These documents may consist of any or all of the following:

1. Purchase money MORTGAGE and bond. See also Chapter 13/BOND.
2. DEED.
3. Affidavit of TITLE. See also Chapter 11/AFFIDAVIT.
4. Estoppel certificate. See also Chapter 11/ESTOPPEL.
5. Assignment of LEASES, if any. See also Chapter 11/ASSIGNMENT.
6. *Indemnity agreement,* whereby one party agrees to repay the other for loss or damages that the other suffers.
7. IRS Form 1099-S (the closing agent's report to the Internal Revenue Service).
8. Letter to tenants, if any, giving notice of the sale.
9. Closing, or settlement, statement.

The deed is the most important closing item, although all papers are examined to make certain that they are in order, signed, and exchanged and that payments are made.

The *closing statement* is an accounting of funds in a real estate sale made by a broker to the seller and buyer, respectively. This statement is prepared by an escrow agent when a title company is used.

Usually, a memo of the closing and a financial statement are prepared.

The transfer of title is complete when the deed has been signed, sealed, and delivered.

A closing in a title insurance state (see Chapter 14/TITLE INSURANCE) is usually not a formal meeting of the parties but rather the reference made regarding the recording of the title transfer in the county recorder's office and the delivery of the deed to the buyer.

REAL ESTATE RECORDS. The files and other records that must be maintained to determine taxes on property held for the production of income. See also Chapter 12/PROPERTY TAX.

Taxes on income-producing property are included in the group of deductions and adjustments that are subtracted from gross income to arrive at adjusted gross income. See also Chapter 12/ADJUSTED GROSS INCOME; DEDUCTIONS/ADJUSTMENTS; GROSS INCOME.

The records that are kept for income-producing property should list all pertinent expenses involved in producing the income.

Examples of expenses that may be deductible in computing net RENT are building maintenance, casualty losses, decorating, depreciation (building and equipment), interest on a MORTGAGE, liability insurance, management fees, real estate taxes, repairs, and theft.

REAL ESTATE TAXES. See Chapter 12/PROPERTY TAX.

REAL PROPERTY. The land, APPURTENANCES, and improvements attached to it. All other property is personal property. See also Chapter 11/PERSONAL PROPERTY.

Real property therefore includes not only the land but also the buildings, natural growth, minerals, and timber that have not been separated from the land, as well as the air space above it. For example, apples on a tree constitute real property, but the harvested apples are personal property.

An interest in real property is an ESTATE and ranges from an estate in FEE SIMPLE (absolute ownership) to a LEASEHOLD (the right to use property during a fixed term for a specific consideration).

An *estate* is a designation of a particular type of interest in property, not a legal entity. Other forms of estate are modifications and limitations of a fee simple estate.

See also JOINT TENANCY; TENANCY BY THE ENTIRETY ; TENANCY IN COMMON.

REALTOR® AND REALTOR ASSOCIATE®. Registered trademarks of the National Association of Realtors® that may be used only in reference to members of that association.

Therefore, not every real estate licensee is a *Realtor®* or *Realtor Associate®*. The following are other terms describing persons or firms that provide real estate services:

A *real estate broker* is an intermediary who, for a fee, COMMISSION, or other valuable consideration, brings parties together and assists them in negotiating a contract involving REAL PROPERTY. (See Chapter 11/CONTRACT.) Generally, a broker acts as an agent for one of the parties.

Help-you-sell brokers usually provide less than full service. For example, the seller rather than the broker may show the property to prospective buyers. For marketing and other assistance, the broker will charge a flat fee or discounted commission.

A *buyer's broker(age)* represents buyers instead of sellers.

RECORDING. The act of entering or recording in the county recorder's office the documents that affect or convey interest in real estate.

A DEED or MORTGAGE generally is not effective against subsequent purchases or mortgages until it is recorded. Normally, the first to record has the first right.

REFINANCING. The renewal of a loan with the same lender. Often, the intent of a borrower in refinancing is to reduce the interest rate of a MORTGAGE if rates have fallen since the original purchase. See also Chapter 13/INTEREST.

RENT. Regular, periodic payments by a tenant to a landlord for the use of REAL PROPERTY. Rent is taxable income.

RIGHT OF SURVIVORSHIP. The right of a survivor to the property of the deceased. This right distinguishes a JOINT TENANCY from a TENANCY IN COMMON. In a joint tenancy, the deceased owner's interest goes to the other, surviving owner rather than to his or her heirs or next of kin.

If an owner sells his or her interest to a new owner, the other owners will continue to share their joint tenancy. But the new owner will hold tenancy in common with them, without the right of survivorship.

RIGHT-OF-WAY. See EASEMENT.

RIPARIAN RIGHTS. A landowner's right of access to and reasonable use of the flowing water located on, under, or adjacent to a landowner's property.

SALE AND LEASEBACK. See LEASE.

TENANCY BY THE ENTIRETY. Also called *tenancy by the entireties.* An estate held by husband and wife by virtue of TITLE acquired by them jointly after marriage. Upon the death of either spouse, his or her interest automatically passes to the other by RIGHT OF SURVIVORSHIP.

A tenancy by the entirety cannot be terminated without the consent of both parties. Thus neither spouse can defeat the right of survivorship by MORTGAGE or CONVEYANCE without the consent of the other.

The courts do not look with disfavor upon a tenancy by the entirety as they do upon a JOINT TENANCY. However, not all states recognize tenancy by the entirety. In many states, an absolute divorce terminates the estate by entirety, converting it into an estate in common.

TENANCY IN COMMON. An estate held by two or more persons by separate and distinct TITLE, with unity of possession only.

Co-ownership. If a DEED is made to two or more persons who are not husband and wife, and nothing is said in the deed concerning the character of the estate it creates, the estate is a *tenancy in common.*

The co-owners are tenants in common. They need not have acquired their titles at the same time or by the same instrument, and their shares need not be equal. For example, one may have an undivided one-tenth interest and the other the remaining undivided nine-tenths interest.

Rights of co-owners. Tenants in common are entitled to share the possession of the property according to their shares in it. Except for their sharing of possession and income, however, the situation is almost as if each one owned a separate piece of real estate.

Each tenant in common may convey or MORTGAGE his or her interest, and the interest of each is subject to the lien or judgments against him or her. See also Chapter 11/LIEN.

Upon death, a tenant's interest passes to his or her heirs and *legatees* (one who inherits something in a will) and not to the other tenant in common. Compare with JOINT TENANCY.

TESTIMONIUM CLAUSE. See Chapter 11/TESTIMONIUM CLAUSE.

TITLE. All of the elements that prove ownership. *Title* to REAL PROPERTY is evidence of ownership and indicates a person's right to possess, use, and dispose of property. See also ADVERSE POSSESSION; CLOUD ON THE TITLE; MARKETABLE TITLE.

Equitable title is ownership of property to which another has title under the law. The term is also used in reference to the right to demand that title to the property be conveyed. See also MORTGAGE.

Title search. A *title search* is common before property is sold or involved in litigation. This involves a thorough investigation of the documented title to, or ownership of, property, along with any liens (see Chapter 11/LIEN) or ENCUMBRANCES against it, as listed in the public records.

Evidence of title. Proof that a seller has apparent good title to property to be conveyed is evidenced by title insurance (see Chapter 14/TITLE INSURANCE), ABSTRACT OF TITLE, CERTIFICATE OF TITLE, or the TORRENS SYSTEM.

Title insurance is customary as evidence in urban centers, an *abstract of title* and opinion is widely used in rural areas of the Midwest, and a *certificate of title* is popular in southern states. The *Torrens system* is used in only a few localities throughout the United States.

TITLE COMPANY. Also known as *abstract company* in some states. A business organization that searches land records and summarizes all recorded instruments that affect title to a particular tract of land. See also ABSTRACT OF TITLE; LAND DESCRIPTION.

TITLE INSURANCE. See ABSTRACT OF TITLE; Chapter 14/TITLE INSURANCE.

TORRENS SYSTEM. A system, named after Sir Robert Torrens in the 1800s, that provides for the registration of a clear TITLE to REAL PROPERTY instead of the recording of evidence of title under the recording system.

The Torrens system is less perilous than the recording system, from which buyers must draw their own conclusions about whether a title is in fact clear—hence the need for a CERTIFICATE OF TITLE or title insurance. See also Chapter 14/TITLE INSURANCE.

Under the Torrens system, a landowner who wants to register first obtains a complete ABSTRACT OF TITLE to the land. He or she then files an application for the registration of title in the proper public office.

After a certain legal procedure, the court orders the registrar of titles to prepare a certificate and register the title.

When land registered under the Torrens system sells, the DEED must be taken to the registrar's office, where the registrar issues a new certificate to the grantee.

A MORTGAGE or judgment lien (see Chapter 11/LIEN) is not effective until a notation has been entered on the certificate of title in the registrar's office.

TOWNHOUSE. A single-family house of two or sometimes three stories that is connected to a similar house by a common sidewall. Townhouses are frequently found in CONDOMINIUM associations.

TRUST DEED. Also called *deed of trust.* An instrument used to arrange financing of real estate (similar to a MORTGAGE). See also DEED; Chapter 11/TRUST DEED.

A trust deed conveys only "naked," or "bare," legal TITLE to property (title without the right of possession) from the grantor (trustor–debtor) to the grantee (trustee) for the benefit of a BENEFICIARY (creditor–lender) as collateral security for a debt.

The trustee holds such title only as is necessary to carry out the terms of the lien document (see Chapter 11/LIEN) until the debt is paid. It is said to be a MORTGAGE with a built-in power of sale.

VARIANCE. Permission to use property for something that is an exception to an existing ZONING ORDINANCE.

VENDEE. One who enters into a PURCHASE AGREEMENT and agrees to purchase the REAL PROPERTY of another (the VENDOR). Every purchase agreement must have a vendee.

The buyer may be an individual, a partnership, a corporation, or a representative, such as an executor or personal representative. See also Chapter 10/CORPORATION; PARTNERSHIP:

If the buyer is an *individual,* he or she must be an adult of sound mind.

If the buyer is a *partnership,* a certificate of partnership must be recorded before the close of ESCROW. This certificate must state the names of the partners, their addresses, and an authorization for the individuals signing.

If the buyer is a *corporation,* the corporation's board of directors must authorize the purchase. See also Chapter 10/BOARD OF DIRECTORS.

If the buyer is a *representative,* the contract should set forth the source of his or her authority.

VENDOR.   One who enters into a PURCHASE AGREEMENT and agrees to sell REAL PROPERTY to another (the VENDEE). Every purchase agreement must have a vendor.

The seller may be an individual, a partnership, a corporation, or a representative, such as an executor or personal representative. See also Chapter 10/CORPORATION; PARTNERSHIP:

If the seller is an *individual,* he or she must be an adult of sound mind.

If the seller is a *partnership,* a certificate of partnership must be recorded before the close of ESCROW. This certificate must state the names of the partners, their addresses, and an authorization for the individuals signing.

If the seller is a *corporation,* the corporation's board of directors must authorize the sale. See also Chapter 10/BOARD OF DIRECTORS.

If the seller is a *representative,* the contract should set forth the source of his or her authority.

ZONING.   A regulation whereby land use is restricted to specific purposes and building construction is controlled as to type, intensity, and volume. The regulation is enforced under police powers by municipalities and states and is applied to the use of both lands and buildings.

Most cities and large towns in the United States have regulatory zoning laws that have a powerful influence on land values.

ZONING ORDINANCE.   The regulation and control of the character and use of property through the exercise of police power by the governing municipality.

PART FOUR

HELPFUL REFERENCE AIDS

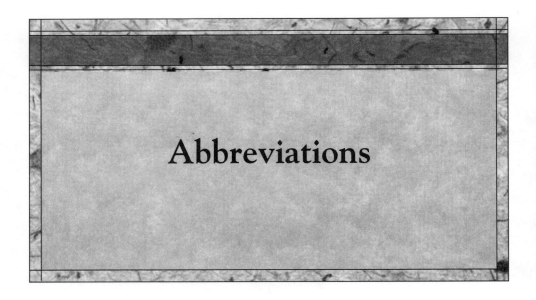

Abbreviations

COMMON ABBREVIATIONS. The following lists consist of selected abbreviations organized in four categories: INFORMATION TECHNOLOGY, ORGANIZATIONS, STATES, and ACADEMIC DEGREES. For additional information, see Chapter 7/ABBREVIATIONS.

See also FOREIGN CURRENCY for a list of currency symbols, THE METRIC SYSTEM for examples of metric prefixes and abbreviations, and FORMS OF ADDRESS for examples of titles, abbreviated or spelled out, that are used in inside addresses and salutations. See also Chapter 8/INSIDE ADDRESS; SALUTATION.

INFORMATION TECHNOLOGY. Although capitalization and punctuation styles vary among organizations, many computer abbreviations, such as *RAM* (random access memory), are written in all capital letters without periods or space between the letters.

Nontechnical abbreviations, however, such as *asap* (as soon as possible), are usually written in small letters.

Technical abbreviations that do not denote proper nouns, such as *AA* (auto attendant), may also be written in small letters (*aa*). Follow the style preferred by your employer. See also the lowercase abbreviation style for weights and measures illustrated in THE METRIC SYSTEM:

AA   Auto attendant

ADC   Analog-to-digital converter

ADSL   Asynchronous digital subscriber loop

AI	Artificial intelligence
ARP	Address Resolution Protocol
ASC	Automatic sequence control
ASCII	American Standard Code for Information Interchange
ASR	Automatic send/receive
ATM	Asynchronous transfer mode
b	Bit
B	Byte
BBS	Bulletin board service/system
BCD	Binary coded decimal
BIOS	Basic input/output system
CD-DA	Compact disk–digital audio
CD-I	Compact disk–interactive
CD-R	Compact disk–recordable
CD-ROM	Compact disk–read-only memory
CDV	Compact disk video
CGI	Common gateway interface
CIX	Commercial Internet exchange
COM	Computer-output microfilm
CPU	Central processing unit
CRT	Cathode ray tube
DAC	Digital-to-analog converter
DB	Database
DBMS	Database management system
DBS	Digital/direct broadcast satellite
DDC	Direct digital control
DDS	Document delivery system
DNS	Domain name server/service
DOD	Digital optical disk
DOR	Digital–optical recording
DRAM	Dynamic random access memory
DRS	Document retrieval system
DSP	Digital signal processor

545

DSS	Digital satellite system
DVD	Digital videodisk
DVI	Digital video interactive
EBCDIC	Extended Binary Coded Decimal Interchange Code
EDI	Electronic data interchange
EDP	Electronic data processing
EDS	Electronic data storage
EM	Electromagnetic
EMS	Electronic messaging system
FAQ	Frequently asked question
FD	Full duplex
FDDI	Fiber-distributed data interface
FDM	Frequency division multiplexing
FMV	Full-motion video
FSN	Full-service network
FTP	File Transfer Protocol
4GL	Fourth-generation language
GDT	Graphic display terminal
GIF	Graphic(s) interchange format
GUI	Graphical user interface
HD	Half duplex
HDSL	High-speed digital subscriber loop
HTML	HyperText Markup Language
HTTP	HyperText Transfer Protocol
IC	Integrated circuit
ICMP	Internet Central Message Protocol
IDA	Integrated digital access
IDE	Integrated drive electronics
IGP	Interior Gateway Protocol
I/O	Input/output
IP	Internet Protocol
IRC	Internet relay chat

ISDN	Integrated Services Digital Network
ISP	Internet service provider
IT	Information technology
IV	Interactive video
IVR	Interactive voice response
LAN	Local area network
LCD	Liquid crystal display
LED	Light-emitting diode
MAN	Metropolitan area network
MBR	Memory buffer register
MHS	Message handling system
MIME	Multipurpose Internet mail extension
MIS	Management information system
MSO	Multiple-system operator
MUD	Multi-User Dimension
MUX	Multiplexer
NAP	Network access point
NFS	Network file system
NIC	Network information center
NIS	Network information service
NOS	Network operating system
OCR	Optical character reader/recognition
OS	Operating system
OSI	Open systems interconnect/interconnection
PAD	Packet assembler/disassembler
PCB	Printed circuit board
PCI	Peripheral component interconnect
PCS	Personal communication service
PDA	Personal digital assistant
PDF	Portable document format
PDN	Public data network
PPP	Point-to-Point Protocol

PRAM	Parameter random access memory
PRI	Primary-rate interface
PROM	Programmable read-only memory
PSTN	Public Switched Telephone Network
PSU	Power-supply unit
QAM	Queued access method
RAM	Random access memory
RIP	Routing Information Protocol
ROM	Read-only memory
RTOS	Real-time operating system
RTV	Real-time video
R/W	Read/write
SAM	Sequential access method
SCSI	Small computer system interface
SDRAM	Synchronous dynamic random access memory
SLIP	Serial Line Internet Protocol
SONET	Synchronous optical network
TAPI	Telephony application programming interface
TCP/IP	Transmission Control Protocol/Internet Protocol
TIFF	Tagged image file format
TTY	Teleprinter/teletype/teletypewriter
TX	Telex
UCS	Universal character set
UPS	Uninterruptible power supply
URL	Uniform Resource Locator
USB	Universal serial bus
VDP	Video display processor
VDT	Video/visual display terminal
VDU	Video/visual display unit
VOX	Voice-operated exchange
VPN	Virtual private network
VR	Virtual reality

VRAM	Video random access memory
WAIS	Wide-area information server/service
WAN	Wide-area network
WATS	Wide-area telecommunications service
WMRM	Write many, read many
WORM	Write once, read many
WWW	World Wide Web

ORGANIZATIONS. As the examples in this list illustrate, acronyms and initialisms (see Chapter 7/ABBREVIATIONS) that denote an official name, such as *AAA* (American Automobile Association), are always written in capital letters, without periods or space between the letters:

AAA	American Automobile Association
AAMA	American Association of Medical Assistants
AAMT	American Association for Medical Transcription
ABA	American Bankers Association; American Bar Association; American Booksellers Association
AFL–CIO	American Federation of Labor–Congress of Industrial Organizations
AID	Agency for International Development
AMA	American Management Association; American Medical Association
ANSI	American National Standards Institute
ARMA	Association of Records Managers and Administrators
ASA	American Standards Association; American Statistical Association
ASTA	American Society of Travel Agents
BOC	Bell Operating Company
CCC	Commodity Credit Corporation
CDC(P)	Centers for Disease Control (and Prevention)
CEA	Commodity Exchange Administration
CEC	Commodity Exchange Commission
CPSC	Consumer Product Safety Commission

CSC	Civil Service Commission
EEOC	Equal Employment Opportunity Commission
EPA	Environmental Protection Agency
EU	European Union
FAA	Federal Aviation Agency
FCC	Federal Communications Commission
FDA	Food and Drug Administration
FDIC	Federal Deposit Insurance Corporation
FHA	Federal Housing Administration
FMC	Federal Maritime Commission
FPC	Federal Power Commission
FRB	Federal Reserve Bank; Federal Reserve Board
FTC	Federal Trade Commission
GAO	General Accounting Office
GPO	Government Printing Office (United States)
GSA	General Services Administration
G-8	Group of Eight
HUD	Housing and Urban Development (U.S. Department of)
IAAP	International Association of Administrative Professionals
IBRD	International Bank for Reconstruction and Development (World Bank)
ICC	Interstate Commerce Commission
IEEE	Institute of Electrical and Electronics Engineers
IFC	International Finance Corporation
IFTU	International Federation of Trade Unions
ILO	International Labor Organization
IMF	International Monetary Fund
INMARSAT	International Maritime Satellite Organization
ISO	International Standards Organization
ISOC	Internet Society
ITC	Independent Telephone Company
ITO	International Trade Organization
ITU	International Telecommunications Union

LC	Library of Congress
LSI	Legal Secretaries International
NAEOP	National Association of Educational Office Personnel
NAM	National Association of Manufacturers
NBS	National Bureau of Standards
NEA	National Education Association
NIH	National Institutes of Health
NIST	National Institute of Standards Technology
NLRB	National Labor Relations Board
NMB	National Mediation Board
NTIA	National Telecommunications and Information Administration
NTSB	National Transportation Safety Board
OECD	Organization for Economic Cooperation and Development
OEO	Office of Economic Opportunity
OMB	Office of Management and Budget
PUC	Public Utilities Commission
RBOC	Regional Bell Operating Company
SBA	Small Business Administration
SEC	Securities and Exchange Commission
SSA	Social Security Administration
TC	Tariff Commission; Tax Court (of the United States)
USIA	United States Information Agency
USPS	United States Postal Service
WHO	World Health Organization
WTrO	World Trade Organization

STATES.   The following list includes, for each state, the capital city, legislative body, and traditional and two-letter postal abbreviations.

Traditional state abbreviations, such as *Calif.,* are used in footnotes, tables, and other supplementary text material. They should be written with an initial capital and followed by a period.

Two-letter postal abbreviations, such as *CA,* are used in the mailing addresses on envelopes and in the inside address of letters. (See Chapter 8/ENVELOPES; INSIDE ADDRESS.) They should be written in capital letters without punctuation:

State Name	State Capital	Legislative Body	Traditional, Postal Abbreviations
Alabama	Montgomery	Legislature	Ala., AL
Alaska	Juneau	Legislature	Alaska, AK
Arizona	Phoenix	Legislature	Ariz., AZ
Arkansas	Little Rock	General assembly	Ark., AR
California	Sacramento	Legislature	Calif., CA
Colorado	Denver	General assembly	Colo., CO
Connecticut	Hartford	General assembly	Conn., CT
Delaware	Dover	General assembly	Del., DE
Florida	Tallahassee	Legislature	Fla., FL
Georgia	Atlanta	General assembly	Ga., GA
Hawaii	Honolulu	Legislature	Hawaii, HI
Idaho	Boise	Legislature	Idaho, ID
Illinois	Springfield	General assembly	Ill., IL
Indiana	Indianapolis	General assembly	Ind., IN
Iowa	Des Moines	General assembly	Iowa, IA
Kansas	Topeka	Legislature	Kans., KS
Kentucky	Frankfort	General assembly	Ky., KY
Louisiana	Baton Rouge	Legislature	La., LA
Maine	Augusta	Legislature	Maine, ME
Maryland	Annapolis	General assembly	Md., MD
Massachusetts	Boston	General court	Mass., MA
Michigan	Lansing	Legislature	Mich., MI
Minnesota	St. Paul	Legislature	Minn., MN
Mississippi	Jackson	Legislature	Miss., MS
Missouri	Jefferson City	General assembly	Mo., MO
Montana	Helena	Legislative assembly	Mont., MT
Nebraska	Lincoln	Legislature	Nebr., NE
Nevada	Carson City	Legislature	Nev., NV
New Hampshire	Concord	General court	N.H., NH
New Jersey	Trenton	Legislature	N.J., NJ

New Mexico	Santa Fe	Legislature	N. Mex., NM
New York	Albany	Legislature	N.Y., NY
North Carolina	Raleigh	General assembly	N.C., NC
North Dakota	Bismarck	Legislative assembly	N. Dak., ND
Ohio	Columbus	General assembly	Ohio, OH
Oklahoma	Oklahoma City	Legislature	Okla., OK
Oregon	Salem	Legislative assembly	Oreg., OR
Pennsylvania	Harrisburg	General assembly	Pa., PA
Rhode Island	Providence	General assembly	R.I., RI
South Carolina	Columbia	General assembly	S.C., SC
South Dakota	Pierre	Legislature	S. Dak., SD
Tennessee	Nashville	General assembly	Tenn., TN
Texas	Austin	Legislature	Tex., TX
Utah	Salt Lake City	Legislature	Utah, UT
Vermont	Montpelier	General assembly	Vt., VT
Virginia	Richmond	General assembly	Va., VA
Washington	Olympia	Legislature	Wash., WA
West Virginia	Charleston	Legislature	W. Va., WV
Wisconsin	Madison	Legislature	Wis., WI
Wyoming	Cheyenne	Legislature	Wyo., WY

ACADEMIC DEGREES. The following are common academic degrees granted in U.S. colleges and universities.

Academic degrees should be written either in all capital letters (*M.D.*) or with a combination of capital and small letters (*Ph.D.*), without a space between the parts. Unlike many other types of abbreviations, such as those in the previous lists, academic degrees should always be punctuated:

A.A.	Associate in arts
A.B.	Bachelor of arts
A.M.	Master of arts
B.A.	Bachelor of arts
B.B.A.	Bachelor of business administration
B.C.	Bachelor of chemistry

B.C.E.	Bachelor of chemical engineering
B.E.	Bachelor of education; bachelor of engineering
B.E.E.	Bachelor of electrical engineering
B.S.	Bachelor of science
B.S.Ed.	Bachelor of science in education
Ch.D.	Doctor of chemistry
D.C.L.	Doctor of canon law; doctor of civil law
D.D.	Doctor of divinity
D.D.S.	Doctor of dental surgery
D.S.; D.Sc.	Doctor of science
D.Th.; D.Theol.	Doctor of theology
D.V.M.	Doctor of veterinary medicine
Ed.B.	Bachelor of education
Ed.D.	Doctor of education
Ed.M.	Master of education
J.D.	Doctor of laws; doctor of jurisprudence; Juris doctor
LL.B.	Bachelor of laws
LL.D.	Doctor of laws
LL.M.	Master of laws
M.A.	Master of arts
M.B.A.	Master in (*or* of) business administration
M.Ed.	Master of education
Ph.B.	Bachelor of philosophy
Ph.D.	Doctor of philosophy
S.B.; Sc.B.	Bachelor of science
S.D.; Sc.D.	Doctor of science
S.M.; Sc.M.	Master of science
Th.D.	Doctor of theology
V.M.D.	Doctor of veterinary medicine

Forms of Address

BUSINESS CORRESPONDENCE. The following lists indicate the proper way to write an official's name and address in business correspondence, including the correct use of personal and professional titles and appropriate salutations.

Examples are provided for individuals affiliated with or employed by the U.S. government, state and local governments, diplomatic services, United Nations, armed forces, religious organizations, and colleges and universities.

For information on social forms, introductions, and so on, consult a regularly updated list available on the Internet (see Chapter 6/INTERNET; WEB SITE) or a current book of etiquette.

For guidelines and examples of the correct forms to use in writing to customers, clients, business associates, and so on, see Chapter 8/ADDRESS, FORMS OF; INSIDE ADDRESS; SALUTATION.

Salutations. In most cases, a relatively informal salutation, such as *Dear Mayor Jones,* is preferred over a more formal one, such as *Dear Mr. Mayor.*

As the following lists indicate, a formal salutation, such as *Dear Mr. Chief Justice,* is used on all occasions only for certain very high ranking officials. For some lower-ranking officials, a formal salutation may be used on strictly official or very formal occasions.

Titles. If an official's title is known, but not the person's name, address the correspondence by title alone, usually preceded by *The: The Lieutenant Governor of Illinois/Dear Sir or Madam.*

When a person is temporarily serving in an official capacity, the words *Acting* (general usage) or *ad Interim* (diplomatic usage) are included.

Acting precedes the title in the address but is omitted in the salutation: *The Honorable Jane Jones, Acting Mayor of Memphis/Dear Mayor Jones.*

Ad Interim follows the title in the address and also is omitted in the salutation: *The Honorable John Jones, Chargé d'Affaires ad Interim of the United States/Dear Dr./Mr. Jones.*

Women officials are addressed the same as men in similar positions, except that *Madam* or *Ms.* replaces *Sir* or *Mr.* However, when addressing women in other countries, use the country's equivalent of *Miss* or *Mrs.,* not *Ms.,* which is rarely used outside the United States.

A person who has held an official position entitling him or her to be addressed as *The Honorable* is still addressed as such after retirement. In most cases, omit any professional title, such as *senator,* in both the address and salutation for a retired person: *The Honorable Jane Jones/Dear Dr./Ms. Jones.*

The same rule applies to a newly elected official who has not yet assumed office, such as a senator-elect: *The Honorable John Jones/Dear Dr./Mr. Jones.*

The title of *judge,* however, is an exception. Someone who was once a judge customarily retains that title: *The Honorable Jane Jones/Dear Judge Jones.*

Retired officers of the armed forces also retain their titles designating rank, with their retirement status indicated immediately after their rank: *Lieutenant General John Jones, USA, Retired/Dear General Jones.*

Address. Send business correspondence to the official's office address. However, when the official is retired, use the individual's home office address or, if none, the home address.

For social-business correspondence, such as an invitation to attend or address a company's anniversary celebration, use the official's office address. For a strictly social invitation, such as an invitation to a private dinner party, and other such nonbusiness correspondence, use the individual's home address.

U.S. GOVERNMENT. When writing to an official included in the following list, add the person's current street address, city, state, and ZIP Code on the lines below his or her name and title in the inside address.

See also DIPLOMATIC SERVICES for additional governmental examples:

Official	Inside Address	Salutation
President of the United States	The President The White House	Dear Mr. President:
Vice President of the United States	The Vice President Old Executive Office Building	Dear Mr. Vice President:
The Chief Justice, U.S. Supreme Court	The Chief Justice of the United States The Supreme Court	Dear Mr. Chief Justice:
Associate Justice, U.S. Supreme Court	Justice Jones The Supreme Court	Dear Justice Jones: Dear Mr. Justice: (*formal*)
Cabinet Officer (Secretary)	The Honorable Jane Jones The Secretary of [Department]	Dear Madam Secretary:
U.S. Attorney General	The Honorable John Jones Attorney General of the United States The Department of Justice	Dear Mr. Attorney General:
Speaker of the U.S. House of of Representatives	The Honorable Jane Jones Speaker of the House of Representatives	Dear Dr./Ms. Jones: Dear Madam Speaker: (*formal*)
Under Secretary (Department)	The Honorable John Jones Under Secretary of [Department]	Dear Dr./Mr. Jones: Dear Mr. Under Secretary: (*formal*)
U.S. Senator	The Honorable Jane Jones United States Senate	Dear Senator Jones:
Member, U.S. House of Representatives	The Honorable John Jones United States House of Representatives	Dear Dr./Mr. Jones:
Chair, Committee or Subcommittee, U.S. Senate	The Honorable Jane Jones Chairman Committee on [Name] United States Senate	Dear Senator Jones:
Head of U.S. Agency or Other Federal Body	The Honorable John Jones Director [Organization]	Dear Dr./Mr. Jones:

DIPLOMATIC SERVICES. The following list includes examples of forms for U.S. diplomatic representatives and for those from other countries.

In both cases, when an ambassador or minister is not at his or her post, add the name of the country to which the person is accredited to his or her title: *The Ambassador of the United States to Great Britain.*

To designate temporary service, include the words *ad Interim* in the title, as explained in BUSINESS CORRESPONDENCE, *Titles.*

When an individual has a military title, use it rather than the complimentary title *The Honorable: Colonel John Jones.*

U.S. representatives. When it might not be clear that an *American* ambassador is from the United States, rather than from a South American country, for example, use the wording *The Ambassador of the United States,* rather than *American Ambassador.*

High officials in the United States are never referred to by the diplomatic title *His/Her Excellency* as they are in other countries.

Foreign representatives. The correct title of ambassadors and ministers from other countries is *Ambassador/Minister of [Country]*, with one exception: For Great Britain, the correct usage is *British Ambassador/Minister.*

When a foreign representative has a royal title, use it rather than the diplomatic title *His/Her Excellency* or the complimentary title *The Honorable: Your Majesty.*

For representatives from Spanish-speaking countries, a courtesy title, such as *Don,* may be used with a diplomatic or complimentary title: *The Honorable Don Cardosa.*

The title *Ms.,* which is common in the United States, should not be used in addressing representatives from other countries. Instead, use *Dr.* if appropriate, or otherwise, use the country's equivalent of *Miss* or *Mrs.*

See also the examples of proper forms in UNITED NATIONS:

Official	Inside Address	Salutation
U.S. Ambassador	The Honorable John Jones The Ambassador of the United States American Embassy	Dear Mr. Ambassador:
U.S. Chargé d'Affaires, Consul General, Consul, Vice Consul	Dr./Ms. Jane Jones Chargé d'Affaires of the United States	Dear Dr./Ms. Jones:

Ambassador to the United States	His Excellency Erik Rolf The Ambassador of [Country]	Dear Mr. Ambassador: Excellency: (*formal*)
Minister to the United States	The Honorable Erik Rolf Minister of [Department]	Dear Mr. Minister:
Prime Minister of Canada or Great Britain	The Right Honorable Brian Chesterfield, P.C., M.P. Prime Minister of Canada	Dear Mr. Prime Minister:
President or Premier of a Foreign Nation	His Excellency Juan Blanco President of the Republic of [Country]	Dear Mr. President: Excellency: (*formal*)

UNITED NATIONS. The following list contains examples of forms of address for high United Nations officials and those with ambassadorial rank. See also DIPLOMATIC SERVICES for additional examples:

Official	Inside Address	Salutation
Secretary General of the United Nations	His Excellency Peter Wilson Secretary General of the United Nations	Dear Mr. Secretary General: Excellency: (*formal*)
Under Secretary of the United Nations	The Honorable Peter Wilson Under Secretary of the United Nations	Dear Mr. Under Secretary:
U.S. Ambassador to the United Nations	The Honorable Jane Jones United States Representative to the United Nations	Dear Madam Ambassador:
Ambassador of a Foreign Nation to the United Nations	His Excellency Michael Harris Representative of [Country] to the United Nations	Dear Mr. Ambassador: Excellency: (*formal*)

STATE AND LOCAL GOVERNMENTS. The following list has examples of the correct forms of address for governmental and court officials at the state and local levels.

Notice that the title *chief judge* is not treated the same as *chief justice:* Whereas it is proper to use the title *Madam* or *Mr.* with *chief justice* (*Mr. Chief*

Justice), one should not use personal titles with *chief judge.* Use the salutation *Dear Judge Jones* instead:

Official	Inside Address	Salutation
Governor of a State or Territory	The Honorable John Jones Governor of [State]	Dear Governor Jones:
Lieutenant Governor	The Honorable John Jones Lieutenant Governor of [State]	Dear Dr./Mr. Jones:
Secretary of State	The Honorable Jane Jones Secretary of the State of [State]	Dear Dr./Ms. Jones: Dear Madam Secretary: (*formal*)
Attorney General	The Honorable John Jones Attorney General State of [State]	Dear Dr./Mr. Jones: Dear Mr. Attorney General: (*formal*)
President, State Senate	The Honorable Jane Jones President of the Senate of the State of [State]	Dear Dr./Ms. Jones:
Speaker, Assembly or House of Representatives	The Honorable John Jones Speaker of the Assembly of the State of [State]	Dear Dr./Mr. Jones:
State Senator	The Honorable Jane Jones The Senate of [State]	Dear Senator Jones:
State Representative	The Honorable John Jones House of Delegates State of [State]	Dear Mr./Dr. Jones:
District Attorney	The Honorable Jane Jones District Attorney State of [State]	Dear Dr./Ms. Jones:
Mayor	The Honorable John Jones Mayor of [City]	Dear Mayor Jones: Dear Mr. Mayor: (*formal*)
Alderman, Alderwoman	Alderman John Jones City Hall	Dear Dr./Mr. Jones:
Chief Justice, State Supreme Court	The Honorable Jane Jones Chief Justice Supreme Court of [State]	Dear Madam Chief Justice:

Associate Justice, State Supreme Court	The Honorable John Jones Associate Justice Supreme Court of [State]	Dear Justice Jones:
Judge of a Court	The Honorable Jane Jones Judge of the United States District Court for the Southern District of [State]	Dear Judge Jones:
Clerk of Court	The Honorable John Jones Clerk of the Superior Court of [State]	Dear Dr./Mr. Jones:

THE ARMED FORCES: U.S. Army, Air Force, and Marine Corps. The titles in these branches of the service are generally the same.

USA signifies the army and *USAR*, the reserve. *USAF* signifies the air force and *USAFR*, the reserve. *USMC* signifies the Marine Corps and *USMCR*, the reserve.

Although members of the military services use capitalized abbreviations, such as *LT* (Lieutenant), for rank, civilians usually spell out the titles in business correspondence.

The full rank is used in the inside address (*Brigadier General John Jones*), and a shortened version is used in the salutation: *Dear General Jones:*

Official	Inside Address	Salutation
General, Lieutenant General, Major General, Brigadier General	Major General John Jones, USA	Dear General Jones:
Colonel, Lieutenant Colonel, Major, Captain	Lieutenant Colonel Jane Jones, USAF	Dear Colonel Jones:
First Lieutenant, Second Lieutenant	Second Lieutenant John Jones, USMC	Dear Lieutenant Jones:
Chief Warrant Officer, Warrant Officer	Chief Warrant Officer Jane Jones, USA	Dear Ms. Jones:
Enlisted Personnel	Private First Class John Jones, USAF	Dear Private Jones:

THE ARMED FORCES: U.S. Navy and Coast Guard. The titles in these branches of the service are generally the same.

USN signifies the navy and *USNR*, the reserve. *USCG* signifies the Coast Guard and *USCGR*, the reserve.

Although members of the military services use capitalized abbreviations, such as *LCDR* (Lieutenant Commander), for rank, civilians usually spell out the titles in business correspondence.

The full rank is used in the inside address (*Vice Admiral John Jones*), and a shortened version is used in the salutation: *Dear Admiral Jones:*

Official	Inside Address	Salutation
Fleet Admiral, Vice Admiral, Rear Admiral	Rear Admiral John Jones, USCG	Dear Admiral Jones:
Captain, Commander, Lieutenant Commander	Lieutenant Commander Jane Jones, USN	Dear Commander Jones:
Lieutenant, Lieutenant Junior Grade, Ensign	Lieutenant John Jones, USCG	Dear Lieutenant Jones:
Chief Warrant Officer, Warrant Officer	Warrant Officer Jane Jones, USN	Dear Ms. Jones:
Enlisted Personnel	Petty Officer First Class John Jones, USCG	Dear Petty Officer Jones:

RELIGION: CATHOLIC FAITH. The following forms of address may vary in certain locations. For example, many religious groups use a title such as *president* instead of *superior* for the head of a congregation. Some groups omit the article *The* before *Reverend, Most Reverend,* and so on.

The address for the head of a brotherhood depends on whether the person is a priest and has a title other than *president, superior,* and so on. The address for the head of a sisterhood depends on the order, which may or may not be included. For such matters, consult a current edition of the *Official Catholic Directory* or a comprehensive book of etiquette.

The examples for sisters and brothers given here use the person's first name in the salutation. Some religious persons prefer the use of the last name with the title or, in the salutation, only the person's title, with no name. Follow the preference of the individual when known:

Official	Inside Address	Salutation
The Pope	His Holiness, Pope [Name] *or* His Holiness the Pope	Your Holiness: *or* Most Holy Father:
Cardinal	His Eminence, John Cardinal Jones Archbishop of [Place]	Dear Cardinal Jones: Your Eminence: (*formal*)
Archbishop, Bishop	The Most Reverend John Jones, D.D. Bishop of [Place]	Dear Bishop Jones: Most Reverend Sir: *or* Your Excellency: (*formal*)
Monsignor	The Right Reverend Monsignor Jones	Dear Monsignor Jones: Right Reverend Monsignor: (*formal*)
Priest (Religious Order)	The Reverend John Jones, S.C.	Dear Dr./Father Jones:
Brother	Brother John, S.J. *or* Brother John Jones, S.J.	Dear Brother John: Dear Brother: (*formal*)
Sister	Sister Jane, H.M. *or* Sister Jane Jones, H.M.	Dear Sister Jane: Dear Sister: (*formal*)

RELIGION: JEWISH FAITH. The following are examples of two principal officials in the Jewish faith. Add the initials for the person's scholastic degree, if any, after the name:

Official	Inside Address	Salutation
Rabbi	Rabbi John Feldman, D.D.	Dear Rabbi Feldman: Dear Rabbi: (*formal*)
Cantor	Cantor John Feldman	Dear Cantor Feldman:

RELIGION: PROTESTANT FAITH. In the following examples, include the initials representing the person's scholastic degree, if any, after the name:

563

Official	Inside Address	Salutation
Episcopal Bishop	The Right Reverend John Jones, D.D., LL.D. Bishop of [Place]	Dear Bishop Jones:
Methodist Bishop	The Reverend John Jones Methodist Bishop	Dear Bishop Jones:
Minister	The Reverend Jane Jones, D.D., Litt.D.	Dear Dr. Jones:
Episcopal Dean	The Very Reverend John Jones, D.D. Dean of [Place]	Dear Dean Jones:

COLLEGES AND UNIVERSITIES. In the following examples, the person's title precedes his or her name: *Dr. Jane Jones.* An alternative form omits the personal or professional title in the inside address and instead adds the initials for the person's scholastic degree after the name: *Jane Jones, Ph.D.:*

Official	Inside Address	Salutation
President	Dr./Mr. John Jones President [Institution]	Dear Dr./Mr. Jones:
Chancellor	Dr./Ms. Jane Jones Chancellor [Institution]	Dear Dr./Ms. Jones:
Dean, Assistant Dean	Dean John Jones [School or Division] [Institution] *or*	Dear Dean Jones:
	Dr. John Jones Dean, [School or Division] [Institution]	Dear Dr./Dean Jones:
Professor, Associate Professor, Assistant Professor	Dr./Ms. Jane Jones Professor of [Subject] [Institution] *or*	Dear Dr./Professor Jones:
	Professor Jane Jones Department of [Subject] [Institution]	Dear Professor Jones:
Instructor	Dr./Mr. John Jones [Institution]	Dear Dr./Mr. Jones:

Foreign Currency

CURRENCY NAMES AND SYMBOLS. The following list gives the commonly recognized names and symbols of monetary units in selected countries.

Some countries, particularly developing nations, change their monetary units from time to time. For recent changes, review one of the regularly updated lists available over the Internet (see Chapter 6/INTERNET; WEB SITE), or check with the international officer or department of your bank.

Some countries also use the same names or symbols for monetary units. Each currency, however, is issued by the individual country and is usually not interchangeable with another country's currency bearing the same name.

For example, a *Taiwanese dollar* is not the same thing as an *American dollar*. However, even though the one is not interchangeable with the other, a Taiwanese dollar may be exchanged for an American dollar, or vice versa, according to the current rate of exchange.

See also Chapter 5/INTERNATIONAL TRAVEL, *Foreign currency*; Chapter 13/FOREIGN EXCHANGE.

STANDARDIZATION OF CURRENCIES. The following list gives the monetary units of individual countries. However, various groups of countries in different parts of the world have formed unions that promote economic advantages for their members.

Such benefits often include simplifying foreign exchange among members or even the adoption of a common currency to be used by all nations within the union.

The European Union, for example, has issued its own currency system, the Euro, with a subcurrency of 100 euro-cents per Euro. This standard currency is intended to replace the individual currencies of member countries such as Austria, Belgium, Denmark, France, Italy, Spain, and the United Kingdom.

LIST OF UNITS AND SYMBOLS. The following list provides a widely adopted wording and spelling for the various monetary units, although the exact form may differ depending on the source consulted.

Also, the issuing country may use accents (see Chapter 7/DIACRITICAL MARKS) that are usually omitted in business writing:

Country	Monetary Unit	Symbol	Subunit
Afghanistan	Afghani	Af	100 puls
Algeria	Dinar	DA	100 centimes
Argentina	Neuvo peso argentino	$	100 centavos
Australia	Dollar	$A	100 cents
Austria	Schilling	AS	100 groschen
Bahamas	Dollar	B$	100 cents
Barbados	Dollar	Bds$	100 cents
Belgium	Franc	BF	100 centimes
Bermuda	Dollar	Bd$	100 cents
Bolivia	Boliviano	$B	100 centavos
Bosnia and Herzegovina	Marka	—	100 pfenniga
Brazil	Real	R$	100 centavos
Bulgaria	Lev	Lv	100 stotinki
Cambodia	New riel	CR	100 sen
Canada	Dollar	Can$	100 cents
Central African Republic	Franc	CFAF	100 centimes
Chile	Peso	Ch$	100 centavos
China	Yuan	¥	10 jiao
Colombia	Peso	Col$	100 centavos
Congo, Dem. Rep. of	Zaire	Z	100 makuta
Congo, Rep. of	Franc	CFAF	100 centimes
Costa Rica	Colon	C	100 centimos
Cuba	Peso	Cu$	100 centavos
Czech Republic	Koruna	Kc	100 haleru
Denmark	Krone	DKr	100 oere
Dominican Republic	Peso	RD$	100 centavos

Ecuador	Sucre	S/	100 centavos
Egypt	Pound	£E	100 piasters
El Salvador	Colon	C	100 centavos
Ethiopia	Birr	Br	100 cents
Finland	Markka *or* Finmark	FMk	100 pennia
France	Franc	F	100 centimes
Germany	Deutsche mark	DM	100 pfennige
Ghana	New cedi	C	100 pesewas
Greece	Drachma	Dr	100 lepta
Guatemala	Quetzal	Q	100 centavos
Haiti	Gourde	G	100 centimes
Honduras	Lempira	L	100 centavos
Hong Kong	Dollar	HK$	100 cents
Hungary	Forint	Ft	100 filler
India	Rupee	Re	100 paise
Indonesia	Ripiah	Rp	—
Iran	Rial	IR	10 rials = 1 toman
Iraq	Dinar	ID	1,000 fils
Ireland	Pound	£Ir	100 pence
Israel	New shekel	NIS	100 new agorot
Italy	Lira	Lit	100 centesimi
Ivory Coast	Franc	CFAF	100 centimes
Jamaica	Dollar	J$	100 cents
Japan	Yen	¥	—
Jordan	Dinar	JD	1,000 fils
Kenya	Shilling	KSh	100 cents
Korea, North	Won	Wn	100 chon
Korea, South	Won	W	100 chun (theoretical)
Kuwait	Dinar	KD	1,000 fils
Laos	New kip	NK	100 at
Lebanon	Pound	£L	100 piasters
Luxembourg	Franc	LuxF	—
Malaysia	Ringgit	M$	100 sen
Mexico	New peso	Mex$	100 centavos
Morocco	Dirham	DH	100 centimes
Myanmar (Burma)	Kyat	K	100 pyas
Nepal	Rupee	NR	100 paisa

Netherlands	Guilder, florin, *or* gulden	f.	100 cents
New Zealand	Dollar	NZ$	100 cents
Nicaragua	Gold cordoba	C$	100 centavos
Nigeria	Naira	N	100 kobo
Norway	Krone	NKr	100 oere
Pakistan	Rupee	PRe	100 paisa
Panama	Balboa	B	100 centesimos
Paraguay	Guarani	G	100 centimos
Peru	Nuevo sol	S/.	100 centimos
Philippines	Peso	P	100 centavos
Poland	Zloty	Zl	100 groszy
Portugal	Escudo	Esc	100 centavos
Romania	Leu	L	100 bani
Russia	Ruble	R	100 kopeks
Saudi Arabia	Riyal	SR	100 halalah
Serbia and Montenegro	New dinar	YD	100 paras
Singapore	Dollar	S$	100 cents
Slovakia	Koruna	Sk	100 halierov
South Africa	Rand	R	100 cents
Spain	Peseta	Pta	100 centimos
Sri Lanka	Rupee	SLRe	100 cents
Sweden	Krona	SKr	100 oere
Switzerland	Franc	SFR	100 centimes, rappen, *or* centesimi
Syria	Pound	£S	100 piastres
Taiwan	New dollar	NT$	100 cents
Thailand	Baht	B	100 satang
Turkey	Lira	TL	—
Ukraine	Hryvnia	—	100 kopiykas
United Arab Emirates	Dirham	Dh	100 fils
United Kingdom	Pound	£	100 pence
Uruguay	Peso	$Ur	100 centesimos
Venezuela	Bolivar	Bs	100 centimos
Vietnam	New dong	D	100 xu

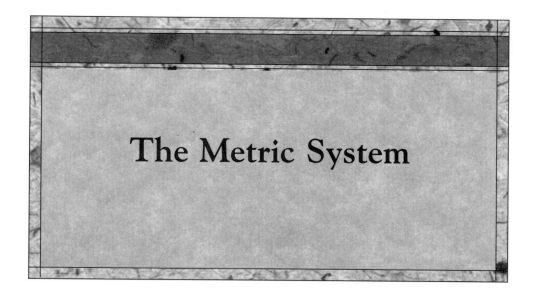

The Metric System

THE METRIC SYSTEM OF WEIGHTS AND MEASURES. The metric system, known worldwide as *SI* (*Système International*), is a decimal system based on the powers of 10. Therefore, a second unit is equal to 10 times the basic unit, a third unit is 10 times the second, and so on.

The fundamental units of the metric system are the *meter* (length), *kilogram* (weight), *liter* (volume), and *degree Celsius* (temperature). Another category, *time*, uses the same system of units as that in the U.S. customary system of weights and measures: hours, minutes, and seconds.

METRIC PREFIXES. The names of the metric units are formed by combining the words *meter, gram,* and *liter* with six numerical prefixes: the Latin prefixes *milli-, centi-,* and *deci-* and the Greek prefixes *deka-, hecto-,* and *kilo-:*

Weight

1 kilogram = 1,000 grams

1 hectogram = 100 grams

1 dekagram = 10 grams

1 gram = 1 gram

1 decigram = 0.1 gram

1 centigram = 0.01 gram

1 milligram = 0.001 gram

Length

1 kilometer = 1,000 meters

1 hectometer = 100 meters

1 dekameter = 10 meters

1 meter = 1 meter

1 decimeter = 0.1 meter

1 centimeter = 0.01 meter

1 millimeter = 0.001 meter

Volume

1 hectoliter = 100 liters

1 dekaliter = 10 liters

1 liter = 1 liter

1 centiliter = 0.01 liter

1 milliliter = 0.001 liter

METRIC ABBREVIATIONS. The following abbreviations are commonly used in expressing metric weights and measures. In general business writing, the names are usually spelled out (*16 millimeters*). However, in technical or scientific writing, the abbreviations are often used (*16 mm*).

The National Bureau of Standards also uses no punctuation in abbreviations of U.S. weights and measures (*ft*), although most business writers add a period (*ft.*). Even when punctuation is generally omitted, a period should be added after an abbreviations such as *in.* (inch) that might be confused with another word that is spelled the same:

Unit	Symbol
are	a
Celsius, degree	°C
centare	ca
centigram	cg
centiliter	cl
centimeter	cm

cubic centimeter	cm^3
cubic decimeter	dm^3
cubic dekameter	dam^3
cubic hectometer	hm^3
cubic kilometer	km^3
cubic meter	m^3
cubic millimeter	mm^3
decigram	dg
deciliter	dl
decimeter	dm
dekagram	dag
dekaliter	dal
dekameter	dam
gram	g
hectare	ha
hectogram	hg
hectoliter	hl
hectometer	hm
kilogram	kg
kiloliter	kl
kilometer	km
liter	l
meter	m
microgram	μg
microliter	μl
micrometer	μm
milligram	mg
milliliter	ml
millimeter	mm
square centimeter	cm^2
square decimeter	dm^2
square dekameter	dam^2

square hectometer	hm²
square kilometer	km²
square meter	m²
square millimeter	mm²
ton, metric	t

METRIC CONVERSION FACTORS. The following list indicates how to convert various customary figures, such as *feet,* into metric equivalents and vice versa:

When You Know	Multiply by	To Find
Length		
inches	2.5400	centimeters
feet	30.4800	centimeters
yards	0.9144	meters
miles	1.6093	kilometers
millimeters	0.0394	inches
centimeters	0.3937	inches
meters	3.2808	feet
meters	1.0936	yards
kilometers	0.6214	miles
Area		
square inches	6.4516	square centimeters
square feet	0.0929	square meters
square yards	0.8361	square meters
square miles	2.5900	square kilometers
acres	0.4047	hectares
square centimeters	0.1550	square inches
square meters	1.1960	square yards
square kilometers	0.3861	square miles
hectares	2.4711	acres

Weight

ounces (avdp.)	28.3500	grams
pounds (avdp.)	0.4536	kilograms
short tons (2,000 lbs.)	0.9072	metric tons
long tons (2,240 lbs.)	1.0160	metric tons
grams	0.0353	ounces (avdp.)
kilograms	2.2046	pounds (avdp.)
metric tons	1.1023	short tons
metric tons	0.9842	long tons

Volume

teaspoons	4.9290	milliliters
tablespoons	14.7870	milliliters
fluid ounces	29.5740	milliliters
cups	0.2366	liters
fluid pints	0.4732	liters
fluid quarts	0.9464	liters
gallons (U.S.)	3.7854	liters
cubic feet	0.0283	cubic meters
cubic yards	0.7646	cubic meters
milliliters	0.0338	fluid ounces
liters	2.1134	fluid pints
liters	1.0567	fluid quarts
liters	0.2642	gallons (U.S.)
cubic meters	35.3150	cubic feet
cubic meters	1.3080	cubic yards

Temperature

$^\circ C = (^\circ F - 32)/1.8$

$^\circ F = (^\circ C \times 1.8) + 32$

METRIC EQUIVALENTS. The following list provides the metric equivalents of various customary figures, such as 1 mile and 1 pound:

Length

1 inch = 2.54 centimeters

1 foot = 30.48 centimeters

1 yard = 0.9144 meter

1 rod = 5.029 meters

1 mile = 1.6093 kilometers

Area

1 square inch = 6.452 square centimeters

1 square foot = 0.0933 square meter

1 square yard = 0.836 square meter

1 acre = 160 square rods

1 square rod = 25.293 square meters

1 acre = 0.405 hectare

1 square mile = 2.59 square kilometers

Volume

1 cubic inch = 16.387 cubic centimeters

1 cubic foot = 0.028 cubic meter

1 cubic yard = 0.765 cubic meter

Capacity: U.S. Liquid Measure

1 fluid ounce = 29.573 milliliters

1 gill = 118.294 milliliters

1 pint = 473.176 milliliters

1 quart = 0.946 liter

1 gallon = 3.785 liters

Capacity: U.S. Dry Measure

1 pint = 0.551 liter

1 quart = 1.101 liters

1 peck = 8.810 liters

1 bushel = 35.239 liters

Weight: Avoirdupois

1 grain = 0.0648 gram
1 dram = 1.772 grams
1 ounce = 28.350 grams
1 pound = 0.454 kilogram
1 hundredweight, short = 45.359 kilograms
1 hundredweight, long = 50.802 kilograms
1 ton, short = 0.907 metric ton
1 ton, long = 1.016 metric tons

Weight: Troy

1 grain = 0.0648 gram
1 pennyweight = 1.555 grams
1 ounce = 31.103 grams
1 pound = 0.373 kilogram

Weight: Apothecaries

1 grain = 0.0648 gram
1 scruple = 1.296 grams
1 dram = 3.888 grams
1 ounce = 31.103
1 pound = 0.373 kilogram

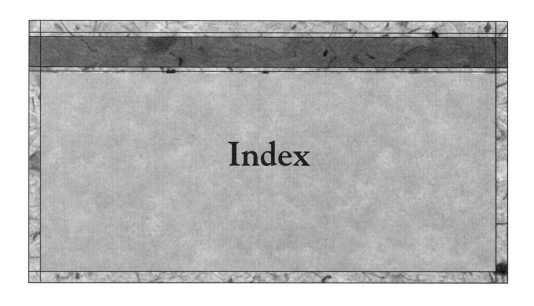

Index